COASTAL CALIFORNIA

STUART THORNTON

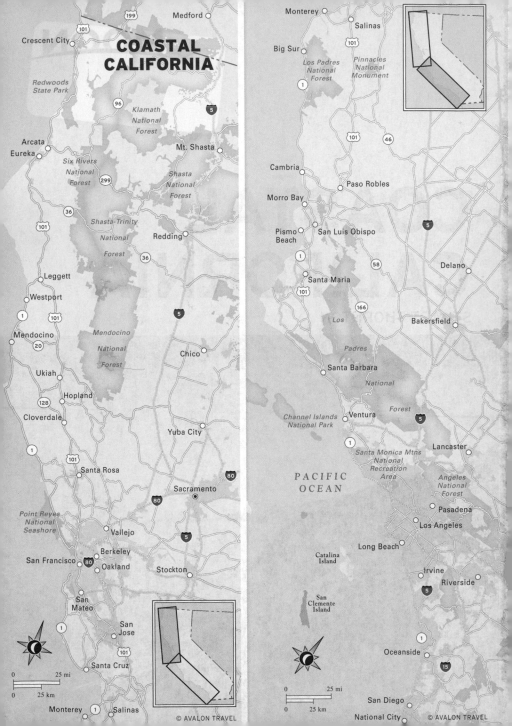

COASTAL CALIFORNIA

Medford

199

101

Crescent City

Redwoods State Park

96

Klamath National Forest

5

Arcata
Eureka

Six Rivers National Forest

299

Mt. Shasta

Shasta National Forest

36

101

Shasta-Trinity National Forest

Redding

36

Leggett

Westport

1

101

Mendocino National Forest

Mendocino

20

5

Chico

Ukiah

Hopland

128

Cloverdale

1

Yuba City

101

Santa Rosa

80

Sacramento

Point Reyes National Seashore

80

Vallejo

5

Berkeley

San Francisco

80

Oakland

Stockton

San Mateo

San Jose

101

1

Santa Cruz

1

0   25 mi
0   25 km

Monterey

1

Salinas

© AVALON TRAVEL

Monterey

Salinas

Big Sur

101

Los Padres National Forest

Pinnacles National Monument

1

Cambria

101

46

Paso Robles

Morro Bay

Pismo Beach

San Luis Obispo

1

5

58

Delano

Santa Maria

101

166

Bakersfield

Los

Padres

Santa Barbara

National

Channel Islands National Park

Ventura

Forest

5

1

Santa Monica Mtns National Recreation Area

Lancaster

PACIFIC OCEAN

Angeles National Forest

Pasadena

Los Angeles

Long Beach

Catalina Island

Irvine

Riverside

5

San Clemente Island

1

Oceanside

0   25 mi
0   25 km

15

San Diego

National City

© AVALON TRAVEL

Contents

Coastal California

California exists on the edge of the continent, where land and sea collide. This primal collision is the source of stunning beauty and singular geologic phenomena like the volcanic dome of Morro Rock, the honeycombs of sea caves along the La Jolla headlands, and the sheer walls of rock falling to the ocean at Big Sur. Waterfalls decorate cliff faces like ribbons, and spring wildflowers paint the hillsides above the blue-green ocean.

This land- and seascape can push you to your physical limits. Catch your first wave in the surf at Santa Cruz. Dive into a Monterey kelp forest. Explore deep into a Channel Islands sea cave by kayak. Trek the wild Lost Coast Trail. You might spot condors swirling in the night sky like embers, elk appearing out of the fog on secluded beaches, or migrating gray whales sounding offshore. You'll never get closer to the natural world than you can here.

Along the more placid sections of the coastline, the crashing surf smooths out into gentle waves lapping soft sands. This is the California coast that people all over the world know through popular culture, where sun worshippers share the shoreline with movie stars. Warm sunshine, colorful boardwalks, and easy access attract visitors seeking pleasure and relaxation.

Clockwise from top left: Golden Gate Bridge from Baker Beach; view from the Pacific Coast Highway; California brown pelican; Monterey coastline; organic wine grapes in Sonoma; golden poppies, Big Sur.

California is also on the cutting edge of art, entertainment, and cuisine. Trends are born here before spreading to the rest of the country and the world. It's where we first heard the music of The Doors, the Grateful Dead, Dr. Dre, and Beck. You can still catch performances by up-and-coming bands of all stripes at venues like The Fillmore in San Francisco, The Echo in Los Angeles, or The Casbah in San Diego. Or see the art of the avant-garde at world-class museums and galleries. California gave the United States its first taste of sushi and its first native-born wines, and it still offers one-of-a-kind culinary experiences. Enjoy authentic dim sum in San Francisco, or sample Mexican street tacos topped with kimchi in Los Angeles. Head to Carmel Valley, Santa Barbara, or Paso Robles to discover your new favorite wine. Or visit one of the North Coast's many microbreweries for your first sip of oatmeal stout or tangerine wheat ale.

Drink it all in. You'll return from your adventures on the edge of the continent with stories at the tip of your tongue.

Clockwise from top left: Mount Tamalpais; Laguna Beach; common warning sign along California's coast; Santa Cruz Beach Boardwalk.

10 TOP EXPERIENCES

1 **San Francisco:** Experience one of the country's most unique cities by exploring its **world-class museums,** plunging city streets, and **iconic sights** (page 49).

2 **Wine-Tasting:** The wines produced in California vineyards are known throughout the world. Sample these creations in **Napa and Sonoma** (page 63), **Carmel Valley** (page 251), **Anderson Valley** (page 157), and **Santa Barbara** (page 291).

3 **California Cuisine:** Whether it's **fresh seafood** in Cayucos (page 320), an **upscale meal** in San Francisco (page 77), or an **inventive taco** served from an LA food truck (page 359), California has a range of flavors as varied as its landscape.

>>>

4 **Redwoods:** Crane your neck at skyscraping redwoods at **Redwood National and State Parks** (page 192), along the **Avenue of the Giants** (page 165), in **Muir Woods** (page 103), and in **Big Sur** (page 258).

<<<

5 **On the Bay in Monterey:** Test your surfing skills in **Santa Cruz** (page 217), kayak or paddle off **Cannery Row** (page 229), or go whale-watching in **Monterey Bay** (page 230).

>>>

6 **Hike Big Sur:** The **Big Sur Coast Highway** (page 254) offers access to some of the state's best parks and hikes.

<<<

7 **Hit the Beach:** Enjoy the solitude and rugged beauty of the **North Coast** (page 137), or opt for sun and sand on the popular beaches of **Los Angeles** (page 355) and **San Diego** (page 408).

8 **Los Angeles:** This world-class city is known for its iconic **Hollywood sights,** a vibrant **culinary scene**, coastal enclaves, and a renewed **downtown** (page 333).

>>>

9 **The Coast Unplugged:** Experience the raw beauty of California's natural world. Camp under redwoods on the **North Coast** (page 162) or in **Big Sur** (page 269). Escape to **Channel Islands National Park** (page 307) to get a feel for the rugged coastline.

10 **Craft Beer:** California's craft beer scene has exploded with excellent breweries across the state. Sample the state's best suds in **San Diego** (page 405) and on the **North Coast** (page 186).

<<<

Planning Your Trip

Where to Go

San Francisco and the Bay Area

The politics, the culture, the food—these are what make San Francisco world-famous. Dine on cutting-edge **cuisine** at high-end restaurants and offbeat food trucks, tour classical and avant-garde **museums,** and bike through **Golden Gate Park** or stroll along **Fisherman's Wharf.** The surrounding region is as diverse as the city itself. To the north, **Marin** offers wilderness seekers a quick respite from the city, while ethnic diversity and intellectual curiosity give the **East Bay** a hip urban edge. Meanwhile, the beaches of **Coastside** are a short drive away.

North Coast

For deserted beaches, towering redwoods, and scenic coastal towns, cruise north along the **Redwood Coast.** Explore Russian history at

Fort Ross on the grassy bluffs of the **Sonoma Coast,** and fall in love with **Mendocino**'s small-town charm and nearby wineries. Detour west to the **Lost Coast** to experience coastline barely touched by human development.

Monterey and Big Sur

Some of the most beautiful and most adventurous coastline in the world is along the **Pacific Coast Highway.** Go surfing in **Santa Cruz.** Witness gray whales and sea lions off rugged **Monterey Bay,** and also explore their environment at the world-class **Monterey Bay Aquarium.** Wander around in the art galleries of **Carmel-by-the-Sea** and then take a stroll on the light sands of **Carmel Beach.** If you are a wine lover, be sure to head out to **Carmel Valley** to taste some of the region's best varietals.

the Monterey Bay Aquarium

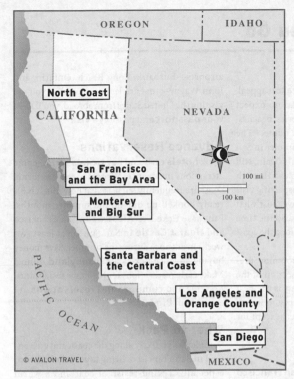

Santa Barbara's abundant sunshine at nearby **Refugio State Beach** on the **Gaviota Coast** or visit the wine-tasting rooms of downtown Santa Barbara and the nearby **Santa Maria Valley.** Farther south, Ventura offers visitors a historic mission, a vibrant downtown, and a reliable surf break. For a relaxing getaway, head to one of the region's beach towns: **Cayucos, Morro Bay,** or **Pismo Beach.**

Los Angeles and Orange County

For a taste of the iconic California dream, you can't beat Los Angeles. From the glitz and glamour of **Hollywood** and **Beverly Hills** to the camp and kitsch of **Santa Monica Pier,** L.A. is all California culture, all the time. Kids of all ages come to visit Walt's original **Disneyland,** while sun and surf worshippers ride the waves or relax on the sugar-sand **beaches.**

Camp and hike the unspoiled wilderness of **Big Sur,** and then tour grandiose **Hearst Castle** in San Simeon.

Santa Barbara and the Central Coast

Take in the picturesque **Santa Barbara Mission** and then stroll down the city's **State Street,** which is lined with shops, restaurants, and bars. Enjoy the lonely coastline of **Jalama Beach County Park** or, to truly get away from it all, take a boat ride out to **Channel Islands National Park.** Bask in

San Diego

For the sun-drenched, soft-sand California beach experience portrayed in endless films and TV shows, come to San Diego. Maritime museums ring the **downtown harbor,** while across the bay in **Coronado,** vibrant and historic Hotel del Coronado creates a centerpiece for visitors to the city. Gorgeous beaches stretch from **Point Loma** north to **La Jolla** and the **North County** coast, begging surfers, swimmers, strollers, and sunbathers to ply their sands.

Know Before You Go

When to Go

California's best feature is its **all-season** appeal. **Summer** is the coast's travel season; expect crowds at popular attractions, wineries, beaches, and campgrounds. (Although the quote, "The coldest winter I ever spent was a summer in San Francisco," falsely attributed to Mark Twain, still holds true, as the wind and fog that blows through the city June-August surprises unsuspecting visitors.) In **fall**, the summer crowds have mostly left but the weather is still warm. It is also the time when some of the best waves occur along the coast for surfers.

Winter is the rainy season, with lots more precipitation falling on the northern section of the coastline than in the south. **Spring** is the best time of year for spotting wildflowers and waterfalls. It's less crowded than summer (except for spring break).

Transportation

The easiest airports to **fly** into are **San Francisco (SFO)** and **Los Angeles (LAX)**. If you're flying into San Francisco, you can avoid some of the hassle by flying into nearby Oakland or San Jose. Similarly, Los Angeles offers several suburban airports—Burbank, Long Beach, Ontario, and John Wayne—that are less congested. If you are visiting the United States from abroad, you'll need your **passport** and possibly a **visa**.

Advance Reservations

Book **hotels** early and buy **tickets** for big-name attractions in advance. Visitors to the California coast are frequently surprised at how much is already booked up during the summer months. Purchase tickets to **Alcatraz** in San Francisco and **Hearst Castle** in San Simeon at least two weeks in advance during the summer. Save money buying advance tickets for **Disneyland** online. Make early reservations for big-name restaurants. Lodging and **campground reservations** are essential in **Big Sur**.

What to Pack

Summer **fog** is likely along the coast, and guaranteed in San Francisco. Bring **layered clothing,** especially a wind-resistant coat and a warm sweater. Expect warm temperatures and even desert heat in Los Angeles and San Diego in the summer. Bring **sunscreen;** that coastal fog doesn't stop UV rays.

Pacific Coast Road Trip

The ideal way to experience the California coast is to hit the road. Following this legendary road trip will take you through California's bustling cosmopolitan cities, small beach towns, redwood forests, and sandy beaches.

For the most part, you'll cover this stunning **850 miles** by following the legendary **Pacific Coast Highway** (Highway 1) and U.S. 101. You can switch back and forth between the two routes depending on your pace and your interests. **Highway 1** is generally more scenic; **U.S. 101** is usually faster. A few diversions onto other routes are necessary to cover the entire coast (for example, you'll be driving I-5 between San Diego and Los Angeles).

The day-by-day routes below begin in **Southern California,** but you can just as easily start in **Central** or **Northern California,** or reverse the route (from driving north to driving south) if that works better for you. Combine all three itineraries to make a 16-day tour of the coast. If you're pressed for time, choose just one or two of the itineraries.

Five Days in Southern California

San Diego
DAY 1

Easygoing San Diego is a great place to start any vacation. Upon arrival, orient yourself by driving to the top of **Mount Soledad Veterans Memorial,** a small mountain that has views of the entire city. After that, head down to **La Jolla Cove** to go kayaking or snorkeling; or just lie on the beach.

In the afternoon, visit **Balboa Park,** where you'll spend most of your time at the **San Diego Zoo.** End your day with a craft beer at one of San Diego's many breweries, like the giant **Stone Brewing Co.,** followed by a meal in the **Gaslamp Quarter.** Try the historic **Grant Grill** or the nearby **Café Chloe.**

DAY 2

The fastest way to reach the **North County** beach towns of **Encinitas, Carlsbad,** and **Oceanside** is to take I-5 north out of San Diego. Or, to cruise along the coast, opt for North Coast Highway 101 (also called Camino del Mar, San Elijo Boulevard, and Carlsbad Boulevard as it travels from Torrey Pines State Beach to Oceanside). Make sure to stop for a surf or a swim since the ocean temperatures cool as you head up the coast.

Continue north on I-5 to visit **Huntington Beach** before turning off toward **Long Beach** for a paranormal ship walk on **The** *Queen Mary,* an ocean liner that is now home to restaurants, a hotel, shops, and a museum. If you are daring enough, book a room for the night in the haunted ship.

Los Angeles
DAY 3

Jump on I-405 to save some time and drive about 30 miles north, exiting toward **Venice Beach.** Park your vehicle and take a stroll along the **Venice Boardwalk** to take in the local wildlife that includes bodybuilders, street performers, and alternative-culture types. Without getting back on the highway, take the local roads paralleling the beach 10 minutes north to **Santa Monica.** Enjoy the amusement park rides of the **Santa Monica Pier** or just take a break on **Santa Monica Beach.** For dinner, get a taste of the Caribbean at Santa Monica's casual but popular **Cha Cha Chicken** or backtrack to Venice for a hearty Italian meal at **C&O Trattoria.**

beach houses north of Malibu

DAY 4

Consider heading inland for a day of culture (and pop culture). For aesthetic stimulation, visit the world-famous **Getty Center** or the **Los Angeles County Museum of Art**. Less rigorous on the mind is a walk down the star-studded **Hollywood Walk of Fame** and a stop at the historic **TCL Chinese Theatre,** where you can find the handprints of your favorite movie stars. End the day in downtown Los Angeles with tacos from **B.S. Taqueria** followed by a cocktail with city views at the **Upstairs Bar**, the rooftop space atop the **Ace Hotel**.

DAY 5

Take the Pacific Coast Highway (Highway 1) out of Santa Monica as it heads away from sprawling Los Angeles and into **Malibu**. Stop at Malibu's **Surfrider Beach** to watch the surfers compete for its famously peeling waves (or catch one yourself). After a morning outdoors, feed your mind with ancient art at **The Getty Villa** in Malibu. (Admission is free, but you'll need to reserve a ticket in advance.) Finish the day by watching the sun slide into the Pacific from the outdoor deck of **Neptune's Net** while enjoying fresh seafood.

If you want to spend more time in the Los Angeles area, you can easily fill a couple of days enjoying **Disneyland Resort**.

SAN FRANCISCO AND THE BAY AREA

- **Point Reyes National Seashore** (page 109) is home to giant **elephant seals** and tiny, endangered **Myrtle's silverspot butterflies.**

- The **Farallon Islands** (page 76) are home to a quarter-million **seabirds** and one of the world's largest **great white shark** populations.

- **Año Nuevo State Reserve** (page 121) is the site of one of the world's largest mainland breeding colonies of **northern elephant seals.**

NORTH COAST

- **Elk Prairie** and **Elk Meadow**, in **Prairie Creek Redwoods State Park** (page 193), are named after their inhabitants.

- **Bodega Head** (page 128) offers views of migrating **gray whales** January-May.

MONTEREY AND BIG SUR

- **Natural Bridges State Beach** (page 216) hosts thousands of migrating **Monarch butterflies** mid-October and mid-February. They also stop at Pacific Grove's **Monarch Grove Sanctuary** (page 236).

- **Elkhorn Slough** (page 222) hosts 340 **bird species,** including brown pelicans and snowy plovers. Paddle toward the bay to spot **sea lions, harbor seals,** and **sea otters,** as well as **bat rays** and **leopard sharks.**

- Walk out on **Monterey's Coast Guard Pier** (page 228) to spot **sea lions** and **harbor seals.**

- Stop along the **Big Sur Coast Highway** (page 254) to spot **California condors,** North America's largest land birds.

- **Piedras Blancas Elephant Seal Rookery** (page 272) is a great place to see the beasts up close.

Monarch butterflies

SANTA BARBARA AND THE CENTRAL COAST

- Unique native species like **island scrub jays** and **island foxes** are prevalent on **Santa Cruz Island** (page 307), especially in the **Scorpion Ranch Campground.**

LOS ANGELES AND ORANGE COUNTY

- A **herd of bison** was introduced to **Catalina Island** (page 382) in the 1920s and has thrived here since.

- Snorkel or a scuba dive at the **Avalon Underwater Park** (page 382) to view **garibaldi** and **gobies.**

- In Los Angeles, **coyotes, foxes, bobcats, mule deer,** and even **mountain lions** have been spotted in **Griffith Park** (page 338).

SAN DIEGO

- **La Jolla Cove** (page 401) is home to **sardines, garibaldi,** and **leopard sharks.**

- Escondido's **San Diego Zoo Safari Park** (page 429) is where giraffes, lions, and elephants enjoy a more natural outdoor space.

Six Days in Central California

Santa Barbara and the Central Coast

DAY 1

Wake up early and drive north on the scenic Pacific Coast Highway. Thirty-five miles from Malibu, at Oxnard, merge onto U.S. 101. Head north on U.S. 101 to Ventura and take the exit toward Ventura Harbor, where you can catch a boat out to **Channel Islands National Park** for a day of hiking, snorkeling, or kayaking on **Santa Cruz Island** or **Anacapa Island.** (Make boat reservations in advance.) Return to **Ventura** and eat dinner at one of its seafood restaurants, such as **Lure Fish House** or **Spencer Makenzie's Fish Company.** Or have an Italian meal and cocktail at hip **Café Fiore.**

DAY 2

Take U.S. 101 north a half hour (28 miles) to **Santa Barbara.** Get a history fix at the **Santa Barbara Mission,** which might be the most

beautiful of the 21 Spanish missions in California. Then taste some local wines on the **Urban Wine Trail,** comprising six tasting rooms on lower State Street, or head north for a day at palm-lined **Refugio State Beach,** 20 miles west of Santa Barbara on U.S. 101.

If your schedule is flexible, you might consider another full day in Santa Barbara, another day of wine-tasting in the nearby **Santa Maria Valley,** or a day on the **Gaviota Coast.** Whatever you do, stop at Santa Barbara's **State Street** for a fine meal or cocktail at a restaurant like the local favorite **Opal.** Or head off State Street for superb Mexican food at **La Super-Rica Taqueria.**

DAY 3

Drive 1.75 hours (92 miles) north of Santa Barbara on U.S. 101 to **San Luis Obispo's Madonna Inn,** where you can take in its kitschy decor during a restroom-and-stretch-the-legs break.

Outdoor enthusiasts will want to head off the

Big Sur's Bixby Bridge

McWay Falls at Julia Pfeiffer Burns State Park

harbor seals in Monterey

highway and go west on Los Osos Valley Road just 20 minutes (12 miles) to **Montaña de Oro State Park,** one of the state's best coastal parks. Picnic at **Spooner's Cove** or hike to the top of 1,347-foot-high **Valencia Peak.** Then head back to U.S. 101 North, but be sure to turn onto Highway 1 north to take in the sunset over **Morro Rock,** known as the "Gibraltar of the Pacific."

Another option is to drive an hour north (44 miles) to opulent **Hearst Castle.** Tours of this "ranch" built for newspaper magnate William Randolph Hearst offer insight into the lifestyle of the rich and infamous.

However you spend your day, end it with a meal in one of the Central Coast's unassuming beach towns: **Morro Bay, Cayucos,** or **Cambria.**

Big Sur
DAY 4
Head north on Highway 1 for what might be the most scenic day of driving on your whole trip. The two-lane highway here winds along the mountains of **Big Sur** with plentiful views of the ocean.

From Cambria to the heart of Big Sur is 75 miles, but the scenery, winding roadway, and frequent road construction can make the drive last well over two hours. Be sure to make multiple stops to take in the scenery at places like **Salmon Creek Falls, Sand Dollar Beach,** and **Julia Pfeiffer Burns State Park.** Or opt for a comfy cabin by the river at **Glen Oaks Big Sur** or a rustic room at the charming **Deetjen's Big Sur Inn.**

Monterey Bay
DAY 5
Continue up Highway 1 for 45 minutes (less than 30 miles) through the northern section of Big Sur to the **Monterey Peninsula.** Take a walk in Carmel's **Point Lobos State Natural Reserve** or head to scenic **Carmel Beach.** Then drive a few miles north into Monterey to spend the afternoon at the **Monterey Bay Aquarium.**

Dine on fresh seafood at Pacific Grove's **Passionfish, The Sandbar & Grill** in Monterey, **The Poke Lab** in Monterey, or **Phil's Fish Market** up Highway 1 in Moss Landing.

If you want to spend another day in this area, wander the galleries in **Carmel-by-the-Sea,** golf at **Pebble Beach,** or head inland to **Carmel Valley** for wine-tasting.

Santa Cruz
DAY 6

Getting to **Santa Cruz** is an easy 50-minute drive (44 miles) up Highway 1 from the Monterey Peninsula. The eclectic beach city is an ideal place for recreation whether you are surfing, stand-up paddleboarding, or hiking redwood-filled **Forest of Nisene Marks State Park** or the coastal bluffs of **Wilder Ranch State Park.** Refuel with a healthy snack at **The Picnic Basket** before ending the day with thrill rides at the **Santa Cruz Beach Boardwalk.**

If your adrenaline is still racing from the Boardwalk rides, calm down with a drink at **Red Restaurant and Bar** or **The Crépe Place.**

Five Days in Northern California

San Francisco
DAY 1

Wake up early for a drive on Highway 1 from Santa Cruz less than two hours (80 miles) to **San Francisco.** In the city, spend a few hours in the thought-provoking **San Francisco Museum of Modern Art** and have a creative snack at the museum's **In Situ;** their menu features popular items from around the world. As the sun goes down, make sure to head out for dinner, whether it's seafood at the **Tadich Grill,** modern Thai food at **Lers Ros,** or pizza at **Tony's Pizza Napoletana.** If you still have energy, make sure to check out some of San Francisco's vibrant nightlife or a concert at a venue like the **Great American Music Hall.**

DAY 2

Head out on San Francisco Bay to take a fascinating tour of the island prison **Alcatraz.** Or secure passage on a ferry to **Angel Island,** which has hiking trails that offer up some of the finest views of the city.

Point Arena-Stornetta Unit of the California Coastal National Monument

Catch of the Day

Some of the state's best seafood can be found in unpretentious eateries just footsteps from the ocean.

SAN FRANCISCO AND THE BAY AREA

• Sit at the long marble bar at Swan Oyster Depot (page 82) to dine on seafood that was swimming in the ocean just hours earlier.

• Enjoy a decadent Dungeness crab roll or a superbly spicy salmon sandwich at Fish (page 99), right on the harbor in Sausalito.

• At Sam's Chowder House (page 118), enjoy both daily fresh catches and a great view of Half Moon Bay.

NORTH COAST

• The smoked wild salmon at tiny Katy's Smokehouse (page 190) in Trinidad may be the best you've ever eaten.

• Salt Fish House (page 185) in Arcata serves local petrale sole, cod, and Humboldt Bay oysters.

• Eureka's Humboldt Bay Provisions (page 181) has a superb raw bar starring delicious Humboldt Bay oysters.

• Bodega Bay's Fishetarian Fish Market (page 130) is almost 600 miles from Baja, but their fresh rockfish tacos topped with two tasty sauces can hold their own with their southern counterparts.

MONTEREY AND BIG SUR

• Monterey's Sandbar & Grill (page 233) serves up the seaside city's best calamari in a laid-back setting over the harbor.

• Get a taste of local Sicilian fishermen's recipes like squid pasta at Monterey's Fish House (page 233).

• Tucked between the harbor and the ocean in Moss Landing, Phil's Fish Market (page 223) serves up hearty and tasty cioppino and sea scallops.

• Opt for raw seafood salads at Monterey's The

Poke Lab (page 233), a fast-casual restaurant on Alvarado Street.

SANTA BARBARA AND THE CENTRAL COAST

• Ventura's Spencer Makenzie's Fish Company (page 306) is known for its fine tempura-battered fish tacos.

• Expect salmon, ahi, and swordfish at local favorite Brophy Brothers (page 296), with locations on both the Santa Barbara and Ventura harbors.

• Just off Cayucos Beach, Rudell's Smokehouse (page 321) serves seafood tacos with big flavors, including smoked salmon, smoked albacore, and an unexpected topping: chopped apples.

• People line up at Splash Café (page 312) in Pismo Beach for a taste of rich, buttery clam chowder.

• Right on the Embarcadero in Morro Bay, Tognazzini's Dockside Restaurant (page 318) is the place for fresh barbecued oysters in garlic butter.

LOS ANGELES AND ORANGE COUNTY

• Enjoy crispy shrimp tacos topped with a pineapple salsa at local hangout Neptune's Net (page 363), overlooking a Malibu surf break.

• The Lobster Trap (page 382) on Catalina Island is all about tasty crustaceans, with options like lobster stuffed with bay shrimp.

SAN DIEGO

• Choose between 13 varieties of fish tacos, including ahi and shark, at San Diego's Blue Water Seafood Market & Grill (page 414).

• Point Loma Seafoods (page 416) is all about the freshest fish, which explains why the menu is full of seafood cocktail, sushi, and sashimi. Visit between October and March for locally caught lobster.

In the afternoon, shop the used clothing stores of **Haight-Ashbury** or the department stores of **Union Square**. Or browse the books at **City Lights** in **North Beach**.

You'll quickly fall in love with San Francisco; you can easily extend your romance to three or four days if you have the time.

North Coast

DAY 3

Your journey north begins with a drive on U.S. 101 over San Francisco's iconic **Golden Gate Bridge**. After five miles, turn off U.S. 101 to Highway 1 at Mill Valley. On the slow, over-four-hour drive up the coast (around 160 miles), make time to stop at places like the tiny but unique **Sea Ranch Chapel,** which is just feet off Highway 1, and take a hike on the stunning cliffside trails in the **Point Arena-Stornetta Unit** of the **California Coastal National Monument.**

End the day in the community of **Mendocino** with a view of the sunset at **Mendocino Headlands State Park** or a pint at the lively **Patterson's Pub** or at the one-of-a-kind dive bar **Dick's Place.**

DAY 4

Drive Highway 1 north of Fort Bragg until the road turns inland to connect with U.S. 101 after about an hour of driving. Opt for the **Avenue of the Giants,** a drive through redwoods by the Eel River. Even though it's only 31 miles, the drive could take a few hours if you decide to get out of your car and ponder the trees.

Get back on U.S. 101 and head an hour north (60 miles) to **Eureka.** Stop to wander the city's Old Town and waterfront. Taste some of the delicious oysters at the **Humboldt Bay Provisions.**

Continue on U.S. 101 another 10 minutes or so to charming **Arcata.** Wander through the redwoods of the **Arcata Community Forest** before sundown. Dine at one of the restaurants surrounding the lively **Arcata Plaza.** Follow it with a craft beer at **Dead Reckoning Tavern.**

DAY 5

Start your morning with a tasty crepe from Arcata's **Renata's Creperie and Espresso** before hitting U.S. 101 North on your final day. About 20 minutes (15 miles) north of Arcata, exit to the scenic coastal city of **Trinidad.** Have your camera handy for photos of **Trinidad Memorial Lighthouse, Trinidad Head,** and **Trinidad State Beach.**

Another half hour up U.S. 101 (26 miles), turn onto Newton B. Drury Scenic Drive to explore **Prairie Creek Redwoods State Park.** If you have the energy, drive out Davison Road to **Gold Bluffs Beach,** where Roosevelt elk roam the sands, and continue on the dirt drive to hike the one-mile round-trip **Fern Canyon Trail,** which passes through a steep canyon draped in bright green ferns.

Head back to U.S. 101 and drive 45 minutes (38 miles) to **Crescent City.** End the journey with a beer, a meal, and some live music at **SeaQuake Brewing.**

Best Beaches

Wide golden beaches with abundant sunshine and legendary surf breaks. Lonely stretches of sand framed by coast redwoods and jagged cliffs. Boardwalks crowded with kids, cotton candy, and roller coasters. California has any kind of beach you could possibly want.

San Francisco and the Bay Area

The Bay Area is one of California's largest urban centers, but sand seekers can still find beaches within—or just outside of—city limits.

OCEAN BEACH
BEST FOR SUNSETS, STROLLS

Ocean Beach runs for miles along the western edge of San Francisco, offering a break from busy streets and crowded tourist attractions (page 72).

BAKER BEACH
BEST FOR SCENERY, PHOTO OPS, SUNBATHING

On the northern tip of San Francisco, this mile-long swath of sand is your best bet for stunning views of the Golden Gate Bridge and San Francisco Bay. Its northernmost end is known for its nude sunbathers (page 73).

MUIR BEACH
BEST FOR SCENERY, WILDLIFE, SUNBATHING

Wildlife enthusiasts flock to Muir Beach. It's a great place to spot migrating whales during the winter, while fall brings Monarch butterflies. The stream that runs into the ocean at Muir Beach provides a habitat for shorebirds, salmon, trout, and amphibians. Meanwhile, the relatively secluded north side provides a habitat for nude sunbathers (page 104).

STINSON BEACH
BEST FOR FAMILIES

In the summer, Stinson has lifeguards, a snack bar, picnic areas, and restrooms that are ideal for a family day at the beach. Surfers, kayakers, and paddleboarders test their skills in the surf (page 107).

Ocean Beach

AÑO NUEVO STATE RESERVE
BEST FOR WILDLIFE
At Año Nuevo, gigantic elephant seals turn the beach into a battleground. You can also catch a glimpse of an eerie, abandoned light station buildings right offshore (page 121).

North Coast
These beaches showcase the wild, rugged beauty that happens when the land meets the sea with little or no human intervention. On these beaches, there is frequently more wildlife than people. The coast up here is perfect for long contemplative walks—as long as you remember to bundle up. Opportunities for recreation include surfing, diving, kayaking, and stand-up paddleboarding, all without the crowds typical of beaches to the south.

MANCHESTER STATE PARK
BEST FOR BEACHCOMBING, SOLITUDE
The long, debris-strewn beach at Manchester State Park is ideal for beachcombers and offers views of the Point Arena Lighthouse in the distance (page 139).

BIG RIVER
BEST FOR KAYAKING, STAND-UP PADDLEBOARDING, BEGINNERS' SURFING
Big River, just south of Mendocino Village, has a range of recreational opportunities. Surf the beach break, launch a kayak to explore the nearby headlands, or paddleboard the river before steering your board into the ocean (page 147).

USAL BEACH
BEST FOR WILDLIFE, SOLITUDE
Follow the mountainous dirt road to Usal Beach, where you may spot Roosevelt elk. Even if you don't see these giant animals, you can bask in the solitude (page 167).

BLACK SAND BEACH
BEST FOR SCENERY
An easier way to take in the rugged beauty of the Lost Coast is to marvel at Shelter Cove's Black Sand Beach, framed by the towering King Range (page 168).

the beautiful Trinidad coast

Surf and Turf

With great weather year-round, lots of ocean access, and a bounty of beaches, the California coast has a plethora of recreational opportunities.

SURFING

After Hawaiians introduced surfing to California, it became an essential part of the state's culture. California offers up waves for every level of surfer. Iconic surf breaks like San Diego's **Black's Beach,** Santa Barbara's **Rincon,** and Santa Cruz's **Steamer Lane** make surfers from around the world drool with anticipation. Beginners can attempt their first waves at the gentle peeling waves of Santa Cruz's **Cowell's Beach** or Malibu's **Surfrider Beach.**

STAND-UP PADDLEBOARDING

California's many bays, inlets, and protected areas are the perfect places to get started in the coast's fastest-growing sport. Hit the water at Orange County's **Dana Point Harbor,** the Central Coast's **Cayucos Beach** or **Santa Cruz Harbor** or offshore along Monterey's **Cannery Row,** and at Mendocino's **Van Damme State Park** on the North Coast.

SCUBA DIVING AND SNORKELING

The best way to see the multitude of sea life, kelp forests, and reefs off the California shoreline is to put on some snorkeling or scuba gear. The clear waters and swaying kelp forests of the **Monterey Peninsula** make it one of the biggest dive destinations in the state. **Santa Catalina Island** offers pristine underwater habitats for the adventurous, while San Diego's **La Jolla Cove** provides easy access to the undersea world.

Explore Mendocino's sea caves by stand-up paddleboard.

BACKPACKING

To get away from the crowds, strap on a backpack and head to the state's more remote areas. The North Coast's **Lost Coast Trail** is a three-day backpacking trip along a 24-mile stretch of rugged coastline. Big Sur's **Ventana Wilderness** offers multiday excursions to hot springs and peaks with fabulous coast views. Or you can get away from it all at backcountry camps on Santa Cruz Island and Santa Rosa Island in **Channel Islands National Park.**

EEL RIVER
BEST FOR SWIMMING
Not all great beaches are on the ocean; beaches line the Eel River as it winds beside the popular Avenue of the Giants, offering motorists a cool dip and a place to bask in the sun (page 166).

TRINIDAD STATE BEACH
BEST FOR SCENERY, PICNICS
This scenic stretch of shore under the rounded knob of Trinidad Head is ideal for a family picnic—especially if you pick up some smoked salmon from nearby Katy's Smokehouse (page 189).

the Central Coast's scenic stretch of sand

GOLD BLUFFS BEACH
BEST FOR WILDLIFE, SOLITUDE
Back in 1850, prospectors found gold flakes on Gold Bluffs Beach, but now the treasures of this coastal area within Prairie Creek Redwoods State Park are its remote beauty and its wildlife (page 194).

SOUTH BEACH
BEST FOR SURFING
Crescent City's South Beach offers one of the state's northernmost surf breaks, where surfers of all abilities can catch easy peeling waves (page 200).

Monterey and Big Sur
Monterey Bay, a National Marine Sanctuary known for its wildlife, has relatively pristine waters and a handful of worthy beaches. The Big Sur coastline is rugged, but there are several places to access the beach—and it's almost always worth the effort.

COWELL'S BEACH
BEST FOR SURFING
Santa Cruz's Cowell's Beach has slow, rolling waves perfect for beginners. Even though it gets crowded, the surfers here are usually friendly (page 216).

SANTA CRUZ BEACH BOARDWALK
BEST FOR FAMILIES
Just feet away from Cowell's, the Santa Cruz Beach Boardwalk makes families happy with its rides, games, and entertainment. The boardwalk's Giant Dipper roller coaster has been thrilling riders since 1924 (page 208).

MOSS LANDING
BEST FOR BEACHCOMBING, SOLITUDE
Usually uncrowded except for a handful of surfers and anglers, Moss Landing State Beach and Zmudowski State Beach offer long stretches of lonesome sand (page 223).

CARMEL BEACH
BEST FOR SCENERY, SUNSETS, DOG LOVERS

With its pale sand and contrasting blue-green ocean water, Carmel Beach is a jewel of the Monterey Bay. It's also one of the friendliest beaches for dogs in the state (page 244).

PFEIFFER BEACH
BEST FOR PHOTO OPS, SUNSETS

Make sure that your camera has fully charged batteries for a trip to Big Sur's windswept Pfeiffer Beach, with picture-perfect rock formations offshore (page 259).

SAND DOLLAR BEACH
BEST FOR PICNICS

Protected by cliffs on windy days, crescent-shaped Sand Dollar Beach is a great spot for a picnic (page 261).

MOONSTONE BEACH
BEST FOR BEACHCOMBING

You can hunt for the eponymous moonstones

on this Cambria beach. Its impressive driftwood structures are also worthy discoveries (page 275).

Santa Barbara and the Central Coast

The last strand of relatively undeveloped coastline before Southern California is north of Santa Barbara. Ventura draws surfers from throughout the Southland. Cayucos, Morro Bay, and Pismo Beach have some of the finest swaths of sand north of Los Angeles County.

ARROYO BURRO BEACH
BEST FOR DOG LOVERS

If you have a dog in tow, head to Santa Barbara's Arroyo Burro Beach. Past the slough, dogs are allowed off leash (page 287).

RINCON
BEST FOR SURFING

Ranked 49th in a *Surfer Magazine* list of the 100 best waves in the world, Rincon can produce a long, peeling right with the right swell (page 292).

Morro Rock

Venice Boardwalk

JALAMA BEACH COUNTY PARK
BEST FOR CAMPING, SOLITUDE
This beach park in the middle of nowhere is a refuge for surfers, anglers, beachcombers, and families who want to unplug from modern life (page 299).

REFUGIO STATE BEACH
BEST FOR SWIMMING, FAMILIES
The best beach on the Gaviota Coast is on this protected cove lined with palm trees. Its ocean waters are calm enough for wading children and beginning kayakers (page 299).

CALIFORNIA STREET BEACH
BEST FOR SURFING, SIGHTSEEING
To catch some hot surfing action, head to Ventura's California Street Beach, known locally as "C Street" (page 304).

PISMO BEACH
BEST FOR FAMILIES
Studded with volleyball courts and lifeguard stands, Pismo Beach feels like a Southern California beach without the massive development. It's ideal for a day with the family (page 310).

SPOONER'S COVE
BEST FOR SCENERY, PICNICS
Soak up the natural beauty of Spooner's Cove, in Montaña de Oro State Park. A scenic arch decorates the bluffs on the south end of the cove (page 313).

MORRO ROCK BEACH
BEST FOR PHOTO OPS, SURFING
Take a photo in front of 576-foot-high Morro Rock. The beach to its north is popular with surfers of all skill levels (page 313).

Los Angeles and Orange County
Los Angeles and neighboring Orange County share a wealth of superb beaches, known to the world from decades of movies and television shows: They're broad, sandy, and packed with people during the summer months. The best of the best have a little something that sets them apart.

LEO CARRILLO STATE PARK
BEST FOR SCENERY, CAMPING, DOG LOVERS
At the northern end of L.A. County, Leo Carrillo feels a world away from bustling Los Angeles. This 1.5-mile-long beach has tide pools, caves, and reefs. The northern section is also a perfect place to take your leashed pooch (page 355).

MALIBU SURFRIDER BEACH
BEST FOR SURFING
Surfers flock to Malibu Surfrider Beach to catch one of California's greatest peeling waves or to soak up the vibe of the surf culture that was born here in the early 1960s (page 356).

SANTA MONICA STATE BEACH
BEST FOR FAMILIES, SUNBATHING
Take in the plentiful Southern California sunshine and the amusements available at the Santa Monica Pier (page 356).

VENICE BEACH
BEST FOR PEOPLE-WATCHING
Venice Beach is a people-watcher's paradise, with a boardwalk filled with weightlifters, skateboarders, musicians, dancers, and vendors hawking their wares (page 346).

HERMOSA BEACH
BEST FOR VOLLEYBALL, FAMILIES
Hermosa Beach has the feel and attitude of a small beach town, even though it's surrounded by metropolitan Los Angeles. Volleyball nets are available for pickup games, and "The Strand" is ideal for a jog or bike ride (page 356).

HUNTINGTON CITY BEACH
BEST FOR SURFING, SUNBATHING
Orange County's Huntington City Beach offers multiple recreation options, including surfing the waves that break on either side of the pier (page 380).

LAGUNA BEACH'S MAIN BEACH
BEST FOR TIDEPOOLING, SUNBATHING
Main Beach is an ideal SoCal stretch of sand with palm trees and abundant sunshine. It gets even better at its north end, where some rocky tide pools are located (page 383).

San Diego
With warmer ocean temperatures and year-round sunshine, San Diego's beaches are the most welcoming in the state.

CORONADO MAIN BEACH
BEST FOR FAMILIES, SUNSETS
Spread out, catch some sun, and take in views of the nearby Hotel del Coronado (page 409).

OCEAN BEACH
BEST FOR PEOPLE-WATCHING, DOG LOVERS
Lying at the end of an eclectic community, this beach is popular with dogs—and their people (page 408).

LA JOLLA COVE
BEST FOR SUNBATHING, SNORKELING, KAYAKING
La Jolla Cove is a pocket beach between two cliffs. Sunbathers take up most of the real estate on crowded weekends. An underwater park with sea caves right offshore is perfect for snorkelers and kayakers (page 401).

BLACK'S BEACH
BEST FOR ADVANCED SURFING, SUNBATHING
Black's Beach is a legendary surf spot and also a nudist beach. Getting here involves an adventurous hiking path down 300-foot-high cliffs (page 408).

Dog owners will have a lot more fun on the California coast with their furry friends along for the ride. Luckily, there are lots of options for people who want to bring their pets.

ACCOMMODATIONS

Kimpton Hotels, a luxury boutique hotel chain with 15 properties along the California coast, goes out of its way to welcome pets. It offers pet beds, food bowls, water bowls, and information about all the pet-friendly attractions and businesses in the area. Some of Kimpton's properties include San Diego's Hotel Palomar, Santa Barbara's Canary Hotel, and San Francisco's Sir Francis Drake.

On the coast, the Crowne Plaza Ventura Beach has a whole floor of pet-friendly rooms.

Carmel-by-the-Sea is a superb place to vacation with your four-legged friend. Many hotels allow dogs including the Tradewinds Carmel, the Coachman's Inn, the Lamp Lighter Inn, and the Cypress Inn, which is co-owned by animal activist Doris Day.

On the North Coast, Fort Bragg's Beachcomber Motel offers pet-friendly rooms, a dog park, and pet suites with doggie doors that open up to a fenced-in enclosure with a doghouse. In nearby Anderson Valley, both the Anderson Valley Inn and the Boonville Hotel reserve a couple of rooms for families with dogs.

BEACHES

A few California beaches permit and even encourage dog visitation. One of the best is Carmel Beach in Carmel-by-the-Sea. On any given day, more dogs roam this beach than people—and they can do so leash-free.

The north end of San Diego's Ocean Beach calls itself "The Original Dog Beach." It's also leash-free. Del Mar City Beach has a dog section that extends from 29th Street to Solana Beach.

Known as "Surf City USA," Orange County's Huntington Beach might as well be called "Dog City USA." The north end between Seapoint Avenue and 21st Street allows pets.

There are lots of dog-friendly beaches on the California Coast.

Santa Barbara's Arroyo Burro Beach permits pets to be off leash past the slough, while Montara State Beach in the Bay Area's Coastside invites dogs as long as they're leashed.

PARKS

The second-largest park in San Francisco, McLaren Park has dog play areas. The Coastside Trail is a paved dog-friendly path that connects various Half Moon Bay beaches and the adjacent shoreline. One of the Monterey Peninsula's best places to hike with your dog is Carmel Valley's Garland Ranch Regional Park. The park has off-leash areas and water fountains designed to hydrate both you and your pet.

The California State Parks on the coast generally allow leashed dogs in the day-use areas but not on the trails. Contact the specific state park that you will be visiting to confirm where your pet is permitted.

Romantic Getaways

Crashing waves, breathtaking views, gourmet restaurants, and luxury hotels make the California coast perfect for romance.

San Francisco and the Bay Area

Have a wonderful meal together at a fine San Francisco restaurant like **State Bird Provisions** or **Farallon** and then take in an opera at the **War Memorial Opera House.** End the night by sipping a cocktail and looking at the lights of the city from **Harry Denton's Starlight Room.** Stay at the **Hotel VIA** and enjoy access to its rooftop bar.

Just north of San Francisco, the **Cavallo Point Lodge** feels a world away from the city but still has all the amenities for a romantic evening, including a fine restaurant, a spa, a pampering staff, and stunning views of the Golden Gate Bridge and the bay.

Down the coast, the Half Moon Bay area offers nice romantic retreats. Spend the night at the castle-like **Ritz-Carlton Half Moon Bay** or the bayside **Beach House at Half Moon Bay.**

North Coast

Pack up a bottle of wine and a blanket for a long walk on a secluded beach. Toward the upper end of the North Coast, **Trinidad State Beach** is a picturesque place to picnic. Farther south, **Manchester State Park**'s beach offers miles of uncrowded coastline and large beached logs perfect for watching the sunset.

Rent one of the four private Victorian cottages at Eureka's **Carter House Inns.** Or spend a night at the lovely **Elk Cove Inn,** where you can walk down to a beautiful cove. Another option is the **Sea Ranch Lodge,** where every room has a view of the serene Sonoma Coast. The village of Mendocino has a variety of romantic bed-and-breakfasts including the **Brewery Gulch Inn.**

Monterey Bay

Romance can blossom on a sunset walk on **Carmel Beach,** followed by an upscale Mexican meal at **Cultura** with its extensive menu of smoky mescals. Stay the night in one of Carmel's

Trinidad State Beach

the Big Sur coast

luxurious accommodations, like the opulent **La Playa Carmel** or the East-meets-West-themed **Tradewinds Carmel.** Or drive a few miles north to Pacific Grove to spend an evening at the **Green Gables Inn,** an ornate Victorian bed-and-breakfast with a view of the aptly named **Lover's Point** protruding into the bay.

Detour inland to Carmel Valley to visit one of the valley's many wine-tasting rooms, such as the luxurious **Bernardus Winery** or the unassuming **Heller Estate Organic Vineyards** with its outdoor sculpture garden. Then relax together at **Refuge Spa,** a collection of hot, warm, and cool water tubs nestled under the Santa Lucia Mountains.

Big Sur

Big Sur is a great place for romantic walks, whether to **Pfeiffer Beach** or to see **McWay Falls** plunge into the Pacific at **Julia Pfeiffer Burns State Park.** Post hike, a posh night at the **Post Ranch Inn** or **Ventana Big Sur** will definitely impress your significant other. A less pricey but cozy alternative is **Deetjen's Big Sur Inn.**

The fascinating guest journals frequently detail romantic encounters.

Farther south, a romantic evening will come easy with a night at Cambria's **Sand Pebbles Inn,** right across the street from Moonstone Beach.

Santa Barbara and the Central Coast

Filled with fragrant flowers and beautiful Spanish-influenced architecture, Santa Barbara is one of the coast's finest spots for romance. Take the **Urban Wine Trail** to wine-taste within the city and then dine on Italian at upscale **Olio e Limone** or enjoy tapas and sangria at **Loquita.**

The **Canary Hotel** is a luxury hotel with a rooftop deck and a fireplace for a romantic evening under the stars. Another option is the elegant **Simpson House Inn,** an elegant historic landmark.

Inland of the Central Coast, visit Paso Robles for wine-tasting and a growing foodie scene. Taste the excellent wines at **Eberle Winery** and then spend a night at the **Paso Robles Inn,** where you

the Scripps Pier in La Jolla, San Diego

can snuggle in a private hot springs mineral pool on the deck of your room.

Los Angeles and Orange County

Enjoy classic French cuisine at Echo Park's **Taix French Restaurant,** then head to Koreatown for a flight of elegant cocktails at **The Walker Inn.** Take a taxi back to your room at the hip **Freehand Los Angeles** in downtown Los Angeles.

In Orange County, **The Inn at Laguna Beach** is perched right above the sand and sea. You can walk from there to **Watermarc** for small bites and wonderful cocktails.

San Diego

San Diego is a great place for relaxing, recharging, and romance. After enjoying the sun on one of the city's many fine beaches, head to the scenic coastal community of **La Jolla** for an afternoon of shopping. If you get hungry, enjoy a meal with ocean views inside **George's at the Cove.**

End the day with cocktails and seaside views at the historic **Hotel del Coronado.** Or opt for a drink at the **Grant Grill,** a restaurant and bar within the historic **US Grant Hotel,** located in the city's Gaslamp Quarter.

San Francisco

San Francisco

San Francisco perches restlessly on an uneven spit of land overlooking the Bay on one side and the Pacific Ocean on the other.

Visitors come for the great art, world-class music, culinary innovation, and a laid-back club scene. Famed for its diversity, liberalism, and dense fog, the city somehow manages to both embody and defy the stereotypes heaped upon it.

Street-corner protests and leather stores are certainly part of the landscape, but farmers markets and friendly communities also abound. English blends with languages from around the world in an occasionally frustrating, often joyful cacophony. Those who have chosen to live here often refuse to live anyplace else, despite the infamous cost of housing and the occasional violent earthquake. Don't call it "San Fran," or worse, "Frisco," or you'll be pegged as a tourist. To locals, this is The City, and that's that.

PLANNING YOUR TIME

Plan to spend at least **two days** in San Francisco, although it's easy to stay longer. Base yourself downtown near Union Square, where you'll have access to public transportation and won't need a car. Don't miss sights include the foodie-friendly **Ferry Building, Golden Gate Park,** and taking a foggy stroll the **Golden Gate Bridge.** Make **reservations** in advance for a trip **Alcatraz** and for any and all **restaurants.**

Summers in San Francisco are typically foggy and cold. Visit in early fall, especially in September, when sunny days often shine down on events like the Folsom Street Fair.

Previous: view of the iconic Painted Ladies; San Francisco skyline. **Above:** Historic Ferry Building.

Look for ★ to find recommended
sights, activities, dining, and lodging.

Highlights

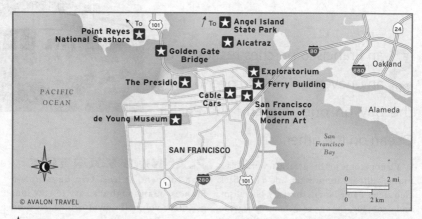

★ **Cable Cars:** Get a taste of free-spirited San Francisco—not to mention great views of Alcatraz and the Bay—via open-air public transit (page 42).

★ **Ferry Building:** The 1898 Ferry Building has been renovated and reimagined as the foodie mecca of San Francisco. The Tuesday and Saturday farmers market is not to be missed (page 42).

★ **San Francisco Museum of Modern Art:** SFMOMA showcases some of modern art's greatest hits and features the largest space dedicated to photographic art in the country (page 43).

★ **Exploratorium:** The exhibits at this innovative and interactive science museum are meant to be touched, heard, and felt (page 48).

★ **Alcatraz:** Spend the day in prison—at the famous former maximum-security penitentiary in the middle of the Bay (page 48).

★ **The Presidio:** The original 1776 El Presidio de San Francisco is now a national park. Tour the historic buildings that formerly housed a military hospital, barracks, and fort—all amid a peaceful and verdant setting (page 54).

★ **Golden Gate Bridge:** Nothing beats the view from one of the most famous and fascinating bridges in the country. Pick a fogless day for a stroll or bike ride across the 1.7-mile span (page 54).

★ **de Young Museum:** The de Young is the showpiece of Golden Gate Park. A mixed collection of media and regions is highlighted by the 360-degree view from the museum's tower (page 58).

★ **Angel Island State Park:** While it once served as a way station for immigrants, today this island offers hiking trails and amazing views of the city, Alcatraz, and the Golden Gate Bridge (page 100).

★ **Point Reyes National Seashore:** At the tip of the Marin coast are acres of hiking, biking, and bird-watching (page 109).

San Francisco and the Bay Area

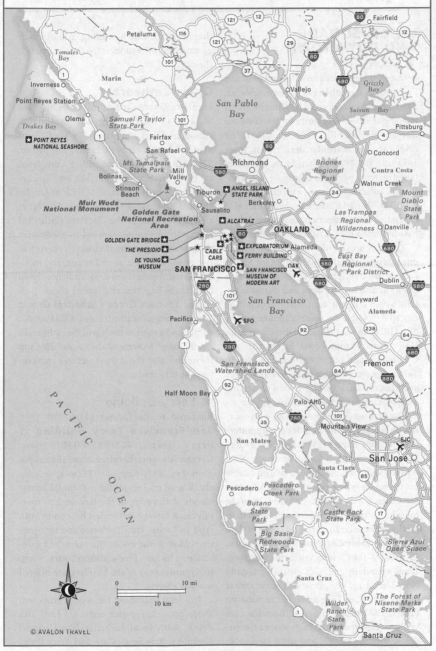

© AVALON TRAVEL

Sights

UNION SQUARE AND DOWNTOWN

★ Cable Cars

Perhaps the most recognizable symbol of San Francisco is the **cable car** (www.sfcablecar.com), originally conceived by Andrew Smith Hallidie as a safer alternative for traveling the steep, often slick hills of San Francisco. The cable cars ran as regular mass transit from 1873 into the 1940s, when buses and electric streetcars began to dominate the landscape. Dedicated citizens, especially "Cable Car Lady" Friedel Klussmann, saved the cable car system from extinction, and the cable cars have become a rolling national landmark.

Today you can ride the cable cars from one tourist destination to another for $5 per ride. A full day "passport" ticket ($13, also grants access to streetcars and buses) is totally worth it if you want to run around the city all day. Cable car routes can take you up Nob Hill from the Financial District, or from Union Square along Powell Street, through Chinatown, and out to Fisherman's Wharf. Take a seat, or grab one of the exterior poles and hang on! Cable cars have open-air seating only, making for a chilly ride on foggy days.

The cars get stuffed to capacity with tourists on weekends and with local commuters at rush hours. Expect to wait an hour or more for a ride from any of the turnaround points on a weekend or holiday. But a ride on a cable car from Union Square down to the Wharf is more than worth the wait. The views from the hills down to the bay inspire wonder even in lifetime residents. To learn a bit more, make a stop at the **Cable Car Museum** (1201 Mason St., 415/474-1887, www.cablecarmuseum.org, 10am-6pm daily Apr.-Oct., 10am-5pm daily Nov.-Mar., free), the home and nerve center of the entire fleet. Here a sweet little museum depicts the life and times of the cable cars while an elevated platform overlooks the engines, winding wheels, and thick steel cable that keeps the cars humming. You can even glimpse the 1873 tunnels that snake beneath the city.

Grace Cathedral

Local icon **Grace Cathedral** (1100 California St., 415/749-6300, www.gracecathedral.org, 7am-6pm Thurs., 8am-6pm Fri.-Wed., 8am-4pm holidays) is many things to many people. The French Gothic-style edifice, completed in 1964, attracts architecture and Beaux-Arts lovers by the thousands with its facade, stained glass, and furnishings. The labyrinths—replicas of the Chartres Cathedral labyrinth in France—appeal to meditative walkers seeking spiritual solace. Concerts featuring world music, sacred music, and modern classical ensembles draw audiences from around the Bay Area and farther afield.

The 1.5-hour **Grace Cathedral Grand Tour** (www.gracecathedral.org, $25) includes a walk up 94 steps to the top of the cathedral's South Tower. Download the GraceGuide app for information about the structure's architecture, history, and art.

★ Ferry Building

Restored to its former glory, the 1898 **San Francisco Ferry Building** (1 Ferry Bldg., 415/983-8030, www.ferrybuildingmarketplace.com, 10am-7pm Mon.-Fri., 8am-6pm Sat., 11am-5pm Sun., check with businesses for individual hours) stands at the edge of the Bay, its 230-foot-tall clock tower serving as a beacon to both land and water traffic. Photos and interpretive plaques just inside the main lobby describe its history. Free **walking tours** (www.sfcityguides.org) of the building are offered one day a week.

Inside, it's all about the food. Permanent shops provide top-tier artisanal food and drink, with local favorites like Cowgirl Creamery, Blue Bottle Café, and Acme Bread

Company, while a few quick-and-easy restaurants offer reasonable meals. The famous **Farmers Market** (415/291-3276, www.cuesa.org/markets, 10am-2pm Tues. and Thurs., 8am-2pm Sat.) draws crowds shopping for produce out front.

On the water side of the Ferry Building, boats come and go from Sausalito, Tiburon, Larkspur, Vallejo, and Alameda each day. Check with the **Blue & Gold Fleet** (www.blueandgoldfleet.com), **Golden Gate Ferry** (www.goldengateferry.org), and **San Francisco Bay Ferry** (http://sanfranciscobayferry.com) for information about service, times, and fares.

★ San Francisco Museum of Modern Art

After a massive three-year renovation, the **San Francisco Museum of Modern Art** (SFMOMA, 151 3rd St., 415/357-4000, www.sfmoma.org, 10am-5pm Sun.-Tues. and Fri., 10am-9pm Thurs., 10am-8pm Sat. summer, 10am-9pm Thurs., 10am-5pm Fri.-Tues., winter, adults $25, seniors $22, youth 19-24 $22, children under 18 free) reopened in 2016 with three times as much gallery space. Modern classics on display include major works by Roy Lichtenstein, Georgia O'Keefe, Jackson Pollock, and Andy Warhol. The 3rd-floor Pritzker Center for Photography is the largest space dedicated to photographic art in the country. Enjoy views of the building's stunning design by walking across the 5th floor's Oculus Bridge, or get a breath of fresh air on the 3rd-floor sculpture terrace.

Contemporary Jewish Museum

The local favorite **Contemporary Jewish Museum** (736 Mission St., 415/655-7800, www.thecjm.org, 11am-5pm Fri.-Tues., 11am-8pm Thurs., adults $14, seniors and students $12, children 18 and under free) curates superb temporary exhibits on pop culture. Recent subjects include filmmaker Stanley Kubrick, Bay Area music promoter Bill Graham, and singer Amy Winehouse. The museum's sleek building is part historic power station and part blue steel structure that spells out the Hebrew word *chai*, meaning life.

CHINATOWN

The massive Chinese migration to California began almost as soon as the news of easy gold in the mountain streams made it to East Asia. And despite rampant prejudice, the Chinese not only stayed, but persevered and eventually prospered. Many never made it to the gold fields, preferring instead to remain in bustling San Francisco to open shops and begin the business of commerce in their new home. They carved out a thriving community at the border of **Portsmouth Square,** then center of the young city, which became known as Chinatown. Along with much of San Francisco, the neighborhood was destroyed in the 1906 earthquake and fire.

Today visitors see the post-1906 visitor-friendly Chinatown that was built after the quake, particularly if they enter through the **Chinatown Gate** (Grant Ave. and Bush St.) at the edge of Union Square. In this historic neighborhood, beautiful Asian architecture mixes with more mundane blocky city buildings to create a unique skyline. Small alleyways wend between the touristy commercial corridors, creating an intimate atmosphere.

NORTH BEACH AND FISHERMAN'S WHARF

North Beach has long served as the Little Italy of San Francisco, a fact still reflected in the restaurants in the neighborhood. North Beach truly made its mark in the 1950s when it was, for a brief time, home to many writers in the Beat Generation, including Jack Kerouac, Gary Snyder, and Allen Ginsburg.

Coit Tower

Built in 1933 as a monument to benefactor Lillie Hitchcock Coit's beloved firefighters, **Coit Tower** (1 Telegraph Hill Blvd., 415/249-0995, http://sfrecpark.org, 10am-6pm daily May-Oct., 10am-5pm daily Nov.-Apr., entrance free) has beautified the city just as Coit

San Francisco

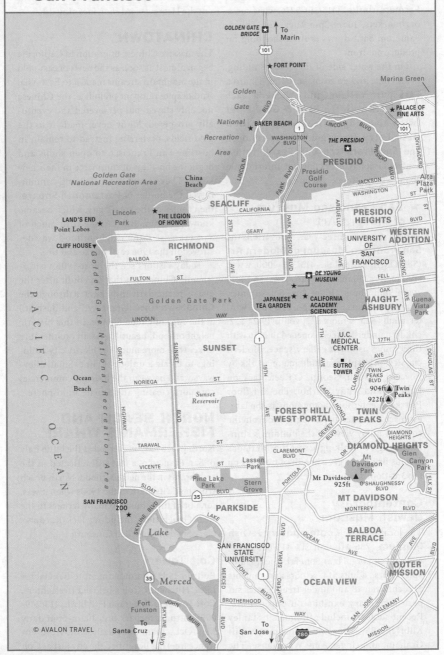

© AVALON TRAVEL

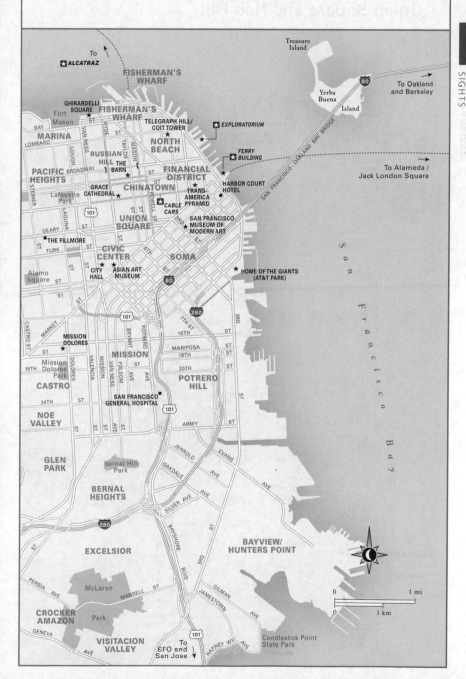

To
★ ALCATRAZ

FISHERMAN'S
WHARF

Treasure
Island

To Oakland
and Berkeley

Yerba
Buena
Island

GHIRARDELLI
SQUARE

FISHERMAN'S
WHARF

Fort
Mason

BAY

LOMBARD

MARINA

TELEGRAPH HILL/
COIT TOWER

★ EXPLORATORIUM

PACIFIC
HEIGHTS

RUSSIAN
HILL

NORTH
BEACH

THE
BARN

BROADWAY

FINANCIAL
DISTRICT

FERRY
BUILDING

To Alameda /
Jack London Square

GRACE
CATHEDRAL

CHINATOWN

TRANS-
AMERICA
PYRAMID

HARBOR COURT
HOTEL

Lafayette
Park

CABLE
CARS

SAN FRANCISCO
MUSEUM OF
MODERN ART

UNION
SQUARE

THE FILLMORE

GEARY

TURK

CIVIC
CENTER

SOMA

Alamo
Square

CITY
HALL

ASIAN ART
MUSEUM

HOME OF THE GIANTS
(AT&T PARK)

S a n

F r a n c i s c o

B a y

MISSION
DOLORES

7TH ST

16TH

ST

Mission
Dolores
Park

19TH

MISSION

MARIPOSA

18TH

ST

CASTRO

24TH

20TH

POTRERO
HILL

SAN FRANCISCO
GENERAL HOSPITAL

NOE
VALLEY

ARMY

GLEN
PARK

Bernal Hill
Park

JERROLD

EVANS

OAKDALE

AVE

BERNAL
HEIGHTS

SILVER AVE

AVE

BAYSHORE

3RD

BAYVIEW/
HUNTERS POINT

EXCELSIOR

PERSIA AVE

McLaren

MANSELL ST

GILMAN

JAMESTOWN

AVE

0   1 mi

0   1 km

CROCKER
AMAZON

Park

GENEVA

VISITACION
VALLEY

AVE

To
SFO and
San Jose

Candlestick Point
State Park

Union Square and Nob Hill

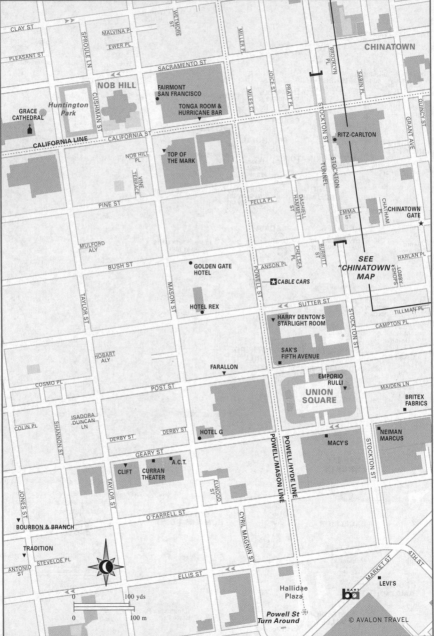

CLAY ST
MALVINA PL
WETMORE ST
EWER PL
PLEASANT ST
SPROULE LN
SACRAMENTO ST
MILLER PL
BROCKYN PL
CHINATOWN
SABIN PL
NOB HILL
FAIRMONT SAN FRANCISCO
JOICE ST
PRATT PL
QUINCY ST
GRACE CATHEDRAL
Huntington Park
CUSHMAN ST
TONGA ROOM & HURRICANE BAR
MILES CT
STOCKTON ST
RITZ-CARLTON
GRANT AVE
CALIFORNIA LINE
CALIFORNIA ST
NOB HILL PL
TOP OF THE MARK
STOCKTON
TUNNEL
VINE TERRACE
PINE ST
FELLA PL
DASHIELL HAMMETT ST
EMMA ST
CHATHAM PL
CHINATOWN GATE
MULFORD ALY
BUSH ST
TAYLOR ST
MASON ST
GOLDEN GATE HOTEL
POWELL ST
CHELSEA PL
ANSON PL
BURRITT ST
HARLAN PL
SEE "CHINATOWN" MAP
LOBBY SHOPS
HOTEL REX
CABLE CARS
SUTTER ST
STOCKTON ST
TILLMAN PL
HARRY DENTON'S STARLIGHT ROOM
CAMPTON PL
HOBART ALY
SAK'S FIFTH AVENUE
FARALLON
EMPORIO RULLI
COSMO PL
POST ST
UNION SQUARE
MAIDEN LN
BRITEX FABRICS
COLIN PL
SHANNON ST
ISADORA DUNCAN LN
DERBY ST
DERBY ST
HOTEL G
MACY'S
STOCKTON ST
NEIMAN MARCUS
GEARY ST
CLIFT
CURRAN THEATER
A.C.T.
TAYLOR ST
POWELL/HYDE LINE
POWELL/MASON LINE
JONES ST
O'FARRELL ST
ELWOOD ST
BOURBON & BRANCH
TRADITION
STEVELOE PL
CYRIL MAGNIN ST
ELLIS ST
MARKET ST
LEVI'S
4TH ST
ANTONIO ST
0   100 yds
0   100 m
Hallidae Plaza
ba
BART
Powell St Turn Around
© AVALON TRAVEL

Financial District and SoMa

intended. Inside the art deco tower, the walls are covered in the restored frescos painted in 1934 depicting city and California life during the Great Depression. For a fee (adults $8, seniors and youth $5, children 5-11 $2, children under 5 free), you can ride the elevator to the top, where on a clear day, you can see the whole city and bay. Part of what makes Coit Tower special is the walk up to it. Rather than contributing to the acute congestion in the area, consider taking public transit to the area and walking up Telegraph Hill Boulevard through Pioneer Park to the tower, and descend down either the Filbert or Greenwich steps toward the Embarcadero. It's long and steep, but there's no other way to see the lovely little cottages and gardens of the beautiful and quaint Telegraph Hill.

Lombard Street

You've no doubt seen it in movies: **Lombard Street** (Lombard St., one way from Hyde St. to Leavenworth St.), otherwise known as "the crookedest street in the world." The section of the street that visitors flock to spans only one block, from Hyde Street at the top to Leavenworth Street at the bottom. However, the line of cars waiting their turn to drive

Chinatown

DELICIOUS
DIM SUM

BECKETT ST

JACKSON AVE

GREAT
EASTERN

ROSS ALLEY

GRANT AVE

WENTWORTH PL

KEARNY AVE

WASHINGTON AVE

★
BANK OF
CANTON

WALTER U LUM PL

Portsmouth
Square Plaza

SPOFFORD ST

WAVERLY PL

CLAY AVE

R&G LOUNGE ▼

BANK OF AMERICA
BUILDING
★

SACRAMENTO AVE

SING CHONG
BUILDING
★

CALIFORNIA AVE

QUINCY ST

St. Mary's
Square

PINE AVE

GRANT AVE

KEARNY AVE

CHINATOWN GATE
★
BUSH AVE

RICKHOUSE ▼

CAFÉ ▼
CLAUDE

CLAUDE LN

0   50 yds

0   50 m

© AVALON TRAVEL

bumper-to-bumper can be just as legendary as its 27 percent grade. Bypass the car and take the hill by foot. The unobstructed vistas of San Francisco Bay, Alcatraz Island, Fisherman's Wharf, Coit Tower, and the city are reason enough to add this walk to your itinerary, as are the brick steps, manicured hydrangeas, and tony residences that line the roadway. To avoid traffic jams, drive the road in the early morning or at night during the summer.

★ Exploratorium

Lauded both as "one of the world's most important science museums" and "a mad scientist's penny arcade," the **Exploratorium** (Pier 15, 415/528-4444, www.exploratorium.edu, 10am-5pm Tues.-Sun. and Fri.-Sun., 10am-6pm Thurs. only, $30 adults, $25 seniors and youth 13-17, $20 children 4-12, children under 4 free) houses 150 playful exhibits on physics, motion, perception, and the senses that utilize its stunning location. Make a reservation ($15) to walk blindly (and bravely) into the Tactile Dome, a lightless space where you can "see" your way only by reaching out and touching the environment around you. Exploratorium "After Dark" targets adults 18 and over (6pm-10pm Thurs., $15). Its location between the Ferry Building and Fisherman's Wharf makes a crowd-free trip impossible, especially on the weekends.

★ Alcatraz

Going to **Alcatraz** (www.nps.gov/alcatraz), one of the most famous landmarks in the city, feels a bit like going to purgatory; this military fortress-turned-maximum-security prison, nicknamed "The Rock," has little warmth or welcome on its craggy, forbidding shores. While it still belonged to the military, the fortress became a prison in the 19th century to house Civil War prisoners. The isolation of the island in the bay, the frigid waters, and the nasty currents surrounding Alcatraz made it a perfect spot to keep prisoners contained, with little hope of escape and near-certain death if the attempt were ever made.

Two Days in San Francisco

San Francisco may only be roughly seven miles long and seven miles wide, but it packs in historic neighborhoods, one of the West Coast's most iconic landmarks, and dozens of stomach-dropping inclines within its small area. Exploring all its hills and valleys takes some planning.

DAY 1

Start your day at the **Ferry Building.** Graze from the many vendors, including **Blue Bottle Café, Cowgirl Creamery,** and **Acme Bread Company,** then walk two blocks to **Yank Sing** for a dim sum lunch. Catch the Muni F line (Steuart St. and Market St., $2) to Jefferson Street and take a stroll along **Fisherman's Wharf.** Stop into the **Musée Mécanique** to play a few coin-operated antique arcade games. Near Pier 39, catch the ferry to **Alcatraz**—be sure to buy your tickets well in advance. Alcatraz will fill your mind with amazing stories from the legendary island prison.

Alcatraz

After you escape from Alcatraz, take the N Judah line ($2) to 9th Avenue and Irving Street, then follow 9th Avenue north into **Golden Gate Park,** where you can delve into art at the fabulous **de Young Museum** or science at the **California Academy of Sciences.** Stroll the scenic **Japanese Tea Gardens** and get a snack at the Tea House.

Catch a cab to North Beach and **Tony's Pizza Napoletana** to get some real sustenance directly from one of its seven pizza ovens. Now you are ready to enjoy the talented performers, silly jokes, and gravity-defying hats of the long-running theater production *Beach Blanket Babylon.* If theater is not your thing, see some live music at the **Great American Music Hall**.

DAY 2

Fortify yourself for a day of sightseeing with a hearty breakfast at **Brenda's French Soul Food,** then drive or take a cab out to the **Land's End Trail,** where you can investigate the ruins of the former Sutro Baths and get views of the city's rocky coastline. Then head back to **Crissy Field** for views of the **Golden Gate Bridge.**

Walk to the adjacent Marina District for oysters at **Swan Oyster Depot** or sushi at **Ace Wasabi's.** Venture back downtown to wander the streets of **Chinatown** and adjacent **North Beach.** Browse through **City Lights,** the legendary Beat Generation bookstore. Wind down with a cocktail at **Vesuvio,** a colorful bar and former Beat writer hangout located next door.

Head to the bustling Mission District, stopping first for a drink at the rooftop bar **El Techo de Lolinda** or **Trick Dog.** Then enjoy dinner at **Tartine Manufactory** or **ICHI Sushi.**

In 1934, after the military closed down its prison and handed the island over to the Department of Justice, construction began to turn Alcatraz into a new style of prison ready to house a new style of prisoner: Depression-era gangsters. A few of the honored guests of this maximum-security penitentiary were Al Capone, George "Machine Gun" Kelly, and Robert Stroud, "the Birdman of Alcatraz." The prison closed in 1963, and in 1964 and 1969 occupations were staged by Indians of All Tribes, an exercise that eventually led to

North Beach and Fisherman's Wharf

© AVALON TRAVEL

RUSSIAN HILL

GHIRARDELLI SQUARE ★
GARY DANKO ★

SAN FRANCISCO MARITIME HISTORICAL PARK
Aquatic Park

THE ARGONAUT
CABLE CAR ✚

FISHERMAN'S WHARF ★
FISHERMAN'S WHARF ★

BISTRO BOUDIN ▼
MADAME TUSSAUDS ★
JEFFERSON ST
MUSÉE MÉCANIQUE ★

LOMBARD STREET ★
LURMONT TERR
Michelangelo Playground
Fay Park

CABLE CAR ✚

COBB'S COMEDY CLUB ▼

SAN REMO HOTEL ●

NORTH BEACH

Coolbrith Park

North Beach Playground

BOUDIN BAKERY & CAFE ▼
PIER 39 ★
AQUARIUM OF THE BAY ★

TRATTORIA CONTADINA ▼
L'OSTERIA DEL FORNO ▼
BEACH BLANKET BABYLON ▼
Washington Square

MAMA'S ON WASHINGTON SQUARE ▼
WASHINGTON SQUARE INN ●

HOTEL BOHÈME ●
CAFFE TRIESTE ▼
TONY'S PIZZA NAPOLETANA/
TONY'S COAL-FIRED PIZZA AND SLICE HOUSE ▼

CITY LIGHTS BOOKSTORE ●
15 ROMOLO ▼
THE BEAT MUSEUM ★
SPEC'S ▼
VESUVIO ▼
TOSCA CAFE ▼

COIT TOWER ★
Pioneer Park
Chestnut/Kearny Park

TELEGRAPH HILL

To
✚ ALCATRAZ
Vallejo, Alameda,
Oakland, Sausalito,
Tiburon, and ✚ ANGEL ISLAND

THE EMBARCADERO

the privilege of self-determination for North America's original inhabitants.

Visit the island on tours offered by **Alcatraz Cruises** (Pier 33, 415/981-7625, www.alcatrazcruises.com, adults $37 and up, seniors $35 and up, children $24 and up, check website for times and prices), departing from Pier 33. Options include the **Day Tour, Night Tour, Behind the Scenes Tour,** and the **Alcatraz and Angel Island Tour.** Tours typically sell out, especially on weekends, so reserve tickets at least two weeks in advance.

Fisherman's Wharf

Welcome to **Fisherman's Wharf** (Beach St. from Powell St. to Van Ness Ave., backs onto Bay St., www.fishermanswharf.org), the tourist mecca of San Francisco! While warehouses, stacks of crab pots, and a fleet of fishing vessels let you know this is still a working wharf, it is also where visitors come and snap photos. Reachable by the Muni F line and the Hyde-Powell cable car, the Wharf sprawls along the waterfront and inland several blocks.

Be prepared to push through a sea of humanity to buy souvenirs, eat seafood, and enjoy fun pieces of San Francisco's heritage, like the **Musée Mécanique** (Pier 45, Fishermen's Wharf, 415/346-2000, www.

museemechaniquesf.com, 10am-8pm daily, free), a strange collection of over 300 working coin-operated machines from the 1800s to today. Machines include a 3-D picture show of San Francisco after the catastrophic 1906 earthquake and fire, along with more modern favorites like Ms. Pac-Man.

Ghirardelli Square

Ghirardelli Square (900 North Point St., www.ghirardellisq.com, winter 10am-6pm Sun.-Thurs., 10am-9pm Fri.-Sat.), pronounced "GEAR-ah-DEL-ee," began its life as a chocolate factory in 1852, but has since reinvented itself as an upscale shopping, dining, and living compound. The **Ghirardelli Chocolate Manufactory** (900 North Point St., 415/474-3938, www. ghirardellisq.com, 9am-11pm Sun.-Thurs., 9am-midnight Fri.-Sat.) anchors the corner of the square. Here you can browse the rambling shop and pick up truffles, wafers, candies, and sauces for all your friends back home. Finally, get in line at the ice cream counter to order a hot fudge sundae. Once you've finished gorging on chocolate, wander out into the square to enjoy more shopping and an unbelievably swank condo complex overlooking the bay.

Exploratorium

San Francisco Maritime National Historical Park

The real gem of the Wharf is the **San Francisco Maritime National Historical Park** (415/561-7000, www.nps.gov/safr), which spreads from the base of Van Ness to Pier 45. At the **visitors center** (499 Jefferson St., 415/447-5000, 9:30am-5pm daily), not only will rangers help you make the most of your visit, but you can also get lost in the labyrinthine museum that houses an immense Fresnel lighthouse lens and engaging displays that recount San Francisco's history. For $5 you can climb aboard the historic ships at permanent dock across the street at the **Hyde Street Pier.** The shiniest jewel of the collection is the 1886 square-rigged *Balclutha*, a three-masted schooner that recalls times gone by, complete with excellent historical exhibits below deck. There are also several steamboats, including the workhorse ferry paddle wheeler *Eureka* and a cool old steam tugboat called the *Eppleton Hall.* Farther down, at Pier 45, World War II buffs can feel the claustrophobia of the submarine **USS *Pampanito*** (415/775-1943, www.maritime.org, 9am-close daily, adults $20, seniors $12, children 6-12 $10, children under 6 free) or the expansiveness of the Liberty ship **SS *Jeremiah O'Brien*** (415/544-0100, www.ssjeremiahobrien.org, 9am-4pm daily, adults $20, seniors and children 5-16 $10, children under 5 free).

The 1939 art deco **Aquatic Bathhouse Building** (900 Beach St., 415/561-7100, www.nps.gov/safr, 10am-4pm daily, adults $5, children free), built in 1939, houses the Maritime Museum, where you can see a number of rotating exhibits alongside its brilliant WPA murals.

MARINA AND PACIFIC HEIGHTS

The Marina and Pacific Heights are wealthy neighborhoods, with a couple of yacht harbors, plenty of open space, great dining, and shopping that only gets better as you go up the hill.

Palace of Fine Arts

The **Palace of Fine Arts** (3301 Lyon St.) was originally meant to be nothing but a temporary structure—part of the Panama-Pacific International Exposition in 1915. But the lovely building designed by Bernard Maybeck won the hearts of San Franciscans, and a fund was started to preserve the palace beyond the exposition. Through the first half of the 20th century, efforts could not

Alcatraz

Marina and Pacific Heights

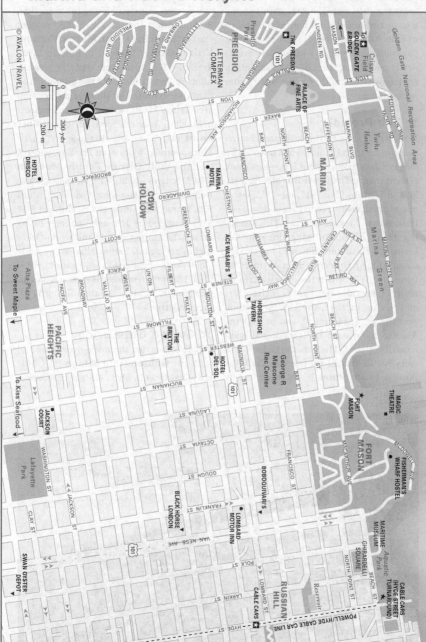

keep it from crumbling, but in the 1960s and 1970s, serious rebuilding work took place, and today the Palace of Fine Arts stands proud, strong, and beautiful. It houses the **Palace of Fine Arts Theatre** (415/563-6504, www. palaceoffinearts.org), which hosts events nearly every day, from beauty pageants to conferences to children's musical theater performances.

★ The Presidio

It seems strange to think of progressive, peace-loving San Francisco as a town with a long military history, yet it is nowhere more evident than at **The Presidio** (Montgomery St. and Lincoln Blvd., 415/561-4323, www. nps.gov/prsf, visitors center 10am-5pm daily, trails dawn-dusk daily, free). This sweeping stretch of land running along the San Francisco Headlands down to the Golden Gate Bridge has been a military installation since 1776, when the Spanish created their El Presidio del San Francisco fort on the site. In 1846, the U.S. Army took over the site (peacefully), and in 1848 the American Presidio military installation formally opened. The Presidio had a role in every Pacific-related war from the Civil War through Desert Storm. It was abandoned by the military and became a national park in 1994.

To orient yourself among the more than 800 buildings that make up the Presidio, start at the **William Penn Mott Jr. Presidio Visitor Center** (Bldg. 210, Lincoln Blvd., 415/561-4323, 10am-5pm daily), where exhibits include a model of the grounds. You can also explore the pioneering aviation area **Crissy Field** (www.parksconservancy. org), Civil War-era fortifications at **Fort Point** (415/556-1693, 10am-5pm Thurs.-Mon. summer, 10am-5pm Fri.-Sun. winter), and the **Walt Disney Family Museum** (104 Montgomery St., 415/345-6800, www. waltdisney.org, 10am-6pm Wed.-Mon., adults $30, seniors and students $25, children 6-17 $20), founded by Disney's daughter to examine the animator's life and work. Other highlights include art installations by Andy Goldsworthy, who works with natural materials. The most renowned is *Spire*, a sculpture that rises 90 feet into the air, utilizing 35 cypress tree trunks.

★ Golden Gate Bridge

People come from the world over to see and walk the **Golden Gate Bridge** (U.S. 101/ Hwy. 1 at Lincoln Blvd., 415/921-5858, www.

Golden Gate Bridge

goldengatebridge.com, southbound cars $7.75, pedestrians free). A marvel of human engineering constructed in 1936 and 1937, the suspension bridge spans the narrow "gate" from which the Pacific Ocean enters the San Francisco Bay. Pedestrians are allowed on the **east sidewalk** (5am-9pm daily mid-Mar.-Oct., 5am-6:30pm daily Nov.-mid-Mar.). On a clear day, the whole bay, Marin Headlands, and city skyline are visible. Cyclists are allowed on both sidewalks (check the website for times), but as the scenery is stunning, be aware of pedestrians and cyclists not keeping their eyes on where they are going.

The Golden Gate National Parks Conservancy has quit offering its Golden Gate Bridge Tours, but the nonprofit **City Guides** (415/557-4266, www.sfcityguides.org) leads bridge walks twice a week. Check the website for days and times.

CIVIC CENTER AND HAYES VALLEY

The Civic Center functions as the heart of San Francisco. Not only is the seat of government here, but so are venerable high-culture institutions: the War Memorial Opera House and Davies Symphony Hall, home of the world-famous San Francisco Symphony. As the Civic Center melts into Hayes Valley, you'll find fabulous hotels and restaurants serving both the city's politicos and the well-heeled.

City Hall

Look at San Francisco's **City Hall** (1 Dr. Carlton B. Goodlett Pl., 415/554-6079, www.sfgov.org, 8am-8pm Mon.-Fri., free) and you'll think you've somehow been transported to Europe. The stately Beaux-Arts building with the gilded dome is the pride of the city and houses the mayor's office and much of the city's government. Enjoy walking through the parklike square in front of City Hall (though this area can get a bit sketchy after dark). Inside you'll find a combination of historical grandeur and modern accessibility and convenience as you tour the Arthur Brown Jr.-designed edifice.

Asian Art Museum

Across from City Hall is the **Asian Art Museum** (200 Larkin St., 415/581-3500, www.asianart.org, 10am-5pm Sat.-Tues. and Thurs., 5pm-9pm Fri. summer, 10am-5pm Tues.-Wed. and Fri.-Sun., 5pm-9pm Thurs. winter, adults $15, seniors and children 13-17 $10, children under 12 free), with enormous Ionic columns. Inside you'll have an amazing window into the Asian cultures that have shaped and defined San Francisco and the Bay Area. The 2nd and 3rd floors of this intense museum are packed with great art from all across Asia, including a Chinese gilded Buddha dating from AD 338. The breadth and diversity of Asian culture may stagger you; the museum's displays come from Japan and Vietnam, Buddhist Tibet, and ancient China. Special exhibitions cost extra—check the website to see what will be displayed on the ground-floor galleries when you're in town. The curators regularly rotate items from the permanent collection, so you'll probably encounter new beauty every time you visit.

Alamo Square

At this area's far western edge sits **Alamo Square** (Hayes St. and Steiner St.), possibly the most photographed neighborhood in San Francisco. Among its stately Victorians are the famous **"painted ladies,"** a row of brilliantly painted and immaculately maintained homes. From the adjacent Alamo Square Park, the ladies provide a picturesque foreground for views of the Civic Center and downtown.

MISSION AND CASTRO

Castro is the heart of gay San Francisco, complete with nightlife, festivals, and LGBT community activism. With its mix of Latino immigrants, working artists, and hipsters, the Mission is a neighborhood bursting at the seams with idiosyncratic energy. Changing from block to block, the zone manages to be blue-collar, edgy, and gentrified all at once. While the heart of the neighborhood is still Latin American, with delicious burritos and *pupusas* around every corner, it is also the

Civic Center, Hayes Valley, Mission, and Castro

RANDALL MUSEUM

MUSEUM WY

FLINT ST

STATES ST

BEAVER ST

LA MEDITERRANEE

INN ON CASTRO

15TH ST

DOUGLASS ST

21ST ST

EUREKA ST

DIAMOND ST

COLLINGWOOD ST

CASTRO

CASTRO ST

CASTRO THEATRE

ANCHOR OYSTER BAR

HARTFORD ST

FRANCES

POND ST

PROSPER ST

MARKET ST

NOE ST

DINOSAURS

© AVALON TRAVEL

300 yds

300 m

NOE VALLEY

JERSEY ST

24TH ST

ELIZABETH ST

23RD ST

ALVARADO ST

22ND ST

HILL ST

21ST ST

SANCHEZ ST

CUMBERLAND

19TH ST

HANCOCK ST

18TH ST

DORLAND ST

17TH ST

CHULA LN

MISSION DOLORES

CHURCH ST

LANDERS ST

DOLORES ST

16TH ST

NELLIE ST

VICKSBURG ST

LIBERTY ST

20TH ST

ST

CHURCH ST

Dolores Park

NAMU GAJI

BI-RITE CREAMERY & BAKESHOP

GUERRERO ST

CHATTANOOGA ST

QUANE ST

CUMBERLAND

OAKWOOD

TARTINE BAKERY

DELFINA

DEARBORN

ALBION ST

FAIR OAKS ST

AMES ST

826 VALENCIA

LINDA ST

LAPIDGE ST

PAYTON GATE

LITTLE STAR PIZZA

PAPALOTE MEXICAN GRILL

SAN JOSE AVE

DEMA

RANGE

VALENCIA ST

SYCAMORE ST

CLARION ALY

BAR TARTINE

POPLAR ST

LOLINDA

LEXINGTON ST

HOFF ST

WIESE ST

ORANGE ALY

BERETTA

BARTLETT ST

SAN CARLOS ST

16th St

OSAGE ALY

MISSION ST

24th St

LILAC ST

CAPP ST

THEATRE RHINOCEROS

CYPRESS ST

SOUTH VAN NESS AVE

MISSION

25TH ST

SHOTWELL ST

LUCKY ST

FOLSOM ST

TREAT AVE

TREAT AVE

HARRISON ST

FAROLITO TAQUERIA

TRICK DOG

ALABAMA ST

18TH ST

MARIPOSA ST

17TH ST

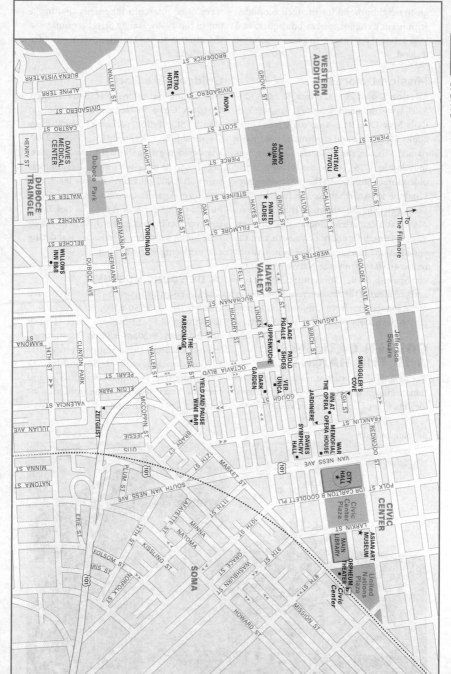

WESTERN ADDITION

METRO HOTEL

BRODERICK ST
WALLER ST
ALPINE TERR
DIVISADERO ST
BUENA VISTA TERR

NOPA

DIVISADERO ST

GROVE ST

CASTRO ST

SCOTT ST

HENRY ST

DAVIES MEDICAL CENTER

Duboce Park

HAIGHT ST

ALAMO SQUARE

PIERCE ST

CHATEAU TIVOLI

PIERCE ST

TURK ST

DUBOCE TRAINGLE

WALTER ST

SANCHEZ ST

BELCHER ST

WILLOWS INN B&B

HERMANN ST

GERMANIA ST

DUBOCE AVE

STEINER ST

PAGE ST

OAK ST

PAINTED LADIES

GROVE ST

FULTON ST

MCALLISTER ST

To The Fillmore

HAYES ST

FILLMORE ST

TORONADO

WEBSTER ST

HAYES VALLEY

GOLDEN GATE AVE

FELL ST

HICKORY ST

LILY ST

IVY ST

BUCHANAN ST

LINDEN ST

SUPPENKUCHE

THE ROSE

THE PARSONAGE

WALLER ST

OCTAVIA BLVD

PLACE PIGALLE

PAOLO SHOES

DARK GARDEN

VER UNICA

BIRCH ST

LAGUNA ST

Jefferson Square

SMUGGLER'S COVE

RAMONA ST

14TH ST

CLINTON PARK

PEARL ST

MCCOPPIN ST

YIELD AND PAUSE WINE BAR

GOUGH ST

ASH ST

THE OPERA

INN AT THE OPERA

JARDINIERE

FRANKLIN ST

REDWOOD ST

MEMORIAL OPERA HOUSE

ELGIN PARK

VALENCIA ST

JULIAN AVE

ZEITGEIST

JESSIE ST

OTIS ST

BRADY ST

12TH ST

MARKET ST

DAVIES SYMPHONY HALL

WAR MEMORIAL

VAN NESS AVE

101

MINNA ST

NATOMA ST

SOUTH VAN NESS AVE

LAFAYETTE ST

PLUM ST

11TH ST

10TH ST

POLK ST

DR CARLTON B GOODLETT PL

CITY HALL

Civic Center Plaza

CIVIC CENTER

ERIE ST

101

FOLSOM ST

IRIS ST

KISSLING ST

12TH ST

MINNA

NATOMA

NORFOLK ST

SOMA

GRACE ST

WASHBURN ST

9TH ST

MISSION ST

HOWARD ST

LARKIN ST

MAIN LIBRARY

ASIAN ART MUSEUM

ORPHEUM THEATER

United Nations Plaza

To Civic Center

8TH ST

go-to neighborhood for the tech economy, with luxury condos, pricey boutiques, and international restaurants in a city famous for its food.

Mission Dolores

Mission Dolores (3321 16th St., 415/621-8203, www.missiondolores.org, 9am-4:30pm daily May-Oct., 9am-4pm daily Nov.-Apr., adults $7, seniors and students $5), formally named Mission San Francisco de Asís, was founded in 1776. Today the mission is the oldest intact building in the city, having survived the 1906 earthquake and fire, the 1989 Loma Prieta quake, and more than 200 years of use. You can attend Roman Catholic services here each Saturday, or you can visit the Old Mission Museum and the Basilica, which house artifacts from the Native Americans and Spanish of the 18th century. The beauty and grandeur of the mission recall the heyday of the Spanish empire in California, as important to the history of the state as it is today.

GOLDEN GATE PARK AND THE HAIGHT

The neighborhood surrounding the intersection of Haight and Ashbury Streets (known locally as "the Haight") is best known for the wave of countercultural energy that broke out in the 1960s. Haight Street terminates at the entrance to San Francisco's gem—Golden Gate Park.

Golden Gate Park

Dominating the western half of San Francisco, **Golden Gate Park** (main entrance at Stanyan St. at Fell St., McLaren Lodge Visitors Center at John F. Kennedy Dr., 415/831-2700, www.golden-gate-park.com, http://sfrecpark. org) is one of the city's most enduring treasures. Its 1,000-plus acres include lakes, forests, formal gardens, windmills, museums, a buffalo pasture, and plenty of activities. Enjoy free concerts in the summer, hike in near solitude in the winter, or spend a day wandering and exploring scores of sights.

★ DE YOUNG MUSEUM

The **de Young Museum** (50 Hagiwara Tea Garden Dr., 415/750-3600, http://deyoung. famsf.org, 9:30am-5:15pm Tues.-Thurs. and Sat.-Sun., 9:30am-8:30pm Fri. summer, 9:30am-5:15pm Tues.-Sun. winter, adults $15, seniors $10, students $6, children 17 and under free) is staggering in its size and breadth: You'll see everything from pre-Columbian art to 17th-century ladies' gowns.

de Young Museum

Japanese Tea Garden

children 4-11 $26) drips with ecological perfection. From the grass-covered roof to the underground **aquarium**, visitors can explore every part of the universe. Wander through a steamy endangered **rainforest** contained inside a giant glass bubble, or travel through an all-digital outer space in the high-tech **planetarium**. More studious nature lovers can spend days examining every inch of the **Natural History Museum,** including favorite exhibits like the 87-foot-long blue whale skeleton. The Academy of Sciences takes pains to make itself kid-friendly, with interactive exhibits, thousands of live animals, and endless opportunities for learning. On **Thursday nights** (6pm-10pm, $15), the academy is an adults-only zone, where DJs play music and the café serves cocktails by some of the city's most renowned mixologists.

JAPANESE TEA GARDEN

The **Japanese Tea Garden** (75 Hagiwara Tea Garden Dr., 415/752-4227, http://japaneseteagardensf.com, 9am-6pm daily Mar.-Oct., 9am-4:45pm daily Nov.-Feb., adults $8, seniors and children 12-17 $6, children 5-11 $2, children under 5 free) is a haven of peace and tranquility that's a local favorite within the park, particularly in the spring. The planting and design of the garden began in 1894 for the California Exposition. Today the flourishing garden displays a wealth of beautiful flora, including stunning examples of rare Chinese and Japanese plants, some quite old. As you stroll along the paths, you'll come upon sculptures, bridges, ponds, and even traditional *tsukubai* (a tea ceremony sink). Take one of the docent-led tours and conclude your visit with tea and a fortune cookie at the tea house. Free admission is available on Monday, Wednesday, and Friday before 10am.

SAN FRANCISCO BOTANICAL GARDEN

Take a bucolic walk in the middle of Golden Gate Park by visiting the **San Francisco Botanical Garden** (1199 9th Ave. at Lincoln

View paintings, sculpture, textiles, ceramics, "contemporary crafts" from all over the world, and rotating exhibits that range from King Tut to the exquisite Jean Paul Gaultier collection. Competing with all of that is the building itself.

The museum's modern exterior is wrapped in perforated copper, while the interior incorporates pockets of manicured gardens. Poking out of the park's canopy is a twisted tower that offers a spectacular 360-degree view of the city and the bay. Entrance to the tower, lily pond, and art garden is free. Surrounded by sphinxes and draping wisteria, you can enjoy an art-filled picnic lunch.

CALIFORNIA ACADEMY OF SCIENCES

A triumph of the sustainable scientific principles it exhibits, the **California Academy of Sciences** (55 Music Concourse Dr., 415/379-8000, www.calacademy.org; 9:30am-5pm Mon.-Sat., 11am-5pm Sun., adults $36, seniors, students, and children 12-17 $31,

Golden Gate Park

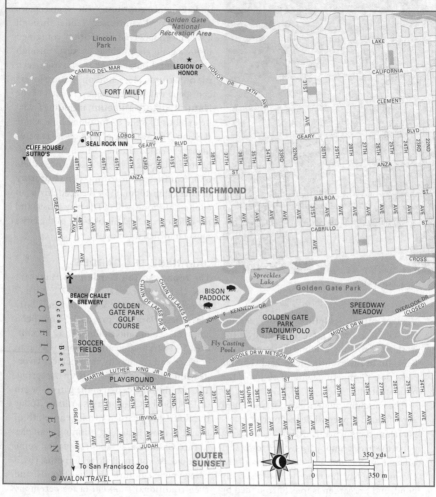

Way, 415/661-1316, www.sfbotanicalgarden. org, 7:30am-6pm mid Mar.-Sept., 7:30am-5pm Oct.-Nov., 7:30am-4pm Nov.-Jan., 7:30am-5pm Feb.-mid Mar., adults $8, students and seniors $6, children 5-11 $2, children under 5 free). The 55-acre gardens are home to more than 8,000 species of plants from around the world, and include a California Natives garden and a shady redwood forest. Fountains, ponds, meadows, and lawns are interwoven with the flowers and trees to create a peaceful, serene setting in the middle of the crowded city.

CONSERVATORY OF FLOWERS

For a trip to San Francisco's Victorian past, step inside the steamy **Conservatory of Flowers** (100 John F. Kennedy Dr., 415/831-2090, www.conservatoryofflowers.org, 10am-6:30pm Tues.-Sun., adults $8, students and seniors $5, children 5-11 $2, children under 5 free). Built in 1878, the striking wood and

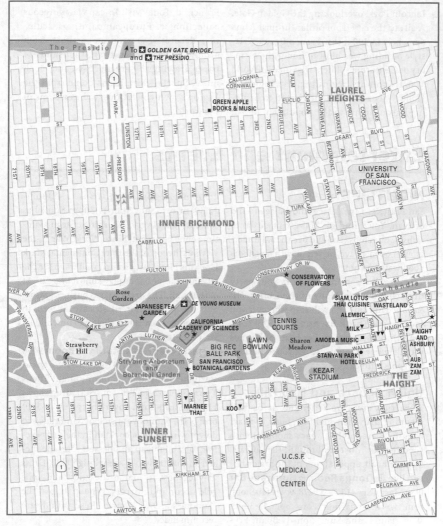

To ✠ GOLDEN GATE BRIDGE, and ✠ THE PRESIDIO

glass greenhouse is home to more than 1,700 plant species that spill out of containers, twine around rainforest trees, climb trellises reaching the roof, and rim deep ponds where eight-foot lily pads float serenely on still waters. Surrounded by the exotic flora illuminated only by natural light, it's easy to transport yourself to the heyday of colonialism when the study of botany was in its first bloom. Plus, it's one of the best places to explore on a rainy day. Strollers are not permitted inside; wheelchairs and power chairs are allowed.

The Legion of Honor

A beautiful museum in a town filled with beauty, the **Legion of Honor** (100 34th Ave. at Clement St., 415/750-3600, http://legionofhonor.famsf.org, 9:30am-5:15pm Tues.-Sun., adults $15, seniors $10, students and ages 13-16 $6, children under 16 free) sits on its lonely promontory in

Lincoln Park, overlooking the Golden Gate. A gift to the city from philanthropist Alma Spreckels in 1924, this French Beaux-Arts-style building was built to honor the memory of California soldiers who died in World War I. From its beginning, the Legion of Honor was a museum dedicated to bringing European art to the population of San Francisco. Today visitors can view gorgeous collections of European paintings, sculpture, decorative arts, ancient artifacts from around the Mediterranean, thousands of paper drawings by great artists, and much more. Special exhibitions come from the Legion's own collections and museums of the world.

Entertainment and Events

NIGHTLIFE

San Francisco isn't a see-and-be-seen kind of town. You'll find gay clubs, vintage dance clubs, Goth clubs, and the occasional underground burner rave, mixed in with neighborhood watering holes.

Several bus services can ferry your party from club to club. Many of these offer VIP entrance to clubs and will stop wherever you want to go. **Think Escape** (800/823-7249, www.thinkescape.com) has buses and limos with drivers and guides to get you to the hottest spots with ease.

Union Square and Nob Hill

These ritzy areas are better known for their shopping than their nightlife, but a few bars hang in there, plying weary shoppers with good drinks. Most tend toward the upscale. Some inhabit upper floors of the major hotels, like the **Tonga Room & Hurricane Bar** (950 Mason St., 415/772-5278, www.fairmont. com, www.tongaroom.com, 5pm-11:30pm Wed.-Thurs. and Sun., 5pm-12:30am Fri.-Sat.), where an over-the-top tiki theme adds a whimsical touch to the stately Fairmont Hotel on Nob Hill. Enjoy the tropical atmosphere with a fruity rum drink topped with a classic paper umbrella. Be prepared for the bar's virtual tropical storms that roll in every once in a while.

Part live-music venue, part elegant bar, **Top of the Mark** (InterContinental Mark Hopkins, 999 California St., 415/392-3434, www.intercontinentalmarkhopkins.com, 4:30pm-11:30pm Mon.-Thurs., 4:30pm-12:30am Fri.-Sat., 5pm-11:30pm Sun.) has something for every discerning taste in nighttime entertainment. Since World War II, the views at the top of the InterContinental Mark Hopkins Hotel have drawn visitors to see the city lights. Live bands play almost every night of the week. The dress code is business casual or better and is enforced, so leave the jeans in your room. Have a top-shelf martini, and let your toes tap along.

Harry Denton's Starlight Room (450 Powell St., 21st Fl., 415/395-8595, www. starlightroomsf.com, 6pm-midnight Tues.-Thurs., 5pm-2am Fri.-Sat., Sun. drag shows 11:30am and 2pm, cover charge up to $20) brings the flamboyant side of San Francisco downtown. Enjoy a cocktail in the early evening or a nightcap and dessert after the theater in this truly old-school nightclub. Dress in your best to match the glitzy red-and-gold decor and mirrors. Whoop it up at the "Sunday's a Drag" shows. Reservations are recommended.

South of the Union Square area in the sketchy Tenderloin neighborhood, brave souls can find a gem: **The Royale** (800 Post St., 415/441-4099, www.theroyalesf.com, 4pm-midnight Sun.-Wed., 4pm-2am Thurs.-Sat.) isn't a typical watering hole by any city's standards, but its intense focus on art fits perfectly with the endlessly eclectic ethos of San Francisco. Local artists exhibit their work in Café Royale on a monthly basis, and a wide range of entertainment is available, from

Side Trip to Wine Country

For oenophiles, no trip to California is complete without an excursion to the state's renowned wine country. Though the main draw is sampling wines at their source, Napa and Sonoma Valleys offer multiple ways to spoil yourself, including spas, fine hotels, revered restaurants, and understated natural beauty. Both are less than 100 miles north of San Francisco, about an hour's drive if traffic is light.

The city of Napa is located on the southern end of Napa Valley, with a scenic downtown perched on the Napa River. For an introduction to the area's vibrant food and wine scene, visit the **Oxbow Public Market** (610 and 644 1st St., 707/226-6529, www.oxbowpublicmarket. com, 9am-8pm Tues., 9am-7pm Wed.-Mon.), which has food vendors, produce markets, and cafés.

organic wine grapes in Sonoma

A multitude of vineyards are strung along the Silverado Trail and CA-29, two roads that head north out of the city of Napa and into serious wine country. Grape vines braid the scenic valley as you drive through the towns of Rutherford, St. Helena, and Calistoga. **Grgich Hills Winery** (1829 St. Helena Hwy., Rutherford, 800/532-3057, www.grgich.com, 9:30am-4:30pm daily, tasting $25) is the winery that put Napa Valley on the map with a win at the Paris Wine Tasting of 1976. It's still known for its chardonnay. **Mumm** (8445 Silverado Trail, Rutherford, 800/686-6272, www.mummnapa.com, 10am-6pm daily, tasting $20-35) produces sparkling wines worth a taste even for wine purists. **Clos Pegase** (1060 Dunaweal Ln., Calistoga, 707/942-4981, www.clospegase.com, 10:30am-5pm daily, tasting $20-30) mixes in some culture with its wine, with over 100 artworks on the grounds, including sculptor Henry Moore's *Mother Earth* and a painting by Francis Bacon.

There is a range of options for staying overnight (and sleeping off an afternoon of wine tasting). One of the more luxurious is **Auberge du Soleil** (180 Rutherford Hill Rd., St. Helena, 707/963-1211, www.aubergedusoleil.com, $875-5,200). Less expensive options include St. Helena's **El Bonita Motel** (195 Main St./CA-29, 800/541-3284, www.elbonita.com, $140-320), which is within walking distance of the historic downtown and has a 1950s motel charm, and Calistoga's **Dr. Wilkinson's Hot Springs Resort** (1507 Lincoln Ave., 707/942-4102, www.drwilkinson. com, $229-350), with an on-site spa.

GETTING THERE

To reach CA-29, the central conduit that runs north into the valley from the city of Napa, from San Francisco, take **US 101 North** across the Golden Gate Bridge to Novato. In Novato, take the exit for **CA-37 East** to Napa. CA-37 skirts the tip of the San Pablo Bay and runs all the way to Vallejo. From Vallejo, take **CA-29 (Sonoma Blvd.) North** for seven miles until you reach downtown Napa. CA-29 will take you as far north as Calistoga.

DJs and live jazz to "The Mildly Intoxicated Spelling Bee." The primary intoxicants are lesser known microbrews and small-batch beers. Also in the Tenderloin, **Tradition** (411 Jones St., 415/474-2284, http://tradbar.com, 6pm-2am Mon.-Sat.) is a two-level bar that takes its cocktails seriously. Eight themed drink menus zero in on cocktail traditions from English pub to tiki. This neighborhood can get dicey after dark; keep your wits (and your valuables) close.

Financial District and SoMa

All those high-powered business suit-clad executive types working in the Financial District need places to drink too. One of these is the **Royal Exchange** (301 Sacramento St., 415/956-1710, http://royalexchange.com, 11am-11pm Mon.-Fri.). This classic pub-style bar has a green-painted exterior, big windows overlooking the street, and a long, narrow barroom. The Royal Exchange serves a full lunch and dinner menu, a small wine list, and a full complement of top-shelf spirits. But most of all, the Exchange serves beer. With 73 taps pouring out 32 different types of beer, the only problem will be choosing one. This watering hole is open to the public only on weekdays; on weekends it hosts private parties.

In SoMa (South of Market), upscale wine bars have become an evening institution. Among the trendiest you'll find is **District** (216 Townsend St., 415/896-2120, www. districtsf.com, 4pm-close Mon.-Fri., 5pm-2am Sat.). A perfect example of its kind, District features bare brick walls, simple wooden furniture, and a big U-shaped bar at the center of the room with wine glasses hanging above it. While you can get a cocktail or even a beer, the point of coming to District is to sip the finest wines from California, Europe, and beyond. With more than 40 wines available by the glass each night, it's easy to find a favorite, or enjoy a flight of three similar wines to compare. While you can't quite get a full dinner at District, you will find a lovely lounge menu filled with small portions of delicacies

to enhance your tasting experience (and perhaps soak up some of the alcohol).

Secret passwords, a hidden library, and an art deco vibe make **Bourbon & Branch** (505 Jones St., 415/346-1735, www. bourbonandbranch.com, 6pm-2am daily, reservations suggested) a must for lovers of the brown stuff. Tucked behind a nameless brown door, this resurrected 1920s-era speakeasy evokes its Prohibition-era past with passwords and secret passages. A business-class elite sips rare bourbon and scotch in dark secluded booths, while those without reservations step into the hidden library.

The **Rickhouse** (246 Kearney St., 415/398-2827, www.rickhousebar.com, 5pm-2am Mon., 3pm-2am Tues.-Fri., 6pm-2am Sat.) feels like a country shack plopped down in the midst of the Financial District. The artisanal cocktail bar draws in the city's plentiful young urban hipsters. It's dimly lit, the walls and floors are wood, and stacks of barrels and old bottles line the mantle. There's also live music on Saturday and Monday nights.

It's dark, it's dank, and it's very Goth. The **Cat Club** (1190 Folsom St., 415/703-8965, www.sfcatclub.com, 9pm-3am Tues.-Sun., cover charge) gets pretty energetic on 1980s dance nights, but it's still a great place to go after you've donned your best down-rent black attire and painted your face deathly pale, especially on Goth-industrial-electronica nights. In fact, there's no dress code at the Cat Club, unlike many local nightspots, which makes it great for travelers who live in their jeans. You'll find a friendly crowd, decent bartenders, strong drinks, and easy access to smoking areas. Each of the two rooms has its own DJ, which somehow works perfectly even though they're only a wall apart from each other. Check the website to find the right party night for you, and expect the crowd to heat up after 11pm.

Monarch (101 6th St., 415/284-9774, www. monarchsf.com, 5:30pm-2am Tues.-Fri., 8pm-2am Sat.-Sun.) is aiming to be a one-stop after-dark venue. Upstairs is a Victorian-inspired cocktail lounge, while the downstairs club hosts international and local DJs. You might also catch offbeat performers like acrobats twirling from the ceilings.

AsiaSF (201 9th St., 415/255-2742, www.asiasf.com, 7:15pm-11pm Sun. and Wed.-Thurs., 7:15pm-2am Fri., 5pm-2am Sat., cover charge) is famous for its transgender performers and servers, "The Ladies of AsiaSF." Weekend reservations for dinner and a show include free admission to the dance floor downstairs.

North Beach and Fisherman's Wharf

Jack Kerouac loved **Vesuvio** (255 Columbus Ave., 415/362-3370, www.vesuvio.com, 8am-2am Mon.-Fri., 6am-2am Sat.-Sun.), which is why it's probably North Beach's most famous saloon. This cozy, eclectic bi-level hideout is an easy place to spend the afternoon with a pint of Anchor Steam. Its eclectic decor includes tables decorated with tarot cards.

Almost across the street from Vesuvio is one of the oldest and most celebrated bars in the city. **Tosca Cafe** (242 Columbus Ave., 415/986-9651, http://toscacafesf.com, 5pm-2am Tues.-Sun.) has an unpretentious yet glam 1940s style. Hunter S. Thompson once tended bar here when the owner was out at the dentist. The jukebox plays grand opera to the patrons clustered in the big red booths. Locals love the lack of trendiness, the classic cocktails, the occasional star sightings, and the chicken marsala.

Dress up for a night out at **15 Romolo** (15 Romolo Pl., 415/398-1359, www.15romolo.com, 5pm-2am Mon.-Fri., 11:30am-2am Sat.-Sun.). You'll have to hike up the steep little alley (Fresno St. crosses Romolo Pl., which can be hard to find) to this hotel bar. You'll love the creative cocktails, edgy jukebox music, and often mellow crowd. The bar is smallish and can get crowded on the weekend, so come on a weeknight if you prefer a quiet drink.

Known for its colorful clientele and cluttered decor, **Specs** (12 William Saroyan Pl., 415/421-4112, 4pm-2am daily, cash only) is a dive bar located in a North Beach alley. Its full name is the Specs' Twelve Adler Museum Café.

Marina and Pacific Heights

Marina and Pacific Heights denizens enjoy a good glass of vino. The **Bacchus Wine Bar** (1954 Hyde St., 415/928-2633, www.bacchussf.com, 5:30pm-midnight daily) is a tiny local watering hole that offers an array of wines, sake cocktails, and craft beers.

The Marina District's Chestnut Street is known for its high-end restaurants and swanky clientele. The **Horseshoe Tavern** (2024 Chestnut St., 415/346-1430, 10am-2am daily) is a place for people to let their hair down, shoot pool, and drink without pretension.

Get to really know your fellow beer drinkers at the tiny **Black Horse London Pub** (1514 Union St., 415/928-2414, www.blackhorselondon.com, 5pm-midnight Mon.-Thurs., 2pm-midnight Fri., 11am-midnight Sat.-Sun., cash only), which can accommodate just nine people. Bottles of beer are served from a claw-foot bathtub located behind the bar.

Civic Center and Hayes Valley

Hayes Valley bleeds into Lower Haight (Haight St. between Divisadero St. and Octavia Blvd.) and supplies most of the neighborhood bars. For proof that the independent spirit of the Haight lives on despite encroaching commercialism, stop in and have a drink at the **Toronado** (547 Haight St., 415/863-2276, www.toronado.com, 11:30am-2am daily), a grimy cathedral to superb beer. This dimly lit haven with a metal- and punk rock-heavy jukebox maintains one of the finest beer selections in the nation, with a changing roster of several dozen microbrews on tap, including Russian River Brewing Company's Pliny the Elder, one of the most sought after beers in the state.

If you'd rather drink a cocktail than a beer, head over to **Smuggler's Cove** (650 Gough St., 415/869-1900, http://smugglerscovesf.com, 5pm-1:15am daily). The drink menu includes

70 cocktails and an impressive number of rare rums.

Mission

These neighborhoods seem to hold a whole city's worth of bars. The Mission still has plenty of no-frills bars, many with a Latino theme. And, of course, men seeking men flock to the Castro's endless array of gay bars. For lesbians, the Mission might be a better bet.

Trick Dog (3010 20th St., 415/471-2999, www.trickdogbar.com, 3pm-2am daily) is shaking up the city's cocktail scene. Named after city landmarks, the drinks use unexpected ingredients like dandelion, lychee, or horseradish (thankfully not all at the same time). The small food menu includes thrice-cooked fries, Scotch eggs, and a standout kale salad.

Expect to hear some old-school vinyl from a lo-fi record player in the dimly lit **Royal Cuckoo** (3202 Mission St., http://royalcuckoo.com, 4pm-2am Mon.-Thurs., 3pm-2am Fri.-Sun.). There's also live music played on a vintage Hammond B3 organ Wednesday-Sunday. The cocktail list includes variations on the classics, including a sour old-fashioned.

Excellent draft beers, tasty barbecue plates, and a motorcycle-inclined crowd give **Zeitgeist** (199 Valencia St., 415/255-7505, 9am-2am daily) a punk-rock edge. This Mission favorite, though, endears itself to all sorts, thanks to its spacious outdoor beer garden, 40 beers on tap, and popular Bloody Marys.

Get a sweeping view of the city with superb South American cocktails at ★ **El Techo de Lolinda** (2518 Mission St., 415/550-6970, http://eltechosf.com, 4pm-10:30pm Mon.-Thurs., 4pm-12:30am Fri., 11pm-12:30am Sat., 11am-10:30pm Sun.), a rooftop bar associated with the Argentinean steak house Lolinda. The bar serves pitchers of margaritas, glasses of *caipirinhas* (a Brazilian cocktail resembling a mojito), and the best Cuba Libre I've ever had. (I know it's a simple drink, but this version is transcendent.) The small food menu includes superb snacks like empanadas, ceviche, and a variety of skewers.

Golden Gate Park and the Haight

Haight Street crowds head out in droves to the **Alembic** (1725 Haight St., 415/666-0822, www.alembicbar.com, 4pm-midnight Mon.-Fri., 2pm-midnight Sat.-Sun.) for artisanal cocktails laced with American spirits. On par with the whiskey and bourbon menu is the cuisine: Wash down the pork belly sliders or chicken liver mousse with a Sazerac.

Hobson's Choice (1601 Haight St., 415/621-5859, www.hobsonschoice.com, 2pm-2am Mon.-Fri., noon-2am Sat.-Sun.) claims the largest selection of rums in the country. Try your rum in everything from a Brazilian *caipirinha* to a Cuban mojito, or in one of Hobson's famous rum punches.

Featured in an episode of Anthony Bourdain's travel show *No Reservations*, **Aub Zam Zam** (1633 Haight St., 415/861-2545, 3pm-2am Mon.-Fri., 1pm-2am Sat.-Sun.) is an old-school bar with an Arabian feel. Zam Zam doesn't take credit cards, but it does have an Arabian mural behind the U-shaped bar, where an interesting mix of locals and visitors congregate for the cheap drinks.

The **Beach Chalet Brewery** (1000 Great Hwy., 415/386-8439, www.beachchalet.com, 9am-11pm Mon.-Thurs., 9am-midnight Fri., 8am-midnight Sat., 8am-11pm Sun.) is an attractive brewpub and restaurant directly across the street from Ocean Beach. Sip a pale ale while watching the sunset, and check out the historical murals downstairs.

Gay and Lesbian

San Francisco's gay nightlife has earned a worldwide rep for both the quantity and quality of options. In fact, the gay club scene totally outdoes the straight club scene for frolicsome, fabulous fun. While the city's queer nightlife caters more to gay men than to lesbians, there's plenty of space available for partiers of all persuasions. For a more comprehensive list of San Francisco's queer bars and clubs, visit http://sanfrancisco.gaycities.com/bars.

You'll have no trouble finding a gay bar in the Castro. One of the best is called simply **Q Bar** (456 Castro St., 415/864-2877, www.qbarsf.com, 4pm-2am Mon.-Fri., 2pm-2am Sat.-Sun.). Just look for the red neon "Bar" sign set in steel out front. Inside, expect to find the fabulous red decor known as "retro-glam," delicious top-shelf cocktails, and thrumming beats spun by popular DJs almost every night of the week. Unlike many Castro establishments, the Q Bar caters to pretty much everybody: gay men, gay women, and gay-friendly straight folks. You'll find a coat check and adequate restroom facilities, and the strength of the drinks will make you want to take off your jacket and stay awhile.

Looking for a stylin' gay bar turned club, Castro style? Head for **Badlands** (4121 18th St., 415/626-9320, www.sfbadlands.com, 2pm-2am daily). This Castro icon was once an old-school bar with pool tables on the floor and license plates on the walls. Now you'll find an always-crowded dance floor, au courant peppy pop music, ever-changing video screens, gay men out for a good time, and straight women who count themselves as regulars at this friendly establishment, which attracts a youngish but mixed-age crowd. The dance floor gets packed and hot, especially on weekend nights. There's a coat check on the bottom level.

The Lookout (3600 16th St., 415/431-0306, www.lookoutsf.com, 3:30pm-2am Mon.-Fri., 12:30pm-2am Sat.-Sun., cover charge) gets its name and much of its rep from its balcony overlooking the iconic Castro neighborhood. Get up there for some primo people-watching as you sip your industrial-strength alcoholic concoctions and nibble on surprisingly edible bar snacks and pizza. Special events come with a cover charge.

Yes, there's a Western-themed gay bar in San Francisco. **The Cinch Saloon** (1723 Polk St., 415/776-4162, http://cinchsf.com, 9am-2am Mon.-Fri., 6am-2am Sat.-Sun.) has a laid-back (no pun intended), friendly,

male-oriented vibe that's all but lost in the once gay, now gentrified Polk Street hood. Expect fewer females and strong drinks to go with the unpretentious decor and atmosphere.

Live Music

In the late 1960s, **The Fillmore** (1805 Geary Blvd., 415/346-6000, www.thefillmore.com, prices vary) became legendary for performances by rock acts like the Grateful Dead, Jefferson Airplane, and Carlos Santana. These days, all sorts of national touring acts stop by, sometimes for multiple nights. The Fillmore is also known for its distinctive poster art: Attendees to certain sold-out shows are given commemorative posters.

With its marble columns and ornate balconies, the **Great American Music Hall** (859 O'Farrell St., 415/885-0750, www.slimspresents.com, prices vary) is one of the nicest places to see a nationally touring act in the city, with bragging for shows by Arcade Fire and the legendary Patti Smith.

The beautiful **Warfield** (982 Market St., 415/345-0900, http://thewarfieldtheatre.com) books all sorts of acts, from John Prine to the Wu-Tang Clan. Choose from limited table seating on the lowest level (mostly by reservation), reserved seats in the balconies, or open standing in the orchestra below the stage.

The **Boom Boom Room** (1601 Fillmore St., 415/673-8040, www.boomboomblues.com, 4pm-2am Sun. and Tues.-Thurs., 4pm-3am Fri.-Sat.) has kept it real in the Fillmore for more than two decades. Today you'll find the latest in a legacy of live blues, boogie, groove, soul, and funk music in this fun, divey joint.

On the other side of town, **Biscuits & Blues** (401 Mason St., 415/292-2583, www.biscuitsandblues.com, hours and days vary) is a local musicians' favorite. Headliners have included Joe Louis Walker, Jimmy Thackery, and Jim Kimo. Dinner is served nightly and features a surprisingly varied and upscale menu.

Bringing jazz to the high culture of Hayes Valley is **SFJazz Center** (201 Franklin St.,

866/920-5299, http://sfjazz.org, hours vary Tues.-Sun.), a stunning 35,000-square-foot space with state-of-the-art acoustics. It's designed to feel like a small club, thanks to steep seating that brings the large audience close to the performers, and has drawn major acts such as Herbie Hancock and the Afro-Cuban All Stars.

Comedy

San Francisco's oldest comedy club, the **Punch Line** (444 Battery St., 415/397-7573, www.punchlinecomedyclub.com, shows 7:30pm, 8pm, 9:45pm, 10:15pm Tues.-Sun., cover varies) is an elegant and intimate venue that earned its top-notch reputation with stellar headliners such as Ellen DeGeneres and Dave Chappelle. An on-site bar keeps the audience primed.

Cobb's Comedy Club (915 Columbus Ave., 415/928-4320, www.cobbscomedy.com, shows 7:30pm, 8pm, 9:45pm, 10:15pm Thurs.-Sun., cover varies, two-drink minimum) has played host to star comedians such as Louis CK, Sarah Silverman, and Margaret Cho since 1982. The 425-seat venue offers a full dinner menu and a bar to slake your thirst. Be sure to check your show's start time—some comics don't follow the usual Cobb's schedule.

THE ARTS
Theater

San Francisco may not be known as a big theater town, but it does boast a number of small and large theaters. A great way to grab last-minute theater tickets (or for music or dance shows) is to walk right up to **Union Square TIX** (Union Square, 415/433-7827, www.tixbayarea.com, 8am-4pm Sun.-Thurs., 8am-5pm Fri.-Sat.) for same-day, half-price, no-refund tickets to all kinds of shows across the city. TIX also sells half-price tickets to same-day shows online—check the website at 11am daily for up-to-date deals. If you really, really need to see a major musical while you're in San Francisco, check out the three venues where big Broadway productions land when they come to town: the Orpheum and Golden Gate Theatres (www.shnsf.com), and the Curran Theatre (www.sfcurran.com).

Just up from Union Square, the traditional San Francisco theater district continues to entertain crowds. The **American Conservatory Theater** (A.C.T., 415 Geary St., 415/749-2228, www.act-sf.org, shows Tues.-Sun., $25-115) puts on a season filled with big-name, big-budget productions, such as high-production-value musicals, American

the legendary SF music venue Biscuits & Blues

Curran Theatre

classics by the likes of Sam Shepard and Somerset Maugham, and intriguing new works. Discount parking is available with a ticket stub from A.C.T. at the Mason-O'Farrell garage around the corner.

The **Curran Theatre** (445 Geary St., 888/746-1799, www.sfcurran.com, $49-285), next door to A.C.T., has a state-of-the-art stage for classic, high-budget musicals, such as *Les Misérables*, *Phantom of the Opera*, and *Chicago*. Expect to pay a premium for tickets to these productions, which can sometimes run for months or even years. Check the schedule for current shows.

There's one live show that's always different, yet it's been running continuously since 1974. It's *Beach Blanket Babylon* (678 Green St., 415/421-4222, www.beachblanketbabylon. com, shows Wed.-Sun., $25-155), which mocks pop culture and continuously evolves to take advantage of tabloid treasures. Although minors are welcome at the Sunday matinees, evening shows are restricted to attendees 21 and over.

Located in the seedy Mid-Market area, both the **Orpheum Theatre** (1192 Market St., 888/746-1799, www.shnsf.com, $50-200) and the **Golden Gate Theatre** (1 Taylor St., 888/746-1799, www.shnsf.com, $50-200) run touring productions of popular Broadway musicals.

Classical Music and Opera

Right around the Civic Center, culture takes a turn for the upscale. This is the neighborhood where the ultra-rich and not-so-rich classics lovers come to enjoy a night out. Acoustically renovated in 1992, **Davies Symphony Hall** (201 Van Ness Ave., 415/864-6000, www. sfsymphony.org) is home to Michael Tilson Thomas's world-renowned San Francisco Symphony. Loyal patrons flock to performances that range from the classic to the avant-garde. Whether you want to hear Mozart and Mahler or classic rock blended with major symphony orchestra, the San Francisco Symphony does it.

The **War Memorial Opera House** (301 Van Ness Ave., 415/621-6600, www.sfwmpac. org), a Beaux-Arts-style building designed by Coit Tower and City Hall architect Arthur Brown Jr., houses the **San Francisco Opera** (415/864-3330, http://sfopera.com) and **San Francisco Ballet** (415/861-5600, www. sfballet.org). Tours are available (415/552-8338, 10am-2pm Mon., $5-7).

Cinema

The **Castro Theatre** (429 Castro St., 415/621-6120, www.castrotheatre.com, $9-12) is a grand movie palace from the 1920s that has enchanted San Francisco audiences for almost a century. The Castro Theatre hosts everything from revival double features (from black-and-white through 1980s classics) to musical movie sing-alongs, live shows, and even the occasional book signing. The Castro also screens current releases and documentaries about queer life in San Francisco and beyond. Once inside, be sure to admire the lavish interior decor. If you get to your seat early, you're likely to be rewarded with a performance of the Mighty Wurlitzer pipe organ before the show.

For a modern movie-going experience, **AMC Kabuki 8** (1881 Post St., www.amctheatres.com) offers reserved seating in eight screens; most show blockbuster Hollywood films, plus a smattering of independents.

FESTIVALS AND EVENTS

San Francisco is host to numerous events year-round. Following are some of the biggest that are worth planning a trip around.

During the **Chinese New Year Parade** (Chinatown, www.chineseparade.com, Feb.), Chinatown celebrates the Lunar New Year with a parade of costumed dancers, floats, and firecrackers.

Join rowdy, costumed revelers for **Bay to Breakers** (Embarcadero to Great Highway, www.baytobreakers.com, May), a 12K run/walk/stumble across the city through Golden Gate Park to a massive street party at Ocean Beach.

One of the year's biggest parades is the **San Francisco LGBT Pride Parade and Celebration** (Market St., www.sfpride.org, June). Hundreds of thousands of people of all orientations take to the streets for this quintessentially San Franciscan party-cum-social justice movement.

Golden Gate Park is host to two wildly popular summer music festivals. **Outside Lands** (www.sfoutsidelands.com, Aug.) is a three-day music festival that floods the park with revelers, food trucks, and hundreds of bands. Headliners have included Radiohead, LCD Soundsystem, Kanye West, Metallica, Neil Young, and Elton John. The park barely recovers in time for **Hardly Strictly Bluegrass** (www.hardlystrictlybluegrass.com, late Sept. or early Oct.), a free music festival celebrating a wide variety of bluegrass sounds, from Lucinda Williams and Emmylou Harris to Ryan Adams and Yo La Tengo.

Shopping

UNION SQUARE

For the biggest variety of department stores and high-end international designers, plus a few select boutiques, locals and visitors alike flock to **Union Square** (bounded by Geary St., Stockton St., Post St., and Powell St.). The shopping area includes more than just the square proper: More designer and brand-name stores cluster for several blocks in all directions.

The big guys anchor Union Square. **Macy's** (170 O'Farrell St., 415/397-3333, www.macys.com, 10am-9pm Mon.-Sat., 11am-8pm Sun.) has two immense locations, one for women's clothing and another for the men's store and housewares. **Neiman Marcus** (150 Stockton St., 415/362-3900, www.neimanmarcus.com, 10am-7pm Mon.-Sat. noon-6pm, Sun.) is a favorite among high-budget shoppers, and **Saks Fifth Avenue** (384 Post St., 415/986-4300, www.saksfifthavenue.com, 10am-7pm Mon.-Wed., 10am-8pm Thurs.-Sat., noon-7pm Sun.) adds a touch of New York style to funky-but-wealthy San Francisco.

Levi's (815 Market St., 415/501-0100, www.levi.com, 9am-9pm Mon.-Sat., 10am-8pm Sun.) may be a household name, but this three-floor fashion emporium offers incredible customization services while featuring new music and emerging art. Levi's got its start outfitting gold miners in 1849, so it's literally a San Francisco tradition.

The bones of fashion can be found at **Britex Fabrics** (146 Geary St., 415/392-2910, www.britexfabrics.com, 10am-6pm Mon.-Sat.), which draws designers, quilters, DIYers, and costume geeks from all over the Bay Area to its legendary monument to fabric. If you're into any sort of textile crafting, a visit to Britex has the qualities of a religious experience. All four floors are crammed floor to ceiling with bolts of fabric, swaths of lace, and rolls of ribbon. From $1-per-yard grosgrain ribbons to $95-per-yard French silk jacquard and $125-per-yard Italian wool coating, Britex has it all.

NORTH BEACH

One of the most famous independent bookshops in a city known for its literary bent is ★ **City Lights** (261 Columbus Ave., 415/362-8193, www.citylights.com, 10am-midnight daily). It opened in 1953 as an all-paperback bookstore with a decidedly Beat aesthetic, focused on selling modern literary fiction and progressive political tomes. As the Beats flocked to San Francisco and to City Lights, the shop put on another hat—that of publisher. Allen Ginsberg's *Howl* was published by the erstwhile independent, which never looked back. Today City Lights continues to sell and publish the best of cutting-edge fiction and nonfiction.

MARINA AND PACIFIC HEIGHTS

The shopping is good in the tony Marina and its elegant neighbor Pacific Heights. **Chestnut and Union Streets** cater to the Marina's young and affluent residents with plenty of clothing boutiques and makeup outlets. Make a stop at **Books Inc.** (2251 Chestnut St., 415/931-3633, www.booksinc.net, 9am-10pm Mon.-Sat., 9am-9pm Sun.), one of the best bookstores in the city. You'll find everything from fiction to travel, as well as a great selection of magazines. **Fillmore Street** is the other major shopping corridor. It's funkier than its younger neighbors in the Marina, probably because of its proximity to Japantown and the Fillmore.

HAYES VALLEY

In Hayes Valley, adjacent to the Civic Center, shopping goes uptown, but the unique scent of counterculture creativity still permeates. This is a fun neighborhood to get your stroll on, checking out the art galleries and peeking into the boutiques for clothing and upscale housewares, and then stopping at one of the lovely cafés for a restorative bite to eat.

Ver Unica (437B Hayes St. and 526 Hayes St., 415/621-6259, 11am-7pm Mon.-Sat., noon-6pm Sun.) is a vintage boutique that attracts locals and celebrities with high-quality men's and women's clothing and accessories dating from the 1920s to the 1980s, along with a small selection of new apparel by up-and-coming designers.

Paolo Iantorno's boutique **Paolo Shoes** (524 Hayes St., 415/552-4580, http://paoloshoes.com, 11am-7pm Mon.-Sat., 11am-6pm Sun.) showcases his collection of handcrafted shoes, for which all leather and textiles are conscientiously selected and then inspected to ensure top quality.

You can hardly walk 10 feet without passing a sweet shop selling macarons. The original is **Miette** (449 Octavia St., 415/626-6221, www.miette.com, 11am-7pm daily), a cheery European-inspired candy shop, sister store to the Ferry Plaza bakery (415/837-0300). From double-salted licorice to handmade English toffee, the quality confections include imports from England, Italy, and France.

MISSION

In a city known for its quirky style, the Mission was the last neighborhood with a funky, easy-on-the-wallet shopping district. Sadly, the days are gone when you could buy cool vintage clothes by the pound, but **Valencia Street** is still the most vibrant and diverse neighborhood for shoppers in the city.

The **Bell Jar** (3187 16th St., 415/626-1749, https://belljarsf.com, 11am-7pm Mon.-Sat., noon-6pm Sun.) has everything you need to make you and your home into stylish trendsetters of the 21st century, from dresses and jewelry to art books and soaps.

Author Dave Eggers's tongue-in-cheek storefront at **826 Valencia** (826 Valencia St., 415/642-5905, www.826valencia.org, noon-6pm daily) doubles as a pirate supply shop and youth literacy center. While you'll find plenty of pirate booty, you'll also find a good stock of literary magazines and books. Almost next door, **Paxton Gate** (824 Valencia St., 415/824-1872, www.paxtongate.com, 11am-7pm Sun.-Wed., 11am-8pm Thurs.-Sat.) takes the typical gift shop to a new level with taxidermy. This quirky spot is surprisingly cheery, with garden supplies, books, and candles filling the cases in addition to the fossilized creatures.

HAIGHT-ASHBURY

The **Haight-Ashbury shopping district** isn't what it used to be, but if you're willing to poke around a bit, you can still find a few bargains in the remaining thrift shops. One relic of the 1960s counterculture still thrives on the Haight: head shops.

Music has always been a part of the Haight. To this day you'll find homeless folks pounding out rhythms on *doumbeks* and congas on the sidewalks and on Hippy Hill in the park.

Located in an old bowling alley, **Amoeba Music** (1855 Haight St., 415/831-1200, www. amoeba.com, 11am-8pm daily) is a larger-than-life record store that promotes every type of music imaginable. Amoeba's staff, many of whom are musicians themselves, are among the most knowledgeable in the business.

Award-winning **The Booksmith** (1644 Haight St., 800/493-7323, www.booksmith. com, 10am-10pm Mon.-Sat., 10am-8pm Sun.) boasts a helpful and informed staff, a fabulous magazine collection, and Northern California's preeminent calendar of readings by internationally renowned authors.

Originally a vaudeville theater, the capacious **Wasteland** (1660 Haight St., 415/863-3150, www.shopwasteland.com, 11am-8pm Mon.-Sat., 11am-7pm Sun.) has a traffic-stopping art nouveau facade, a distinctive assortment of vintage hippie and rock-star threads, and a glamour-punk staff.

Sports and Recreation

BEACHES
Ocean Beach

San Francisco boasts of being a city that has everything, and it certainly comes close. This massive urban wonderland even claims several genuine sand beaches within its city limits. No doubt the biggest and most famous of these is **Ocean Beach** (Great Hwy., parking at Sloat Blvd., Golden Gate Park, and the Cliff House, www.parksconservancy.org). This four-mile stretch of sand forms the breakwater for the Pacific Ocean along the whole west side of the city. Because it's so large, you're likely to find a spot to sit down and maybe even a parking place along the beach, except perhaps on that rarest of occasions in San Francisco—a sunny, warm day. Don't go out for an ocean swim at Ocean Beach: Extremely dangerous rip currents cause fatalities every year.

It may be hard to believe that you can surf in San Francisco, but Ocean Beach has a series

of beach breaks that are good in the fall and monstrous in the winter. It's not for beginners, and even accomplished surfers can find it difficult to paddle out. Five blocks from the beach, **Aqua Surf Shop** (3847 Judah St., 415/242-9283, www.aquasurfshop.com, 10am-5:30pm Sun.-Tues., 10am-7pm Wed.-Sat., surfboard rentals $25-35 per day, wetsuits $15 per day) rents shortboards, longboards, and the very necessary 4/3 wetsuit.

Aquatic Park

The beach at **Aquatic Park** (Beach St. and Hyde St., www.nps.gov/safr) sits at the west end of the Fisherman's Wharf tourist area. This makes Aquatic Park incredibly convenient for visitors who want to grab a picnic on the Wharf to enjoy down on the beach. It was built in the late 1930s as a bathhouse catering to wealthy San Franciscans, and today, swimming remains one of Aquatic Park's main attractions: Triathletes and hard-core swimmers brave the frigid waters to swim for miles in the protected cove. More sedate visitors can find a seat and enjoy a cup of coffee, a newspaper, and some people-watching.

Baker Beach

Baker Beach (Golden Gate Point and the Presidio, www.parksconservancy.org) is best known for its scenery, and that doesn't just mean the lovely views of the Golden Gate Bridge. Baker is San Francisco's own clothing-optional (that is, nude) beach. But don't worry, plenty of the denizens of Baker Beach wear clothes while flying kites, playing volleyball and Frisbee, and even just strolling on the beach. Because Baker is much smaller than Ocean Beach, it gets crowded in the summer. Whether you choose to sunbathe nude or not, don't try to swim here. The currents get seriously strong and dangerous because it's so close to the Golden Gate.

PARKS
Golden Gate Park

The largest park in San Francisco is **Golden Gate Park** (main entrance at Stanyan St. and Fell St., McLaren Lodge Visitors Center at John F. Kennedy Dr., 415/831-2700, www.golden-gate-park.com). In addition to housing popular sights like the **Academy of Sciences,** the **de Young,** and the **Japanese Tea Garden,** Golden Gate Park is San Francisco's unofficial playground. There are three botanical gardens, a **children's playground** (Martin Luther King Jr. Dr. and Bowling Green Dr.), tennis courts, and a golf course. **Stow Lake** (415/386-2531, http://stowlakeboathouse.com, 10am-6pm daily, $22-38 per hour) offers paddleboats for rent, and the park even has its own bison paddock. Weekends find the park filled with locals inline skating, biking, hiking, and even Lindy Hopping. John F. Kennedy Drive east of Transverse Drive is closed to motorists every Saturday April-September and Sunday year-round for pedestrian-friendly fun.

Crissy Field

Crissy Field (Marina Blvd. and Baker St., 415/561-4700, www.parksconservancy.org), with its beaches, restored wetlands, and wide promenade, is the playground of the **Presidio** (415/561-4323, www.nps.gov/prsf, free). It's part of the Golden Gate National Recreation Area and is dedicated to environmental education. At the **Crissy Field Center** (1199 E. Beach, 415/561-7690, 8:30am-4:30pm daily) you'll find a list of classes, seminars, and fun hands-on activities for all ages. Many of these include walks out into the marsh and the Presidio.

Lands End

The **Lands End Trail** (Merrie Way, 415/561-4700, www.nps.gov/goga) is part of the Golden Gate National Recreation Area. Rising above rugged cliffs and beaches, Lands End feels wild, but the three-mile trail, which runs from El Camino Del Mar near the Legion of Honor to the ruins of the Sutro Baths, is perfect for any hiking enthusiast. For a longer adventure, there are plenty of auxiliary trails to explore that lead down to little beaches. Be sure to look out for the remains of three shipwrecks on the rocks of Point Lobos at low tide. Grab a cup of hot chocolate at the stunning **Lands End Lookout visitors center** (680 Point Lobos Ave., 415/426-5240, www.parksconservancy.org, 9am-5pm daily) when your hike is finished.

Mission Dolores Park

If you're looking for a park where the most strenuous activity is people-watching, then head to **Mission Dolores Park** (Dolores St. and 19th St., 415/554-9521, http://sfrecpark.org). Usually called Dolores Park, it's a favorite of Castro and Mission District denizens. Bring a beach blanket to sprawl on the lawn and a picnic lunch supplied by one of the excellent nearby eateries. On weekends, music festivals and cultural events often spring up at Dolores Park.

BIKING

In other places, bicycling is a sport or a mode of transportation. In San Francisco, bicycling is a religion. Some might say that the high church of this religion is the **San Francisco Bike Coalition** (415/431-2453, www.sfbike. org). In addition to providing workshops and hosting events, the Bike Coalition is an excellent resource for anyone who wants to cycle through the city. Check out its website for tips, maps, and rules of the road.

Newcomers to biking in the city may want to start off gently, with a guided tour that avoids areas with dangerous traffic. **Blazing Saddles** (2715 Hyde St., 415/202-8888, www. blazingsaddles.com, $8-15 per hour) rents bikes and offers tips on where to go. There are five locations, most in the Fisherman's Wharf area. If you prefer the safety of a group, take the guided tour (10am daily, three hours, adult $55, child $35, reservations required) through San Francisco and across the Golden Gate Bridge into Marin County. One of the most popular treks is the easy and flat nine-mile ride across the **Golden Gate Bridge** and back. This is a great way to see the bridge and the bay for the first time, and it takes only an hour or two to complete. Another option is to ride across the bridge and into the town of Sausalito (8 miles) or Tiburon (16 miles), enjoy an afternoon and dinner, and then ride the ferry back into the city (bikes are allowed on board).

Another easy and low-stress option is the paved paths of **Golden Gate Park** (main entrance at Stanyan St. and Fell St., McLaren Lodge Visitors Center at John F. Kennedy Dr., 415/831-2700, www.golden-gate-park. com) and the **Presidio** (Montgomery St. and Lincoln Blvd., 415/561-4323, www.nps. gov/prsf). A bike makes a perfect mode of transportation to explore the various museums and attractions of these two large parks, and you can spend all day and never have to worry about finding parking. At the entrance of Golden Gate Park, **Golden Gate Tours & Bike Rentals** (1816 Haight St., 415/922-4537, www.goldengateparkbikerental.com, 9:30am-6:30pm daily, $8-15 per hour, $30-60 per day) has a kiosk. Another choice is **Golden Gate Park Bike and Skate** (3038 Fulton St., 415/922-4537, http:// goldengateparkbikeandskate.com, 9:30am-6:30pm daily, $5-15 per hour, $15-75 per day), located just north of the park on Fulton near the de Young Museum.

Lands End

Twin Peaks

Twin Peaks rises up from the center of San Francisco and is the second-highest point in the city. Twin Peaks divides the city between north and south, catching the fog bank that rolls in from the Golden Gate and providing a habitat for lots of wild birds and insects, including the endangered Mission blue butterfly.

While you barely need to get out of your car to enjoy the stunning 360-degree views of the city from the peaks, the best way to enjoy the view is to take a hike. To scale the less traveled South Peak, start at the pullout on the road below the parking lot. You'll climb a steep set of stairs up to the top of the South Peak in less than 0.2 mile. Stop and marvel at human industry: the communications tower that's the massive eyesore just over the peak. Carefully cross the road to access the red-rock stairway up to the North Peak. It's only 0.25 mile, but as with the South Peak, those stairs seem to go straight up! It's worth it when you look out across the Golden Gate to Mount Tamalpais in the north and Mount Diablo in the east.

If you're seeking an amazing view along with your exercise, head to Twin Peaks on a sunny day. If the fog is in, as so often happens in the summertime, you'll have trouble seeing five feet in front of you. Don't expect a verdant paradise—the grass doesn't stay green long in the spring, so most visitors get to see the dried-out brush that characterizes much of the Bay Area in the summertime and fall.

GETTING THERE

Drive west up **Market Street** (eventually turning into **Portola Drive**) and turn right onto **Twin Peaks Boulevard** and past the parade of tour buses to the parking lot past the North Peak. Parking is free, and Twin Peaks is open year-round.

WHALE-WATCHING

With day-trip access to the marine sanctuary off the Farallon Islands, whale-watching is a year-round activity in San Francisco. **San Francisco Whale Tours** (Pier 39, Dock B, 415/706-7364, www.sanfranciscowhaletours. com, tours daily, $60-89, advance purchase required) offers six-hour trips out to the Farallons almost every Saturday and Sunday, with almost-guaranteed whale sightings on each trip. Shorter whale-watching trips along the coastline run on weekdays, and 90-minute quickie trips out to see slightly smaller local wildlife, including elephant seals and sea lions, also go out daily. Children ages 3-15 are welcome on boat tours (for reduced rates), and kids often love the chance to spot whales, sea lions, and pelicans. Children under age three are not permitted for safety reasons.

SPECTATOR SPORTS

Lovers of the big leagues will find fun in San Francisco. Major League Baseball's **San Francisco Giants** (http://sanfrancisco.giants. mlb.com), winners of the 2014 World Series, play at **AT&T Park** (24 Willie Mays Plaza, 3rd St. and King St., 415/972-2000). Come out to enjoy the game, the food, and the views at San Francisco's ballpark. Giants games take place on weekdays and weekends, both day and night. It's not hard to snag last-minute tickets to a regular-season game. Check out the gourmet restaurants that ring the stadium; it wouldn't be San Francisco without top-tier cuisine.

The National Football League's **San Francisco 49ers** (www.49ers.com) left behind their longtime home at Candlestick Park in 2014 and now play at **Levi's Stadium** (4900 Marie P. DeBartolo Way, at Tasman Ave., 415/464-9377, www.levisstadium.com) in Santa Clara, 45 minutes south of the city.

Go Wild on the Farallon Islands

On one of those rare clear San Francisco days, you might catch a glimpse of something far offshore in the distance. It's not a pirate ship or an ocean-based optical illusion. It's the **Farallon Islands,** a series of jagged islets and rocks 28 miles west of the Golden Gate Bridge.

At certain times, humans have attempted to make a living on these harsh rocky outcroppings. In the 1800s, Russians hunted the Farallons' marine mammals for their pelts and blubber. Following the Gold Rush, two rival companies harvested murre eggs on the Farallons to feed nearby San Francisco's growing population.

Now the islands have literally gone to the birds. The islands have been set aside as a national wildlife refuge, allowing the region's bird populations to flourish. The Farallons are home to the largest colony of western gulls in the world and has half the world's ashy storm petrels.

But this wild archipelago is also known for its robust population of great white sharks that circle the islands looking for seal and sea lion snacks. The exploits of a group of great white shark researchers on the island were detailed in Susan Carey's gripping 2005 book *The Devil's Teeth.*

Nature lovers who want to see the Farallons' wildlife up close can book an all-day boat trip through **San Francisco Whale Tours** (415/706-7364, www.sanfranciscowhaletours.com) or **SF Bay Whale Watching** (415/331-6267, www.sfbaywhalewatching.com). Don't fall overboard.

Food

From near and far, people come to San Francisco to eat. Some of the greatest culinary innovations in the world come out of the kitchens in the city. The only problem is to narrow down the choices for dinner tonight.

UNION SQUARE AND NOB HILL
California Cuisine

Make reservations in advance if you want to dine at San Francisco legend **Farallon** (450 Post St., 415/956-6969, www.farallonrestaurant.com, 5:30pm-9:30pm Mon.-Thurs., 5:30pm-10pm Fri.-Sat., 5:30pm-9pm Sun., $27-65). Dark, cave-like rooms are decorated in an under-the-sea theme complete with the unique Jellyfish Bar. The cuisine, on the other hand, is out of this world. Chef Mark Franz has made Farallon a 20-year fad that just keeps gaining ground. The major culinary theme, seafood, dominates the pricey-but-worth-it menu.

Chinese

It may not be in Chinatown, but the dim sum at ★ **Yank Sing** (101 Spear St., 415/781-1111, www.yanksing.com, 11am-3pm Mon.-Fri., 10am-4pm Sat.-Sun., $4-11) is second to none. They even won a prestigious James Beard Award in 2009. The family owns and operates both this restaurant and its sister location (49 Stevenson St., 415/541-4949), and now the third generation is training to take over. Expect traditional steamed pork buns, shrimp dumplings, and egg custard tarts. Note that it's open for lunch only.

French

Tucked away in a tiny alley that looks like it might have been transported from Saint-Michel in Paris, **Café Claude** (7 Claude Ln., 415/392-3505, www.cafeclaude.com, 11:30am-10:30pm Mon.-Sat., 5:30pm-10:30pm Sun., $21-28) serves classic brasserie cuisine to French expatriates and Americans alike. Much French is spoken here, but the simple food tastes fantastic in any language. Café Claude is open for lunch through dinner (dinner only on Sun.), serving an attractive post-lunch menu for weary shoppers looking for sustenance at 3 or 4pm. In the evening it can get crowded, but reservations aren't strictly necessary if you're willing to order a classic French cocktail or a glass of wine and enjoy the bustling atmosphere and live music (on weekends) for a few minutes.

Thai

Located in the Parc 55 Wyndham Hotel, **Kin Khao** (55 Cyril Magnin St., 415/362-7456, http://kinkhao.com, 11:30am-2pm and 5:30pm-10pm Sun.-Thurs., 11:30am-2pm and 5:30pm-11pm Fri.-Sat., $10-25) offers cuisine far beyond peanut sauces, with dishes like caramelized pork belly, vegetables in a sour curry broth, and green curry with rabbit meatballs. The curries are made from scratch, and the seafood is never frozen.

Just outside of the Union Square area, **Lers Ros Thai** (730 Larkin St., 415/931-6917, http://lersros.com, 11am-midnight daily, $9-18) is a great place to expand your knowledge of Thai cuisine. Daily specials might include stir-fried alligator or venison, while specialties include shredded green papaya salads, garlic quail, and stir-fried pork belly. Bring a handkerchief to mop up the sweat caused by these spicy dishes! Other locations are in Hayes Valley (307 Hayes St., 415/874-9661, 11am-11pm daily) and the Mission District (3189 16th St., 415/923-8983, 11:30am-10pm Sun.-Thurs., 11:30am-11pm Fri.-Sat.).

Breakfast

Even on a weekday morning, there will be a line out the door of ★ **Brenda's French Soul Food** (652 Polk St., 415/345-8100, http://frenchsoulfood.com, 8am-3pm Mon.-Tues., 8am-10pm Wed.-Sat., 8am-8pm Sun., $12-17). People come in droves to this Tenderloin eatery for its delectable and filling New Orleans-style breakfasts. Unique offerings include crawfish beignets, an Andouille sausage omelet, and beef cutlet and grits. Entrées like chicken étouffée and red beans and rice top the dinner menu.

Bakeries and Cafés

Blue Bottle Café (66 Mint Plaza, 415/495-3394, www.bluebottlecoffee.net, 7am-7pm daily, $5-10), a popular local chain with multiple locations around the city, takes its equipment seriously. Whether you care about the big copper thing that made your mocha or not, you can get a good cup of joe and a small if somewhat pretentious meal at the Mint Plaza, which is Blue Bottle's only café with a full food program. Other locations can be found at the Ferry Building (1 Ferry Bldg., Ste. 7 and Kiosk #4 at Ste. 56), Market Square (1355 Market St.), Pacific Heights (2453 Fillmore St.), and Hayes Valley (315 Linden St.). Expect a line.

FINANCIAL DISTRICT AND SOMA
California Cuisine

★ **Michael Mina** (252 California St., 415/397-9222, www.michaelmina.net, 11:30am-2pm and 6pm-9pm Mon.-Thurs., 11:30am-2pm and 5:30pm-10pm Fri., 5:30pm-10pm Sat.-Sun., $135-195) finds the celebrity chef using Japanese ingredients and French influences to create bold California entrées. This sleek, upscale restaurant with attentive service is where Mina showcases his signature dishes, including his ahi tuna tartare and his Maine lobster pot pie, an inventive take where the lobster, lobster cream sauce, and vegetables are ladled over a flaky pastry crust. With the only dinner options available being the five-course menu and the eight-course chef's tasting menu, expect to spend some money.

International

Located in the San Francisco Museum of Modern Art, **In Situ** (151 3rd St., 415/941-6050, http://insitu.sfmoma.org, 11am-3:30pm Mon.-Tues., 11am-3:30pm and 5pm-9pm Thurs.-Sun., $12-28) is almost an art piece unto itself. The concept behind the dining room and lounge: Chef Corey Lee re-creates popular dishes from fine restaurants around the world. The à la carte menu of mostly small plates features the stories of the chefs behind the creations, immersing diners in their creative process. Reservations for the dining room are recommended, but if you can't get in, opt for the 29-seat lounge.

Gastropub

★ **The Cavalier** (360 Jessie St., 415/321-6000, http://thecavaliersf.com, 7am-10pm Mon.-Wed., 7am-11pm Thurs.-Fri., 10am-11pm Sat., 10am-9pm Sun., $16-34) serves a California take on upscale British pub food. The restaurant is decorated like a British hunting lodge, with mounted game heads on the walls. A stuffed fox named Floyd reclines on a bookcase in the back. As for the food, it is inventive, tasty, sometimes rich, and surprisingly well priced. The golden-fried lamb scrumpets are worth the trip, while other entrées include classics like fish-and-chips and meat pies.

Seafood

It's easy to see why the ★ **Tadich Grill** (240 California St., 415/391-1849, www.tadichgrill.com, 11am-9:30pm Mon.-Fri., 11:30am-9:30pm Sat., $15-38), claiming to be the oldest restaurant in the city, has been around for over 160 years. Sit at the long wooden bar, which stretches from the front door back to the kitchen, and enjoy the attentive service by the white-jacketed waitstaff. The food is classic and hearty, and the seafood-heavy menu has 75 entrées, including a dozen daily specials. One of the standouts is the restaurant's delectable seafood cioppino, which might just be the best version of this Italian-American stew out there.

Steak

Alexander's Steakhouse (448 Brannan St., 415/495-1111, www.alexanderssteakhouse.com, 5:30pm-9pm Mon.-Thurs., 5:30pm-10pm Fri., 5pm-10pm Sat., 5pm-9pm Sun., $48-190) describes itself as "where East meets beef." It's true: The presentation at Alexander's looks like something you'd see on *Iron Chef*, and the prices of the *wagyu* beef look like the monthly payment on a small Japanese car. This white-tablecloth steak house is the antithesis of a bargain, but the food, including the steaks, is more imaginative than most, and the elegant dining experience will make you feel special as your wallet quietly bleeds out.

Italian

For fine Italian-influenced cuisine, make

Tadich Grill

a reservation at **Quince** (470 Pacific Ave., 415/775-8500, www.quincerestaurant.com, 5:30pm-9:30pm Mon.-Thurs., 5pm-9:30pm Fri.-Sat., $210-250). Chef-owner Michael Tusk blends culinary aesthetics to create his own unique style of cuisine. There are three options: the single extended tasting menu, the abbreviated seasonal tasting menu, or ordering à la carte from the salon menu.

Japanese

Forget your notions of the plain-Jane sushi bar; **Ozumo** (161 Steuart St., 415/882-1333, www.ozumosanfrancisco.com, 11:30am-2pm and 5:30pm-10:30pm Mon.-Thurs., 11:30am-2pm and 5:30pm-11pm Fri., 5:30pm-11pm Sat., 5:30pm-10pm Sun., $28-46) takes Japanese cuisine upscale, San Francisco-style. Order some classic *nigiri*, tempura battered dishes, or a big chunk of meat off the traditional *robata* grill. High-quality sake lines the shelves above the bar and along the walls. For non-imbibers, choose from a selection of premium teas. If you're a night owl, enjoy a late dinner on weekends and drinks in the lounge nightly.

Vietnamese

Probably the single most famous Asian restaurant in a city filled with eateries of all types is **The Slanted Door** (1 Ferry Plaza, Ste. 3, 415/861-8032, www.slanteddoor.com, 11am-2:30pm and 5:30pm-10pm Mon.-Sat., 11:30am-3pm and 5:30pm-10pm Sun., $11-45). Owner Charles Phan, along with more than 20 family members and the rest of his staff, pride themselves on welcoming service and top-quality food. Organic local ingredients get used in both traditional and innovative Vietnamese cuisine, creating a unique dining experience. Even experienced foodies remark that they've never had green papaya salad, glass noodles, or shaking beef like this before. The light afternoon-tea menu (2:30pm-4:30pm daily) can be the perfect pick-me-up for weary travelers who need some sustenance to get them through the long afternoon until dinner, and Vietnamese coffee is the ultimate Southeast Asian caffeine experience.

Bakeries and Cafés

One of the Ferry Building mainstays, the **Acme Bread Company** (1 Ferry Plaza, Ste. 15, 415/288-2978, http://acmebread.com, 7am-7:30pm Mon.-Fri., 8am-7pm Sat.-Sun.) remains true to its name. You can buy bread here, but not sandwiches, croissants, or pastries. All the bread that Acme sells is made with fresh organic ingredients in traditional style; the baguettes are traditionally French, so they start to go stale after only 4-6 hours. Eat fast!

The motto of **Café Venue** (67 5th St., 415/546-1144, www.cafevenue.com, 7am-3:30pm Mon.-Fri., 8am-2:30pm Sat., $6-10) is "real food, fast and fresh." This simple strategy is clearly working: On weekdays, you can expect a long line of local workers grabbing a salad or a sandwich for lunch. The warm chicken pesto sandwich is a highlight.

Farmers Markets

While farmers markets litter the landscape in just about every California town, the **Ferry Plaza Farmers Market** (1 Ferry Plaza, 415/291-3276, www.ferrybuildingmarketplace.com, 10am-2pm Tues. and Thurs., 8am-2pm Sat.) is special. At the granddaddy of Bay Area farmers markets, you'll find a wonderful array of produce, cooked foods, and even locally raised meats and locally caught seafood. Expect to see the freshest fruits and veggies from local growers, grass-fed beef from Marin County, and seasonal seafood pulled from the Pacific beyond the Golden Gate. Granted, you'll pay for the privilege of purchasing from this market—if you're seeking bargain produce, you'll be better served at one of the weekly suburban farmers markets. Even locals flock downtown to the Ferry Building on Saturday mornings, especially in the summer when the variety of California's agricultural bounty becomes staggering.

CHINATOWN
Chinese Banquets

Banquet restaurants offer tasty meat, seafood, and veggie dishes along with rice, soups, and appetizers, all served family-style. Tables are often round, with a lazy Susan in the middle to facilitate the passing of communal serving bowls around the table. In the city, most banquet Chinese restaurants have at least a few dishes that will feel familiar to the American palate, and menus often have English translations.

The **R&G Lounge** (631 Kearny St., 415/982-7877, www.rnglounge.com, 11am-9:30pm daily, $12-40, reservations suggested) takes traditional Chinese American cuisine to the next level. The menu is divided by colors that represent the five elements, according to Chinese tradition and folklore. In addition to old favorites like moo shu pork, chow mein, and lemon chicken, you'll find spicy Szechuan and Mongolian dishes and an array of house specialties. Salt-and-pepper Dungeness crab, served whole on a plate, is the R&G signature dish, though many of the other seafood dishes are just as special. Expect your seafood to be fresh since it comes right out of the tank in the dining room. California-cuisine mores have made their way into the R&G Lounge in the form of some innovative dishes and haute cuisine presentations. This is a great place to enjoy Chinatown cuisine in an American-friendly setting.

Dim Sum

The Chinese culinary tradition of dim sum is translated as "touch the heart," meaning "order to your heart's content" in Cantonese. In practical terms, it's a light meal composed of small bites of a wide range of dishes. Americans tend to eat dim sum at lunchtime, though it can just as easily be dinner or even Sunday brunch. In a proper dim sum restaurant, you do not order anything or see a menu. Instead, you sip your oolong and sit back as servers push loaded steam trays out of the kitchen one after the other. Servers and trays make their way around the tables; you pick out what you'd like to try as it passes, and enough of that dish for everyone at your table is placed before you.

One of the many great dim sum places in Chinatown is the **Great Eastern** (649 Jackson St., 415/986-2500, www. greateasternrestaurant.net, 10am-11pm Mon.-Fri., 9am-11pm Sat.-Sun., $15-25), which serves its dim sum menu 10am-2:30pm daily. It's not a standard dim sum place; instead of the steam carts, you'll get a menu and a list. You must write down everything you want on your list and hand it to your waiter, and your choices will be brought out to you, so family style is undoubtedly the way to go here. Make reservations or you may wait 30-60 minutes for a table. This restaurant jams up fast, right from the moment it opens, especially on weekends. The good news is that most of the folks crowding into Great Eastern are locals. You know what that means.

Ordering dim sum at **Delicious Dim Sum** (752 Jackson St., 415/781-0721, 7am-6pm Thurs.-Tues., $3) may pose challenges. The signs are not in English, and they don't take credit cards. Also, there is only one table inside so you'll probably be getting your dim sum to go. The inexpensive dim sum, with popular pork buns and shrimp and cilantro dumplings, among other options, is worth rising to the challenge.

NORTH BEACH AND FISHERMAN'S WHARF
California Cuisine

San Francisco culinary celebrity Gary Danko has a number of restaurants, but the finest is the one that bears his name. **Gary Danko** (800 North Point St., 415/749-2060, www.garydanko.com, 5:30pm-10pm daily, prix fixe $87-124) offers the best of Danko's California cuisine, from the signature horseradish-crusted salmon medallions to the array of delectable fowl dishes. The herbs and veggies come from Danko's own farm in Napa. Choose 3-5 courses. Make reservations in advance to get a table, and dress up for your sojourn in the elegant white-tablecloth dining room.

Italian

North Beach is San Francisco's own version of Little Italy. Poke around and find one of the local favorite mom-and-pop pizza joints, or try a bigger, more upscale Italian eatery.

Want a genuine world-champion pizza while you're in town? Tony Gemignani, winner of 11 World Pizza Champion awards, can hook you up. ★ **Tony's Pizza Napoletana** (1570 Stockton St., 415/835-9888, www. tonyspizzanapoletana.com, noon-10pm Mon., noon-11pm Wed.-Sun., $15-30) has seven different pizza ovens that cook by wood, coal, gas, or electric power. You can get a classic American pie loaded with pepperoni, a California-style pie with quail eggs and chorizo, or a Sicilian pizza smothered in meat and garlic. The chef's special Neapolitan-style pizza margherita is a simple-sounding pizza made to perfection. The wood-fired atmosphere of this temple to the pie includes marble-topped tables, dark woods, and white linen napkins stuck into old tomato cans. The long full bar dominates the front dining room, so grab a fancy bottle of wine or a cocktail to go with that champion pizza. For a slice to go, head next door to **Tony's Coal-Fired Pizza and Slice House** (1556 Stockton St., 11:30am-8pm Tues., 11:30am-11pm Wed.-Sun., $3-6).

Trattoria Contadina (1800 Mason St., 415/982-5728, www.trattoriacontadina. com, 5pm-9pm Mon.-Thurs., 5pm-9:30pm Fri., 4pm-9:30pm Sat.-Sun., $18-35) presents mouthwatering Italian fare in a fun, eclectic dining room. Dozens of framed photos line the walls, and fresh ingredients stock the kitchen in this San Francisco take on the classic Italian trattoria. Menu items include veal, spaghetti, and gnocchi. Kids are welcome, and vegetarians will find good meatless choices on the menu.

A teensy neighborhood place, **L'Osteria del Forno** (519 Columbus Ave., 415/982-1124, www.losteriadelforno.com, 11:30am-10pm Sun.-Mon. and Wed.-Thurs., 11:30am-10:30pm Fri.-Sat., $6-19) serves up a small menu to match its small dining room and small tables and small (but full) bar. The delectable northern Italian-style pizzas and pastas paired with artisanal cocktails go a long way toward warming up frozen, fog-drenched visitors from the Wharf and the beach. Locals love L'Osteria, which means it's next to impossible to get a table at lunchtime or dinnertime, and doubly impossible on weekends. Your best bet is to drop by during the off-hours; L'Osteria stays open all afternoon and makes a perfect haven for travelers who find themselves in need of a late lunch.

Greek

In the Greek fishing village of Kokkari, wild game and seafood hold a special place in the local mythology. At **Kokkari Estiatorio** (200 Jackson St., 415/981-0983, www.kokkari.com, 11:30am-2:30pm and 5:30pm-10pm Mon.-Thurs., 11:30am-2:30pm and 5:30pm-11pm Fri., 5pm-11pm Sat., 5pm-10pm Sun., $22-49), patrons enjoy Mediterranean delicacies made with fresh California ingredients amid rustic elegance, feasting on such classic dishes as crispy zucchini cakes, moussaka, and grilled lamb chops.

Steak House

A New York stage actress wanted a classic steak house in San Francisco, and so **Harris' Restaurant** (2100 Van Ness Ave., 415/673-1888, www.harrisrestaurant.com, 5:30pm-close Mon.-Fri., 5pm-close Sat.-Sun., $49-198) came to be. The fare runs to traditional steaks and prime rib as well as upscale features, with a Kobe *wagyu* beef and surf-and-turf featuring a whole Maine lobster. Music lovers can catch live jazz in the lounge most evenings.

Breakfast

Smack-dab in the middle of North Beach, **Mama's on Washington Square** (1701 Stockton St., 415/362-6421, www.mamas-sf. com, 8am-3pm daily, $8-10) is perched right across from the green lawn of Washington

Square. This more that 50-year-old institution is the perfect place to fuel up on gourmet omelets, freshly baked breads that include a delectable cinnamon brioche, and daily specials like crab Benedict before a day of sightseeing. Arrive early, or be prepared to wait . . . and wait.

Bakeries and Cafés

Widely recognized as the first espresso coffeehouse on the West Coast, family-owned **Caffé Trieste** (601 Vallejo St., 415/392-6739, www.caffetrieste.com, 6:30am-11pm daily, cash only) first opened its doors in 1956. It became a hangout for Beat writers in the 1950s and 1960s and was where Francis Ford Coppola penned the screenplay for his classic film *The Godfather* in the 1970s. Sip a cappuccino, munch on Italian pastries, and enjoy frequent concerts at this treasured North Beach institution. There are now four locations, from Berkeley to Monterey.

Serving some of the most famous sourdough in the city, the **Boudin Bakery & Café** (Pier 39, Space 5-Q, 415/421-0185, www.boudinbakery.com, 7:30am-9pm daily, $6-8) is a Pier 39 institution. Grab a loaf of bread to take with you, or order in one of the Boudin classics. Nothing draws tourists like the fragrant clam chowder in a bread bowl, but if you prefer, you can try another soup, a signature sandwich, or even a fresh salad. For a more upscale dining experience with the same great breads, try **Bistro Boudin** (160 Jefferson St., 415/351-5561, 11:30am-10pm Sun.-Thurs., 11:30am-10:30pm Fri.-Sat., $13-38).

MARINA AND PACIFIC HEIGHTS

New American

The Brixton (2140 Union St., 415/409-1114, www.brixtonsf.com, 11am-midnight daily, entrées $13-23) might have rock posters on the wall and loud music blaring overhead, but that doesn't mean you shouldn't try the food. The dinner menu goes late into the night and includes items like half a chicken and a tasty burger. The appetizer menu, including

a chorizo clam dish and a crab cake plate, is worth grazing, and the "Tacos of the Day" can sate smaller appetites.

Seafood

Anytime you come to the tiny ★ **Swan Oyster Depot** (1517 Polk St., 415/673-1101, 10:30am-5:30pm Mon.-Sat., $10-25, cash only), there will be a line out the door. With limited stools at a long marble bar, Swan, which opened in 1912, is an old-school seafood place that serves fresh seafood salads, seafood cocktails, and clam chowder, the only hot item on the menu. The seafood is so fresh that you pass it resting on ice while waiting for your barstool.

Steak House

The Marina is a great place to find a big thick steak. One famed San Francisco steak house, **Boboquivari's** (1450 Lombard St., 415/441-8880, www.boboquivaris.com, 5pm-11pm daily, $23-150) prides itself on its dry-aged beef and fresh seafood. In season, enjoy whole Dungeness crab. But most of all, enjoy "The Steak," thickly cut and simply prepared to enhance the flavor of the beef. The 49-ounce porterhouse costs a pretty penny: $150.

Japanese

With rolls named after rock acts U2 and Elvis, it's no surprise that **Ace Wasabi's** (3339 Steiner St., 415/567-4903, www.acewasabisf.com, 5:30pm-10pm Mon.-Wed., 5:30pm-10:30pm Thurs., 5:30pm-11pm Fri.-Sat., 5pm-10pm Sun., $6-18 per item) advertises itself as a "rock 'n' roll sushi" joint. Some of the fish is flown in from Tokyo's Tsukiji Fish Market, and the menu includes unusual offerings like tuna tostadas.

If you're in Pacific Heights, give **Kiss Seafood** (1700 Laguna St., 415/474-2866, 5:30pm-9:30pm Wed.-Sat., $38-78) a try. This tiny restaurant (12 seats total) boasts some of the freshest fish in town, which is no mean feat in San Francisco. The lone chef prepares all the fish himself, possibly due to the tiny size of the place. If you're up for sashimi, you'll be in raw-fish heaven. Round off your meal with a glass of chilled premium sake. Reservations are a good idea.

Breakfast

Sweet Maple (2101 Sutter St., 415/655-9169, www.sweetmaplesf.com, 8am-3pm daily, $11-22) takes breakfast to the next level. The varied menu takes eggs in new directions with morning pizzas, egg tacos, and creations including a *wagyu* sliders Benedict. Wash it down with a morning cocktail. It's all served in an airy space with orchids and hanging lamps.

CIVIC CENTER AND HAYES VALLEY

California Cuisine

Housed in a former bank, **Nopa** (560 Divisadero St., 415/864-8643, http://nopasf.com, 6pm-midnight Sun.-Thurs., 6pm-1am Fri.-Sat., $16-32) brings together the neighborhood that the restaurant is named after with a whimsical mural by a local artist, a communal table, and a crowd as diverse as the surrounding area. A creative and inexpensive menu offers soul-satisfying dishes and keeps tables full into the wee hours. The cocktails are legendary.

State Bird Provisions (1529 Fillmore St., 415/795-1272, http://statebirdsf.com, 5:30pm-10pm Sun.-Thurs., 5:30pm-11pm Fri.-Sat., $14-22) burst onto the San Francisco dining scene in a big way, winning two James Beard Awards (Best New Restaurant in the Whole of the USA in 2013 and the Best Chef in the West in 2015). Part of the unique menu is devoted to "Pancakes and Toast," with items like a beef tongue and horseradish buckwheat pancake. Of course, they also serve the state bird (quail) with provisions.

French

★ **Jardinière** (300 Grove St., 415/861-5555, www.jardiniere.com, 5pm-close daily, $25-95) was the first restaurant opened by local celebrity chef Traci Des Jardins. The bar and dining room blend into one another and

feature stunning art deco decor. The ever-changing menu is a masterpiece of French California cuisine, and Des Jardins has long supported the sustainable restaurant movement. Eating at Jardinière is not only a treat for the senses, it is also a way to support the best of trends in San Francisco restaurants. Make reservations if you're trying to catch dinner before a show.

Absinthe (398 Hayes St., 415/551-1590, www.absinthe.com, 11:30am-11pm Mon.-Wed., 11:30am-midnight Thurs.-Fri., 11am-midnight Sat., 11am-10pm Sun., $15-37) takes its name from the notorious "green fairy" drink made of liquor and wormwood. Absinthe indeed does serve absinthe, including locally made St. George Spirits Absinthe Verte. It also serves upscale French bistro fare, including what may be the best french fries in the city. The French theme carries on into the decor as well, so expect the look of a Parisian brasserie or perhaps a café in Nice, with retro-modern furniture and classic prints on the walls. The bar is open until 2am on Thursday, Friday, and Saturday, so if you want drinks or dessert after a show at the Opera or Davies Hall, just walk around the corner.

German

Suppenküche (525 Laguna St., 415/252-9289, www.suppenkuche.com, 5pm-10pm Mon.-Sat., 10am-2:30pm and 5pm-10pm Sun., $12.50-20) brings a taste of Bavaria to the Bay Area. The beer list is a great place to start, since you can enjoy a wealth of classic German brews on tap and in bottles, plus a few Belgians thrown in for variety. For dinner, expect German classics with a focus on Bavarian cuisine. Spaetzle, pork, sausage—you name it, they've got it, and it will harden your arteries right up. They now serve a Sunday brunch that's almost as heavy as its dinners. Suppenküche also has a **Biergarten** (424 Octavia St., 415/252-9289, http://biergartensf.com, 3pm-9pm Mon.-Sat., 1pm-7pm Sun. summer, 2pm-8pm Mon.-Sat., 1pm-7pm Sun. winter), two blocks away.

MISSION AND CASTRO
Mexican and Latin American

Much of the rich heritage of the Mission District is Latino, thus leading to the Mission being *the* place to find a good taco or burrito. **Farolito Taqueria** (2950 24th St., 415/641-0758, www.elfarolitoinc.com, 10am-1:30am Mon.-Thurs. and Sun., 10am-2:30am Fri.-Sat., $10) has found favor with the picky locals who have dozens of taqueria options within a few blocks. It seems that every regular has a different favorite: the burritos, the enchiladas, the quesadillas. Whatever your pleasure, you'll find a tasty version of it at Farolito. A totally casual spot, you order at the counter and sit at picnic-style tables to chow down on the properly greasy Mexican fare. (Don't confuse this Farolito with the taqueria with the same name on Mission Street.)

Argentina is known for tango, wine, and beef. The latter is done superbly at ★ **Lolinda** (2518 Mission St., 415/550-6970, http://lolindasf.com, 5:30pm-midnight Fri.-Sat., 5:30pm-11pm Sun.-Thurs., $14-78). The six-ounce skirt steak has a big flavor for its modest size, while the "Gaucho," a 26-ounce bone-in ribeye is the largest and priciest cut. All meat is cooked on a wood-fired *asador* (grill). The menu makes room for ceviche, empanadas, and grilled skewers. It's all served in a lit space decorated with a bull mural and a trio of mounted bull heads above the open kitchen.

Seafood

For great seafood in a lower-key atmosphere, locals eschew the tourist traps on the Wharf and head for the **Anchor Oyster Bar** (579 Castro St., 415/431-3990, www.anchoroysterbar.com, 11:30am-10pm Mon.-Sat., 4pm-9:30pm Sun., $14-39) in the Castro. The raw bar features different ways to have oysters, including an oyster *soju* shot. The dining room serves seafood, including local favorite Dungeness crab. Service is friendly, as befits a neighborhood spot, and it sees fewer large crowds. This doesn't diminish its quality, and it makes for a great spot to get a delicious meal before heading out to the local clubs for a late night out.

Italian

Sometimes even the most dedicated culinary explorer needs a break from the endless fancy food of San Francisco. When the time is right for a plain ol' pizza, head for **Little Star Pizza** (400 Valencia St., 415/551-7827, www.littlestarpizza.com, 5pm-10pm Mon.-Tues., noon-10pm Wed.-Thurs. and Sun., noon-11pm Fri.-Sat., $12-23). A jewel of the Mission District, this pizzeria specializes in Chicago-style deep-dish pies, but also serves thin-crust pizzas for devotees of the New York style. Once you've found the all-black building and taken a seat inside the casual eatery, grab a beer or a cocktail from the bar if you have to wait for a table. Pick one of Little Star's specialty pizzas, or create your own variation from the toppings they offer. Can't get enough of Little Star? They've got a second location in the city (846 Divisadero St., 415/441-1118).

Delfina (3621 18th St., 415/552-4055, www.delfinasf.com, 5pm-9:30pm Mon.-Thurs., 4pm-10:30pm Fri., 3pm-10:30pm Sat., 3pm-9:30pm Sun., $10-32) gives Italian cuisine a hearty California twist. From the antipasti to the entrées, the dishes speak of local farms and ranches, fresh seasonal produce, and the best Italian-American taste that money can buy. With both a charming, warm indoor dining room and an outdoor garden patio, there's plenty of seating at this lovely restaurant.

Korean

Owned and operated by three brothers, **Namu Gaji** (499 Dolores St., 415/431-6268, www.namusf.com, 5:30pm-10pm Tues., 11:30am-3pm and 5:30pm-10pm Wed.-Thurs., 11:30am-3pm and 5:30pm-10:30pm Fri., 10:30am-4pm and 5pm-10:30pm Sat., 10:30am-4pm and 5pm-10pm Sun., $13-21) presents a new take on Korean food. One standout dish is the *okonomiyaki*, a pan-fried entrée made with kimchee and oysters. The adventurous can try beef tongue, while the less courageous might opt for salmon or a burger.

Sushi

ICHI Sushi & Ni Bar (3369 Mission St., 415/525-4750, http://ichisushi.com, 5:30pm-10pm Mon.-Tues., 11:30am-2pm and 5:30pm-10pm Wed.-Thurs., 11:30am-2pm and 5:30pm-11pm Fri., 11am-2:30pm and 5:30pm-11pm Sat., 11am-2:30pm and 5:30pm-9:30pm Sun., $4.50-14.50) started out as a Bernal Heights food stall and evolved into a sleek restaurant. The emphasis is on sustainable sashimi. There are also rolls, a unique cold ramen with pesto, and some perfectly golden-brown chicken wings. Get good deals on appetizers and drinks at the bar's happy hour (5:30pm-6:30pm Mon.-Fri.).

Bakeries and Cafés

A line snakes into the ★ **Tartine Bakery** (600 Guerrero St., 415/487-2600, www.tartinebakery.com, 8am-7pm Mon., 7:30am-7pm Tues.-Wed., 7:30am-8pm Thurs.-Fri., 8am-8pm Sat.-Sun.) almost all day long. You might think that there's an impromptu rock show or a book signing by a prominent author, but the eatery's baked goods, breads, and sandwiches are the stars. A slab of the transcendent quiche made with crème fraîche, Niman Ranch smoked ham, and organic produce is an inspired way to start the day, especially if you are planning on burning some serious calories. Meanwhile, there is nothing quite like a piece of Passion Fruit Lime Bavarian Rectangle, a cake that somehow manages to be both rich in flavor and light as air. Its latest endeavor is **Tartine Manufactory** (595 Alabama St., 7:30am-5pm and 5:30pm-10pm Mon.-Fri., 8am-5pm and 5:30pm-10pm Sat.-Sun.), a big industrial building with a bread baking operation, a coffee bar, a bar, and a café serving breakfast, lunch, and dinner.

You can also satisfy your sweet tooth at **Bi-Rite Creamery & Bakeshop** (3692 18th St., 415/626-5600, http://biritecreamery.com, 11am-10pm daily). The ice cream is made by hand with organic milk, cream, and eggs; inventive flavors include honey lavender, salted caramel, and white chocolate raspberry swirl. Pick up a scoop to enjoy at nearby Mission Dolores Park. They also have a location at 550 Divisadero (415/551-7900, 9am-9pm daily).

GOLDEN GATE PARK AND THE HAIGHT

California Cuisine

One of the most famous restaurant locations on the San Francisco coast is the **Cliff House.** The high-end eatery inhabiting the famed facade is **Sutro's** (1090 Point Lobos Ave., 415/386-3330, www.cliffhouse.com, 11:30am-9:30pm Mon.-Sat., 11am-9:30pm Sun., $25-39). The appetizers and entrées are mainly seafood in somewhat snooty preparations. Although the cuisine is expensive and fancy, in all honesty it's not the best in the city. What *is* amazing are the views from the floor-to-ceiling windows out over the vast expanse of the Pacific Ocean. These views make Sutro's a perfect spot to enjoy a romantic dinner while watching the sun set over the sea.

The Cliff House also houses the more casual **Bistro** (1090 Point Lobos Ave., 415/386-3330, www.cliffhouse.com, 9am-3:30pm and 4:15pm-9:30pm Mon.-Sat., 8:30am-3:30pm and 4:15pm-9:30pm Sun., $15-30).

Japanese

Sushi restaurants are immensely popular in these residential neighborhoods. **Koo** (408 Irving St., 415/731-7077, www.sushikoo.com, 5:30pm-10pm Tues.-Thurs., 5:30pm-10:30pm Fri.-Sat., 5pm-9:30pm Sun., $30-50) is a favorite in the Sunset. While sushi purists are happy with the selection of *nigiri* and sashimi, lovers of fusion and experimentation will enjoy the small plates and unusual rolls created to delight diners. Complementing the Japanese cuisine is a small but scrumptious list of premium sakes. Only the cheap stuff is served hot, as high-quality sake is always chilled.

Thai

Dining in the Haight? Check out the flavorful dishes at **Siam Lotus Thai Cuisine** (1705 Haight St., 415/933-8031, noon-4pm and 5pm-9pm Mon. and Thurs., 5pm-9pm Wed., noon-4pm and 5pm-9:30pm Fri., noon-9:30pm Sat., noon-9pm Sun., $7-13). You'll find a rainbow of curries, pad thai, and all sorts of Thai meat, poultry, and vegetarian dishes. Look to the lunch specials for bargains, and to the Thai iced tea for a lunchtime pick-me-up. Locals enjoy the casually romantic ambience, and visitors make special trips down to the Haight just to dine here.

Vietnamese

Thanh Long (4101 Judah St., 415/665-1146, http://thanhlongsf.com, 5pm-9pm Tues.-Thurs. and Sun., 5pm-9:30pm Fri.-Sat., $20-30) was the first family-owned Vietnamese restaurant in San Francisco. Since the early 1970s, Thanh Long has been serving one of the best preparations of local Dungeness crab in the city: roasted crab with garlic noodles. This isn't a $5 pho joint, so expect white tablecloths and higher prices at this stately small restaurant in the outer Sunset neighborhood. Fans include actors Harrison Ford and Danny Glover.

Accommodations

Both the cheapest and the most expensive places tend to be in Union Square and downtown. Cheaper digs can be had in the neighborhoods surrounding Fisherman's Wharf. You'll find the most character in small boutique hotels, but plenty of big chain hotels have at least one location in town. Valet parking and overnight garage parking can be expensive. Check to see if your hotel has a "parking package" that includes this expense.

UNION SQUARE AND NOB HILL

In and around Union Square and Nob Hill, you'll find approximately a zillion hotels. As a rule, those closest to the top of the Hill or to Union Square proper are the most expensive. For a one- or two-block walk away from the center, you get more personality and a genuine San Francisco experience for less money and less prestige. There are few inexpensive options in these areas. Hostels are located to the southwest, closer to the gritty Tenderloin neighborhood, where safety becomes an issue after dark.

$150-250

One of the best deals in town is at the ★ **Golden Gate Hotel** (775 Bush St., 415/392-3702, www.goldengatehotel.com, $150-225), centrally located between Union Square and the top of Nob Hill. This narrow yellow building has 25 rooms decorated with antiques, giving it a bed-and-breakfast feel. The cheapest option is a room with a shared bath down the hall, though there are rooms with their own baths. The Golden Gate serves a fine continental breakfast with fresh croissants.

Despite its location in the seedier Tenderloin neighborhood—or perhaps because of it—the ★ **Phoenix Hotel** (601 Eddy St., 415/776-1380, www.phoenixsf.com, $229-329) has serious rock-and-roll cred. A former motor lodge, the Phoenix has hosted a who's who of rock music, including the Red Hot Chili Peppers, Debbie Harry, and Sublime. When a Kurt Cobain letter was found mocking his wedding vows to Courtney Love, it was written on Phoenix letterhead. The main draw is the large deck with an inlaid, heated pool that has a mosaic on the bottom. Palm trees rising overhead make the Phoenix feels like it's a beachside oasis rather than sited in a gritty urban neighborhood. At night, the sounds of the surrounding Tenderloin remind you of the hotel's true location, but most guests don't come here to catch up on their sleep.

Over $250

★ **Hotel G** (386 Geary St., 877/828-4478, http://hotelgsanfrancisco.com, $279-499) comes on like an unassuming cool kid that impresses with understated style. The rooms in this boutique hotel are all simple, clean, and serene with accouterments like smart TVs, Nespresso coffeemakers, Tivoli clock radios, and comfy beds with denim headboards (a nod to Levi's San Francisco roots). The lower-level rooms have bathrooms with subway-tiled floors and showers, while the upper-floor bathrooms utilize marble flooring and shower walls. Choose a room on the 8th floor if you enjoy rooms with high ceilings. There's also three drinking and dining establishments within the building. Best of all, your room will feel like a homey apartment or studio even though the hotel is located just a block from bustling Union Square.

Just blocks from Union Square, **Hotel Rex** (562 Sutter St., 415/433-4434, www.jdvhotels. com/rex, $250-300) is an ideal writer's retreat. The spacious guest rooms all have wooden writing desks and are decorated with the work of local artists. The downstairs Library Bar is a fine place to sip a cocktail or glass of wine while browsing its shelves of hardback books. Live jazz acts perform on Friday.

A San Francisco legend, the **Clift** (495 Geary St., 415/775-4700, www. morganshotelgroup.com, $269-2,100) has a lobby worth walking into, whether you're a guest of the hotel or not. The high-ceilinged, gray industrial space is devoted to modern art, including a Salvador Dalí coffee table. By contrast, the big Philippe Starck-designed guest rooms are almost Spartan in their simplicity, with colors meant to mimic the city skyline. Stop in for a drink at the **Redwood Room,** done in brown leather and popular with a younger crowd. the **Velvet Room** serves breakfast and dinner. The Clift is perfectly located for theatergoers, and the square is an easy walk away.

Certain names just mean luxury in the hotel world. The **Fairmont San Francisco** (950 Mason St., 415/772-5000, www.fairmont. com, $499-4,999) is among the best of these. With a rich history, above-and-beyond service, and spectacular views, the Fairmont makes any stay in the city memorable. Check online for package specials, including "Room with a Vroom," which includes parking, starting at $299 when available. While on-site, head downstairs for a Mai Tai at the Tonga Room & Hurricane Bar.

The **Ritz-Carlton** (600 Stockton St.,

the exterior of San Francisco's Hotel G

415/296-7465, www.ritzcarlton.com, $399-1,000) provides patrons with ultimate pampering. From the high-thread-count sheets to the five-star dining room and the full-service spa, guests at the Ritz all but drown in sumptuous amenities. Even the "standard" guest rooms are exceptional, but if you've got the bread, spring for the Club Floors, where they'll give you an iPod, a personal concierge, and possibly the kitchen sink if you ask for it.

FINANCIAL DISTRICT AND SOMA

Top business execs make it their, well, business to stay near the towering offices of the Financial District, down by the water on the Embarcadero, or in SoMa. Thus, most of the lodgings in these areas cater to the expense-account set. The big-name chain hotels run expensive; book one if you're traveling on an unlimited company credit card. Otherwise, look for smaller boutique and indie accommodations that won't tear your wallet to bits.

$150-250

For something small but upscale, check out **Hotel Griffon** (155 Steuart St., 800/321-2201, www.hotelgriffon.com, $230-500), a boutique business hotel with a prime vacation locale on the Embarcadero, just feet from the Ferry Building. The Griffon offers business and leisure packages to suit any traveler's needs. Although they're pricey, the best guest rooms have views of the Bay Bridge and Treasure Island.

Over $250

Entering the bright lobby exploding with color, you'll realize the ★ **Hotel Triton** (342 Grant Ave., 844/808-0290, www.hoteltriton.com, $389-529) celebrates San Francisco's independent spirit. The rooms are wallpapered with text from Jack Kerouac's *On the Road*, while copies of Allen Ginsberg's *Howl* take the place of the Gideon Bibles found in most other hotels across the country. There are three specialty suites, including one designed by musician Jerry Garcia. The Häagen-Dazs "Sweet Suite" comes stocked with a fridge of the gourmet ice creams. The environmentally friendly practices developed at the Triton are being adopted by sister hotels all over the world. Guest rooms are small but comfortable and well stocked with ecofriendly amenities and bath products.

★ **Hotel Zetta** (55 5th St., 415/543-8555, www.viceroryhotelgroup.com/en/zetta, $299-1,214) embraces San Francisco's reputation as a technology hub. The ultra-modern rooms are equipped with a gaggle of gadgets, including a G-Link station for mobile devices and a device that streams content from your smartphone onto the large flat-screen TVs. There are also espresso machines and a large butcher-block desk for those who need to get work done. The hotel's common rooms are more playful, with shuffleboard, a pool table, and an oversize game of Jenga. Recycled art throughout the building includes chandeliers made of old eyeglasses, located in the lobby. The upscale on-site restaurant **The Cavalier** features British-meets-California cuisine.

Hotel Vitale (8 Mission St., 888/890-8688, www.hotelvitale.com, $309-900) professes to restore guests' vitality with its lovely guest rooms and exclusive spa, complete with rooftop hot soaking tubs and a yoga studio. Many of the good-size guest rooms also have private deep soaking tubs. The Vitale's **Americano Restaurant** serves Italian fare.

Le Méridien San Francisco (333 Battery St., 415/296-2900, www.starwoodhotels.com, $362-843) stands tall in the Embarcadero Center, convenient to shopping, dining, and cable car lines. This expensive luxury hotel pampers guests with Frette sheets, down duvets, and stellar views. Expect nightly turndown service and 24-hour room service. A pedestrian bridge connects the hotel to the Federal Reserve Building.

For a true San Francisco hotel experience, book a room at the famous **Hotel Palomar** (12 4th St., 415/348-1111, www.hotelpalomar-sf.com, $268-549). You'll find every amenity imaginable, from extra-long beds for taller guests to in-room spa services and temporary pet goldfish. Get drinks and dinner at the on-site restaurant **Dirty Habit,** which names *Project Runway* finalist Melissa Fleis as a "muse and collaborator." Join a wellness ambassador for a group run on weekday mornings at 7am or borrow one of the hotel's complimentary bikes to tool around town.

The modern minimalism of ★ **Hotel VIA** (138 King St., 415/200-4977, www.hotelviasf.com, $300-650) is sleek yet functional and comfortable. Rooms come with rain showerheads in the elegantly tiled bathrooms and electronic tablets that guests can use to request services, play music, or browse *The New York Times.* Enjoy views of the downtown skyline, the bay, and the Bay Bridge from the **Rooftop at VIA,** a rooftop bar and lounge open to overnight guests. It's across the street from AT&T Park, so you can soak up the excitement of a Giants game some nights.

NORTH BEACH AND FISHERMAN'S WHARF

Perhaps it's odd, but the tourist mecca of San Francisco is not a district of a zillion hotels. Most of the major hostelries sit down nearer to Union Square. But you can stay near the Wharf or in North Beach if you choose; you'll find plenty of chain motels here, plus a few select boutique hotels in all price ranges.

Under $150

The unexpected **Fisherman's Wharf Hostel** (Fort Mason, Bldg. 240, 415/771-7277, www.sfhostels.com/fishermans-wharf, dorm $44-60, private room $120-170) sits in bucolic Fort Mason, far from the problems that plague other SF hostels but within walking distance of frenetic downtown. The best amenities (aside from the free parking, free continental breakfast, and no curfews or chores) are the sweeping lawns, mature trees, and the views of Alcatraz and the Bay.

The **San Remo Hotel** (2237 Mason St., 800/352-7366, www.sanremohotel.com, $99-179) is one of the best bargains in the city. The blocky old yellow building has been around since just after the 1906 earthquake, offering inexpensive guest rooms to budget-minded travelers. One of the reasons for the rock bottom pricing is the baths: You don't get your own. Four shared baths with shower facilities located in the hallways are available to guests day and night. The guest rooms boast the simplest of furnishings and decorations as well as clean, white-painted walls and ceilings. Some rooms have their own sinks, all have either

the rooftop deck at Hotel VIA

double beds or two twin beds, and none have telephones or TVs, so this might not be the best choice of lodgings for large media-addicted families. Couples on a romantic vacation can rent the Penthouse, a lovely room for two with lots of windows and a rooftop terrace boasting views of North Beach and the Bay.

$150-250

Located in a quieter section of the Embarcadero, the ★ **Harbor Court Hotel** (165 Steuart St., 415/882-1300, www. harborcourthotel.com, $219-430) is housed in an attractive brick building just a block from the Ferry Building. Spring for a harbor-view room to watch ships passing by during the day and the pulsing lights of the Bay Bridge after dark. Modern touches include iPod docks and flat-screen TVs. Guests can get a day pass to the adjacent Embarcadero YMCA, which has a gym, a spa, and a swimming pool.

Hotel Bohème (444 Columbus Ave., 415/433-9111, www.hotelboheme.com, $194-320) offers comfort, history, and culture at a pleasantly low price for San Francisco. Guest rooms are small but comfortable, Wi-Fi is free, and the spirit of the 1950s bohemian Beats lives on. The warmly colored and gently lit guest rooms are particularly welcoming to solo travelers and couples, with their retro brass beds covered by postmodern geometric spreads. All guest rooms have private baths, and the double-queen room can sleep up to four people for an additional charge.

The **Washington Square Inn** (1660 Stockton St., 415/981-4220, www.wsisf. com, $209-359) doesn't look like a typical California B&B. With its city-practical architecture and canopy out on the sidewalk, it's more a small, elegant hotel. The inn offers 15 guest rooms with private baths, elegant appointments, and fine linens. Some guest rooms have spa bathtubs, and others have views of Coit Tower and Grace Cathedral. Only the larger guest rooms and junior suites are spacious; the standard guest rooms are "cozy" in the European urban style. Amenities include a generous

continental breakfast brought to your room daily, afternoon tea, a flat-screen TV in every guest room, and free Wi-Fi. To stay at the Washington Square Inn is to get a true sense of the beauty and style of San Francisco.

Over $250

For a luxurious stay in the city, save up for a room at **The Argonaut** (495 Jefferson St., 800/790-1415, www.argonauthotel.com, $249-849). With stunning Bay views from its prime Fisherman's Wharf location, in-room spa services, and a yoga channel, The Argonaut is all San Francisco. The rooms feature exposed brick walls and nautical-inspired decor. Guest rooms range from cozy standards to upscale suites with separate bedrooms and whirlpool tubs. The SF Maritime National Historical Park's visitors center and interactive museum is located in the same building as The Argonaut.

MARINA AND PACIFIC HEIGHTS

These areas are close enough to Fisherman's Wharf to walk there for dinner, and the lodgings are far more affordable than downtown digs.

$150-250

Staying at the ★ **Marina Motel** (2576 Lombard St., 415/921-9406 or 800/346-6118, www.marinamotel.com, $209-349) feels like you have your own apartment in the fancy Marina District. This European-styled motor lodge features rooms above little garages where you can park your car. More than half the rooms have small kitchens with a stove, fridge, microwave, and dishes for taking a break from eating out. Though the Marina Motel was built in the 1930s, the rooms are updated with modern amenities, including sometimes-working Wi-Fi and TVs with cable. With major attractions like the Exploratorium and the Palace of Fine Arts within walking distance, this reasonably priced motel is a great place to hunker down for a few days and see the nearby sights.

Reserve a room away from Lombard Street if you are a light sleeper.

Pack the car and bring the kids to the **Hotel del Sol** (3100 Webster St., 877/433-5765, www.jdvhotels.com, $230-340). This unique hotel-motel embraces its origins as a 1950s motor lodge, with the guest rooms decorated in bright, bold colors with whimsical accents, a heated courtyard pool, palm trees, hammocks, and parking for $25 a night, which is a deal in this city. The Marina locale offers trendy cafés, restaurants, bars, and shopping within walking distance, as well as access to major attractions.

Another Pacific Heights jewel, the **Jackson Court** (2198 Jackson St., 415/929-7670, www.jacksoncourt.com, $219-255) presents a lovely brick facade in the exclusive neighborhood. The 10-room inn offers comfortable, uniquely decorated queen rooms and a luscious continental breakfast each morning.

The exterior and interior amenities of the **Hotel Majestic** (1500 Sutter St., 415/441-1100, www.thehotelmajestic.org, $200-448) evoke the grandeur of early 20th-century San Francisco. It is said that one of the former hotel owner's daughters haunts the Edwardian-style 1902 building, which boasts antique furnishings and decorative items from England and France. Cozy guest rooms, junior suites, and one-bedroom suites are available. The on-site **Cafe Majestic** serves breakfast and dinner, with a focus on local, healthful ingredients.

Over $250

Tucked in with the money-laden mansions of Pacific Heights, **Hotel Drisco** (2901 Pacific Ave., 800/634-7277, www.hoteldrisco.com, $379-949) offers elegance to discerning visitors. Away from the frenzied pace and noise of downtown, at the Drisco you get quiet, comfy guest rooms with overstuffed furniture, breakfast with a latte, and a glass of wine in the evening. Families and larger parties can look into the hotel's suite with two bedrooms and two baths. They also have a morning car service to downtown on weekdays.

The stately **Queen Anne Hotel** (1590 Sutter St., 800/227-3970, www.queenanne.com, $249-305) brings the elegance of downtown San Francisco out to Pacific Heights. Sumptuous fabrics and rich colors in the guest rooms and common areas add to the feeling of decadence and luxury in this boutique hotel. Small, moderate guest rooms offer attractive accommodations on a budget, while superior rooms and suites are more upscale. Continental breakfast is included, as are high-end services such as courtesy car service in the morning and afternoon tea and sherry.

The **Lombard Motor Inn** (1475 Lombard St., 415/441-6000, www.lombardmotorinn.com, $262-285) has the standard-issue amenities: reasonable-size guest rooms, flat-screen TVs, Internet, free parking, and location, location, location. Of course, the location means there's plenty of nighttime noise pouring in through the windows, especially on weekends.

The aptly named **Inn at the Presidio** (42 Moraga Ave., 415/800-7356, www.innatthepresidio.com, $295-450) is just minutes from the heart of the city, but its location in the Presidio's green space makes it feel a world away. The inn offers immediate access to the national park's hiking trails and cultural attractions along with panoramic views of the Bay and Alcatraz in the distance. Most of the rooms are within a former housing unit for bachelor officers. While the inn is modernized, it nods to its past with military decorations on the lobby's walls. Continental breakfast is served in the former mess hall. Suites are spacious for the city, including a bedroom with an adjoining room, a pullout sofa, and a gas fireplace. The nearby four-bedroom **Funston House** is available for large groups.

CIVIC CENTER AND HAYES VALLEY

You'll find a few reasonably priced accommodations and classic inns in the Civic Center and Hayes Valley areas.

Under $150

Take a step back into an older San Francisco at

the **Chateau Tivoli** (1057 Steiner St., 800/228-1647, www.chateautivoli.com, $150-300). The over-the-top colorful exterior matches perfectly with the American Renaissance interior decor. Each unique guest room and suite showcases an exquisite style evocative of the Victorian era. Some furnishings come from the estates of the Vanderbilts and J. Paul Getty. Most guest rooms have private baths, although the two least expensive share a bath.

Located in Hayes Valley a few blocks from the Opera House, the **Inn at the Opera** (333 Fulton St., 888/298-7198, www.shellhospitality.com, $179-323) promises to have guests ready for a swanky night of San Francisco culture. Clothes-pressing services count among the inn's many amenities. French interior styling in the guest rooms and suites that once impressed visiting opera stars now welcomes guests from all over the world. The on-site restaurant **Plaj** serves Scandinavian fare.

The Metro Hotel

GOLDEN GATE PARK AND THE HAIGHT

Accommodations around Golden Gate Park are surprisingly reasonable. Leaning toward Victorian and Edwardian inns, most lodgings are in the middle price range for well above average guest rooms and services. However, getting downtown from the quiet residential spots can be a trek; ask at your inn about car services, cabs, and the nearest bus lines.

Out on the ocean side of the park, motor inns of varying quality cluster on the Great Highway. They've got the advantages of more space, low rates, and free parking, but they range from drab all the way down to seedy; choose carefully.

Under $150

Just west of the Haight-Ashbury neighborhood, ★ **The Metro Hotel** (319 Divisadero St., 415/861-5364, www.metrohotelsf.com, $107-182) is one of the best priced lodging options in the city. It's a huge plus that the rooms in this wonderful three-story building are also clean and comfy. Some units have bay windows that bulge out over the bustling Divisadero Street below, but don't worry, street noise is near nonexistent due to triple-paned windows. Enjoy the tranquil courtyard garden out back or pepper the friendly, 24-hour-staffed front desk with questions. The only real negative here for discerning budget travelers is the lack of designated parking.

$150-250

The **Stanyan Park Hotel** (750 Stanyan St., 415/751-1000, www.stanyanpark.com, $179-284) graces the Upper Haight across the street from Golden Gate Park. This renovated 1904-1905 building, listed on the National Register of Historic Places, shows off its Victorian heritage both inside and out. Guest rooms can be small but are elegantly decorated. Multiple-room suites are available. Ask for a room overlooking the park. A stay includes a morning continental breakfast and a late afternoon wine and cheese reception.

To say the **Seal Rock Inn** (545 Point Lobos

Ave., 888/732-5762, www.sealrockinn.com, $170-217) is near Golden Gate Park pushes even the fluid San Francisco neighborhood boundaries. In fact, this pretty place perches near the tip of Land's End, only a short walk from the Pacific Ocean. All guest rooms at the Seal Rock Inn have ocean views, private baths, free parking, and free Wi-Fi. With longer stays in mind, the Seal Rock offers rooms with

kitchenettes (two-day minimum stay to use the kitchen part of the room; weird but true). You can call and ask for a fireplace room that faces the Seal Rocks, so you can stay warm and toasty while training your binoculars on a popular mating spot for local sea lions. The restaurant downstairs serves breakfast and lunch; on Sunday you'll be competing with brunch-loving locals for a table.

Transportation and Services

AIR

San Francisco International Airport

(SFO, 800/435-9736, www.flysfo.com) is actually about 12 miles south of the city center, near the town of Millbrae. You can easily get a taxi, Lyft, Uber, or other ground transportation into the heart of the city from the airport. BART is available from SFO's international terminal, but Caltrain is only accessible via a BART connection from SFO. Some San Francisco hotels offer complimentary shuttles from the airport as well. You can also rent a car here.

As one of the 30 busiest airports in the world, SFO has long check-in and security lines much of the time and dreadful overcrowding on major travel holidays. Plan to arrive at the airport two hours prior to departure for domestic flights and three hours prior to an international flight.

TRAIN AND BUS

Amtrak does not run directly into San Francisco. You can ride into the San Jose, Oakland, or Emeryville stations and then take a connecting bus into San Francisco.

Greyhound (200 Folsom St., 415/495-1569, www.greyhound.com, 5:30am-1am daily) offers bus service to San Francisco from all over the country.

CAR

The **Bay Bridge** (toll $6) links I-80 to San Francisco from the east, and the **Golden**

Gate Bridge (toll $7.75) connects CA-1 from the north. From the south, US 101 and I-280 snake up the peninsula and into the city. Be sure to get a detailed map and good directions to drive into San Francisco—the freeway interchanges, especially surrounding the east side of the Bay Bridge, can be confusing, and the traffic congestion is legendary. For traffic updates and route planning, visit **511.org** (www.511.org).

If you have your car with you, try to get a room at a hotel with a parking lot and either free parking or a parking package for the length of your stay.

Car Rental

All the major car rental agencies have a presence at the **San Francisco Airport** (SFO, 800/435-9736, www.flysfo.com). In addition, most reputable hotels can offer or recommend a car rental. Rates tend to run $50-100 per day and $200-550 per week (including taxes and fees), with discounts for weekly and longer rentals.

Parking

Parking a car in San Francisco can easily cost $50 per day or more. Most downtown and Union Square hotels do not include free parking with your room. Expect to pay $35-65 per night for parking, which may not include in-and-out privileges.

Street parking meters cost up to $2 per hour, often go late into the night, and charge during the weekends. At least many now take credit cards. Unmetered street parking spots are as rare as unicorns and often require residential permits for stays longer than two hours during the day. Lots and garages fill up quickly, especially during special events.

MUNI

The **Muni** (www.sfmta.com, adults $2.75, youth and seniors $1.35, children under 4 free) transit system can get you where you want to go as long as time isn't a concern. Bus and train tickets can be purchased from any Muni driver; underground trains have ticket machines at the entrance. Exact change is required, except on the cable cars, where drivers can make change for up to $20. See the website for a route map, tickets, and schedules.

BART

Bay Area Rapid Transit, or **BART** (www.bart. gov, fees vary), is the Bay Area's late-coming answer to major metropolitan underground railways like Chicago's L trains and New York's subway system. Sadly, there's only one arterial line through the city. However, service directly from San Francisco Airport into the city runs daily, as does service to Oakland

Airport, the cities of Oakland and Berkeley, and many other East Bay destinations. BART connects to the Caltrain system and San Francisco Airport in Millbrae. See the website for route maps, schedules (BART usually runs on time), and fare information.

To buy tickets, use the vending machines found in every BART station. If you plan to ride more than once, you can add money to a single ticket and then keep that ticket and reuse it for each ride.

CALTRAIN

This traditional commuter rail line runs along the peninsula into Silicon Valley, from San Francisco to San Jose, with limited continuing service to Gilroy. **Caltrain** (www.caltrain. com, one-way $3.75-13.75) Baby Bullet trains can get you from San Jose to San Francisco in an hour during commuting hours. Extra trains are often added for San Francisco Giants, San Francisco 49ers, and San Jose Sharks games.

You must purchase a ticket in advance at the vending machines found in all stations. The main Caltrain station in San Francisco is at the corner of 4th and King Streets, within walking distance of AT&T Park and Moscone Center.

BART station

TAXIS AND RIDE SHARES

Ride-sharing drivers abound in the Bay Area. Download the apps for **Lyft** (www.lyft.com) or **Uber** (www.uber.com) on your smartphone and secure a ride. You'll find some taxis scooting around all the major tourist areas of the city. If you have trouble hailing a cab, try **City Wide Dispatch** (415/920-0700).

TOURS

San Francisco City Guides (415/557-4266, www.sfcityguides.org, free) is a team of enthusiastic San Francisco tour guides who want to show you more about their beloved city. Opt to learn about San Francisco sights like Fort Mason and Fisherman's Wharf, or choose a walk where you'll hear about the local locales used by famed director Alfred Hitchcock in his films, including *Vertigo*. Visit the website for a complete schedule of the current month's offerings.

One of the most popular walking tour companies in the city is **Foot** (415/793-5378, www.foottours.com, $20-40 pp). Foot was founded by stand-up comedian Robert Mac and hires comics to act as guides for its many different tours around San Francisco. The two-hour "San Francisco in a Nutshell" tour offers a funny look at the basics of city landmarks and history, and the three-hour "Whole Shebang" is a comprehensive if speedy look at Chinatown, Nob Hill, and North Beach. For visitors who are back for the second or third time, check out the more in-depth neighborhood tours that take in Chinatown, the Castro, or the Haight. You can even hit "Full Exposure," a look at the rise of 18-and-up entertainment in North Beach. Tour departure points vary, so check the website for more information about your specific tour and about packages of more than one tour in a day or two.

For an inside look at the culinary delights of Chinatown, sign up for a spot on **"I Can't Believe I Ate My Way Through Chinatown"** (650/355-9657, www.wokwiz. com, $90 pp). This three-hour bonanza will take you first for a classic Chinese breakfast, then out into the streets of Chinatown for a narrated tour around Chinatown's food markets, apothecaries, and tea shops. You'll finish up with lunch at one of Chef Shirley's favorite hole-in-the-wall dim sum places. For folks who just want the tour and lunch, or the tour alone, check out the standard "Wok Wiz Daily Tour" ($50 pp with lunch, $35 pp).

The **Chinatown Ghost Tour** (888/440-7976, www.sfchinatownghosttours.com, 7:30pm-9:30pm Fri.-Sat., adults $48) delves into the neighborhood's mysticism and rich history. The whole thing burned down more than a century ago, and it was rebuilt in exactly the same spot, complete with countless narrow alleyways. This tour will take you into these alleys after the sun sets, when the spirits are said to appear on the streets. You'll start out at Utopia Cafe (139 Waverly Pl.) and follow your loquacious guide along the avenues and side streets of Chinatown. As you stroll, your guide will tell you the stories of the neighborhood spirits, spooks, and ancestors. The curious get to learn about the deities worshipped by devout Chinese to this day, along with the folklore that permeates what was until recently a closed and secretive culture. Then you head into a former gambling den where a magician will attempt to conjure the soul of a long-dead gambler.

TOURIST INFORMATION

The main San Francisco **Visitor Information Center** (900 Market St., 415/391-2000, www. sftravel.com, 9am-5pm Mon.-Fri., 9am-3pm Sat.-Sun. May-Oct., 9am-5pm Mon.-Fri., 9am-3pm Sat. Nov.-Apr.) can give you information about attractions and hotels, and discounted tickets for various museums and attractions. The Market Street location (just below Hallidie Plaza at Powell St.) has brochures in 14 different languages and a few useful coupons.

MEDICAL SERVICES

The **San Francisco Police Department** (766 Vallejo St., 415/553-0123, http://

sanfranciscopolice.org) is headquartered in Chinatown, on Vallejo Street between Powell and Stockton Streets. For life-threatening emergencies or to report a crime in progress, dial 911.

San Francisco boasts a large number of full-service hospitals. The **UCSF Medical Center at Mount Zion** (1600 Divisadero St., 415/567-6600, www.ucsfhealth.org) is renowned for its research and advances in cancer treatments and other important medical breakthroughs. The main hospital is at the corner of Divisadero and Geary Streets. Right downtown, **St. Francis Memorial Hospital** (900 Hyde St., 877/649-7525, www.saintfrancismemorial.org), at the corner of Hyde and Bush Streets, has an emergency department.

North Bay

The North Bay is San Francisco's backyard. From the Marin Headlands at the terminus of the Golden Gate Bridge, a nearly unbroken expanse of wildlands extends from San Francisco Bay to Tomales Bay. Rugged cliffs plunge into the Pacific, towering redwoods loom above hiking trails, and verdant pastures are home to grass-fed beef cattle and award-wining, cheese-producing dairy cows.

MARIN HEADLANDS

The Marin Headlands lie north of San Francisco at the north end of the Golden Gate Bridge. The land encompasses a wide swath of virgin wilderness, former military structures, and a historic lighthouse.

Once over the bridge, the Alexander Avenue exit offers two options for exploring the headlands. Turn left onto Bunker Road for the Marin Headlands.

Vista Point

Vista Point (north end of Golden Gate Bridge) offers views from the Marin Headlands toward San Francisco. If you dream of walking across the **Golden Gate Bridge** (877/229-8655, http://goldengate.org, gates 5am-6:30pm daily Nov.-Apr., 5am-9pm daily Apr.-Oct.), bring a warm coat: The wind can really whip across the span. The bridge is 1.7 miles long, so a round-trip walk will turn into a 3.4-mile excursion. Bikes are allowed daily 24 hours, though after 9pm they must be buzzed through a gate.

Vista Point is the first exit after crossing the Golden Gate Bridge Note that this small parking lot fills early.

Marin Headlands Visitors Center

Start your exploration at the **Marin Headlands Visitors Center** (Field Rd. and Bunker Rd., 415/331-1540, www.nps.gov/goga, 9:30am-4:30pm daily), in the old chapel at Fort Barry. Ask park rangers for the lowdown on the best trails, beaches, and campgrounds.

Point Bonita Lighthouse

The **Point Bonita Lighthouse** (415/331-1540, www.nps.gov/goga, 12:30pm-3:30pm Sat.-Mon., free) has been protecting the headlands for over 150 years and remains an active light station to this day. You need some dedication to visit Point Bonita, since it's only open a few days each week and there's no direct access by car. A 0.5-mile trail with steep sections leads from the trailhead on Field Road. Along the way, you'll pass through a hand-cut tunnel chiseled from the hard rock by the original builders of the lighthouse, and then you'll cross the dramatic suspension bridge that leads to the building. Point Bonita was the third lighthouse built on the West Coast and was the last staffed lighthouse in California. Today, the squat hexagonal building shelters automatic lights, horns, and signals.

Marine Mammal Center

The **Marine Mammal Center** (Fort Cronkite, 2000 Bunker Rd., 415/289-7325, www.marinemammalcenter.org, 10am-4pm daily, free) is a hospital for sick and injured seals and sea lions. Educational displays descirbe more about what the center does. The one-hour docent-led **tours** (11am, 1pm, 3pm daily June-Aug.; 1pm and 3pm Fri. and Mon., 11am, 1pm, 3pm Sat.-Sun. Sept.-May; adults $7, seniors and ages 5-17 $5, under age 5 free) explain the program in greater depth. Visitors will also get an education on the impact of human activity on marine mammals, and maybe a chance for close encounters with some of the center's patients.

Nike Missile Site

Military history buffs jump at the chance to tour a restored Cold War-era Nike missile base, known in military speak as SF-88. The **Nike Missile Site** (Field Rd. 415/331-1453, www.nps.gov/goga) is the only such restored Nike base in the United States. Volunteers continue the restoration and lead **tours** (12:45pm and 1:45pm first Sat. of the month, free) of the fueling area and the testing and assembly building. You can even take a ride on the missile elevator down into the pits that once stored missiles built to defend the United States from the Soviet Union.

Hiking

Numerous trails thread through the Marin Headlands, with unparalleled views of the Golden Gate Bridge and the Pacific Ocean.

From the Marin Headlands Visitors Center parking lot (Field Rd. and Bunker Rd.), the **Lagoon Trail** (1.75 miles round-trip, easy) encircles Rodeo Lagoon and gives bird-watchers an eagle's-eye view of the egrets, pelicans, and other seabirds that call the lagoon home. The trailhead is near the restrooms.

Rodeo Beach draws many visitors on summer weekends—do not expect solitude on the beach or the trails, or even in the water. Locals come to surf when the break is going, while beachcombers look for the unique red and green pebbles on the shore. Note that the wind can really howl out here. The Lagoon Trail accesses the beach, but there is also a fairly large parking lot on Bunker Road that is much closer.

At Rodeo Beach is a trailhead for the **Coastal Trail.** To explore some of the battery ruins that pockmark these hills, follow Coastal Trail (1.5 miles one-way, easy) north to its intersection with Old Bunker Road Trail and return to Bunker Road near the Marine Mammal Center. Or extend this hike by continuing 2.3 miles up the Coastal Trail to the summit of Hill 88 and stellar views. Loop this trail by linking it with Wolf Ridge Trail to Miwok Trail for a moderate 5.5-mile round-trip hike.

To reach the trailheads and parking lots, follow Bunker Road west to either Rodeo Beach or the Marin Headlands Visitors Center.

Biking

If you prefer two wheels to two feet, you'll find the road and trail biking in the Marin Headlands both plentiful and spectacular. From the Tennessee Valley Trailhead, there are many multiuse trails designated for bikers as well as hikers. The **Valley Trail** (4 miles round-trip) takes you down the Tennessee Valley and all the way out to Tennessee Beach. A longer ride runs up the **Miwok Trail** (2 miles) northward. Turn southwest onto the **Coyote Ridge Trail** (0.9 miles), then catch the **Coastal Fire Road** (2 miles) the rest of the way west to Muir Beach. Another fun ride leads from just off U.S. 101 at the Rodeo Avenue exit. Park your car on the side of Rodeo Avenue and then bike down the short **Rodeo Avenue Trail,** which ends in a T intersection after 0.7 miles at **Alta Trail.** Take a left, and access to **Bobcat Trail** is a few yards away. Continue on Bobcat Trail for 2.5 miles straight through the headlands to the **Miwok Trail** for just 0.5 miles, and you'll find yourself out at Rodeo Beach.

To rent a bicycle, visit San Francisco's **Blazing Saddles** (2715 Hyde St.,

415/202-8888, www.blazingsaddles.com, $8-9/hour, $32-60/day).

Camping

Camping here requires advance planning (book sites up to three months in advance). Bring your warm camping gear, even during summer.

The most popular campground is tent-only **Kirby Cove** (Conzelman Rd., 877/444-6777, www.recreation.gov, reservations required Apr.-Nov., $30). Five secluded and shaded campsites provide a beautiful respite. Make your reservations well in advance for summer weekends, as this popular campground fills up fast. To get there, hike the one-mile trail from Battery Spencer on Conzelman Road.

The **Bicentennial Campground** (Battery Wallace parking lot, 877/444-6777, www. recreation.gov reservations required Mar.-Dec., $20) boasts a whopping three campsites easily accessible from the parking lot. Each site can accommodate a maximum of three people, and there's no water available or fires allowed on-site. A nearby picnic area has barbecue grills that campers can use to cook a hot dinner.

The Tennessee Valley trailhead accesses **Hawk Campground** (415/331-1540, reservations required, free) with three primitive sites. Amenities include chemical toilets but no water.

Transportation and Services

Fort Baker and the Marin Headlands are just north of the Golden Gate Bridge on Highway 1 and U.S. 101. To get to the headlands from San Francisco, take the Alexander Avenue exit, the second exit after you cross the bridge. From the north, Alexander Avenue is the last Sausalito exit. If the visitors center is the first stop on your itinerary, turn left onto Bunker Road and go through the one-way tunnel. If you want to hit Fort Barry and the Bonita Lighthouse first, follow Alexander Avenue right and travel under the highway to Conzelman Road, which leads up the hill along the edge

of the headlands. Keep in mind that many of the roads are very narrow and become one-way in places.

Traffic in this area, particularly in the headlands, can be heavy on beautiful weekend days, so try and plan to get here early and spend the time that other people are stuck in their cars exploring the area on foot. Another option is to take bus route 76 of the **Muni** (415/701-2311, www.sfmta.com, Sun. 10am-7pm, $2.25 one-way). Making stops throughout downtown San Francisco and the north end of the city, this Sunday-only Muni line crosses the Golden Gate and ventures as far as Rodeo Cove in the headlands. It makes frequent trips, and you can even load bikes on the front.

SAUSALITO

The affluent town of Sausalito wraps around the north end of San Francisco Bay. The main drag runs along the shore, and the concrete boardwalk is perfect for strolling and biking. A former industrial fishing town, Sausalito still has a few old cannery buildings and plenty of docks, most now lined with pleasure boats. Sausalito has a community of people living on 400 houseboats along its northern end.

Once over the Golden Gate, take the Alexander Avenue exit to Fort Baker and the Bay Area Discovery Museum.

Fort Baker

Fort Baker (435 Murray Circle, 415/331-1540, www.nps.gov/goga, sunrise-sunset daily, free) is a 335-acre former army post established in 1905. Fort Baker is part of the Golden Gate National Recreation Area and is open to visitors. The location, just east of the Golden Gate Bridge, makes it great for city views and a wind-free beach. The fort is the best example of military architecture from the Endicott Period. It includes many elegant homes with large sweeping porches arrayed around the oval parade grounds.

Fort Baker houses the **Cavallo Point Lodge** and two restaurants. The Bay Area

Discovery Museum is also nearby, along with the tiny Presidio Yacht Club.

Bay Area Discovery Museum

The **Bay Area Discovery Museum** (557 McReynolds Rd., 415/339-3900, www.baykidsmuseum.org, 9am-4pm Tues.-Fri., 10am-5pm Sat., 9am-5pm Sun., adults $15, seniors and children age 6-11 months $14) offers kids of all ages a chance to explore the world they live in. Most of the permanent exhibits are geared toward small children, with lots of interactive components and places to play. Kids can check out easy-to-understand displays that describe the natural world, plus lots of Bay Area-specific exhibits. The Discovery Museum also has a theater and a café.

San Francisco Bay Model

The **San Francisco Bay Model** (2100 Bridgeway, 415/332-3871, www.spn.usace.army.mil, 9am-4pm Tues.-Sat., free) is a scale model of the way the bay works, complete with currents and tides. Scientists and engineering types love to see how the waters of the bay move and work.

Food

Snag a blanket and a seat on the porch to watch the fog roll in over the Golden Gate Bridge at ★ **Farley Bar** (Cavallo Point Lodge, 601 Murray Circle, Fort Baker, 415/339-4750, www.cavallopoint.com, 11am-11pm Sun.-Thurs., 11am-midnight Fri.-Sat., $10-28). The bar boasts one of the most classic and contemporary cocktail menus around. Options from the bar menu include steamed mussels and a burger made from Marin-raised beef. There's live music on Monday nights (7:30pm-9:30pm).

The excellent **Murray Circle Restaurant** (Cavallo Point Lodge, 601 Murray Circle, Fort Baker, 415/339-4751, www.cavallopoint.com, 7am-11am, 11:30am-2pm, and 5:30pm-9pm Mon.-Thurs.; 7am-11am, 11:30am-2pm, and 5:30pm-10pm Fri.; 7am-2:30pm, and 5:30pm-10pm Sat.; 7am-2:30pm and 5:30pm-9pm Sun.; $25-60) has a menu based on the best

Marin produce, seafood, meat, and dairy. Simple dishes are executed with French technique.

★ **Fish** (350 Harbor Dr., 415/331-3474, www.331fish.com, 11:30am-8:30pm daily, $9-23, cash only) serves sustainable seafood right on the water. Its rich Dungeness crab roll is drenched in butter while the spicy Saigon salmon sandwich explodes with the taste of carrots, jalapeños, and cilantro.

For California-influenced Chinese food, go to **Tommy's Wok Chinese Cuisine** (3001 Bridgeway, 415/332-5818, http://tommyswok.com, 11:30am-3pm and 4pm-9pm Mon.-Thurs., 11:30am-3pm and 4pm-9:30pm Fri.-Sat., 4pm-9pm, Sun. $14-20). The menu includes organic free-range chicken, organic tofu, and a heavy emphasis on fresh vegetables—even in the meat dishes.

Accommodations

Lodging options are fairly limited in the Marin Headlands except for one luxurious lodge. Many luxury-minded travelers stay in Tiburon or Sausalito.

Travelers who want budget accommodations indoors often choose the **Marin Headlands Hostel** (Bldg. 941, Fort Barry, 415/331-2777, www.norcalhostels.org/marin, dorm $31-37, private room $105-132). Surprisingly cozy and romantic, the hostel is sheltered in the turn-of-the-20th-century buildings of Fort Barry. Facilities include a full kitchen, Internet access, laundry, and a rec room.

The ★ **Cavallo Point Lodge** (601 Murray Circle, Fort Baker, Sausalito, 415/339-4700, www.cavallopoint.com, $429-1,000) is on the old military installation's grounds. Stay in beautiful historic homes (former officers' residences) that feature elegant early-20th-century woodwork, box-beam ceilings, and wraparound porches. Cavallo Point Lodge also has rooms and suites in two-story, environmentally friendly buildings situated on a hillside. All rooms have luxury amenities including gas fireplaces and large flat-screen TVs; contemporary rooms include stone bathroom floors and deep soaking tubs. The high-end restaurant Murray Circle and Farley Bar are on-site.

The **Gables Inn** (62 Princess St., or 800/966-1554, www.gablesinnsausalito.com, $190-545) opened in 1869 and is the oldest B&B in the area. Each of the 16 rooms is appointed in tasteful earth tones, with white linens and several baths. Although this inn honors its long history, it has also kept up with the times, adding cable TV and Internet access. Genial innkeepers serve a continental breakfast and host a wine and cheese soiree each evening.

With a checkered history dating back to 1915, the **Hotel Sausalito** (16 El Portal, 415/332-0700, www.hotelsausalito.com, $175-395) was a speakeasy, a bordello, and a home for the writers and artists of the Beat Generation. Today, this tiny boutique hotel, with its yellow walls, cozy rooms, and locally built furnishings, evokes the Mediterranean coast.

For a taste of the good life, stay at Sausalito's **Inn Above Tide** (30 El Portal, 415/332-9435 or 800/893-8433, www.innabovetide.com, $405-885). The inn sits over the edge of the water looking out at the San Francisco skyline. Most rooms have private decks with sublime views (except when it's foggy) and upscale appointments. The shops, spas, and restaurants of Sausalito are within walking distance.

Transportation and Services

Sausalito is north of San Francisco just over the Golden Gate Bridge; it is easily accessible by bicycle on side roads or by car on U.S. 101. To get there, take the Alexander Avenue exit and stay right for downtown Sausalito. Once in town, park your car and walk to minimize (and avoid) traffic congestion. Street parking is mostly metered.

A great way to get to Sausalito from San Francisco is by ferry. Two companies make the trip daily, which takes up to an hour. The **Blue & Gold Fleet** (415/705-8200, www.blueandgoldfleet.com, 11am-6:15pm Mon.-Fri., 11am-7:30pm Sat.-Sun.,

adults $12.50, children and seniors $7.50, under age 5 free) makes the trip from Pier 41. Largely serving commuters, the **Golden Gate Ferry** (415/455-2000, http://goldengate.org, 7:10am-7:50pm Mon.-Fri., 10:40am-6:45pm Sat.-Sun., adults $12, children and seniors $6, under age 5 free) leaves from the Ferry Building, closer to downtown San Francisco.

Get your visit started with a stop at the **Sausalito Visitors Center** (780 Bridgeway, 415/332-0505, www.sausalito.org, 11:30am-4pm Tues.-Sun.).

TIBURON

Tiburon's downtown area that backs onto the marina is popular with the young and affluent crowd as well as longtime yacht owners. Aside from the views, one of the greatest draws to Tiburon is its proximity to Angel Island, the largest in the bay and a unique state park.

★ Angel Island State Park

The long history of **Angel Island** (415/435-1915 or 415/435-5390, www.parks.ca.gov, 8am-sunset daily, admission rates vary) begins with regular visits (though no permanent settlements) by the Coastal Miwok people. During the Civil War the U.S. Army created a fort on the island in anticipation of Confederate attacks from the Pacific. The attacks never came, but the army maintained a base here. Today, many of the 19th-century military buildings remain and can be seen on the **tram tour** (415/897-0715 or 415/435-3392, http://angelislandsf.com, daily Apr.-Oct., Sat.-Sun. Nov.-Feb., adults $16.50, seniors $15, ages 6-12 $10.50), on foot, or on a docent-led **Segway tour** (415/897-0715 or 415/435-3392, http://angelislandsf.com, daily, $68).

IMMIGRATION STATION

Angel Island's history also has a sobering side. It served as an immigration station for Chinese emigrants from 1910 to 1940, a holding center for prisoners of war during World War II, and a Japanese internment camp.

During its time as an immigration checkpoint, Europeans were waved through with little more than a head-lice check, while the Chinese were herded into barracks while government officials scrutinized their papers. After months and sometimes years of waiting, many were shipped back to China. Today, poetry covers the walls of the barracks, expressing the despair of the immigrants who had hoped for a better life and found little more than prison. Docent-led **tours** (415/435-5537, 11am-3pm Wed.-Sun., adults $5, ages 6-17 $3, under 6 free) is open to visitors; docent-led tours are also available (11am and 12:30pm Wed.-Sun., adults $7, ages 5-11 $5) show this poetry and the buildings of the camps.

RECREATION

Angel Island is a major destination for both casual and serious hikers. Adventurous trekkers can scale Mount Livermore via either the **North Ridge Trail** or the **Sunset Trail** (4.5 miles round-trip, moderate). Stop at the summit's picnic tables and wooden benches for a rest and to soak in the expanse of the bay region and the skyscrapers of San Francisco. For the best experience, make a loop by taking one trail up the mountain and the other back down.

For a long paved-road hike or bike ride, take the **Perimeter Road** (5 miles, moderate) all the way around the island. **Bike rentals** (415/435-3392, http://angelisland.com, daily, $15-25/hour, $60-90/day) are available at Ayala Cove.

FOOD

The **Angel Island Café** (415/435-3392, http://angelislandsf.com, 10am-2pm Mon.-Tues., 10am-3pm Wed.-Fri., 10am-4pm Sat.-Sun. Apr. and Oct., 10am-3pm Mon.-Fri., 11am-4pm Sat.-Sun. May-Sept., $8-14) serves hot sandwiches, wraps, salads, and even a gourmet cheese platter from Cowgirl Creamery. Craving oysters and a beer? Stroll next door to the **Angel Island Cantina** (11:30am-4:30pm Sat.-Sun., $8-14).

CAMPING

Camping (800/444-7275 or www. reservecalifornia.com, $30) is available at nine primitive sites that fill up quickly (reserve six months in advance). Each "environmental site" is equipped with food lockers, surprisingly nice outhouses, running water, and a barbecue. You must bring your own charcoal or camp stove, as wood fires are strictly prohibited. The three **Ridge Sites** sit on the southwest side of the island, known to be fairly windy. The six **East Bay** and **Sunrise Sites** face the East Bay. Plan on walking 0.5-1.75 miles from the ferry to your campsite.

GETTING THERE

The harbor at Tiburon is the easiest place to access Angel Island, located in the middle of San Francisco Bay. The private **Angel Island-Tiburon Ferry** (415/435-2131, http://angelislandferry.com, 10am-3pm Mon.-Fri. 10am-5pm Sat.-Sun. May-Sept., 10am-1pm Mon.-Tues. 10am-3pm Wed.-Fri. 10am-5pm Sat.-Sun. Oct., 10am-3pm Sat.-Sun. Nov.-Feb., 10am-1pm Wed.-Fri., 10am-3pm Sat.-Sun. Mar., 10am-1pm Mon.-Tues. 10am-3pm Wed.-Fri., 10am-4pm Sat.-Sun. Apr., adults $15, seniors $14, ages 6-12 $13, ages 3-5 $5, under 3 free, bicycles $1, cash only) can get you out to the island in about 10 minutes and runs several times a day.

You can also take the **Blue & Gold Fleet** (415/705-8200, www.blueandgoldfleet.com, one-way adult $9.75, seniors and ages 5-11 $5.50, under 5 free) to Angel Island from San Francisco's Pier 41. Blue and Gold ferries sail from San Francisco at 9:45am daily; the last ferry back departs at 3:40pm (Mon.-Fri.) and 4:15pm (Sat.-Sun.). Both ferries accommodate bicycles.

Food and Accommodations

For a good Italian meal, head for **Servino** (9 Main St., 415/435-2676, www.servino.com, 11:30am-4pm and 5pm-11pm Mon.-Fri., 11:30am-3:30pm and 5pm-11pm Sat., 11:30am-3:30pm and 5pm-11pm Sun., $18-30) on the waterfront. A huge outdoor patio offers stunning views of the bay and the service is warm and friendly. The menu runs to hearty, Americanized Italian dishes. The full bar makes a great place to wait for a table, and Servino hosts live music on Friday nights.

A Tiburon mainstay is **Sam's Anchor Café** (27 Main St., 415/435-4527, www.samscafe.com, 11am-5pm Mon., 11am-11pm Tues.-Thurs., 11am-midnight Fri., 9:30am-midnight Sat., 9:30am-11am Sun., $18-29) sits on the water with a large glassed-in deck. Sam's specializes in seafood and wine. Catch some rays over oysters on the half shell, fish-and-chips, or a burger. At night, the fare becomes a bit fancier as dining moves indoors amid low lighting.

It would be difficult to find a place to stay closer to the water than the ★ **Waters Edge Hotel** (25 Main St., 415/789-5999, www.marinhotels.com, $289-519). This boutique hotel is actually perched on a historic dock over the bay. Most rooms have views of the bay and sights like Angel Island and San Francisco in the distance. They also include luxurious beds and wood-burning fireplaces. The staff delivers a full continental breakfast to your room every morning.

Transportation

Tiburon is on a peninsula about eight miles north of the Golden Gate Bridge. From San Francisco, take U.S. 101 north to the Tiburon Boulevard exit. Stay to the right and follow the road along the water for nearly six miles until you reach the small downtown area.

Like Sausalito, Tiburon is very walkable and is a great destination via the ferry from San Francisco. The **Blue & Gold Fleet** (415/705-8200, http://blueandgoldfleet.com, 9:45am-10pm Mon.-Fri., 11am-10pm Sat.-Sun., adults $12.50, seniors and ages 5-11 $7.50, under age 5 free) runs daily trips to Tiburon from San Francisco's Pier 41.

MILL VALLEY

Mill Valley is a great base for an exploration of Marin County's many attractions. The upscale city has a walkable downtown with great restaurants, a state-of-the-art music venue, and a theater that hosts all sorts of events. Recreational opportunities include the Dipsea Trail, which climbs out of the valley and eventually ends at Muir Beach, and nearby Mount Tamalpais.

Entertainment and Events

Mill Valley Beerworks (173 Throckmorton Ave., 415/888-8218, www.millvalleybeerworks.com, 5:30pm-9pm Mon., 5:30pm-9:30pm Tues.-Thurs., 5:30pm-10:30pm Fri., 11:30am-3pm and 5:30pm-10:30pm Sat., 11:30am-3pm and 5:30pm-9pm Sun.) is a great place to sip a beer after a hike. Beerworks has a rotating menu of seasonally brewed beers made in-house as well as an extensive list of bottled beer from around the world. Sip your suds at the bar or at the long wooden tables.

In 2012, the Grateful Dead's Bob Weir helped to open the state-of-the-art **Sweetwater Music Hall** (19 Corte Madera Ave., 415/388-3850, www.sweetwatermusichall.com), which hosts rock, blues, funk, and New Orleans acts on a good-sized stage with pristine sound. A café serves creative small bites.

The **Throckmorton Theatre** (142 Throckmorton Ave., 415/383-9600, https://throckmortontheatre.org) is the place to see all sorts of plays, musicals, and concerts. It's probably best known though for its Tuesday comedy nights, where locals like Dana Carvey frequently stop in to perform.

Founded in 1978 by the California Film Institute, the **Mill Valley Film Festival** (www.mvff.com, Oct.) showcases films from more than 200 filmmakers in Mill Valley and the surrounding area. Mill Valley's other big event happens is the **Dipsea Race** (www.dipsea.org, 2nd Sun. in June), the oldest footrace in the nation.

Food

The **Dipsea Café** (200 Shoreline Hwy., 415/381-0298, www.dipseacafe.com, 7am-3pm Mon.-Fri., 7am-4pm Sat.-Sun., $11-30) is a great place to fuel up for a day of hiking. Go hearty with a chicken-fried steak and egg platter or opt for a more delicate pear-walnut omelet. With a farm scene painted on the wall and plaid tablecloths, the Dipsea has a country feel.

A partnership between celebrity chef Tyler Florence and rocker Sammy Hagar, **El Paseo** (17 Throckmorton Ave., 415/388-0741, www.elpaseomillvalley.com, 5pm-9pm Sun.-Thurs., 5pm-10pm Fri.-Sat., $20-50) serves meaty entrees like veal chops and steak frites.

Bungalow 44 (44 E. Blithedale Ave., 415/381-2500, www.bungalow44.com, Sun.-Mon. 5pm-9:30pm, Tues.-Thurs. 5pm-10pm, Fri.-Sat. 5pm-10:30pm, $20-35) cooks up salmon and coffee-crusted ribeye on an old-fashioned wood-burning grill. They also offer vegetarian entrées like roasted stuffed peppers.

Accommodations

Situated in Mill Valley's downtown, ★ **Mill Valley Inn** (165 Throckmorton Ave., 415/389-6608 or 855/334-7946, www.marinhotels.com, $279-340) has rooms in the modern main building and a historic creekside house. For more seclusion, opt for one of the two single-bedroom cottages shaded by towering redwoods. The rooms in the main building are decorated with repurposed wood furniture and have small balconies overlooking Throckmorton Street or a small redwood forest. Nice touches include a deluxe continental breakfast and free use of a fleet of mountain bikes for tooling around town.

Situated on sparkling Richardson Bay, **Acqua Hotel** (555 Redwood Hwy., 415/380-0400, www.marinhotels.com, $269-300) has serene rooms and suites. A night's stay includes a hot breakfast buffet and complimentary use of the hotel's mountain bikes. Acqua is two miles from downtown Mill Valley.

Transportation

To get to Mill Valley, take U.S. 101 north across the Golden Gate Bridge. Take the East Blithedale/Tiburon Boulevard exit. Turn left on East Blithedale and follow the road into downtown Mill Valley.

There is usually parking to be found in Mill Valley, but it's best to leave your car as the downtown is small and everything is walkable.

MUIR WOODS NATIONAL MONUMENT

Giant coast redwoods are located not far outside San Francisco's city limits. Some of the finest examples of these towering trees can be found at **Muir Woods National Monument** (1 Muir Woods Rd., 415/388-2596, www.nps.gov/muwo, 8am-sunset daily, $10). More than six miles of trails wind through the lush forest and cross verdant creeks. Begin your exploration at the **Muir Woods Visitors Center** (1 Muir Woods Rd., 415/388-2595, from 8am daily, closing time varies). In addition to maps, information, and advice about hiking, you'll also find a few amenities.

First-time visitors should follow the wheelchair- and stroller-accessible **Main Trail Loop** (1 mile), an easy and flat walk with an accompanying interpretive brochure that identifies and describes the flora and fauna. Serious hikers can continue the loop on the **Hillside Trail** for an elevated view of the valley.

After your hike, fill up on a hearty lunch of British comfort food at **The Pelican Inn** (10 Pacific Way, Muir Beach, 415/386-6000, www.pelicaninn.com, 11:30am-9pm Mon.-Fri., 8am-9pm Sat.-Sun., $15-30). Dark wood and a long trestle table give a proper Old English feel to the dimly lit dining room. It's just a short drive from the restaurant to lovely **Muir Beach** (www.nps.gov/goga, sunrise-sunset daily), perfect for wildlife-watching and beachcombing.

End the day with oysters and drinks at the Farley Bar at **Cavallo Point Lodge** (601 Murray Circle, Fort Baker, Sausalito, 415/339-4750, www.cavallopoint.com, 11am-11pm

Sun.-Thurs., 11am-midnight Fri.-Sat., $12-56). Snag a blanket and a seat on the porch to watch the fog roll in over the Golden Gate Bridge.

Getting There

Take **US 101 North** out of San Francisco and over the Golden Gate Bridge. Once on the north side of the Bay, take the **Stinson Beach/CA-1 exit.** On CA-1, also named the **Shoreline Highway,** follow the road under the freeway and proceed until the road splits at a T junction at the light. Turn left, continuing on Shoreline Highway for 2.5 miles. At the intersection with **Panoramic Highway,** make a sharp right turn and continue climbing uphill. At the junction of Panoramic Highway and **Muir Woods Road,** turn left and follow the road 1.5 twisty miles down to the Muir Woods parking lots on the right. **Parking reservations** (www.gomuirwoods. com, $8) are required in advance. Take the **Muir Woods Shuttle** (www.marintransit. org, $3) to avoid parking congestion, especially in summer.

MUIR BEACH

Few coves on the California coast can boast as much beauty as **Muir Beach** (south of the town of Muir Beach, www.nps.gov/goga, sunrise-sunset daily). From the overlook above Highway 1 to the edge of the ocean beyond the dunes, Muir Beach is a haven for both wildlife and beachcombers. (In summer, the north end of the cove is clothing-optional).

Food and Accommodations

One fine Marin lodging is **The Pelican Inn** (10 Pacific Way, Muir Beach, 415/383-6000, www.pelicaninn.com, $242-316). Inside the Tudor structure, the guest room decor continues the historic ambience, with big-beam construction, canopy beds, and historic portrait prints. The seven mostly small rooms each come with a private bath and full English-style breakfast, but no TVs or phones. (There is free Wi-Fi.)

Muir Woods National Monument

Enjoy a hearty plate of food at the Pelican Inn's **restaurant** (11:30am-9:30pm Mon.-Fri., 8am-9:30pm Sat.-Sun., $11-36). Dark wood and a long trestle table give the proper old English feeling to the dimly lit dining room. The cuisine brings home the flavors of old England, with dishes like beef Wellington, shepherd's pie, and fish-and-chips. True fans of the British Isles will round off the meal with a pint of Guinness.

Getting There

Muir Beach is directly off Highway 1. The most direct route is to take U.S. 101 to the Stinson Beach/Highway 1 exit and follow Highway 1 (also called Shoreline Highway) for 6.5 miles to Pacific Way (look for the Pelican Inn). Turn left onto Pacific Way and continue straight to the Muir Beach parking lot. If arriving from Muir Woods, simply continue following Muir Woods Road down to the junction with Highway 1 and turn left onto Pacific Way.

MOUNT TAMALPAIS STATE PARK

Mount Tamalpais State Park (801 Panoramic Hwy., Mill Valley, 415/388-2070, www.parks.ca.gov, 7am-sunset daily, day-use parking $8) boasts stellar views of the San Francisco Bay Area—from Mount St. Helena in Napa down to San Francisco and across to the East Bay. The Pacific Ocean peeks from around the corner of the western peninsula, and on a clear day you can just make out the foothills of the Sierra Nevada to the east. This park is the Bay Area's backyard, with hiking, biking, and camping opportunities widely appreciated for both their beauty and easy access. Ample parking, interpretive walks, and friendly park rangers make a visit to Mount Tam a hit even for less outdoorsy travelers.

Mount Tam also provides the perfect setting for the arts. The **Mountain Theater** (E. Ridgecrest Blvd. at Pan Toll Rd., Mountain Play Association: 415/383-1100, www.mountainplay.org, May-June, ticket prices vary), also known as the Cushing Memorial Amphitheater, was built in the 1930s and still hosts plays amid its outdoor stone seating. Performances and dates vary; contact the Mountain Play Association for information and tickets. Arrive early, as both parking and seating fill completely well before the show starts. The Mountain Theater also serves as the meeting place for the **Mount Tam Astronomy Program** (E. Ridgecrest Blvd. at Pan Toll Rd., 415/388-2070 or 415/455-5370, www.mttam.net, Sat. Apr.-Oct.). The group hosts a talk by an astronomer that lasts about 45 minutes, followed by a tour of the night sky and star viewing through telescopes. Bring flashlights.

The **East Peak Visitors Center** (11am-4pm Sat.-Sun.) at the top of Mount Tam contains a small museum and gift shop as well as a picnic area with tables and restrooms and a small refreshment stand. The on-site staff can assist with hiking tips or guided walks. The **Pantoll Ranger Station** (3801 Panoramic Hwy. at Pantoll Rd., 415/388-3653, 8am-4pm daily), which anchors the western and larger edge of the park, provides hikers with maps and camping information.

Enjoy the views without setting out on the trail at the **Bootjack Picnic Area** (Panoramic Hwy.), which has tables, grills, water, and restrooms. The small parking lot northeast of the Pantoll Ranger Station fills quickly and early in the day.

Hiking

Mount Tam's hiking areas are divided into three major sections: the East Peak, the Pantoll area, and the Rock Springs area. Each of these regions offers a number of beautiful trails, so you'll want to grab a map from the visitors center or online to get a sense of the mountain and its hikes.

For additional hikes, visit the **Friends of Mount Tam** (www.friendsofmttam.org).

EAST PEAK

The charming interpretive **Verna Dunshee Trail** (0.75 mile, easy) offers a short, mostly flat walk along a wheelchair-accessible trail. The views are fabulous, and you can get a leaflet at the visitors center that describes many of the things you'll see along the trail. Turn this into a loop hike by continuing on Verna Dunshee counterclockwise; once back at the visitors center, make the climb up to **Gardner Lookout** for stellar views from the top of Mount Tam's East Peak (elev. 2,571 ft.).

PANTOLL

The Pantoll Ranger Station is ground zero for some of the best and most challenging hikes in the park. The **Old Mine Trail** (0.5 mile, easy) leads up to the Mountain Theater via the **Easy Grade Trail** (2 miles, easy-moderate). Eager hikers can continue on the **Rock Springs Trail** to West Point Inn and back via **Old Stage Road** for 4.7 more challenging miles.

The **Steep Ravine Trail** (3.8 miles, moderate) descends through lush Webb Creek and gorgeous redwoods to meet with the Dipsea Trail. To return to the Pantoll parking area, turn left onto Dipsea Trail and climb the demanding steps back to the **Coastal Fire**

Road. Turn left again, then right on the Old Mine Trail for an exhilarating 3.8-mile hike.

The **Dipsea Trail** (7.3 miles round-trip, strenuous) is part of the famous Dipsea Race (second Sun. in June), renowned for both its beauty and its challenging stairs. The trailhead begins in Muir Woods, near the parking lot, and leads through Mount Tam all the way to Stinson Beach. Hikers can pick up the Dipsea on the Old Mine Trail or at its intersection with the Steep Ravine Trail in Mount Tam, but a common loop is to take the **Matt Davis Trail** (across Panoramic Hwy. from the Pantoll parking area) west all the way to Stinson Beach and then return via the Dipsea Trail to Steep Ravine Trail. This is a long, challenging hike, especially on the way back, so bring water.

ROCK SPRINGS

Rock Springs is conveniently near the Mountain Theater, and a variety of trails radiate from this historic venue. Cross Ridgecrest Boulevard and take the **Mountain Theater Fire Trail** to Mountain Theater. Along the top row of the stone seats, admire the vistas while looking for **Rock Springs Trail** (it's a bit hidden). Once you find it, follow Rock Springs Trail all the way to the historic West Point Inn. The views here are stunning, and you'll see numerous cyclists flying downhill on Old Stage Road below. Cross this road to pick up Nora Trail, following it until it intersects with **Matt Davis Trail.** Turn right to reach the Bootjack day-use area. Follow the **Bootjack Trail** right (north) to return to the Mountain Theater for a 4.6-mile loop.

Visit waterfalls via the lovely **Cataract Trail** (3 miles, easy-moderate). From the trailhead, follow Cataract Trail for a short bit before heading right on **Bernstein Trail.** Shortly, turn left onto **Simmons Trail** and continue to Barth's Retreat, site of a former camp that is now a small picnic area with restrooms. Turn left on **Mickey O'Brien Trail** (a map is helpful), returning to an intersection with the Cataract Trail. It's worth the short excursion to follow Cataract Trail to the right

through the Laurel Dell picnic area and up to Cataract Falls. Enjoy a picnic at Laurel Dell before returning to Cataract Trail to follow it down to the Rock Springs trailhead.

Biking

To bike up to the peak of Mount Tam is a mark of local cyclists' strength and endurance. Rather than driving up to the East Peak or the Mountain Home Inn, sturdy cyclists pedal up the paved road to the **East Peak.** It's a long, hard ride, but for an experienced cyclist the challenge and the views make it more than worthwhile. Just take care: This road is open to cars, many of which may not realize that bikers frequent the area.

Food and Accommodations

At **Mountain Home Inn** (810 Panoramic Hwy., 415/381-9000, www.mtnhomeinn.com, $179-329), the innkeepers would prefer that you relax as much as possible. With 10 rooms, many with jetted tubs, wood-burning fireplaces, and private decks, it would be hard to exert yourself. Opt for a massage, slip downstairs for a complimentary breakfast, or dine on a three-course prix fixe dinner (11:30am-7pm Mon.-Tues., 11:30am-8:30pm Wed.-Fri., 8am-11am and 11:30am-8:30pm Sat.-Sun., prix fixe 5:30pm-8:30pm Wed.-Sun., $15-29) in the cozy and warmly lit dining room. The **Wine Bar** (11:30am-7pm daily) is open between meals.

Reaching the **West Point Inn** (100 Old Railroad Grade Fire Rd., Mill Valley, 415/388-9955, www.westpointinn.com, Tues.-Sat., adult $50, children $25) requires hiking two miles on a dirt road to the entrance. The inn, which was built in 1904, has no electricity. It is lit by gaslights and warmed by fires in the large fireplaces in the downstairs lounge and parlor, where guests are encouraged to read, play games, and enjoy each other's company. There are seven rooms upstairs and five rustic cabins nearby. All guests must bring their own linens, flashlights, and food, which can be prepared in the communal kitchen. One Sunday a month during the summer, the inn hosts a **pancake breakfast** (9am-1pm, adults $10, children $5) that draws local hikers. The wait can be long, but it is a lot of fun.

Camping

With spectacular views of the Pacific Ocean, it's no wonder that the rustic accommodations at ★ **Steep Ravine** (800/444-7275, www.reservecalifornia.com, cabins $100, campsites $25) stay fully booked. On the steep ravine (the name is no exaggeration) there are seven primitive campsites and 10 cabins adjacent to a small cove. Each rustic cabin comes equipped with a small woodstove, a table, a sleeping platform, and a grill; the campsites are also spare but each has a table, a fire pit, and a food locker. Restrooms and drinking water are nearby. To book either a cabin or a campsite, call at 8am six months before the date you intend to go.

The **Pantoll** and **Bootjack Campgrounds** (Panoramic Hwy., 415/388-2070, www.parks.ca.gov, first-come first-serve, $25) each have 15 sites with drinking water, firewood, and restrooms nearby. The sites are pleasantly removed from the parking lot, which means that once you have gone to the trouble of hauling in all your gear, you will enjoy the quiet of car-free camping.

Transportation

Panoramic Highway is a long and winding two-lane road across the Mount Tamalpais area and extending all the way to Stinson Beach. Take Highway 1 to the Stinson Beach exit, then follow the fairly good signs up the mountain. Turn right at Panoramic Highway at the top of the hill. Follow the road for five winding miles until you reach the Pantoll Ranger Station. To get to the East Peak Visitors Center, take a right on Pantoll Road and then another right on East Ridgecrest Boulevard. To access the park from Stinson Beach, take a right on Panorama Highway at the T intersection with Highway 1 just south of town.

STINSON BEACH

The primary attraction at **Stinson Beach** (415/388-2595, www.nps.gov, 9am-sunset, daily) is the tiny town's namesake: a broad 3.5-mile-long sandy stretch of coastline with weather that's unusually congenial. Although it's as plagued by fog as anywhere else in the Bay Area, on rare clear days Stinson Beach is the favorite destination for San Franciscans seeking some surf and sunshine.

To get out on the water, swing by **Stinson Beach Surf and Kayak**

the cabins at Steep Ravine in Mount Tamalpais State Park

(3605 Hwy. 1, 415/868-2739, www. stinsonbeachsurfandkayak.com, weekdays by appointment, 9:30am-6pm Sat.-Sun., $20-45 per day) rents surfboards, kayaks, boogie boards, and stand-up paddleboards. Wetsuits and surf lessons are available.

Food and Accommodations

The best of the few small restaurants that dot the town of Stinson Beach is the **Sand Dollar Restaurant** (3458 Hwy. 1, 415/868-0434, www.stinsonbeachrestaurant.com; 11am-9pm daily, bar open later, $19-26). This so-called fish joint actually serves more land-based dishes than seafood.

The **Sandpiper Inn** (1 Marine Way, 415/868-1632, www.sandpiperstinsonbeach. com, $145-300) has six rooms and five cabins. Choose between motel-style accommodations with comfortable queen beds, private baths, and gas fireplaces or the individual redwood cabins, which offer additional privacy, bed space for families, and full kitchens.

Stinson Beach Motel (3416 Shoreline Hwy. 1, 415/868-1712, www. stinsonbeachmotel.com, $105-259) features eight vintage-y beach bungalow-style rooms that sleep 2-4 guests each. Some rooms have substantial kitchenettes; all have private baths, garden views, flat-screen TVs, and blue decor.

Getting There

Stinson Beach is an unbelievably beautiful place to get to. First, take the Stinson Beach exit off U.S. 101. Follow the Shoreline Highway (Hwy. 1) as it snakes up the hill past the turnoffs for Tennessee Valley, Muir Woods, and Mount Tamalpais State Park. The road will pass through Green Gulch, where produce is grown for the legendary Greens Restaurant in San Francisco; Muir Beach; and eventually along cliffs high above the Pacific. After about five miles, the highway descends into Stinson Beach. Most of the town is strung along the highway, and signs make it easy to navigate to the beach.

With only one lane in each direction and a couple of intersections with stop signs, traffic backups that stretch for miles are all too common, especially on summer weekends. Your best bet is to drive in on a weekday or in the evening when everyone else is leaving.

An alternative to driving is the route 61 bus from **West Marin Stagecoach** (415/226-0855, www.marintransit.org, daily, $2), which runs from Mill Valley into Stinson Beach.

BOLINAS

Situated alongside the Bolinas Lagoon, the unincorporated community of Bolinas is one of the North Bay's most idyllic spots. And the town's reclusive residents want it to stay that way: They've been known to steal any road signs indicating how to get to their community from Highway 1. Bolinas is worth a stop for its beach, tide pools, old-timey saloon, and renowned art museum—that is, if you can find it.

Bolinas Museum

The **Bolinas Museum** (48 Wharf Rd., 415/868-0330, www.bolinasmuseum.org, 1pm-5pm Fri., noon-5pm Sat.-Sun., free) has a rotating gallery that showcases the work of one coastal Marin artist for two months at a time. It also has a fine arts photography exhibit and a history gallery that illuminates the past of Bolinas and coastal Marin.

Agate Beach Park

Offshore of **Agate Beach Park** (end of Elm St., www.marincounty.org, dawn-dusk daily) is Duxbury Reef, one of the largest shale reefs in North America. Onshore is a coastline dotted with tide pools and bird habitats that are ripe for exploration by wildlife lovers.

Smiley's Schooner Saloon

Built back in 1851, **Smiley's Schooner Saloon** (41 Wharf Rd., 415/868-1311, http:// smileyssaloon.com, 11am-2am Mon.-Fri., 10am-2am Sat.-Sun.) has an Old West feel, a pool table, and live entertainment Thursdays-Saturdays. It's a good place to soak up the eccentric character of Bolinas.

Transportation

To find Bolinas, drive 4.5 miles north on Highway 1 and turn left onto Olema-Bolinas Road, which may be unmarked. Then drive into town. Once in town, street and beach parking can be a challenge. The town itself is easily walkable.

★ POINT REYES NATIONAL SEASHORE

The Point Reyes area boasts acres of unspoiled forest and beach country. Cool weather presides even in the summer, but the result is lustrous green foliage and spectacular scenery. **Point Reyes National Seashore** (1 Bear Valley Rd., 415/464-5100, www.nps.gov/pore, dawn-midnight daily) stretches for miles between Tomales Bay and the Pacific, north from Stinson Beach to the tip of the land at the end of the bay. Dedicated hikers can trek from the bay to the ocean, or from the beach to land's end. The protected lands shelter a range of wildlife. In the marshes and lagoons, a wide variety of birds—including three different species of pelicans—make their nests. Over a thousand elephant seals call these beaches home, while endangered Myrtle's Silverspot butterflies can be found in the dunes and grasslands. The pine forests shade shy deer and larger elk.

There are also a number of ranches and dairy farms that still operate inside the park. Grandfathered in at the time the park was created, these sustainable, generations-old family farms give added character and historical depth to Point Reyes. Another remnant of past times is the historic Point Reyes Lighthouse, which is on the cliffs of the Point Reyes Headlands, a point of land that is supposed to be the windiest place on the West Coast and the second-foggiest spot in North America.

The Point Reyes area includes the tiny towns of Olema, Point Reyes Station, and Inverness.

Visitors Centers

The **Bear Valley Visitors Center** (1 Bear Valley Rd., 415/464-5100; 10am-5pm Mon.-Fri., 9am-5pm Sat.-Sun., Mar.-Nov.; 10am-4:30pm Mon.-Fri., 9am-4:30pm Sat.-Sun., Nov.-Feb.) acts as the central visitors center for Point Reyes National Seashore. In addition to its maps, fliers, and interpretive exhibits, you can watch a short video introducing the Point Reyes region. You can also talk to the park rangers, either to ask advice or to obtain beach fire permits and backcountry camping permits.

Two other visitors centers are at different spots in the vast acreage of Point Reyes. The **Ken Patrick Visitors Center** (Drakes Beach, 415/669-1250, 9am-5pm daily summer; 9:30am-4:30pm Sat.-Sun. fall-spring) sits right on the beach in a building made of weathered redwood. Its small museum focuses on the maritime history of the region, and it acts as the host area for the annual Sand Sculpture event held on the beach every Labor Day Sunday.

Point Reyes Historic Lighthouse

The jagged, rocky shores of Point Reyes make for great sightseeing but incredibly dangerous maritime navigation. In 1870 the first lighthouse was constructed on the headlands. Its first-order Fresnel lens threw light far enough for ships to see and avoid the treacherous granite cliffs.

The **Point Reyes Historic Lighthouse** (Sir Francis Drake Blvd., 415/669-1534, www.nps.gov/pore, 10am-4:30pm Thurs.-Mon.) still stands today on the point past the visitors center, accessed by descending a sometimes treacherous, cold, and windblown flight of more than 300 stairs. It's worth a visit; the Fresnel lens and original machinery all remain in place, and the adjacent equipment building contains foghorns, air compressors, and other safety implements from decades past. Check the website for special events when the light is switched on.

Point Reyes National Seashore

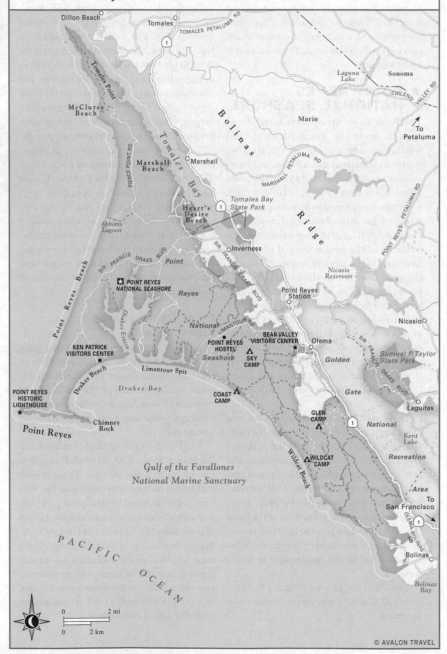

Dillon Beach

Tomales

TOMALES PETALUMA RD

Laguna Lake

Sonoma

Marin

To Petaluma

CHILENO VALLEY RD

McClures Beach

B o l i n a s

Tomales Point

PIERCE POINT RD

Marshall Beach

Marshall

MARSHALL PETALUMA RD

POINT REYES PETALUMA RD

Tomales Bay

R i d g e

Abbotts Lagoon

Heart's Desire Beach

Tomales Bay State Park

Inverness

SIR FRANCIS DRAKE BLVD

SIR FRANCIS DRAKE BLVD

Point

Point Reyes Beach

POINT REYES NATIONAL SEASHORE

Reyes

Nicasio Reservoir

Point Reyes Station

Nicasio

Drakes Estero

National

LIMANTOUR RD

BEAR VALLEY VISITORS CENTER

KEN PATRICK VISITORS CENTER

POINT REYES HOSTEL

Olema

SIR FRANCIS DRAKE BLVD

Samuel P. Taylor State Park

Drakes Beach

Limantour Spit

Seashore

SKY CAMP

Golden

POINT REYES HISTORIC LIGHTHOUSE

Drakes Bay

COAST CAMP

Gate

Laguitas

Point Reyes

Chimney Rock

GLEN CAMP

National

Kent Lake

Gulf of the Farallones
National Marine Sanctuary

Wildcat Beach

WILDCAT CAMP

Recreation

Area

To San Francisco

OLEMA BOLINAS RD

P A C I F I C

O C E A N

Bolinas

Bolinas Bay

0   2 mi
0   2 km

© AVALON TRAVEL

GETTING THERE

The lighthouse is 19 miles west of the Bear Valley Visitor Center on Sir Francis Drake Boulevard. Parking can be difficult. To alleviate congestion, the park closes Sir Francis Drake Boulevard at the South Beach Junction on weekends. Visitors to the lighthouse must take a **shuttle** (9:30am-3pm Sat.-Sun. late-Dec.-mid-Apr., adults $7, under 16 free) from Drakes Beach. Tickets are available at the Kenneth C. Patrick Visitor Center.

Tomales Bay State Park

Tomales Bay State Park (1100 Pierce Point Rd., 415/669-1140, www.park.ca.gov, 8am-sunset daily, $8) lies within the northern Point Reyes area and is home to four popular beaches, all accessible via scenic walks from the parking lots. Trails cross the tiny park, which serves as a popular put-in for kayaks and canoes into Tomales Bay. Kayak rentals are available at **Blue Waters** (12944 Sir Francis Drake Blvd., Inverness, 415/669-2600, www.bwkayak.com, 9am-4pm Sat.-Sun., weekdays by appointment).

Food

OLEMA

The **Farm House Restaurant and Bar** (Point Reyes Seashore Lodge, 10021 Hwy. 1, 415/663-1264, www.pointreyesseashore. com, 11:30am-9pm Mon.-Thurs., 11:30am-10pm Fri.-Sun., $12-32) is the oldest operating business in Olema. Diners enjoy a pleasant range of fresh California cuisine in the elegant, bright dining room. There is an emphasis on seafood, but there are also pasta dishes, pork chops, steaks, and roast chicken. The bar menu features specialty cocktails, locally brewed beer, and oysters prepared half a dozen different ways.

The **Sir and Star** (11180 Hwy. 1, Point Reyes Station, 415/663-1515, www. stationhousecafe.com, 8am-8pm Sun.-Tues. and 8am-9pm Thurs.-Sat., $17-29) intrigues diners with it taxidermy interior and a menu of locally sourced meals.

POINT REYES STATION

The **Station House Café** (11180 Hwy. 1, 415/663-1515, www.stationhousecafe.com, 8am-9pm Thurs.-Mon., $15-30) serves food with ingredients that reflect the area's agrarian culture. The California cuisine is top-notch, more comfort food than haute cuisine. The oyster stew is not to be missed. The dining room's large multi-paned windows let in tons of light, while bartenders deftly mix cocktails in the full bar. There is also an outside patio.

Osterina Stellina (11285 Hwy. 1, 415/663-9988, http://osteriastellina.com, 11:30am-2:30pm and 5pm-9pm daily, $16-30) has plenty of local items on the menu prepared in a rustic yet elegant Mediterranean fashion. There are thin-crust pizzas, robust pastas with seafood and organic vegetables, and hearty main dishes of pan-roasted pork loin and whole roasted local sole.

For a drink (and a bit of local color), slip through the swinging doors of the **Old Western Saloon** (11201 Hwy. 1, 415/663-1661, 10am-2am daily). At this crusty old West Marin haunt you'll see ranchers yukking it up with park rangers, patrons young and old, longtime natives, and recent transplants. Live music goes down on Friday and Saturday nights.

Nick's Cove (23240 Hwy. 1, Marshall, 415/663-1033, www.nickscove.com, 11am-9pm Sun.-Thurs., 11am-9pm Fri.-Sat., $30-36) overlooks the bay in an expansive redwood building. The menu accommodates all types of diners, from those who want a light nibble with their Bloody Mary to those eager for a high-end meal. Out back is a long deck and a boathouse, perfect to explore with the little ones.

There is no better place to stock a picnic basket than the **Bovine Bakery** (11315 Hwy. 1, 415/663-9420, http://thebovinebakery. wordpress.com, 6:30am-5pm Mon.-Fri., 7am-5pm Sat.-Sun.), where you can pick up a cup of coffee, loaves of bread, cookies, pizza, quiche, and salads.

Around the corner is **Cowgirl**

Creamery (80 4th St., 415/663-9335, www.cowgirlcreamery.com, 10am-6pm Wed.-Sun.), which produces the best cheese in the Bay Area. All cheese is made on-site in the French brie style. Tours are available Friday mornings by appointment only.

The **Tomales Bay Oyster Co.** (15479 Hwy. 1, Marshall, 415/663-1243, http://tomalesbayoysters.com, noon-5pm Fri., 9am-5pm Sat.-Sun.) is a low-key affair where you can buy a wide selection of oysters, clams, and mussels in an open-air market a few feet from where they are harvested.

Hog Island Oyster Co. (20215 Hwy. 1, 415/663-9218, www.hogislandoysters.com, 9am-5pm daily) has an open-air stand where you can buy and barbecue oysters. Hog Island gets insanely busy on weekends and parking can be tricky. Reserve a table and/or grill (10am-5pm) online.

INVERNESS

Vladimir's Czechoslovakian Restaurant (12785 Sir Francis Drake Blvd., 415/669-1021, 4pm-10pm Tues., noon-9pm Wed., noon-10pm Thurs.-Sun., $17-27, cash only) is a family-serving serious Czech food: borscht, rabbit, duck, and all manner of delicious things. The bar menu offers Americanized items such as burgers and quesadillas. Vladimir's has a no-children policy, which makes it a perfect retreat for romantic couples.

The **Saltwater Oyster Depot** (12781 Sir Francis Drake Blvd., 415/669-1244, www.saltwateroysterdepot.com, 5pm-9pm Mon. and Thurs.-Fri., noon-9pm Sat.-Sun., $29-31) is an oyster bar, a wine shop, and a beloved restaurant serving plenty of oysters and wine along with small plates and seafood entrées.

The **Inverness Park Market Deli** (12301 Sir Francis Drake Blvd., 415/663-1491, https://invernessparkmarket.com, 7am-8pm Mon. and Wed., 7am-8pm Thurs.-Sat., 8am-8pm Sun.) serves killer breakfast sandwiches and Reubens.

Accommodations

Accommodations are a bit limited. Vacation homes in the area are represented by **Point Reyes Vacation Rentals** (415/663-6113, http://pointreyesvacationrentals.com).

OLEMA

The **Point Reyes Seashore Lodge** (10021 Hwy. 1, 415/663-9000 or 800/404-5634, www.pointreyesseashorelodge.com, $200-440) offers budget and luxury lodging in its 22 rooms and two cottages. Attractive floral patterns mix with clean white walls and attractive wooden accents. All rooms have private baths, some with whirlpool tubs, and a couple of suites with special amenities are located away from the main lodge for extra privacy. Attractive gardens with winding brick pathways roll out to Olema Creek. The Farm House Restaurant, Bar, and Deli adjoin the hotel, providing plenty of food and drink options.

Quiet **Olema Druid's Hall** (9870 Hwy. 1, 415/663-8727, www.olemadruids.com, $245-355) has only three rooms and one cottage. Housed in the 1885 meeting hall of the Druids Association, the inn has a distinct architectural charm, and the surrounding gardens are sculpted with lush flower beds, stands of mature cypresses and pines, and green lawns. Keep warm with the inn's radiant floor heating while wrapped in the 300-thread-count sheets. Each of the rooms is decorated in a style that melds with the Victorian building but is modern. Three of the four rooms have soaking tubs. There is a complimentary continental breakfast composed of local ingredients. Two-night minimum stays are required.

POINT REYES STATION

Point Reyes Station Inn (11591 Hwy. 1, 415/663-9372, www.pointreyesstationinn.com, $135-225) is a five-room inn with light and airy turn-of-the-20th-century charm. Rooms are decorated in heavy antique furnishings that are lightened by the vaulted ceilings, large windows, and glass doors leading to private porches. All but one have fireplaces and private en suite baths. There is a communal hot tub, and the continental breakfast features eggs from the inn's own chickens and seasonal homegrown fruit.

Lingonberry Farm B&B (12430 Hwy. 1, 415/663-1826, www.lingonberryfarm. com, $125-225) is outfitted in bright, simple Swedish style. Each of the three rooms is distinctively decorated in blues, yellows, and crisp whites with trim farm-style furniture and minimalist artwork. All have private baths. Downstairs in the sunny dining area, guests are treated to a breakfast buffet.

The ★ **Point Reyes Hostel** (1390 Limantour Spit Rd., 415/663-8811, www. norcalhostels.org/reyes, $29-130) is steps from fantastic hiking and lush natural scenery. Dorm accommodations are spare but comfortable. Pick the affordable dorm rooms or a private room in one of two converted historic ranch buildings. These are very popular so try and book well in advance. The hostel also has a communal kitchen and a nice outdoor space on a brick patio.

INVERNESS

★ **Manka's Inverness Lodge** (30 Callendar Way, 415/669-1034, www.mankas.com, $225-635) has a woodsy charm that has made it a favorite of Bay Area weekenders. The lodge has four upstairs rooms decked out with deep reading chairs, plush beds with tree-limb posts, and antique fixtures. Four similar rooms are in the annex. Two of the four cabins are perched on Inverness Ridge to make the most of the views. All feature large sitting rooms with stone fireplaces. Some have private hot tubs or luxurious outdoor showers. Two more modern lodgings can be found a few miles from the main compound hanging over the edge of Tomales Bay: The Boat House is akin to a small, lushly appointed loft, with two baths and multiple sleeping spaces. The smaller Boatman's Quarters has lovely views of the bay, a private deck, and a fireplace. The celebrated dining room features a prix fixe multicourse dinner ($58).

Ten Inverness Way (10 Inverness Way, 415/669-1648, www.teninvernessway.com, $160-190) is a 1904 craftsman building in which each of the five rooms are dressed in antiques and colorful quilts. Part of the charm are the coved ceilings, multi-paned windows, and built-in benches. Each room has a queen featherbed and a private bath. In the morning, enjoy coffee, a newspaper, and a full breakfast; evenings see complimentary wine and refreshments.

Constructed of natural wood with lovely and fanciful flourishes, **Motel Inverness** (12718 Sir Francis Drake Blvd., 415/236-1967 or 866/453-3839, www.motelinverness.com, $135-345) is more like a classic lodge than a typical motel. There are rooms and suites with full kitchens, and all are decorated in light colors with minimal fuss. Inside the main lodge is a grand lounge, where you can play pool on the antique pool table, read in front of the stone fireplace, or sip a glass of wine on the expansive deck.

Camping

The only camping is in the **Point Reyes National Seashore** (415/663-8054, www. recreation.gov, $20). All are hike-in sites that require reservations months in advance. Campsites have a pit toilet, a water faucet, a picnic table, a charcoal grill, and a food locker.

Sky Camp is accessed via a 1.4-mile trail on Limantour Road. The campground includes 11 individual sites and 1 group site. From its location at 1,025 feet elevation, you'll get great views of the Pacific Ocean and Drakes Bay (if it's not foggy).

Near the end of Limantour Road is the trailhead for **Coast Camp.** The campground is in a quiet valley of coastal scrub and willow trees, 200 yards from the beach. There are 12 individual campsites and 2 group sites. There are two routes to get here: one that is 1.8 miles uphill along the Laguna and Firelane Trails, and the longer 2.7-mile Coast Trail route, which is flat and considerably easier when carrying camping gear.

Wildcat Camp has five individual sites and three group sites. It it is set away from the beach on an open bluff-top meadow. From Bear Valley it is a 5.5-mile hike or an easier but longer 6.7-mile stroll on the Coast Trail.

Secluded **Glen Camp** is hidden deep within a valley and protected from ocean winds. The campground is a healthy 4.6 miles from the Bear Valley Trailhead. There are 12 individual sites and no group sites.

Transportation

Point Reyes is an hour north of San Francisco by car but getting here can be quite a long drive. From the Golden Gate Bridge, take U.S. 101 north to the Sir Francis Drake Boulevard exit toward San Anselmo. Follow Sir Francis Drake Boulevard west for 20 miles to the small town of Olema and Highway 1. At the intersection with Highway 1, turn right (north) to Point Reyes Station and the Bear Valley Visitors Center.

The Peninsula

The Peninsula's coastal area is popular for weekend vacations. Many enjoy the small-town atmosphere in Half Moon Bay and Pescadero along with the unspoiled beauty of the undeveloped coastline. Peak seasons and events include October's pumpkin season and winter, when elephant seals return to Año Nuevo.

MOSS BEACH

Moss Beach is one of several towns that line the coast south of San Francisco. There is little here besides stunning scenery, a few small businesses, and the Fitzgerald Marine Reserve. North of Moss Beach is the lovely Montara, while south is the Half Moon Bay Airport, El Granada, Princeton, and then Half Moon Bay.

Fitzgerald Marine Reserve

For tide-pooling on the coast, the **Fitzgerald Marine Reserve** (200 Nevada Ave., 650/728-3584, http://parks.smcgov.org, 8am-sunset daily, free) is the place to go. The 32-acre reserve, a marine protected area, is considered one of the most diverse intertidal zones in the Bay Area. On its rocky reefs you can hunt for sea anemones, starfish, eels, and crabs—there's even a small species of red octopus. The reserve is also home to egrets, herons, an endangered species of butterfly, and a slew of sea lions and harbor seals that enjoy sunning themselves on the rocks. Rangers are available to answer any questions and, if need be, to remind you of the strict tide pool etiquette. Persistent ocean spray and blankets of seaweed can keep the reefs slick, so wear shoes with good traction. For the best viewing, come at low tide and on weekdays, as this is a popular destination. For a more leisurely experience, numerous trails crisscross the windswept bluffs and go through sheltering groves of cypress and eucalyptus trees. There is a strict no-dog policy.

Montara State Beach

North of Moss Beach is **Montara State Beach** (2nd St. and Hwy. 1, Montara, www.parks.ca.gov, 650/726-8819, 8am-sunset daily), one of the most beautiful beaches in this area. It is as popular with tide-poolers, surfers, and anglers as it is with picnickers and beachcombers. It is also dog-friendly, which is a big plus as many state beaches have restrictions on canines in the interest of preserving the endangered snowy plover. Thankfully, the beach also remains relatively uncrowded compared to many of the other beaches to the south; it has a tendency to get windy, and there is limited parking.

McNee Ranch State Park

For sweeping views of the coast as well as a heart-pounding hike, **McNee Ranch** (Hwy. 1, across from Montara State Beach, 650/726-8819, www.parks.ca.gov, 8am-sunset daily) fits the bill. The big hike is eight miles up

Montara Mountain, through dry California chaparral along a series of fire roads. The peak itself is 1,900 feet high (the parking lot is at 100 feet), and it is an arduous but worthwhile climb to the top. Although the trail is unmarked, there are maps at the information board just past the parking lot. Still, it's easy to wing it—just follow the roads uphill. From the top, you can see all the way across the Golden Gate and south past Half Moon Bay. The mountain is also home to the endemic Montara manzanita. There is no loop trail, so you must return down the mountain. But with the crisscrossing trails, you won't have to come back the same way. Free parking is in a small and poorly marked dirt lot directly across Highway 1 from Montara State Beach. An easier option, also free, is to park at the beach and walk across the road to the trailhead. McNee Ranch is also a popular mountain biking area, and dogs are welcome on leash.

Hiking

The Devil's Slide was once a pesky section of Highway 1 between Montara and Pacifica known for its frequent landslides, car wrecks, and road closures. The former traffic headache is now the paved and stunning 1.3-mile **Devil's Slide Trail** (Hwy. 1 between Pacifica and Montara, 650/355-8289, http://parks. smcgov.org/devils-slide-trail, 8am-sunset daily). Along the bicycle and pedestrian lanes are observation scopes, interpretive plaques, and stellar coastal views. There are two small parking areas. To reach them, drive north of Montara on CA-1. At the stoplight before the Tom Lantos Tunnels, take a left and then look for the two small parking areas.

Food

As many people come to the **Moss Beach Distillery** (140 Beach Way, Moss Beach, 650/728-5595, www.mossbeachdistillery.com, noon-8pm Mon.-Thurs., noon-8:30pm Fri.-Sat., 11am-8pm Sun., $16-37) for the ghost stories as for the hearty food and terrific ocean views. The restaurant operated as a speakeasy during Prohibition and was also frequented by mystery writer Dashiell Hammett. Folks who want to soak up the old-school atmosphere like to sit in the bar, while visitors who want to stare out over the ocean prefer the terrace, where plenty of blankets are on hand to ward off the Pacific chill.

Swing by **Gherkin's Sandwich Shop** (171 7th St., Montara, 650/728-2211, http://www. eatgherkins.com, 9am-7pm daily, $4-10) for

La Costanera, near Montara State Beach

everything you can imagine between two slices of bread. You'll find oddities like breakfast frittata sandwiches and the Ooey Gooey, with peanut butter, Nutella, and marshmallows. There are also classics like BLTs, burgers, and pastrami and swiss cheese.

Poised above Montara State Beach, ★ **La Costanera** (8150 Cabrillo Hwy., Montara, 650/728-1600, www.lacostanerarestaurant. com, 5pm-9pm Tues.-Thurs. and Sun., 5pm-10pm Fri.-Sat., 5pm-9pm Sun., $21-39) is a sophisticated Peruvian restaurant and the only eatery on this part of the coast to earn a Michelin star. There are a variety of ceviches to choose from as well as slow-cooked pork shoulder and lobster gnocchi, all accented in Peruvian sauces and spices. The bar menu offers hearty plates that could serve as a light dinner.

Accommodations

Tucked away in the cypress and pine forest of Moss Beach, **Seal Cove Inn** (221 Cypress Ave., Moss Beach, 650/728-4114 or 800/995-9987, www.sealcoveinn.com, $325-425) is a highly regarded 10-room B&B that bills itself a "European sanctuary." Outside, the gabled roof, climbing ivy, and expansive gardens let guests know they have entered the inn's rarified world, as do the interior's warm colors, creamy soft linens, private decks, pre-breakfast coffee, and real wood-burning fireplaces.

The **Point Montara Lighthouse Hostel** (16th St. and Hwy. 1, Montara, 650/728-7177, www.norcalhostels.org, dorm $33-36, private room $83-128, nonmembers add $3 per night) offers even better views at a fraction of the price, albeit with a bit less luxury. Stay in the shared dorm rooms, each with 3-6 beds and either coed or gender-specific. Or spring for a private room. Either way, enjoy use of the shared kitchen, common areas with wood-burning fireplaces, the eclectic garden perched on the cliff, and the private cove beach. Other amenities include Wi-Fi, laundry facilities, an espresso bar, and complimentary linens.

Transportation

Moss Beach is 23 miles directly south of San Francisco on Highway 1 (Cabrillo Hwy.). From San Francisco, the easiest and most direct—not to mention scenic—route is to follow Highway 1 south all the way to Moss Beach.

Alternatively, if you are coming from I-280 on the peninsula, take Highway 92 west to Half Moon Bay and Highway 1. From Half Moon Bay, Moss Beach is only seven miles north on Highway 1.

HALF MOON BAY

The coastal city of Half Moon Bay is an agricultural town. The locals all know each other, even though the majority of residents commute "over the hill" to peninsula and Silicon Valley jobs. Strawberries, artichokes, and Brussels sprouts are the biggest crops, along with flowers, pumpkins, and Christmas trees, making the coast the place to come for holiday festivities. Half Moon Bay enjoys a beautiful natural setting and earns significant income from tourism, especially during the world-famous Pumpkin Festival each October.

Onshore is the Pillar Point Harbor and the neighboring town of **Princeton-by-the-Sea,** the other workhorse on the coast. Here, anglers haul in crab, salmon, and herring, and local businesses cater to their needs. This is the place to rent kayaks, go on a chartered fishing trip, and buy fresh fish, sometimes straight off the boat (especially during crab season).

Beaches

The beaches of Half Moon Bay draw visitors from over the hill and farther afield all year long. As with most of the North Pacific region, summer can be a chilly, foggy time on the beaches. For the best beach weather, plan your Half Moon Bay trip for September-October. **Half Moon Bay State Beach** (www.parks. ca.gov, 650/726-8819 or 650/726-8820, parking $10) actually encompasses three discrete beaches stretching four miles down the coast, each with its own access point and parking lot. **Francis Beach** (95 Kelly Ave.) has the most developed amenities, including a good-size **campground** (50 sites, reservations 800/444-7275 or www.reservecalifornia.com, $35) with grassy areas to pitch tents and enjoy picnics, a visitors center, and indoor hot showers. **Venice Beach** (Venice Blvd., off Hwy. 1) offers outdoor showers and flush toilets. **Dunes Beach** (Young Ave., off Hwy. 1) is the southernmost major beach in the chain and the least developed.

Half Moon Bay Art & Pumpkin Festival

The biggest annual event in this small agricultural town is the **Half Moon Bay Art & Pumpkin Festival** (www.miramarevents.com, Oct.). Nearly 250,000 people trek to Half Moon Bay to pay homage to the big orange squash. The festival includes live music, food, artists' booths, contests, activities for kids, an adults lounge area, and a parade. Perhaps the best-publicized event is the pumpkin weigh-off, which takes place before the festivities begin. Farmers bring their tremendous squash in on flatbed trucks from all over the country to determine which is the biggest of all. If anyone breaks the current world record, they'll take home an impressive $5,000.

Sports and Recreation

SURFING

Perhaps the most famous beach in the area is one that has no name. At the end of West Point Avenue in Princeton is the Pillar Point Marsh and a long stretch of beach that wraps around the edge of the point. This beach is the launchpad for surfers paddling out to tackle the infamous **Mavericks Break** (Pillar Point Marsh parking lot, past Pillar Point Harbor). Formed by unique underwater topography, the giant waves are the site of the legendary **Mavericks Surf Contest** (http://maverickssurf.com). The competition is always held in winter, when the swells reach their peak, and scheduling left until the last minute to ensure that the waves are the biggest of the year. When perfect conditions present themselves, the best surfers in the world are given 48 hours' notice to make it to Mavericks to compete. Mavericks is not a beginner's break, especially in winter, and the giant breakers can be deadly.

HIKING AND BIKING

There are plenty of great trails around Half Moon Bay. **Purisima Creek Redwoods** (4.4 miles up Higgins Canyon Rd., 650/619-1200, www.openspace.org, sunrise-sunset daily) has a multitude of trails; many ascend to Skyline Boulevard. Take a leisurely stroll through the redwoods, complete with dripping ferns, flowering dogwood, and wood sorrel, along **Purisima Creek Trail** (3.9 miles, easy-strenuous) until it turns steep and eventually takes you to its literally breathtaking Skyline terminus.

Fortunately for mountain bikers, nearly all the trails in the preserve are open to cyclists. The trails are steep and knotted with rocks and tree roots, which makes for an exhausting, exhilarating, or terrifying ride, depending on your experience and attitude.

The most popular trail in Half Moon Bay is the **Coastside Trail** (650/726-8819, www.parks.ca.gov). Extending five miles from Miramar Beach to Poplar Beach, this flat, paved trail follows the coast and is filled with joggers, dog walkers, and bikes. There are a multitude of beach-access points along the way. To go downtown, jump off at Kelly Avenue and take it across Highway 1 to the heart of Half Moon Bay. Beyond the Poplar Beach parking lot, the trail crosses a wooden bridge and turns into a dirt trail. This area is known as the **Wavecrest Open Space** and goes all the way down to the Ritz-Carlton. It is a great place to spot herons, egrets, and gray whales off the coast during their spring migration. Parking is plentiful at Poplar Beach ($2 per hour), at the end of Poplar Street on the south end of town.

KAYAKING AND WHALE-WATCHING

The *Queen of Hearts* (Pillar Point Harbor, 510/581-2628, www.fishingboat.com, reservations strongly recommended) offers whale-watching trips (Jan.-Apr., $50) in addition to deep-sea fishing trip (Apr.-Nov., $100).

One of the coolest ways to see the coast is from the deck of a sea kayak or stand-up paddleboard. Many tours with the **Half Moon Bay Kayaking Company** (2 Johnson Pier, 650/773-6101, www.hmbkayak.com, 10am-4pm daily late May-early Sept., 10am-4pm Wed.-Mon. mid-Sept.-mid-May, $85-150) require no previous kayaking experience. For an easy first paddle, try the Pillar Point tour, the full-moon tour, or the sunset paddle. Classes and rentals are available.

HORSEBACK RIDING

Sea Horse Ranch (1828 Hwy. 1, 650/726-9903, www.seahorseranch.org, 8am-close daily, $70-90) offers one-hour, 90-minute, and two-hour guided tours that take you along the cliffs and down onto the sands at Half Moon Bay's Poplar Beach. Children over the age of seven are welcome, as are riders of all ability levels. Beginners can ask to have their horses led by a guide or can request to ride Tardy, an extremely laid-back horse known for his slow speed and gentle disposition.

Food

For seafood, go to ★ **Sam's Chowder House**

(4210 N. Cabrillo Hwy., Pillar Point Harbor, 650/712-0245, www.samschowderhouse.com, 11:30am-9pm Mon.-Thurs., 11:30am-9:30pm Fri., 11am-9:30pm Sat., 11am-9pm Sun., $15-38), a fusion of an East Coast chowder and lobster shack with West Coast sensibilities and a view of the Pacific. The lobster clambake for two is a splurge, but it's an excellent introduction to Sam's seafood-heavy menu. Many other dinners opt for the buttery lobster roll.

Pasta Moon (315 Main St., 650/726-5125, www.pastamoon.com, 11:30am-2pm and 5:30pm-9pm Mon.-Thurs., 11:30am-2pm and 5:30pm-9:30pm Fri., noon-3pm and 5:30pm-9:30pm Sat., noon-3pm and 5:30pm-9pm Sun., $19-40) is the area's godmother of fine dining, serving updated Italian cuisine with an emphasis on fresh, light dishes. The wood-fired pizzas are particularly good and affordable, as are any of the pasta dishes, made with house-made noodles. The bar and lounge offers a more urbane evening out.

In the historic San Benito House, the **Garden Deli Café** (356 Main St., 650/726-9507, www.sanbenitohouse.com, 10am-5pm daily, $7) serves sandwiches like turkey, roast beef, and ham that stand out due to the slabs of tasty homemade bread that the ingredients

Take a horseback tour with Sea Horse Ranch.

lie between. Get your sandwich to go or eat it in the adjacent courtyard.

★ **Half Moon Bay Brewing Co.** (390 Capistrano Rd., 650/728-2739, www. hmbbrewingco.com, 11am-close Mon.-Fri. 10am-close Sat.-Sun. $12-24) is a fine place to watch the sunset over Pillar Point Harbor. This landmark has a worn and comfy interior along with some outdoor seating for sunny days. The beers made on-site include five standard brews and five seasonal brews; the amber ale is the most popular. The golden-fried artichoke heart appetizer is a favorite, but the fish tacos are where the kitchen does its best work.

Accommodations

Half Moon Bay offers several lovely bed-and-breakfasts along with one luxury resort hotel and a suites hotel right by the harbor, among other options.

Tthe ★ **Ritz-Carlton Half Moon Bay** (1 Miramontes Point Rd., 650/712-7000, www. ritzcarlton.com, $700) resembles a Scottish castle transported to the California coast. Surrounding the luxury hotel are two emerald-green golf courses perched above the Pacific. The sprawling grounds are dotted with always-lit fire pits and chairs for taking in the marvelous ocean views. Guests enjoy

the finest modern amenities: Bathrooms have marble floors and countertops, while many of the posh rooms overlook the sea. The hotel also has a spa, restaurant, two fitness rooms, a pool, tennis courts, and a basketball court. Guests can also enjoy top-tier restaurant **Navio,** which has an extensive wine list.

The **Beach House at Half Moon Bay** (4100 N. Cabrillo Hwy., 650/712-0220 or 800/315-9366, www.beach-house.com, $295-195) is situated in an ideal location a few feet from Pillar Point Harbor. All the rooms are multilevel lofts and have a private patio. On fog-shrouded days, the Beach House has in-room wood-burning fireplaces and an outdoor hot tub and heated pool on the pool deck.

Transportation and Services

Half Moon Bay is on Highway 1 about 45 minutes south of San Francisco. From San Francisco, take I-280 south to Highway 92 west to Half Moon Bay and Highway 1.

Parking in downtown Half Moon Bay is usually a fairly easy proposition—except, of course, if you're in town for the Pumpkin Festival, when parking is a nightmare of epic proportions. Your best bet is to stay in town with your car safely stowed in a hotel parking lot before the festival.

Sam's Chowder House

There is a 24-hour emergency room at the **Seton Coastside Hospital** (600 Marine Blvd., Moss Beach, 650/563-7100, www.setoncoastside.org). For less serious health services visit the **Coastside Clinic** (Shoreline Station, Suite 100A, 225 S. Hwy. 1, Half Moon Bay, 650/573-3941, www.sanmateomedicalcenter.org).

PESCADERO

South of Half Moon Bay is Pescadero with one main street, one side street, and several smallish farms. Despite its tiny size, many Bay Area denizens visit Pescadero for the twisty roads that challenge motorcyclists and bicyclists, fresh produce, the town's 19th-century buildings and, of course, the legendary Duarte's Tavern.

Sights

San Gregorio is a tiny, picturesque town of rolling rangeland, neat patches of colorful crops, and century-old homes, including a one-room schoolhouse and an old brothel. Its beating heart is the **San Gregorio General Store** (Hwy. 84 and Stage Rd., 650/726-0565, www.sangregoriostore.com, 10:30am-6pm Mon.-Thurs., 10:30am-7pm Fri., 10am-7pm Sat., 10am-6pm Sun.), open since 1889. The store has an eclectic book section and a variety of cast-iron cookery, oil lamps, and raccoon traps. In the back are coolers stocked with homemade deli sandwiches. The real centerpiece is the bar, which serves beer, wine, and spirits. On the weekends the store is packed with out-of-towners, and the live music keeps things moving.

South of Pescadero is **Pigeon Point Lighthouse** (210 Pigeon Point Rd., at Hwy. 1, 650/879-2120, www.parks.ca.gov, 8am-sunset daily, visitor center 10am-4pm Wed.-Mon. June-Aug., 10am-4pm Thurs.-Mon. Sept.-May, free). First lit in 1872, Pigeon Point is one of the most photographed lighthouses in the United States. Its hostel still shelters travelers, and visitors still marvel at the incomparable views from the point. In winter, look for migrating whales from the rocks beyond the tower.

Beaches

Pescadero State Beach (Hwy. 1 at Pescadero Rd., 650/879-2170, www.parks.ca.gov, 8am-sunset daily, $8) is a great spot to walk in the sand and stare out at the Pacific. Near-constant winds make it less than ideal for picnics or sunbathing. It does have public restrooms.

Beach House at Half Moon Bay

Bird lovers flock to **Pescadero Marsh Natural Preserve** (Hwy. 1, www.smcnha. org), right across the highway from Pescadero State Beach. This protected wetland is home to a variety of avian species, including blue herons, great and snowy egrets, and northern harriers. For the best birding, visit the marsh early in the morning or in late fall or early spring, when migration is in full swing.

San Gregorio State Beach (650/726-8819, www.parks.ca.gov, 8am-sunset daily, $8) stretches beyond the cliffs that bound it to create a long stretch of beach. San Gregorio is a local favorite in the summer, despite the regular appearance of thick, chilly fog over the sand. Brave beachgoers can even swim and bodysurf here, although wearing a wetsuit is advisable. Picnic tables and restrooms cluster near the parking lot, although picnicking can be hampered by the wind.

Año Nuevo State Reserve

Año Nuevo State Reserve (1 News Years Creek Road at Hwy. 1, south of Pescadero, 650/879-2025, reservations 800/444-4445, www.parks.ca.gov, 8am-sunset daily, $10) is world famous as the winter home and breeding ground of the once-endangered elephant seal. The reserve also has extensive dunes and marshland. The beaches and wilderness are open year-round. The elephant seals start showing up in December and stay to breed, birth pups, and loll on the beach until early March. Visitors are not allowed down to the elephant seal habitats on their own and must sign up for a guided walking tour. Book your tour at least a day or two in advance; the seals are popular with both locals and travelers.

Food

★ **Duarte's Tavern** (202 Stage Rd., Pescadero, 650/879-0464, www.duartestavern. com, 7am-8pm Sun.-Thurs., 7am-8:30pm Fri.-Sat., $8-26) has been honored by the James Beard Foundation as "An American Classic," and once you walk through the doors you'll see why. The rambling building features sloping floors and age-darkened wooden walls.

The food is good, the service friendly, and the coffee plentiful. And while almost everybody comes to Duarte's for a bowl of artichoke soup or a slice of olallieberry pie, it's really the atmosphere that's the biggest draw.

The **Pescadero Country Store** (251 Stage Rd., 650/879-0410, daily 9am-7pm, $11-18) is as converted grocery store with a pizza counter serving wood-fired pies, a full-service deli, and a beer and wine bar decorated in a deepblue nautical theme.

Harley Farms (205 North St., 650/879-0480, www.harleyfarms.com, 10am-5pm daily summer, 11am-3pm Fri.-Sun., 10am-4pm Mon.-Thurs. winter) is the last working dairy on the San Mateo coast. Its locally famous goat cheese is sold in its farm store. During your stop, you can even assist in the cheese-making process, taking a tour that teaches you how to milk a goat and then create fresh artisanal cheese.

Drop by **Arcangeli Grocery** (287 Stage Rd., 650/879-0147, www.normsmarket.com, 10am-6pm daily) to pick up the delicious, homemade breads, including the Italian artichoke herb bread and the garlic-herb sourdough loaf. The pastries—especially the raspberry twists—are also great.

Bob's Vegetable Stand (Hwy. 1, 5 miles south of Half Moon Bay, 650/712-7740) has a selection of local produce rivaling any grocery store.

Accommodations

Pigeon Point Hostel (210 Pigeon Point Rd. at Hwy. 1, 650/879-0633, http://norcalhostels. org/pigeon, dorm adult $28-32, children $14-16, private room $82-186) has simple but comfortable accommodations, both private and dorm-style. Amenities include three kitchens, free Wi-Fi, linens, and beach access. But the best amenity of all is the cliff-top hot tub (4pm-10:30pm, max. four people, $8 pp.).

At **Costanoa Lodge and Campground** (2001 Rossi Rd., at Hwy. 1, 650/879-1100 or 877/262-7848, www.costanoa.com, campsite $42-55, rooms $80-385), you can pitch a tent in the campground or rent a whirlpool suite in the lodge. Other options include log-style cabins with shared baths, small tent cabins with shared baths, and private rooms. Costanoa's many nature programs educate visitors about the ecology of the San Mateo coast and the preservation efforts that are underway. A small general store offers s'mores fixings and souvenirs, while "comfort stations" provide outdoor fireplaces, private indoor-outdoor showers, bathrooms with heated floors, and saunas that are open daily 24 hours to all guests.

For a little more luxury, the **Pescadero Creek Inn Bed & Breakfast** (393 Stage Rd., 888/307-1898, www.pescaderocreekinn. com, $175-210) is conveniently located in downtown Pescadero. While the century-old house isn't completely soundproof, the rooms have high ceilings and are prettily appointed; amenities include down-feather bed tops. The owner serves a delectable breakfast each morning, and pours his homemade award-winning wines in the afternoon

Camping

Butano State Park (1500 Cloverdale Rd., Pescadero, 650/879-2040, www.parks.

ca.gov, reservations 800/444-7275 or www. reservecalifornia.com, Apr.-Nov., $35) offers 21 drive-in and 18 walk-in campsites. While there are no showers, there are clean restrooms, fire pits, and drinking water. Perhaps the best amenity is the proximity to fantastic strolls through the canopy of redwoods or more athletic treks up dusty ridgelines.

Farther inland, past the tiny town of Loma Mar, is **Memorial Park** (9500 Pescadero Creek Rd., 650/363-4021, https://parks. smcgov.org, year-round, $25-30) and its 158 campsites. Each site accommodates as many as eight people, with a fire pit, picnic tables, and a metal locker to store food and sundries. There is also drinking water, flush toilets, and a general store. Memorial boasts an amphitheater and swimming holes in Pescadero Creek.

Transportation

Pescadero is 17 miles south of Half Moon Bay. At Pescadero State Beach, Highway 1 intersects Pescadero Road. Turn east on Pescadero Road and drive two miles to the stop sign (the only one in town). Turn left onto Stage Road to find the main drag. Parking is free and generally easy to find on Stage Road.

North Coast

Look for ★ to find recommended
sights, activities, dining, and lodging.

Highlights

★ **California Coastal National Monument:** The monument's Point Arena-Stornetta Unit is a stunning coastline that showcases sheer cliffs, giant tide pools, and several sea arches (page 137).

★ **Mendocino:** Spend an afternoon or a weekend wandering this arts-filled community and its headlands, which jut out into the Pacific (page 143).

★ **Avenue of the Giants:** The towering coast redwoods in Humboldt Redwoods State Park are a true must-see. Simply gaze at the silent giants or head to the nearby Eel River for a quick dip (page 165).

★ **Arcata Plaza:** Arcata is Humboldt County's cultural hub, and its Arcata Plaza is a vibrant, grassy square circled by bars, bookstores, and restaurants (page 183).

★ **Trinidad:** This tiny town perched above an idyllic bay is one of the most photogenic coastal communities in the state (page 188).

★ **Prairie Creek Redwoods State Park:** With big trees, impressive wildlife, a long, lonely beach, and one-of-a-kind Fern Canyon, this park is worth a stop (page 193).

★ **Jedediah Smith Redwoods State Park:** The park showcases the rugged beauty of the North Coast with its stunning old-growth redwoods (page 196).

★ **Battery Point Lighthouse:** This lighthouse on an island off Crescent City is only accessible at low tide. If you time it right, you can take an insightful tour from the lighthouse keeper (page 198).

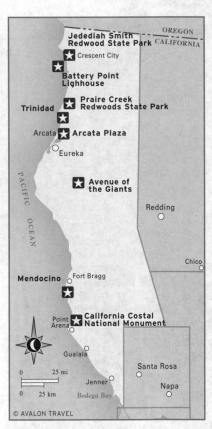

The rugged North Coast of California is spectacular, its wild beauty in many places unspoiled and almost desolate. The cliffs are forbidding, the beaches are rocky and windswept, and the surf thunders in with formidable authority.

This is not the California coast of surfer movies, though hardy souls do ride the chilly Pacific waves as far north as Crescent City.

From Bodega Bay, Highway 1 twists and turns north along hairpin curves that will take your breath away. The Sonoma and Mendocino Coasts offer lovely beaches and forests, top-notch cuisine, and a friendly, uncrowded wine region. Along the way, tiny coastal towns—Jenner, Gualala, Point Arena, Mendocino, Fort Bragg—dot the hills and valleys, beckoning travelers with bed-and-breakfasts, organic farms, and relaxing respites from the road. Between the towns are a wealth of coastal access areas where you can take in the striking meeting of land and sea. Inland, Mendocino's hidden wine region offers the rural and relaxed pace missing from that other famous wine district. Anderson Valley and Hopland can quench your thirst, whether it's for beer at the local microbrewery or wine at one of many tasting rooms.

Where Highway 1 merges with U.S. 101 is the famous Lost Coast, accessed only via steep, narrow roads or by backpacking the famous Lost Coast Trail. This is California at its wildest.

For most travelers, the North Coast means redwood country, and U.S. 101 marks the gateway to those redwoods. The famous, immense coastal sequoias loom along the highway south of the old logging town of Eureka and the hip college outpost of Arcata. A plethora of state and national parks lure travelers with numerous hiking trails, forested campgrounds, kitschy tourist traps, and some of the tallest and oldest trees on the continent; you can pitch a tent in Humboldt Redwoods State Park, cruise the Avenue of the Giants, and gaze in wonder at the primordial Founders Grove. Crescent City, marking the northern terminus of the California Coast, is a seaside town known for fishing, seafood—and for surviving a tsunami.

Previous: scenic Highway 101; Avenue of the Giants. **Above:** Trinidad Memorial Lighthouse.

North Coast

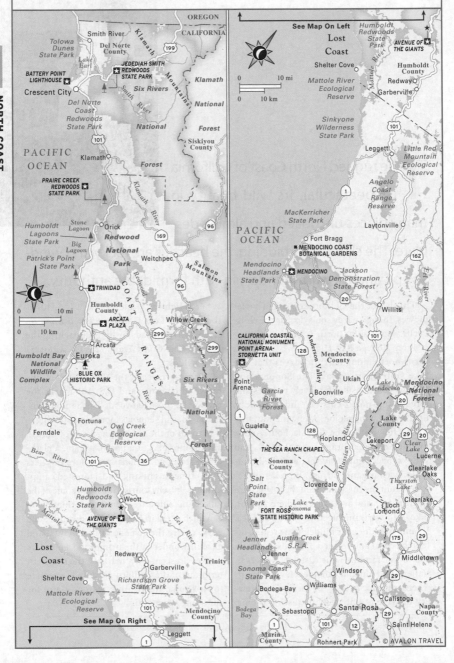

OREGON
CALIFORNIA

See Map On Left

Lost
Coast

Humboldt
Redwoods
State
Park

AVENUE OF
THE GIANTS

Tolowa
Dunes
State Park

Smith River
Del Norte
County

199

Klamath

Six Rivers

Klamath

Shelter Cove

Humboldt
County

Lake
Earl

Redway

BATTERY POINT
LIGHTHOUSE

JEDEDIAH SMITH
REDWOODS
STATE PARK

Mattole River
Ecological
Reserve

Garberville

Crescent City

Smith River

Six Rivers

National

0   10 mi

0   10 km

Del Norte
Coast
Redwoods
State Park

National

Forest

Sinkyone
Wilderness
State Park

101

PACIFIC
OCEAN

101

Klamath

Forest

Siskiyou
County

Leggett

Little Red
Mountain
Ecological
Reserve

PRAIRE CREEK
REDWOODS
STATE PARK

Klamath River

1

Angelo
Coast
Range
Reserve

MacKerricher
State Park

Laytonville

Humboldt
Lagoons
State Park

Stone
Lagoon

Orick

Redwood
National

169

96

PACIFIC
OCEAN

Fort Bragg

MENDOCINO COAST
BOTANICAL GARDENS

162

Big
Lagoon

Patrick's Point
State Park

Weitchpec

Park

Salmon
Mountains

Mendocino
Headlands
State Park

MENDOCINO

Jackson
Demonstration
State Forest

El River

0   10 mi

0   10 km

TRINIDAD

96

Redwood Creek

COAST

20

Willits

Humboldt
County

ARCATA
PLAZA

Willow Creek

1

101

Humboldt Bay
National
Wildlife
Complex

Arcata

299

299

CALIFORNIA COASTAL
NATIONAL MONUMENT
POINT ARENA-
STORNETTA UNIT

Anderson Valley

128

Mendocino
County

Eureka

BLUE OX
HISTORIC PARK

RANGES

Six Rivers

Point
Arena

Garcia
River
Forest

Ukiah

Lake
Mendocino

Mendocino
National
Forest

Mud River

Boonville

20

Fortuna

National

1

Lake
County

29

20

Ferndale

Owl Creek
Ecological
Reserve

Gualala

128

Hopland

Russian River

Lakeport

Clear
Lake

Lucerne

Bear River

101

36

Forest

THE SEA RANCH CHAPEL

Sonoma
County

Cloverdale

Lake
Sonoma

Clearlake
Oaks

Thurston
Lake

Clearlake

Humboldt
Redwoods
State Park

Weott

Salt
Point
State
Park

FORT ROSS
STATE HISTORIC PARK

Loch
Lomond

AVENUE OF
THE GIANTS

Mattole River

El River

175

29

Jenner
Headlands

Austin Creek
S.R.A.

Middletown

Lost
Coast

Redway

Garberville

Trinity

Jenner

29

Sonoma Coast
State Park

Windsor

Calistoga

Shelter Cove

Richardson Grove
State Park

Williams

Santa Rosa

29

Napa
County

Mattole River
Ecological
Reserve

101

Mendocino
County

Bodega
Bay

Bodega Bay

Sebastopol

101

12

Saint Helena

See Map On Right

Leggett

1

Marin
County

Rohnert Park

© AVALON TRAVEL

PLANNING YOUR TIME

If you're planning a road trip to explore the North Coast in depth and want to make stops in more than one destination, plan to spend a **full week.** Driving is the way to get from place to place, unless you're a hard-core backpacker. **Highway 1** winds along the North Coast from Bodega Bay to above Fort Bragg, where it heads east to connect with U.S. 101 at its northern terminus near Leggett. U.S. 101 then heads inland through southern Humboldt County before heading back to the coast at Eureka. North of Eureka, U.S. 101 continues through Arcata, Trinidad, and Crescent City, along with the Redwood National and State Parks.

If you are heading to Mendocino or a section of the coast north of there, take **U.S. 101,** which is a great deal faster than Highway 1, and then take one of the connector roads from U.S. 101 to Highway 1. One of the best and most scenic connector roads is **Highway 128,** which heads west off U.S. 101 at Cloverdale and passes through the scenic Anderson Valley, with its many wineries, before joining Highway 1 just south of the town of Mendocino.

Driving times on Highway 1 tend to be longer on the North Coast due to the roadway's twists, turns, and many spectacular ocean vistas. On U.S. 101 north of Leggett, expect to share the road with logging vehicles. A lot of the roads off U.S. 101 or Highway 1 are worthwhile excursions, but expect mountainous terrain.

Many Bay Area residents consider **Mendocino** ideal for a weekend getaway or romantic retreat. A **weekend** is about the perfect length of time to spend on the Mendocino Coast or in the Anderson Valley wine country. There are at least 3-4 days' worth of intriguing hikes to take in Redwood National and State Parks.

Along the **Lost Coast,** the most lodging and dining options can be found in Shelter Cove. If you want to explore the Lost Coast Trail, consider hiking it north to south, with the wind at your back. Spend the night in Ferndale or camp at the Mattole Recreation Site, where the trail begins, so that you can get an early start for the first day of backpacking.

If you're exploring the **redwood parks,** consider staying in the small towns of Arcata or Trinidad. The campgrounds at Patrick's Point State Park and Prairie Creek State Park are superb places to pitch a tent.

Summer on the North Coast has average daily temperatures in the mid-60s, which is comparable to the temps in Southern California during the winter. Expect rain on the North Coast from November to May. The chances of fog or rain are significantly lower in the **fall,** making it one of the best times to visit. Frequent visitors to the area know this, so many popular hotels book quickly for fall weekends.

Sonoma Coast

One good way to begin your meanders up the coast is to take U.S. 101 out of San Francisco as far as Petaluma, and then head west toward Highway 1. This stretch of Highway 1 is also called the Shoreline Highway. As you travel toward the coast, you'll leave urban areas behind for a while, passing through some of the most pleasant villages in California.

BODEGA BAY

Bodega Bay is popular for its coastal views, whale-watching, and seafood—but it's most famous as the filming locale of Alfred Hitchcock's *The Birds.* The town sits on the eastern side of the harbor, while Bodega Head is a peninsula that shields the bay from the ocean. The tiny town with a population of just over 1,000 has kite shops, marinas, and

Local Favorites

Many strange and hidden attractions can be found in the small communities of the North Coast.

★ **The Sea Ranch Chapel:** (Hwy. 1, Sea Ranch, www.thesearanchchapel.org, sunrise-sunset daily) This stunning and intimate place of worship is an art piece and sanctuary, decorated with stained-glass windows, seashells, and sea urchins.

★ **Schooner Gulch State Beach:** (Schooner Gulch Rd. and Hwy. 1, 707/937-5804, www.parks.ca.gov) Hike to the coast, descend to the beach, and walk 0.25 mile north to **Bowling Ball Beach** where giant bowling ball-shaped boulders are lined in rows on the beach.

★ **Triangle Tattoo Museum:** (356B N. Main St., Fort Bragg, 707/964-8814, www.triangletattoo.com, noon-6pm daily, free) Exhibits include everything from the heavily inked New Zealand Maori to circus sideshow workers.

---

unassuming seafood restaurants. The whole town shuts down around 7pm, even on summer evenings.

Whale-Watching

The best sight you could hope to see is a close-up view of Pacific gray whales migrating home to Alaska with their newborn calves. The whales head past the area January-May on their way from their summer home off Mexico. If you're lucky, you can see them from the shore. **Bodega Head,** a promontory just north of the bay, is a place to get close to the migration route. To get to this prime spot, travel north on Highway 1 about one mile past the visitors center and turn left onto Eastshore Road; make a right at the stop sign, and then drive three more miles to the parking lot.

On weekends from January to Mother's Day weekend, volunteers from **Stewards of the Coast and Redwoods** (707/869-9177, www.stewardscr.org) are available to answer questions. Contact them for organized whale-watching tours or to learn more about their various educational programs. Or go out on a whale-watching trip with **Bodega Bay Sport Fishing** (707/875-3344, www.bodegabaysportfishing.com, Dec.-Mar., $50-60/half day) on their 60- or 65-foot boat.

Doran Regional Park

When you arrive in Bodega Bay, you'll see a sign pointing left for **Doran Regional Park** (201 Doran Beach Rd., 707/875-3540, http://parks.sonomacounty.ca.gov, 7am-sunset daily, day use $7 per vehicle). It is less than one mile down the road and worth the trip. The wide and level two-mile-long beach has a small boardwalk. You can even swim at Doran Beach; although it's cold, the water is protected from the open ocean waves, so it's much safer than most of the beaches along the coast.

Bodega Head

Bodega Bay looks like an open safety pin on maps; **Bodega Head** (3799 Westshore Rd., 707/875-3483, www.parks.ca.gov, sunrise-sunset daily, free) is the thicker side, a knob that protects the bay from the open ocean. A part of Sonoma Coast State Park, it's the best place for a hike that gives you an overview of the area. The **Bodega Head Trail** (1.9 miles, 136-foot elevation change) showcases rock arches, sandy coves, and migrating gray whales before hitting the high point and winding back to views of Doran Beach, Bodega Bay, and Bodega Harbor.

Sonoma Coast

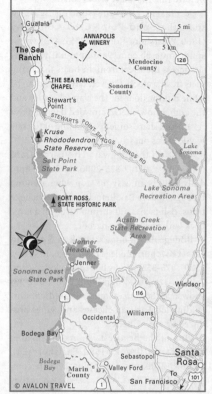

Coast State Park (707/875-3483, www. parks.ca.gov, sunrise-sunset daily, day use $8 per vehicle). The park's boundaries extend from Bodega Head at the south up to the Vista Trailhead, four miles north of Jenner. As you drive north along Highway 1, you'll see signs for various beaches. Although they're lovely places to walk, fish, and maybe sunbathe on the odd hot day, it is not advisable to swim here. If you go down to the water, bring your binoculars and camera. The cliffs, crags, inlets, whitecaps, mini-islands, and rock outcroppings are fascinating in any weather, and their looks change with the shifting tides and fog.

Sports and Recreation

With a usually calm bay and a protected harbor, Bodega Bay is a great place to kayak or stand-up paddleboard. Stop into the **Bodega Bay Surf Shack** (Pelican Plaza, 1400 Hwy. 1, 707/875-3944, www. bodegabaysurf.com, 10am-6pm Mon.-Fri., 9am-7pm Sat.-Sun., kayaks $45/four hours, SUPs $40/five hours) to rent your SUP or kayak, then set out in Bodega Bay, Salmon Creek, or the nearby lower portion of the Russian River. They also give private lessons ($145) and group lessons ($109) and rent surfboards ($17/day) and wetsuits ($17/day). Doran Beach has an unintimidating wave for beginners. Just north of town is Salmon Creek, a series of powerful and exposed beach breaks.

Long, rugged beaches with few people mean that the Sonoma Coast is a terrific place to go horseback riding. Just north of town at the 378-acre Chanslor Ranch, **Horse N Around Trail Rides** (2660 N. Hwy. 1, 707/875-3333, www.horsenaroundtrailrides. com, $40-250) offers 30-minute wetlands trail rides and 1.5-hour beach rides. Choose between group rides and slightly pricier private rides.

Shopping

Gourmet au Bay (1412 Bay Flat Rd., 707/875-9875, www.gourmetaubay.com, 11am-8pm

Bodega Seafood, Art, and Wine Festival

The annual **Bodega Seafood, Art, and Wine Festival** (16855 Bodega Hwy., Bodega, 707/824-8717, www.bodegaseafoodfestival. com, Aug., adults $15-20, seniors $10-15, children 12-18 $8-10, children under 12 free) takes place the last weekend in August, combining all the best elements of the Bodega lifestyle with live music, wine-tastings, and special dinners. The proceeds benefit two worthy organizations: the Bodega Volunteer Fire Department and Stewards of the Coast and Redwoods.

Sonoma Coast State Park

Seventeen miles of coast are within **Sonoma**

Thurs.-Mon., 11am-7pm Tues.-Wed., $15/ tasting) is a shop and tasting bar that offers the chance to taste wines from different vintners: some are major players in the Napa wine scene, and some are from wineries so small they don't have tasting rooms of their own. You might even get to taste the odd French or Australian wine when you "wine surf," tasting three wines poured and presented on a miniature surfboard for you to carry out to the deck to admire the view of Bodega Harbor. Inside, peruse the gift shop, which includes some local artisanal foods plus plenty of handmade ceramics and pottery and an array of toys for wine lovers.

Food

The ★ **Fishetarian Fish Market** (599 Hwy. 1, 707/875-9092, www.fishetarianfishmarket. com, 11am-7pm Fri.-Sun., 11am-6pm Mon.-Thurs., $6-15) nails the Baja-style fish taco with rockfish, a cabbage slaw, and a zingy sauce. They also do Point Reyes oysters and an award-winning clam chowder. Order at the counter above display cases of smoked salmon, oysters, and octopus salad, then dine casually inside or outside at one of the limited tables. Fishetarian has a few well-chosen craft beers on tap along with a fridge filled with

bottled beers, sodas, and other cold beverages. Beware that this place closes early.

A classic and unassuming seafood spot, the **Spud Point Crab Company** (1860 Westshore Rd., 707/875-9472, www. spudpointcrab.com, 9am-5pm daily, $7-11) sits across the street from the boats that bring in its fresh seafood. On weekdays, there can be a line out the door for the clam chowder and the crab sandwich. On crowded days, make a friend and share some space at one of the few picnic tables out front.

Right on the highway, **The Birds Café** (1407 Hwy. 1, 707/875-2900, 11:30am-6pm daily, $10) is an easy pit stop when driving through Bodega Bay. Refuel on fried artichoke tacos, fish tacos, and shrimp tacos on a large deck with views of the harbor.

Bodega Bay Lodge's **Drakes Sonoma Coast Kitchen** (Bodega Bay Lodge, 103 Hwy. 1, 707/875-3525, www.bodegabaylodge.com, 7:30am-11am and 6pm-9pm daily, $22-38) showcases Sonoma County ingredients including local artisan cheeses and wines produced by area wineries.

One of the best restaurants in the area is **Terrapin Creek** (1580 Eastshore Dr., 707/875-2700, www.terrapincreekcafe.com, 4:30pm-9pm Thurs.-Mon., $23-32) where they

Benches overlook the water at Doran Regional Park.

make creative use of the abundance of fresh seafood available and cook up tasty pasta, duck, and beef entrées.

Accommodations and Camping

The ★ **Bodega Bay Lodge & Spa** (103 Hwy. 1, 707/875-3525 or 888/875-2250, www.bodegabaylodge.com, $279-669) is on a seven-acre property that sits high enough to overlook the bay and harbor, Doran Beach, the bird-filled marshes, and Bodega Head in the distance. Most rooms have views of the water, while all the units in the seven separate buildings have their own private balconies or terraces. Warm up on a foggy day in the heated pool, sauna, and oversized infinity soaking tub. There's a fitness center and spa in the same facility. Dine at the lodge's upscale **Drakes Sonoma Coast Kitchen** (7:30am-11am and 6pm-9pm daily, $22-40) or the casual **Drakes Fireside Lounge** (5pm-9pm daily, $6-17).

For a B&B experience, head to the **Bay Hill Mansion** (3919 Bay Hill Rd., 877/468-1588, www.bayhillmansion.com, $269-354) on the north side of Bodega Bay. Be spoiled in one of just four rooms and wake up to a family-style sit-down brunch.

Sonoma Coast State Park (707/875-3483 or 707/865-2391, www.parks.ca.gov, day use $8 per vehicle) encompasses several campgrounds along its 17-mile expanse. Both **Bodega Dunes Campground** (2485 Hwy. 1, www.reservecalifornia.com, $35) and **Wright's Beach Campground** (7095 Hwy. 1, www.reservecalifornia.com, $35-45) are developed, with hot showers and flush toilets.

Doran Regional Park (201 Doran Beach Rd., 707/565-2267, http://sonomacountycamping.org, $32-35) has 120 campsites for tents, trailers, and RVs. Amenities include restrooms with coin-operated showers.

Transportation

Bodega Bay is on Highway 1 north of Point Reyes National Seashore and west of Petaluma. From the Bay Area, it's a beautiful drive north, but the road's twists and turns require taking it slow. A faster way to get here is to take U.S. 101 north to Petaluma. Take the exit for East Washington Street and follow Bodega Avenue to Valley Ford Road, cutting across to the coast. You'll hit Bodega Bay about two miles after you pass through Valley Ford. The latter route takes about 1.5 hours, with some of the route slow and winding.

Bodega Bay Lodge & Spa

JENNER

Jenner is on Highway 1 at the mouth of the Russian River. It's a beautiful spot for a quiet honeymoon or a paddle in a kayak. **Goat Rock State Beach** (Goat Rock Rd., 707/875-3483, www.parks.ca.gov, day use $8 per vehicle) is at the mouth of the Russian River inside Sonoma Coast State Park. A colony of harbor seals breed and frolic here, and you may also see gray whales, sea otters, elephant seals, and a variety of sealife. Pets are not allowed, and swimming is prohibited.

Food and Accommodations

Both the food and the views are memorable at ★ **River's End** (11048 Hwy. 1, 707/865-2484, www.ilovesunsets.com, 11:30am-3pm and 5pm-8:30pm daily, $19-42). The restaurant is perched above the spot where the Russian River flows into the Pacific, and it's a beautiful sight to behold over seafood or filet mignon. Prices are high, but if you get a window table at sunset, you may forget that.

The renovated **Jenner Inn** (10400 Hwy. 1, 707/865-2377, www.jennerinn.com, $169-549) has a variety of quiet, beautifully furnished rooms mere steps from the river. Some rooms have hot tubs and private decks, and breakfast is included.

Fourteen miles north of Jenner is the large and luxurious **Timber Cove Inn** (21780 N. Hwy. 1, 707/847-3231 or 800/987-8319, www.timbercoveinn.com, $340-930), with a spacious bar and lounge, an oceanfront patio, rooms with spa tubs and fireplaces, and hiking trails nearby. You can't miss the inn from the road thanks to the 93-foot-tall obelisk rising above the building. Dine on-site at **Coast Kitchen** (8am-11am and noon-9:30pm daily, $21-46), which pairs Sonoma wines with organic seasonal fare.

Transportation

Jenner is on the ocean along Highway 1. There is no public transportation, but it is a pretty drive from just about anywhere. The fastest route from San Francisco (about 1.75 hours) is to drive north along U.S. 101 and make a left onto Washington Street in Petaluma. Washington Street becomes Bodega Avenue and then Valley Ford Road before you make a slight left onto Highway 1 and head north toward Jenner. From Sacramento (2.5 hours) or points in the East Bay, take I-80 west and then navigate to Petaluma, where you continue west to Highway 1.

FORT ROSS STATE HISTORIC PARK

There is no historic early American figure named Ross who settled here: "Ross" is short for "Russian," and this park commemorates the history of Russian settlement on the North Coast. In the 19th century Russians came to the wilds of Alaska and worked with native Alaskans to develop a robust fur trade, harvesting seals, otters, sea lions, and land mammals for their pelts. The enterprise required sea travel as the hunters chased the animals as far as California. Eventually, a group of fur hunters and traders came ashore on what is now the Sonoma Coast and developed a fortified outpost that became known as **Fort Ross State Historic Park** (19005 Hwy. 1, Jenner, 707/847-3286, www.fortross.org, 10am-4:30pm Fri.-Mon., visitors center days/hours vary, parking $8). The area gradually became not only a thriving Russian American settlement but also a center for agriculture and shipbuilding and the site of California's first windmills. Learn more at the park's large visitors center, which provides a continuous film and a roomful of exhibits.

You can walk into the reconstructed fort buildings to see how the settlers lived. The only original building still standing is the captain's quarters—a large, luxurious house for that time and place. The other buildings, including the large bunkhouse, the chapel, and the two cannon-filled blockhouses, were rebuilt using much of the original lumber used by the Russians. Be aware that a serious visit to the whole fort and the beach beyond entails a level but long walk; wear comfortable shoes and bring water.

Camping

Part of Fort Ross State Historic Park, the **Reef Campground** (19005 Hwy. 1, 707/847-3708, www.parks.ca.gov, Apr.-Nov., $35) has 21 first-come, first-served campsites within a small canyon winding down toward the coast. There are paths here to a couple of scenic coves.

SALT POINT STATE PARK

Stretching for miles along the Sonoma coastline, **Salt Point State Park** (25050 Hwy. 1, Jenner, 707/847-3221, www.parks.ca.gov, sunrise-sunset daily, $8 per vehicle) provides easy access from U.S. 101 to more than a dozen sandy state beaches. You don't have to stop at the visitors center to enjoy this park and its many beaches—just follow the signs along the highway to the turnoffs and parking lots.

If you're looking to scuba dive or free dive, head for **Gerstle Cove,** accessible from the visitors center just south of Salt Point proper. The cove was designated one of California's first underwater parks, and divers who can deal with the chilly water have a wonderful time exploring the diverse undersea wildlife.

Kruse Rhododendron State Reserve

For a genteel experience, head east off Highway 1 to the **Kruse Rhododendron State Reserve** (Hwy. 1 near milepost 43, 707/847-3221, www.parks.ca.gov, sunrise-sunset daily, free), where you can meander along the **Chinese Gulf Trail** in the spring, admiring the profusion of pink rhododendron flowers blooming beneath the second-growth redwood forest. If you prefer a picnic, you'll find tables at many of the beaches—though it can be quite windy in the summer.

Camping

Salt Point State Park (25050 Hwy. 1, 800/444-7275, www.reservecalifornia.com, $25-35) has scenic **Gerstle Cove Campground** on the west side of the highway and **Woodside Campground** on the eastern side.

THE SEA RANCH

The last 10 miles of the Sonoma Coast before entering Mendocino County are the property of The Sea Ranch, a private coastal community known for its distinctive buildings with wood siding and shingles. One of its structures, Condominium 1, won the American

The Sea Ranch Chapel

Institute of Architects Gold Medal in 1991 and is now on the National Register of Historic Places.

The community's hard-won coastal access points make The Sea Ranch a good place to take a break from driving for a short beach stroll. Visitors who want to linger here can spend the night at the Sea Ranch Lodge.

Annapolis Winery

You'll find a pleasant coastal climate and a short list of classic California wines at **Annapolis Winery** (26055 Soda Springs Rd., Annapolis, 707/886-5460, www.annapoliswinery.com, noon-5pm daily, free). At this small, family-owned winery seven miles east of Sea Ranch, you can taste pinot, cabernet, zinfandel, and port, depending on what they've made this year and what's in stock. Take a glass outside to enjoy the views from the estate vineyards out over the forested mountains.

Sports and Recreation

With its front nine holes perched above the Pacific, the **Sea Ranch Golf Links** (42000 Hwy. 1, 707/785-2468, www.searanchgolf. com, $57-67) are like the legendary golf courses at Pebble Beach except without the crowds. Designed by Robert Muir Graves, the course also allows you to putt past redwood trees.

Food and Accommodations

Situated on 52 acres of prime coastal real estate, ★ **Sea Ranch Lodge** (2.5 miles north of Stewart's Point on Hwy. 1, 707/785-2371, http://searanchlodge.com, $276-414) offers 19 rooms, all with simple 1960s throwback decor and ocean vistas that evoke paintings. Hiking trails on the grounds offer a self-guided wildflower walk and a short walk to Black Point Beach. Most rooms are equipped with gas fireplaces for those foggy days on the Sonoma Coast. Guests are treated to a complimentary hot breakfast at the lodge's **Black Point Grill** (2.5 miles north of Stewart's Point on Hwy. 1, 707/785-2371, 8am-11am and 11:30am-9pm daily, $13-27). Black Point Grill is open to the public, serving everything from burgers to local seafood in a dining area with large windows facing the sea.

Mendocino Coast

The Mendocino Coast is a popular retreat for those who've been introduced to its specific charms. On weekends, Bay Area residents flock north to their favorite hideaways to enjoy windswept beaches, secret coves, and luscious cuisine. This area is ideal for deep-sea anglers, wine aficionados, and fans of luxury spas. Art is especially prominent in the culture; from the 1960s onward, aspiring artists have found supportive communities, sales opportunities, and homes in Mendocino County, and a number of small galleries display local artwork.

Be aware that the most popular inns fill up fast many weekends year-round. Fall-winter is the high season, with the Crab Festival, the Mushroom Festival, and various harvest and after-harvest wine celebrations. If you want to stay someplace specific on the Mendocino Coast, book your room at least a month in advance for weekday stays and six months or more in advance for major festival weekends.

GUALALA

With a population of 585, Gualala (wa-LA-la) feels like a metropolis along the Highway 1 corridor in this region. While it's not the most charming coastal town, it does have some of the services other places lack.

Since 1961, the **Art in the Redwoods Festival** (46501 Gualala Rd., 707/884-1138, www.gualalaarts.org, mid-Aug., adults $6, children under 17 free) and its parent organization, Gualala Arts, have been going strong. Taking place over the course of a long weekend in mid-August, the festival features gallery exhibitions, special dinners, a champagne preview, bell ringers, a quilt raffle, and awards for the artists.

Food

Breakfast is big at **Trinks Café** (39140 Hwy. 1, 707/884-1713, http://trinkscafe.com, 7am-4pm Sat. and Mon.-Tues., 7am-4pm and 5pm-8pm Wed.-Fri., 8am-4pm Sun., $5-14), led by graduates of the California Culinary Academy. They also do lunch and dinner (Wed.-Fri.).

Locals and visitors rave about the tacos at **Antonio's Tacos** (38820 S. Hwy. 1, 707/884-1789, 8am-7pm Mon.-Fri., 8am-6pm Sat., $2-12). Carne asada and carnitas are the favorite meat options. Gussy up your tacos with toppings from the salsa bar.

MendoViné (39145 S. Hwy. 1, 707/896-2650, www.mendovinelounge.com, 6pm-9pm Thurs.-Sun., $9-12) is a wine lounge with a curated selection of local reds and whites. They also do small plates with an international flair, served up to the sounds of the occasional jazz band.

The Gualala **farmers market** (47950 Center St., 707/884-3726, www.sonomacounty.com, 9:30am-12:30pm Sat. late May-early Nov.) is at the Gualala Community Center. The **Surf** (39250 S. Hwy. 1, 707/884-4184, www.surfsuper.com, 7:30am-8pm Sat.-Wed., 7:30am-9pm Thurs.-Fri. summer; 7:30am-8pm daily winter) supermarket sells flatbread pizzas and sandwiches.

Accommodations

When it comes to food and lodging in Gualala, you're not going to hear so many of those Sonoma and Mendocino County adjectives (luxurious, elegant, pricey), but you will find choices.

For the budget-conscious, a good option is **The Surf Motel** (39170 Hwy. 1, 707/884-3571 or 888/451-7873, www.surfinngualala.com, $139-259). Only a few of the more expensive

Mendocino Coast

© AVALON TRAVEL

rooms have ocean views, but a full hot breakfast, flat-screen TVs with DVD players, and wireless Internet access are included for all guests.

The **Whale Watch Inn** (35100 Hwy. 1, 800/942-5342, www.whalewatchinn.com, $220-300) specializes in romance. Each of its 18 individually decorated, luxuriously appointed rooms has an ocean view and a wood-burning stove. Most also have whirlpool tubs. Every morning, a hot breakfast is delivered to your room. Explore the beach below via a staircase on the grounds.

Four miles north of Gualala, the **North Coast Country Inn** (34591 S. Hwy. 1, 707/884-4537, www.northcoastcountryinn. com, $190-245) was once part of a coastal sheep ranch. Six rooms are outfitted with antique furnishings and fireplaces; three also have kitchenettes. Mornings begin with a hot breakfast buffet. An antiques store and art gallery are on the inn's grounds.

Camping

Two nearby parks provide good camping options: **Gualala River Redwood Park** (46001 Gualala Rd., 707/884-3533, www. gualalapark.com, May-Oct., day use $5 pp, $42-49) and **Gualala Point Regional Park** (42401 Hwy. 1, 707/785-2377, http://parks. sonomacounty.ca.gov, day use $7, camping $35), one mile south of the town of Gualala. Both places offer access to redwoods, the ocean, and the river.

Transportation

Gualala is 115 miles north of San Francisco on Highway 1, and 60 miles south of Fort Bragg. The **Mendocino Transit Authority** (800/696-4682, http://mendocinotransit.org) has a bus line that connects Gualala to Fort Bragg.

POINT ARENA

A small coastal town 1.5 miles south of its namesake point, Point Arena might be one of the North Coast's best secrets. The town's Main Street is Highway 1, which has a couple of bars, restaurants, markets, and the Arena Theater. One mile from the downtown section is the scenic Point Arena Cove, which has a small fishing pier with rocky beaches on either side. The cove feels like the town's true center, a meeting place where fisherfolk take in the conditions of the ocean. Just north of Point Arena Cove is the California Coastal

National Monument Point Arena-Stornetta Unit, a stunning coastal park.

Sights
POINT ARENA LIGHTHOUSE

Although its magnificent Fresnel lens no longer turns through the night, the **Point Arena Lighthouse** (45500 Lighthouse Rd., 707/882-2809 or 877/725-4448, www. pointarenalighthouse.com, 10am-4:30pm daily summer, 10am-3:30pm daily winter, adults $7.50, children $1) remains a Coast Guard light and fog station. But what makes this beacon special is its history. When the 1906 earthquake hit San Francisco, it jolted the land all the way up the coast, severely damaging the Point Arena Lighthouse. When the structure was rebuilt two years later, engineers devised an aboveground foundation that gives the lighthouse both its distinctive shape and additional structural stability.

The lighthouse's extensive interpretive museum, which is housed in the fog station beyond the gift shop, includes the lighthouse's Fresnel lens. Docent-led **tours** climb 145 steep steps to the top of the lighthouse and are well worth the trip, both for the views of the lighthouse from the top and for the fascinating story of its destruction and rebirth through the 1906 earthquake as told by the knowledgeable staff. Catch your breath by taking in the surrounding coastline from Manchester State Beach to the north to the California Coastal National Monument Point Arena-Stornetta Unit to the south.

B. BRYAN PRESERVE

Antelope, zebras, and giraffes wander around the 110-acre **B. Bryan Preserve** (130 Riverside Dr., 707/882-2297, http:// bbryanpreserve.com, 9:30am-4pm daily Mar.-Oct., 9:30am-3pm daily Nov.-Feb., adults $35, children under 11 $20). Take a 1.5-hour tour of the preserve or choose to spend a night in one of three **lodging options** on-site ($165-235).

Recreation

★ CALIFORNIA COASTAL NATIONAL MONUMENT

The 1,655-acre **Point Arena-Stornetta Unit** of the **California Coastal National Monument** (Point Arena Cove north to Manchester State Park, 707/468-4000, www.blm.gov, sunrise-sunset daily) is like a greatest-hits compilation of the California coast: vertigo-inducing cliffs, far-ranging ocean views, sea arches, rocky points, and tide pools.

The area can be explored by eight miles of trails including a superb hike that starts from behind the Point Arena City Hall and continues 3.5 miles to Lighthouse Road. Walk another 0.5 mile on the road to visit the Point Arena Lighthouse. Parking is available at Point Arena City Hall and at the pullouts along Lighthouse Road.

SCHOONER GULCH STATE BEACH

The area around Point Arena is filled with coastal access points. A local favorite is **Schooner Gulch State Beach** (intersection of Schooner Gulch Rd. and Hwy. 1, three miles south of Point Arena, 707/937-5804, www.parks.ca.gov). From a pullout north of Schooner Gulch Bridge, trails lead to two different beaches. The southern trail leads to **Schooner Gulch Beach,** a wide, sandy expanse with rocky headlands and a stream flowing into the sea. The northern trail, though, leads to a more memorable destination: **Bowling Ball Beach.** At low tide, the ocean recedes to reveal small spherical boulders lined up in rows. The end section of the trail is steep and has a rope to help your descent. Once on the beach, hike north about 0.25 mile to find the photo-worthy sight.

Entertainment and Events

The onetime vaudeville **Arena Theater** (214 Main St., 707/882-3272, www.arenatheater.org) was also a movie palace when it opened in 1929. In the 1990s, the old theater got a facelift that returned it to its art deco glory. Today, you can see recent box-office films, new documentaries, and unusual independent films, or a live musical or theatrical show.

Right on the main drag, **215 Main** (215 Main St., 707/882-3215, http://215main.com, 3pm-10pm Sun.-Tues., 3pm-11pm Wed.-Sat.) is a venue for artists, with local art, poetry nights, live music, and Wednesday night open mics. The friendly staff pours California wines and craft beers, and there is a small bar menu.

Despite the fact that local dive bar **Sign of**

a cliffside trail at the Point Arena-Stornetta Unit of the California Coastal National Monument

the Whale (194 Main St., 707/882-2259, 2pm-10pm Sun.-Thurs., 2pm-2am Fri.-Sat., cash only) has only bottled beer, it has a surprisingly sophisticated cocktail menu. Locals hold court at the long bar, and there's a jukebox, arcade game, and two pool tables. Bar patrons can order food from the adjacent restaurant Pacific Plate.

The annual **Whale and Jazz Festival** (707/884-1138, www.gualalaarts.org/whalejazz, Apr.) takes place around Mendocino County. Some of the nation's finest jazz performers play in a variety of venues, while the whales put on their own show out in the Pacific. Point Arena Lighthouse offers whale-watching from the shore daily, and the wineries and restaurants provide refreshment on festival evenings.

Food

Arena Market & Café (183 Main St., 707/882-3663, www.arenaorganics.org, 7am-7pm Mon.-Sat., 8am-6pm Sun.) is a co-op committed to local, sustainable, and organic food, and they do their best to compensate farmers fairly and keep money in the community. Stock up on staples or sit at one of the tables out front and enjoy a cup of coffee or homemade soup. They're one of the only places in town with Wi-Fi.

The **Uneda Eat Cafe** (206 Main St., 707/882-3800, www.unedaeat.com, 5:30pm-8:30pm Wed.-Sat., $13-32, cash only) has preserved the sign of the former owner, an Italian butcher: The storefront still says "Uneda Meat Market." Now a dine-in, take-out, and catering operation run by Jill and Rob Hunter, the locavore menu offers international items like Indian-style cauliflower and clay-pot pork. The small, narrow restaurant is crowded on weekends when diners occupy the colorful tables and a small counter overlooking the kinetic kitchen.

Blue on the outside, pink on the inside, ★ **Franny's Cup and Saucer** (213 Main St., 707/882-2500, www.frannyscupandsaucer. com, 8am-4pm Wed.-Sat., $2-6, cash/check only) is whimsical and welcoming. The owners, Franny and her mother, Barbara, do all the baking—they even make truffles and candies from scratch. Heartier options include mini-pizzas, croque monsieurs, and mind-blowing bacon slippers. It's take-out only, perfect for a picnic.

Slightly north of town, **Rollerville Café** (22900 S. Hwy. 1, 707/882-2077, www. rollervillecafe.com, 8am-2pm Mon.-Thurs., 8am-7:30pm Fri.-Sun. summer, 8am-2pm Sun.-Thurs., 8am-6:30pm Fri.-Sat. winter, lunch $8-10, dinner $20-24) is a small, homey place catering to resort guests, locals, and travelers. Dinner may seem a little pricey, but lunch is available all day. Breakfast (order the crab cakes Benedict) is served until 11am.

The **Pier Chowder House & Tap Room** (790 Port Rd., 2nd fl., 707/882-3400, www. thepierchowderhouse.net, 11am-9pm daily summer, 11am-8pm Fri.-Tues. winter, $12-30) has an outside deck perfect for taking in the sunset over Point Arena's scenic cove. The menu focuses on seafood: Go for the salmon or rock cod, both caught by local anglers, when they're in season. A long bar has 31 beers on tap.

Cove Coffee and Tackle (790 Port Rd., 707/882-2665, 7am-3pm daily, $6-10) attracts locals with tasty items like "Nate's Special," an egg sandwich with pesto, cream cheese, sausage, onion, and Swiss cheese. It's the perfect place for morning coffee.

Accommodations

From 1901 to 1957, the **Coast Guard House** (695 Arena Cove, 707/882-2442 or 800/524-9320, www.coastguardhouse.com, $185-295) was a working Coast Guard life-saving station. Now the main building hosts overnight guests who enjoy views of Point Arena Cove. Four rooms are available, including a suite with two bedrooms. Two detached cottages offer more privacy. The friendly and informative innkeepers serve a hot breakfast in the main house every morning, and restaurants are just a short walk away.

Next door to the Coast Guard House

is the **Wharf Master's Inn** (785 Iverson Ave., 707/882-3171 or 800/392-4031, www.wharfmasters.com, $109-499). Many rooms have a fireplace, a two-person spa, and a private deck. Twelve of the units have ocean views. The Wharf Master's House has a kitchen and can accommodate up to eight people.

For a unique overnight, stay in the old lightkeepers' quarters at ★ **Point Arena Lighthouse** (877/725-4448, www.pointarenalighthouse.com, $150-350, cleaning fee, 2-night min. weekends). Located on a spit of land with views of the ocean, these lodging options are a real deal, especially since any room or cottage includes a free tour of the nearby lighthouse, a small bottle of wine, and chocolates. The assistant keepers' homes have three bedrooms, two baths, a kitchen, and a wood-burning fireplace. It makes a great base for exploring the North Coast.

Transportation and Services

Point Arena is 10 miles north of Gualala on Highway 1, and about 120 miles north of San Francisco.

The **Mendocino Transit Authority** (800/696-4682, https://mendocinotransit.org, $1.50) runs the route 75 bus to connect Point Arena south to Gualala and north to Fort Bragg.

The **Coast Community Library** (225 Main St., 707/882-3114, www.coastcommunitylibrary.org, noon-6pm Mon. and Fri., 10am-6pm Tues., 10am-8pm Wed., noon-8pm Thurs., noon-3pm Sat.) offers free Internet access.

Many places in Point Arena are cash-only. The **Redwood Credit Union** (280 Main St.) has an ATM.

Manchester State Park

Seven miles north of the town of Point Arena, **Manchester State Park** (44500 Kinney Ln., Manchester, 707/882-2463, www.parks.ca.gov, day use free) is a wild place perfect for a long, solitary beach walk. The 3.5-mile-long coast is littered with bleached white driftwood and logs that lie on the dark sand like giant bones amid crashing waves. Even the water offshore is protected as part of the 3,782-acre Point Arena State Marine Reserve. At the southwestern tip of the park is Arena Rock, a nautical hazard known for sinking at least six ships before the construction of the nearby Point Arena Lighthouse to the south. Part of the 1,500 acres of onshore parkland was once a dairy ranch.

coastline of Manchester State Park

Today, there's beach, dunes, a wetlands trail, and a **campground** (Fri.-Sun. late May-early Sept., first-come, first-served, $25) with 41 sites and basic amenities, including fire pits, picnic tables, and pit toilets. Some environmental campsites in the dunes are accessible via a one-mile hike.

ELK

The town of Elk used to be called Greenwood, after the family of Caleb Greenwood, who settled here in about 1850. Details of the story vary, but it is widely believed that Caleb was part of a mission to rescue survivors of the Donner Party after their rough winter near Truckee.

Greenwood State Beach

From the mid-19th century until the 1920s, the stretch of shore at **Greenwood State Beach** (Hwy. 1, 707/937-5804, www.parks. ca.gov, visitors center 10am-4pm Wed.-Sun. Mar.-Nov.) was a stop for large ships carrying timber to points of sale in San Francisco and sometimes even China. The visitors center displays photographs and exhibits about Elk's past in the lumber business. It also casts light on the Native American heritage of the area and the natural resources that are still abundant.

A short hike demonstrates what makes this area so special. From the parking lot, follow the trail down toward the ocean. You'll soon come to a fork; to the right is a picnic area. Follow the left fork to another picnic site and then, soon afterward, the beach. Turn left and walk about 0.25 mile to reach Greenwood Creek. Shortly past it is a cliff, at which point you have to turn around and walk back up the hill. Even in the short amount of time it takes to do this walk, you'll experience lush woods, sandy cliffs, and dramatic ocean overlooks. In winter, the walk can be dark and blustery and even more intriguing, although it's a pleasure in any season.

Greenwood State Beach is alongside the town of Elk, 10-15 miles north of Point Arena and about 17 miles south of Mendocino.

Food and Accommodations

With a perfect location in the center of town and across the street from the ocean, **Queenie's Roadhouse Café** (6061 Hwy. 1, 707/877-3285, http://queeniesroadhousecafe. com, 8am-3pm Thurs.-Mon., $9-18) is the place to go for hot food and a friendly atmosphere. Expect to be full for a while after leaving.

The **Beacon Light by the Sea** (7401 S. Hwy. 1, south of Elk, 707/877-3311, 5pm-11pm Fri.-Sat.) is the best bar in the area. Its colorful owner, R. D. Beacon, was born in Elk and has run the Beacon Light since 1971. He claims it's the only place you can get hard liquor for 14 miles in any direction. With 85 different brands of vodka, 20 whiskeys, and 15 tequilas, there's something for every sort of drinker. On clear days, the views stretch all the way to the Point Arena Lighthouse.

Housed in a little blue cottage attached to the resort, **Bridget Dolan's Pub & Restaurant** (5910 S. Hwy. 1, 707/877-1820, 4:30pm-8:30pm Thurs.-Mon., $9-16) is a terrific place to hole up with a draft beer on a rainy winter day or foggy summer afternoon. The tables are draped in white tablecloths and the small bar is lined with locals. The menu includes burgers, pizzas, and hearty pub fare like cottage pie.

Perched on a hillside over the stunning Greenwood State Beach cove, the ★ **Elk Cove Inn** (6300 S. Hwy. 1, 800/275-2967, www.elkcoveinn.com, $195-395) offers luxury accommodations, generous hospitality, and superb views of the nearby Pacific, studded with islands and a scattering of offshore rocks. Check-in comes with a complimentary cocktail or glass of wine and a welcome basket filled with wine, fruit, popcorn, and fresh-baked cookies. Choose from rooms in the main house, cozy cabins with an ocean view, or luxurious suites with jetted soaking tubs and private balconies or patios. A private staircase leads down to the beach below. There's also a full-service day spa with a sauna and aromatherapy steam shower. The innkeepers make your stay top notch, from port wine and chocolates in the rooms to the big morning breakfast buffet of Southern comfort food with a glass of champagne.

The **Sacred Rock Resort** (5910 S. Hwy. 1, 707/877-3422, www.sacredrockresort.com, $138-260) has five cottages, three of which have private decks overlooking Elk Cove. Full breakfast can be delivered to your room, but there's also a lively dining room.

ALBION AND LITTLE RIVER

Tiny Albion is along Highway 1 almost 30 miles north of Point Arena and about 8 miles south of Mendocino. Little River is about five miles farther north, also on Highway 1. There is a state park and several plush places to stay.

Van Damme State Park

The centerpiece of **Van Damme State Park** (Hwy. 1, 3 miles south of Mendocino, 707/937-5804, www.parks.ca.gov, 8am-9pm daily, $8) is the **Pygmy Forest,** where you'll see a true biological rarity: mature yet tiny cypress and pine trees perpetually stunted by a combination of always-wet ground and poor soil-nutrient conditions. To get there, drive along Airport Road to the trail parking lot (opposite the county airport) and follow the

wheelchair-accessible loop trail (0.25 mile, easy). You can also get there by hiking along the **Fern Canyon Trail** (7 miles round-trip, difficult).

Kayak Mendocino launches four **Sea Cave Nature Tours** (707/813-7117, www. kayakmendocino.com, 9am, 11:30am, 2pm, and sunset, $60 pp) from Van Damme State Park. No previous experience is necessary; the expert guides provide all the equipment you need and teach you how to paddle your way through the sea caves and around the harbor seals.

Food

★ **Ledford House Restaurant** (3000 N. Hwy. 1, Albion, 707/937-0282, www. ledfordhouse.com, 5pm-close Wed.-Sun., $19-30) is beautiful even from a distance; you'll see it on the hill as you drive up Highway 1. With excellent food and nightly jazz performances, it's one of the true "special occasion" choices in the area. Try to reserve a table for sunset.

A fine restaurant with stunning coast views, the **5200 Restaurant & Lounge** (Heritage House Resort, 5200 N. Hwy. 1, Little River, 707/202-9000, http://heritagehouseresort. com, 8am-10:30am and 5pm-9pm Mon.-Fri., 8am-11:30am and 5pm-9pm Sat.-Sun., lounge

Bridget Dolan's Pub & Restaurant

4pm-9pm daily, $12-33) has farm-to-fork cuisine for breakfast and dinner. The lounge has a great happy hour (4pm-6pm) in a comfortable setting that includes a fireplace, couches, and board games.

Start the day at ★ **Circa '62** (7051 N. Hwy. 1, Little River, 707/937-5525, www.schoolhousecreek.com, 8am-11am Mon. and Wed.-Fri., 8am-1pm Sat.-Sun., $9-16). Housed within a cozy blue-and-white former schoolhouse on the grounds of the Inn at Schoolhouse Creek, the building oozes charm, from its fireplace to its ocean-facing windows. Yet it's the glorious food that makes this place worthwhile. The creative, changing menu offers steak-and-egg tacos, kimchi pancakes, and a hash-brown waffle drenched in sausage gravy.

Wild Fish (7750 N. Hwy. 1, Little River, 707/937-3055, www.wild-fish.com, 11:30am-2:30pm and 5pm-9pm Sun. and Tues.-Thurs., 5pm-9pm Mon., 11:30am-2pm and 5pm-9:30pm Fri.-Sat., $28-38) utilizes local assets, from organic produce to wild-caught seafood, on an ever-changing menu. The wild king salmon and petrale sole are caught right out of Fort Bragg's Noyo Harbor.

Tucked into a corner of a convenience store, the **Little River Market Grill & Gourmet**

Deli (7746 N. Hwy. 1, Little River, 707/937-5133, grill: 9am-2:50pm daily; deli: 9am-3:50pm daily, $8) is a local favorite. This better-than-average deli has a wide range of options, including burgers, pulled pork sandwiches, and fish tacos. Vegetarian options include the tasty pesto veggie and avocado sandwich. Grab a sandwich for a picnic on the coast.

Accommodations

There's no place quite like ★ **The Andiron** (6051 N. Hwy. 1, Little River, 707/937-1543, www.theandiron.com, $119-274). The one- and two-room cabins in a meadow above Highway 1 are filled with curiosities and kitsch. Every room is different. One has a unique camel-shaped bar, while another has a coin-operated vibrating bed. Most have vintage board games, View-Masters, and an eclectic library of books. Standard amenities include small wooden decks and small flat-screen TVs. A hot tub is available for guests. The fun-loving owners throw happy hour parties every weekend, including "Fondue Fridays," when they also serve local beers and wines.

A longtime lodging destination, the ★ **Heritage House Resort** (5200 Hwy.

the steak-and-egg tacos at Circa '62

1, Little River, 707/202-9000, http:// heritagehouseresort.com, $289-400) has a rich history that includes being the past hideout of bank robber "Baby Face" Nelson and the setting of the 1978 film *Same Time, Next Year*. Perched on stunning cliffs pocked with coves, the numerous buildings spread across 37 acres. The rooms are top tier: Each is enhanced by private decks, rain showers, and wood-burning or gas fireplaces. The units are priced according to proximity to the water and quality of the view. The resort has a full-service spa and restored garden.

The **Albion River Inn** (3790 N. Hwy. 1, Albion, 707/937-1919 or 800/479-7944, www. albionriverinn.com, $195-355) is a gorgeous and serene setting for an away-from-it-all vacation. This cliffside inn is all about romance. A full breakfast is included in the room rates; pets and smoking are not allowed, and there are no TVs.

The **Little River Inn** (7901 N. Hwy. 1, Little River, 707/937-5942 or 888/466-5683, www.littleriverinn.com, $205-369) appeals to coastal vacationers who like a little luxury. It has a nine-hole golf course and two lighted tennis courts. All recreation areas overlook the Pacific, which crashes on the shore just across the highway from the inn. The sprawling white Victorian house and barns hide the expansiveness of the grounds, which also have a great restaurant and a charming sea-themed bar. Relax even more at the in-house Spa at Little River Inn.

Camping

There's camping on the coast at **Van Damme State Park** (Hwy. 1, Little River, 707/937-5804, www.parks.ca.gov, reservations 800/444-7275, www.reservecalifornia.com, $35), three miles south of Mendocino. The appealing campground offers picnic tables, fire rings, and food lockers, as well as restrooms and hot showers. The park's 1,831 acres include beaches as well as forest, so there's lots of natural beauty to enjoy. Reservations are strongly encouraged.

★ MENDOCINO

Perched on a headland surrounded by the Pacific, Mendocino is one of the most picturesque towns on the California coast. Quaint bed-and-breakfasts, art colonies, and local sustainable dining add to its charm, making it a favorite for romantic weekend getaways.

Once a logging town, Mendocino was reborn as an artist community in the 1950s. One of its most striking buildings is the town's

Heritage House Resort

Mendocino

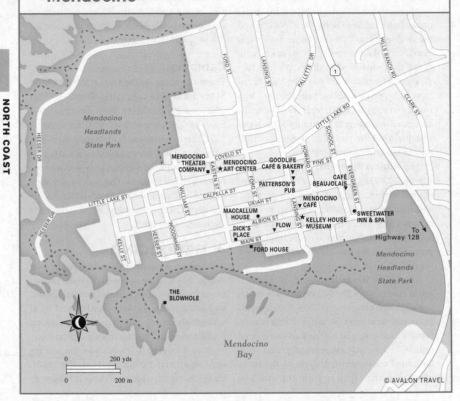

Mendocino Headlands State Park

Mendocino Bay

0   200 yds
0   200 m

© AVALON TRAVEL

Masonic Hall, dating from 1866 and adorned with a redwood statue of Father Time on its roof. Many New Englanders settled in the region in its early years. With its old water towers and historic buildings, it resembles a New England fishing village—so much so that it played one in the long-running TV series *Murder, She Wrote*. It was also a stand-in for Monterey in the 1955 James Dean film *East of Eden*.

Sights
MENDOCINO ART CENTER

The town of Mendocino has long been an inspiration and a gathering place for artists of many varieties, and the **Mendocino Art Center** (45200 Little Lake St., 707/937-5818 or 800/653-3328, www.mendocinoartcenter.

org, 11am-4pm daily, donation) gives these diverse artists a community, provides them with opportunities for teaching and learning, and displays contemporary works. Since 1959, the center has offered artist workshops and retreats. Today it has a flourishing schedule of events and classes, five galleries, and a sculpture garden. You can even drop in and make some art of your own. Supervised open studios in ceramics, jewelry making, watercolor, sculpture, and drawing take place throughout the year (call for specific schedules, $12-15 per session).

KELLEY HOUSE MUSEUM

The mission of the lovely, stately **Kelley House Museum** (45007 Albion St., 707/937-5791, www.kelleyhousemuseum.org,

11am-3pm Fri.-Mon., free) is to preserve the history of Mendocino for future generations. The permanent exhibits chronicle a notorious local shipwreck and the Native American population, while a collection of photos details the town in present times and 100 years ago. Ask about the town's water-rights issues for a great lesson in the untold history of the Mendocino Coast. On weekends, docents lead two-hour **walking tours** (11am Sat.-Sun., $10) that detail Mendocino's history. Self-guided audio tours ($10) are available when the museum or research office (1pm-4pm) is open.

MENDOCINO HEADLANDS STATE PARK

No trip to Mendocino is complete without a walk along the rugged coastline of **Mendocino Headlands State Park** (west of town, 707/937-5804, www.parks.ca.gov, sunrise-sunset daily). A series of trails along the seaside cliffs west of town offer views of the area's sea caves and coves. It's a favorite spot for painters and photographers hoping to capture the majesty of the coast. In winter, the park is a great vantage point for viewing migrating gray whales. In town, the **Historic Ford House** (735 Main St., 707/937-5397, www.mendoparks.org, daily 11am-4pm, free, donations encouraged) doubles as the Mendocino Headlands State Park Visitor Center. A favorite display in the center is a scale model of the town, constructed in 1890.

POINT CABRILLO LIGHT STATION

Located between Mendocino and Fort Bragg, the beautiful **Point Cabrillo Light Station Historic Park** (45300 Lighthouse Rd., 707/937-6122, www.pointcabrillo.org, park: sunrise-sunset daily; light station and museum: 11am-4pm daily, $5) has been functioning since the early 1900s. The light station was absorbed into the California State Parks system in 2002 and is currently managed by a volunteer organization, the Point Cabrillo Lightkeepers Association. Take a tour of the famous Fresnel lens, learn about the infamous *Frolic* shipwreck of 1850, and explore the tide-pool aquarium. For an overnight stay, rent the **lightkeeper's house** or two cottages on the grounds (800/262-7801, www.mendocinovacations.com, $307-1,163 2-night stays).

Mendocino

Entertainment and Events

BARS AND LIVE MUSIC

For a place to hunker down over a pint, head to cozy **Patterson's Pub** (10485 Lansing St., 707/937-4782, www.pattersonspub.com, 10am-midnight daily). This traditional Irish-style pub is in the former rectory of a 19th-century Catholic church. It nods to the 21st century with six plasma TVs that screen current sporting events. Order a simple, filling meal at the tables or at the bar, where you'll find 14 beers on tap, a full-fledged wine list, and liquor imported from around the world.

So where do the locals go for a drink in Mendocino? That would be **Dick's Place** (45080 Main St., 707/937-6010, 11:30am-2am daily, cash only), an old-school bar with a mounted buck head draped in Christmas lights as decor. Dick's is easy to find: Look for the only neon sign on Main Street, in the shape of a martini glass.

THEATER

The **Mendocino Theater Company** (45200 Little Lake St., 707/937-4477, www. mendocinotheatre.org, 8pm Thurs.-Sat., 2pm Sun., adults $25, students $12) offers a genuine small-theater experience. Plays are staged in the 75-seat Helen Schoeni Theater for an intimate night of live drama or comedy. The small, weathered old building exudes just the right kind of charm to draw in lovers of quirky community theater. But this little theater company has big goals, and it tends to take on thought-provoking work by contemporary playwrights.

EVENTS

For two weekends every March, the Point Cabrillo Light Station is host to the annual **Whale Festival** (707/937-6123, www. pointcabrillo.org, Mar., $5), a chance to get expert guidance as you scan the sea for migrating gray whales headed north for the summer.

In July, musicians descend on the coast for the **Mendocino Music Festival** (707/937-2044, www.mendocinomusic.com, July, prices vary). For 2.5 weeks, live performances are held at venues around the area. There's always chamber music, orchestral concerts, opera, jazz, and bluegrass, and there's usually world music, blues, singer-songwriters, and dance performances. A centerpiece of the festival is the famed big-band concert. In addition to 13 evenings of music, there are three series of daytime concerts: piano, jazz, and village chamber concerts. No series passes are available; all events require separate tickets.

Patterson's Pub

If restaurants are the heart of the Mendocino food scene, festivals are its soul. **Taste of Mendocino** (888/636-3624, http://winecrab.com) comprises a couple of subfestivals. **Mendocino Crab, Wine & Beer Days** (Jan., prices vary) offers a burst of crab-related events. The **Beer, Wine & Mushroom Festival** (Nov., prices vary) focuses on the wild mushroom season. Come for classes, tastings, and tours, learn to cook, or just eat.

Shopping

The galleries and boutiques of **Mendocino Village** are welcoming and fun, plus the whole downtown area is beautiful. It seems that every shop in the Main Street area has its own garden, and each fills with a riotous cascade of flowers in the summer.

Panache (45120 Main St., 707/937-1234, www.thepanachegallery.com, 10:30am-5pm daily) displays and sells beautiful works of art in all sorts of media—paintings, jewelry, sculpture, and art glass. Much of the artistic focus is inspired by the sea crashing just outside the large multi-room gallery. The wooden furniture and boxes are a special treat: Handmade treasures using rare woods are combined and then sanded and polished to silky-smooth finishes.

If you love fine woodworking and handcrafted furniture, don't miss the **Highlight Gallery** (45094 Main St., 707/937-3132, www.thehighlightgallery.com, 10am-5pm daily). Its roots are in woodwork, which it maintains as a focus, although the gallery also features glasswork, ceramics, painting, and sculpture.

The **Gallery Bookshop** (Main St. and Kasten St., 707/937-2665, www.gallerybookshop.com, 9:30am-6pm Sun.-Thurs., 9:30am-9pm Fri.-Sat.) is a large store with fiction from around the world along with the works of local authors. They host an array of literary events, too.

Sports and Recreation

HIKING

Russian Gulch State Park (Hwy. 1, 2 miles north of Mendocino, 707/937-5804, www.

parks.ca.gov, $8) has its own **Fern Canyon Trail** (3 miles round-trip), which winds into a second-growth redwood forest filled with lush green ferns. At the four-way junction, turn left to hike another 0.75 mile to the ever-popular waterfall. You'll likely be part of a crowd on summer weekends. Making a right at the four-way junction will take you on a three-mile loop, for a total hike of six miles that leads to the top of the attractive little waterfall. If you prefer the shore to the forest, hike west to take in the lovely, wild headlands and see blowholes, grasses, and trawlers out seeking the day's catch. The biggest attraction is the **Devil's Punchbowl,** a collapsed sea cave 100 feet across and 60 feet deep. There's also a nice beach.

KAYAKING AND STAND-UP PADDLEBOARDING

The shoreline on the Mendocino Coast is pocked with caves and coves that are ideal for kayaking or stand-up paddling. Some of the best can be accessed in the waters off Van Damme State Park. A short paddle north are some impressive sea caves that adventurous paddlers can pass through. **Kayak Mendocino** (707/813-7117, www.kayakmendocino.com, SUP rentals $25/two hours) has a bus parked by the beach that rents kayaks and SUPs. From there, guides lead SUP and kayak sea cave tours (9am, 11:30am, and 2pm daily, adults $60, children under 12 $40).

To explore the relatively sedate waters of the Big River estuary, rent an outrigger or a sailing canoe from **Catch a Canoe & Bicycles Too** (Stanford Inn, 1 S. Big River Rd., 707/937-0273, www.catchacanoe.com, 9am-5pm daily, adults $35 pp for three hours, children 6-17 $15 pp). Guided **tours** (June-Sept., $65 pp) include an estuary excursion with a naturalist and a ride on an outrigger that utilizes solar energy.

SURFING

Big River is a beach break surf spot just south of the town of Mendocino where the Big River flows into the ocean. It's a place you can check out from Highway 1, and on most days, all levels of surfers try their hand at surfing the break. More experienced surfers should try **Smuggler's Cove,** in Mendocino Bay on the south side of Big River. It's a reef break that usually only works during winter swells.

DIVING

A good spot for abalone is **The Blowhole** (end of Main St.), a favorite summer lounging spot for locals. In the water, you'll find abalone and their empty shells; colorful, tiny nudibranchs; and occasionally, overly friendly seals. The kelp beds just offshore attract divers who don't fear cold water and want to check out the complex ecosystem. Abalone is strictly regulated; most species are endangered and can't be harvested. Check with the state Department of Fish and Game (916/445-0411, www.wildlife.ca.gov) for abalone season opening and closing dates, catch limits, licensing information, and the best spots to dive each year.

SPAS

Relax on the Mendocino Coast at one of the many nearby spas. The **Sweetwater Spa & Inn** (44840 Main St., 800/300-4140, www. sweetwaterspa.com, 11am-10pm daily summer, 11am-9pm daily winter, $15-19/half hour, $18-23/hour) rents indoor hot tubs and has a range of massage services ($90-154). They also have group tub and sauna rates ($10-12). The rustic buildings and garden setting complete the experience. Appointments are required for massage and private tubs, but walk-ins are welcome to use the communal tub and sauna.

Food

Mendocino has a weekly **farmers market** (Howard St. and Main St., www.mcfarm.org. noon-2pm Fri. May-Oct.), where you can find seasonal produce, flowers, fish, wine, honey, and more.

AMERICAN

Publications including the *Wall Street Journal* rave about **Trillium Café** (10390 Kasten St.,

707/937-3200, 11:30am-2:30pm and 5:30pm-8:30pm Sun.-Thurs., 11:30am-2:30pm and 5:30pm-9pm Fri.-Sat., $22-36). The shellfish fettuccine is a favorite. Dine inside by the fireplace or out on the deck overlooking a garden where many of the restaurant's ingredients grow.

CAFES

The **Goodlife Café & Bakery** (10483 Lansing St., 707/937-0836, www. goodlifecafemendo.com, 8am-4pm daily, $5-13) is a great place for an espresso drink, a freshly made pastry, or a sandwich on delicious, pillowy focaccia. There are lots of gluten-free options as well. The busy café has seating inside and outside.

One of the most appealing and dependable places is the **Mendocino Café** (10451 Lansing St., 707/937-6141, www.mendocinocafe.com, 11am-4pm and 5pm-9pm daily, $14-32). The café has good, simple, well-prepared food, a small kids menu, a wine list, and a beer list. Enjoy a Thai burrito, fresh local rockfish, or a steak in the warm, well-lit dining room. The café is in the gardens of Mendocino Village, and thanks to a heated patio, you can enjoy outdoor dining any time of day.

FRENCH

★ **Café Beaujolais** (961 Ukiah St., 707/937-5614, www.cafebeaujolais.com, 5:30pm-9pm Mon.-Tues., 11:30am-2:30pm and 5:30pm-9pm Wed.-Sun., $23-38) is a standout French-California restaurant in an area dense with great upscale cuisine. This charming, out-of-the-way spot is a few blocks from the center of Mendocino Village in an old vine-covered house. Despite the white tablecloths and crystal, the atmosphere is casual at lunch and only slightly formal at dinner. The giant salads and delectable entrées are made with organic produce, humanely raised meats, and locally caught seafood. The portions are enormous, but come half-size by request. The waitstaff are friendly, helpful, and knowledgeable about the menu and wine list. Reservations are available online.

VEGETARIAN

Vegetarians and carnivores alike rave about **Ravens Restaurant** (Stanford Inn, 44850 Comptche Ukiah Rd., 0707/937-5615 or 800/331-8884, www.ravensrestaurant.com, 8am-10:30am and 5:30pm-close daily, $12-27). Inside the lodge, which is surrounded by lush organic gardens, you'll find a big, open dining room. Many of the vegetarian and vegan dishes use produce from the inn's own organic farm. At breakfast, enjoy delicious vegetarian (or vegan, with tofu) scrambles, omelets, and Florentines, complete with homemade bread and English muffins. At dinner, try one of the seasonal vegetarian entrées. The wine list reflects organic, biodynamic, and sustainable-practice wineries.

Accommodations

$150-250

The warm and welcoming ★ **Blackberry Inn** (44951 Larkin Rd., 707/937-5281 or 800/950-7806, www.blackberryinn.biz, $125-225) is in the hills beyond the center of Mendocino. The inn looks like a town from the Old West. Each of the 16 charmingly decorated rooms has a different storefront outside, including the bank, the saloon, the barbershop, and the land-grant office. Amenities include plush, comfortable bedding cozied up with colonial-style quilts, along with microwaves, fridges, and free wireless Internet. The manager-hosts are the nicest you'll find anywhere.

Sweetwater Inn & Spa (44840 Main St., 800/300-4140, www.sweetwaterspa.com, $140-295) harks back to the days when Mendocino was a colony of starving artists. A redwood water tower was converted into a guest room, joined by a motley collection of detached cottages that guarantee privacy. Every guest room and cottage has its own style—you'll find a spiral staircase in one of the water towers, a hot tub on a redwood deck in the Garden Cottage, and fireplaces in many of the units. The eclectic decor makes each room different. Thick gardens surround the building complex, and a path leads back to the Garden Spa. The location, just past downtown on Main Street, is perfect for dining, shopping, and art walks. They also run **Sweetwater Vacation Home Rentals** (800/300-4140, http://sweetwatervacationrentals.com, $229-499), which rents apartments and home in town.

The 1882 **MacCallum House** (45020 Albion St., 800/609-0492, www.maccallumhouse.com, $169-359) is the king of luxury on the Mendocino Coast. The facility includes several properties in addition to the main building in Mendocino Village. Choose from private cottages with hot tubs, suites with jetted tubs, and rooms with opulent antique appointments. There's a two-night minimum on weekends, and a three-night minimum for most holidays. Room rates include a cooked-to-order breakfast.

The **Blue Door Inn** (10481 Howard St., 707/937-4892, www.bluedoorinn.com, $159-349) aims to spoil you. Five sleek, modern rooms come with flat-screen TVs and gas fireplaces. The two-course breakfast features homemade pastries and egg dishes.

OVER $250

Set amid redwoods, the **Stanford Inn** (44850 Comptche Ukiah Rd., 707/937-5615 or 800/331-8884, www.stanfordinn.com, $355-555) is an upscale forest lodge. The location is convenient to hiking and only a short drive from Mendocino Village and the coast. Rooms have beautiful, honey wood-paneled walls, pretty furniture, and fluffy down comforters. Amenities include a wood-burning fireplace, Internet access, a pool, sauna and hot tub, and free use of mountain bikes. Gardens surrounding the resort are perfect for strolling after a complimentary vegan breakfast at the on-site Ravens Restaurant.

A mile south of the village, the ★ **Brewery Gulch Inn** (9401 Hwy. 1, 800/578-4454, www.brewerygulchinn.com, $350-495) provides a lot of amenities to guests staying in its 11 rooms, including a made-to-order hot breakfast and a light dinner buffet with wine. The rooms are modern and calming, with plush carpets, feather beds, and gas fireplaces; all have ocean views. Downstairs is a wonderful common area with a steel fireplace. Relax with a newspaper, book, or magazine from the extensive collection. There's also a collection of more than 500 DVDs to watch in the comfort of your room. Another option is the Serenity Cottage ($625/three-night minimum), a standalone oceanfront studio.

The beautifully restored 1909 **Point Cabrillo Head Lightkeeper's House** (45300 Lighthouse Rd., 707/937-5033, www. mendocinovacations.com, 2-night minimum, $307-1,163 for 2 nights) sits atop a cliff beside the Pacific, so you can watch for whales, dolphins, and seabirds without leaving the porch. Four bedrooms sleep eight people, with 4.5 baths and a very modern kitchen. Larger groups can rent two of the cottages nearby.

Transportation

It's simplest to navigate Mendocino with your own vehicle. From U.S. 101 near Cloverdale, take Highway 128 northwest for 60 miles. Highway 128 becomes Highway 1 on the coast; Mendocino is another 10 miles north. A slower, more scenic alternative is to take Highway 1 from San Francisco to Mendocino; this route takes at least 4.5 hours.

Mendocino has a fairly compact downtown area, Mendocino Village, with a concentration of restaurants, shops, and inns just a few blocks from the beach.

The **Mendocino Transit Authority** (800/696-4682, http://mendocinotransit. org) operates a dozen bus routes that connect Mendocino and Fort Bragg with larger cities like Santa Rosa and Ukiah.

FORT BRAGG

Fort Bragg is the Mendocino Coast's largest city. With fast-food joints and chain hotels lining Highway 1 through town, it lacks the immediate charm of its neighbor to the south. But it does offer some great restaurants, interesting downtown shops, and proximity to coastal landmarks.

Sights
SKUNK TRAIN

The California Western Railroad, popularly called the **Skunk Train** (depot at end of Laurel St., 707/964-6371, www.skunktrain. com, 9am-3pm daily), is perfect for rail buffs and traveling families. The brightly painted trains appeal to children, and the historic aspects and scenery call to adults.

There are two rides on these restored

the front deck of the Brewery Gulch Inn

steam locomotives. The Northspur Flyer (four hours, adults $84, children 2-12 $42, children under 2 $10) travels 40 miles from Fort Bragg through majestic redwood forest to the town of Willits and back. The Pudding Creek Express (one hour, adults $25, children 2-12 $15, children under 2 $10) does a run up to Pudding Creek. Board in either Fort Bragg or Willits and make a round-trip return to your lodgings for the night.

Another option is to take the Skunk Train to **Camp Noyo** ($100-220), a former logging camp on the Noyo River where you can bed down in a campsite or a chalet. Check the train's website for special events like a Halloween pumpkin patch excursion and a special Zombie Train.

The **Mendocino Coast Model Railroad and Navigation Company** (behind the Skunk Train Depot, www.mendorailhistory. org, 10:30am-2:30pm Wed. and Sat.-Sun, adults $5, children $3, Skunk Train ticketholders free) is an operational train yard that recreates Fort Bragg's logging past in miniature. The large room is full of noise as model trains chug, bells ding, and lumber splashes into water.

GLASS BEACH
Fascinating **Glass Beach** (Elm St. and Glass Beach Dr.) is strewn with sea glass that has been polished and smoothed by the pounding surf. At the tideline, amber, green, and clear sea glass color the shore. It's against the park rules to remove the glass, though you can take photos. The trail down to Glass Beach is short but steep and treacherous; wear good walking or hiking shoes.

PACIFIC STAR WINERY
Pacific Star Winery (33000 N. Hwy. 1, 707/964-1155, www.pacificstarwinery.com, 11am-5pm Thurs.-Mon., tasting free) makes the most of its location 12 miles north of Fort Bragg. Barrels of wine are left out in the salt air to age, incorporating a hint of the Pacific into each vintage. Wines are tasty and reasonably priced, and you can bring your own

picnic to enjoy on the nearby bluff, which overlooks the ocean.

MENDOCINO COAST BOTANICAL GARDENS
Stretching 47 acres down to the sea, **Mendocino Coast Botanical Gardens** (18220 N. Hwy. 1, 707/964-4352, www. gardenbythesea.org, 9am-5pm daily Mar.-Oct., 9am-4pm daily Nov.-Feb., adults $15, seniors $12, children 6-14 $8, children under 6 free) offer miles of walking through careful plantings and wild landscapes. The star of the gardens is the rhododendron, with 125 species on the grounds. Children can pick up "Quail Trail: A Child's Guide" and enjoy an exploratory adventure.

Entertainment and Events
The **Gloriana Musical Theatre** (Eagles Hall Theatre, 210 N. Corry St., 707/964-7469, www. gloriana.org) seeks to bring music and theater to young people, so they produce major musicals that appeal to kids, such as *Peter Pan,* while *Into the Woods* and *Chicago* appeal mostly to people past their second decade. Local performers star in the two major shows and numerous one-off performances each year.

The Mendocino Coast hosts a number of art events each year. **Art in the Gardens** (18220 N. Hwy. 1, Fort Bragg, www.gardenbythesea.org, Aug., adults $15-20, children under 16 free) takes place at the Mendocino Coast Botanical Gardens. The gardens are decked out with the finest local artwork, food, and wine, and there is music to entertain the crowds who come to eat and drink, and to view and purchase art.

North Coast Brewery's Sequoia Room (444 N. Main St., 707/964-3400, www. northcoastbrewing.com) hosts jazz shows featuring national touring acts or the local house band in a cabaret environment. The venue holds a crowd of 60 people.

Shopping
Stop in at the **Glass Beach Museum and**

Gift Shop (17801 N. Hwy. 1, 707/962-0590, www.glassbeachjewelry.com, 10am-5pm daily) and you can see a wide array of found treasures; hear stories from Captain Cass, a retired sailor and expert glass scavenger; and buy sea glass set in pendants and rings.

Vintage clothing enthusiasts will love **If the Shoe Fits** (337 N. Franklin St., 707/964-2580, 11am-5:30pm Mon.-Thurs. and Sat., 11am-6pm Fri., 11am-2pm Sun.), an eclectic collection of used clothing and accessories for men and women with well-preserved, interesting pieces in good condition.

The Bookstore and Vinyl Cafe (353 Franklin St., 707/964-6559, 10:30am-5pm Mon.-Sat., 11am-3pm Sun.) is a small shop with a well-curated selection of new and used books likely to please discriminating readers. Music lovers can head upstairs where there is a selection of used records for sale.

Sports and Recreation
SPORTFISHING
The Mendocino Coast is an ideal location to watch whales do acrobatics, or to try to land the big one (salmon, halibut, rock cod, or tuna). During Dungeness crab season, you can go out on a crab boat, learn to set pots, and catch your own delectable delicacy.

Many charters leave out of Noyo Harbor in Fort Bragg. The **Trek II** (Noyo Harbor, 707/964-4550, www.anchorcharterboats. com, fishing trips $80-125, two-hour whale-watching $40) offers fishing trips and whale-watching jaunts (Dec.-May). They'll take you rockfishing in summer, crabbing in winter, and chasing after salmon and tuna in season.

The **Noyo Fishing Center** (32440 N. Harbor Dr., Noyo Harbor, 707/964-3000, www.fortbraggfishing.com, half-day fishing trips $100-250, two-hour whale-watching excursion $35) can take you out for salmon or halibut fishing. They'll help you fish for cod and various deep-sea dwellers in season. The twice-daily trips are an intimate experience, with a maximum of six passengers.

HORSEBACK RIDING
What better way to enjoy the rugged cliffs, windy beaches, and quiet forests of the coast than on the back of a horse? **Ricochet Ridge Ranch** (24201 N. U.S. 101, 707/964-9669 or 888/873-5777, www.horse-vacation.com, 9:30am, 11:30am, 1:30pm, and 3:30pm, $60) has one-hour beach trail rides departing four times daily. They also offer longer beach and trail rides, sunset beach rides, and full-fledged riding vacations by reservation.

SURFING
Just south of town is **Hare Creek** (southwest of the intersection of Hwy. 1 and Hwy. 20, north end of the Hare Creek Bridge), one of the region's most popular spots. North of town is **Virgin Creek** (1.5 miles north of Fort Bragg on Hwy. 1), another well-known break. The **Lost Surf Shack** (319 N. Franklin St., 707/961-0889, 10am-6pm daily, surfboards $25/day, wetsuits $15/day) in downtown Fort Bragg rents surfboards and wetsuits.

SPAS
The **Bamboo Garden Spa** (303 N. Main St., Ste. C, 707/962-9396, www.bamboogardenspa. com, 11:30am-8pm Tues.-Sat., massages $95-245) pampers its guests with a wide array of massage, skin, and beauty treatments.

Food
Fort Bragg hosts a **farmers market** (Franklin St. between Laurel and Pine, www.mcfarm. org, 3pm-6pm Wed. May-Oct., 3pm-5pm Nov.-Apr. inside Old Recreation Center Gym) that sells wild-caught seafood, free-range beef, and fresh-baked bread.

BAKERIES AND CAFÉS
Cowlick's Ice Cream (250 N. Main St., 707/962-9271, www.cowlicksicecream.com, 11am-9pm daily) serves delectable handmade ice cream in a variety of flavors. They even serve mushroom ice cream during the famous fall mushroom season. Get the perennial favorites such as vanilla, chocolate, coffee, and strawberry, or try a seasonal flavor (banana

daiquiri, cinnamon, green tea). Ice cream from this local, family-owned chain is also sold at the **Mendocino Coast Botanical Gardens** (18220 N. Hwy. 1, 707/964-4352 ext. 20); at **Frankie's Ice Cream Parlor** (44951 Ukiah St., Mendocino, 707/937-2436, www. frankiesmendocino.com, 11am-9pm daily) in Mendocino Village; on the Skunk Train; and at **J. D. Redhouse** (212 S. Main St., Willits, 707/459-1214, 10am-6pm daily).

The **Headlands Coffeehouse** (120 Laurel St., 707/964-1987, www.headlandscoffeehouse. com, 7am-10pm Mon.-Sat., 7am-7pm Sun. summer; 7am-10pm Mon.-Sat., 7am-5pm Sun. winter) is the place to go for a cup of joe. They have 15 different self-serve roasts of coffee, as well as food ranging from breakfast burritos to paninis. There is free live music in the evenings and free Internet access (but no electrical outlets for customers).

Egghead's (326 N. Main St., 707/964-5005, 7am-2pm daily, $6-19) has been serving an enormous menu of breakfast, lunch, and brunch items to satisfy diners for more than 30 years. The menu includes every imaginable omelet combination, cinnamon raisin toast, burritos, Reuben sandwiches, and "flying-monkey potatoes," derived from the *Wizard of Oz* theme that runs through the place.

AMERICAN

The ★ **North Coast Brewing Company** (444 N. Main St., 707/964-3400, www. northcoastbrewing.com, 11:30am-9pm Sun.-Thurs., 11:30am-10pm Fri.-Sat., $15-33) serves seafood, steak, and creative salads, all washed down with a North Coast microbrew. Taste the magic in their Red Seal Ale, Old Rasputin Russian Imperial Stout, and Scrimshaw Pilsner. Sit at the cozy wooden bar in the taproom if you're here for the beer.

Jenny's Giant Burger (940 N. Main St., 707/964-2235, http://jennysgiantburger.com, 10:30am-9pm daily, $4-7) has a 1950s hamburger-stand feel. The burgers are fresh and antibiotic-free, with garden burger and veggie sandwich options. Jenny's followers are devoted, so it can get crowded, but there are a few outdoor tables, and you can always get your order to go.

ITALIAN

Small and almost always packed, the ★ **Piaci Pub & Pizzeria** (120 W. Redwood Ave., 707/961-1133, www.piacipizza.com, 11am-9:30pm Mon.-Thurs., 11am-10pm Fri.-Sat., 4pm-9:30pm Sun., $9-26) has an L-shaped bar and just a few tables, so you may share a table with some strangers. The 16 delicious

North Coast Brewing Company

pizzas range from traditional pepperoni to more creative combinations like pesto, chèvre, pears, prosciutto, and herbs. The Nonnie is a flavorful combination of prosciutto, grilled chicken, mozzarella, herbs, and a garlic sauce on a thin crust. Piaci's has an extensive list of brews, from Belgian-style beers to hearty ales.

Cucina Verona (124 E. Laurel St., 707/964-6844, www.cucinaverona.com, 8am-9pm Mon.-Thurs., 8am-9:30pm Fri.-Sat., 9am-9pm Sun., $12-35) does northern Italian food with touches of Northern California. Menu items run the gamut from butternut squash lasagna to grilled local salmon. Complement your meal with a local wine or beer. Frequent live music provides entertainment.

MEXICAN

Inside a Fort Bragg strip mall, **Los Gallitos** (130 S. Main St., 707/964-4519, 11am-8pm Mon.-Sat., 10am-7pm Sun., $7-16, cash only) doesn't look like much. But you know this is a better-than-average taqueria when the thick, fresh tortilla strips and superb salsa hit your table. Everything on the menu, from burritos to tostadas, is what you'd expect, but the attention to little details like the grilled onions and beans on the tasty carne asada torta make this place special.

SEAFOOD

With the small fishing and crabbing fleet of Fort Bragg's Noyo Harbor, it's natural that lots of seafood restaurants are clustered nearby. One spot known for its fish-and-chips is the **Sea Pal Cove Restaurant** (32390 N. Harbor Dr., 707/964-1300, 10am-11pm daily, $6-13, cash only). They also have 18 beers on tap.

THAI

Small and unassuming, **Nit's Café** (322 Main St., 707/964-7187, 11am-2pm and 5pm-9pm Tues.-Sun., $14-26, cash only) specializes in Thai and Asian fusion. Noted for its beautiful presentations of both classic and creative dishes, Nit's gets rave reviews. They have a special of the day and a fresh daily catch of the day.

Accommodations
UNDER $150

A budget option, the **Surf Motel** (1220 S. Main St., 707/964-5361, www.surfmotelfb.com, $95-199) provides a bike-washing station, a fish-cleaning station, an outdoor shower for divers, a garden to stroll through, and an area set aside for horseshoes and barbecues. Your spacious modern guest room comes with breakfast, free wireless Internet

pizza at Piaci Pub & Pizzeria

access, a microwave, a fridge, and a blow dryer. The two apartments have a kitchen and room for four people.

The stately **Grey Whale Inn** (615 N. Main St., 707/964-0640 or 800/382-7244, www.greywhaleinn.com, $135-190) was once a community hospital. The blocky craftsman-style building was erected by the Union Lumber Company in 1915. Today, 13 spacious, simple rooms offer views of the water or the city. The lovely, individually decorated rooms feature a private bath and queen or king bed, perhaps covered by an old-fashioned quilt. The inn prides itself on simplicity and friendliness, and its location in downtown Fort Bragg makes visitors feel at home walking to dinner or the beach. It also has a game room with a pool table and foosball.

$150-250

★ **Weller House** (524 Stewart St., 707/964-4415, www.wellerhouse.com, $150-320) is a picture-perfect B&B with elegant Victorian-style rooms, ocean views, and sumptuous home cooking. There are even a few secluded rooms in the old water tower. The manager, Vivien LaMothe, is a tango dancer, and the third floor of the main building—a gorgeous 1886 mansion listed on the National Register of Historic Places—is a ballroom. (There are dance events four times a week.) Weller House is one block west of Main Street and an easy walk to good restaurants and shopping.

The **Beachcomber Motel** (1111 N. Main St., 707/964-2402, www.thebeachcombermotel.com, $139-309) is just north of town right behind Pudding Creek Beach. It's one of the most pet-friendly motels along the coast. Not only are there pet-friendly rooms, but there is a dog park and suites with doggie doors that open up to a fenced-in enclosure with a doghouse. Rooms are equipped with private balconies and decks to take in the bluffs and ocean. Some units even have hot tubs. A deck on the northern end of the property has fire pits and barbecue grills. The motel rents beach cruisers for use on the Coastal Trail at adjacent MacKerricher State Park.

Next door, the ★ **Surf & Sand Lodge** (1131 N. Main St., 707/964-9383, www.surfsandlodge.com, $169-299) is the slightly more upscale sister property of the Beachcomber. Most of the rooms in the six blue buildings have views of headlands and ocean. The trails, tide pools, crashing waves, and broad beaches of MacKerricher State Park are right out front. Every room has a balcony

Surf & Sand Lodge

or a porch to take in the view. Opt for a room with a Jacuzzi spa tub to soak in while looking out at the chilly Pacific.

Transportation and Services

Fort Bragg is on Highway 1; driving from San Francisco takes about four hours. The road in any direction is narrow and full of curves; be prepared to make the scenic journey part of the fun. From Willits, take Highway 20 (Fort Bragg-Willits Road) west for 30 miles. The sun pops in and out among the redwood forest and makes you want to use all the pullouts to take photos. There is no cell-phone service along this road, so fill your gas tank before the drive and allow plenty of time to travel these 30 miles.

Fort Bragg has great access to public transportation. The most enjoyable way to get here is to take the **Skunk Train** (707/964-6371, www.skunktrain.com, adults $84, children 2-12 $42, children under 2 $10) from Willits. The **Mendocino Transit Authority** (800/696-4682, http://mendocinotransit.org, $1.50-5.25) has a number of bus lines that pass through Fort Bragg. It also offers **Dial-a-Ride Curb-to-Curb Service** (707/462-3881, 7am-6pm Mon.-Fri., 10am-5pm Sat., adults $6, seniors $3, children under 6 $1.25).

The **Mendocino Coast Chamber of Commerce and Visitors Center** (217 S. Main St., 707/961-6300, www.mendocinocoast.com, 10am-5pm Mon.-Fri., 10am-3pm Sat.) also serves as the Mendocino County film office, which strongly encourages filmmaking in the area. Get the inside story on where to see the filming locations of *Summer of '42*, in which the bluffs of Fort Bragg play the role of Long Island; *East of Eden*; *Karate Kid III*; and *Humanoids from the Deep*.

The **Mendocino Coast District Hospital** (700 River Dr., at Cypress St., 707/961-1234, www.mcdh.org) has the nearest full-service emergency room.

MACKERRICHER STATE PARK

Three miles north of Fort Bragg, **MacKerricher State Park** (Hwy. 1, 707/964-9112, district office 707/937-5804, www.parks. ca.gov, sunrise-10pm daily, day use free) offers the small, duck-filled Cleone Lake, six miles of sandy ocean beaches, four miles of cliffs and crags, and camping. The main attraction is a gigantic, almost complete skeleton of a whale near the park entrance. If you're lucky, you can also spot live whales and harbor seals

Pudding Creek Beach in MacKerricher State Park

frolicking in the ocean. The coast can be rough here, so don't swim or wade unless it's what the locals call a "flat day"—no big waves and undertow. If the kids want to play in the water, take them to **Pudding Creek Beach** in the park, about 2.5 miles south of the campground, where they can enjoy the relatively sheltered area under the trestle bridge.

The hike to take is the **Ten Mile Beach Trail** (10 miles round-trip, moderate), starting at the Laguna Point Parking Area at the north end of Fort Bragg and running five miles up to the Ten Mile River. Most of this path is fairly level and paved. It's an easy walk, and you can turn around whenever you want. Street bikes and inline skates are also allowed.

Campground (800/444-7275, www.reservecalifornia.com, $35) reservations are recommended April 1-October 15, and they're site-specific. In winter, camping is first-come, first-served. The park has 107 sites suitable for tents and RVs (up to 35 feet) in its wooded and pleasant West Pinewood and East Pinewood Campgrounds; there are also a group campground and walk-in hike-and-bike sites. Restrooms with flush toilets as well as hot showers are provided, and each campsite has a fire ring, picnic table, and food storage locker.

WESTPORT

Westport is 16 miles north of Fort Bragg, with its own patch of ocean, a few essential services, and one lodging gem. It's the last settlement before the wild Lost Coast.

Food and Accommodations

Inside the Westport Hotel is the **Old Abalone Pub** (3892 Hwy. 1, 707/964-3688 or 877/964-3688, www.westporthotel.us, 5pm-9pm Thurs.-Fri., 3pm-9pm Sat., 10am-2pm and 5pm-9pm Sun., $10-25). Thanks to a large mirror over the bar, everyone in the dining room gets an ocean view.

The motto at the ★ **Westport Hotel** (3892 Hwy. 1, 707/964-3688 or 877/964-3688, www.westporthotel.us, $150-225) is, "At last, you've found nowhere." The Westport Hotel is marvelous and private, perfect for a honeymoon spent in luxury and comfort. Each of the six rooms has one bed and a bath with fixtures that blend perfectly into the historic 1890 house. Some rooms have small private balconies overlooking the waves, and all guests have access to the redwood sauna. Fresh scones, fruit, and coffee are delivered to your room in the morning, and a full hot breakfast is served in the dining room.

Camping is available two miles north of Westport at **Westport-Union Landing State Beach** (Hwy. 1, 707/937-5804, www.parks.ca.gov, $25), with 86 first-come, first-served sites. There are no showers or other amenities—just the cliffs, the waves, the sunsets, and the views.

INLAND MENDOCINO COUNTY

About 60 miles east of the coast (a 1.5-hour scenic drive), Mendocino's interior valley is home to history, art, and wine. The Anderson Valley is the apex of Mendocino's wine region, the tiny town of Hopland also has its share of tasting rooms, and Ukiah is home to several microbreweries.

The interior valleys of Mendocino get hot in the summer. Bring shorts, a swimsuit, and an air-conditioned car if you plan to visit June-September.

TOP EXPERIENCE

Anderson Valley
WINERIES AND BREWERIES

The **Anderson Valley Wine Trail** (Hwy. 128) begins in Boonville and continues northwest toward the coast, with most of the wineries clustered between Boonville and Navarro.

A big name in the Anderson Valley, **Scharffenberger Cellars** (8501 Hwy. 128, Philo, 707/895-2957, www.scharffenbergercellars.com, 11am-5pm daily, $3) makes wine in Mendocino. Its tasting room is elegant and child-friendly, decorated with the work of local artists.

A broad-ranging winery with a large estate vineyard and event center, **Navarro**

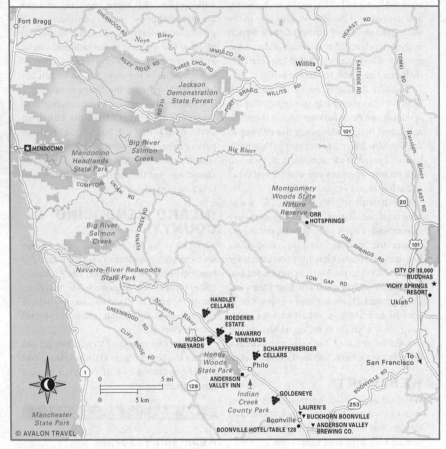

Mendocino Wine Country

Vineyards (5601 Hwy. 128, Philo, 707/895-3686 or 800/537-9463, www.navarrowine.com, 8am-6pm daily summer, 8am-5pm daily winter, free) offers a range of tasty wines as well as some interesting specialty products such as the nonalcoholic verjus.

Roederer Estate (4501 Hwy. 128, Philo, 707/895-2288, www.roedererestate.com, 11am-5pm daily, $6) sparkling wines are some of the best of the state. The large tasting room features a bar with sweeping views of the estate vineyards and huge cases filled with well-deserved awards. Pourers are knowledgeable, and you'll get to taste from magnum bottles—a rarity at any winery. Ask for a taste of Roederer's rarely seen still wines.

Handley Cellars (3151 Hwy. 128, Philo, 800/733-3151, www.handleycellars.com, 10am-6pm daily summer, 10am-5pm daily winter, free) offers a complimentary tasting of handcrafted wines. The intriguing tasting room features folk art from around the world. Books on wine are sold, especially those that focus on women making and drinking wine.

Toulouse Vineyards (8001 Hwy. 128, Philo, 707/895-2828, http://toulousevineyards.com, 11am-5pm daily) is the kind of small operation where the winemaker's dog will greet you upon arrival. Known for pinot noir, they also do a pinot gris and a gewürztraminer.

Anderson Valley Brewing Company (17700 Hwy. 253, Boonville, 707/895-2337, www.avbc.com, 11am-6pm Sat.-Thurs., 11am-7pm Fri. summer; winter hours vary) serves up an array of microbrews that change each season and year. The warehouse-size beer hall feels like a wine-tasting room, with a bar, tables, and a good-size gift shop. A beer garden out back is comfortable in spring and fall, and the disc golf course is popular with travelers and locals.

FOOD

The Buckhorn (14081 Hwy. 128, Boonville, 707/895-3224, kitchen: 11am-9pm Mon. and Wed.-Fri., 10am-9pm Sat.-Sun., bar: 11am-11pm Sun.-Mon. and Wed.-Thurs., 11am-midnight Fri.-Sat., $11-32) has more than 40 local wines and 14 beers on tap, many from nearby Anderson Valley Brewing Company. They also do big portions of good food including burgers and hot sandwiches such as a worthwhile French dip.

Farmers markets and farm stands abound in the Anderson Valley. The **Boonville Farmers Market** (14050 Hwy. 128, Boonville, www.mcfarm.org, 10am-12:30pm Sat. May-Oct.) draws a crowd, so be prepared to hunt for parking. **Gowan's Oak Tree Farm Stand** (6600 Hwy. 128, 2.5 miles north of Philo, 707/895-3353, www.gowansoaktree.com, 8am-7pm daily June-Aug., 8am-6pm daily Sept.-Oct., 8:30am-5:30pm daily Nov.-May) belongs to the local Gowan's Oak Tree Farm and sells in-season local produce and homemade products made with the same fruits and veggies.

ACCOMMODATIONS

The **Anderson Valley Inn** (8480 Hwy. 128, Philo, 707/895-3325, www.avinn.com, $95-190), between Boonville and Philo, makes the perfect spot from which to divide your time between the Anderson Valley and the Mendocino Coast. Six small rooms are done up in bright colors, homey bedspreads, and attractive appointments. A butterfly-filled garden invites guests to sit out on the porches. Two suites have full kitchens and are perfect for longer stays. The friendly owners welcome children and dogs in the suites and can offer hints about how best to explore the region. This inn often fills quickly on summer weekends, as it's one of the best values in the region. There's a two-night minimum on weekends April-November.

The quaint **Boonville Hotel** (14050 Hwy. 128, 707/895-2210, www.boonvillehotel.com, $155-395) has a rough, weathered exterior that contrasts with the 15 contemporary rooms, each of which is bright and airy and has earthtone furniture and mismatched decorations. Downstairs are spacious common areas and a huge garden. Amenities include a bookshop and a gift shop, a good-size bar, and a dining room. Book one of the rooms with a balcony, which comes with a hammock, or a guest room with an outdoor bathtub. Child- and pet-friendly rooms are available on request.

CAMPING

The campgrounds at **Indian Creek County Park** (Hwy. 128 at mile marker 23.48, 1 mile east of Philo, 707/463-4291, www.co.mendocino.ca.us, $25) are budget-friendly. Eight miles northwest of Boonville is **Hendy Woods State Park** (18599 Philo-Greenwood Rd., Philo, 800/444-7275, www.reservecalifornia.com, campsites $40, cabins $55), with woodsy, shaded campsites along with four rustic cabins with wood-burning stoves.

TRANSPORTATION

Highway 128 departs the Mendocino Coast approximately 10 miles south of Mendocino. From Mendocino, drive south on Highway 1 to the junction with Highway 128 and turn east. Follow Highway 128 east for 30 miles to the town of Boonville.

From Boonville, it's possible to continue east to U.S. 101, which accesses Ukiah (north) and Hopland (south).

Many of the major wine-country

touring outfits operate in the Anderson Valley. **Mendo Wine Tours** (707/937-0289 or 800/609-0492, http://www.maccallumhouse.com/wine-tours, group tours $175 pp, private tours for two $500-650) is a regional specialist that offers a Lincoln Town Car for small groups and an SUV limo for groups of up to 10.

Hopland

This small farming town is on the upper section of the Russian River. The **Solar Living Center** (13771 S. U.S. 101, 707/472-2460, http://solarliving.org, 9am-6:30pm daily) is a "12-acre sustainable living demonstration site," showing, among other things, what life might be like without petroleum. Exhibits include permaculture, an organic garden, and a demonstration of solar-powered water systems. Guided **tours** (707/472-2460, 11am and 3pm Sat.-Sun. Apr.-Oct., $5/person, $10/family) are available.

The on-site **Real Goods** (707/472-2403, 10am-6pm daily summer, 10am-5pm daily winter) is also a draw for visitors; the completely recycled restrooms are worth a look. If your vehicle happens to run on biodiesel, you can fill your tank here.

WINERIES

Hopland's wineries are the perfect place to relax, enjoy sipping each vintage, and chat with the pourer, who just might be the winemaker and owner. Most of the tasting rooms are along U.S. 101, which runs through the center of town.

The star is **Brutocao Cellars** (13500 S. U.S. 101, 800/433-3689, www.brutocaocellars.com, 10am-5pm daily, free), which has vineyards that surround the town. The wide, stone-tiled tasting room and restaurant complex house exceptional wines poured by knowledgeable staff. A sizable gift shop offers gourmet goodies under the Brutocao label, and there are six regulation bocce ball courts. A second tasting room is in the Anderson Valley (7000 Hwy. 128, Philo, 800/661-2103, www.brutocaocellars.com, 10am-5pm daily, free).

Heading north, the highway passes through acres of vineyards, many of which belong to **Jeriko** (12141 Hewlett and Sturtevant Rd., 707/744-1140, www.jerikoestate.com, 10am-5pm daily summer, 11am-4pm daily winter, $10). A glass wall exposes the barrel room, stacked high with aging wines.

FOOD

The casual **Bluebird Café & Catering Company** (13340 S. U.S. 101, 707/744-1633, 7am-2pm Wed.-Mon., $17-20) does wild game, including bison burgers. The **Hopland Tap House** (13551 S. Hwy. 101, 707/744-1255, http://hoplandtaphouse.com, noon-9pm Wed.-Sat., noon-6pm Sun., $9-14) is located within a historic brick building. The eight craft beers on tap go nicely with the small menu of burgers, hot dogs, paninis, and salads.

TRANSPORTATION

Hopland is inland on U.S. 101, about 15 miles south of Ukiah and 28 miles east of the Anderson Valley via Highway 253.

Ukiah

Ukiah's low-key, historic downtown has some worthwhile restaurants and shops. The surrounding area is home to organic wineries, the largest Buddhist monastery in the country, and historic mineral springs.

CITY OF 10,000 BUDDHAS

The **City of 10,000 Buddhas** (4951 Bodhi Way, 707/462-0939, www.cttbusa.org, 8am-6pm daily) is an active Buddhist college and monastery. The showpiece is the temple, which contains 10,000 golden Buddha statues. An extensive gift shop sells souvenirs as well as scholarly texts on Buddhism. For a treat, stop in for lunch at the **Jyun Kang Vegetarian Restaurant** (707/468-7966, 11:30am-3pm Wed.-Mon., $7), which is open to the public.

The monastery asks that guests wear modest clothing and keep their voices down out of respect for the nuns and monks who live here.

GRACE HUDSON MUSEUM AND SUN HOUSE

The **Grace Hudson Museum** (431 S. Main St., 707/467-2836, www.gracehudsonmuseum. org, 10am-4:30pm Wed.-Sat., noon-4:30pm Sun., adults $4, seniors and students $3, family $10) focuses on the life and work of the artist Grace Hudson and her husband, Dr. John Hudson. The museum's permanent collection includes many of Grace's paintings, a number of Pomo baskets, and the works of dozens of other California artists. The 1911 craftsman-style **Sun House** (docent-guided tours available with museum ticket, noon-3pm Wed.-Sun.) was the Hudsons' home.

VICHY SPRINGS RESORT

Established in 1854, **Vichy Springs Resort** (2605 Vichy Springs Rd., 707/462-9515, www. vichysprings.com, 9am-dusk daily, baths $35/ two hours, $65/day) has been patronized by Mark Twain, Jack London, Ulysses S. Grant, Teddy Roosevelt, and California governor Jerry Brown. The hot springs, mineral-heavy and naturally carbonated, closely resemble the world-famous waters of their namesake at Vichy in France and spill into indoor and outdoor concrete tubs. Services include the baths, a hot pool, and an Olympic-size swimming pool as well as a day spa. The serene 700-acre property also has 12 miles of trails.

FOOD

Local favorite **Stan's Maple Restaurant** (295 S. State St., 707/462-5221, www. stansmaplecafe.com, 7am-2pm daily, $6-14) serves tasty breakfasts and lunches. Excellent service complements good, American-style food. Shockingly good coffee is a charming final touch.

For a cool, relaxing breather on a hot day, visit one of the three locations of **Schat's Bakery Café** (www.schats.com; 113 W. Perkins St., 707/462-1670, 5:30am-6pm Mon.-Fri., 5:30am-5pm Sat.; 1255A Airport Park Blvd., 707/468-5850, 7am-8pm Mon.-Fri., 7am-7pm Sat., 8am-7pm Sun.; 1000 Hensley Creek Rd., 707/468-3145, 7am-8:15pm Mon.-Thurs., 7am-3pm Fri., $5-12) for a quick, filling sandwich on fresh-baked bread. Enjoy it in the large, airy dining room.

Ellie's Mutt Hut & Vegetarian Café (732 S. State St., 707/468-5376, http://elliesmutthutukiahca.com, 6:30am-8pm Mon.-Sat., $8-15) has great vegetarian entrées and an impressive hot dog list. The atmosphere is hamburger-stand casual, and the food is mostly healthy.

historic soaking tubs at Vichy Springs Resort

At **Patrona** (130 W. Standish St., 707/462-9181, www.patronarestaurant.com, 11am-9pm Mon.-Fri., 10am-9pm Sat.-Sun., $13-29), innovative California cuisine is served in a bistro-casual atmosphere by solicitous servers. The kitchen's attention to detail is impressive. The wine list features Mendocino County vintages, plus a good range of European wines.

Ukiah Brewing Company & Restaurant (102 S. State St., 707/468-5898, http:// ukiahbrewing.com, 11am-9pm Sun.-Thurs., 11am-10pm Fri.-Sat., $11-28) has a wide menu that includes pizzas, sandwiches, salads, steak frites, and a chef's tasting menu, but it's the house-blended burgers on brioche buns that shine. Order the burger with bacon jam, white cheddar, and aioli. They also serve Ukiah Brewing Co. beer, which is brewed on-site.

ACCOMMODATIONS

Lodgings in Ukiah tend to be standard chain motels. Out by the airport, the **Fairfield Inn** (1140 Airport Park Blvd., 707/463-3600, www.marriott.com, $179) is a good choice, with an indoor pool and spa, a small exercise room, laundry facilities, and a generous complimentary continental breakfast. Rooms are what you'd expect: floral bedspreads, durable, nondescript carpet, and clean baths.

For a peaceful retreat, the best choice is ★ **Vichy Springs Resort** (2605 Vichy Springs Rd., 707/462-9515, www.vichysprings. com, $175-445). Rooms in the genteel and rustic inn and nearby cottages are small but comfortable, with private baths, warm bedspreads, and cool breezes; many have views of the mountains or creek. Two of the cottages date to 1852. Use of the pools and hiking trails is included in the rates, as are Internet access and a buffet breakfast.

TRANSPORTATION AND SERVICES

Ukiah is located on U.S. 101, about 15 miles north of Hopland, 22 miles east of Boonville, and 60 miles east of the Mendocino Coast.

To reach Ukiah from Boonville, turn east at the junction of Highways 128 and 253, and continue 22 miles to U.S. 101.

The **Mendocino Transit Authority** (800/696-4682, http://mendocinotransit.org) runs bus service throughout the county, with Ukiah as the hub; you can catch buses here and in Mendocino and Fort Bragg. Private pilots can land at **Ukiah Municipal Airport** (UKI, 1411 S. State St., 707/467-2817, www.cityofukiah.com).

The **Ukiah Valley Medical Center** (275 Hospital Dr., 707/462-3111, www.uvmc.org) has a 24-hour emergency room as part of its full-service facility.

The Redwood Coast

TOP EXPERIENCE

Of all the natural wonders California has to offer, the one that seems to inspire the purest and most unmitigated awe is the giant redwood. The coast redwood, *Sequoia sempervirens*, grows along the California coast from around Big Sur in the south and into southern Oregon in the north. Coast redwoods hold the records for the tallest trees ever recorded, and are among the world's oldest and all-around most massive living things. The two best places to experience extensive wild groves of these gargantuan treasures are Humboldt Redwoods State Park, in Humboldt County, and Redwood National and State Parks, near the north end of California around Eureka and Crescent City.

Most of the major park areas along the Redwood Coast can be accessed via U.S. 101 and U.S. 199. Follow the signs to the smaller roads that lead farther from civilization. To get to the redwood parks from the south, drive up U.S. 101 or the much slower but prettier Highway 1. The two roads merge at Leggett, north of Fort Bragg, and continue north as U.S. 101.

LEGGETT

As Highway 1 heads inland toward Leggett, the ocean views are replaced with redwoods. This part of the road is curvy, winding, and sun-dappled. It's a beautiful drive, so take it slow.

At the junction of Highway 1 and U.S. 101, you'll enter Leggett, famed for the local attraction **Chandelier Drive-Thru Tree** (67402 Drive-Thru Tree Rd., 707/925-6464, www.drivethrutree.com, hours and dates vary, $5). The tree opening is about six feet wide and a little over six feet high. Kids will be thrilled. And of course, there's a gift shop.

The Peg House (69501 U.S. 101, 707/925-6444, http://thepeghouse.com), which was built with pegs instead of nails, gets raves for its burgers, tri-tip, Humboldt Bay oysters, and deli sandwiches. Sometimes there is live music.

GARBERVILLE AND REDWAY

Garberville is the first real town in Humboldt County. Just three miles northwest is the slightly larger town of Redway, with just a few hundred more residents. Known as the "Gateway to the Avenue of the Giants," both towns are good places to get a meal or fill your tank with gas before heading west to the coast or north to the redwoods.

Richardson Grove State Park

Richardson Grove State Park (1600 U.S. 101, 707/247-3318, www.parks.ca.gov, daily sunrise-sunset, $8) is the first with old-growth redwoods along U.S. 101. This park has special features, like a tree you can walk through and the ninth-tallest coast redwood. The Eel River flows through the park, offering good fishing as well as camping, swimming, and hiking. The visitors center (May-Sept.) in the 1930s Richardson Grove Lodge has cool exhibits and a nature store. Richardson Grove State Park is seven miles south of Garberville.

Festivals and Events

The **Mateel Community Center** (59 Rusk

The Redwood Coast

Ln., Redway, 707/923-3368, www.mateel.org) brings music, theater, dance, comedy, film, and craft events to southern Humboldt. They also put on local annual events, including the Summer Arts & Music Festival, the Humboldt Hills Hoedown, and Winter Arts Faire.

Food

The restaurant at the ★ **Benbow Inn** (445 Lake Benbow Dr., Garberville, 707/923-2124 or 800/355-3301, www.benbowinn.com,

8am-3pm and 5pm-9:30pm daily, $19-45) serves upscale California cuisine (a vegan menu is available on request) and features an extensive wine list with many regional wineries represented. The white-tablecloth dining room is exquisite, and the expansive outdoor patio overlooking the water is the perfect place to sit as the temperature cools on a summer evening.

An easy place to stop for a pick-me-up, **Flavors Coffeehouse** (767 Redwood Dr., Garberville, 707/923-7717, 7am-7pm daily, $5-11) refuels with a menu of caffeine drinks, sandwiches, paninis, and salads. The build-your-own-grilled-cheese-sandwich option lets you add ingredients including bacon and roasted bell peppers. A good breakfast and lunch stop is the **Eel River Café** (801 Redwood Dr., 707/923-3783, 6am-2pm Tues.-Sat., $6-12), a diner with black-and-white checkerboard floors and a long counter with red stools. Try the chicken-fried steak with biscuits and gravy. You can't miss the old-school sign towering above the establishment.

You can enjoy a taste of local Humboldt-roasted coffee at **Signature Coffee** (3455 Redwood Dr., Redway, 707/923-2661, www.signaturecoffeecompany.com, 7am-5pm Mon.-Fri.), which takes pride in its organic products and sustainable practices.

Enjoy a classic roadhouse experience at **The Riverwood Inn** (2828 Avenue of the Giants, Phillipsville, 707/943-3333, https://theriverwoodinn.com, 3pm-midnight Mon.-Thurs., 11am-midnight Fri.-Sun., $80-98), six miles north of Garberville. This classic tavern was one of the few buildings that survived the Eel River flood of 1964. Come for the tasty Mexican food and stay for the live music Friday and Saturday nights. There's also five hotel rooms upstairs.

Ray's Food Place (875 Redwood Dr., 707/923-2279, www.gorays.com, 7am-11pm daily) is a supermarket in Garberville.

Accommodations

The best place to stay is the ★ **Benbow Inn** (445 Lake Benbow Dr., Garberville, 707/923-2124 or 800/355-3301, www.benbowinn.com, $195-400). A swank resort backing onto Lake Benbow, this inn has it all: a gourmet restaurant, a nine-hole golf course, an outdoor swimming pool, and a woodsy atmosphere that blends perfectly with the ancient redwood forest surrounding it. Rooms glow with dark polished woods and jewel-toned carpets. Wide king and comfy queen beds beckon guests tired after a long day of hiking in the redwoods or golfing beside the inn.

Several small motels offer reasonable rooms, and many have outdoor pools. The best of these is the **Best Western Humboldt House Inn** (701 Redwood Dr., Garberville, 707/923-2771, www.bestwestern.com, $179-239). Rooms are clean and comfortable, the pool is sparkling and cool, the breakfast is hot, and the location is convenient to restaurants and shops in Garberville. Most rooms have two queen beds.

Camping

Richardson Grove State Park (1600 U.S. 101, 800/444-7275, www.reservecalifornia.com, camping $35) has 169 campsites in three campground areas surrounded by redwoods and the Elk River.

You can park your RV year-round at the 112 sites of the posh **Benbow RV Park** (7000 Benbow Dr., Garberville, 707/923-2777, www.benbowrv.com, campsites $46-85, cabins $75-400). Premium sites come with complimentary tea and scones at the nearby Benbow Inn.

Transportation and Services

Garberville is 65 miles south of Eureka and 200 miles north of San Francisco on U.S. 101. From Garberville, take Redwood Drive just three miles to Redway. The best way to get to Humboldt Redwoods State Park is via U.S. 101. Road signs point to the Avenue of the Giants. Bicycles are not permitted on U.S. 101, but you can ride on the Avenue of the Giants.

The towns in this region can be short on necessary services such as gas stations. There

redwood trees along the Avenue of the Giants

is a **76 Gas Station** (790 Redwood Dr.) just off the highway.

The **Redwood County Transit** (707/443-0826, https://humboldttransit.org) bus system offers limited service to Garberville from the north.

The nearest hospital with an emergency room is **Redwood Memorial Hospital** (3300 Renner Dr., Fortuna, 707/725-3361, www.stjoehumboldt.org).

HUMBOLDT REDWOODS STATE PARK

The largest stand of unlogged redwood trees is in Humboldt, bisected by U.S. 101. A drive along the Avenue of the Giants with a stop at the **Humboldt Redwoods State Park Visitors Center** (Hwy. 254, 707/946-2263, www.parks.ca.gov or www.humboldtredwoods.org, 9am-5pm daily Apr.-Oct., 10am-4pm daily Nov.-Mar., free) and a quick nature walk or picnic can give you a taste of the lovely southern end of the coastal redwoods region.

★ Avenue of the Giants

The most famous stretch of redwood trees is the **Avenue of the Giants** (www.avenueofthegiants.net), paralleling U.S. 101 and the Eel River for about 33 miles between Garberville and Fortuna; look for signs on U.S. 101. Visitors drive this stretch of road and gaze in wonder at the sky-high old-growth redwoods along the way. Campgrounds and hiking trails sprout amid the trees off the road. It's easy to park your car at various points along the way and get out to walk among the giants or down to the nearby Eel River for a cool dip.

The Avenue's highest traffic volume is in July-August, when you can expect bumper-to-bumper traffic along the entire road. That's not necessarily a bad thing: Going slow is the best way to see the sights. But if crowds aren't your thing, visit in spring or fall, or brave the rains of winter to gain a more secluded redwood experience.

To enhance your Avenue of the Giants drive, there's an eight-stop audio tour along the route. Pick up an audio tour card at the visitors center or on either side of the drive.

Hiking and Biking

Start with the **Founder's Grove Nature Loop Trail** (0.6 mile, easy), at mile marker 20.5 on the Avenue of the Giants. This sedate, flat nature trail gives a taste of the big old-growth trees in the park. Sadly, the onetime tallest tree in the world, the Dyerville Giant, fell in 1991 at the age of about 1,600. But it's still doing its part in this astounding ecosystem, decomposing before your eyes on the forest floor and feeding new life in the forest.

Right at the visitors center, you can enjoy the **Gould Grove Nature Trail** (0.6 mile, easy), a wheelchair-accessible interpretive nature walk with helpful signs describing the denizens of the forest.

For a longer walk, try the lovely **River Trail** (Mattole Rd., 1.1 miles west of Ave. of the Giants, 7 miles round-trip, moderate) as it follows the South Fork Eel River. Check with the visitors center to be sure that the summer bridges have been installed before hiking this trail.

Hard-core hikers can get their exercise on the **Grasshopper Multiuse Trailhead** (Mattole Rd., 5.1 miles west of Ave. of the Giants), which accesses the **Johnson Camp Trail** (10.5 miles round-trip, difficult) to the abandoned cabins of railroad tie makers. Or pick another fork from the same trailhead to climb more than 3,000 feet to **Grasshopper Peak** (13.5 miles, difficult). From the peak, you can see 100 miles in any direction.

You can bring your street bike to the park and ride the Avenue of the Giants or Mattole Road. A number of the trails around Humboldt Redwoods State Park are designated multiuse, which means that mountain bikers can make the rigorous climbs and then rip their way back down.

Swimming and Kayaking

The **Eel River**'s forks meander through the Humboldt redwoods, creating great opportunities for cooling off on hot summer days. Reliably good spots include **Eagle Point**, near Hidden Valley Campground; **Gould Bar**; and **Garden Club of America Grove**. In addition to the usual precautions for river swimming, a blue-green algae (poisonous if ingested) can bloom August-September, making swimming in certain parts of the river hazardous.

Events

Humboldt Redwoods State Park is the site of a couple of excellent marathons and half-marathons. These events are also less crowded than more famous marathons, and you can camp right in the park where they begin. October has the **Humboldt Redwoods Marathon** (www.redwoodsmarathon.org, Oct., $75-95) with a related half-marathon ($65-75) and a 5K ($25-35). The **Avenue of the Giants Marathon** (www.theave.org, marathon $75-95, half-marathon $65-85, 10K $40-60) is held each May.

Camping

Humboldt Redwoods State Park (707/946-2263, www.reservecalifornia.com, $35) has three developed, car-accessible campgrounds; there are also primitive backcountry campsites ($5). Each developed campground has its own entrance station, and reservations are strongly recommended, as the park is quite popular with weekend campers.

Burlington Campground (707/946-1811, year-round) is adjacent to the visitors center and is a convenient starting point for the marathons and races that traverse the park in May and October. It's shaded and comfortable, engulfed in trees, and has ample restroom facilities and hot showers. **Albee Creek** (Mattole Rd., 5 miles west of Ave. of the Giants, 707/946-2472, mid-May-mid-Oct.) offers some redwood-shaded sites and others in open meadows. ★ **Hidden Springs Campground** (Ave. of the Giants, 5 miles south of the visitors center, 707/943-3177, early May-Labor Day) is large and popular. Nearby, a trail leads to a great Eel River swimming hole. Minimalist campers will enjoy the seclusion of hike-in trail camps at **Johnson Camp** and **Grasshopper Peak.**

Equestrians can make use of the multiuse trails, and the **Cuneo Creek Horse Camp** (old homestead on Mattole Rd., 8 miles west of Ave. of the Giants, May-mid-Oct., 1 vehicle and 2 horses $35) provides a place for riders.

Transportation and Services

Humboldt Redwoods State Park is 21 miles north of Garberville on U.S. 101. The Avenue of the Giants parallels U.S. 101, and there are several marked exits along the highway to reach the scenic redwood drive.

Fill your gas tank in the nearby towns of Piercy, Garberville, Redway, Redcrest, Miranda, and Rio Dell. Markets to stock up on supplies are in Garberville, Redway, Miranda, Phillipsville, Redcrest, Myers Flat, Scotia, and Rio Dell.

The nearest hospital with an emergency room is **Redwood Memorial Hospital** (3300 Renner Dr., Fortuna, 707/725-3361, www.stjoehumboldt.org).

The Lost Coast

The Lost Coast is one of California's last undeveloped coastlines. Encompassing northern Mendocino County and southern Humboldt County, this coast is "lost" because the rugged terrain makes it impractical—some might say impossible—to build a highway here. An arduous trek along its wilderness trails is worthwhile to soak up the raw beauty of its rugged beaches.

The small fishing community of Shelter Cove is situated between the King Range Conservation Area and Sinkyone Wilderness State Park. The town has a few restaurant and lodging options and is also home to Black Sand Beach and the Cape Mendocino Lighthouse.

SINKYONE WILDERNESS STATE PARK

Encompassing the southern section of the Lost Coast, the **Sinkyone Wilderness State Park** (707/247-3318, www.parks.ca.gov, sunrise-sunset daily, $6) is a wild region of steep coastal mountains and surf-pounded beaches spotted with wildlife, including bears and elk. The Roosevelt elk had disappeared from the region until a herd from Prairie Creek State Park was reintroduced here. With their impressive antlers, the elk bulls usually weigh 700-1,100 pounds and can be quite a sight to see in the wild.

The Sinkyone Wilderness has a 16-mile **Lost Coast Trail** that starts at Bear Harbor, south of Needle Rock, and ends at Usal Beach. This trail takes backpackers 2-3 days and has more climbing than the Lost Coast Trail to the north. The rigorous hike is mostly on bluffs above the coastline. It passes through virgin redwood groves and mixed forest with beach access at **Wheeler Beach.**

Needle Rock

The most easily accessible spot in the northern Sinkyone is **Needle Rock,** the former site of a small settlement and the current location of a park visitors center. The area's namesake rock is nearby on a black-sand beach. Visitors can camp at three environmental **campsites** (first-come, first-served, $25), three miles from the visitors center, as well as at an old barn (first-come, first-served, $30) close to the visitors center. Camping is done by self-registration. Needle Rock's visitors center was once a ranch house. Now it is staffed by a volunteer year-round. The visitors center has information on the region's history and various artifacts. You can also purchase maps and firewood.

To reach Needle Rock, head off U.S. 101 at the Garberville exit and take Redwood Road to Redway. Drive Briceland Road in Redway until it becomes Mendocino County Road 435. The road dead-ends into the state park. The last 3.5 miles are unpaved, steep, and narrow.

Usal Beach

At the southern tip of Sinkyone Wilderness State Park, **Usal Beach** is a remote, two-mile-long black-sand beach situated under cliffs bristling with massive trees. It's accessible to adventurous coastal explorers via a steep, unpaved six-mile dirt road that is not for the fainthearted or the squeamish. Passenger cars can make the drive until the winter rainy season, when four-wheel drive becomes necessary.

When you reach the beach, you can fish from shore or beachcomb the sandy expanse. Watch sea lions torpedo through the ocean and pelicans splash into the water looking for food. Facilities include 35 primitive drive-in **campsites** (first come, first served, $25) with picnic tables, fire pits, and pit toilets. The rangers come here to collect the camping fees on some days, but otherwise you self-register to camp. Be aware that although firearms are not allowed in

Hiking the Lost Coast

Start: Mattole Beach
End: Black Sand Beach (Shelter Cove)
24 Miles One-Way / 3 Days
To fully experience one of the country's most remote and rugged coastal areas, backpackers head out on the **Lost Coast Trail.** This 24-mile beach hike stretches from the Mattole River south to Shelter Cove's Black Sand Beach. This is a once-in-a-lifetime experience that offers hiking along-side primal, mostly wild coastline, interrupted only by the abandoned Punta Gorda Lighthouse and numerous shipwrecks along the shore. Waterfalls feather the coastal bluffs, shorebirds fly above the crashing surf, sea lions congregate at the aptly named Sea Lion Gulch, and migrating whales surface along the horizon. On land, you might encounter deer and bears.

This is a strenuous hike, challenging even for experienced hikers. It demands both preparation and stamina. While scenic, the ocean along the trail is also cold, rough, and unforgiving. Use caution, as multiple people have been swept out to sea.

Planning: You can hike the trail anytime between **spring and fall.** Spring is notable for blooming wildflowers. Summer is the most crowded. Fall is the least crowded and often has the most pleasant weather. During winter, the trail can be impassable due to massive surf or flooding streams.

Most hikers **begin at the Mattole River** and head south so that you are hiking with the wind at your back, rather than in your face. Allow **three days** and **two nights** to complete the trail, hiking around eight miles a day. Be prepared to walk on sand, cobblestones, and boulders. Plan on carrying in everything you'll need (tents, sleeping bags, equipment, food, and water). Carry it all (including any trash) back out to keep the area wild. There are creeks every 1.5-2 miles along the trail, but you need to purify the water before drinking it.

This is a wilderness hike, so there are few signs. You'll mostly just be hiking the beach except at a few spots. Two sections of the trail are impassable at high tide: The first is from Sea Lion Gulch to Randall Creek, and the second is from south of Big Flat down to Gitchell Creek. It's critical that you **consult a tide chart** and manage your time to make sure you pass through these areas of the trail during low tide.

the park, locals sometimes shoot guns at night here.

From Fort Bragg, drive 25 miles north on Highway 1 to Rockport. Usal Beach is accessible from a dirt road that leaves Highway 1 three miles north of Rockport. Turn left on an unmarked road at mile marker 90.88.

SHELTER COVE

Get a taste of the Lost Coast in Shelter Cove, a fishing community with a scattering of restaurants and accommodations and access to the shoreline.

Black Sand Beach

One of the most beautiful and accessible features of the Lost Coast, the 3.5-mile **Black Sand Beach** (King Range National Conservation Area, www.blm.gov) is named for its unusually dark sand and stones, which contrast with the deep-blue ocean water and the towering King Range Mountains in the background. The main beach parking lot has interpretive panels about the region as well as bathrooms and a drinking fountain. It's just north of the town of Shelter Cove; to get there, follow Shelter Cove Road and then take a right onto Beach Road, which dead-ends at Black Sand Beach. The long walk across the dark sands to either Horse Creek or Gitchell Creek is relatively easy. This beach also serves as the south end of the Lost Coast Trail.

Cape Mendocino Lighthouse

At Mal Coombs Park, the 43-foot tower of the **Cape Mendocino Lighthouse** (www.

Dogs are allowed on the trail as long as they are under voice control or on a leash. Dogs should be outfitted with booties so that their paws don't get scraped by the rocks on the trail.

Transportation: You'll need to park a vehicle at either end of the trail. Parking at the Mattole Trailhead is free. (There have been vehicle break-ins, so don't leave valuables in your car.) There's also free parking at Black Sand Beach at the southern end of the trail. The drive between the two trailheads is 1 hour and 45 minutes. Or leave your car in Shelter Cove and contact **Lost Coast Adventures** (707/986-9895, http://lostcoastadventures.com, $85/person) for a ride.

Permits: Hikers need a free backcountry permit that also doubles as a fire permit. Reserve a permit online at www.recreation.gov ($10) or get a permit at a self-service box at the trailheads, at the King Range office (768 Shelter Cove Rd., Whitethorn, 707/986-5400, 8am-4:30pm Mon.-Fri.), or at the Bureau of Land Management (BLM) Arcata Field Office (1695 Heindon Rd., Arcata, 707/825-2300, www.blm.gov, 7:45am-4:30pm Mon.-Fri.).

Bear canisters: Bear canisters ($5) are mandatory for storing food and scented items while on the trail. They can be rented near the Mattole Trailhead from the **Petrolia General Store** (40 Sherman Rd., Petrolia, 707/629-3694). They're also available in Shelter Cove at the BLM Whitethorn Office (768 Shelter Cove Rd., 707/986-5400,) or in Arcata at the BLM Arcata Field Office (1695 Heindon Rd., 707/825-2300).

Camping: The **Mattole Campground** (end of Lighthouse Rd., 707/825-2300, www.blm.gov, $8) has 14 first-come, first-served sites that allow you to camp near the Mattole Trailhead the night before heading out. There are no developed campgrounds or facilities along the trail. Dispersed camping is allowed at Cooksie Creek, Randall Creek, Big Creek, Big Flat Creek, Buck Creek, Shipman Creek, and Gitchell Creek.

Maps: Before heading to the area, get your hands on a copy of Wilderness Press's Lost Coast Map (www.wildernesspress.com, $7.46). Check trail conditions by visiting the U.S. Department of the Interior website (www.blm.gov) and searching "Lost Coast Trail." More information is available at the King Range Information Line (707/825-2300).

lighthousefriends.com, tours 11am-3pm daily Memorial Day-Labor Day) is quiet and dark. It began life on Cape Mendocino—a 400-foot cliff that marks the westernmost point of California—in 1868. In 1951 the tower was abandoned in favor of a light on a pole, and in 1999 the tower was moved to Shelter Cove, becoming a museum in 2000. When docents are available, you can take a tour of the lighthouse. The original first-order Fresnel lens is now on display in nearby Ferndale.

Sports and Recreation
HIKING
For a great hike, take the **King Crest Trail,** a mountain hike from the southern Saddle Mountain Trailhead to stunning King Peak and on to the North Slide Peak Trailhead. A good, solid, 10-mile one-day round-trip can be done from either trailhead. To reach Saddle Mountain Trailhead from Shelter Cove, drive up Shelter Cove Road and turn left onto King Peak Road. Bear left on Saddle Mountain Road and turn left on a spur road to the trailhead. Only high-clearance, four-wheel-drive vehicles are recommended.

Accessible from the Saddle Mountain Trailhead, **Buck Creek Trail** includes an infamous grade, descending more than 3,000 vertical feet on an old logging road to the beach.

An arduous but gorgeous loop trail, the eight-mile **Hidden Valley-Chinquapin-Lost Coast Loop Trail** can be done in one day, or in two days with a stop at water-accessible Nick's Camp. Access it by driving out of Shelter Cove and turning right onto Chemise

Mountain Road. The trailhead will be less than a mile on your right.

FISHING

The Lost Coast is a natural fishing haven. The harbor at Shelter Cove offers charter services for ocean fishing. Kevin Riley of **Outcast Sportfishing** (Shelter Cove, 707/223-0368, www.outcastsportfish.com, Apr.-Sept., $225 pp per day) can help plan a charter fishing trip chasing whatever is in season. The cost includes gear, tackle, and filleting and packaging your fish at the end of the day, but you must bring your own lunch. A reputable charter service is **Shelter Cove Sport Fishing** (707/923-1668, www.codking.com, fishing trips $175-250 pp), offering excursions to hunt halibut, albacore, salmon, or rockfish. The largest kayak fishing event on the west coast is **Gimme Shelter** (www.norcalkayakanglers. com, May).

SURFING

Big Flat is a legendary surf spot about eight miles north of Shelter Cove on the Lost Coast Trail. While the hike in is challenging, hard-core surfers will find it worth the effort. Local surfers are very protective of this break: Even a writer for *National Geographic Adventure* who wrote about the break refused to name it for fear of retaliation. He referred to it as "Ghost Point." Be careful: Big Flat is in the middle of nowhere, and help is a ways off.

Food

The **Delgada Pizza and Bakery** (Inn of the Lost Coast, 205 Wave St., 707/986-7672, https://innofthelostcoast.com, 4pm-9pm daily, $9-30) is the place for pizza and pasta. The appropriately named Lost Coast Pizza is a favorite. Bottled beer and wine complements your meal. This is a small place with just one table inside and three tables outside. Next door, go for coffee, breakfast, or a sandwich at the **Fish Tank Espresso Gallery** (205 Wave Dr., 707/986-7850, 7am-2pm Thurs.-Tues.).

Mario's Marina Bar (53 Machi Rd., 707/986-7600, http://mariosofsheltercove. com, 4pm-11pm Mon.-Thurs., 4pm-midnight Fri., noon-midnight Sat., 10am-11pm Sun.) is the only bar in Shelter Cove. They do a full breakfast on Sunday mornings (10am-2pm).

Accommodations

Shelter Cove offers several nice motels for those who aren't up for roughing it in the wilderness overnight. **The Tides Inn of Shelter Cove** (59 Surf Point, 707/986-7900 or 888/998-4337, www.sheltercovetidesinn. com, $170-220) has standard rooms as well as luxurious suites. The suites come with fireplaces and full kitchens. All rooms face the sea, which is only steps from the inn. The Tides Inn is within walking distance of the airstrip, local shops, and restaurants.

The **Inn of the Lost Coast** (205 Wave Dr., 707/986-7521 or 888/570-9676, www. innofthelostcoast.com, $225-345) has an array of large, airy rooms and suites with stellar views to suit even luxurious tastes. While all rooms take in the coastline, the corner king bedrooms are the most popular.

The **Cliff House at Shelter Cove** (141 Wave Dr., 707/986-7344, www. cliffhouseatsheltercove.com, $225-250) is perched atop the bluffs overlooking the black-sand beaches. Only two suites are available; they're perfect for a romantic vacation or family getaway. Each has a full kitchen, living room, bedroom, gas fireplace, and satellite TV.

Camping

There are developed campsites in the King Range National Conservation Area with amenities like restrooms, grills, fire rings, picnic tables, bear boxes, and potable water. For developed camping in Shelter Cove, the **Shelter Cove RV Campground** (492 Machi Rd., Whitethorn, 707/986-7474, RVs $45, tents $35) is just feet away from the airport and has views of the ocean. They have a deli and store (grill 10am-5pm daily) on-site so you don't have to bring all your own food.

Transportation and Services

To reach Shelter Cove from U.S. 101 North, take the second Garberville exit. After exiting, look for the Shelter Cove signs and turn west on Briceland Road, which becomes Shelter Cove Road. Though the trip on Shelter Cove Road is just 23 miles, it takes an hour because it's windy and goes down to one lane at one section.

Pilots can fly into the **Shelter Cove Airport** (707/986-7447, www.sheltercove-ca.gov) if weather conditions cooperate. There are live webcams on the airport's website to check the current weather.

There are no medical facilities in Shelter Cove, but emergency services are coordinated through the **Shelter Cove Fire Department** (9126 Shelter Cove Rd., Whitethorn, 707/986-7507, www.sheltercove-ca.gov). The nearest hospital with an emergency room is **Redwood Memorial Hospital** (3300 Renner Dr., Fortuna, 707/725-3361, www.stjoehumboldt.org).

KING RANGE NATIONAL CONSERVATION AREA

The **King Range National Conservation Area** encompasses the northern section of the Lost Coast. Here, King Peak rises more than 4,000 feet from the sea in less than three miles. It's also home to the most popular version of the **Lost Coast Trail:** a 24-mile backpacking excursion along the region's wild beaches that begins at the mouth of the Mattole River and traverses beaches right by the ocean to end at Shelter Cove's Black Sand Beach.

Trails in the Kings Range National Conservation Area near Shelter Cove include **Rattlesnake Ridge, Kinsey Ridge, Spanish Ridge,** and **Lightning.** Before heading to the area, try to obtain a copy of Wilderness Press's Lost Coast Map (www.wildernesspress.com).

Mattole Road

Mattole Road, a narrow, mostly paved two-lane road, affords views of remote ranchland, unspoiled forests, and a few short miles of barely accessible cliffs and beaches. It's one of the few paved, drivable routes that allow you to view the Lost Coast from your car (the other is Shelter Cove Road, farther south). In sunny weather, the vistas are spectacular. This road also serves as access to the even smaller tracks out to the trails and campgrounds of the Sinkyone Wilderness. The most common way to get to Mattole Road is from the Victorian village of Ferndale, where you take a right on Ocean Avenue and follow the signs toward the community of Petrolia.

Mattole Beach

At the northern end of the Lost Coast, **Mattole Beach** (end of Lighthouse Rd., 707/825-2300, www.blm.gov) is a broad length of sand that's perfect for an easy, contemplative stroll. It's also popular for picnicking and fishing. Mattole Beach is the northern entry point to the Lost Coast Trail, and the start of a shorter, six-mile round-trip day hike to the **Punta Gorda Lighthouse.** The lighthouse was built in 1911 after the coast and its rocks caused multiple shipwrecks. It was shut down in 1951 due to high maintenance costs.

To reach Mattole Beach from U.S. 101, take the Garberville, Honeydew, or Ferndale exits. Follow the signs to Petrolia on Mattole Road. Turn off Mattole Road onto Lighthouse Road, which is south of the Mattole River Bridge. Follow Lighthouse Road for five miles to the beach.

Camping

Developed campsites in the King Range National Conservation Area (no permit required) include amenities like restrooms, grills, fire rings, picnic tables, bear boxes, and potable water. Campgrounds are open year-round. Reservations are not available but the odds of getting a site are pretty good, given the small number of people who come here, even in high season. Some of the larger BLM camping areas (707/986-5400, www.ca.blm.gov) are **Wailaki** (Chemise Mountain Rd., 13 sites, $8), **Nadelos** (Chemise Mountain Rd., tents only, 8 sites, $8), **Tolkan** (King Peak Rd., 5 RV sites,

4 tent sites, $8), and **Horse Mountain** (King Peak Rd., 9 sites, no water, $5). Trailers and RVs (up to 24 feet) are allowed at most sites except Nadelos. If you are driving an RV, check road conditions beforehand.

There is a campground at **Mattole Beach** (end of Lighthouse Rd., 707/825-2300, www.blm.gov, $8) with 14 first-come, first-served sites for those who are preparing to hike the Lost Coast Trail.

FERNDALE

Ferndale was built in the 19th century by Scandinavian immigrants who came to California to farm. Little has changed since the immigrants constructed their fanciful gingerbread Victorian homes and shops. Many cows still munch grass in the dairy pastures that surround the town.

The main sight in Ferndale is the town itself, which has been designated a historical landmark. Ferndale is all Victorian, all the time: Ask about the building you're in and you'll be told all about its specific architectural style, its construction date, and its original occupants. Main Street's shops, galleries, inns, and restaurants are all set into scrupulously maintained and restored late-19th-century buildings, and even the public restrooms are housed in a small Victorian-esque structure.

Sights

The **Ferndale History Museum** (515 Shaw St., 707/786-4466, www.ferndale-museum.org, 11am-4pm Wed.-Sat., 1pm-4pm Sun., $1), one block off Main Street, tells the story of the town. Life-size dioramas depict period life in a Victorian home, and an array of antique artifacts brings history to life. Downstairs, the implements of rural coast history vividly display the reality that farmers and artisans faced in the preindustrial era. The museum owns its own seismograph and records the many earthquakes that occur near town.

To cruise farther back into the town's history, wander into the **Ferndale Cemetery** (Bluff St.). Well-tended tombstones and mausoleums wend up the hillside behind the town. Genealogists will love reading the scrupulously maintained epitaphs that tell the human history of the region.

Beaches

Ferndale locals love that they have their own beach just five miles outside of their quaint village. West of Ferndale, the **Centerville County Park and Beach** (4000 Centerville Rd., 707/445-7651, www.humboldtgov.org, 5am-11:45pm daily, free) stretches for an impressive nine miles and is home to a winter congregation of tundra swans. You can drive your four-wheel-drive vehicle on the sand, ride a horse, or build a big beach bonfire at night here.

Entertainment and Events

Ferndale is a quiet town where the sidewalks roll up early, but for visitors who like to be out after 6pm, there are a few options. The **Ferndale Repertory Theater** (447 Main St., 707/786-5483, www.ferndalerep.org, $13-18), the oldest and largest of the North Coast's community theaters, puts on a number of shows each year. Some are suitable for the whole family, like *Annie*, while others, including *In the Next Room (Or the Vibrator Play)*, feature more adult subject matter.

The Palace (353 Main St., 707/786-4165, 11am-1am Mon.-Thurs., 11am-1:30am Fri., 10am-1:30am Sat.-Sun.) is the local bar with pool tables, shuffleboard, and a jukebox.

Ferndale has hosted the **Humboldt County Fair** (1250 5th St., 707/786-9511, www.humboldtcountyfair.org, Aug., adults $8, seniors $6, children $5) since 1896. For 10 days, the old-fashioned fair hosts livestock exhibits, horse racing, competitions, a carnival, nightly musical entertainment, and a variety of shows for kids and adults.

Every Memorial Day weekend, moving sculptures race 42 miles in three days from Arcata's plaza to Ferndale's Main Street. It's the **Kinetic Grand Championship Sculpture Race** (www.kineticgrandchampionship.com, May).

Shopping

Ferndale's Main Street makes for an idyllic morning stroll. The Victorian storefronts house antiques stores, jewelry shops, clothing boutiques, and art galleries. Ferndale is also a surprisingly good place to buy a hat.

The **Golden Gait Mercantile** (421 Main St., 707/786-4891, www.goldengaitmercantile. com, 10am-5pm Mon.-Sat., noon-4pm Sun.) has it all: antiques, candies, gourmet foodstuffs, clothing, hats, souvenirs, and more. Antiques and collectibles tend to be small and reasonably priced.

Silva's Fine Jewelry (400 Ocean Ave., 707/786-4425 or 888/589-1011, www. silvasjewelry.com, 8am-9pm daily), on the bottom floor of the Victorian Inn, is not a place for the faint of wallet. But the jewels, both contemporary and antique, are classically gorgeous.

The **Blacksmith Shop** (455 Main St., 707/786-4216, www.ferndaleblacksmith.com, 9:30am-5pm daily) displays a striking collection of useful art made by top blacksmiths and glassblowers from around the country. The array of jewelry, furniture, kitchen implements, fireplace tools, and metal defies description.

Food

Tucked into the bottom floor of the Victorian Inn, the **VI Restaurant & Tavern** (400 Ocean Ave., 707/786-4950, https:// victorianvillageinn.com, 8am-10am, 11:30am-3pm, and 4:30pm-9pm Tues.-Sun., 8am-10am and 4:30pm-9pm Mon., $12-36) feels like a spruced-up Western saloon. Perch yourself at the bar for casual options like fish-and-chips or sit down at a table for sophisticated dinner entrées like Portuguese paella or cold water lobster. Sundays are prime rib nights, complete with piano music.

Locals come from as far away as Eureka to dine at the restaurant at the **Hotel Ivanhoe** (315 Main St., 707/786-9000, http://hotel-ivanhoe.com, 5pm-9pm Thurs.-Sun., bar open from 4pm Thurs.-Sun., $16-37), where it's all about the hearty homemade Italian dishes

and friendly personal service. A more casual Italian dining experience can be had at the **Ferndale Pizza Co.** (607 Main St., 707/786-4345, 11:30am-9pm Tues.-Thurs., 11:30am-9:30pm Fri.-Sat., noon-9pm Sun., $16-21).

For breakfast, stop in at local favorite **Poppa Joe's** (409 Main St., 707/786-4180, 6am-2pm Mon.-Fri., 6am-noon Sat.-Sun., $5.50-9). The interior is dim and narrow, but the breakfast and lunch offerings are delicious.

Valley Grocery (339 Main St., 707/786-9515, 7am-10pm daily) stocks staples and maintains a deli; it's a perfect last stop on the way out to a beach picnic. Don't forget to drop in at the heavenly candy store **Sweetness and Light** (554 Main St., 707/786-4403 or 800/547-8180, www.sweetnessandlight.com, 10am-5pm Mon.-Fri., 11am-4pm Sat.).

Accommodations

In Ferndale, lodgings tend to be Victorian-style inns, mostly bed-and-breakfasts. Guests of the **Shaw House Inn** (703 Main St., 707/786-9958 or 800/557-7429, www. shawhouse.com, $142-275) must walk a block or two to get to the heart of downtown Ferndale, but the compensation is a spacious garden on the inn's grounds. Huge shade trees and perfectly positioned garden benches make a lovely spot to sit and enjoy the serene beauty. The inn has eight rooms and three common parlor areas. A lush morning breakfast fortifies guests.

The historic ★ **Victorian Inn** (400 Ocean Ave., 707/786-4949 or 888/589-1808, www. victorianvillageinn.com, $139-359) is an imposing structure at the corner that also houses Silva's Fine Jewelry. The inn comprises 13 rooms, all decorated with antique furnishings, luxurious linens, and pretty knickknacks. For a special treat, rent the Ira Russ Suite, a spacious room with a tower alcove that takes in the town below. A full hot breakfast is served downstairs.

In a town full of history, the **Hotel Ivanhoe** (315 Main St., 707/786-9000, www. ivanhoe-hotel.com, $95-145) is the oldest extant hostelry. Plaques on the building's exterior describe its rich legacy. The four rooms are done in rich colors that evoke the Western-Victorian atmosphere of the original hotel.

An inexpensive option is the **Redwood Suites** (332 Ocean Ave., 707/786-5000 or 888/589-1863, www.redwoodsuites.com, $120-185). Only a block off Main Street, the property has modern rooms that are simple but comfortable. Family suites with full kitchens are available. A stay includes a hot breakfast at the nearby Victorian Inn.

Transportation

Ferndale is not directly accessible from U.S. 101; you must get off U.S. 101 at Fernbridge and then follow Highway 211 south to Ferndale. Mattole Road leads out of town south toward the Sinkyone Wilderness area, while Centerville Road heads out to the beach. Walking provides the best views and feel of the town.

If you need medical care, the **Redwood Memorial Hospital** (3300 Renner Dr., Fortuna, 707/725-3361, www.stjoehumboldt. org) is 10 miles away in Fortuna.

Eureka

The town of Eureka began as a seaward access point to the remote gold mines of the Trinity area. Once settlers realized the value of the redwood trees, the town's logging industry was born.

Visitors can wander the town's five-block-long boardwalk on Humboldt Bay and the charming downtown shopping area, or enjoy the colorful murals and sculptures along the city streets. Outdoors enthusiasts can fish and hike, while history buffs can explore museums, Victorian mansions, and even a working Victorian-era lumber mill.

SIGHTS

For an introduction to Old Town Eureka, take a horse-drawn carriage tour of the historic district with the **Old Town Carriage Co.** (1st St. and F St., 646/591-2058, www. oldtowncarriageco.com, 12:30pm-6:30pm Wed.-Mon., $40-80). The carriage is usually downtown near the gazebo around the small square at 2nd and F Streets. Tours last 25 minutes, 45 minutes, or one hour.

Blue Ox Millworks and Historic Park

Blue Ox Millworks and Historic Park (1 X St., 707/444-3437 or 800/248-4259, www. blueoxmill.com, self-guided tours 9am-5pm Mon.-Fri., 9am-4pm Sat. Apr.-Nov., 9am-5pm Mon.-Fri. Nov.-Apr., adults $12, seniors $11, children $7, children under 6 free, guided tour $12.50 pp) has a working lumber mill, an upscale wood and cabinetry shop, a blacksmith forge, an old-fashioned print shop, a shipbuilding yard, a rose garden, and a historic park. It also has the world's largest collection of human-powered woodworking tools made by the historic Barnes Equipment Company. Today, the rambling buildings are filled with purchased, donated, and rehabbed tools of all kinds. Workshops feature a glassblowing kiln and a darkroom where students can learn nondigital photography methods, making their own photosensitive paper and developing black-and-white and sepia prints.

Visitors to the Blue Ox learn about the real lives and times of craftspeople of the late 1800s and early 1900s as they tour the facilities and examine the equipment. If you ask, you might be allowed to touch and even work a piece of wood of your own. Stop in at the gift shop—a converted lumberjack barracks—to check out the ceramics and woodwork the students have for sale.

Carson Mansion

Gables, turrets, cupolas, and pillars: the **Carson Mansion** (143 M St., www.ingomar.

Clarke Historical Museum

The privately owned **Clarke Historical Museum** (240 E St., 707/443-1947, www. clarkemuseum.org, 10am-6pm Tues.-Sat., 10am-3pm Sun., adults $5, families $10), housed in a regal old bank building, is dedicated to preserving the history of Eureka and the surrounding area. Changing exhibitions illuminate the Native American history of the area as well as the gold rush and logging eras. The Nealis Hall annex displays one of the best collections of Native American artifacts in the state.

Fort Humboldt State Historic Park

Established in 1853 to protect white settlers—particularly gold miners—from the local Native Americans, the original Fort Humboldt lasted only 17 years as a military installation. Today, **Fort Humboldt State Historic Park** (3431 Fort Ave., 707/445-6567, www.parks.ca.gov, 8am-5pm daily, free) gives visitors a glimpse into the lives of 19th-century soldiers and loggers. The original hospital is the only remaining building from the fort; it now serves as a museum. A gravel trail circles the grounds, where interpretive plaques depict the fort's frequently dark history. Come on the third Saturday of the month (May-Sept.) to take a five-minute ride on a steam locomotive.

Sequoia Park Zoo

The **Sequoia Park Zoo** (3414 W St., 707/441-4263, www.sequoiaparkzoo.net, 10am-5pm daily summer, 10am-5pm Tues.-Sun. winter, adults $10, seniors $7, children 3-12 $6) seeks to preserve local species and educate the public about their needs. The Secrets of the Forest exhibit recreates the ecology of a Northern California forest.

Humboldt Botanical Gardens

Humboldt Botanical Gardens (7707 Tompkins Hill Rd., 707/442-5139, www.hbgf. org, 10am-4pm Wed.-Sun. Apr.-Oct., 10am-2pm Wed.-Sat., 11am-3pm Sun. Nov.-Mar.,

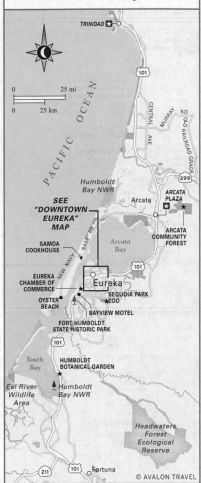

Humboldt Bay

TRINIDAD

PACIFIC OCEAN

0   25 mi
0   25 km

101

CENTRAL AVE

MURRAY RD

OLD RAILROAD GRADE RD

Humboldt Bay NWR

299

SEE "DOWNTOWN EUREKA" MAP

ARCATA PLAZA

Arcata

ARCATA COMMUNITY FOREST

SAMOA COOKHOUSE

Arcata Bay

BASE RD

NEW NAVY

101

EUREKA CHAMBER OF COMMERCE

Eureka

SEQUOIA PARK ZOO

OYSTER BEACH

BAYVIEW MOTEL

FORT HUMBOLDT STATE HISTORIC PARK

101

South Bay

HUMBOLDT BOTANICAL GARDEN

Eel River Wildlife Area

Humboldt Bay NWR

Headwaters Forest Ecological Reserve

211   101   Fortuna

© AVALON TRAVEL

org, closed to the public) has all these architectural flourishes. The elaborate three-story, 18-room Victorian mansion was built by William Carson in 1884 and 1885 after he struck it rich in the lumber business. Almost demolished in the 1940s, it was purchased and renovated by the Ingomar Club, which now uses it for private dinner parties. It's touted as one of the most photographed buildings in the country. The building and grounds are not open to the public, but you can take photos.

Downtown Eureka

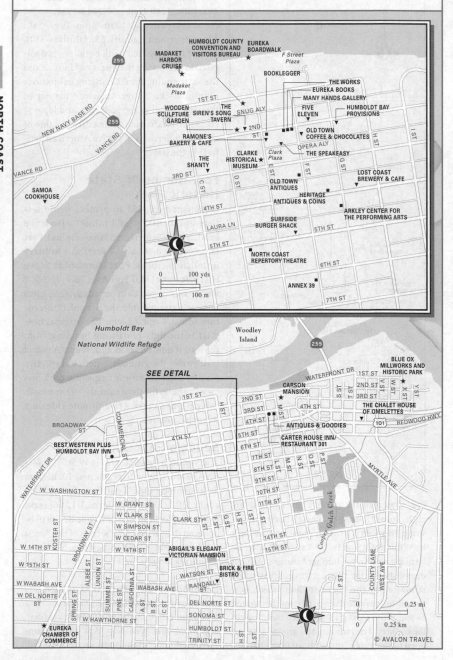

MADAKET HARBOR CRUISE

HUMBOLDT COUNTY CONVENTION AND VISITORS BUREAU

EUREKA BOARDWALK

F Street Plaza

Madaket Plaza

BOOKLEGGER

THE WORKS
EUREKA BOOKS
MANY HANDS GALLERY

1ST ST

WOODEN SCULPTURE GARDEN

THE SIREN'S SONG TAVERN

SNUG ALY

FIVE ELEVEN

HUMBOLDT BAY PROVISIONS

2ND

RAMONE'S BAKERY & CAFE

OLD TOWN COFFEE & CHOCOLATES

OPERA ALY

THE SHANTY

CLARKE HISTORICAL MUSEUM

Clark Plaza

THE SPEAKEASY

3RD ST

LOST COAST BREWERY & CAFE

OLD TOWN ANTIQUES

4TH ST

HERITAGE ANTIQUES & COINS

ARKLEY CENTER FOR THE PERFORMING ARTS

LAURA LN

SURFSIDE BURGER SHACK

5TH ST

5TH ST

NORTH COAST REPERTORY THEATRE

6TH ST

0   100 yds
0   100 m

ANNEX 39

7TH ST

Humboldt Bay National Wildlife Refuge

Woodley Island

255

SEE DETAIL

WATERFRONT DR

BLUE OX MILLWORKS AND HISTORIC PARK

1ST ST

2ND ST

3RD ST

1ST ST

CARSON MANSION

THE CHALET HOUSE OF OMELETTES

BROADWAY ST

4TH ST

ANTIQUES & GOODIES

101

REDWOOD HWY

BEST WESTERN PLUS HUMBOLDT BAY INN

5TH ST

6TH ST

CARTER HOUSE INN/ RESTAURANT 301

7TH ST

8TH ST

9TH ST

10TH ST

11TH ST

MYRTLE AVE

W WASHINGTON ST

W GRANT ST

W CLARK ST

W SIMPSON ST

W CEDAR ST

CLARK ST

Cooper Gulch Creek

KOSTER ST

W 14TH ST

W 14TH ST

14TH ST

15TH ST

ABIGAIL'S ELEGANT VICTORIAN MANSION

W 15TH ST

W WABASH AVE

W DEL NORTE ST

BRICK & FIRE BISTRO

WATSON ST

RANDALL ST

WABASH AVE

DEL NORTE ST

SONOMA ST

HUMBOLDT ST

EUREKA CHAMBER OF COMMERCE

W HAWTHORNE ST

TRINITY ST

COUNTY LANE

WEST AVE

0   0.25 mi
0   0.25 km

© AVALON TRAVEL

adults $8, seniors and children $5) celebrates the ecosystems of Humboldt County. The 44-acre site includes native plants, ornamental plants, and plants that grow in riparian regions.

ENTERTAINMENT AND EVENTS

Bars

The biggest and most popular bar is the **Lost Coast Brewery & Café** (617 4th St., 707/445-4480, www.lostcoast.com, 11am-10pm Sun.-Thurs., 11am-11pm Fri.-Sat.). The tall cream-and-green building is perched by itself on the main drag, easy to spot as you pass through town. The brewery draws crowds, especially on weekends, and makes popular microbrews including Great White and Downtown Brown, which are on tap. Try the tasty brewpub-style food and a few of the delicious beers. Free tours are available at Lost Coast's off-site brewery (1600 Sunset Dr., www.lostcoast.com).

The Speakeasy (411 Opera Alley, 707/444-2244, 4pm-11pm Mon.-Thurs., 4pm-1am Fri.-Sat.) is the place to go for tasty cocktails. This dark, narrow bar, which sometimes has live music, serves up Southern-style drinks, including a great mint julep.

One of the best dive bars on the North Coast, **The Shanty** (213 3rd St., 707/444-2053, noon-2am Mon.-Sat., 9am-2am Sun.) impresses with friendly clientele, a superbly curated jukebox, and a lot of eclectic character. Head outdoors to play table tennis or pool or smoke a cigarette. The extended happy hour (4pm-7pm Mon.-Fri., noon-4pm Sat.-Sun.) offers top-shelf beers and liquors and rock-bottom prices.

The cool, worn-feeling Victorian space at **The Siren's Song Tavern** (325 2nd St., 707/442-8778, www.sirenssongtavern.com, 3pm-10pm Tues.-Thurs., 3pm-midnight Fri.-Sat.) hosts bands that perform on a rug in front of the window. Siren's Song has a superb craft beer list including 18 brews on tap.

Live Music

The **Arkley Center for the Performing Arts** (412 G St., 707/442-1956 or 888/859-8797, www.atlpublishing.com) is the home of the Eureka Symphony and North Coast Dance. The elegant venue, with its striking mural of musicians and dancers on the back of the building, also hosts rock, country, and jazz acts.

Events

Music lovers flock to Eureka each year for a number of big music festivals. One of the biggest is the **Redwood Coast Jazz Festival** (various venues around town, 707/445-3378, www.rcmfest.org, Apr., $25-85). For four days in spring, music lovers can enjoy every style of jazz imaginable, including Dixieland, zydeco, and big band. The festival also features dance lessons and contests.

Experience what Eureka was like during its logging heyday at the **Dolbeer Steam Donkey Days** (Fort Humboldt State Historic Park, 3431 Fort Ave., 707/445-6567, www. parks.ca.gov, Apr.). This two-day event features working logging equipment, train rides, and logging skill competitions.

The **Kinetic Grand Championship** (707/786-3443, http://kineticgrandchampionship. com, Memorial Day weekend) is a pedal-powered moving sculpture race that originates in Arcata and ends in Ferndale. The second day of this event takes place on Eureka's waterfront.

SHOPPING

Eureka boasts the largest California antiques scene north of the Bay Area. **Annex 39** (610 F St., 707/443-1323, noon-5:30pm Tues.-Sat.) specializes in vintage linens and laundry products and also has a great selection of art deco and midcentury modern pieces. **Heritage Antique & Coins** (521 4th St., 707/444-2908, 10am-5pm Tues.-Fri., 10am-3pm Sat.) is a coin shop that also carries jewelry and Native American artifacts. Generalists will love rooting through **Old Town Antiques** (318 F St., 707/442-3235, 10:30am-6pm Mon.-Sat.).

For an afternoon of shopping, head down toward the water to 2nd Street. Most of the buildings are historic, and you might find an unassuming brass plaque describing the famous brothel that once occupied what is now a toy store. Literature lovers have a nice selection of independent bookstores: **Eureka Books** (426 2nd St., 707/444-9593, www.eurekabooksellers.com, 10am-6pm daily) has a big, airy room in which to browse a selection of new and used books. **Booklegger** (402 2nd St., at E St., 707/445-1344, 10am-5:30pm Mon.-Sat., 11am-4pm Sun.) is a small but well-organized new-and-used bookshop that specializes in antique books.

Galleries and gift shops abound. **Many Hands Gallery** (438 2nd St., 707/445-0455, www.manyhandsgallery.net, 10am-9pm Mon.-Sat., 10am-6pm Sun.) represents approximately 100 local artisans and also displays work from national and international artists cooperatives, fair-trade organizations, and commercial importers. You'll find plenty of humor and whimsy, and prices range from 10 cents to $10,000.

The Works (434 2nd St., 707/442-8121, www.theworkseureka.com, 11am-6pm daily) has been providing Humboldt County music fans with vinyl records and CDs since 1971.

SPORTS AND RECREATION
Fishing
Eureka is a serious fishing destination. Oodles of both ocean- and river-fishing opportunities are available, and several fishing tournaments are held each year. In California, you must have a valid state fishing license to fish in either the ocean or the rivers. Check with your charter service or guide to be sure they provide a day license with your trip. If they don't, you will have to get your own.

For deep-sea fishing, **Greenwater Fishing Adventures** (707/845-9588, www.eurekafishing.net, fishing trips $170-250, crabbing $75) heads out on the 36-foot *Shellback* to catch salmon, rockfish, halibut, tuna, and crab. **Full Throttle Sportfishing** (601 Startare Dr., 707/498-7473, www.fullthrottlesportfishing.com, $180-275) supplies all needed tackle and can take you out to fish for salmon, rockfish, tuna, or halibut. Trips last all day, and most leave at 6:30am. If you're launching your own boat, public launches are the **Samoa Boat Ramp** (New Navy Base Rd., 707/445-7651, www.humboldtgov.org, 5am-11:45pm daily) and the **Fields Landing Boat Ramp** (Railroad Ave., 707/445-7651, www.humboldtgov.org, 5am-midnight daily).

Eureka has good spots for pier fishing. In town, try the K Street Pier, the pier at the east end of Commercial Street, or the pier at the end of Del Norte Street. Farther north, the north jetty (Hwy. 255, across Samoa Bridge) also has a public pier open for fishing.

Bird-Watching
The national, state, and county parks lacing the area are ideal bird-watching havens. The **Humboldt Bay National Wildlife Refuge Complex** (1020 Ranch Rd., Loleta, 707/733-5406, www.fws.gov) encompasses several wildlife-refuge sites where visitors are welcome. At the Salmon Creek Unit, you'll find the **Richard J. Guadagno Headquarters and Visitors Center** (8am-5pm daily), which is an excellent starting place for a number of wildlife walks. To get to the visitors center from U.S. 101, take the exit for Hookton heading north and turn left onto Eel River Drive. Take the first right onto Ranch Road, and you'll find the visitors center parking lot.

Hiking and Biking
There is a vast system of trails in the state and national parks, and the city of Eureka maintains a number of multiuse biking and hiking trails as well. Most familiar is the Old Town Boardwalk, part of the **Waterfront Trail** that comprises disconnected sections along Humboldt Bay. **Sequoia Park Trail** begins at the Sequoia Park Zoo and wends through redwood forests, past a duck pond, and through a meadow. This trail is paved and friendly for strollers and wheelchairs. The unpaved **Elk**

River Trail (end of Hilfiker Ln.) stretches for one mile through wild meadows along the coast. **Cooper Gulch Trail** is more a sedate stroll than a strenuous hike, circling the Cooper Gulch park playing fields.

Kayaking, Rafting, and Stand-Up Paddleboarding

The water is cold, but getting out on it in a kayak can be exhilarating. Guided paddles, lessons, rentals, and kayak-fishing trips are available through **Humboats Kayak Adventures** (Woodley Island Marina, 601 Startare Dr., 707/443-5157, www.humboats. com, canoe, kayak, and SUP rentals $30-110, tours $55-95). Guides lead a huge variety of tours, from serene paddles in the harbor suitable for children to a kayaking trip among the Avenue of the Giants redwoods.

River rafters and kayakers have great opportunities for rapids fun on the inland Klamath and Trinity Rivers. **Bigfoot Rafting Company** (Willow Creek, 530/629-2263, www.bigfootrafting.com, adults $89, children $79) leads half-day, full-day, and multiday trips on both rivers as well as on the Cal-Salmon and Smith Rivers. Experts can take inflatable kayaks down the Class IV rapids, while newcomers can find a gentle paddle.

Harbor Cruises

For a great introduction to Eureka and Humboldt Bay, book a tour on the *Madaket* (dock at end of C St., 707/445-1910, www. humboldtbaymaritimemuseum.com, May-Sept.), the oldest continuously operating passenger vessel in the country, with the smallest licensed bar in California. The ferry, built in 1910, offers three tours: a narrated **history cruise** (75 minutes, adults $22, seniors and children 13-17 $18, children 5-12 $12, children under 5 free), a **cocktail cruise** (one hour, $10), or a **wildlife tour** (1.5 hours, adults $26, seniors and children 13-17 $22, children 5-12 $12, children under 5 free). The historic cruise follows a scenic 8.5-mile loop in Humboldt Bay and the adjoining Arcata Bay. Passengers learn about the area's history and the stories behind local landmarks, and visit an egret colony.

Drag Racing

For a down-home American experience, take in a car race at the **Samoa Drag Strip** (New Navy Base Rd., 707/845-5755, www. samoadragstrip.com, May-Sept., adults $10, children under 13 free). The 0.25-mile track is on the Samoa Peninsula. Special nights feature Harley motorcycles or diesel trucks.

FOOD

Breakfast

One of the older restaurants in downtown Eureka, ★ **The Chalet House of Omelettes** (1935 5th St., 707/442-0333, http://thechaleteureka.com, 7am-3pm daily, $8-11) has been serving delicious omelets in a homey atmosphere since 1975. The build-your-own-omelet (four ingredients and three eggs, $10.25) is a favorite. The Chalet Special Omelet is recommended, filled with bacon, cheese, and avocado slices. Attentive servers fill your cup of coffee to the brim for the duration of your meal.

Bakeries and Cafés

Ramone's Bakery & Café (209 E St., 707/445-2923, http://ramonesbakery.com, 7am-6pm Mon.-Fri., 8am-5pm Sat., 8am-4pm Sun.) is a local chain, selling fresh baked goods and candies. Enjoy a fresh cup of coffee roasted in-house with a Danish or scone, or get a whole tart, cake, or loaf of bread to take away.

Old Town Coffee & Chocolates (211 F St., 707/445-8600, http://oldtowncoffeeeureka. com, 7am-8pm Sun.-Mon., 7am-9pm Tues.-Thurs., 7am-10pm Fri.-Sat.) does more than caffeinate their customers. They also sell chocolate and fudge made on-site, as well as bagels, waffles, wraps, and grilled cheese sandwiches. Many evenings feature live music, open mics, or book readings.

American

The ★ **Samoa Cookhouse** (511 Vance Rd.,

Samoa, 707/442-1659, www.samoacookhouse. net, 7am-9pm daily summer, 7am-3pm and 5pm-8pm daily winter, adults $18, children 8-11 $9) is a Eureka institution. Red-checked tablecloths cover long, rough tables to create the atmosphere of a logging-camp dining hall. All-you-can-eat meals are served family-style from huge serving platters. Diners sit on benches and pass the hearty fare down in turn. Think hunks of roast beef, mountains of mashed potatoes, and piles of cooked vegetables for lunch and dinner, or a giant plate of eggs, hash browns, sausage, and toast for breakfast. This is the place to bring your biggest appetite. After dinner, browse the small Historic Logging Museum and gift shop.

Restaurant 301 (301 L St., 800/404-1390, www.carterhouse.com, 5pm-8:30pm daily, $23-47) at the Carter House Inns seems like a big-city spot. The chef creates an ever-changing menu of delectable delicacies, along with tasting menus. Menu options include exotic duck dishes, local seafood preparations, and items from the restaurant's on-site garden. For a treat, try the wine flights suggested with the menus. Restaurant 301 is known for its extensive wine list, with more than 3,400 selections.

A turquoise floor and jade lighting give **Five Eleven** (511 2nd St., 707/268-3852, 5pm-9pm Mon.-Thurs., 5pm-9:30pm Fri.-Sat., 5pm-8pm Sun. summer; 5pm-9:30pm Fri.-Sat., 5pm-9pm Tues.-Thurs. winter; $10-35) a bold, metropolitan feel. The food changes frequently, but the Southern fried chicken and fresh oysters are staples. They also serve specialty craft cocktails, a few choice craft beers, and a wide variety of wines at the long stone bar.

The **Surfside Burger Shack** (445 5th St., 707/268-1295, 11am-7pm Sun.-Mon. and Wed.-Thurs., 11am-8pm Fri.-Sat., $6-8) is nowhere near the ocean, but it does have surfing decor and darn good burgers made from grass-fed Humboldt cows. The classic cheeseburger hits the spot, but the shack also gets creative with the Surfside Sunrise, a burger topped with cheese, bacon, an egg, and maple syrup.

Italian

Brick & Fire Bistro (1630 F St., 707/268-8959, www.brickandfirebistro.com, 11:30am-9pm Mon. and Wed.-Fri., 5pm-9pm Sat.-Sun., $14-22) updates Italian classics with a menu that includes fire-roasted polenta lasagna and pizzas with locally smoked salmon and quail eggs. The wild mushroom cobbler appetizer is one of the most talked-about menu items.

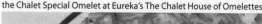
the Chalet Special Omelet at Eureka's The Chalet House of Omelettes

Seafood

Sample the products of Humboldt County at **Humboldt Bay Provisions** (205 G St., 707/672-3850, www.humboldtbayprovisions. com, 3pm-9pm daily, $10-48). Sit at the reclaimed redwood bar where you can nibble on salmon from nearby Blue Lake and slurp tasty oysters from Humboldt Bay while drinking local brews.

ACCOMMODATIONS
Under $150

Originally built by one of the town's founders, **Abigail's Elegant Victorian Mansion** (1406 C St., 707/444-3144, www.eureka-california.com, $135-145) offers an authentic Victorian experience, having retained many of the large home's original fixtures. Each of the two rooms comes with its own story and an astonishing collection of antiques; both have detached bathrooms. Guests can request a tour of Eureka in one of the inn's 1928 Fords. There are a few quirks: no reservations (rooms are first-come, first-served); no breakfast; and no credit cards (the owners only take cash).

If B&Bs aren't your style, get a room at the **Bayview Motel** (2844 Fairfield St., 707/442-1673 or 866/725-6813, www.bayviewmotel. com, $130-220). This hilltop motel has lovely views of Humboldt Bay. Rooms are spacious and decorated in elegant colors and fabrics. You'll find whirlpool suites, free Wi-Fi, cable TV, wet bars, and coffeemakers. If you're traveling with the family, rent a double suite—two rooms with an adjoining door and separate baths. Downtown Eureka is within an easy drive.

$150-250

The ★ **Carter House Inns** (301 L St., 800/404-1390, www.carterhouse.com, $179-595) have a range of accommodations in a cluster of butter-yellow Victorian buildings near the Carson Mansion. The main building has 23 rooms and suites, a number of which have gas fireplaces and soaking tubs. Across the street, a reproduction of a Victorian mansion has six rooms, including a family suite with two bedrooms, while **The Bell Cottage** has three rooms and a full common kitchen. For a splurge, rent **The Carter Cottage**, which has two bathrooms, a deck with a fountain, a soaking tub, and a large den and kitchen area. All guests are treated to a hot breakfast and an afternoon wine and appetizer hour. Dine at the inn's renowned Restaurant 301.

There's no place along the California

a hearty breakfast at the Samoa Cookhouse

coast quite like ★ **Oyster Beach** (865B New Navy Base Rd., 707/834-6555, www. humboldtbaysocialclub.com, $175-295), a set of refurbished buildings on the Samoa Peninsula. The 22-acre property has its own beach on Humboldt Bay and impressive eucalyptus groves. Five units range from The Loft, with reclaimed wood walls, to the Mid-Century Waterfront, mere feet from the bay. Just eight minutes from downtown Eureka, Oyster Beach feels like it's a world away.

★ **Best Western Plus Humboldt Bay** (232 W. 5th St., 707/443-2234, www. humboldtbayinn.com, $185-250) is a pleasant surprise. What sets it apart is its Oasis Spa Area, a tropical-themed courtyard with tiki torches, island music, fire pits, and a hot tub grotto that stand in contrast to the industrial neighborhood location. Within the enclosure are a heated pool, 24-hour fitness center, and billiards table. A complimentary continental breakfast is served daily. An unexpected amenity is an on-site limo and driver that will drive guests to any restaurant in Eureka. The rooms are modern and clean, too.

TRANSPORTATION AND SERVICES

Eureka is on U.S. 101, easily accessed by car from north or south. From Crescent City, Eureka is less than an hour's drive south on U.S. 101.

Driving is the only option if you're not staying downtown. Parking downtown is metered or free on the streets, and not too difficult to find except on holiday or event weekends.

Bus service in and around Eureka is operated by the **Humboldt Transit Authority** (HTA, http://humboldttransit.org, adults $1.70, seniors and children $1.30). The HTA's **Eureka Transit System** (ETS, 707/443-0826, https://humboldttransit.org) runs within town limits, and the **Redwood Transit System** (RTS, 707/443-0826, https:// humboldttransit.org, adults $1.65-5.50, seniors and children $1.40-5) can take you around the area; it runs from Eureka north to Trinidad, south to Scotia, and east to Willow Creek.

Eureka has a small commercial airport, **California Redwood Coast-Humboldt County Airport** (ACV, 3561 Boeing

the Oasis Spa Area at Eureka's Best Western Plus Humboldt Bay

Ave., McKinleyville, 707/839-5401, www. humboldtgov.org), which serves the North Coast region with expensive but convenient flights on United Airlines.

The full-service **St. Joseph Hospital** (2700 Dolbeer St., 707/445-8121, www. stjoehumboldt.org) has an emergency room and an urgent care center.

Arcata

Arcata has a distinctly small-town feel, different from its southern neighbor. The hippie daughter of blue-collar Eureka, Arcata is home to Humboldt State University. Students make up almost half of the city's population, and the town is known for its liberal politics.

Arcata has a lively arts and music scene along with a handful of restaurants that you might expect in a bigger city. It makes a great home base for exploring the wild North Coast.

SIGHTS
★ Arcata Plaza
The heart of downtown is **Arcata Plaza** (9th and G Sts., www.arcatamainstreet.com), which has been the epicenter of town since the 1850s when it was a freight and passenger stop. The park has a William McKinley statue, a couple of palm trees, and a grassy lawn where folks hang out. Circling the plaza are independent restaurants, bars, coffee shops, and stores. The plaza hosts many events, from the Saturday farmers market to the start of the annual Kinetic Grand Championship race.

Arcata Community Forest
The first city-owned forest in California, the 2,134-acre **Arcata Community Forest** (east ends of 11th St., 14th St., and California St., 707/822-5951, www.cityofarcata.org, sunrise-sunset daily) has trails winding through second-growth redwoods, open for hiking, mountain biking, and horseback riding. Just east of the city's downtown and behind Humboldt State University, the forest is an ideal place to stroll between the silent giants, many of which are cloaked in moss, and take in stumps the size of compact cars

and vibrant-green waist-high ferns. The park also has a section with picnic tables and a playground.

ENTERTAINMENT AND EVENTS
Bars
A strip of dive bars lines the edge of Arcata Plaza on 9th Street. The best of the bunch, **The Alibi** (744 9th St., 707/822-3731, www. thealibi.com, 8am-2am daily), dates to the 1920s. The Alibi serves cheap, well-crafted cocktails with infused liquors, including a wide range of Bloody Marys. It also has an extensive breakfast, lunch, and dinner menu with specialty burgers and entrées.

The North Coast is known for its microbrews, and **Dead Reckoning Tavern** (815 J St., 707/630-5008, 2pm-8pm Sun.-Mon., 2pm-10pm Tues.-Thurs., 2pm-11pm Fri.-Sat.) is a great place to try one. They have 34 rotating beers on tap along with one kombucha tap and a root beer tap for non-imbibers. The tavern's back room has a few arcade games and a small record store to enjoy while sipping suds.

Humboldt Brews (856 10th St., 707/826-2739, www.humboldtbrews.com, noon-11pm daily, open until 2am for live music) serves food and 25 beers on tap. This popular hangout has a pool table and an adjacent room that serves as a concert space for midsize national jam bands, indie acts, and reggae outfits.

Richard's Goat Tavern & Tea Room (401 I St., 707/630-5000, http://richardsgoat.com, 3pm-2am Tues.-Sun., 3pm-midnight Mon.) is an oasis of culture and cocktails blocks away from the plaza's dive bar scene. The liquors are house infused, and there's craft beer on tap. The bar has its own tiny theater dubbed the Miniplex, where art house movies are screened and the occasional live act performs.

Live Music

Music legends like Elvis Costello, John Prine, Melissa Etheridge, The Growlers, and Jake Shimabukuro play at Humboldt State University's **John Van Duzer Theatre** (1 Harpst St., 707/826-4411, www.humboldt. edu). Up-and-coming acts typically perform at **The Depot** (University Center, 1 Harpst St., 707/826-4411) and the **West Gym** (top of Union St.).

Cinema

Dating to 1938, the art deco **Arcata Theatre Lounge** (1036 G St., 707/822-1220, www. arcatatheatre.com) screens movies, hosts concerts, and puts on events like Sci-Fi Pint and Pizza Night, where they show old science-fiction movies. The theater seats have been replaced by circular tables and chairs, and the full bar serves food as well as drinks.

A few blocks away, the 1914 **Minor Theatre** (1001 H St., 707/822-3456, www. minortheatre.com) is one of the oldest operating movie theaters in the country, showing independent movies as well as Hollywood films. Enjoy your film with food (from empanadas to pizza), draft beer, and wine served to your seat.

Festivals and Events

Arcata Plaza is the starting line of the **Kinetic Grand Championship** (707/786-3443, http://kineticgrandchampionship.com, Memorial Day weekend), a three-day, 42-mile race featuring human-powered art sculptures that continues to Eureka and Ferndale.

In the plaza is the annual **Arcata Main Street Oyster Festival** (707/822-4500, www.arcatamainstreet.com/oyster-fest, June), which celebrates the local Kumamoto oyster with—you guessed it—oysters. This is the largest one-day event in Humboldt County. There's live music and microbrews to enjoy with the bivalves.

SPORTS AND RECREATION

The 18-hole **Redwood Curtain Disc Golf Course** (accessible from Humboldt State University's Redwood Science Lab, though parking is only available in the lot after 5pm) winds its way through massive redwood trees. On the second hole, the tee is atop a 10-foot-high redwood stump.

For local sports action, get a ticket to see the

Arcata Plaza

Humboldt Crabs (Arcata Ball Park, F St. and 9th St., 707/840-5665, http://humboldtcrabs.com), the oldest continually active collegiate summer baseball team in the country.

Arcata Marsh and Wildlife Sanctuary

One of Arcata's most popular places to take a hike is in a section of the town's wastewater treatment facility. The **Arcata Marsh Interpretive Center** (569 S. G St., 707/826-2359, www.arcatamarsh.org, visitor center: 1pm-5pm Mon., 9am-5pm Tues.-Sun.; grounds: 4am-sunset daily) holds a small museum that explains how the city transformed an industrial wasteland into a 307-acre wildlife sanctuary using Arcata's wastewater. Hike the sanctuary's five miles of hiking and biking paths, or try to spot some of the 270 bird species that use the marsh as a migratory stop.

SHOPPING

Around Arcata Plaza and along H Street are a number of unique stores. Head into **Pacific Paradise** (1087 H St., 707/822-7143, 10am-6pm Mon.-Sat., 10:30am-5:30pm Sun.) to stock up on golf discs, hoodies, tie-dyes, and smoking equipment.

Across the street, the **Tin Can Mailman**

Used & Rare Books Store (1000 H St., 707/822-1307, www.tincanbooks.com, 10am-6pm Sun.-Thurs., 10am-7pm Fri.-Sat.) crams together two floors full of used books. For the latest fiction or memoir, head to **Northtown Books** (957 H St., 707/822-2834, www.northtownbooks.com, 10am-7pm Mon.-Thurs. and Sat., 10am-9pm Fri., noon-5pm Sun.), which also has an extensive magazine collection.

Solutions (858 G St., 707/822-6972, 10am-5:30pm Mon.-Sat.) is the place to pick up hemp clothing, organic bedding, and eco-goods.

A few blocks from the plaza, **Holly Yashi** (1300 9th St., 877/607-8361, www.hollyyashi.com, 10am-6pm Mon.-Sat., noon-5pm Sun.) specializes in niobium jewelry. Niobium is a metal that gains streaks of color after being dipped in an electrically charged bath. Watch artists at work crafting the jewelry in the attached studio.

FOOD

There's a lot of water around Arcata and **Salt Fish House** (761 8th St., 707/630-5300, www.saltfishhouse.com, 11:30am-10pm Tues.-Fri., 4pm-10pm Sat.-Sun., $15-32) always has local sustainable seafood—the cod and chips are a favorite. The weekday happy hour (3pm-5pm Mon.-Fri.) sees fish tacos, raw oysters, grilled oysters, and margaritas at nice prices.

The Alibi

North Coast Breweries

California's North Coast is known for its beer. Local craft beer and microbrews are served in restaurants and line the beer aisles of local supermarkets. One way to taste these beers or sample their smaller batches is to visit a North Coast brewery.

For beer fans, the **Anderson Valley Brewing Company's Tap Room and Brewery** (17700 Hwy. 253, Boonville, 707/895-2337, www.avbc.com, 11am-6pm daily) is worth a visit. With its high ceilings and copper bar, the taproom feels more like an informal tasting room in a winery. The 20 taps serve Anderson Valley favorites like Boont Amber Ale, along with 10 rotating taps of small-batch brews, including a sour stout. Brewery tours (1:30pm and 3pm, $5) are offered when the taproom is open. You can also head outdoors to the brewery's 18-hole disc golf course (8am-6pm daily, free).

Since opening in 1988, the **North Coast Brewing Company** (444 N. Main St., Fort Bragg, 707/964-3400, www.northcoastbrewing.com, 11:30am-10pm Fri.-Sat., 11:30am-9pm Sun.-Thurs.) has expanded to a city block

beers on tap at the Mad River Brewing Company Tasting Room

with the actual brewery, a brewery shop, and a taproom and grill. Head into the popular taproom to try North Coast favorites like the Red Seal Ale or the more potent Brother Thelonious, a Belgian-style abbey ale.

If you crave sustainable suds, visit the **Eel River Brewing Company's Taproom & Grill** (1777 Alamar Way, Fortuna, 707/725-2739, http://eelriverbrewing.com, 11am-11pm daily), where you can sip organic beer made with renewable energy. Drink the Organic IPA or Organic Acai Berry Wheat Ale inside at the taproom's long wooden bar or head out to the adjacent beer garden. Tours (707/764-1772) of the brewing facilities are in the nearby town of Scotia.

The **Lost Coast Brewery & Café** (617 4th St., Eureka, 707/445-4480, www.lostcoast.com, 11am-10pm Sun.-Thurs., 11am-11pm Fri.-Sat.) feels like a local's bar and is filled with people even on weeknights. The brewery's Great White and Lost Coast Pale Ale are the most popular brews, but the smooth Downtown Brown is recommended for darker beer fans. Free half-hour tours are at their brewery (1600 Sunset Dr., Eureka, 707/267-9651).

Fifteen miles from downtown Arcata, the **Mad River Brewing Company Tasting Room** (101 Taylor Way, Blue Lake, 707/668-4151, www.madriverbrewing.com, 11:30am-9pm Sun.-Thurs., 11:30am-10pm Fri.-Sat.) is a favorite with Humboldt County beer drinkers. Not only do they brew award-winning beers like Steelhead Extra Pale Ale and Jamaica Red Ale, they also have tasty pub food, frequent live music, and an outdoor beer garden on sunny days.

A local favorite, **The Redwood Curtain Brewing Company Tasting Room** (550 S. G St., Arcata, 707/826-7222, www.redwoodcurtainbrewing.com, noon-11pm Sun.-Tues., noon-midnight Wed.-Sat.) is in an industrial park a few blocks south of downtown. This unassuming spot is the place to try their Imperial Golden Ale, their award-winning Dusseldorf Altbier, or their creative Cerise Coup, which is aged in a French oak chardonnay barrel and then infused with cherries for six months. Sit at the bar overlooking the brew room or play a game of shuffleboard.

★ **Renata's Creperie and Espresso** (1030 G St., 707/825-8783, 8am-3pm Sun.-Thurs., 8am-9pm Fri.-Sat., $4-12) is the best place to start the day. Their organic buckwheat crepes are artfully decorated with drizzled sauces and well-placed garnishes, and deliver on their promising looks with sweet and savory fillings. Expect a wait on weekends. Renata's is open for dinner on Friday and Saturday nights.

The Big Blue Café (846 G St., 707/826-7578, 8am-3pm Sun.-Thurs., 7am-3pm Fri.-Sat., $6-16) is an appropriately colored diner on Arcata Plaza with a menu that skews toward breakfast basics like omelets, French toast, and breakfast burritos. The organic house coffee is flavorful.

Abruzzi (780 7th St., 707/826-2345, www.abruzziarcata.com, 5pm-9pm Wed.-Sun., $12-40) is the place to go for fine dining. The menu includes free-range chicken dishes, seafood offerings, and classic pastas like Bolognese, primavera, and Alfredo.

A local institution for more than 30 years, ★ **Tomo Japanese Restaurant** (708 9th St., 707/822-1414, www.tomoarcata.com, 11:30am-2pm and 4pm-9pm Mon.-Sat., 4pm-9pm Sun., $10-22) serves sushi rolls and entrées that are as eclectic as its hometown. Get a spicy tofu roll or a unique locally smoked albacore roll. Tomo has a list of sakes, and there's also a full bar.

Arcata locals swear by **Taqueria La Barca** (5201 Carlson Park Dr., 707/822-6669, 10am-8pm Mon.-Fri., $7-11) for the house-made horchata, chile rellenos, and carnitas.

Stop in **Wildberries Marketplace** (747 13th St., 707/822-0095, www.wildberries.com, 6am-10pm daily) to stock up for a picnic. They also have a café, a juice bar, a coffee shop, and a farmers market (3:30pm-6:30pm Tues.). The Arcata Plaza hosts a Saturday **farmers market** (www.humfarm.org, 9am-2pm Sat. Apr.-mid-Nov., 10am-2pm Sat. mid-Nov.-Mar.) that has live music.

ACCOMMODATIONS

Downtown lodging options are limited. The **Hotel Arcata** (708 9th St., 707/826-0217, www.hotelarcata.com, $102-172) has a superb location right on the plaza. The rooms are small, but the bathrooms have claw-foot tubs outfitted with showerheads. The hallways are decorated with framed historic photos of Arcata Plaza and other local landmarks. A stay includes complimentary Wi-Fi and continental breakfast. Secure a free pass to the Arcata Community Pool from the front desk.

The Lady Anne Bed and Breakfast (902 14th St., 707/822-2797, http://ladyanneinn.com, $150-185) has a little more character, with five rooms in an old Victorian built in 1888. All have private bathrooms, and most include gas-burning woodstoves. A music room is decorated with instruments including a piano, an accordion, and a bass guitar that guests can play. The Lady Anne serves a continental breakfast.

A few miles from the plaza, the **Best Western Arcata Inn** (4827 Valley West Blvd., 707/826-0313, http://bestwesterncalifornia.com, $101-160) is a well-regarded chain motel in the area. The rooms have satellite TV and Wi-Fi, and there's an indoor/outdoor heated swimming pool and hot tub. Fuel up with a complimentary breakfast.

TRANSPORTATION AND SERVICES

Arcata is eight miles north of Eureka on U.S. 101. Once there, it's easiest to just park your car and walk around the small city. The **Arcata & Mad River Transit System** (www.humboldttransit.org, adults $1.50, seniors and children $1.25) runs a fleet of red-and-yellow buses that travel all over Arcata.

A small commercial airport, **California Redwood Coast-Humboldt County Airport** (ACV, 3561 Boeing Ave., McKinleyville, 707/839-5401, http://humboldtgov.org) serves the region via United Airlines. Flights are expensive but convenient.

North of downtown, the **Mad River Community Hospital** (3800 Janes Rd., 707/822-3621, http://madriverhospital.com) has an emergency room and urgent care department.

Trinidad Bay

Perched on a bluff over boat-studded Trinidad Bay, Trinidad has a wealth of natural assets, including scenic headlands and wild beaches on either side of town. It also has a long history: The town was named by two Spanish Navy men who came to the area on Trinity Sunday in 1775. Right off U.S. 101, Trinidad is worth a visit, whether it's for a stop to stretch your legs or a tranquil weekend getaway.

★ TRINIDAD

With a population of just 360 people, Trinidad is one of the smallest incorporated cities in California; it's also one of the most beautiful.

Trinidad Memorial Lighthouse

Not an actual lighthouse but a replica of the one on nearby Trinidad Head, **Trinidad Memorial Lighthouse** (Trinity St. and Edwards St.) is the local photo opportunity. It was built by the Trinidad Civic Club in 1949. The small red-and-white building sits on a bluff above the bay where boats bob in the water. A marble slab and a series of plaques list names of people who have been lost at sea. To the left of the lighthouse is the old Trinidad fog bell.

Trinidad Head

A rocky promontory north of the bay, the 380-foot-high **Trinidad Head** (end of Edwards St.) affords great views of the area's beaches, bay, and town. A one-mile-long loop trail on the headlands goes under canopies of vegetation and then out to a series of clear spots with benches. A large stone cross on the west end of Trinidad Head marks where Spanish seamen initially erected a wooden cross. Below the cross is a small wooden deck where you can glimpse the top of the Trinidad Head Lighthouse. The squat lighthouse on a 175-foot-high cliff was activated in 1871. In 1914, the lighthouse made news when, according to the lighthouse keeper, a huge wave extinguished the light.

Trinidad State Beach

Below the bluffs of Trinidad Head, **Trinidad**

Hotel Arcata

State Beach (end of Edwards St., 707/677-3570, www.parks.ca.gov, sunrise-sunset daily, free) runs north for a mile to Elk Head. Spruce-tufted Pewetole Island and a scattering of scenic coastal islets lie offshore. The northern end has caves, an arch, and tide pools. It's a great place for a contemplative walk.

Humboldt State University Marine Laboratory

Students come to the **HSU Marine Laboratory** (570 Ewing St., 707/826-3671, www2.humboldt.edu/marinelab, 9am-4:30pm Mon.-Fri., 10am-5pm Sat.-Sun., tours by appointment, self-guided tours $1, guided tours $2) to learn about the area's coastal critters. A tour of the lab includes looks at invertebrates from nearby intertidal zones, like sea cucumbers, tube worms, giant green anemones, and red octopi. Visitors can also sign up to explore the area's tide pools with a marine naturalist ($3).

SPORTS AND RECREATION
Kayaking and Whale-Watching

Protected Trinidad Bay is an ideal spot for a scenic sea-kayaking excursion. **Humboats**

Kayak Adventures (707/443-5157, www.humboats.com, $45-110) runs guided whale-watching tours in the spring and early summer when gray whales migrate right through the protected harbor area.

Sportfishing

Head out to sea with one of two Trinidad-based fishing outfits. Fish for rockfish, salmon, or Dungeness crab with **Trinidad Bay Charters** (707/499-8878, www.trinidadbaycharters.net, $120). Trips leave daily at 6:15am and 12:15pm. **Patrick's Point Charters** (707/445-4106, www.patrickspointcharters.com, $120/half day) leaves out of Trinidad Harbor for rockfish, salmon, and Dungeness crab.

Surfing

South of Trinidad are some of Humboldt County's best-known surf spots. **Moonstone Beach** (3 miles south of Trinidad on Scenic Dr.) is a popular surf break where the Little River pours into Trinidad Bay. Up the road 0.5 mile, **Camel Rock** (about 2.3 miles south of Trinidad on Scenic Dr.) has right breaks that peel inside of a distinct, double-humped offshore rock.

Trinidad State Beach

Salty's Supply Co. (332 Main St., 707/677-0300, https://saltystrinidad.com, 7am-6pm daily summer, 10am-6pm daily fall, 10am-5pm Tues.-Sun. winter, surfboards $30/day, wetsuits $30/day) rents surf gear along with kayaks, bikes, books, and magazines (seriously!).

FOOD

Stock up on delicious, locally smoked seafood at ★ **Katy's Smokehouse** (740 Edwards St., 707/677-0151, www.katyssmokehouse.com, 9am-6pm daily). There are smoked oysters and salmon jerky, but you can't go wrong with the smoked king salmon. It's not a sit-down restaurant, so you'll need to get your order to go.

The friendly, spunky staff at the **Beachcomber Café** (363 Trinity St., 707/677-0106, http://trinidadbeachcomber. blogspot.com, 7am-4pm Mon.-Fri., 8am-4pm Sat.-Sun.) serve coffee, cookies, paninis, and bagels. The café also has free Wi-Fi with purchase.

North of Trinidad, the ★ **Larrupin Café** (1658 Patrick's Point Dr., 707/677-0230, www. thelarrupin.com, 5pm-9pm daily, $26-50) is probably the most-loved restaurant in the area. They put their legendary mesquite barbecue sauce on everything from tofu kebabs to creole prawns and are known for their mustard dill and red sauces. Enjoy the heated patio June through September.

ACCOMMODATIONS

The only lodging in Trinidad proper is the **Trinidad Bay Bed & Breakfast** (560 Edward St., 707/677-0840, www.trinidadbaybnb.com, $300-400), across the street from the Trinidad Memorial Lighthouse. Each of the four rooms has a view of Trinidad Bay; two rooms have private entrances, and all have private bathrooms. A hot three-course breakfast is served.

Between the main section of Trinidad and Patrick's Point State Park, **The Lost Whale Bed & Breakfast Inn** (3452 Patrick's Point Dr., 707/677-3425, http://lostwhaleinn.com, $275-335) has five rooms with great views of the Pacific and four with garden views. Two rooms have lofts to accommodate up to four people. There's a private trail to the beach, an oceanview hot tub, and a wood-burning sauna. A seven-course breakfast buffet is served.

The Emerald Forest (753 Patrick's Point Dr., 707/677-3554, www.cabinsintheredwoods.

Pick up some smoked salmon at Katy's Smokehouse.

com, $179-349) has a variety of rustic cabins for rent. The higher-end cabins have full kitchens and amenities like wood-burning stoves. RV and tent campsites are also available ($35-48), although those at nearby Patrick's Point State Park are more spacious.

TRANSPORTATION

Trinidad is 15 miles north of Arcata on U.S. 101. Take exit 728 off the highway. The **Redwood Transit System** (707/443-0826, www.redwoodtransit.org, adults $3, seniors and children $2.75) has buses that connect from Arcata and Eureka to Trinidad.

Trinidad is a small city, so don't expect too many services. Most major services can be found in nearby Arcata.

PATRICK'S POINT STATE PARK

Patrick's Point State Park (4150 Patrick's Point Dr., 707/677-3570, www.parks.ca.gov, sunrise-sunset daily, day use $8) is a rambling coastal park 25 miles north of Eureka, replete with beaches, historic landmarks, trails, and campgrounds. The climate remains cool year-round, making it perfect for hiking and exploring.

Get a map and information at the **Patrick's Point State Park Visitors Center** (707/677-1945, 9am-5pm daily summer, 10am-4pm daily winter), immediately to the right of the entry gate. Information about nature walks and campfire programs is posted on the bulletin board.

Sights

Prominent among the local landmarks is **Patrick's Point**, which can be reached by a brief hike from a convenient parking lot. Adjacent to Patrick's Point in a picturesque cove is **Wedding Rock**, a promontory sticking out into the ocean like an upturned thumb. (People really do hike the narrow trail out to the rock to get married.)

The most fascinating area is **Sumeg Village**, a re-creation of a native Yurok village based on an archaeological find east of here. Visitors can crawl through the perfectly round doors into semi-subterranean homes, meeting places, and storage buildings. Check out the native plant garden, a collection of local plants the Yurok people used for food, basketry, and medicine. (The local Yurok people use Sumeg Village as a gathering place; please tread lightly).

Trinidad Bay Bed & Breakfast

Patrick's Point has a number of accessible beaches. A steep trail leads down to **Agate Beach,** a wide stretch of coarse sand bordered by cliffs shot through with shining quartz veins. The semiprecious stones for which it is named really do appear here.

Hiking

Six miles of trails thread through the park, including the **Rim Trail** (4 miles round-trip), which will take you along the cliffs for a view of the sea and migrating whales (Sept.-Jan., Mar.-June). Tree lovers might prefer the **Octopus Tree Trail,** which provides a great view of an old-growth Sitka spruce grove.

Camping

Three campgrounds (reservations 800/444-7275, www.reservecalifornia.com, $35) have a total of 124 sites. It can be difficult to determine the difference between **Agate Beach, Abalone,** and **Penn Creek,** so get directions from the park rangers. Most campsites are pleasantly shaded by the groves of trees. All include a picnic table, fire pit, and food storage cupboard, and you'll find running water, restrooms, and showers nearby.

Transportation

Patrick's Point State Park is on the coast, 25 miles north of Eureka and 15 miles south of Orick on U.S. 101.

Redwood National and State Parks

The lands of Redwood National and State Parks (www.nps.gov/redw) meander along the coast and include three state parks—Prairie Creek Redwoods, Del Norte Coast Redwoods, and Jedediah Smith. This complex of parkland encompasses most of California's northern redwood forests. The main landmass of Redwood National Park is just south of Prairie Creek State Park along U.S. 101, stretching east from the coast and the highway.

REDWOOD NATIONAL PARK

The **Thomas H. Kuchel Visitors Center** (U.S. 101, west of Orick, 707/465-7765, 9am-5pm daily spring-fall, 9am-4pm daily winter) is a large facility with a ranger station, clean restrooms, and a path to the shore. Get advice, maps, backcountry permits, and books. In the summer, rangers run patio talks and coast walks that provide a great introduction to the area for children and adults. Picnic at one of the tables outside the visitors center, or walk a short distance to Redwood Creek.

Hiking

One of the easiest, most popular ways to get close to the trees is to walk the **Lady Bird Johnson Trail** (Bald Hills Rd., 1.4 miles, easy). This nearly level loop provides an intimate view of the redwood and fir forests that define this region. Another easy-access trail is **Trillium Falls** (Davison Rd. at Elk Meadow, 2.8 miles, easy). The redwood trees along this cool, dark trail are striking, and the small waterfall is a nice treasure in the woods. This little hike is lovely any time of year but best in spring, when the water volume over the falls is at its peak.

The **Lost Man Creek Trail** (east of Elk Meadow, 1 mile off U.S. 101, 0.5-22 miles, easy-difficult) has it all. The first 0.5 mile is perfect for wheelchair users and families with small children. But as the trail rolls along, the grades get steeper and more challenging. Customize the length of this out-and-back trail by turning around at any time. If you reach the Lost Man Creek picnic grounds, your total round-trip distance is 22 miles with more than 3,000 feet of elevation gain and several stream crossings.

The **Redwood Creek Trail** (Bald Hills Rd. spur off U.S. 101, difficult) follows Redwood Creek for 8 miles to the **Tall Trees Grove.** If you have a shuttle car, pick up the **Tall Trees Trail** and walk another 6 miles (a total of 14 miles) to the **Dolason Prairie Trail,** which takes you back out to Bald Hills Road.

Camping

There are no designated campgrounds in Redwood National Park; free backcountry camping is allowed, but permits may be necessary. The **Elam Camp** and the **44 Camp** are both hike-in primitive campgrounds along the Dolason Prairie Trail.

Transportation

The Redwood National and State Parks line U.S. 101 from Prairie Creek Redwoods north to Jedediah Smith near Crescent City. The Thomas H. Kuchel Visitors Center at the south end of the park is 40 miles north of Eureka on U.S. 101.

★ PRAIRIE CREEK REDWOODS STATE PARK

In addition to the silent majesty of the redwoods, the 14,000 acres of **Prairie Creek Redwoods State Park** (Newton B. Drury Dr., 25 miles south of Crescent City, 707/488-2039, www.parks.ca.gov, sunrise-sunset daily, day use $8) offer miles of wild beach, roaming wildlife, and a popular hike through a one-of-a-kind fern-draped canyon.

The **Visitors Center** (Newton B. Drury Dr., 707/488-2039, 9am-5pm daily summer, 9am-4pm daily winter) includes a small interpretive museum describing the history of the redwood forests. A tiny bookshop adjoins the museum, well stocked with books describing the history, nature, and culture of the area. Many ranger-led programs originate at the visitors center, and permits are available for backcountry camping.

One of the many reasons to visit is a chance to view a herd of **Roosevelt elk.** This subspecies of elk can stand up to five feet high and can weigh close to 1,000 pounds. These big guys usually hang out at—where else?—the Elk Prairie, a stretch

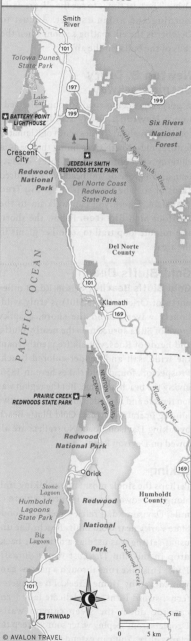

of open grassland along the highway, and off the southern end of the Newton B. Drury Drive. The best times to see the elk are early morning and around sunset. August to October is the elk mating season, when the calls of the bulls fill the air.

Newton B. Drury Scenic Parkway

A gorgeous scenic road through the redwoods, **Newton B. Drury Scenic Parkway** (off U.S. 101 about 5 miles south of Klamath) features old-growth trees lining the roads, a close-up view of the redwood forest ecosystem, and a grove or trailhead every hundred yards or so. The turnoff is at the **Big Tree Wayside,** where you can walk up to the 304-foot-high **Big Tree.** Follow the short, five-minute loop trail to see other giants in the area.

Gold Bluffs Beach

Gold Bluffs Beach (Davison Rd., 3 miles north of Orick off U.S. 101) is truly wild. Lonely waves pound the shore, a spiky grove of Sitka spruce tops the nearby bluffs, and herds of Roosevelt elk frequently roam the wide, salt-and-pepper-colored beach. Prospectors found gold flakes here in 1850, giving the beach its name. But the region was too remote and rugged to maintain a lucrative mining operation. Access Gold Bluffs Beach by taking Davison Road. No trailers are allowed on Davison Road.

Hiking

Perhaps the single most famous hiking trail along the redwood coast is **Fern Canyon** (1 mile, Davison Rd., Prairie Creek Redwoods State Park), near Gold Bluffs Beach. The unusual setting was used as a dramatic backdrop in the film *The Lost World: Jurassic Park.* This hike runs through a narrow canyon carved by Home Creek. Five-fingered ferns, sword ferns, and delicate lady ferns cascade down the steep canyon walls. Droplets from seeping water sources keep the plants alive. You can extend this hike into a

longer loop (6.5 miles, moderate): When the trail intersects with James Irvine Trail, bear right and follow that spur. Bear right again onto **Clintonia Trail** and walk to Miners Ridge Trail. Bear right onto Miners Ridge and follow it down to the ocean. Walk 1.5 miles along Gold Bluffs Beach to complete the loop.

To get to the trailhead, take U.S. 101 three miles north of the town of Orick. At the Prairie Creek visitors center, turn west onto Davison Road (no trailers allowed) and travel two miles. This rough dirt road takes you through the campground and ends at the trailhead in 1.5 miles.

Miners Ridge and **James Irvine Loop** (12 miles, moderate) starts from the visitors center instead of the Fern Canyon trailhead, avoiding the rough dirt terrain of Davison Road. Start out on **James Irvine Trail** and bear right when you can, following the trail all the way until it joins Fern Canyon Trail. Turn left when you get to the coast and walk along Gold Bluffs Beach for 1.5 miles. Then make a left onto the Clintonia Trail and head back toward the visitors center.

The **California Coastal Trail** (www. californiacoastaltrail.info) runs along the park's northern coastline and can be accessed via the **Ossagon Creek Trail** (north end of Newton B. Drury Dr., 2 miles round-trip, moderate). It's not long, but the steep grade makes it a tough haul in spots, and the stunning trees along the way make it worth the effort.

Camping

The **Elk Prairie Campground** (127011 Newton B. Drury Dr., Orick, campground 707/488-2039, reservations 800/444-7275, www.reservecalifornia.com, reservations recommended Memorial Day-Labor Day, vehicles $35, hikers and cyclists $5) has 75 sites for tents or RVs and a full range of comfortable camping amenities, including showers and firewood. Several campsites are wheelchair-accessible (request at reservation). A big campfire area, an easy walk north of the campground, has evening programs put on by rangers and volunteers.

For beach camping, head to **Gold Bluffs Beach Campground** (Davison Rd., 3 miles north of Orick, www.nps.gov/redw, $35 regular sites, $20 environmental sites). There are 26 first-come, first-served sites for tents or RVs and 3 environmental sites. Amenities include flush toilets, water, solar showers, and wide ocean views. The surf can be quite dangerous here, so be extremely careful if you go in the water.

Backcountry camping is allowed in two designated camping areas: Ossagon Creek and Miners Ridge (3 sites each, $5). Permits are available at the campground kiosk or the Prairie Creek visitors center (Newton B. Drury Dr., 707/488-2171, 9am-5pm daily).

Transportation

Prairie Creek Redwoods is 50 miles north of Eureka and 25 miles south of Crescent City on U.S. 101. Newton B. Drury Drive traverses the park and can be accessed from U.S. 101 north or south.

Trees of Mystery

Generations of kids have enjoyed spotting the gigantic wooden sculptures of Paul Bunyan and his blue ox, Babe, from U.S. 101. The **Trees of Mystery** (15500 U.S. 101 N., 707/482-2251 or 800/638-3389, www.treesofmystery.net, 8am-7pm daily June-Aug., 8:30am-6:30pm daily Sept.-Oct., 9am-5pm daily Nov.-May, adults $18, seniors $14, children 6-12 $9, children under 5 free) is a great place to let the family out for some good cheesy fun. Visitors can enjoy the original Mystery Hike, the SkyTrail gondola ride through the old-growth redwoods, and the palatial gift shop. Perhaps best of all, at the left end of the gift shop is a little-known gem: the Native American museum. A large collection of artifacts from both tribes across the country and those indigenous to the redwood forests graces several crowded galleries. The restrooms here are large and well maintained, which makes Trees of Mystery a nice rest stop.

DEL NORTE COAST REDWOODS STATE PARK

Del Norte Coast Redwoods State Park (Mill Creek Campground Rd., off U.S. 101, 707/465-7335, www.parks.ca.gov, $8) encompasses a variety of ecosystems, including eight miles of wild coastline, second-growth redwood forest, and virgin old-growth forests. One of the largest in this system of parks, Del Norte is a great place to get lost in the backcountry with just your knapsack.

Del Norte state park has no visitors center, but you can get information from the **Crescent City Information Center** (1111 2nd St., Crescent City, 707/465-7306, 9am-5pm daily spring-fall, 9am-4pm Thurs.-Mon. winter).

Hiking

Several rewarding yet gentle and short excursions start and end in the Mill Creek Campground. The **Trestle Loop Trail** (1 mile, easy) begins across from the campfire center in the campground. Notice the trestles and other artifacts along the way; the loop follows the route of a defunct railroad from the logging era. Another easy stroll is the nearby **Nature Loop Trail** (1 mile, easy), which begins near the campground entrance gate. Interpretive signage teaches you about the varieties of impressive trees you'll pass.

Camping

The **Mill Creek campground** (U.S. 101, 7 miles south of Crescent City, 800/444-7275, www.reservecalifornia.com, May-Sept., vehicles $35, hikers and cyclists $5) is in an attractive setting along Mill Creek. There are 145 sites for RVs and tents, and facilities include restrooms, fire pits, and a dump station. There are no designated backcountry campsites and backcountry camping is not allowed.

Transportation

Del Norte Coast Redwoods is seven miles

California Coastal Trail

The northern section of the great **California Coastal Trail** (CCT, www.californiacoastaltrail. info) runs right through Del Norte Coast Redwoods State Park. The trail is reasonably well marked; look for signs with the CCT logo. The **"last chance"** section of the California Coastal Trail (Enderts Beach-Damnation Creek, 14 miles, strenuous) makes a challenging day hike. To reach the trailhead, turn west from U.S. 101 onto Enderts Beach Road in Del Norte, three miles south of Crescent City. Drive 2.3 miles to the end of the road.

The trail follows the historic route of U.S. 101 south to Enderts Beach. You'll walk through fields of wildflowers and groves of trees twisted by the wind and saltwater. Eventually, the trail climbs about 900 feet to an overlook with a great view of Enderts Beach. At just over two miles, the trail enters Del Norte Coast Redwoods State Park, where it meanders through Anson Grove's redwood, fir, and Sitka spruce trees. At 4.5 miles, cross Damnation Creek on a footbridge, and at 6.1 miles, cross the Damnation Creek Trail. (For a longer hike, take the four-mile round-trip side excursion down to the beach and back.) After seven miles, a flight of steps leads up to milepost 15.6 on U.S. 101. At this point, you can turn around and return the way you came, making for a gloriously varied day hike of about 14 miles round-trip.

One alternative is to make this a point-to-point hike, either by dropping a car off at one end to get you back at the end of the day, or by having one group of hikers start at each end of the trail and exchange keys at a central meeting point.

If you've made arrangements for a lift back at the end of the day, continue on to the DeMartin section of the Coastal Trail. From here, descend through a lush grove of ferns and take a bridge over a tributary of Wilson Creek, enjoying views of the rocky coast far below. The wildflowers continue as you enter Redwood National Park and wander through the grasslands of DeMartin Prairie. The southern trailhead (where you pick up your vehicle if you're doing the trail one-way north-south) is at the Wilson Creek Picnic Area on the east side of U.S. 101 at the north end of DeMartin Bridge.

---

south of Crescent City on U.S. 101. The park entrance is on Hamilton Road, east of U.S. 101.

★ JEDEDIAH SMITH REDWOODS STATE PARK

There's nowhere better to experience the majesty of the North Coast's redwoods than at **Jedediah Smith Redwoods State Park** (1440 U.S. 199, 9 miles east of Crescent City, 707/465-7335 or 707/458-3496, www. parks.ca.gov, sunrise-sunset daily, $8/vehicle). The most popular redwood grove in the park is the **Stout Memorial Grove,** a 44-acre grove of 300-foot-tall redwoods and waist-high sword ferns. These are some of the biggest and oldest trees on the North Coast, somehow spared the loggers' saws. The quiet grove lacks visitors, since its far-north latitude makes it harder to reach than some of the other big redwood groves in California.

There are two visitors centers, about five minutes apart: **Jedediah Smith Visitors Center** (U.S. 101, Hiouchi, 707/465-7306, 9am-5pm daily summer) and the **Hiouchi Information Center** (U.S. 199, Hiouchi, 707/458-3294, 9am-5pm daily summer, 9am-4pm daily winter). Both offer information and materials about all of the nearby parks.

Hiking

The shaded trails make for wonderfully cool summer hiking. Many trails run along the river and the creeks, offering beach access and plenty of lush scenery to enjoy. The **Simpson Reed Trail** (U.S. 199, 6 miles east of Crescent City, 1 mile, easy) takes you from U.S. 199 down to the banks of the Smith River.

To get a good view of the Smith River, hike the **Hiouchi Trail** (2 miles, moderate). From the Hiouchi Information Center and campgrounds on U.S. 199, cross the Summer Footbridge and then follow the river north. The Hiouchi Trail then meets the Hatton Loop Trail and leads away from the river and into the forest.

For a longer and more aggressive trek, try the **Mill Creek Trail** (7.5 miles round-trip, difficult). Start at the Summer Footbridge (seasonal) and follow the creek down to the unpaved Howland Hill Road. The trail winds through ferns, maples, pines, and stunning redwoods. (Just off the trail is the Grove of the Titans, said to be the home of the world's largest coast redwood.) There's also a pristine swimming hole with a rope swing near the southeast end of the trail.

The **Boy Scout Tree Trail** (5.2 miles, moderate) is usually quiet, with few hikers, and the gargantuan forest will make you feel truly tiny. To get to the trailhead, drive a rugged, unpaved road for a couple of miles. About three miles into the trail, you'll come to a fork. If you've got time, take both forks: first the left, which takes you to the small, mossy, and very green Fern Falls, and then the right, which takes you to the eponymous Boy Scout

Tree, one of the impressively huge redwoods. Check at the visitors center first to make sure the road to the trailhead is open.

Boating and Swimming

You'll find two boat launches in the park: one at Society Hole and one adjacent to the Summer Footbridge (winter only). Down by the River Beach Trail, you'll find **River Beach** (immediately west of the Hiouchi Information Center), a popular spot for swimming. Swimming is allowed throughout the park, but be very careful—rivers and creeks move unpredictably, and you might not notice deep holes until you're on them.

Fishing

With the Smith River and numerous feeder creeks running through Jed Smith, fishing a popular activity. Chilly winter fishing draws a surprising number of anglers to vie for king salmon up to 30 pounds and steelhead up to 20 pounds. Seasons for both species run October-February. In the summer, cast into the river to catch cutthroat trout.

Camping

The ★ **Jedediah Smith Campground** (U.S. 199, Hiouchi, 800/444-7275, www.

the trail through Jedediah Smith Redwoods State Park's Stout Memorial Grove

reservecalifornia.com, vehicles $35, hike-in or cycle-in primitive sites $5) is beautifully situated on the banks of Smith River, with most sites near the River Beach Trail. There are 106 RV and tent sites. Facilities include restrooms, fire pits, and coin-operated showers. Reservations (accepted Memorial Day-Labor Day) are advised, especially for summer and holiday weekends. Jedediah Smith has no designated backcountry campsites; camping outside the developed campgrounds is not allowed.

Transportation

Jedediah Smith Redwoods State Park is northeast of Crescent City along the Smith River, next door to the immense Smith River National Recreation Area (U.S. 199 west of Hiouchi). Get to the park by taking U.S. 199 nine miles east of Crescent City.

Crescent City

The northernmost city on the California coast perches on the bay that provides its name. Cool and windswept, Crescent City is a perfect place to put on a parka, stuff your hands deep into your pockets, and wander along a wide, beautiful beach. The small city also has a vibrant surf scene centered on South Beach, which frequently has good waves for longboarders.

Crescent City is also known for surviving tsunamis. In 1964, a tsunami caused by an Alaskan earthquake wiped out 29 city blocks and killed 11 people. It was the most severe tsunami on the U.S. West Coast in modern history. In 2011, a devastating earthquake in Japan resulted in a tsunami that laid waste to the city's harbor. The old, rusted warning sirens on the tops of the city's utility poles still work; when they sound, there's a chance of massive waves coming to shore.

SIGHTS
Point St. George

Wild, lonely, beautiful **Point St. George** (end of Washington Blvd., sunrise-sunset daily) epitomizes the glory of the North Coast. Walk out onto the cliffs to take in the deep blue sea, wild salt- and flower-scented air, and craggy cliffs and beaches. On a clear day, you can see all the way to Oregon. Short, steep trails lead across wild beach prairie land down to broad, flat, nearly deserted beaches. In spring and summer, wildflowers bloom on the cliffs, and swallows nest in the cluster of buildings on the point. On rare and special clear days, you can almost make out the **St. George Reef Lighthouse** alone on its perch far out in the Pacific.

★ Battery Point Lighthouse

On an island just north of Crescent City Harbor, the **Battery Point Lighthouse** (end of A St., 707/464-3089, www.delnortehistory. org, 10am-4pm daily Apr.-Sept., 10am-4pm Sat.-Sun. Oct.-Mar. tides permitting, adults $3, children 8-15 $1) is only accessible at low tide, when a rocky spit littered with tide pools emerges, serving as a walkway for visitors. The 1856 lighthouse's current keepers reside on the island in one-month shifts; they also lead tours. You'll see a Fresnel lens and a working clock that was used by Battery Point's first lighthouse keeper. After you view the building's two residential floors, the docent leads any adventurous visitors up a metal ladder and through a small hole into the lantern room, where you'll be able to feel the heat of the still-working light just feet away. On a clear day, you'll also be able to see the pencil-like outline of the St. George Reef Lighthouse in the distance. St. George is situated on a small, wave-washed rock seven miles from shore, and its dangerous location resulted in the deaths of four keepers who worked there.

Crescent City

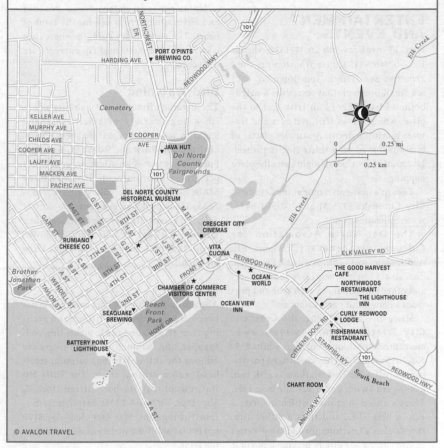

© AVALON TRAVEL

Ocean World

A great family respite is **Ocean World** (304 U.S. 101 S., 707/464-4900, www. oceanworldonline.com, 9am-6pm daily, adults $13, children 3-11 $8). Tours of the small sea park depart about every 15 minutes and last about 40 minutes. Featured attractions are the shark-petting tank, the 500,000-gallon aquarium, and the sea lion show. An immense souvenir shop sells gifts with nautical themes.

Del Norte County Historical Society Museum

The **Del Norte County Historical Society Museum** (577 H St., 707/464-3922, www. delnortehistory.org, 10am-4pm daily, free) maintains this small museum that features the local history of both the Native Americans who were once the only inhabitants of Del Norte County and the encroaching white settlers. Exhibits include the wreck of the *Brother Jonathan* at Point St. George, the story of the

1964 tsunami, and artifacts of the local Yurok and Tolowa people.

ENTERTAINMENT AND EVENTS

Port O'Pints Brewing Co. (1215 Northcrest Dr., 707/460-1154, http://portopints.com, 2pm-9pm Sun.-Thurs., 1pm-10pm Fri.-Sat.) is a small brewpub that resembles a neighborhood bar. There's an Irish feel to the place, which serves Irish red beer and features maritime decor. A sampler platter of brews is served on a ship's steering wheel. Live music on weekend nights gets the place hopping.

Take in a first-run movie at the **Crescent City Cinemas** (375 M St., 707/570-8438, www.catheatres.com).

The **Del Norte Association for Cultural Awareness** (Crescent Elk Auditorium, 994 G St., 707/464-1336, www.dnaca.net) hosts several live musical acts and other performances each year and provides a community arts calendar.

Since the early 1980s, the **Crescent City Triathlon** (707/465-3995, www.crescentcitytriathlon.com, Aug., adults $55-65, children $20-25) has challenged participants of all ages. This triathlon is a 5K run, a 500-yard swim, and a 12-mile bike ride. There's also a duathlon, which involves a run, a bike ride, and then another run; there's also a triathlon for kids that varies in intensity by age group, making it possible for anyone ages 5-12 to join the fun.

SPORTS AND RECREATION

Beaches
The sands of Crescent City are a beachcomber's paradise. **South Beach** (Hwy. 1 between Anchor Way and Sand Mine Rd.), at the south end of town, is long, wide, and flat—perfect for a romantic stroll, as long as you're bundled up. Two miles south of town, **Crescent Beach** (Enderts Rd.) is a wide, sandy strip. Down a 0.5-mile dirt trail, **Enderts Beach** (Enderts Rd.) is a superb

pocket beach with a creek flowing into the ocean and an onshore rock arch.

No lifeguards patrol these beaches and swimming here is not for the faint of heart. The water is icy cold, the shores are rocky, and undertow and rip currents are dangerous.

Bird-Watching
The diverse climates and habitats nourish a huge variety of avian residents. Right in town, check out **Battery Point Lighthouse Park** and **Point St. George.** For a rare view of an Aleutian goose or a peregrine falcon, journey to **Tolowa Dunes State Park** (1375 Elk Valley Rd., 707/465-7335, www.parks.ca.gov, sunrise-sunset daily, free), specifically the shores of Lake Earl and Kellogg Beach. South of town, **Enderts Beach** is home to another large bird habitat.

Fishing
Anglers on the North Coast can choose between excellent deep-sea fishing and exciting river trips. The Pacific yields ling cod, snapper, and salmon, while the rivers are famous for chinook (king) salmon, steelhead, and cutthroat trout. The *Tally Ho II* (Crescent City Harbor, Citizen Dock R, Slip D29, 707/464-1236, http://tally-ho-sportfishing.com, May-Oct., half-day $120 pp) is available for a variety of deep-sea fishing trips.

River fishers have a wealth of guides to choose from. **Ken Cunningham Guide Service** (50 Hunter Creek, Klamath, 707/391-7144, www.salmonslayer.net, $200-250) will take you on a full-day fishing trip; the price includes bait, tackle, and the boat.

Hiking
The redwood forests that nearly meet the wide, sandy beaches make the Crescent City area a fabulous place to hike. The hikes at **Point St. George** aren't strenuous and provide stunning views of the coastline and surrounding landscape. **Tolowa Dunes**

State Park (1375 Elk Valley Rd., 707/465-7335, www.parks.ca.gov, sunrise-sunset daily, free), north of Point St. George, offers miles of trails winding through forests, across beaches, and meandering along the shores of Lake Earl.

Horseback Riding
Casual riders can enjoy a guided riding adventure through redwoods or along the ocean with **Crescent Trail Rides** (2002 Moorehead Rd., 707/951-5407, www.crescenttrailrides.com, 1.5 hours $70, 3 hours $135). **Fort Dick Stable** (2002 Moorehead Rd., 707/951-5407) offers boarding and riding lessons.

A great place to ride is **Tolowa Dunes State Park** (1375 Elk Valley Rd., 707/465-7335, www.parks.ca.gov, sunrise-sunset daily, free), which maintains 20 miles of trails accessible to horses. Serious equestrians with their own mounts can ride in to a campsite with corrals at the north end of the park off Lower Lake Road.

Surfing
Crescent City has a collection of surf breaks. Pioneering big-wave surfer Greg Noll even lives here. Just south of the harbor is the most popular break in town, **South Beach** (Hwy. 1 between Anchor Way and Sand Mine Rd.), with peeling waves perfect for longboarders and beginners. North of town, **Point St. George** (end of Washington Blvd.) has a reef and point break that comes alive during winter.

FOOD
Seafood is standard fare in Crescent City, but family restaurants and one or two ethnic eateries add some variety.

★ **SeaQuake Brewing** (400 Front St., 707/465-4444, www.seaquakebrewing.com, 3pm-10pm Tues.-Sat., $10-19) has revolutionized Crescent City's drinking and dining scene. The giant brewery and restaurant pours tasty brews, including a Citra IPA, enjoyed outside or in one of the cavernous

building's two floors. The menu showcases Del Norte County's assets, from fish tacos made with locally caught rock cod, to burgers with local organic beef, to brick-oven pizzas topped with Crescent City's own Rumiano cheese. Live music on Saturday night makes this the city's ideal stop for great beer, local food, and good music.

The **Java Hut** (437 U.S. 101 N., 707/465-4439, 5am-10pm daily, $5) is a drive-through and walk-up coffee stand that serves a wide array of coffee drinks. Beware of long lines during the morning hours.

The small, family-owned, award-winning **Rumiano Cheese Co.** (511 9th St., 707/465-1535 or 866/328-2433, www.rumianocheese.com, 9:30am-5pm Mon.-Fri., 9am-3pm Sat. June-Dec., 9am-5pm Mon.-Fri. Jan.-May) has been part of Crescent City since 1921. Come to the tasting room for the cheese and stay for, well, more cheese. The dry jack cheese is a particular favorite.

Enjoy an impressive variety of fresh and healthy food at **The Good Harvest Cafe** (575 U.S. 101 S., 707/465-6028, 7:30am-9pm Mon.-Sat., 8am-8pm Sun., $10-35). It serves the best breakfast in town, with vegetarian options like tofu rancheros and veggie frittata. Steak entrées are at the pricier end of the dinner menu, which also includes burgers, pasta, vegetarian entrées, and big salads. Kitschy Native American decorations abound.

Fishermans Restaurant (700 U.S. 101 S., 707/465-3474, 6am-9pm daily, $11-26) is a casual place to grab delicious breakfasts—biscuits and gravy, pancakes, and thick, juicy bacon—and a diverse dinner menu of fresh localt seafood.

The chef/owners behind **Vita Cucina** (1270 Front St., Ste. A, 707/464-1076, www.vitacucina.com, 7am-4pm Mon.-Thurs., 7am-7pm Fri., $4-15) up the city's casual dining cred with *bahn mi* sandwiches and pulled pork. On Thursday and Friday, they do pizzas, calzones, and whole smoked chickens.

For seafood at a reasonable price, the best

bet is **The Chart Room** (130 Anchor Way, 707/464-5993, https://ccchartroom.com, 11am-4pm Tues., 7am-7pm Wed.-Thurs. and Sun., 7am-8pm Fri.-Sat., $10-23). It's very casual, the food is excellent, and it's right on the ocean.

Crescent City runs a **farmers market** (Del Norte County Fairgrounds, 451 U.S. 101 N., 707/464-7441, www.delnorte.org, 9am-1pm Sat. June-Oct.).

ACCOMMODATIONS

The aptly named **Curly Redwood Lodge** (701 U.S. 101 S., 707/464-2137, www.curlyredwoodlodge.com, $75-107) is constructed of a single rare curly redwood tree. You'll see the lovely color and grain of the tree in your large, simply decorated room. A 1950s feel pervades this friendly, unpretentious motel even though it offers free Wi-Fi. Some rooms even have antique TVs from the 1950s; others have flat screens.

The **Lighthouse Inn** (681 U.S. 101 S., 707/464-3993 or 877/464-3993, http://thelighthouseinncrescentcity.com, $89-145) has an elegant yet whimsical lobby to welcome guests, and the enthusiastic staff can help with restaurant recommendations and sights. Stylish appointments and bold colors grace each guest room. Corner suites with oversize whirlpool tubs make a perfect romantic retreat for couples; standard double rooms are downright cheap.

The "harbor view" inn may be a more apt name for **Ocean View Inn** (270 U.S. 101 S., 707/465-1111 or 855/623-2611, http://oceanviewinncrescentcity.com, $120-165), but the west-facing rooms do overlook a body of water. The lobby is a bit over the top with model sailboat decorations and a large mural of Crescent City's sights, but the rooms are big and worth the price. A complimentary continental breakfast is served in the morning to sweeten the deal. Pay a bit more for a two-room family suite or a room with a Jacuzzi tub and fireplace.

TRANSPORTATION

The main routes in and out of town are U.S. 101 and U.S. 199. Both are well maintained but are twisty in spots, so take care, especially at night. From San Francisco, the drive to Crescent City is about 350 miles (6.5 hours). It is 85 miles (under two hours) from Eureka north to Crescent City on U.S. 101. Traffic isn't a big issue in Crescent City, and parking is free and easy to find throughout town.

Crescent City's Ocean View Inn

Jack McNamara Field (CEC, 250 Dale Rupert Rd., 707/464-7288, http://flycrescentcity.com) is the only airport in Crescent City. Alaska Airlines and PenAir have two daily flights to Portland, Oregon.

Redwood Coast Transit (RCT, 707/464-6400, www.redwoodcoasttransit. org, adults $1, seniors and people with disabilities $0.75) handles bus travel in Crescent City. Have exact change handy. Four in-town routes and a coastal bus from Smith River to Arcata provide ample public-transit options. Pick up a schedule at the visitors center (1001 Front St.).

Monterey and Big Sur

T he Monterey and Big Sur area is a favorite getaway for locals as much as visitors. The wild and rugged coastline provides ample opportunities to explore marine ecosystems, historic sights, and charming small towns.

Monterey Bay is the largest marine sanctuary in the country. Dive into its pristine waters to explore the bay's swaying kelp forests, or visit the Monterey Bay Aquarium for close-up views of local sea creatures. Santa Cruz is home to a seaside amusement park that offers roller coasters, bumper cars, and family-friendly beaches. Victorian architecture and butterfly migrations are the draws at Pacific Grove. Exclusive Pebble Beach offers some of the most-photographed scenery in the state. Artsy Carmel-by-the-Sea is an idyllic village gently descending to a white-sand beach. Inland Carmel Valley offers a burgeoning wine industry with enough tasting rooms to fill a long, relaxing afternoon.

Big Sur's 90 miles of rugged coastline begin just south of Carmel on the Monterey Peninsula and stretch south to San Simeon. Here, the mountains rise up suddenly and drop just as dramatically into the sea. Highway 1 twists and turns like a two-lane snake, trying to keep up with the land- and seascape.

South of Big Sur, San Simeon is home to one of California's biggest attractions: the magnificent Hearst Castle, a monument to the incredible wealth of newspaper magnate William Randolph Hearst. Farther south, Cambria has a pleasant downtown and Moonstone Beach, where you can pick up pieces of the gemstone right off the sand.

PLANNING YOUR TIME

For a relaxed **weekend** without much travel, focus your trip on Santa Cruz or the Monterey Peninsula. If you've got more than a couple of days, start in either Santa Cruz or Monterey and work your way down the coast.

Many people drive through Big Sur in one day, taking **Highway 1** south from Carmel and pulling off at the road's many turnouts. Outdoors enthusiasts who want to *really* experience Big Sur will need at least a couple of

---

Previous: Carmel Beach; Santa Cruz shoreline. **Above:** lifeguard tower on a Santa Cruz beach.

Look for ★ to find recommended
sights, activities, dining, and lodging.

Highlights

★ **Santa Cruz Beach Boardwalk:** With thrill rides, carnival games, and retro-cool live music, this is the best old-time boardwalk in the state (page 208).

★ **Surfing in Santa Cruz:** If there's anywhere in Northern California to don a wetsuit and go surfing, it's Santa Cruz. Breaks range from easy-rolling beginner waves at **Cowell's Beach** to more powerful breakers at **Steamer Lane** (page 217).

★ **Elkhorn Slough:** There's no better place to view the marine mammals of Monterey Bay than from a kayak in the Elkhorn Slough (page 222).

★ **Monterey Bay Aquarium:** This mammoth aquarium astonishes with a vast array of sealife and exhibits on the local ecosystem (page 224).

★ **Scuba Diving, Kayaking, and Stand-Up Paddleboarding:** Experience Monterey Bay's calm water and unique wildlife by getting into the water (page 229).

★ **Carmel Beach:** A great place for a stroll, a surf, or a picnic, this is one of the finest beaches on Monterey Bay (page 244).

★ **Point Lobos State Natural Reserve:** The crown jewel of California's impressive state park system has pocket coves, tide pools, forests of Monterey cypress, and diverse marine and terrestrial wildlife (page 244).

★ **Point Sur Light Station:** Crowning a 361-foot-high rock towering above the sea, this

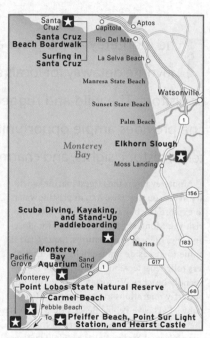

lighthouse is arguably California's most stunning light station (page 256).

★ **Pfeiffer Beach:** With rock formations offshore and purple sand, Pfeiffer Beach is one of Big Sur's most picturesque spots (page 259).

★ **Hearst Castle:** Newspaper magnate William Randolph Hearst's 56-bedroom mansion is the closest thing that the United States has to a castle (page 274).

Monterey and Big Sur

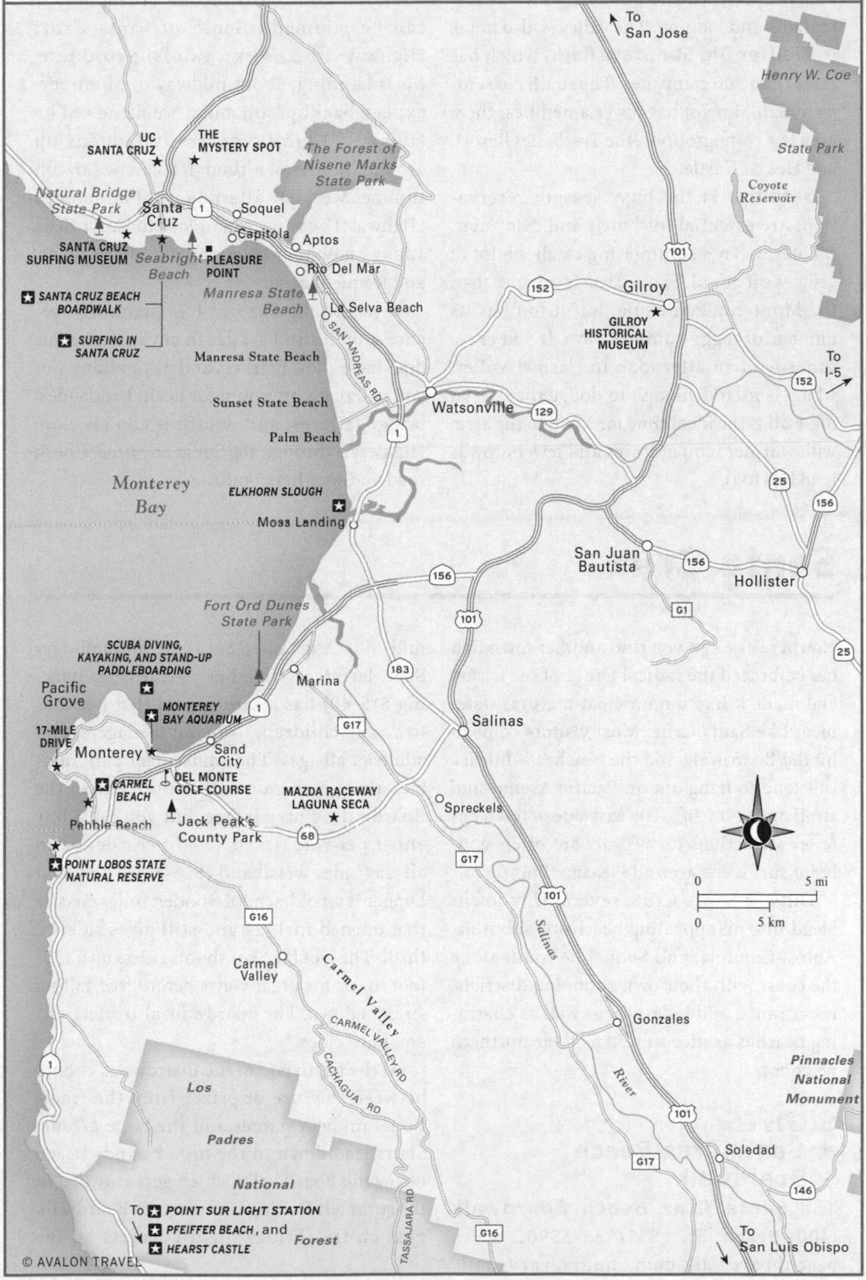

To San Jose

Henry W. Coe

State Park

Coyote Reservoir

UC SANTA CRUZ
THE MYSTERY SPOT
The Forest of Nisene Marks State Park

Natural Bridge State Park

Santa Cruz
Soquel
SANTA CRUZ SURFING MUSEUM
Capitola
Aptos
Seabright Beach
PLEASURE POINT
Rio Del Mar

101

SANTA CRUZ BEACH BOARDWALK
Manresa State Beach
La Selva Beach

152

Gilroy

SURFING IN SANTA CRUZ
GILROY HISTORICAL MUSEUM

Manresa State Beach

To I-5

Sunset State Beach
Watsonville
129
152

Palm Beach

1

25

Monterey Bay

ELKHORN SLOUGH

156

Moss Landing

San Juan Bautista
156

156

Hollister

Fort Ord Dunes State Park

G1

25

SCUBA DIVING, KAYAKING, AND STAND-UP PADDLEBOARDING

Marina
183

Pacific Grove

MONTEREY BAY AQUARIUM

Salinas

17-MILE DRIVE

Sand City

Monterey
DEL MONTE GOLF COURSE

CARMEL BEACH
MAZDA RACEWAY LAGUNA SECA

G17

Spreckels

Pebble Beach
Jack Peak's County Park
68

POINT LOBOS STATE NATURAL RESERVE

G16

101

Carmel Valley

CARMEL VALLEY RD

Gonzales

CACHAGUA RD

Los

Padres

Pinnacles National Monument

National

To POINT SUR LIGHT STATION
PFEIFFER BEACH, and
HEARST CASTLE

Soledad
146

Forest

TASSAJARA RD

To San Luis Obispo

0   5 mi
0   5 km

© AVALON TRAVEL

days. The **Big Sur Valley** (26 miles south of Carmel) is a good place to stay for a great outdoors experience and amenities such as restaurants and lodging. The valley is also home to **Pfeiffer Big Sur State Park,** which has more than 200 campsites. The south coast toward San Simeon has fewer amenities; there are a few campgrounds, the Treebones Resort, and Hearst Castle.

Summer is the busy season; reservations are essential for hotels and campsites. Monterey Bay's summer fog catches a lot of visitors off guard. Santa Cruz is warmer than the Monterey Peninsula, but it too has its number of foggy summer days. If you crave sun, spend an afternoon in Carmel Valley, which is inland enough to dodge the coastal fog. **Fall** is the ideal time for a trip to the area, with warmer temperatures and fewer crowds (and less fog).

Highway 1 connects Santa Cruz south to Carmel. (In morning and afternoon rush hour, the Santa Cruz section of Highway 1 can be jammed.) South of Santa Cruz, Highway 1 becomes a two-lane road near Moss Landing, about midway to Monterey; expect backups on busy weekends. The Highway 1 traffic generally lightens up around Monterey, although it can be slow on summer weekday afternoons. Mountainous Highway 17 connects San Jose to Santa Cruz and is known for heavy traffic, sharp turns, and frequent accidents.

A trip to Big Sur involves planning—secure supplies and get gas in advance. Big Sur does have a few markets and gas stations, but you will pay a premium for both. Landslides, bridge failures, and wildfires can all close Highway 1 through Big Sur at any time. Check road and weather conditions.

Santa Cruz

Nowhere else can you find another town that has embraced the radical fringe of the nation and made it into a municipal-cultural statement like Santa Cruz. Most visitors come to hit the Boardwalk and the beaches, while locals tend to hang out on Pacific Avenue and stroll on West Cliff. The east side of town has fewer attractions for visitors but offers a vibrant surf scene around Pleasure Point.

Outside Santa Cruz, several tiny towns blend into an appealing beachside suburbia. Aptos, Capitola, and Soquel lie south along the coast with their own shopping districts, restaurants, and lodgings, as well as charming beaches as nice to visit as their northern neighbors.

SIGHTS
★ **Santa Cruz Beach Boardwalk**

The **Santa Cruz Beach Boardwalk** (400 Beach St., 831/423-5590, www.beachboardwalk.com, hours vary daily mid-May-Aug., open Sat.-Sun. and holidays Sept.-late May, weather permitting, parking $15-40) has a rare appeal that beckons to young children, too-cool teenagers, and adults of all ages. The amusement park rambles along each side of the south end of the Boardwalk. Entry is free, but you must buy either per-ride tickets ($4-7 per ride) or an all-day rides wristband ($28-36). The Giant Dipper is an old-school wooden roller coaster that opened in 1924 and still gives riders a thrill. The Double Shot shoots riders up a 125-foot tower for great views before free-falling straight down. The Boardwalk also offers several kids' rides.

At the north end of the Boardwalk, choose between the lure of prizes from the traditional midway games and the large arcade. Stairs lead down to the broad, sandy beach below the Boardwalk, which gets crowded in the summer. During summer, the Boardwalk puts on free Friday-night concerts on the

Santa Cruz and Vicinity

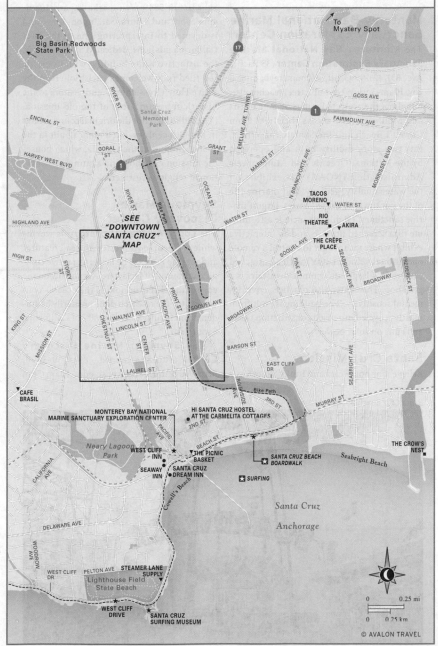

To
Big Basin Redwoods
State Park

To
Mystery Spot

17

GOSS AVE

FAIRMOUNT AVE

ENCINAL ST

RIVER ST

CORAL ST

GRANT ST

HARVEY WEST BLVD

EMELINE AVE TUNNEL

Santa Cruz
Memorial
Park

MARKET ST

N BRANCIFORTE AVE

MORRISSEY BLVD

TACOS
MORENO

WATER ST

RIO
THEATRE

AKIRA

THE CRÊPE
PLACE

HIGHLAND AVE

RIVER ST

Bike Path

SEE
"DOWNTOWN
SANTA CRUZ"
MAP

WATER ST

OCEAN ST

SOQUEL AVE

PINE ST

SEABRIGHT AVE

BROADWAY

FREDERICK ST

HIGH ST

STOREY ST

FRONT ST

PACIFIC AVE

SOQUEL AVE

KING ST

CHESTNUT ST

WALNUT AVE

LINCOLN ST

CENTER ST

BROADWAY

MISSION ST

BARSON ST

EAST CLIFF
DR

SEABRIGHT AVE

LAUREL ST

RIVERSIDE AVE

Bike Path

3RD ST

MURRAY ST

CAFE
BRASIL

MONTEREY BAY NATIONAL
MARINE SANCTUARY EXPLORATION CENTER

HI SANTA CRUZ HOSTEL
AT THE CARMELITA COTTAGES

2ND ST

THE CROW'S
NEST

Neary Lagoon
Park

PACIFIC AVE

WEST CLIFF
INN

BEACH ST

THE PICNIC
BASKET

SANTA CRUZ BEACH
BOARDWALK

Seabright Beach

CALIFORNIA AVE

SEAWAY
INN

SANTA CRUZ
DREAM INN

SURFING

DELAWARE AVE

Cowell's Beach

Santa Cruz

Anchorage

WOODROW AVE

WEST CLIFF
DR

PELTON AVE

STEAMER LANE
SUPPLY

Lighthouse Field
State Beach

0   0.25 mi

0   0.25 km

WEST CLIFF
DRIVE

SANTA CRUZ
SURFING MUSEUM

© AVALON TRAVEL

beach featuring retro acts like Warrant and A Flock of Seagulls.

Monterey Bay National Marine Sanctuary Exploration Center

The **Monterey Bay National Marine Sanctuary Exploration Center** (35 Pacific Ave., 831/421-9993, https://montereybay.noaa. gov, 10am-5pm Wed.-Sun., free) teaches visitors about the protected waters off Santa Cruz and Monterey. Just across the street from Cowell's Beach and the Santa Cruz Wharf, this two-story facility built and operated by the National Oceanic and Atmospheric Administration (NOAA) has exhibits on the water quality, geology, and marine life of the continental United States' largest marine sanctuary. Highlights include a 15-minute film screened upstairs and an interactive exhibit where visitors get to control a remote operational vehicle (ROV) with an attached camera in a large aquarium. Downstairs is a gift shop. The center also practices environmental sensitivity: The building is built from mostly recycled or reused construction waste and runs on solar power.

Santa Cruz Mission

Believe it or not, weird and funky Santa Cruz started out as a mission town. **Santa Cruz Mission State Historic Park** (130 Emmet St., 831/425-5849, www.parks.ca.park, 10am-4pm Mon. and Thurs.-Sat., noon-4pm Sun.) is devoted to interpreting one of the later California missions, dedicated in 1791. Today, the attractive white building with its classic red-tiled roof welcomes parishioners to the active Holy Cross church and visitors to the historic museum areas of the old mission. (The building is not the original complex built in the 18th century, but a replica built in the 1930s.) Stop in at the Galeria, which houses the mission gift shop and a stunning collection of religious vestments.

Seymour Marine Discovery Center

The **Long Marine Laboratory** is worthwhile for people interested in sea creatures and marine issues. The large, attractive complex at the end of Delaware Avenue sits on the edge of the cliff overlooking the ocean—convenient for the research done primarily by students and faculty of University of California, Santa Cruz.

The **Seymour Marine Discovery Center** (100 Shaffer Rd., 831/459-3800, http://seymourcenter.ucsc.edu, 10am-5pm

Santa Cruz Beach Boardwalk

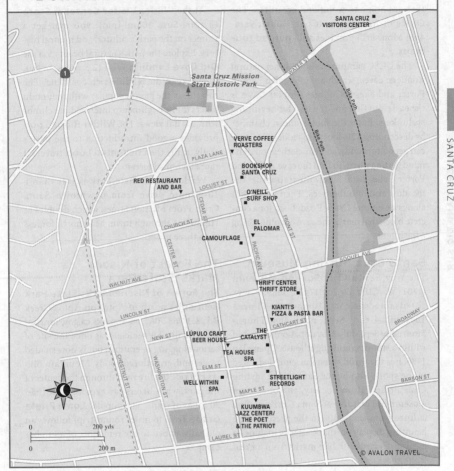

Downtown Santa Cruz

SANTA CRUZ
VISITORS CENTER

Santa Cruz Mission
State Historic Park

VERVE COFFEE
ROASTERS

BOOKSHOP
SANTA CRUZ

RED RESTAURANT
AND BAR

O'NEILL
SURF SHOP

EL
PALOMAR

CAMOUFLAGE

THRIFT CENTER
THRIFT STORE

KIANTI'S
PIZZA & PASTA BAR

LÚPULO CRAFT   THE
BEER HOUSE   CATALYST

TEA HOUSE
SPA

WELL WITHIN   STREETLIGHT
SPA   RECORDS

KUUMBWA
JAZZ CENTER/
THE POET
& THE PATRIOT

0   200 yds
0   200 m

© AVALON TRAVEL

PLAZA LANE · LOCUST ST · CEDAR ST · CHURCH ST · CENTER ST · WALNUT AVE · LINCOLN ST · NEW ST · CHESTNUT ST · WASHINGTON ST · ELM ST · MAPLE ST · LAUREL ST · PACIFIC AVE · FRONT ST · SOQUEL AVE · BROADWAY · BARSON ST · CATHCART ST · WATER ST · Bike Path

Tues.-Sun., adults $8, seniors, students, and children $6) is the part of the lab that's open to the public. Outside the door, a blue whale skeleton lights up at night. Inside is a marine laboratory similar to those used by scientists elsewhere in the complex. The aquariums showcase fascinating creatures including monkeyface eels and speckled sand dabs, while displays highlight environmental issues like shark finning. Kids love the touch tanks; check out the seasonal tank that contains the wildlife that's swimming around outside in the bay. **Tours** run at 11am, 1pm, 2pm, and 3pm each day; sign up an hour in advance to be sure of getting a slot.

University of California, Santa Cruz

The **University of California, Santa Cruz** (UCSC, 1156 High St., 831/459-0111, www.ucsc.edu) might be the most beautiful college campus in the country. Set in the hills above downtown Santa Cruz, the classrooms and dorms sit underneath groves of coast redwoods, among tangles of ferns and vines that are home to woodland creatures. The Office of Admissions (Cook House, 9am-4pm Mon.-Fri.) provides **self-guided tour maps.**

The UCSC campus has some other natural wonders: caves, which are in a gulch behind Porter and Kresge Colleges. **Porter Cave** is the easiest to find and the best for beginning spelunkers. Enter the subterranean chamber by descending a 20-foot steel ladder. The cave can get quite muddy, so wear clothes you don't mind getting dirty. To find the cave, go behind Porter College and follow the trail across the meadow and into the trees. Then head right alongside Empire Grade Road. Look for a concrete block that marks the cave opening. Bring a flashlight.

Santa Cruz Surfing Museum

The tiny **Santa Cruz Surfing Museum** (1701 W. Cliff Dr., 831/420-6289, www.cityofsantacruz.com, 10am-5pm Thurs.-Tues. July 4-early Sept.; noon-4pm Thurs.-Mon. early Sept.-July 3, by donation) is housed within a still-operating lighthouse. Opened in 1986, it is the world's first museum dedicated to the sport. Run by the Santa Cruz Surfing Club Preservation Society, the one-room museum has pictures of Santa Cruz's surfing culture from the 1930s to the present. One haunting display on shark attacks includes a local surfboard with bite marks from a great white shark.

Wilder Ranch State Park

North of Santa Cruz's city limits, the land on both sides of Highway 1 suddenly gives way to farmland perched atop coastal terraces. The best place to get a feel for this stretch of coastline is to visit **Wilder Ranch State Park** (1401 Coast Rd., 831/423-9703, www.parks.ca.gov, 8am-sunset daily, $10/vehicle). Visitors can step back in time and discover what it was like to live on this ranch through its many living-history demonstrations. Annual events include gardening demonstrations

and the Old-Fashioned Independence Day Celebration.

At the **Wilder Visitor Center & Store** (Thurs.-Sun. 10am-4pm), you can get a primer on the park's cultural and natural history. Explore the park's natural beauty via the **Old Cove Landing Trail** (2.5 miles), a flat, easy hike to the wildlife-rich coastline. The east side of the park is popular with mountain bikers for its beginner to intermediate climbs with coastal views. The **Wilder Ridge Loop** provides a good introduction to the park's trails, while the **Enchanted Loop** traverses more technical terrain.

Wilder Ranch State Park is less than a 10-minute drive from downtown Santa Cruz. From Mission Street, which doubles as Highway 1 through town, head north for less than three miles.

The Forest of Nisene Marks State Park

The Forest of Nisene Marks State Park (four miles north of Aptos on Aptos Creek Rd., 831/763-7062, www.parks.ca.gov, sunrise-sunset daily, $8/vehicle) was once the site of serious logging operations but is now shaded by second-growth redwoods. Mountain bikers can ride the fire road through the center of the park, while hikers can explore more than 30 miles of trails. The popular **Loma Prieta Grade Trail** (6 miles round-trip) follows an old railway bed to the remnants of a lumber camp.

The Mystery Spot

Santa Cruz has its own kitschy tourist trap: **The Mystery Spot** (465 Mystery Spot Rd., 831/423-8897, www.mysteryspot.com, 10am-6pm Mon.-Fri., 10am-8pm Sat.-Sun. summer, 10am-4pm daily winter, adults $8, children under 3 free, $5 parking), a tiny piece of land just outside of Santa Cruz where gravity fails. Balls roll uphill and people can stand off the side of a wall. It may be an area of spatial distortion where the laws of physics don't apply . . . or it may be a collection of optical illusions.

Surf City

the Santa Cruz Surfing Museum

There's a plaque outside the **Santa Cruz Surfing Museum** that explains how three Hawaiian princes introduced surfing to California in 1885. Apparently, they rode redwood planks from a nearby lumber mill on waves at the mouth of the San Lorenzo River in Santa Cruz.

While Santa Cruz's claim to be the birthplace of surfing on the mainland is not disputed, the popular surfing town calling itself "Surf City" has raised the hackles of Southern California's Huntington Beach, which also likes to have its tourist T-shirts adorned with "Surf City." In 2006, Huntington Beach was awarded exclusive use of the title "Surf City" by the U.S. Patent and Trademark Office and went after Santa Cruz beachwear stores that sold T-shirts with the words "Santa Cruz" and "Surf City."

Despite Huntington Beach's aggressive legal action, the residents of Santa Cruz might have the last laugh. In 2009, *Surfer Magazine* proclaimed that Santa Cruz is "The Real Surf City, USA" in a piece about the top 10 surf towns. To Huntington Beach's chagrin, it didn't even make the magazine's top 10 list.

ENTERTAINMENT AND EVENTS
Bars and Clubs

Lovers of libations should grab a drink at **Red Restaurant and Bar** (200 Locust St., 831/425-1913, www.redrestaurantandbar.com, 5pm-1:30am daily), upstairs in the historic Santa Cruz Hotel Building. Creative cocktails include signature creations like the Jean Grey, a mix of house-infused Earl Grey organic gin, lemon, and simple syrup. They also have a nice selection of 30 craft and Belgian beers on tap. With its dark wood paneling and burgundy barstools, Red feels like an old speakeasy. It also serves a comprehensive late-night menu until 1am for those who need some food to soak up their alcohol.

The Crêpe Place (1134 Soquel Ave., 831/429-6994, http://thecrepeplace.com, Mon.-Thurs. 11am-midnight, Fri. 11am-1am, Sat.-Sun. 9am-midnight) has recently emerged as a hangout for the hipster crowd, who are drawn in by the high-profile indie rock acts and popular Bay Area bands that perform in its intimate front room. There is also outdoor seating and a comprehensive menu of creative crepes.

Beer fans should make their way to the **Lúpulo Craft Beer House** (233 Cathcart St., 831/454-8306, www.lupulosc.com, 11:30am-10pm Mon.-Thurs., 11:30am-11:30pm Fri., 11am-11:30pm Sat., 11am-10pm Sun.). A small drinking establishment with a hip industrial feel, Lúpulo has 16 rotating craft beers on tap and over 300 types of bottled beer to consume on premises or take to go. There is also a small-bites menu featuring tacos, salads, and sandwiches. This husband-and-wife-owned business also conducts brewing demos, tastings, and other beer-related events.

Set in an alley, **The Poet & The Patriot** (320 Cedar St., 831/426-8620, daily 1pm-2am) is a popular watering hole that was opened by a Santa Cruz politician and playwright. The bar has two main rooms including one where there is frequently live music and another one that has four regulation dartboards. Both rooms feature framed memorabilia on the walls and banners on the ceiling.

Live Music

The Catalyst (1011 Pacific Ave., 831/423-1338, www.catalystclub.com), right downtown on Pacific Avenue, hosts a variety of reggae, rap, and punk acts from Snoop Dogg to Agent Orange. Check the calendar when you buy tickets—some shows are 21 and over. The 800-person main concert hall is a standing-room-only space, while the balconies offer seating. The bar sits downstairs adjacent to the concert space. The vibe tends to be low-key, but it depends on the night and the event. The **Catalyst Atrium,** a smaller room in the same building, snags some superb national touring bands. Buy tickets online or by phone; purchasing in advance is recommended, especially for national acts.

The Crow's Nest (2218 E. Cliff Dr., 831/476-4560, www.crowsnest-santacruz.com) is as a venue for all kinds of live musical acts. Rock, soul, reggae, and funk bands typically play Tuesday-Saturday. Sundays are live comedy evenings, and Tuesdays are reggae jam nights.

A former 1940s movie house, the **Rio**

Theatre (1205 Soquel Ave., 831/423-8209, www.riotheatre.com) hosts everything from film festivals to performances by international touring acts like Ladysmith Black Mambazo and Built to Spill. Check the theater's website for a full list of upcoming events.

Named one of the great jazz venues in the world by *Downbeat Magazine*, the **Kuumbwa Jazz Center** (320 Cedar St., 831/427-2227, http://kuumbwajazz.org) is a 200-seat treasure of a venue. It puts on 120 intimate concerts a year, aided by a superb sound and lighting setup. Past performers have included Bobby Hutcherson, Pharaoh Sanders, Christian McBride, and David Grisman.

Breweries

Since 2013, Santa Cruz's craft brewing scene has exploded. Sample Santa Cruz's suds by booking a seat on the **Brew Cruz** (831/222-0120, www.scbrewcruz.com, $69 pp), an army-green bus with a refrigerated cooler on board. The bus stops at three local breweries over a four-hour period.

One of the city's best breweries is **Discretion Brewing** (2703 41st Ave., Ste. A, Soquel, 831/316-0662, www.discretionbrewing.com, 11:30am-9pm daily). Their tasting menu includes the award-winning and widely popular Uncle Dave's Rye IPA and Oh Black Lager. The indoor and outdoor space also serves farm-to-table comfort food.

Comedy

For a good laugh in Santa Cruz, **The Crow's Nest** (2218 East Cliff Dr., 831/476-4560, www.crowsnest-santacruz.com) hosts a weekly **stand-up comedy show** (Sun. 9pm, $7). Because the show runs on Sunday nights, The Crow's Nest takes advantage of the opportunity to hire big-name comics who have been in San Francisco or San Jose for weekend engagements. This lets folks see headliners in a more casual setting for a fraction of the cost of the big-city clubs. The Crow's Nest, with its great views out over the Pacific, also has a full bar and restaurant. Enjoy drinks and dinner while you get your giggle on.

Bookshop Santa Cruz

the (slightly seedy) south end, visitors can purchase body jewelry or tattoos. The sidewalks are often jammed with shoppers, street performers, panhandlers, and sightseers. It's a good idea to park in one of the structures a block or two off Pacific Avenue and walk.

Bookshop Santa Cruz (1520 Pacific Ave., 831/423-0900, www.bookshopsantacruz.com, Sun.-Thurs. 9am-10pm, Fri.-Sat. 9am-11pm) is a superb independent bookstore that hosts regular readings by literary heavy hitters like Jonathan Franzen and Daniel Handler. Browse new books and used books, as well as an extensive collection of magazines.

Santa Cruz's Jack O'Neill is credited with making cold-water surfing possible with the invention of the wetsuit. His **O'Neill Surf Shop** (110 Cooper St., 831/469-4377, 10am-9pm Sun.-Thurs., 10am-10pm Fri.-Sat. summer; 10am-8pm Sun.-Thurs., 10am-9pm Fri.-Sat. winter) specializes in surfboards, brand-name clothing, and, of course, wetsuits.

One of the largest secondhand-clothing shops sits only a block off Pacific Avenue—the **Thrift Center Thrift Store** (504 Front St., 831/429-6975, Mon.-Sat. 9am-8pm, Sun. 10am-6pm). This big, somewhat dingy retail space offers a wide array of cheap secondhand clothes.

Camouflage (1329 Pacific Ave., 831/423-7613, www.shopcamoflauge.com, 10am-10pm Mon.-Sat., 10am-8pm Sun.) is an independent, family-owned, and women-friendly adult store. The first room contains mostly lingerie and tame items. Walk through the narrow black-curtained passage and you'll find the *other* room, which is filled with grown-up toys.

Stop in to **Streetlight Records** (939 Pacific Ave., 831/421-9200, www.streetlightrecords.com, Sun.-Mon. noon-8pm, Tues.-Thurs. 11am-9pm, Fri.-Sat. 11am-10pm) to pick up the latest music. With records and turntables making a serious comeback, Streetlight is also the place in Santa Cruz to find new and used vinyl.

Theater

When the long-running Shakespeare Santa Cruz went belly-up in 2013, the nonprofit **Santa Cruz Shakespeare** (The Sinsheimer-Stanley Festival Glen, UCSC Performing Arts Center, Meyer Dr., 831/460-6396, box office 831/460-6399, www.santacruzshakespeare.org, July-Aug., adults $40-52, seniors and military $36-48, children 18 and under $16, previews $20) was formed in 2014 so Bard lovers could still get their fix. Recent productions, presented in The Grove at DeLaveaga Park (501 Upper Park Rd.) have included *A Midsummer Night's Dream* and *Hamlet*.

SHOPPING

Santa Cruz's bustling downtown is centered on **Pacific Avenue** (Water St. to Laurel St.). At the north end, shoppers peruse antiques, clothing, and kitchenware. In the middle, grab a cappuccino, a cocktail, or a bite to eat in one of the many independent eateries. At

SPORTS AND RECREATION

Beaches

NATURAL BRIDGES STATE BEACH

At the tip of the West Side, picturesque **Natural Bridges State Beach** (2531 W. Cliff Dr., 831/423-4609, www.parks.ca.gov, 8am-sunset daily, $10) has a beach that doesn't stretch wide but falls back deep, crossed by a creek that feeds into the sea. An inconsistent break makes surfing at Natural Bridges fun on occasion, while the near-constant winds bring out windsurfers every weekend. Hardy sun-worshippers brave the breezes, bringing out their beach blankets, umbrellas, and sunscreen on rare sunny days (usually in late spring and fall). A wooded picnic area has tables and grills for small and larger parties. The park's Monarch butterfly preserve is where the migrating insects take over the eucalyptus grove during the fall and winter months. Rangers offer guided tours of the tide pools that range out to the west side of the beach. Access is by a scrambling short hike (0.25-0.5 mile) on the rocky cliffs.

COWELL'S BEACH

Cowell's Beach (350 W. Cliff Dr.) is where lots of beginning surfers rode their first waves.

This West Side beach sits right at a crook in the coastline that joins with underwater features to create a reliable small break that lures new surfers by the dozens.

SEABRIGHT BEACH

At the south end of Santa Cruz, down by the harbor, beachgoers flock to **Seabright Beach** (E. Cliff Dr. at Seabright Ave., 831/427-4868, www.thatsmypark.org, 6am-10pm daily, free). This miles-long stretch of sand, protected by the cliffs from the worst winds, is a favorite retreat for sunbathers and loungers. While there's little in the way of facilities, there is soft sand, plenty of room to play football or set up a volleyball net, and, of course, easy access to the chilly Pacific Ocean. There's no surfing here—Seabright has a shore break that delights skim-boarders but makes wave riding impossible. Beach fires are allowed in fire rings.

NEW BRIGHTON STATE BEACH

One of the most popular sandy spots is **New Brighton State Beach** (1500 Park Ave., Capitola, 831/464-6330, www.thatsmypark. org, 8am-sunset daily, $10/vehicle). This forest-backed beach has everything: a strip of sand perfect for lounging and swimming,

Natural Bridges State Beach

a forest-shaded campground for both tents and RVs, hiking trails, and ranger-led nature programs. New Brighton can get crowded on sunny summer days, but it's nothing like the wall-to-wall people of the popular Southern California beaches.

SEACLIFF STATE BEACH
Seacliff State Beach (1500 Park Ave., Capitola, 831/685-6500, www.parks.ca.gov, 8am-sunset daily, $10/vehicle) is known as the final resting place of the *SS Palo Alto,* a concrete ship that was once an amusement park. The vessel is visible, but inaccessible. The surrounding beach makes a fine sunning and swimming spot.

TOP EXPERIENCE

★ Surfing
The coastline of Santa Cruz has more than its share of great surf breaks. The water is cold, demanding full wetsuits year-round, and the shoreline is rough and rocky.

The best place for beginners is **Cowell's** (stairs at W. Cliff Dr. and Cowell's Beach). The waves rarely get huge, and they typically provide long, mellow rides, perfect for surfers just getting their balance. Because the Cowell's

break is acknowledged as the newbie spot, the often-sizable crowd tends to be polite to newcomers and visitors.

For more advanced surfers looking for smaller crowds in the water, **Manresa State Beach** (San Andreas Rd., Aptos, 831/724-3750, www.parks.ca.gov, 8am-sunset daily, $10/vehicle) is a nice beach break south of Santa Cruz. Manresa is several minutes' drive toward Aptos. During summer, it's a great place to surf and then recline on the beach.

Visitors who know their surfing lore will want to surf the more famous spots along the Santa Cruz shore. **Pleasure Point** (between 32nd Ave. and 41st Ave.) encompasses a number of different breaks. You may have heard of **The Hook** (steps at 41st Ave.), a well-known, experienced longboarder's paradise. But don't mistake The Hook for a beginner's break; the locals feel protective of the waves here and aren't always friendly toward inexperienced tourists. The break at **36th and East Cliff** (steps at 36th Ave.) can be a better place to go on weekdays—on the weekends, the intense crowding makes catching your own wave a challenge. Up at **30th and East Cliff** (steps at 36th Ave.), you'll find shortboarders catching larger, long peeling sets if there is a swell in the water.

the iconic surf break Steamer Lane

The most famous break in all of Santa Cruz can also be the most hostile to newcomers. **Steamer Lane** (W. Cliff Dr. between Cowell's and the Santa Cruz Surfing Museum) has a fiercely protective crew of locals. But if you're experienced and there's a swell coming in, Steamer Lane can have some of the best waves on the California coast.

Yes, you can learn to surf in Santa Cruz. Check out either **Club Ed Surf School and Camps** (831/464-0177, https://club-ed.com, beginner group lesson $90 pp, beginner/private lessons for children $120/hour) or the **Richard Schmidt School** (849 Almar Ave., 831/423-0928, www.richardschmidt.com, 2-hour class $90 pp, private lessons $100-180/hour) to sign up for lessons.

Stand-Up Paddleboarding

Stand-up paddleboarders vie for waves with surfers at Pleasure Point and can also be found in the Santa Cruz waters with less wave action. **Covewater Paddle Surf** (726 Water St., 831/600-7230, www.covewatersup.com, 2-hour lesson $65) conducts beginner stand-up paddleboarding (SUP) classes in the relatively calm waters of the Santa Cruz Harbor. They also rent paddleboards ($40/two hours, $75/all day).

Hiking and Biking

Winding **West Cliff Drive** has a full-fledged sidewalk trail running its length on the ocean side; it's the town's favorite walking, dog walking, jogging, skating, scootering, and biking route. Start at Santa Cruz Municipal Wharf and go 2.75 miles to Natural Bridges State Beach (the west end of West Cliff). You'll pass the *To Honor Surfing* statue along with views of the ocean studded with sea stacks. Watch for fellow path-users, as it can get crowded.

To rent a bike, head to **Pacific Ave Cycles** (320-322 Pacific Ave., 831/471-2453, 10am-6pm daily, hourly $8-15, daily $25-45). The small shop with single- and multiple-speed bikes is just a few blocks east of the start of West Cliff Drive.

Spas

The **Tea House Spa** (112 Elm St., 831/426-9700, www.teahousespa.com, 11am-11pm Mon.-Thurs., 11am-midnight Fri.-Sun., spa rooms $12-35/hour, massages $55-140) is a half-block off Pacific Avenue and offers private hot tubs with views of a bamboo garden. It's not fancy, but the tubs will warm you up and mellow you out. The **Well Within Spa** (417 Cedar St., 831/458-9355, http://wellwithinspa.com, 11am-midnight daily) has indoor spa rooms and outdoor spas ($16-47/hour) and offers massages ($50-115).

FOOD
California Cuisine

The **Shadowbrook Restaurant** (1750 Wharf Rd., Capitola, 831/475-1511, www.shadowbrook-capitola.com, 5pm-8:45pm Mon.-Fri., 4:30pm-9:45pm Sat., 4:30pm-8:45pm Sun., $20-55) is where to celebrate a special occasion. The adventure begins with a cable car ride down to the restaurant, which is perched on a steep slope above Soquel Creek. Entrées include a slow-roasted, bone-in pork prime rib, a one-pound surf-and-turf dish, and several vegetarian options. If you're staying within a three-mile radius of the restaurant, you can be shuttled to the restaurant in a 1950 Dodge (free, tips appreciated). Reserve a ride when you make dinner reservations.

Breakfast

Just a few feet away from legendary surf spot Steamer Lane, the ★ **Steamer Lane Supply** (698 W. Cliff Dr., 831/621-7361, http://steamerlanesc.com, 7:30am-sunset daily, $4-10) has everything a surfer needs before hitting the waves: hot coffee, breakfast quesadillas, surf wax, surf leashes, and more. This small, takeout concession stand within Lighthouse Field State Park is an ideal place to take in the surf by Santa Cruz's West Cliff Drive. On Saturday and Sunday, they do fish tacos from a food truck.

Coffee and Bakeries

For a casual sandwich or pastry, head to

Kelly's French Bakery (402 Ingalls St., 831/423-9059, www.kellysfrenchbakery.com, 7am-7pm daily, $8-20). This popular bakery makes its home in an old industrial warehouse-style space, and its domed shape constructed out of corrugated metal looks like anything but a restaurant. It has both indoor and outdoor seating, and serves full breakfasts and luncheon sandwiches.

★ **Verve Coffee Roasters** (1540 Pacific Ave., 831/600-7784, www.vervecoffeeroasters. com, 6:30am-9pm daily) offers a hip, open space with lots of windows at the eastern edge of Pacific Avenue. Order a drink at the counter and then grab a seat in this frequently crowded coffee shop. They also have locations on the East Side (846 41st Ave., 831/475-7776, 6am-8pm daily; 104 Bronson St., Ste. 19, 831/471-8469, 6am-5pm daily).

Italian

Kianti's Pizza & Pasta Bar (1100 Pacific Ave., 831/469-4400, www.kiantis.com, 11am-10pm Mon.-Fri., 10am-10pm Sat.-Sun., $13-21) draws in crowds with pastas, pizzas, and salads. Pizza toppings range from traditional Italian ingredients to more creative options (one pie is covered with seasoned beef, lettuce, tomato, avocado, and tortilla chips). Kianti's

full bar and outdoor seating area are right on Pacific Avenue.

Japanese

South of downtown, **Akira** (1222 Soquel Ave., 831/600-7093, www.akirasantacruz.com, 11am-11pm daily, $6-21) is a modern sushi bar with interesting creations. Some rolls employ unconventional ingredients like skirt steak and spicy truffled shoestring yams; more traditional rolls are served at the sushi bar or tableside. Akira's happy hour (4pm-6pm and 9:30pm-10:30pm daily) offers appetizers to go with your beer, sake, or wine.

Mexican

At **El Palomar** (1336 Pacific Ave., 831/425-7575, http://elpalomarsantacruz.com, 11am-9pm Mon.-Wed., 11am-10pm Thurs., 11am-10:30pm Fri., 10am-10:30pm Sat., 10am-9pm Sun., $13-27), enjoy shrimp enchiladas or chicken mole while a roving mariachi band plays. Jose's Special Appetizer can be a light meal for two. The informal taco bar is great for a quick bite and drink. El Palomar also has a happy hour (3pm-6pm Mon.-Fri.).

Sandwiches

Just feet from the Santa Cruz Beach Boardwalk

a sandwich from The Picnic Basket

is a casual eatery with a simple menu that utilizes locally sourced, tasty goodness: ★ **The Picnic Basket** (125 Beach St., 831/427-9946, http://thepicnicbasketsc.com, 7am-9pm daily summer, 7am-4pm daily winter, $3-9). Its attention to detail shines through even on a simple turkey, cheese, and avocado sandwich. Options include breakfast items, salads, mac and cheese, and local beer and wine.

South American

Cafe Brasil (1410 Mission St., 831/429-1855, www.cafebrasil.us, 8am-3pm daily, $6-11) serves up the Brazilian fare its name promises. Thanks to a building painted jungle green with bright yellow and blue trim, you can't miss this totally Santa Cruz breakfast and lunch joint. In the morning, the fare runs to omelets and Brazilian specialties. Lunch includes pressed sandwiches, meat and tofu dishes, and Brazilian house specials.

ACCOMMODATIONS
Under $150

The **Hostelling International Santa Cruz Hostel** (321 Main St., 831/423-8304, www.hi-santacruz.org, dorm beds $28, private rooms $48-113) offers the area's only budget lodging.

The historic cottages, just two blocks from the Santa Cruz Beach Boardwalk, are clean, cheap, friendly, and close to Cowell's Beach. There's a big, homey kitchen open for guest use and a garden, outdoor deck, free linens, laundry facilities, and a free Internet kiosk. The hostel is closed 11am-5pm daily, so there is no access to guest rooms or indoor common areas. Guests are allowed to leave their luggage inside or in outdoor lockers.

$150-250

The ★ **West Cliff Inn** (174 W. Cliff Dr., 831/457-2200, www.westcliffinn.com, $209-399) is a gleaming white mansion topping the hill above Cowell's Beach and the Boardwalk. This three-story historic landmark was constructed back in 1877 and was the first of the bluff's Millionaires' Row residences. The nine rooms in the main house have stunning white-marble bathrooms, some of which have oversize soaking tubs. The more moderately priced and pet-friendly Little Beach Bungalow is behind the main house. Fill up on a morning breakfast buffet and an afternoon wine and appetizer hour. The inn's veranda and second-floor balcony provide wonderful views.

The ★ **Seaway Inn** (176 W. Cliff Dr.,

The Seaway Inn is one of Santa Cruz's best overnight bargains.

831/471-9004, www.seawayinn.com, $204-330) offers a night's stay across from Cowell's Beach. Rooms are clean, but not fancy, and have a shared patio or deck with chairs; the bathrooms are small. The 18 units in the main building have TVs with DVD players, microwaves, and mini-fridges. Family suites accommodate up to five adults. The complimentary breakfast boasts make-your-own waffles. The friendly staff also operate a nearby building that has five studio apartments, each with a full kitchen. Pets are welcome ($15 for the first night, $5 each additional night).

Over $250

Perched over Cowell's Beach and the Santa Cruz Wharf, **Santa Cruz Dream Inn** (175 W. Cliff Dr., 831/426-4330, www.dreaminnsantacruz.com, $421-669) has 165 rooms with striking ocean views and either a private balcony or a shared common patio. The retro-chic rooms match perfectly with the vibrant colors of the nearby Boardwalk. The Dream Inn's sundeck is right on Cowell's Beach; among the inn's amenities are a heated swimming pool, a large hot tub, and a poolside bar.

The **Ocean Echo Inn & Beach Cottages** (410 Johans Beach Dr., 831/462-4192, www.oceanecho.com, $375-630) is a secluded gem on the East Side, just 53 footsteps down to a locals' pocket beach. The inn's water tower, chicken coop, and carriage house have all been converted into cozy cottages. There are 15 units, including the cottages and inn rooms (11 have full kitchens), and multiple decks along with a Ping-Pong table and grills. A modest continental breakfast is put out in the morning.

TRANSPORTATION AND SERVICES

Navigating the winding, broken-up streets of this oddly shaped town isn't for the faint of heart. Highway 1 (Mission St. on the West Side) is the main artery through Santa Cruz down to Capitola, Soquel, and Aptos.

Highway 1 at the interchange to Highway 17 is a parking lot most of the time.

Car

From San Francisco, Santa Cruz is 75 miles south, about 1.5 hours away. Take either **U.S. 101** or I-280 south (101 can be slightly faster, but less scenic and more prone to traffic) to **Highway 17** toward Santa Cruz. Most locals take this 50-mile-per-hour corridor fast—probably faster than they should. Each year, several people die in accidents on Highway 17, so keep to the right and take it slow, no matter what the traffic to the left of you is doing. Check traffic reports before you head out; Highway 17 is known as one of the worst commuting roads in the Bay Area, and weekend beach traffic in the summer jams up fast in both directions.

For a more leisurely drive, opt for two-lane **Highway 1.** Once in town, Highway 1 becomes Mission Street on the West Side and acts as the main artery through Santa Cruz and down to Capitola, Soquel, Aptos, and coastal points farther south.

Another option for a more leisurely drive is two-lane **Highway 9.** The tight curves and endless switchbacks will keep you at a reasonable speed; use the turnouts to let the locals pass and watch for bicyclists and motorcyclists.

Parking in Santa Cruz can be challenging. Downtown, head straight for the parking structures one block away from Pacific Avenue on either side. They're much easier to deal with than trying to find street parking. The same goes for the beach and Boardwalk areas. At the Boardwalk, just pay the fee to park in the big parking lot adjacent to the attractions. You'll save an hour and a possible car break-in or theft trying to find street parking in the sketchy neighborhoods that surround the Boardwalk.

Public Transit

Buses are run by the **Santa Cruz Metro** (831/425-8600 www.scmtd.com, adults $2 per ride, passes available). In the summer, take advantage of the **Santa Cruz Trolley** (831/420-5150, http://santacruztrolley.com, noon-8pm daily late May-early Sept., $0.25). The vintage trolley car connects the Boardwalk and downtown via a three-stop route running every 15-20 minutes.

Services

While it can be fun to explore Santa Cruz just by using your innate sense of direction, those who want a map can hit the **Santa Cruz County Visitors Center** (303 Water St., Ste. 100, 800/833-3494, www.santacruz.org, 9am-noon and 1pm-4pm Mon.-Fri., 11am-3pm Sat.-Sun.) or stop by the **Downtown Information Kiosk** (1130 Pacific Ave., K2, 831/332-7422 Ext. 2, www.downtownsantacruz.com, 11am-6pm Sun.-Thurs., 11am-8pm Fri.-Sat.). Medical treatment is available at **Dominican Hospital** (1555 Soquel Ave., 855/489-4580).

Moss Landing

Moss Landing is a picturesque, working fishing village (just ignore the rising smokestacks of the towering Moss Landing Power Plant). The main drag, Moss Landing Road, has a scattering of antiques stores and art galleries, and Moss Landing Harbor is home to a fleet of fishing vessels. To the south, Salinas River State Beach offers miles of wild, undeveloped shoreline. North of the inlet, Zmudowski State Beach is popular with local surfers during the winter months. Offshore, the Monterey Submarine Canyon is one of North America's largest submarine canyons. It's the reason that the Moss Landing Marine Laboratories and Monterey Bay Aquarium Research Institute have local addresses.

SIGHTS
★ Elkhorn Slough

Elkhorn Slough is the second-largest section of tidal salt marsh in California after San Francisco Bay. The estuary hosts an amazing amount of wildlife that includes marine mammals and over 340 bird species, which makes it one of the state's best birding spots. The best way to explore the slough is by kayak, where you can view rafts of lounging sea otters and a barking rookery of California sea lions from water level. In Moss Landing's North Harbor, which connects to the slough, **Monterey Bay Kayaks** (2390 Hwy. 1, 831/373-5357, www.montereybaykayaks.com, 9am-7pm daily summer, 9am-6pm daily spring and fall,

9am-5pm winter, SUP rental $35/day) rents kayak ($30-35/day) and has a range of guided tours ($45-80), from a 1.5-hour paddle around the harbor to monthly full-moon tours.

Elkhorn Slough Safari (Moss Landing Harbor, Dock A, 7881 Sandholdt Rd., 831/633-5555, www.elkhornslough.com, adults $38, children $28, seniors $35) offers a 1.5- to 2-hour tour of the estuary by boat.

ENTERTAINMENT AND EVENTS

The **Moss Landing Inn** (7902 Hwy. 1, 831/633-9803, http://wenchilada.com, 1pm-2am Mon.-Thurs., noon-2am Fri.-Sun.) is a dive bar where dollar bills hang off the ceiling. Spend a few hours getting acquainted with the local characters. It's connected to The Whole Enchilada restaurant and offers live music on weekends.

On the last Sunday of July, Moss Landing is flooded with antiques enthusiasts for the annual **Moss Landing Antique Street Fair** (831/633-4501, www.mosslandingchamber.com, July, adults $5, children under 12 free). The giant outdoor antiques market has more than 200 booths selling collectibles; other booths serve local foods.

SHOPPING

Located behind the Haute Enchilada Café, the **Haute Enchilada Gallery** (7902 Moss Landing Rd., 831/633-3743, www.

hauteenchilada.com, 11am-5pm daily) has multiple rooms filled with sculptures, watercolors, woodworks, and ceramic items. **Driftwood** (8071-B Moss Landing Rd., 831/632-2800, www.driftwoodstore.com, noon-5pm Sun.-Thurs., 11am-6pm Fri.-Sat.) bills itself as an "artisan gift boutique." Expect hipster-approved jewelry, home furnishings, and candles.

SPORTS AND RECREATION
Beaches
Just north of Moss Landing's harbor, **Moss Landing State Beach** (Jetty Rd., 831/649-2836, www.parks.ca.gov, 8am-sunset daily) and **Zmudowski State Beach** (20 miles north of Monterey on Hwy. 1, 831/649-2836, www.parks.ca.gov, 8am-sunset daily) stretch for miles. They're mostly enjoyed by locals who fish, surf, or ride horses on the beach. To get to the beaches from Highway 1, take Struve Road and turn onto Giberson Road.

Just south of Moss Landing is the **Salinas River State Beach** (Potrero Rd., 831/649-2836, www.parks.ca.gov, 8am-sunset daily). Expect some serenity among a few horseback riders or anglers.

Whale-Watching
For a glimpse of gray whales or orcas, catch a ride with **Sanctuary Cruises** (7881 Sandholt Rd., 831/350-4090, www.sanctuarycruises.com, adults $55, children under 13 $45). Running on biodiesel, the 43-foot ocean vessel *Sanctuary* takes passengers out daily for 4-5-hour cruises. **Blue Ocean Whale Watch** (7881 Sandholt Rd., 831/600-5103, www.blueoceanwhalewatch.com, adults $50, children 4-12 $40) heads into the bay for 3-4-hour whale-watching expeditions.

Fishing
Anglers can cast a line for rockfish, lingcod, salmon, halibut, or albacore on the 50-foot *Kahuna*, run by **Kahuna Sportfishing** (7881 Sandholdt Rd., 831/633-2564, www.kahunasportfishing.com, $85-180 per person).

FOOD
Moss Landing is best known for its seafood restaurants. The most popular is ★ **Phil's Fish Market** (7600 Sandholt Rd., 831/633-2152, www.philsfishmarket.com, fish market: 8:30am-8pm daily in summer, 8:30am-7pm Sun.-Wed., 8:30am-8pm Thurs.-Sat. in winter; eatery: 10am-9pm daily in summer, 10am-8pm Sun.-Wed., 10am-9pm Thurs.-Sat. in winter, $9-26), known for its cioppino—a hearty Italian American seafood stew that includes clams, mussels, fish, Dungeness crab, prawns, and scallops. A heaping bowl comes with salad and garlic bread, while blackened sea scallops are served in a lemon-caper butter sauce. This informal market/eatery has a bluegrass band playing Monday-Thursday nights.

The Whole Enchilada (7902 Hwy. 1, 831/633-3038, http://wenchilada.com, 11:30am-8:15pm daily, $10-24) does seafood with a Mexican slant. Dine on seafood enchiladas, Mexican-style cioppino, or chile relleno stuffed with crab, shrimp, and cheese in the brightly colored dining room or on the outdoor patio.

Part art gallery, part eatery, fanciful **Haute Enchilada Café & Galleries** (7902 Moss Landing Rd., 831/633-5843, www.hauteenchilada.com, 11am-9pm daily, $17-26) serves Peruvian empanadas and skirt steaks in Oaxacan black bean sauce.

ACCOMMODATIONS AND CAMPING
The ★ **Captain's Inn** (8122 Moss Landing Rd., 831/633-5550, www.captainsinn.com, $188-287) is the perfect place to spend an evening in the fishing village. Rooms are in two buildings: a historic structure, once the site of the Pacific Coast Steamship Company, and the Boathouse, where every room has a superb view of the nearby tidal marsh. Wildlife watchers might be able to catch a glimpse of marine mammals or birds in the nearby tidal marsh, while maritime fans will love the bed sets crafted out of boat parts. Wake up to a home-cooked breakfast that can be taken to-go.

The **Monterey Dunes Company** (407 Moss Landing Rd., 831/633-4883 or 800/553-8637, www.montereydunes.com, from $733/night) rents 2-4-bedroom homes on the beach south of Moss Landing. Guests have access to the development's tennis courts, swimming pool, saunas, and hot tub.

The **Moss Landing KOA Express** (7905 Sandholt Rd., 831/633-6800 or 800/562-3390, https://koa.com, $75-85) has almost 50 RV sites right in the Moss Landing Harbor area.

TRANSPORTATION

Moss Landing is 25 miles south of Santa Cruz and 15 miles north of Monterey on Highway 1.

Monterey

Monterey has roots as a fishing town. Native Americans were the first to ply the bay's waters, and fishing became an economic driver with the arrival of European settlers in the 19th century. Author John Steinbeck immortalized this unglamorous industry in his novel *Cannery Row*. Monterey's blue-collar past is still evident in its architecture, even though the cannery workers have been replaced by visiting tourists.

There are two main sections of Monterey: the old downtown area and "New Monterey," which includes Cannery Row and the Monterey Aquarium. The old downtown is situated around Alvarado Street and includes the historic adobes that make up Monterey State Historic Park. New Monterey bustles with tourists during the summer. The six blocks of Cannery Row are packed with businesses, including the must-see Monterey Bay Aquarium, seafood restaurants, shops, galleries, and wine-tasting rooms. One way to get from one section to the other is to walk the Monterey Bay Coastal Recreation Trail, a paved path that runs right along a stretch of coastline.

SIGHTS
Cannery Row

Cannery Row (www.canneryrow.com) did once look and feel as John Steinbeck described it in his famed novel of the same name. In the 1930s and 1940s, fishing boats docked here and offloaded their catches straight into the huge, warehouse-like cannery buildings.

But overfishing took its toll, and by the late 1950s Cannery Row was deserted. A slow renaissance began in the 1960s, driven by new interest in preserving the historic integrity of the area, as well as by a few savvy entrepreneurs who understood the value of beachfront property. Today, what was once a worker's wharf is now an enclave of boutique hotels, big seafood restaurants, and souvenir stores selling T-shirts adorned with sea otters. Cannery Row is anchored at one end by the aquarium and runs for several blocks that include a beach; it then leads into the Monterey Harbor area.

★ Monterey Bay Aquarium

The **Monterey Bay Aquarium** (886 Cannery Row, 831/648-4800, www.montereybayaquarium.org, 9:30am-6pm daily, adults $50, seniors and students $40, children 3-12 $30) displays a dazzling array of local sealife. First-class exhibits include the Kelp Forest, which mimics the environment just outside; the Open Sea exhibit, with its deepwater tank that's home to giant bluefin tuna and hammerhead sharks; Wild About Otters, which gives an up-close view of rescued otters; and the Jellies Experience, which illuminates the delicate creatures. Check the feeding schedules when you arrive, and show up in advance to get a good spot near the critters for the show. The aquarium is wildly popular, and in the summer, the crowds can be forbidding. Weekdays can be less crushing (though you'll run into school groups much

Cannery Row

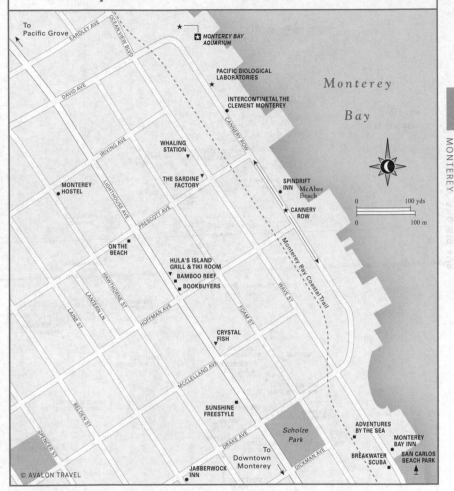

of the year), and the off-season is always a better time to visit. Most exhibits at the aquarium are wheelchair-accessible.

Monterey State Historic Park

Monterey State Historic Park (20 Custom House Plaza, 831/649-2907, www.parks. ca.gov, 9am-5pm daily May-Sept., 10am-4pm daily Oct.-Apr., free) pays homage to the long and colorful history of the city of Monterey. This busy port town acted as the capital of California when it was under Spanish and Mexican rule. Today, the park is a collection of old buildings scattered about downtown Monterey, and it provides a peek into the city as it was in the mid-19th century.

Built in 1827, the **Custom House** (east of Fisherman's Wharf, 10am-4pm daily, $5) is the oldest government building still standing in the state. Wander the adobe building and check out the artifacts on display, meant to resemble the building's goods when it was under

Downtown Monterey

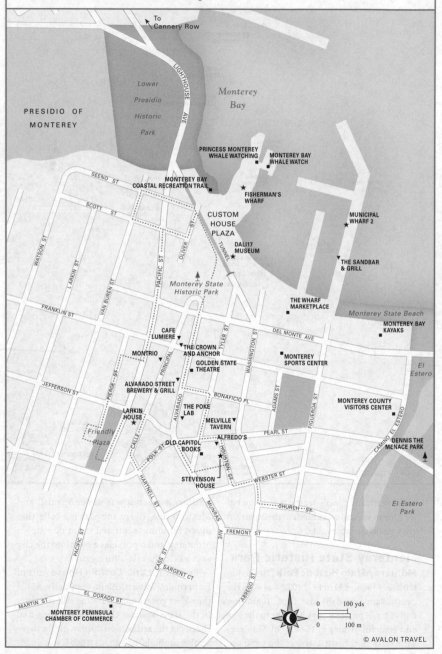

To Cannery Row

LIGHTHOUSE AVE

Lower
Presidio
Historic
Park

Monterey
Bay

PRESIDIO OF
MONTEREY

PRINCESS MONTEREY
WHALE WATCHING

MONTEREY BAY
WHALE WATCH

SEENO ST

MONTEREY BAY
COASTAL RECREATION TRAIL

FISHERMAN'S
WHARF

SCOTT ST

OLIVER ST

CUSTOM
HOUSE
PLAZA

MUNICIPAL
WHARF 2

WATSON ST

LARKIN ST

VAN BUREN ST

PACIFIC ST

TUNNEL

DALI17
MUSEUM

THE SANDBAR
& GRILL

Monterey State
Historic Park

FRANKLIN ST

THE WHARF
MARKETPLACE

Monterey State Beach

DEL MONTE AVE

MONTEREY BAY
KAYAKS

CAFE
LUMIERE

TYLER ST

WASHINGTON ST

El
Estero

PIERCE ST

PRINCIPAL

MONTRIO

THE CROWN
AND ANCHOR

MONTEREY
SPORTS CENTER

GOLDEN STATE
THEATRE

JEFFERSON ST

ALVARADO STREET
BREWERY & GRILL

ALVARADO

BONAFICIO PL

ADAMS ST

FIGUEROA ST

MONTEREY COUNTY
VISITORS CENTER

CAMINO EL ESTERO

LARKIN
HOUSE

CALLE

THE POKE
LAB

MELVILLE
TAVERN

PEARL ST

DENNIS THE
MENACE PARK

Friendly
Plaza

POLK ST

OLD CAPITOL
BOOKS

ALFREDO'S

HOUSTON ST

HARTNELL ST

STEVENSON
HOUSE

WEBSTER ST

El Estero
Park

MUNRAS AVE

CHURCH ST

El Estero
Park

PACIFIC ST

FREMONT ST

CASS ST

SARGENT CT

ABREGO ST

MARTIN ST

EL DORADO ST

MONTEREY PENINSULA
CHAMBER OF COMMERCE

0   100 yds

0   100 m

© AVALON TRAVEL

Steinbeck

John Ernst Steinbeck was born in Salinas, California, in 1902 and grew up in its tiny, isolated agricultural community. He somehow managed to escape life as a farmer, a sardine fisherman, or a fish canner, and ended up living the glamorous life of a writer for his too-short 66 years.

Steinbeck's experiences in the Salinas Valley farming community and in the fishing town of Monterey informed many of his novels. The best known of these is *Cannery Row*, but *Tortilla Flat* is also set in working-class Monterey (though no one knows exactly where the fictional "Tortilla Flat" neighborhood was supposed to be). The Pulitzer Prize-winning novel *The Grapes of Wrath* takes more of its inspiration from the Salinas Valley. Steinbeck used the valley as a model for farming in the Dust Bowl during the Great Depression.

Steinbeck was fascinated by the plight of workingmen and women; his novels and stories generally depict ordinary folks going through tough and terrible times. Steinbeck lived and worked through the Great Depression, thus it's not surprising that many of his stories do *not* feature happy Hollywood endings. Steinbeck was a realist in almost all of his novels, portraying the good, the bad, and the ugly of human life and society. His work gained almost immediate respect: In addition to his Pulitzer, Steinbeck also won the Nobel Prize for Literature in 1962. Almost every American high school student from the 1950s onward has read at least one of Steinbeck's novels or short stories; his body of work forms part of the enduring American literary canon.

As the birthplace of California's most illustrious literary son in the 20th century, Salinas became equally famous for spawning the author and inspiring his work. You'll find a variety of Steinbeck maps online (www.mtycounty.com) that offer self-guided tours of the regions made famous by his various novels. Poor Steinbeck's name is taken in vain all over now-commercial Cannery Row, where even the cheesy wax museum tries to draw customers in by claiming kinship with the legendary author.

Serious scholars of Steinbeck prefer the **National Steinbeck Center** (1 Main St., Salinas, 831/796-3833, www.steinbeck.org, 10am-5pm daily, $11) and the **Steinbeck House** (132 Central Ave., Salinas, 831/424-2735, www.steinbeckhouse.com, monthly tours: 11pm-1pm Sun. May-Sept., $10), both in the still-agricultural town of Salinas. And if the museums aren't enough, plan to be in Monterey County in early August for the annual **Steinbeck Festival** (www.steinbeck.org), a big shindig put on by the Steinbeck Center that celebrates the great man's life and works in fine style.

Mexican rule. On the nearby plaza, enter the first floor of the **Pacific House Museum** (hours and days vary seasonally) to see a range of Monterey's history from the Native Californians to the American Period. The second floor has a plethora of Native American artifacts.

The other buildings that compose the park were built mostly with adobe and/or brick between 1834 and 1847. These include the **Casa del Oro** (210 Oliver St., 831/649-3364, 11am-3pm Thurs.-Sun.); the **First Brick House** (10am-4pm daily); the **Larkin House** (464 Calle Principal, 831/649-7172, private tours: $75 for up to 12 people); the **Old Whaling Station** (391 Decatur St., 831/375-5356, 10am-2pm Tues.-Fri.); the **Sherman**

Quarters (closed to the public); and the **Stevenson House** (530 Houston St., hours and days vary seasonally), once a temporary residence of Robert Louis Stevenson.

For an introduction to the park and its history, take a **guided tour** (Pacific House Museum, hours and days vary, $5). The one-hour walk includes the Pacific House, the Custom House, the First Brick House, the Old Whaling Station (with its whalebone sidewalk out front), California's First Theatre, Casa del Oro, and the Memory Garden. A **cell phone tour** (831/998-9458) offers a two-minute rundown on each building.

Fisherman's Wharf

Monterey's scenic harbor is a great place to

stroll along the shore, spot marine life, and explore the area's three wharves. Most popular is **Fisherman's Wharf** (1 Old Fisherman's Wharf, 831/238-0777, www.montereywharf.com, hours vary daily, free), which hosts a collection of seafood restaurants, touristy gift shops, and whale-watching boats. It has also been featured in the HBO series *Big Little Lies*.

The **Coast Guard Pier,** a 1,700-foot-long breakwater on the north end of the harbor, is one of Monterey's best wildlife-viewing areas. Look for sea lions and harbor seals as you walk out on the structure.

Municipal Wharf II is on the eastern edge of the harbor. It still has working fishing operations along with a few wholesale fish companies, a couple of restaurants, an abalone farm underneath its deck, and fine views of the harbor and nearby Del Monte Beach.

Dalí 17 Museum

One does not usually associate Salvador Dalí with Monterey; however, in 1941 the artist lived at Monterey's Hotel Del Monte, where he threw a legendary, surreal party. The **Dalí 17 Museum** (5 Custom House Plaza, 831/372-2608, www.dali17.com, 10am-5pm Sun.-Thurs., 10am-6pm Fri.-Sat., adults $20, seniors and students $16, children 6-17 $10, children under 6 free) has the second-largest collection of his works in the country, including 557 lithographs and 230 originals. Take a stroll through the two-floor museum, which portrays well this one-of-a-kind artist and his many quirks.

Dennis the Menace Park

The brainchild of Hank Ketcham, the creator of the *Dennis the Menace* comic strip, **Dennis the Menace Park** (777 Pearl St., 831/646-3860, 10am-dusk daily May-Sept., 10am-dusk Wed.-Mon Sept.-May) opened in 1956. The park has a nine-foot climbing wall, a suspension bridge, curvy slides, brightly colored jungle gyms, and a (fenced-in, nonworking) locomotive, as well as a bronze sculpture of the little menace near the entrance.

ENTERTAINMENT AND EVENTS
Bars and Clubs

Descending into **The Crown & Anchor** (150 W. Franklin St., 831/649-6496, www.crownandanchor.net, 11am-1:30am daily) feels a bit like entering a ship's hold. Along with the maritime theme, The Crown & Anchor serves up 20 international beers on tap. They also have good pub fare, including

Monterey Bay Aquarium

cottage pies and curries; the curry fries are a local favorite.

Microbrew fans should make for ★ **Alvarado Street Brewery & Grill** (426 Alvarado St., 831/655-2337, www.alvaradostreetbrewery.com, 11:30am-10pm Sun.-Thurs., 11:30am-11pm Fri.-Sat.). The boisterous, big modern space has more than 20 beers on tap, including their own sours, ales, and Mai Tai PA, a Great American Beer Festival gold-medal winner. Enjoy sipping the tasty brews out front on their sidewalk patio or in the beer garden in back.

A distinct stone building just a couple of blocks off Alvarado Street, **Alfredo's Cantina** (266 Pearl St., 831/375-0655, 10am-midnight Sun.-Thurs., 10am-2am Fri.-Sat., cash only) is a cozy dive bar. This comfortable drinking establishment has dim lighting, a gas fireplace, cheap drinks, and a good jukebox.

Live Music

Downtown Monterey's historic **Golden State Theatre** (417 Alvarado St., 831/649-1070, www.goldenstatetheatre.com) hosts live music, a speaker series, and dance, comedy, and theater productions. The theater dates to 1926 and was designed to resemble a Moorish castle. Performers have included music legends like Patti Smith, Willie Nelson, and "Weird Al" Yankovic.

Festivals and Events

The annual **Monterey Wine Festival** (Custom House Plaza, 360/693-6023, http://montereywine.com, June) celebrates wine with a generous helping of food on the side. The outdoor festival is the perfect introduction to Monterey and Carmel wineries, many of which have not yet hit the "big time" in major wine magazines. It is also, incongruously, home to the West Coast Chowder Competition.

One of the biggest music festivals in California is the **Monterey Jazz Festival** (Monterey County Fairgrounds, 2004 Fairground Rd., 831/373-3366, www.montereyjazzfestival.org, Sept.). As the site of the longest-running jazz festival on earth, Monterey attracts 500 artists from around the world to the fest's eight stages. Past acts to grace the stage include Herbie Hancock, Booker T. Jones, and The Roots.

Monterey Car Week (www.seemonterey.com, Aug.) lures car enthusiasts to the Monterey Peninsula for seven days of car shows, races, and high-end automobile auctions. An event with a big sense of humor, the **Concours d'Lemons** (Seaside City Hall, 440 Harcourt Ave., Seaside, https://24hoursoflemons.com, Aug.) showcases clunkers, junkers, and automotive oddities.

SPORTS AND RECREATION
★ Scuba Diving

There's one great place to get certified in scuba diving: Monterey Bay. Accordingly, dozens of dive schools cluster in and around the city of Monterey. Locals' favorite **Bamboo Reef** (614 Lighthouse Ave., 831/372-1685, www.bambooreef.com, 9am-6pm Mon.-Fri., 7am-6pm Sat.-Sun.) offers scuba lessons and rents equipment just a few blocks from popular dive spots, including Breakwater Cove. The aquamarine storefront has been helping people get underwater since 1980.

Aquarius Dive Shop (2040 Del Monte Ave., 831/375-1933, www.aquariusdivers.com, 9am-6pm Mon.-Thurs., 9am-7pm Fri., 7am-7pm Sat., 7am-6pm Sun.) offers air and nitrox fills, equipment rental, and certification courses, and can help book a trip on a local dive boat. Aquarius works with five boats to create great trips for divers of all interests and ability levels. Call 831/657-1020 for local dive conditions.

TOP EXPERIENCE

★ Kayaking and Stand-Up Paddleboarding

The coast off Monterey is an ideal place for paddling: It is less exposed than other spots along the coast, and if the swells are big, you

Sea Sanctuary

Monterey Bay is in a federally protected marine area known as the **Monterey Bay National Marine Sanctuary** (MBNMS). Designated a sanctuary in 1992, the protected waters stretch far past the confines of Monterey Bay to a northern boundary seven miles north of the Golden Gate Bridge and a southern boundary at Cambria in San Luis Obispo. The sanctuary was created for resource protection, education, public use, and research. The MBNMS is the reason so many marine research facilities, including the Long Marine Laboratory, the Monterey Bay Marine Laboratory, and the Moss Landing Marine Laboratories, dot the Monterey Bay shoreline.

Among the many marine treasures of the MBNMS is the Monterey Bay Submarine Canyon, which is right offshore of the fishing village of Moss Landing. The canyon is similar in size to the Grand Canyon and has a rim-to-floor depth of 5,577 feet. In 2009, the MBNMS expanded to include another fascinating underwater geographical feature: the Davidson Seamount. Located 80 miles southwest of Monterey, the undersea mountain rises an impressive 7,480 feet, yet its summit is still 4,101 feet below the ocean's surface.

can duck into Monterey Harbor and paddle past moored boats and harbor seals. When the surf is manageable, the paddle from San Carlos Beach to the aquarium and back (1.16 miles round-trip) guarantees you will see an otter or a harbor seal. Note that Monterey Bay National Marine Sanctuary regulations require all paddlers to stay 150 feet from all sea otters, sea lions, and harbor seals.

Adventures by the Sea (299 Cannery Row, 831/372-1807, www.adventuresbythesea. com, 9am-8pm daily summer, 9am-5pm daily winter, kayak tours $60-85 pp, kayak rentals $35/day, SUP rentals $50/day) rents kayaks and SUPs and lets you choose your own route around the Monterey Bay kelp forest. Adventures also offers tours (2.5 hours, 10am and 2pm daily in summer) from Cannery Row. Guides can tell you all about the wildlife you'll see: harbor seals, sea otters, pelicans, gulls, and maybe even a whale in the winter. The tandem sit-on-top kayaks make it a great experience for children. They also run a tour of Stillwater Cove at Pebble Beach. Reservations are recommended for all tours. The company has other locations in Monterey (685 Cannery Row, 32 Cannery Row, and 210 Alvarado St.).

Rent a kayak or SUP from **Monterey Bay Kayaks** (693 Del Monte Ave., 831/373-5357, www.montereybaykayaks.com, 9am-7pm daily summer, 9am-6pm daily spring, 9am-5pm daily fall/winter; kayak tours $450-100, kayak rentals $30-50 pp, SUP rentals $35 pp) and paddle into the bay from the beach just south of the Municipal Wharf. Tours include kayak fishing, Sunday sunrise excursions, and a Point Lobos paddle. There's also a branch in Moss Landing on the Elkhorn Slough.

TOP EXPERIENCE

Whale-Watching

Whales pass quite near the shores of Monterey year-round. Although you can sometimes even see them from the beach, boats can take you out for a closer look. The area hosts many humpbacks, blue whales, and gray whales, plus the occasional killer whale, minke whale, fin whale, and pod of dolphins. Bring your own binoculars for a better view, but the experienced boat captains will do all they can to get you as close as possible to the whales and dolphins. Most tours last 2-3 hours and leave from Fisherman's Wharf.

Monterey Bay Whale Watch (84 Fisherman's Wharf, 831/375-4658, www. montereybaywhalewatch.com, adults $40-145, children 4-12 $29-39, children under 4 $15) leaves from an easy-to-find red building on Fisherman's Wharf and runs tours in every season. You must make a reservation in advance, even for regularly scheduled tours. Afternoon tours are available.

***Princess Monterey* Whale Watching** (96 Fisherman's Wharf, 831/372-2203, www. montereywhalewatching.com, adults $45-65, children 3-11 $35-55) prides itself on its knowledgeable guides and its comfortable, spacious cruising vessels. It costs a bit extra to secure a space on the ship's upper deck. The *Princess Monterey* offers morning and afternoon tours, and you can buy tickets online or by phone.

Fast Raft Ocean Safaris (Monterey Harbor and Moss Landing Harbor, 408/659-3900, www.fastraft.com, $150/pp) offers an intimate way to explore the coast and wildlife. The "fast raft" is a 33-foot-long inflatable boat with a rigid hull that accommodates six passengers. The outfit does whale-watching trips out of Moss Landing and coastal safaris that depart from Monterey and head south to Pebble Beach's Stillwater Cove and Point Lobos. Note that the fast raft does not have a restroom.

Fishing

J&M Sport Fishing (66 Fisherman's Wharf, 831/372-7440 or 800/251-7440, https:// jmsportfishing.com, $80-90) took over the longtime Randy's Fishing fleet. The new operation leaves shore for salmon, rock cod, and a fishing/crabbing combo trip.

To catch your own seafood, head out with **Westwind Charter Sport Fishing & Excursions** (66 Fisherman's Wharf, 831/392-7867, http://montereysportfishing.com). Depending on what's in season, you can catch salmon ($650/up to four people), rock cod, lingcod, or halibut ($550/up to four people).

Hiking

The 18-mile paved **Monterey Bay Coastal Recreation Trail** (831/646-3866, https:// monterey.org) stretches from Pacific Grove north to the town of Castroville. The most scenic section is from Monterey Harbor down to Pacific Grove's Lovers Point Park. It's a great way to take in Monterey's coastline, sea otters, and harbor seals.

Jack's Peak County Park (25020 Jacks Peak Park Rd., 831/775-4895, www. co.monterey.ca.us, 10am-close daily, $4-5) is home to the highest point on the Monterey Peninsula. The park has picnic sites and 8.5 miles of walking paths, including the 0.8-mile-long **Skyline Trail.** The trail passes through a rare Monterey pine forest and offers glimpses of fossils from the Miocene epoch

the Monterey Bay Coastal Recreation Trail

before reaching the summit, which offers an overview of the whole peninsula.

Fort Ord Dunes State Park was home to a U.S. Army post from 1917 to 1994, (831/649-2836, www.parks.ca.gov, 8am-sunset daily, free). Across the park, paths lead to remnants of the military past plus four miles of beach access. To get there from Monterey, head north on Highway 1 and take the Lightfighter Drive exit. Turn left onto 2nd Avenue and then take a left on Divarty Street. Turn right on 1st Avenue and follow the signs to the park entrance at the 8th Street Bridge over Highway 1.

Golf

The **Monterey Pines Golf Course** (Fairground Rd. and Garden Rd., 831/656-2167, www.montereypeninsulagolf.com, Mon.-Fri. $18-34, Sat.-Sun. $20-37) is a beginner-friendly 18 holes next to the Monterey County Fairgrounds. The Pebble Beach Company manages the **Del Monte Golf Course** (1300 Sylvan Rd., 800/654-9300, www.montereypeninsulagolf.com, $110), an 18-hole course that claims to be the oldest continuously operating course west of the Mississippi.

Motor Sports

The **Mazda Raceway Laguna Seca** (1021 Monterey-Salinas Hwy., 831/242-8200, www.mazdaraceway.com) is one of the country's premier road-racing venues. You can see historic auto races, superbikes, speed festivals, and an array of Grand Prix events. Laguna Seca also hosts innumerable auto clubs and small sports car and stock car races. The major racing season runs May-October. You can camp here, and you'll find plenty of concessions during big races.

FOOD

The Monterey Bay Seafood Watch program (www.montereybayaquarium.org) is the definitive resource for sustainable seafood, while the Salinas Valley inland hosts a number of organic farms. The primary farmers market in the county, the **Monterey Farmers Market**

(Alvarado St. between Del Monte Ave. and Pearl St., 831/655-8070, www.oldmonterey.org, 4pm-7pm Tues. Oct.-Apr., 4pm-8pm Tues. May-Sept.) takes over downtown Monterey with fresh-produce vendors, restaurant stalls, jewelry booths, and live music.

Cafes

Connected to the Osio Cinemas, Monterey's art-house movie theater, **Café Lumiere** (365 Calle Principal, 831/920-2451, http://cafe-lumieremonterey.com, 7am-9pm Sun.-Thurs., 7am-10pm Fri.-Sat.) is where Monterey's old Sicilian anglers hang out in the morning while sipping coffee drinks and munching on pastries. There are a lot of tempting options behind the counter's glass case, but the café also offers breakfast, lunch, and Sunday brunch dishes. In addition, the café has weekday lunch specials including a very popular giant bowl of pho (Vietnamese noodle soup) on Thursday. The tasty coffee is from Acme Coffee Roasting Company, a local favorite.

American

Inside an old brick firehouse, **Montrio** (414 Calle Principal, 831/648-8880, www.montrio.com, 4:30pm-close daily, $19-46) is an elegantly casual Monterey eatery. The ever-changing menu includes meat and seafood entrées, but Montrio is also an ideal place for a lighter dinner. Dine inside under ceilings decorated with art that resembles clouds, or out front on the patio. Executive chef Tony Baker is known for his dry-cured bacon. Happy Hour (4:30pm-6:30pm daily, $6.50) is worth a visit for cocktails and well-priced snacks.

A cozy locals' spot in a brick building a block off Alvarado Street, ★ **Melville Tavern** (484 Washington St., 831/643-9525, www.melvilletav.com, 11am-9pm Mon.-Fri., 10:30am-9pm Sat.-Sun., $11-30) does a bit less damage on the wallet. The straightforward but well-executed menu of sandwiches, salads, tacos, and a green chile cheeseburger will hit the spot. There's a nicely curated mix of beers on tap and wine by the glass or the bottle (look for the $3 beer of the week and the $6 wine of the week).

Seafood

On weekends, there is typically a line out the door at **Monterey's Fish House** (2114 Del Monte Ave., 831/373-4647, http://monterey-fishhouse.com, 11:30am-2:30pm and 5pm-9:30pm Mon.-Fri., 5pm-9:30pm Sat.-Sun., $11-30), one of the peninsula's most popular seafood restaurants with a fun, old-school Italian vibe. Inside, expect attentive service and fresh seafood including snapper, albacore tuna, and calamari fished right out of the bay.

The Sandbar & Grill (Municipal Wharf II, 831/373-2818, www.sandbarandgrillmonterey.com, 11am-9pm Mon.-Sat., 10:30am-9pm Sun., $12-30) has the best fried calamari around. They are also known for their fresh sand dabs and Dungeness crab sandwich with bacon. The restaurant hangs off the Municipal Wharf over Monterey Harbor.

For a South Pacific spin on seafood, head to ★ **Hula's Island Grill & Tiki Room** (622 Lighthouse Ave., 831/655-4852, www.hulastiki.com, 4pm-9:30pm Mon., 11:30am-9:30pm Tues.-Thurs., 11:30am-10pm Fri.-Sat., 4pm-9pm Sun., $12-23). Hula's is Monterey's most fun casual restaurant, with tasty and sometimes imaginative food. In addition to fresh fish and a range of tacos, the menu has land-based fare like Jamaican jerk chicken. The happy hours (4pm-6pm Sun.-Mon., 2pm-9:30pm Tues., 2pm-6pm Wed.-Sat.) feature tiki drinks and pupus (appetizers) for just six bucks a pop.

The Sardine Factory (701 Wave St., 831/373-3775, http://sardinefactory.com, 5pm-10:30pm Sun.-Thurs., 5pm-11pm Fri.-Sat., $26-59) is the area's iconic seafood and steak house. Its abalone bisque was served at one of President Ronald Reagan's inaugural dinners, and part of Clint Eastwood's directorial debut *Play Misty for Me* was filmed in the restaurant. This place oozes old-school cool, complete with a piano player in the lounge (Tues.-Sat.). The menu includes pasta, steak, and wild abalone medallions. Ask for a tour of the building, which has a glass-domed conservatory and an exclusive wine cellar that feels transported from a European castle.

★ **The Poke Lab** (475 Alvarado St., 831/200-3474, www.thepokelab.com, 11am-8pm daily, $11-15) dishes up poke (raw seafood) salads in a fast-casual setting. There may be a line out the door for the small eatery's build-your-own poke bowls or the namesake bowl (spicy tuna, ahi tuna, salmon,

the giant beached boat outside of The Sardine Factory

avocado, and toppings on sushi rice, brown rice, or salad).

Steak House
The Whaling Station (763 Wave St., 831/373-3778, www.whalingstation.net, 5pm-9pm Sun.-Thurs., 5pm-10:30pm Fri.-Sat., $24-58) has been a local institution since 1970. Waiters present different cuts of meat on a tray and answer questions about the best qualities of each piece. Options include a New York steak, beef Wellington, and red-wine braised beef short ribs. Non-beef items include rack of lamb, seafood, and pasta. The moderately priced bar menu offers a steak sandwich or a burger made with ground filet mignon.

Sushi
Fresh seafood and creative rolls make **Crystal Fish** (514 Lighthouse Ave., 831/649-3474, http://crystalfishmonterey.com, 11:30am-2pm and 5pm-9:30pm Mon.-Thurs., 11:30am-2pm and 5pm-10pm Fri., 1pm-10pm Sat., 1pm-9:30pm Sun., $14-27) the Monterey go-to for sushi. There's not a lot of ambience, but there are a lot of rolls, including fresh salmon, tuna, eel, octopus, calamari, and unusual ingredients like asparagus and eggplant.

ACCOMMODATIONS
Under $150
The **Monterey Hostel** (778 Hawthorne St., 831/649-0375, http://montereyhostel.org, dorm bed $39, private room $139-184, family room $174-184) offers inexpensive accommodations within walking distance of the major attractions of Monterey. Accommodations include a men's dorm room, women's dorm room, private rooms, a five-person family room, and a coed dorm room with 16 beds; linens are included. A self-service laundry is within walking distance. Common areas include a large, fully stocked kitchen and spaces with couches and a piano. The kitchen serves a free pancake breakfast every morning.

$150-250
Jabberwock Inn (598 Laine St.,

831/372-4777, www.jabberwockinn.com, $209-599) is named after a nonsense poem written by Lewis Carroll as part of his novel *Through the Looking Glass*. Despite its name, the amenities of this comfortable former convent turned eight-room bed-and-breakfast are no-nonsense. The common area has a covered wraparound sun porch with views of Monterey Bay and two fireplaces. There are no TVs or telephones. Breakfasts are tasty and filling, while the innkeepers are warm and knowledgeable. Perks include free parking and late-afternoon wine and appetizers, along with evening milk and cookies. The B&B is just a short walk to Cannery Row, the aquarium, and Lighthouse Avenue.

The ★ **Spindrift Inn** (652 Cannery Row, 831/646-8900, www.spindriftinn.com, $239-529) is a boutique hotel towering above the golden sand and clear green waters of scenic McAbee Beach. This 45-room establishment has been called the country's most romantic hotel. Most of the hardwood-floored rooms have wood-burning fireplaces and full or half canopy beds. The very friendly staff serves a wine and cheese reception daily (4:30pm-6pm) and delivers a complimentary continental breakfast to your room.

The greatest asset of **Monterey Tides** (2600 Sand Dunes Rd., 831/394-3321 or 800/242-8627, https://www.jdvhotels.com, $200-400) is its proximity to the sand and surf. The four-story building sits right over Monterey State Beach; 102 of its 196 rooms face Monterey Bay. At night, take in the tapered triangle of lights on the Monterey peninsula from the wooden patios off the hotel's lobby. There's a heated pool (year-round) alongside a spa, and bikes and stand-up paddleboards are available for rent. The lobby bar, Bar Sebastian, and the top-floor Vizcaino restaurant have stellar views to accompany meals and drinks. The hotel also offers something most don't: fires on the beach (firewood, $25; bonfire kit with s'mores, $30).

Over $250
Luxury hotel **InterContinental The**

Clement Monterey (750 Cannery Row, 831/375-4500, www.ictheclementmonterey. com, $250-850) has a can't-be-beat location just a splash away from the bay and aquarium. The hotel has 208 rooms and 12 luxury suites decorated with tasteful Asian elements such as a bonsai tree, a tiny Zen garden, and live orchids. Most of the bathrooms have a separate soaking tub and walk-in shower. Oceanside rooms have views of the bay, while units on the other side of Cannery Row have fireplaces. There are a lot of amenities, including a fitness room, an outdoor whirlpool, **The Spa** (831/642-2075, 9am-7pm daily, massages $80-175), **The C Restaurant & Bar** (831/375-4800, 6:30am-10pm daily, $29-58), a sliver of an outdoor pool to swim laps in, and an artsy, jellyfish-inspired staircase connecting the first and second floors.

Located between San Carlos Beach and Cannery Row, the ★ **Monterey Bay Inn** (242 Cannery Row, 831/373-6242 or 800/424-6242, www.montereybayinn.com, $309-600) has oceanfront rooms with private balconies that overlook Monterey Bay and in-room binoculars for spotting wildlife. The hotel's rooftop hot tub offers another vantage point to take in the action offshore. Enjoy a continental breakfast delivered to your room in the morning and cookies in the evening.

Camping

One mile up a hill from downtown Monterey, the 50-acre **Veterans Memorial Park** (Via Del Rey and Veterans Dr., 831/646-3865, www.monterey.org, $30/single vehicle, $38/ two vehicles) has 40 first-come, first-served campsites with views of Monterey Bay.

TRANSPORTATION AND SERVICES

Most visitors drive into Monterey via scenic Highway 1. Inland, U.S. 101 allows access into Salinas from the north and south. From Salinas, Highway 68 travels west into Monterey.

For a more leisurely ride, **Amtrak's** *Coast Starlight* train (11 Station Pl., Salinas, 10am-2pm and 3pm-8pm daily) travels through Salinas.

The **Greyhound** bus station (3 Station Pl., Salinas, 831/424-4418, www.greyhound.com, 9am-noon and 1pm-4pm Mon.-Sat.) is 18.5 miles east of Monterey. To get to Monterey, walk two blocks to the **Salinas Transit Center** (110 Salinas St., 888/678-2871, https://

Monterey Bay Inn

mst.org) and hop on a Monterey-Salinas Transit bus to the coast.

In Monterey, take advantage of the free **Monterey Trolley** (Waterfront Area Visitor Express, 888/678-2871, https://mst.org, hours vary daily late May-early Sept., 10am-7pm Sat.-Sun. early Sept.- late May), which loops between downtown Monterey and the aquarium. **Monterey-Salinas Transit** (888/678-2871, www.mst.org, $1.25-2.50) has routes throughout Monterey.

For medical needs, the **Community Hospital of the Monterey Peninsula** (CHOMP, 23625 Holman Hwy., 831/624-5311 or 888/452-4667, www.chomp.org) provides emergency services to the area.

Pacific Grove

Sandwiched between historic Monterey and exclusive Pebble Beach, Pacific Grove makes a fine base for exploring the peninsula. It's also worth a visit for its colorful turn-of-the-20th-century Victorian homes and its striking strand of coastline. Founded in 1875 as a Methodist summer retreat, this quiet city is perfect for a relaxing afternoon of strolling among the yellow, purple, and green Victorian homes and cottages on Lighthouse Avenue. (There's a different Lighthouse Avenue in adjacent Monterey.)

Pacific Grove's "Poor Man's 17-Mile Drive" winds around a piece of coastal real estate between Lover's Point Park and Asilomar Beach that's almost as striking Pebble Beach's 17-Mile Drive. Start on Ocean View Boulevard by Lover's Point and continue onto Sunset Drive to get the full experience. In the spring, flowering ice plant right along the road adds a riot of color to the landscape.

SIGHTS
Lover's Point Park
Aptly named **Lover's Point Park** (Ocean View Blvd. and 17th St., 831/648-3100, www.cityofpacificgrove.org) is one of the area's most popular wedding sites. A finger of land with a jumble of rocks at its northernmost point, Lover's Point offers expansive views of the interior section of Monterey Bay. The park also has a sheltered pocket beach that is ideal for a dip. A kelp forest right offshore offers a superb spot for snorkelers to get a feel for Monterey Bay's impressive underwater ecosystem. During summer, an old-fashioned hamburger stand operates above the beach, and a vendor rents kayaks, bikes, and snorkeling equipment.

Point Pinos Lighthouse
Surrounded by a golf course, **Point Pinos Lighthouse** (80 Asilomar Ave. between Lighthouse Ave. and Del Monte Ave., 831/648-3176, www.pointpinoslighthouse. org, 1pm-4pm Thurs.-Mon., adults $2, children $1) is the oldest continuously operating lighthouse on the West Coast, in service since 1855. Point Pinos is also notable for the two female lighthouse keepers who served there during its long history. The light was automated in 1975, but it is still an active aid to local marine navigation. Lighthouse lovers will enjoy walking through the building's two floors and cellar.

Monarch Grove Sanctuary
Pacific Grove is also known as "Butterfly Town U.S.A." An impressive migration of Monarch butterflies descends on the town each year. The small **Monarch Grove Sanctuary** (Ridge Rd. between Lighthouse Ave. and Short St., 831/648-5716, www.cityofpacificgrove.org, free) offers stands of eucalyptus and pine trees that are cloaked with colorful insects during the migration period (Oct.-Feb.). The best time to visit is in the early afternoon, when sunlight illuminates the butterflies and docents can answer your questions.

Local Favorites

While the Monterey Bay Aquarium and the Santa Cruz Beach Boardwalk draw many visitors to the coast, lesser-known attractions appeal to adventurous travelers.

★ **Pacific Biological Laboratories:** (800 Cannery Row, 831/646-5648, www.monterey. org, free tours monthly) The former residence and workplace of Ed Ricketts, one of Cannery Row's most colorful literary characters, opens to the public once a month for free tours.

★ **Land of the Medicine Buddha:** (5800 Prescott Ave., Soquel, 831/462-8383, http://landofmedicinebuddha.org, 7am-8pm Mon.-Fri., noon-8pm Sun.) At this Buddhist meditation and retreat center in the Santa Cruz foothills, visitors can wander the grounds to spin an ornate prayer wheel or enjoy a contemplative walk on Eight Verses Trail, which features eight Buddhist verses posted at signs along the path.

★ **Pinnacles National Park:** (5000 Hwy. 146, Paicines, 831/389-4486, www.nps.gov/pinn, 7:30am-8pm daily, $25 entrance fee) A one-hour drive inland is this wonderland of rock spires and caves, with California condors sailing overhead. Take a satisfying day hike or spend the night in the campground.

Asilomar State Beach

One of the Monterey Peninsula's most popular beaches, **Asilomar State Beach** (Sunset Dr., 831/646-6440, www.parks.ca.gov) draws beachgoers, walkers, and surfers. The beach is a narrow, one-mile-long strip of coastline with a boardwalk trail on the dunes behind it. Keep walking on the trail to get to nearby Pebble Beach.

Right across Sunset Drive, visitors can explore the **Asilomar Dunes Natural Preserve** and the **Asilomar Conference Grounds** (800 Asilomar Ave., 831/372-8016, www.visitasilomar.com). The dunes preserve is 25 acres of restored sand dune ecosystem that can be accessed via a 0.25-mile boardwalk. The conference grounds are shaded by Monterey pines and studded with arts and crafts-style structures designed by Hearst Castle architect Julia Morgan. Enjoy the facilities, including the Phoebe A. Hearst Social Hall, which has pool tables, a fireplace, and some comfy seats. One-hour **ranger-guided tours** of the grounds (831/646-6443) focus on the architecture, the dunes, the forest, and the coast.

To reach Asilomar, take the Route 68 West exit off Highway 1 and turn left onto Sunset Drive.

Pacific Grove Museum of Natural History

Stop into the **Pacific Grove Museum of Natural History** (165 Forest Ave., 831/648-5716, www.pgmuseum.org, 10am-5pm Tues.-Sun., adults $9, military, students, and children $6) and learn how to identify the animal and plant species of the Monterey Peninsula. The museum provides a fairly comprehensive overview of the region's biodiversity. One room is dedicated to feathered friends and includes 300 mounted birds found around the county, among them the gigantic California condor. Other rooms highlight large terrestrial mammals (mountain lions, bears) and whales. There's also a space devoted to the Monarch butterfly. Out front is a life-sized gray whale statue, while out back is a native plant garden.

ENTERTAINMENT AND EVENTS

A couple of family-friendly annual events occur in "America's Last Hometown."

Pacific Grove

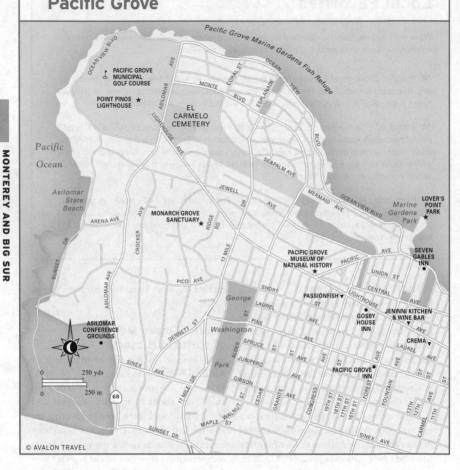

© AVALON TRAVEL

Recalling another era, Pacific Grove's **Good Old Days** (831/373-3304, www.pacificgrove.org, Apr.) is a weekend of good clean fun that includes a parade, a quilt show, pony rides, and live entertainment. For more than 70 years, kids have been getting dressed up like butterflies at the **Butterfly Parade and Bazaar** (www.pacificgrove.org, first Sat. of Oct.), which welcomes the wintering Monarch butterflies to the area every fall.

SPORTS AND RECREATION
Scuba Diving and Snorkeling

Some of the best scuba diving and snorkeling spots lie off Pacific Grove. **Lover's Point Park** (Ocean View Blvd. and 17th St., novice to advanced, 10-40 feet) has a protected cove and kelp forest right off its shores. The cove's protected, sandy beach makes an easy entry point for scuba divers and snorkelers. **Sunshine Freestyle** (443 Lighthouse

Ave., Monterey, 831/375-5015, http://sunshinefreestyle.com, 10am-6pm Mon.-Sat., 11am-5pm Sun., surfboard rental $30/day, wetsuit rental $15/day) and a few blocks away, **Otter Cove** (Ocean View Blvd. and Sea Palm Ave., novice to advanced, 10-60 feet) is a dive spot best explored during days of calm seas. One of the highlights is an underwater pinnacle that rises from 50 feet to just 18 feet below the surface. Nearby **Coral Street Cove** (Coral St. and Ocean View Blvd., advanced, 20-50 feet) is known for its fish population.

For equipment, visit **Bamboo Reef** (614 Lighthouse Ave., 831/372-1685, www.bambooreef.com, 9am-6pm Mon.-Fri., 7am-6pm Sat.-Sun.), **Aquarius Dive Shop** (2040 Del Monte Ave., 831/375-1933, www.aquariusdivers.com, 9am-6pm Mon.-Fri., 7am-6pm Sat.-Sun.), or **Breakwater Scuba** (225 Cannery Row, Monterey, 831/717-4546, http://breakwaterscuba.com, 9am-6pm Mon.-Fri., 7am-6pm Sat.-Sun.).

Surfing

During the summer and fall, clean swells produce fun waves at **Asilomar State Beach** (Sunset Dr., 831/646-6440, www.parks.ca.gov), making it one of the peninsula's most popular surf spots. Winter produces big, often dangerous swells, so stay out of the water during that time of the year. To get there, take the Route 68 West exit off Highway 1 and turn left onto Sunset Drive.

During big swells, **Lovers Point** (Ocean View Blvd. and 17th St.) turns into a nice left. There are some rocks in the lineup, so it is probably best that first-timers go out with someone who knows the break.

On the Beach (693 Lighthouse Ave., Monterey, 831/646-9283, http://onthebeachsurfshop.com, 10am-6pm Sun.-Thurs., 10am-7pm Fri.-Sat., surfboard rental $30/day, wetsuit rental $15/day) rents surfboards and wetsuits.

Golf

The **Pacific Grove Golf Links** (77 Asilomar Blvd., 831/648-5775, www.playpacificgrove.

com, daily sunrise-sunset, Mon.-Thurs. $46, Fri.-Sun. and holidays $52) doesn't have the acclaim of the nearby Pebble Beach courses, but it's on a similarly gorgeous length of coastline just a few miles away.

FOOD
American
★ **Crema** (481 Lighthouse Ave., 831/324-0347, http://cremapg.com, 7am-4pm daily, $7-15) is a gourmet comfort food restaurant in a multilevel building that feels like someone's house. Dine on oversize burgers or chicken sandwiches beside a fireplace or a piano. They also offer a stout beer float (stout beer, ice cream, and espresso) and weekend pitchers of mimosas and sangria.

In the cavernous American Tin Cannery shopping mall, **First Awakenings** (125 Oceanview Blvd., 831/372-1125, www.firstawakenings.net, 7am-2pm Mon.-Fri., 7am-2:30pm Sat.-Sun., $6-12) serves oversize versions of classic breakfast fare including huevos rancheros, eggs Benedict, crepes, and omelets. Locals frequently vote this place the county's top breakfast spot. On sunny days, dine outside on the large patio while surrounded by the sounds of nearby Monterey Bay.

Italian
Il Vecchio (110 Central Ave., 831/324-4282, noon-1:30pm and 5pm-9pm Mon.-Thurs., noon-1:30pm and 5pm-9:30pm Fri., 5pm-9:30pm Sat., 5pm-9pm Sun., $13-22) is a Pacific Grove favorite. The name Il Vecchio means "the old" and refers to traditional Italian fare like gnocchi with pesto. They make their pasta daily and offer traditional Italian takes on meats and seafood. Mondays are Piatti at Vecchio (5pm-9pm, $18), where you can sample three popular dishes in smaller portions. The Lunch for the Workers Special (noon-1:30pm Mon.-Fri., $9) offers diners a salad and two pastas.

Mediterranean
The **Jeninni Kitchen & Wine Bar** (542 Lighthouse Ave., 831/920-2662, 4pm-close

Thurs.-Tues., $18-30) has elevated Pacific Grove's dining scene. The menu changes frequently, but the wagyu bullfighter's steak and the eggplant fries are favorites. Sit in the dining area in the front of the building or walk up a few stairs to the bar area for small plates, wine, and craft beers.

Seafood

One of the Monterey Peninsula's most lauded seafood restaurants is ★ **Passionfish** (701 Lighthouse Ave., 831/655-3311, www.passionfish.net, Sun.-Thurs. 5pm-9pm, Fri.-Sat. 5pm-10pm, $16-36), which is on a mission to spread the gospel about sustainable seafood. Passionfish does great food, especially creative and flavorful sustainable seafood. Their menu starts with a nice scallop appetizer and includes seared albacore tuna in a bacon sauce or basil-stuffed rainbow trout entrées. They are also known for their extensive, moderately priced wine list. The knowledgeable waitstaff could teach a course on seafood.

Crema offers gourmet comfort food.

ACCOMMODATIONS

Pacific Grove is known for bed-and-breakfasts in nice Victorian buildings.

Under $150

The ★ **Gosby House Inn** (643 Lighthouse Ave., 800/527-8828, www.gosbyhouseinn.com, $125-280) has been taking care of visitors since the 1880s. The white-and-yellow Queen Anne-style Victorian, which sits on downtown Pacific Grove's main street, is a welcome cross between a boutique hotel and a B&B. Amenities include free Wi-Fi, flat-screen TVs in most rooms, and a complimentary breakfast. The photo- and antique-heavy main house has 22 rooms, some with gas fireplaces. The two deluxe rooms in the adjacent Carriage House have a balcony, a gas fireplace, a roomy bathroom, and a nice-sized soaking tub.

$150-250

Staying overnight at the ★ **Asilomar Conference Grounds** (804 Crocker Ave., 831/372-8016, www.visitasilomar.com, $190-335) can feel like going back to summer camp. Common areas on the 107 acres include the Phoebe Apperson Hearst Social Hall, where visitors can relax by a roaring fire or play pool at one of two billiards tables. Accommodations range from historic rooms to family cottages to modern rooms with a view of nearby Asilomar Beach, but purposefully lack TVs and telephones. Rooms with an ocean view and a fireplace are definitely recommended. The lodging hosts a multitude of conferences, so expect to see corporate types walking through the forests of Monterey pine, Monterey cypress, and coast live oaks.

The **Old St. Angela Inn** (321 Central Ave., 831/372-3246, www.oldstangelainn.com, $165-290) spoils with cozy accommodations, a friendly staff, and terrific food. The nine homey rooms have pine antiques, live plants, and comfortable beds. Comfy common areas are downstairs, while out back is a brick patio area with a fire pit and a waterfall fountain. One of the best features of The Old St. Angela Inn is its house-made food. Afternoon teatime offers wine, a dessert, and an appetizer. The scrumptious breakfast includes yogurt, granola, muffins, and a hot sweet or savory item.

One of the finest and most notable Queen Anne Victorian buildings is the dark green and white **Green Gables Inn** (301 Ocean View Blvd., 831/375-2095 or 800/722-1774, www.greengablesinnpg.com, $169-309). The main building, which was built in 1888, has a downstairs common area with ocean views—it's the place to stay, with a throwback feel and antique furnishings. Behind the main inn, the Carriage House has five spacious rooms, all with a gas fireplace, a jetted tub, and ocean views. The inn offers afternoon wine and appetizers, a morning breakfast buffet, and a few bikes that can be borrowed for a spin on the nearby Monterey Bay Coastal Recreation Trail.

Over $250
The most striking bed-and-breakfast on the Pacific Grove coast, the **Seven Gables Inn** (555 Ocean View Blvd., 831/372-4341, www.sevengablesinn.com, $329-469) is perched just feet away from Lover's Point. Every room has superb ocean views. Decorated with antique furniture and artwork, the inn is for those who want to step back in time and experience ornate Victorian- and Edwardian-style lodging.

TRANSPORTATION AND SERVICES
Most visitors drive into the area via scenic Highway 1. From Highway 1, take the Route 68 West exit to reach downtown Pacific Grove. For medical needs, the **Community Hospital of the Monterey Peninsula** (CHOMP, 23625 Holman Hwy., 831/624-5311 or 888/452-4667, www.chomp.org) in Monterey provides emergency services to the area.

Pebble Beach

Between Pacific Grove and Carmel, the gated community of Pebble Beach lays claim to some of the Monterey Peninsula's best and highest-priced real estate. Pebble Beach is famous for the scenic 17-Mile Drive and its collection of high-end resorts, restaurants, spas, and golf courses, owned by the Pebble Beach Company, a partnership that included golf legend Arnold Palmer and film legend Clint Eastwood. Pebble Beach also hosts the annual **AT&T Pebble Beach National Pro-Am** (831/649-1533, www.attpbgolf.com, Feb., event prices vary)., a charity golf tournament that pairs professional golfers with celebrities.

SIGHTS
17-Mile Drive
The best way to take in the stunning scenery of Pebble Beach is the **17-Mile Drive** ($10.25/vehicle). Pay the fee at the gatehouse and receive a map of the drive that describes the parks and sights you'll pass along the winding coastal road: the much-photographed Lone Cypress, the beaches of Spanish Bay, and Pebble Beach's golf course, resort, and housing complex. If you're in a hurry, you can get from one end of the 17-Mile Drive to the other in 20 minutes. But go slowly and stop often to enjoy the natural beauty of the area. Plenty of turnouts let you stop to take photos, and you can picnic at many of the beaches; most have basic restroom facilities and ample parking lots. The only food and gas are at the Inn at Spanish Bay and the Lodge at Pebble Beach.

SPORTS AND RECREATION
Spa at Pebble Beach (1518 Cypress Dr., 831/649-7615 or 800/877-0597, www.pebblebeach.com, 8:30am-7:30pm daily, $165-470) has specialty massages for golfers before or after a day on the greens.

Biking

Traveling the **17-Mile Drive** by bike means you don't have to pay the $10 vehicle admission fee. It's also a great bike route. Expect fairly flat terrain with lots of twists and turns, and a ride that runs . . . about 17 miles. Foggy conditions can make this ride a bit slick in the summer, but spring and fall weather are perfect for pedaling.

Bay Bikes (3600 The Barnyard Shopping Center, Carmel, 831/655-2453, www.baybikes. com, 10am-5pm Sun.-Mon., 10am-6pm Tues.-Fri., 9am-6pm Sat., $8-16/hour, $24-48/four hours) is the closest place to rent a cruiser, hybrid bike, road bike, or tandem.

Golf

Golf has been a major pastime here since the late 19th century; today avid golfers come from around the world to tee off (and pay $200 or more for a single round of golf). The 18-hole, par-72 **Spyglass Hill** (1700 17-Mile Dr., 800/654-9300, www.pebblebeach.com, $395) gets its name from the Robert Louis Stevenson Novel *Treasure Island*. Spyglass Hill boasts some of the most challenging play in this golf course-laden region. Expect a few bogeys, and tee off from the championship level at your own (ego's) risk.

A favorite with the Pebble Beach crowd is the famed 18-hole, par-72 **Poppy Hills Golf Course** (3200 Lopez Rd., 831/622-8239, www. poppyhillsgolf.com, $210). Poppy Hills shares amenities with the other Pebble Beach golf courses. Expect the same level of care and devotion to the maintenance of the course and your experience as a player.

The **Pebble Beach Golf Links** (1700 17-Mile Dr., 800/877-0597, www.pebblebeach. com, $495) has been called the nation's best golf course by *Golf Digest*. The high ranking might have something to do with the fact that some of the fairways are perched above the Pacific Ocean. The course will host its sixth men's U.S. Open championship in 2019 and is one of three courses utilized during the popular AT&T Pro-Am.

Less pricey than the Pebble Beach Golf Links, **The Links at Spanish Bay** (2700 17-Mile Dr., 831/647-7495 or 800/877-0597, $155-270) is on native sand dune habitat. Due to the environmental sensitivity of the grounds, the course caps the number of players and spectators on the greens.

FOOD AND ACCOMMODATIONS

You need to drop some serious money to stay in Pebble Beach. To experience the luxury of Pebble Beach without spending your savings, consider having lunch, dinner, or a drink here and then head back to a less expensive lodging in nearby Pacific Grove or Monterey.

The Hawaiian fusion cuisine of celebrity chef Roy Yamaguchi takes center stage at **Roy's at Pebble Beach** (The Inn at Spanish Bay, 2700 17-Mile Dr., 831/647-7423, www.pebblebeach.com, 6:30am-10pm daily, $27-50). Island-inspired dishes include seafood and sushi, all with an Asian flair. Head to **Peppoli** (The Inn at Spanish Bay, 2700 17-Mile Dr., 831/647-7433, www. pebblebeach.com, 6pm-10pm daily, $25-110) for a hearty Italian dinner of gnocchi with black truffle cream sauce or seared local halibut.

The Bench Restaurant (The Lodge at Pebble Beach, 1700 17-Mile Dr., 800/654-9300, 11am-10pm daily, $25-36) overlooks the famed 18th hole of the Pebble Beach Golf Links. The chef employs wood-roasting and open-flame cooking techniques to create wood-fired Brussels sprouts and grilled steaks. **The Tap Room** (The Lodge at Pebble Beach, 1700 17-Mile Dr., 831/625-8535, 11am-midnight daily, $22-79) bar serves burgers, bratwurst, Wagyu beef filet mignon, and fresh Maine lobster (the prime rib chili is worth your time), and 14 beers on tap at an inflated price ($10.75). Bill Murray is an occasional customer.

Porter's in the Forest (3200 Lopez Rd., 831/622-8240, http://poppyhillsgolf.com/porters, 6am-6pm daily, $13-25), beside the Poppy Hills Golf Course, serves ingenious twists on clubhouse fare with items like a

Korean Philly cheesesteak and carne asada fries. They serve breakfast, lunch, and a twilight menu.

Expect luxury amenities at **The Lodge at Pebble Beach** (1700 17-Mile Dr., 831/647-7500 or 800/654-9300, www.pebblebeach.com, $900-4,400), by the 18th hole of the Pebble Beach Golf Links. Most rooms and suites have wood-burning fireplaces as well as private patios or balconies. Some high-end rooms have their own spas. A stay includes access to The Beach & Tennis Club, which has a heated outdoor pool, a whirlpool spa, and a tennis pavilion. **The Inn at Spanish Bay** (2700 17-Mile Dr., 831/647-7500 or 800/654-9300, www.pebblebeach.com, $790-4,450) has rooms with fireplaces and decks or patios. There's also a fitness center and tennis pavilion on-site.

TRANSPORTATION

Pebble Beach is a gated community and entry requires a fee ($10.25). There are several gates to get into Pebble Beach, including three in Pacific Grove and one in Carmel. You can get the fee waived if you are dining at a Pebble Beach restaurant. Just make a reservation and tell the guard at the entry gate.

Carmel-by-the-Sea

There are no addresses in Carmel-by-the-Sea (frequently referred to as simply Carmel). There are lots of trees and no streetlights, and street signs are wooden posts with names written perpendicularly, to be read while walking along the sidewalk, rather than driving down the street. There's little to do at night. These are a few clues as to how this village facing the Pacific Ocean maintains its lost-in-time charm.

Formerly a Bohemian enclave where local poets George Sterling and Robinson Jeffers hung out with literary heavyweights including Jack London and Mary Austin, Carmel-by-the-Sea is now a popular vacation spot for the moneyed, the artistic, and the romantic. People come to enjoy the small coastal town's almost European appeal. They stroll its sidewalks, peering into the windows of upscale shops and art galleries that showcase the work

the white sand of Carmel Beach

of sculptors, plein air painters, and photographers. Between the galleries are some of the region's most revered restaurants. The main thoroughfare, Ocean Avenue, slopes down to Carmel Beach, one of the finest on the Monterey Peninsula.

The old-world charms of Carmel can make it a little confusing for drivers. Because there are no addresses, locations are sometimes given via directions, for example: on 7th Avenue between San Carlos and Dolores Streets; or the northwest corner of Ocean Avenue. The town is compact, laid out on a plain grid system, so you're better off getting out of your car and walking anyway. Expect to share everything from Carmel's sidewalks to its restaurants with our canine friends. Carmel is very pro-pup.

SIGHTS
★ Carmel Beach
Carmel Beach (Ocean Ave., 831/624-4909, http://ci.carmel.ca.us/carmel, 6am-10pm daily) is one of the Monterey Bay region's best beaches. Under a bluff dotted with twisted, skeletal cypress trees, it's a long, white, sandy beach that borders a usually clear blue-green Pacific. In the distance to the south, Point Lobos juts out from the land like a pointing finger, while just north of the beach, the green-as-billiard-table-felt golf courses cloak the grounds of nearby Pebble Beach. Like most of Carmel, Carmel Beach is very dog friendly. On any given day, all sorts of canines fetch, sniff, and run on the white sand.

One of the best places to access the beach is at the west end of Ocean Avenue. There's a parking lot here, along with four beach volleyball courts, a wooden observation deck, and restrooms.

For surfers, Carmel Beach is one of the Monterey area's most consistent breaks.

Carmel Mission
San Carlos Borromeo de Carmelo Mission (3080 Rio Rd., 831/624-1271, www.carmelmission.org, 9:30am-7pm daily, adults $6.50, seniors $4, children $2) was Father Junípero Serra's favorite among his California mission churches. He lived, worked, and died here; visitors can see a replica of his cell. An active Catholic parish remains part of the complex, so please be respectful when taking the self-guided tour. The rambling buildings and courtyard gardens show some wear, but restoration work makes them attractive and eminently visitor friendly.

The Carmel Mission has a small memorial museum in a building off the second courtyard that shows a slice of the lives of the 18th- and 19th-century friars. The highlight is the church with its gilded altar front, its shrine to the Virgin Mary, the grave of Junípero Serra, and an ancillary chapel dedicated to his memory. Round out your visit by walking the gardens to admire the flowers and fountains and to read the grave markers in the small cemetery.

Tor House
Local poet Robinson Jeffers penned nature poems to the uncompromising beauty of Carmel Point and nearby Big Sur. He built this rugged-looking castle on the Carmel coast in 1919. Jefffers named it **Tor House** (26304 Ocean View Ave., 831/624-1813, www.torhouse.org, tours 10am-3pm Fri.-Sat., adults $10, students $5) after its rocky setting, and he added the majestic Hawk Tower a year later.

Volunteer docents offer tours of the property that include a walk through the original home, which was hand built by Jeffers with giant stones. The poet once hosted luminaries like Ansel Adams, Charlie Chaplin, Edna St. Vincent Millay, and Dylan Thomas within the dining room, which offers fine views of Carmel Point and Point Lobos. The highlight of the tour is a visit to **Hawk Tower,** a four-story stone structure crowned with an open-air turret.

★ Point Lobos State Natural Reserve
Said to be the inspiration behind the setting

Carmel-by-the-Sea

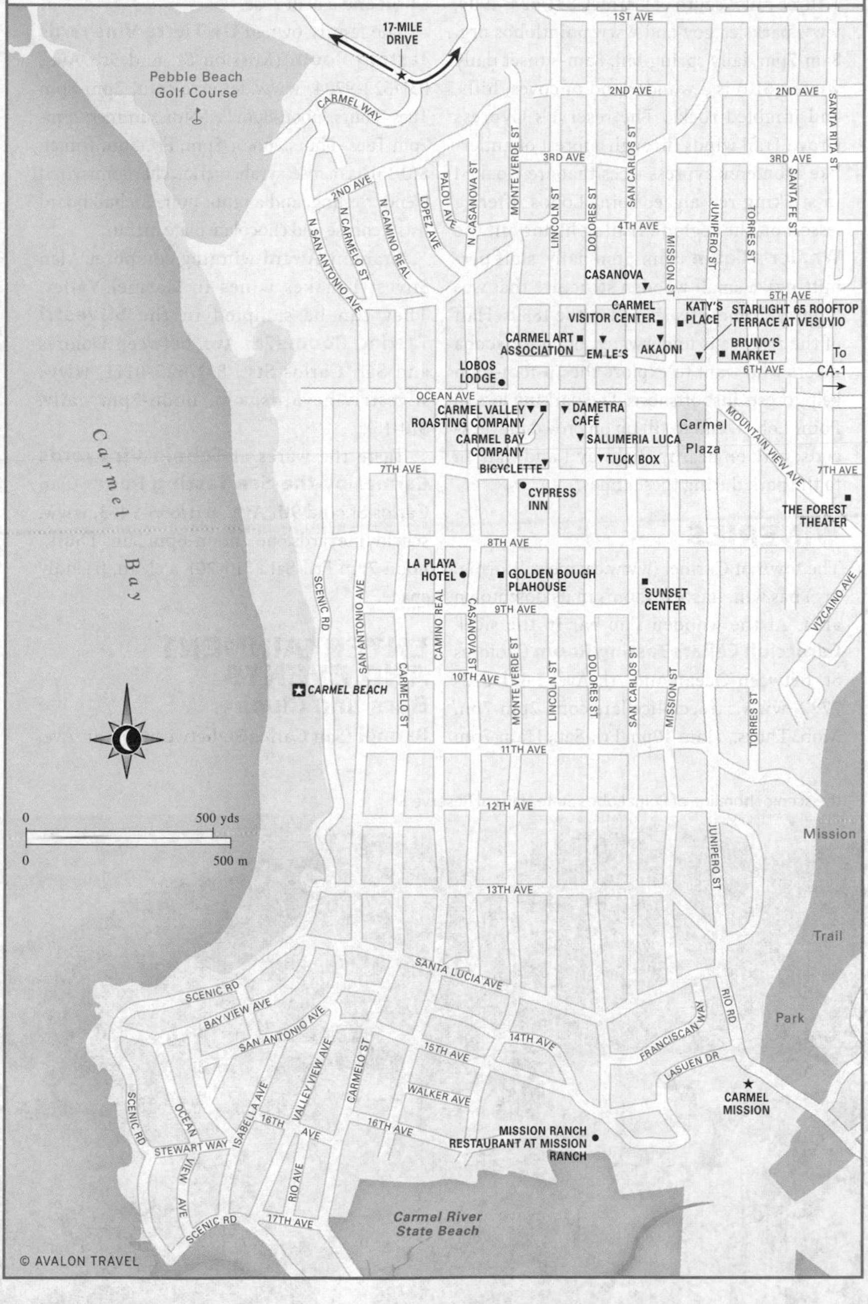

17-MILE DRIVE

Pebble Beach Golf Course

1ST AVE

CARMEL WAY

2ND AVE

2ND AVE

SANTA RITA ST

2ND AVE

3RD AVE

3RD AVE

SANTA FE ST

N SAN ANTONIO AVE

N CARMELO ST

N CAMINO REAL

PALOU AVE

LOPEZ AVE

N CASANOVA ST

MONTE VERDE ST

LINCOLN ST

DOLORES ST

SAN CARLOS ST

MISSION ST

JUNIPERO ST

TORRES ST

4TH AVE

CASANOVA

5TH AVE

CARMEL VISITOR CENTER

KATY'S PLACE

STARLIGHT 65 ROOFTOP TERRACE AT VESUVIO

CARMEL ART ASSOCIATION

EM LE'S

AKAONI

BRUNO'S MARKET

To CA-1

6TH AVE

LOBOS LODGE

OCEAN AVE

CARMEL VALLEY ROASTING COMPANY

DAMETRA CAFÉ

Carmel Plaza

MOUNTAIN VIEW AVE

CARMEL BAY COMPANY

SALUMERIA LUCA

TUCK BOX

7TH AVE

BICYCLETTE

7TH AVE

Carmel Bay

CYPRESS INN

THE FOREST THEATER

8TH AVE

LA PLAYA HOTEL

GOLDEN BOUGH PLAHOUSE

SCENIC RD

SAN ANTONIO AVE

CAMINO REAL

CASANOVA ST

9TH AVE

SUNSET CENTER

VIZCAINO AVE

CARMELO ST

10TH AVE

MONTE VERDE ST

LINCOLN ST

DOLORES ST

SAN CARLOS ST

MISSION ST

TORRES ST

CARMEL BEACH

11TH AVE

0   500 yds
0   500 m

12TH AVE

JUNIPERO ST

Mission

13TH AVE

Trail

SANTA LUCIA AVE

Park

SCENIC RD

BAY VIEW AVE

SAN ANTONIO AVE

VALLEY VIEW AVE

CARMELO ST

15TH AVE

14TH AVE

FRANCISCAN WAY

RIO RD

LASUEN DR

SCENIC RD

OCEAN VIEW AVE

ISABELLA AVE

16TH AVE

WALKER AVE

16TH AVE

CARMEL MISSION

STEWART WAY

RIO AVE

17TH AVE

SCENIC RD

MISSION RANCH RESTAURANT AT MISSION RANCH

Carmel River State Beach

of Robert Louis Stevenson's *Treasure Island*, **Point Lobos State Natural Reserve** (Hwy. 1, three miles south of Carmel, 831/624-4909, www.parks.ca.gov and www.pointlobos.org, 8am-7pm daily spring-fall, 8am-sunset daily winter, $10) is a wonderland of coves, hills, and jumbled rocks. The reserve's Cypress Grove Trail winds through a forest of antler-like Monterey cypress trees that are cloaked in striking red algae. Point Lobos offers a lesson on the region's fishing history in the **Whaler's Cabin** (9am-5pm daily, staff permitting), a small wooden structure that was built by Chinese fishermen in the 1850s. Half of the reserve is underwater, open for scuba divers who want to explore the 70-foot-high kelp forests just offshore. The parking lots in Point Lobos tend to fill up on crowded weekends; park on nearby Highway 1 and walk in to the park during these times.

WINERIES

The town of Carmel (www.carmelcalifornia. org) has wine-tasting rooms in its downtown area. At the wooden slab bar in the sleek **Caraccioli Cellars Tasting Room** (Dolores St. between Ocean and 7th Aves., 831/622-7722, www.caracciolicellars.com, 2pm-7pm Mon.-Thurs., 11am-10pm Fri.-Sat., 11am-7pm Sun., $10-15), taste wines made from pinot noir and chardonnay grapes. They also pour a brut and a brut rosé.

The family-owned **De Tierra Vineyards Tasting Room** (Mission St. and 5th Ave., 831/622-9704, www.detierra.com, 2pm-8pm Tues.-Thurs., noon-8pm Fri.-Sun. summer; 2pm-7pm Tues.-Thurs., noon-8pm, Fri.-Sun. winter, $10-15) has a rosé, syrah, merlot, chardonnay, red blend, riesling, and a pinot noir. A chalkboard lists a cheese and chocolate plate menu.

Grammy Award-winning composer Alan Silvestri makes wines in Carmel Valley. They can be sampled in the **Silvestri Tasting Room** (7th Ave. between Dolores and San Carlos Sts., 831/625-0111, www. silvestrivineyards.com, noon-7pm daily, $10-15).

Taste the wares at **Scheid Vineyards Carmel-by-the-Sea Tasting Room** (San Carlos St. and 9th Ave., 831/656-9463, www. scheidvineyards.com, noon-6pm Sun.-Thurs., noon-7pm Fri.-Sat., $10-20), a clean, friendly space.

ENTERTAINMENT AND EVENTS
Bars and Clubs

Barmel (San Carlos St. between Ocean Ave.

the scenic shoreline of Point Lobos State Natural Reserve

and 7th Ave., 831/626-3400, 2:30pm-midnight daily) has live music Thursday-Saturday with a DJ on weekend nights.

Live Music

The **Chamber Music Monterey Bay** (831/625-2212, www.chambermusicmontereybay.org) society brings talented ensembles and soloists from around the world to perform on the lovely Central Coast. String quartets rule the small stage. Shows are performed at the **Sunset Cultural Center** (San Carlos St. at 9th Ave., 831/620-2048, www.sunsetcenter.org), a state-of-the-art performing center with more than 700 seats. Chamber Music Monterey Bay reserves up-front seats for children and their adult companions.

Theater

The **Pacific Repertory Theater** (831/622-0100, www.pacrep.org, adults $15-39, seniors $15-28, military, students, and teachers $10-15, children $7.50) is the only professional theater company on the Monterey Peninsula. Shows travel the region, but most are in the **Golden Bough Playhouse** (Monte Verde St. and 8th Ave.), the company's home theater. Other venues include the **The Forest Theater** (Mountain View St. and Santa Rita St.) and the **Circle Theater** (Casanova St. between 8th and 9th Aves.) within the Golden Bough complex. The company puts on dramas, comedies, and musicals both new and classic. Buy tickets online or by phone to guarantee a seat.

Festivals and Events

One of the biggest events of the year is the **Carmel Art Festival** (Devendorf Park at Mission St., www.carmelartfestivalcalifornia.com, May). This three-day event celebrates visual arts in all media with shows by internationally acclaimed artists at galleries, parks, and other venues all across town. This wonderful festival also sponsors here-and-now contests, including the prestigious plein air (outdoor painting) competition. A wealth of children's activities help even the youngest festivalgoers become budding artists.

One of the most prestigious festivals in Northern California is the **Carmel Bach Festival** (831/624-1521, www.bachfestival.org, July). For 15 days each July, Carmel-by-the-Sea and its surrounding towns host dozens of classical concerts. You can also hear Mozart, Vivaldi, Handel, and other heavyweights of Bach's era. Concerts and recitals take place every day of the week.

SHOPPING

It is easy to spend an afternoon poking into Carmel's many art galleries. Sample Carmel's art scene at the monthly **Carmel Art Walk** (www.carmelartwalk.com, 5pm-8pm second Sat. of the month), a self-guided tour of the town's art galleries. Talk to the artists, sip wine, and listen to live music.

The paintings at the **Joaquin Turner Gallery** (Dolores St. between 5th and 6th Sts., 831/869-5564, www.joaquinturnergallery.com, 11am-5pm Thurs.-Mon., by appointment Tues.-Wed.) are a nod to the works of early-20th-century Monterey Peninsula artists.

At the **Steven Whyte Sculpture Gallery** (Dolores St. between 5th and 6th Sts., 831/620-1917, www.stevenwhytesculptor.com, 9:30am-4pm Mon. and Wed.-Thurs., 9:30am-5pm Fri., 10am-5pm Sat., 10:30am-4pm Sun.), you can watch the artist create amazing life-size sculptures in his open studio.

One of the best galleries in town is the **Weston Gallery** (6th Ave., 831/624-4453, www.westongallery.com, 11am-5pm Tues.-Sun.), which highlights the photographic work of 20th-century masters including Ansel Adams, Diane Arbus, Robert Mapplethorpe, and Edward Weston.

A tiny art gallery owned by two local photographers, **Exposed** (Carmel Sq., San Carlos St. and 7th Ave., 831/238-0127, http://galleryexposed.blogspot.com, 1pm-3pm Sat., 5pm-8pm first Fri. of the month) is worth a peek.

Carmel Plaza (Ocean Ave. and Mission

St., 831/624-0138, www.carmelplaza.com, 10am-6pm Mon.-Sat., 11am-5pm Sun.) is an outdoor mall with luxury fashion shops like Tiffany & Co. as well as the hip clothing chain Anthropologie. Don't miss locally owned establishment **The Cheese Shop** (800/828-9463, www.thecheeseshopinc.com, 10am-6pm Mon.-Sat., 11am-5:30pm Sun.), which sells delicacies like cave-aged gruyère cheese.

SPORTS AND RECREATION

Devendorf Park (Ocean Ave. and Junipero Ave., 831/624-3543, https://ci.carmel.ca.us) is downtown Carmel-by-the-Sea's best public place. This block-long park features a grassy lawn rimmed by live oaks, benches, and monuments honoring U.S. service people. It's the site of many Carmel-by-the-Sea events, including a Fourth of July celebration, a Halloween parade, and an annual tree-lighting ceremony. It is also home to one of downtown's only public restrooms.

Carmel Beach (Ocean Ave., 831/624-4909, 6am-10pm daily) has some of the area's most consistent beach breaks. Being a beach break, the sandbars shift, so the best spot on the beach frequently changes. The waves are usually at their finest from spring to late summer. The winds blow out a lot of area breaks in the spring, but Carmel Beach really comes alive during this time of year.

Carmel Surf Lessons (831/915-4065, www.carmelsurflessons.com) can teach you to surf at Carmel Beach. **On the Beach** (693 Lighthouse Ave., 831/646-9283, http://onthebeachsurfshop.com, 10am-6pm Sun.-Thurs., 10am-7pm Fri.-Sat., surfboard rental $30/day, wetsuit rental $15/day) rents surfboards and wetsuits.

FOOD
American
★ **Carmel Belle** (Doud Craft Studios, Ocean Ave. and San Carlos Sts., 831/624-1600, www.carmelbelle.com, 8am-6pm daily, $6-15) is a little eatery with big attention to detail. The superb breakfast menu includes an open-face breakfast sandwich featuring a slab of toasted bread topped with a poached egg, strips of thick bacon, a bed of arugula, and wedges of fresh avocado. Its slow-cooked Berkshire pork sandwich with red onion-currant chutney is a perfect example of what can happen when savory meets sweet.

Aubergine (Monte Verde St. at 7th Ave., 831/624-8578, www.auberginecarmel.com, 6pm-9:30pm daily, $175) has been racking up accolades, among them coveted awards from the James Beard Foundation. The Tasting Menu includes eight courses and changes daily.

Italian
On paper, **Vesuvio** (6th Ave. and Junipero St., 831/625-1766, http://chefpepe.com, 4pm-11pm daily, $16-32) dishes out cannelloni, gnocchi, and wood-oven pizzas, but there's a lot more going on. A popular rooftop bar has fire pits, heat lamps, and love seats. There's also a great eight-ounce burger topped with caramelized onions, oozing cambozola cheese, and chipotle aioli on a house-made mini-sub roll. Order it as a "Grown-up Happy Meal" with fries and a well cocktail or glass of wine.

Mediterranean
Dametra Café (Ocean Ave. at Lincoln St., 831/622-7766, www.dametracafe.com, 11am-11pm daily, $11-27) has a wide-ranging international menu that includes the all-American cheeseburger and Italian dishes like spaghetti alla Bolognese. Still, it's best to go with the lively restaurant's signature Mediterranean food. The Greek chicken kebab is a revelation with two chicken-and-vegetable kebabs drizzled with aioli sauce over yellow rice and a Greek salad. The owner and his staff have been known to serenade evening diners.

Mexican
★ **Cultura Comida y Bebida** (Dolores St. between 5th and 6th Sts., 831/250-7005, www.culturacarmel.com, 5:30pm-midnight Mon.-Fri., 10:30am-midnight Sat.-Sun., $18-28) satisfies adventurous diners with superb upscale Mexican cuisine. Try the *chapulines*

(toasted grasshoppers) appetizer or skip ahead to the relleno-style abalone. The restaurant's large mescal menu offers the smoky spirit in cocktails or one-ounce pours. The late-night menu (10pm-midnight daily) includes $2 street tacos.

Seafood

The **Flying Fish Grill** (Mission St. between Ocean Ave. and 7th Ave., 831/625-1962, http://flyingfishgrill.com, 5pm-10pm daily, $21-36) serves Japanese-style seafood with a California twist. Entrées include rare, peppered ahi and black bean halibut. You might even be able to score a market-price meal of Monterey abalone. Relax over your meal in the dimly lit, wood-walled establishment.

Sushi

Akaoni (Mission St. and 6th Ave., 831/620-1516, 5:30pm-8:30pm Mon.-Tues., 11:30am-1pm and 5:30pm-8:30pm Wed.-Sat., $7-40) is a superb hole-in-the-wall sushi restaurant. Sit at the bar (or one of the few tables) and order tempura-fried oysters, soft-shell crab rolls, and an unagi donburi (eel bowl). Daily specials showcase the freshest seafood including items flown in from Japan. Adventurous diners can opt for the live Monterey spot prawn.

ACCOMMODATIONS
$150-250

Just two blocks from the beach, the ★ **Lamp Lighter Inn** (Ocean Ave. and Camino Real, 831/624-7372 or 888/375-0770, www.carmellamplighter.com, $225-425) has 11 rooms in five cottages with a comfortable, beachy decor. The cottages encircle a courtyard area that has two fire pits. Guests are treated to an afternoon wine and cheese reception and a morning continental breakfast. This is a pet-friendly property; two of the units have fenced-in backyards.

Outside of downtown Carmel, **Mission Ranch** (26270 Dolores St., 831/624-6436, www.missionranchcarmel.com, $165-380) is a sprawling old ranch complex with views of sheep-filled pastures and Point Lobos in the distance. If you get a glimpse of Mission Ranch's owner, it might just make your day: It's none other than Hollywood icon and former Carmel-by-the-Sea mayor Clint Eastwood. On the grounds is a restaurant with a nightly sing-along piano bar.

Over $250

Touted by *Architectural Digest*, **Tradewinds Carmel** (Mission St. and 3rd Ave., 831/624-2776, www.tradewindscarmel.com,

La Playa Carmel

$250-550) brings a touch of the Far East to California. The 28 serene hotel rooms are decorated with Asian antiquities and live orchids. Outside, the grounds have a water fountain that passes through bamboo shoots and horsetails along with a meditation garden, where an oversize Buddha head overlooks a trio of cascading pools. A continental breakfast includes French pastries and fruit.

Coachman's Inn (San Carlos St. and 8th Ave., 831/624-6421, www.coachmansinn.com, $249-329) is a small downtown motel with 30 clean, well-appointed rooms. The rooms have large flat screens, mini-fridges, microwaves, and Keurig coffeemakers. Some also have gas fireplaces and jetted spa tubs. A stay includes access to a hot tub, sauna, and exercise bike. The inn's staff will deliver a light continental breakfast to your room ($10).

The initial structure at ★ **La Playa Carmel** (Camino Real at 8th Ave., 831/293-6100 or 800/582-8900, www.laplayahotel.com, $399-849) was a mansion built for a member of the Ghirardelli family. It still has many features from an earlier era, including the dark, wood-walled bar, stained glass windows, and a tiled staircase. Half of the 75 rooms at La Playa look out onto nearby Carmel Beach, only two blocks away. Wander the grounds and stop by the library, the heated outdoor pool, and the courtyard with its oversize chessboard. The staff will treat you to an afternoon wine reception, a dessert of fresh-baked cookies, and a champagne breakfast with made-to-order omelets and waffles.

The landmark **Cypress Inn** (Lincoln St. and 7th Ave., 831/624-3871 or 800/443-7443, www.cypress-inn.com, $279-699) welcomes human and canine guests in a white, ornate Mediterranean-inspired building. This is one of the most pro-pup hotels in the state. They have dog cookies at the desk, water bowls are situated around the hotel, and they provide dog beds and dog towels by request. The rooms come with complimentary cream sherry, fruit, and snacks for guests, while some also have fireplaces and/or jetted tubs. Human visitors are treated to a breakfast that includes several hot items.

TRANSPORTATION

The quick way to get to Carmel from the north or the south is via Highway 1. From Highway 1, take Ocean Avenue into the middle of downtown Carmel.

There are no street addresses in Carmel-by-the-Sea, so pay close attention to the street names and the block you're on. To make things even more fun, street signs can be difficult to see in the mature foliage, and a dearth of streetlights can make signs nearly impossible to find at night. Show up during the day to get the lay of the land before trying to navigate after dark.

The nearest major medical center is in Monterey at the **Community Hospital of the Monterey Peninsula** (CHOMP, 23625 Holman Hwy., Monterey, 831/624-5311, www.chomp.org).

Carmel Valley

The landscape changes quickly as you leave the coast. You'll see the mountains rising above you, as well as farms, ranches, and orchards. Thirteen miles east of Highway 1 is the unincorporated Carmel Valley Village. In the small strip of businesses hugging Carmel Valley Road is a collection of wineries, tasting rooms, restaurants, and even an Old West saloon.

SIGHTS
Earthbound Farm

One of the largest purveyors of organic produce in the United States, Earthbound Farm began at **Earthbound Farm's Farm Stand** (7250 Carmel Valley Rd., 831/625-6219, www.earthboundfarm.com, 8am-6:30pm Mon.-Sat., 9am-6pm Sun.). This 2.5-acre farm and roadside stand offers visitors easy access to the company's smallish facility in the Carmel Valley. Browse a variety of organic fruits, veggies, and flowers or ramble the fields, checking out the chamomile labyrinth and the kids' garden (yes, your kids can look *and* touch). Select and harvest your own fresh herbs from the cut-your-own-herb garden, or purchase delicious prepared organic dishes at the farm stand. Scheduled walks offer a guided tour of the fields.

TOP EXPERIENCE

WINERIES

This small, charming wine region makes for a perfect wine-tasting day trip from Carmel, Monterey, or Big Sur. Small crowds, light traffic, and meaningful tasting experiences categorize this area, which still has many family-owned wineries.

The **Bernardus Winery** (5 W. Carmel Valley Rd., 831/298-8021 or 800/223-2533, www.bernardus.com, 11am-5pm daily, tasting $15-35) sits on a vineyard estate that also hosts a luxurious lodge and gourmet restaurant.

Bernardus creates a small list of wines, but the pride of the winery is the Bordeaux-style blended red Marinus Vineyard wine. Other varietals (chardonnay, pinot noir, and sauvignon blanc) come from cool coastal vineyards.

Tiny **Parsonage Village Vineyard** (19 E. Carmel Valley Rd., 831/659-7322, www.parsonagewine.com, 11am-5pm daily, tasting $10-20) has a tasting room in a little strip of shops, the space glowing with light that bounces off the copper of the bar. At the bar, you'll taste wonderful syrahs, hearty cabernet sauvignons, and surprisingly deep and complex blends—the Snosrap (that's Parsons spelled backward) table wine is inexpensive and incredibly tasty.

In the same strip of wineries, the **Cima Collina** (19 E. Carmel Valley Rd., Ste. A, 831/620-0645, http://cimacollina.com, noon-6pm daily, tasting $5) tasting room looks like a farmhouse with a front porch. Inside, enjoy pinot noir, chardonnay, sauvignon blanc, pinot blanc, and Cima Collina wines like the Howlin' Good Red.

A smaller, well-regarded Carmel winery, **Heller Estate Organic Vineyards** (69 W. Carmel Valley Rd., 831/659-6220, www.hellerestate.com, 11am-5pm daily, tasting $15-18) is a completely organic winery that uses natural methods, including predatory wasps, to rid the vineyard of pests rather than resorting to chemical-laden sprays. After visiting the tasting room, sit outdoors in Heller's sculpture garden.

Folktale Winery and Vineyards (8940 Carmel Valley Rd., 831/293-7500, www.folktalewinery.com, 11am-8pm daily, tasting $20) aims to be an "extension of your backyard" with bocce, horseshoes, and cornhole. Winery events include yoga, stand-up comedy, and concerts featuring musical acts like Lukas Nelson.

Talbott Vineyards (25 Pilot Rd., 831/659-3500, www.talbottvineyards.com, 11am-5pm

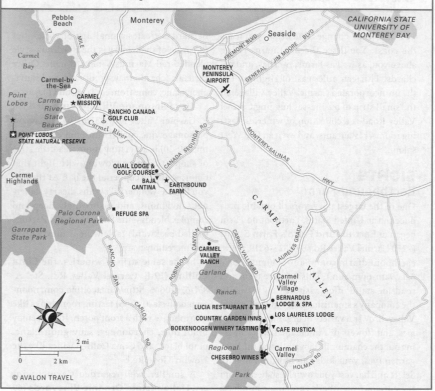

Carmel Valley

daily, tasting $10-15) utilizes two vineyards 18 miles apart to produce their chardonnays and pinot noirs. At the Carmel Valley tasting room, they pour six of their chardonnays and six of their pinot noirs alongside an impressive collection of vintage motorcycles. There's another tasting room near Salinas (1380 River Rd., 831/675-0409, 11am-4:30pm Thurs.-Mon., tasting $10-15).

The **Boekenoogen Vineyard & Winery** (24 W. Carmel Valley Rd., 831/659-4215, www.boekenoogenwines.com, 11am-5pm daily, tasting $15-20) tasting room offers pinot noirs, chardonnays, and syrahs, as well as a garden patio for those sunny Carmel Valley afternoons.

One fun way to get around the wineries is to hitch a ride on the **Happy Trails Wagon Tour** (831/970-8198, http://carmelvalleyhappytrailswagontours.com, noon-4pm Wed.-Sun., adult $25, child $10). Cowboy Pete pulls a 10-passenger wagon behind an antique tractor to wineries and restaurants in the immediate area.

Carmel Valley Village shows off its local wines and locally produced art at the daylong **Carmel Valley Art & Wine Celebration** (831/659-4000, www.carmelvalleychamber.com, June, free).

SPORTS AND RECREATION
Hiking

The 4,462-acre **Garland Ranch Regional Park** (700 W. Carmel Valley Rd.,

831/372-3196, www.mprpd.org, sunrise-sunset daily, free) boasts the best hiking trails in Carmel Valley. The **Lupine Loop** (1.4 miles, easy) is a level, dog-friendly trail that circles a flat part of the park, while **Snively's Ridge Trail-Sky Loop** (6 miles, difficult) involves a very steep hike to a ridge that offers views of the ocean and mountains. The **Mesa Trail** (1.6 miles, moderately strenuous) climbs to a saddle with valley views and a small pond.

Golf

The **Quail Lodge Golf Club** (8505 Valley Greens Dr., 866/675-1101, www.quaillodge.com, $185) has an 18-hole course with 10 lakes, as well as an academy to improve your game.

Spas

Sprawled over two acres in the shadow of the Santa Lucia Mountains, **Refuge Spa** (27300 Rancho Carlos Rd., 831/620-7360, www.refuge.com, 10am-10pm daily, admission $49, treatments $129-239) features warm waterfalls tumbling into soaking pools and two kinds of cold plunge pools. Don't miss the eucalyptus steam room, where a potent cloud of steam will purge all of your body's impurities.

FOOD

Led by revered local chef Cal Stamenov, the **Lucia Restaurant & Bar** (Bernardus Lodge & Spa, 415 W. Carmel Valley Rd., 831/658-3400, www.bernarduslodge.com, 7am-2:30pm and 5pm-9pm daily, $21-62) uses herbs from the garden out front and serves wines created from the adjacent vineyard. The menu features meat-centric dishes, while oenophiles should consider wine pairings, including the superb Bernardus Pisoni pinot noir and the Bernardus Ingrid's chardonnay. The knowledgeable and friendly staff will properly guide you.

With a large outdoor dining area, **Café Rustica** (10 Del Fino Pl., 831/659-4444, www.caferusticacarmel.com, 11am-2:30pm and 5pm-9pm Tues.-Sun., $13-30) is known for its nightly fish specials and herb-roasted half chicken.

Sip a wide range of tasty, intoxicating margaritas on the large wooden deck at ★ **Baja Cantina** (7166 Carmel Valley Rd., 831/625-2252, www.carmelcantina.com, 11:30am-11pm Mon.-Fri., 11am-midnight Sat.-Sun., $13-20). The menu includes hearty Americanized Mexican cuisine, like rosemary chicken burritos and wild mushroom and spinach enchiladas. The nachos have so much baked cheese that they resemble a casserole.

The Running Iron Restaurant & Saloon (24 E. Carmel Valley Rd., 831/659-4633, www.runningironrestaurantandsaloon.com, 11am-9pm daily, $12-25) keeps Carmel Valley's cowboy culture alive in the face of all the area's wineries. Named for a type of branding iron, The Running Iron is decorated with cowboy memorabilia. Enjoy stick-to-yer-ribs fare and a full bar at this classic California saloon.

ACCOMMODATIONS

Country Garden Inns (102 W. Carmel Valley Rd., 831/659-5361, www.countrygardeninns.com, $179-249) offers a perfect spot to rest and relax. Composed of two inns, the Acacia and the Hidden Valley, this small B&Bs offers French country-style charm in the violet and taupe rooms, as well as a pool, a self-serve breakfast bar, and strolling gardens. Rooms run from romantic king-bed studios to big family suites; most sleep at least four people (with daybeds in the window nooks).

Hosting guests on and off since 1915, the former ranch at **Los Laureles Lodge** (313 W. Carmel Valley Rd., 831/659-2233, www.loslaureles.com, $160-290, three-bedroom house $650) can put you up in a room, a honeymoon cottage, or a three-bedroom house. Enjoy the property's restaurant, saloon, and, most of all, its swimming pool and adjacent pool bar.

The spacious suites at the 500-acre ★ **Carmel Valley Ranch** (1 Old Ranch Rd., 831/625-9500, www.carmelvalleyranch.com, $430-800) are 650-1,200-square feet and have fireplaces and decks. An activity calendar comes with your stay and includes everything from a beekeeping class to nightly s'mores over an open fire. Don't miss the amazing pool deck with a saltwater swimming pool and an infinity pool hot tub that overlooks some beautiful oak trees and the resort's vineyard.

TRANSPORTATION

From Highway 1 south of Monterey, take Carmel Valley Road east for 13 miles to Carmel Valley Village, where most of the area's restaurants and wineries are.

Big Sur

Big Sur welcomes many types of visitors. Nature lovers come to camp and hike the pristine wilderness areas, to don thick wetsuits and surf often-deserted beaches, and even to hunt for jade in rocky coves. On the other hand, some of the wealthiest people from California visit to relax at unbelievably posh hotels and spas with dazzling views of the ocean. Whether you prefer a low-cost camping trip or a luxury resort, Big Sur offers its beauty and charm to all. Part of that charm is Big Sur's determination to remain peacefully apart from the Information Age (this means that your cell phones may not work in many parts of Big Sur).

SIGHTS

TOP EXPERIENCE

Big Sur Coast Highway

Even if you're not up to tackling the endless hiking trails and deep wilderness backcountry of Big Sur, you can still get a good sense of the glory of this region just by driving through it. The **Big Sur Coast Highway,** a 90-mile stretch of Highway 1, is quite simply one of the most picturesque roads in the country. A two-lane road, Highway 1 twists and turns with Big Sur's jagged coastline, running along precipitous cliffs and rocky beaches, through dense redwood forests, over historic bridges, and past innumerable parks. In winter, you might spot migrating whales offshore spouting fountains of air and water, while spring finds yucca plants feathering the hillsides and wildflowers coloring the landscape. Construction on this stretch of road was completed in the 1930s, connecting Cambria to Carmel.

Start out at either town and spend a whole day making your way to the other end of the road. The road has plenty of wide turnouts

Big Sur coast

Big Sur

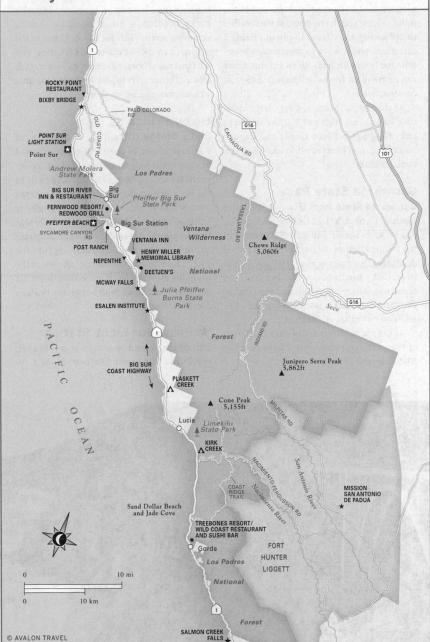

ROCKY POINT RESTAURANT
BIXBY BRIDGE
PALO COLORADO RD
OLD COAST RD
POINT SUR LIGHT STATION
Point Sur
CACHAGUA RD
G16
101
Andrew Molera State Park
Los Padres
BIG SUR INN & RESTAURANT
Big Sur
FERNWOOD RESORT/ REDWOOD GRILL
Pfeiffer Big Sur State Park
PFEIFFER BEACH
SYCAMORE CANYON RD
Big Sur Station
TASSAJARA RD
POST RANCH
VENTANA INN
Ventana Wilderness
NEPENTHE
HENRY MILLER MEMORIAL LIBRARY
Chews Ridge 5,060ft
DEETJEN'S
MCWAY FALLS
National
Julia Pfeiffer Burns State Park
ESALEN INSTITUTE
G16
Seco
PACIFIC OCEAN
Forest
1
BIG SUR COAST HIGHWAY
INDIANS RD
Junipero Serra Peak 5,862ft
PLASKETT CREEK
MILPITAS RD
Cone Peak 5,155ft
Lucia
Limekiln State Park
San Antonio River
KIRK CREEK
NACIMIENTO-FERGUSSON RD
Nacimiento River
MISSION SAN ANTONIO DE PADUA
COAST RIDGE TRAIL
Sand Dollar Beach and Jade Cove
TREEBONES RESORT/ WILD COAST RESTAURANT AND SUSHI BAR
FORT HUNTER LIGGETT
Gorda
Los Padres
National
Forest
0   10 mi
0   10 km

SALMON CREEK FALLS

© AVALON TRAVEL

set into picturesque cliffs to make it easy to stop to admire the glittering ocean and stunning wooded cliffs running right out to the water. (Please use the turnouts to park, rather than looking away from the road.) Bring a camera as you'll want to take photos every mile for hours on end. Be aware that there can be frequent highway delays due to road construction.

At time of publication, a very large landslide had closed Highway 1 at the southern end of Big Sur between Gorda and Ragged Point. The road is expected to reopen in late summer 2018.

Garrapata State Park

Garrapata State Park (Hwy. 1, 6.7 miles south of Carmel, 831/624-4909, www.parks.ca.gov, 8am-sunset daily, free) has most of the features that make Big Sur such a famed destination for outdoor enthusiasts: redwood trees, rocky headlands, pocket beaches, and ocean vistas from steep hills and mountains. **Garrapata Beach** is northern Big Sur's finest, with two miles of coastline.

At time of publication, the eastern section of the park remained closed following the 2016 Soberanes Fire.

HIKING
The **Soberanes Point Trail** (2 miles round-trip) is a mild hike up and around the park's rocky headlands. Stroll along the beach, scramble up the cliffs for a better view of the ocean, or check out the seals, sea otters, and sea lions near Soberanes Point. In winter, grab a pair of binoculars to look for migrating gray whales passing close to shore.

Bixby Bridge

Bixby Bridge (Hwy. 1, 15 miles south of Carmel) is one of the most-photographed bridges in the nation. The picturesque, open-spandrel arched cement bridge was built in the early 1930s as part of the massive government works project that completed Highway 1 through Big Sur. Pull out north of the bridge to take photos or just look out at the attractive span and Bixby Creek flowing into the Pacific far below. Get another great view of the bridge by driving a few hundred feet down the dirt Old Coast Road, which is on the bridge's northeast side.

★ Point Sur Light Station

Sitting lonely and isolated out on its cliff, the **Point Sur Light Station** (Hwy. 1, 19

Big Sur's Bixby Bridge

miles south of Carmel, 831/625-4419, www. pointsur.org, tours: 1pm Wed., 10am Sat.-Sun. Oct.-Mar.; 10am and 2pm Wed. and Sat., 10am Sun., Apr.-Sept., adults $15, children $5) crowns the 361-foot-high volcanic rock Point Sur. It's the only complete 19th-century light station in California that you can visit, and even here access is severely limited. First lit in 1889, this now fully automated light station still provides navigational aid to ships off the coast.

TOURS

Take one of the **moonlight tours** (call 831/625-4419 for information) to learn about the haunted history of the light station buildings.

You can't make a reservation for a Point Sur tour, so just show up and park your car off Highway 1 on the west side by the farm gate. Your guide will meet you there and lead you up the paved road 0.5 mile to the light station. Once there, you'll climb the stairs up to the light, explore the restored keepers' homes and service buildings, and walk out to the cliff edge. Expect to see a great variety of flora and fauna, from brilliant wildflowers in the spring to gray whales in the winter to

flocks of pelicans flying in formation at any time of year. Dress in layers; it can be sunny and hot or foggy and cold, winter or summer, and sometimes both on the same tour! Tours last three hours and require more than a mile of walking, with a bit of slope, and more than 100 stairs.

If you need special assistance for your tour or have questions about accessibility, call 831/649-2836 as far in advance as possible of your visit to make arrangements.

Andrew Molera State Park

Andrew Molera State Park (Hwy. 1, 21 miles south of Carmel, 831/667-2315, www. parks.ca.gov, sunrise-sunset daily, $10/vehicle) has several hiking trails that run down to the beach and up into the forest along the river.

At the park entrance, you'll find bathrooms but no drinking water or food concessions.

HIKING

The beach is a one-mile walk down the easy, multiuse **Trail Camp Beach Trail** (2 miles round-trip, easy). From there, climb out to the headlands on the **Headlands Trail** (0.5 mile round-trip, easy) for a beautiful view of

Point Sur Light Station, atop Point Sur

the Big Sur River emptying into the sea. In the distance is Pico Blanco, one of the region's most distinctive mountains, rising like a pyramid from behind a ridgeline. For a better look at the river, take the flat, moderate **Bobcat Trail** (5.5 miles round-trip, easy) and perhaps a few of its ancillary loops. You'll walk right along the riverbank, enjoying the local microhabitats.

For a longer and more difficult trek up the mountains and down to the beach, the **Ridge Trail and Panorama Trail Loop** (8 miles round-trip, moderate) is one of the best coastal hikes in Big Sur. Start at the parking lot on the **Creamery Meadow Beach Trail,** then make a left onto the long and fairly steep **Ridge Trail** to get a sense of the local ecosystem. Then turn right onto the **Panorama Trail,** which has sweeping views of the coast, including Molera Point and Point Sur, as it runs down to the coastal scrublands. Take the small **Spring Trail** (0.2 mile round-trip, easy) down a driftwood-littered gully to a scenic stretch of beach. Hike back out and take a left connecting to the **Bluffs Trail,** which takes you back to Creamery Meadow along the top of a marine terrace.

Pfeiffer Big Sur State Park

The most developed park in Big Sur, **Pfeiffer Big Sur State Park** (Hwy. 1, 26 miles south of Carmel, 831/667-2315, www.parks.ca.gov, sunrise-sunset daily, $10/vehicle) is home to a lodge, a restaurant and café, hiking trails, and lovely redwood-shaded **campsites**. This is one of the best parks in the area to see Big Sur's redwoods and a great place to dip into the cool Big Sur River.

HIKING

Pfeiffer Big Sur has the tiny **Ernst Ewoldsen Memorial Nature Center** (open seasonally), which features taxidermy examples of local wildlife. The historic **Homestead Cabin,** off the Big Sur Gorge Trail, was once the home of part of the Pfeiffer family, who were the first European immigrants to settle in Big Sur.

The **Nature Trail** (0.7 mile round-trip, easy) leaves from Big Sur Lodge and provides an introduction to the park's natural assets. No bikes or horses are allowed on trails in this park, which makes it quite peaceful for hikers.

The **Buzzard's Roost Trail** (3 miles round-trip, moderate) explores the park's

beach off Highway 1

west side. Climb from the river's edge through redwoods and oak trees on the way up to the summit of Pfeiffer Ridge, where you'll have a view of the coastline.

Big Sur Station

The ranger station at **Big Sur Station** (Hwy. 1, 27 miles south of Carmel, 831/667-2315, 9am-4pm daily) offers maps and brochures for all the major parks and trails of Big Sur, plus a minimal bookshop. This is where the trailhead for the popular backcountry **Pine Ridge Trail** is located. Get a free backcountry fire permit as well as pay for Pine Ridge Trailhead parking.

★ Pfeiffer Beach

Pfeiffer Beach (end of Sycamore Canyon Rd., http://campone.com, 9am-8pm daily, $10/vehicle) is one of the coastline's most picturesque spots. This frequently windswept beach has two looming rock formations right where the beach meets the surf, and both of these rocks have holes that look like doorways, allowing waves and sunlight to pass through. Occasionally, purple sand colors the beach; it is eroded manganese garnet from the bluffs above. It can be incredibly windy here some days.

Getting to Pfeiffer Beach is a bit tricky. It is at the end of the second paved right south of the Big Sur Station. Motorists (no motor homes) must then travel down a narrow, windy, two-mile road before reaching the entrance booth and the beach's parking lot. It's part of the adventure. This road gets very busy during the summer and on weekends. Plan a trip to Pfeiffer Beach when it's less busy. Otherwise, the two-mile drive might take a lot longer than expected.

Henry Miller Memorial Library

Henry Miller lived and wrote in Big Sur for 18 years, and his 1957 novel *Big Sur and the Oranges of Hieronymus Bosch* describes his time here. Today, the **Henry Miller Memorial Library** (Hwy. 1, 31 miles south of Carmel, 831/667-2574, www.henrymiller.org, 10am-5pm Wed.-Mon., free) celebrates the life and work of Miller and his brethren in this quirky community center, museum, coffee shop, and gathering place. Inside is a well-curated bookstore featuring the works of Miller as well as other authors like Jack Kerouac and Richard Brautigan. The small redwood-shaded lawn hosts concerts and literary events. During summer, the library puts

Henry Miller Memorial Library

on an international short-film series every Thursday night.

Julia Pfeiffer Burns State Park

One of Big Sur's best postcard-perfect views can be attained at **Julia Pfeiffer Burns State Park** (Hwy. 1, 37 miles south of Carmel, 831/667-2315, www.parks.ca.gov, sunrise-sunset daily, $10/vehicle)—the scenic, if crowded, walk to McWay Falls. To get to the stunning view of **McWay Falls,** take the **Overlook Trail** (0.6 mile round-trip) along a level, wheelchair-accessible boardwalk. Stroll under the highway, past the Pelton wheelhouse, and out to the observation deck. The 80-foot-high waterfall cascades year-round off a cliff and onto the beach of a remote cove, where the water wets the sand and trickles out into the sea. You'll look down on a pristine and empty stretch of sand—there's no way down to the cove that is even remotely safe.

McWay Falls at Julia Pfeiffer Burns State Park

HIKING

The west side of the road is where you pick up the **Partington Cove Trail** (2 miles round-trip, easy), an underrated walk that goes to a striking, narrow coastal inlet. It begins as a steep dirt road and continues through a 60-foot-long tunnel blasted into the rock. The trail arrives at a cove where John Partington used to ship out the tanbark trees that he had harvested in the canyon above. There is a bench at the end of the trail with views of the cove and the coastline to the south. To reach the trailhead from the north, drive nine miles south of Pfeiffer Big Sur State Park on Highway 1. Look for a big bend in the road to the east with dirt pullouts on either side. Park here and then begin your hike where the gated road departs from the west side.

The **Waters Trail** (1.2 miles one-way, easy) connects the Tanbark Trail to the Ewoldsen Trail. Begin either at the main park entrance—where you'll find the trailhead off the Ewoldsen Trail—or start from the Tanbark Trail. The path cuts across the hillside while offering postcard-worthy coastal views along most of its route. In the spring, this area is painted purple by fields of flowering lupine. Unless you use two cars, you will have to walk along the highway a short distance to return to your vehicle. This hike is worth all of the effort.

Limekiln State Park

The 716-acre **Limekiln State Park** (Hwy. 1, 56 miles south of Carmel, 805/434-1996, www.parks.ca.gov, 8am-sunset daily, $10/vehicle) is home to redwoods, an impressive waterfall, a campground, ruins from the region's rugged past, and a nice beach on the stunning coastline. The park is named for four large, rusted limekilns accessed via the **Limekiln Trail.** From 1887 to 1890, the Rockland Lime and Lumber Company extracted and processed the land's limestone rock deposits in kilns, which used hot wood fires to purify the stones.

It's worth hiking the trail to **Limekiln Falls,** a 100-foot-high waterfall that splashes down a rock face in two distinct prongs. A sandy stretch of beach is littered with boulders, with the Limekiln Creek Bridge as a backdrop. A single picnic table plopped in the sand provides a terrific place for lunch. The park also has a **campground** with 32 sites.

Nacimiento-Fergusson Road

The only road that traverses Big Sur's Santa Lucia Mountains, the **Nacimiento-Fergusson Road** (58 miles south of Carmel) offers spectacular coastal views to those who are willing to wind their way up this twisty, paved, 1.5-lane road. Simply drive a few miles up to get an eyeful of the expansive Pacific Ocean or to climb above Big Sur's summer fog. It also heads in and out of infrequent redwood forests on the way up. The road connects Highway 1 to U.S. 101, passing through Fort Hunter Liggett army base on its journey.

The road is frequently closed during the winter months. It is not recommended for those who get carsick.

Sand Dollar Beach

Sand Dollar Beach (60 miles south of Carmel, www.fs.usda.gov, sunrise-sunset daily, $10/vehicle) is one of Big Sur's biggest and best beaches. This half-moon-shaped beach is tucked under cliffs that keep the wind down. Though frequently strewn with rocks, the beach is a great place to plop down for a picnic or an afternoon in the sun. From the beach, enjoy a striking view of Big Sur's south coast mountains including Cone Peak, rising like a jagged fang from a long ridgeline. A series of uncrowded beach breaks offer waves for surfers even during the flatter summer months.

The area around the parking lot has picnic tables with raised grills, pit toilets, and a pay phone. If the parking lot is full, park on the dirt pullout to the south of the entrance.

Jade Cove Recreation Area

It's easy to miss **Jade Cove Recreation Area** (Hwy. 1, 61 miles south of Carmel). A road sign marks the area, but there's not much in the way of a formal parking lot or anything

else to denote the treasures of this jagged, rough part of the Big Sur coastline. Park in the dirt/gravel strip off the road and head past the fence. It's fun to read the unusual signs along the narrow, beaten path that seems to lead to the edge of a cliff. Once you get to the edge of the cliff, the short trail gets rough. It's only 0.25 mile, but it's almost straight down a rocky, slippery cliff. Don't try to climb down if you're not in reasonable physical condition, and even if you are, don't be afraid to use your hands to steady yourself. At the bottom, you'll find huge boulders and smaller rocks and very little sand. But most of all, you'll find the most amazing minerals in the boulders and rocks. Search the smaller rocks beneath your feet for chunks of sea-polished jade. If you're a hardcore rock nut, join the locals in scuba diving for jewelry-quality jade. As long as you find it in the water or below the high-tide line, it's legal for you to take whatever you find here.

Jade Cove has no water, no restrooms, no visitors center, and no services of any kind.

Salmon Creek Falls

One of the best natural attractions is **Salmon Creek Falls** (Hwy. 1, 71 miles south of Carmel). A pair of waterfalls flow year-round down rocks over 100 feet high, their streams joining halfway down. For a great perspective of the falls, take an easy 10-minute walk over a primitive trail littered with rocks fallen from the highway. The unmarked parking area is a pullout in the middle of a hairpin turn on Highway 1.

Note: At time of publication, the area south of the landslide remained blocked.

SPORTS AND RECREATION
Horseback Riding

Take a guided horseback ride into the forests or out onto the beaches of Andrew Molera State Park with **Molera Horseback Tours** (831/625-5486, http://molerahorsebacktours.com, $75). The 1-2.5-hour tours depart daily at 9am, 11am, 1pm, and 3pm. Call ahead to guarantee a spot or to book a private guided ride. Each ride begins at the modest corral area, from which you'll ride along multiuse trails through forests or meadows, or along the Big Sur River, and down to Molera Beach. There you'll guide your horse along the solid sands as you admire the beauty of the wild Pacific Ocean.

Molera Horseback Tours are suitable for children over age six and riders of all ability levels; you'll be matched to the right horse for you. All but one of the rides go down to the beach. Tours can be seasonal, so call ahead if you want to ride in the fall or winter.

Backpacking

If you long for the lonely peace of backcountry camping, the **Ventana Wilderness** (www. ventanawild.org) area is ideal for you. This area comprises the peaks of the Santa Lucia Mountains and the dense growth of the northern reaches of the Los Padres National Forest. It has 167,323 acres of steep, V-shaped canyons and mountains that rise to over 5,000 feet. You'll find many trails beyond the popular day hikes of the state parks, especially as Big Sur stretches down to the south.

One of the most popular hikes is the 10-mile-long climb on the **Pine Ridge Trail** (Big Sur Station, 0.25 mile south of Pfeiffer Big Sur State Park) to **Sykes Hot Springs,** a cluster of warm mineral pools at a backcountry camp on the Big Sur River. The trail closes periodically; check trail access and secure a campfire permit and parking pass from the Big Sur Station.

Farther south, the **Vicente Flat Trail** (4 miles south of Lucia on Hwy. 1, across from the Kirk Creek Campground, 10 miles roundtrip) heads up toward Cone Peak, the jagged mountain rising in the distance, while gaining sweeping views of the coast. Do this one as a grueling up-and-back day hike to the Vincente Flat Camp or backpack it. Check the Ventana Wilderness Alliance website (www. ventanawild.org) in advance to find reports on the conditions of the trails you've decided to tackle, and stop in at Big Sur Station to get the latest news on the backcountry areas.

Fishing

The region offers your choice of shore or river fishing. Steelhead run up the Big Sur River to spawn each year, and a limited fishing season follows them up the river into **Pfeiffer Big Sur State Park** and other accessible areas. Check with Fernwood Resort (831/667-2422, www.fernwoodbigsur.com) and the lodges around Highway 1 for the best spots this season.

The numerous creeks that feed into and out of the Big Sur River also play home to their fair share of fish. The California Department of Fish and Game (www.wildlife.ca.gov) can give you specific locations for legal fishing, season information, and rules and regulations.

If you prefer the fish from the ocean, cast off several of the beaches for the rockfish that scurry about in the near-shore reefs. **Garrapata State Beach** has a good fishing area, as do the beaches at **Sand Dollar.**

Scuba Diving

There's not much for beginner divers in Big Sur. Expect cold water and an exposure to the ocean's swells and surges. Temperatures are in the mid-50s in the shallows, dipping into the 40s as you dive deeper down. Visibility is 20-30 feet, though rough conditions can diminish this significantly; the best season for clear water is September-November.

The biggest and most interesting dive locale here is **Julia Pfeiffer Burns State Park** (Hwy. 1, 37 miles south of Carmel, 831/667-2315, www.parks.ca.gov, sunrise-sunset, $10/ vehicle). You'll need to acquire a special permit at Big Sur Station and prove your experience to dive at this protected underwater park. You enter the water from the shore, which gives you the chance to check out all the ecosystems, beginning with the busy life of the beach sands before heading out to the rocky reefs and then into the lush green kelp forests.

Divers at access-hostile **Jade Cove** (Hwy. 1, 61 miles south of Carmel) come to stalk the wily jade pebbles and rocks that cluster in this special spot. The semiprecious stone striates the coastline right here, and storms

California Condors

With wings spanning 10 feet from tip to tip, the California condors soaring over the Big Sur coastline are some of the area's most impressive natural treasures. But, in 1987, there was only one bird left in the wild, and it was taken into captivity as part of a captive breeding program. The condors' population had plummeted due to their susceptibility to lead poisoning along with deaths caused by electric power lines, habitat loss, and being shot by indiscriminate humans.

Today the reintroduction of the high-flying California condor, the largest flying bird in North America, to Big Sur and the Central Coast is truly one of conservation's greatest success stories. In 1997, the Monterey County-based nonprofit Ventana Wildlife Society (VWS) began releasing the giant birds back into the wild. Currently, 70 wild condors soar above Big Sur and the surrounding area, and in 2006, a pair of condors were found nesting in the hollowed-out section of a redwood tree.

The species' recovery in the Big Sur area means that you may be able to spot a California condor flying overhead while visiting the rugged coastal region. Look for a tracking tag on the condor's wing to determine that you are actually looking at a California condor and not just a big turkey vulture. Or take a two-hour tour with the **Ventana Wildlife Society** (831/455-9514, $50/person), which uses radio telemetry to track the released birds. You can also visit the **VWS Discovery Center** (Andrew Molera State Park, Hwy. 1, 22 miles south of Carmel, 831/624-1202, www.ventanaws.org, 10am-4pm Sat.-Sun. Memorial Day-Labor Day), where an exhibit details the near extinction of the condor and the attempts to restore its population.

tear clumps of jade out of the cliffs and into the sea. Much of it settles just off the shore of the tiny cove, and divers hope to find jewelry-quality stones to sell for a huge profit.

If you're looking for a guided scuba dive, contact **Adventure Sports Unlimited** (303 Potrero St., Santa Cruz, 831/458-3648, https://asudoit.com, $200-918).

Bird-Watching

The Big Sur coast is home to innumerable species, from the tiniest bushtits up to grand pelicans and beyond. The most famous avian residents of this area are the rare and endangered California condors. Once upon a time, condors were all but extinct, with only a few left alive in captivity and conservationists struggling to help them breed. Today, around 70 of these birds soar above the trails and beaches of Big Sur. You might even see one swooping down low over your car as you drive down Highway 1!

The **Ventana Wildlife Society** (VWS, www.ventanaws.org) watches over many of the endangered and protected avian species in Big Sur. As part of their mission to raise awareness of the condors and many other birds, the VWS offers bird-watching expeditions.

Spas

Spa Alila at Ventana Big Sur (Ventana Big Sur, 48123 Hwy. 1, 28 miles south of Carmel, www.ventanainn.com, 10am-6:30pm daily, massages $175-615) offers a large menu of spa treatments to both hotel guests and visitors. Indulge in a soothing massage, purifying body treatment, or rejuvenating or beautifying facial. Take your spa experience a step further in true Big Sur fashion with an astrological reading, essence portrait, or a jade stone massage. Hotel guests can choose to have a spa treatment in the comfort of their own room or out on a private deck.

Across the highway from the Ventana, the **Post Ranch Inn's Spa** (Post Ranch Inn, 47900 Hwy. 1, 30 miles south of Carmel, 831/667-2200, www.postranchinn.com, 10am-7pm daily, massages $165-495) is an ultra-high-end resort spa only open to those spending the evening at the luxurious resort. Shaded by redwoods, the relaxing spa offers massages and facials along with more unique treatments including Big Sur jade stone therapy and craniosacral therapy. They also offer sessions inspired by Native American shamanism ($315-365), including a shamanic session, a fire ceremony, and a drum journey.

ENTERTAINMENT AND EVENTS
Live Music
Big Sur has become an unexpected hotbed of concerts. More than just a place to down a beer and observe the local characters, **Fernwood Tavern** (Fernwood Resort, 47200 Hwy. 1, 27 miles south of Carmel, 831/667-2422, www.fernwoodbigsur.com, 11am-11pm Sun.-Thurs., 11am-1am Fri.-Sat.) also has live music. Most of the big-name acts swing through in the summer and fall, but a wide range of regional acts perform on Saturday night starting at 10pm.

Down the road, the **Henry Miller Memorial Library** (48603 Hwy. 1, 31 miles south of Carmel, 831/667-2574, www.henrymiller.org) hosts concerts, book readings, and film screenings.

The manager of the **Big Sur River Inn** (46480 Hwy. 1, 25 miles south of Carmel, 831/667-2700, www.bigsurriverinn.com, 1pm-5pm Sun. late Apr.-early Oct.) jokes that they have been doing Sunday afternoon concerts on their back deck since "Jesus started riding a bicycle." The live music tradition here began in the 1960s with famed local act Jack Stock and the Abalone Stompers. Now mostly local jazz bands play on the restaurant's sunny deck, while a barbecue is set up on the large green lawn.

Bars
Fernwood Tavern (Fernwood Resort, 47200 Hwy. 1, 27 miles south of Carmel, 831/667-2422, www.fernwoodbigsur.com, 11am-11pm Sun.-Thurs., 11am-1am Fri.-Sat.) is a classic watering hole with redwood timbers and a fireplace that warms the place in the chilly months. Enjoy a beer or cocktail inside or out back on the deck under the redwoods.

The **Big Sur Taphouse** (47250 Hwy. 1, 29 miles south of Carmel, 831/667-2197, www.bigsurtaphouse.com, noon-10pm daily) has 10 rotating beers on tap, with a heavy emphasis on West Coast microbrews. The cozy interior has wood tables, a gas fireplace, and board games. With two big-screen TVs, the Taphouse is also a good place to catch your favorite sports team in action. Out back is a large patio with picnic tables and plenty of sun. They serve better-than-average bar food, including tacos and pork sliders.

The **Big Sur River Inn Restaurant** (46840 Hwy. 1, 831/667-2700, www.bigsurriverinn.com, 8am-11am, 11:30am-4:30pm, and 5pm-9pm daily) is a fine place for a cocktail or beer. In the late afternoon and early evening, the intimate bar area gets a fun local crowd.

Festivals and Events
The **Big Sur International Marathon** (831/625-6226, www.bsim.org, $175-200, Apr.) is one of the most popular marathons in the world, due in no small part to the scenery. Begin at the Big Sur Station and then wind, climb, and descend again on the way to Carmel's Rio Road.

Throughout the summer, the **Henry Miller Memorial Library** (48603 Hwy. 1, 831/667-2574, www.henrymiller.org, June-Aug.) hosts the **Big Sur International Short Film Screening Series,** where free films from all over the globe are shown on Thursday nights.

The **Big Sur Food & Wine Festival** (831/596-8105, www.bigsurfoodandwine.org, Nov.) celebrates cuisine and vino in stunning settings. Events include live music, dinner, and hiking with stemware.

FOOD
In Big Sur, a ready meal isn't something to take for granted. Pick up supplies in Cambria or Carmel before you enter the area to avoid paying premiums at the few mini-marts.

Casual Dining
The **Fernwood Bar & Grill** (Fernwood

Resort, 47200 Hwy. 1, 27 miles south of Carmel, 831/667-2129, www.fernwoodbigsur.com, 11am-10pm daily, $10-25) looks and feels like a grill in the woods ought to. Even in the middle of the afternoon, the aging, wood-paneled interior is dimly lit and strewn with casual tables and chairs. Walk up to the counter to order tacos, burgers, or pizzas, then head to the bar to grab a soda or a beer.

One of Big Sur's most popular attractions is ★ **Nepenthe** (48510 Hwy. 1, 29 miles south of Carmel, 831/667-2345, www.nepenthebigsur.com, 11:30am-4:30pm and 5pm-10:30pm daily July 4-early Sept., 11:30am-4:30pm and 5pm-10pm daily early Sept.-early July, $15-44), a restaurant built on the site where Rita Hayworth and Orson Welles owned a cabin until 1947. The deck offers stellar views. Sit under multicolored umbrellas on long, bar-like tables with stunning south-facing views. Order a basket of fries with Nepenthe's signature Ambrosia dipping sauce and wash them down with a potent South Coast margarita. The restaurant's most popular item is the Ambrosia burger, a ground steak burger drenched in tasty Ambrosia sauce.

If there's a line, consider dining at **Café Kevah** (weather permitting, 9am-4pm daily mid-Feb.-Jan.1, $9-16), an outdoor deck below the main restaurant that serves brunch, salads, and paninis.

The **Big Sur Bakery** (47540 Hwy. 1, 29 miles south of Carmel, 831/667-0520, www.bigsurbakery.com, bakery 8am daily; restaurant dinner 5:30pm-8:30pm Wed.-Sun., $18-32) might sound like a casual establishment, and the bakery part is. Stop in beginning at 8am for a fresh-baked scone, a homemade jelly doughnut, or a flaky croissant sandwich. On the dining room side, an elegant surprise awaits. Make reservations or you might miss out on the creative wood-fired pizzas, wood-grilled meats, and seafood. At brunch, they serve their unique wood-fired bacon and three-egg breakfast pizza.

The locals know ★ **Deetjen's** (48865 Hwy. 1, 31 miles south of Carmel, 831/667-2378, www.deetjens.com, 8am-noon and 6pm-9pm daily, $10-32) for its breakfast—an almost required experience for visitors to the area. Among fanciful knickknacks and framed photos of inn founder "Grandpa" Deetjen, diners can fill up on Deetjen's popular eggs Benedict dishes or the equally worthy Deetjen's dip, a turkey and avocado sandwich with hollandaise dipping sauce. In the evening, things get darker and more romantic

the outdoor deck at Nepenthe

as entrées, including the spicy seafood paella and an oven-roasted rack of lamb, are served at your candlelit table.

If it's a warm afternoon, get a table on the sunny back deck of the ★ **Big Sur River Inn Restaurant** (46840 Hwy. 1, 25 miles south of Carmel, 831/667-2700, http://bigsurriverinn.com, 8am-11am, 11:30am-4:30pm, and 5pm-9pm daily, $12-32). On summer Sundays, bands perform on the crowded deck, and you can take your libation to one of the chairs situated right in the middle of the cool Big Sur River. If it's chilly out, eat in the wood-beamed main dining room. The restaurant serves sandwiches, burgers, and fish-and-chips for lunch along with steak, ribs, seafood, and the recommended Noelle's salad at dinner. For dessert, they still do the famous apple pie that put them on the map back in the 1930s. The bar is known for its popular spicy Bloody Mary cocktails.

The unassuming **Ripplewood Café** (47047 Hwy. 1, 26 miles south of Carmel, 831/667-2242, www.ripplewoodresort.com, daily 8am-2pm, $9-16) may save the day on summer weekends when Deetjen's is flooded. Dine inside at the classic breakfast counter or on the outside brick patio among flowering plants. The breakfast menu includes pancakes, three-egg omelets, and a worthwhile chorizo and eggs. The grilled potato gratin is a highlight. Ripplewood shifts to lunch at 11:30am; offerings include sandwiches, Mexican food items, and salads.

The Big Sur Roadhouse (47080 Hwy. 1, 26 miles south of Carmel, 831/667-2370, www.glenoaksbigsur.com, 8am-2:30pm daily, $7-16) is one of the best bets for affordable, creative California dining in Big Sur for breakfast and lunch. The decor is homegrown modernism, with contemporary art hanging on the walls. The outdoor seating area has heating lamps and two fire pits. The menu skews toward Mexican items, including huevos rancheros and chilaquiles.

Oceanview Sushi Bar (Treebones Resort, 71895 Hwy. 1, 64 miles south of Carmel, 805/927-2390, 4:30pm-8pm Wed.-Sun. Mar.-Dec., $8-19) offers an intimate place to eat artfully prepared sushi. Just 10 seats are available at a redwood sushi bar within a tent-like structure. The menu includes simple rolls, garden rolls, specialty rolls, and hearty rolls designed to resemble burritos. There are two beers on tap along with sake, Japanese beer, and California wine. Seating priority is given to Treebones' guests.

Big Sur Bakery

Fine Dining

Enjoy a fine gourmet dinner at **The Sur House** (Ventana Big Sur, 48123 Hwy. 1, 28 miles south of Carmel, 800/628-6500, www.ventanainn.com, 7:30am-10:30am, 11:30am-4:30pm, and 6pm-close daily, $80-90). The spacious dining room boasts a warm wood fire, an open kitchen, lodge-like wood beams, and comfortable banquettes with plenty of throw pillows. Request a table outside to enjoy stunning views on the expansive patio. Chef Paul Corsentino has upped the quality of the menu, which at times has wild boar and Monterey sardine courses. Choose an à la carte main course or go for the vegetarian or chef's tasting menus.

The **Sierra Mar** (Post Ranch Inn, 47900 Hwy. 1, 28 miles south of Carmel, 831/667-2800, www.postranchinn.com, 12:15pm-3pm and 5:30pm-9pm daily) restaurant offers a decadent four-course prix-fixe dinner menu every night ($125) or a nine-course tasting menu ($175). There's also a less formal three-course lunch ($65) every day. With floor-to-ceiling glass windows overlooking the plunging ridgeline and the Pacific below, this is a good place to schedule dinner during sunset. The daily menu rotates, but some courses have included farm-raised abalone in brown butter and a succulent short rib and beef tenderloin duo.

Markets

The best of the local markets is the ★ **Big Sur Deli** (47520 Hwy. 1, 29 miles south of Carmel, 831/667-2225, www.bigsurdeli.com, 7am-8pm daily). Very popular with locals, the deli has large, made-to-order sandwiches, burritos, tamales, tacos, and pasta salads. If the line is long at the counter, opt for a premade sandwich for a quicker exit. They also have cold drinks, wine, beer, and some basic supplies.

River Inn Big Sur General Store (46840 Hwy. 1, 25 miles south of Carmel, 831/667-2700, 11am-7pm daily) has basic supplies, along with beer and a nice selection of California wines. Even better, it has a

wonderful burrito bar and smoothie counter in the back. There are also simple premade turkey and ham sandwiches in a nearby fridge for taking out on a hike or picnic.

ACCOMMODATIONS

$100-150

New Camaldoli Hermitage (Hwy. 1, 51 miles south of Carmel, 831/667-2456, www.contemplation.com, $135-291) offers a quiet stay in the mountains above Lucia. The Hermitage is home to Roman Catholic monks who offer overnight accommodations for people of any or no religious denomination. The five private hermitages are basically trailers decorated with religious iconography and outfitted with a bed, desk, bathroom, and kitchen with a gas stove. There are also nine private rooms with a half bath and garden. Male guests can stay overnight in a monk's cell within the monastic enclosure; there are also a few units outside the enclosure for groups of two guests. Meals from the monastery's kitchen are included in the price. In addition to being a unique experience, staying at the Hermitage is one of the region's best deals. The accommodations can be rustic, but they are worth it if it's solitude you're after. Radios and musical instruments are not permitted.

$150-250

You'll find a couple of small motels along Highway 1 in the valley of Big Sur. One of the more popular is the **Fernwood Resort** (47200 Hwy. 1, 27 miles south of Carmel, 831/667-2422, www.fernwoodbigsur.com, motel rooms $155-200, cabins $250). The cluster of buildings includes a 12-room motel, a small convenience store, a restaurant, and a bar that is a gathering place for locals and a frequent host of live music. The motel units are on either side of the restaurant-bar-convenience store. The nicely priced units start at a simple queen bedroom and go up to a queen bedroom with a fireplace and a two-person hot tub on an outdoor back deck. Near the Big Sur River, the cabins have fully equipped kitchens and a refrigerator. The cabins are a good deal for groups of two to six people.

Your guest room at ★ **Deetjen's Big Sur Inn** (48865 Hwy. 1, 31 miles south of Carmel, 831/667-2378, www.deetjens.com, $155-290) will be unique, still decorated with the art and collectibles chosen and arranged by Grandpa Deetjen. The historic inn prides itself on its rustic construction, so expect thin, weathered walls, funky cabin construction, and no outdoor locks on the doors. Five rooms have shared baths, but you can request a room with private bath when you make reservations. Deetjen's prefers a serene environment and does not permit children under 12. The inn has no TVs or stereos, no phones in rooms, and no cell phone service, but you can have a night's worth of entertainment by reading your room's guest journals.

Over $250

The best part about staying at the **Big Sur Lodge** (Pfeiffer Big Sur State Park, 47225 Hwy. 1, 26 miles south of Carmel, 800/424-4787, www.bigsurlodge.com, $309-479) is leaving your room and hitting the trail. Set on a sunny knoll, the lodge has 62 units, with the majority being two-bedroom options; 12 units have kitchenettes. All rooms have a deck. There are no TVs and Internet access is an extra fee, but stays come with a pass to all of Big Sur's state parks, including Pfeiffer Big Sur State Park, Andrew Molera State Park, and Julia Pfeiffer Burns State Park. Several amenities are a short walk down from the rooms, including the **Big Sur Lodge Restaurant**, the **Deli & Café**, and the **Gift Shop & General Store**. Take advantage of the lodge's pool (9am-9pm daily Mar.-Oct.) and watch for the semi-wild turkeys that roam the property.

The **Big Sur River Inn** (46480 Hwy. 1, 25 miles south of Carmel, www.bigsurriverinn.com, $260-400) has 14 rooms on the east side of Highway 1 and six suites on the west side of the road. The east-side rooms are cozy, with knotty pine walls and small porches. The west-side suites each have two rooms, one with a king bed and the other with a trundle bed, which is good for families and small groups. The suites have decks overlooking the Big Sur River. Also on-site is a seasonally heated outdoor pool.

Filled with creative touches and thoughtful amenities, ★ **Glen Oaks Big Sur** (47080 Hwy. 1, 26 miles south of Carmel, 831/667-2105, www.glenoaksbigsur.com, $275-650)

the rustic accomodations at Deetjen's Big Sur Inn

offers the region's best lodging for the price. Its 16 units bring the motor lodge into the new millennium with heated stone bathroom floors, in-room yoga mats, spacious showers, and elegant gas fireplaces. Glen Oaks also has two cottages and eight cabins by the Big Sur River. The cabins are clean, with a modern rustic feel, and have kitchenettes along with outdoor fire pits. Guests have access to two on-site beaches on scenic sections of the Big Sur River.

At **Ventana Big Sur** (48123 Hwy. 1, 28 miles south of Carmel, 800/628-6500, www. ventanainn.com, $1,000-1,500), one of Big Sur's two luxury resorts, the panoramic views begin on the way to the parking lot. Rooms range from "modest" standard rooms—with king beds, tasteful exposed cedar walls and ceilings, and attractive green and earth-tone appointments—to gorgeous suites to multi-bedroom houses. The property has an infinity tub overlooking redwoods. Another option for staying at Ventana is in their Glamping Tents ($325-500), safari-style canvas tents on wooden decks with amenities including beds, electricity, and USB ports.

A night at **Post Ranch Inn** (47900 Hwy. 1, 28 miles south of Carmel, 831/667-2200 or 888/524-4787, www.postranchinn.com, $925-3,000), staring at the stars over the Pacific from one of the stainless-steel hot soaking tubs, can temporarily cause all life's worries to ebb away. Situated on a 1,200-foot-high ridgeline, the rooms at this luxury resort have striking views of the ocean or the jagged peaks of the nearby Ventana Wilderness. The units blend in with the natural environment, including the seven tree houses, which are perched 10 feet off the ground. Each one has a king bed, an old-fashioned wood-burning fireplace, a spa tub, and a private deck. Take advantage of complimentary activities including yoga classes, nature hikes, garden tours, and stargazing. Breakfast includes made-to-order omelets and French toast as well as a spread of pastries, fruit, and yogurt served in the Sierra Mar Restaurant with its stellar ocean views.

Camping

The **Fernwood Resort** (47200 Hwy. 1, 25 miles south of Carmel, 831/667-2422, www. fernwoodbigsur.com, tent site $60, campsite with electrical hookup $80, tent cabin $110, adventure tent $150) offers a range of options. There are 66 campsites around the Big Sur River, some with electrical hookups for RVs. Fernwood also has tent cabins with room for four in a double and two twins. Bring your own linens or sleeping bags, pillows, and towels. The rustic Adventure Tents are canvas tents draped over a solid floor with fully made queen beds and electricity courtesy of an extension cord. All camping options have easy access to the river. Hot showers and restrooms are a short walk away.

The biggest and most developed campground in Big Sur is at ★ **Pfeiffer Big Sur State Park** (Hwy. 1, 26 miles south of Carmel, 800/444-7275, www.parks.ca.gov, www.reservecalifornia.com, $35-50), with more than 150 sites, each of which can handle two vehicles and eight people or an RV (maximum 32 feet, trailers maximum 27 feet, dump station on site). A grocery store and laundry facility operate within the campground, and plenty of flush toilets and hot showers are scattered throughout. In the evenings, walk down to the Campfire Center for entertaining and educational programs. Pfeiffer Big Sur fills up fast in the summer, especially on weekends. Reservations are recommended.

★ **Julia Pfeiffer Burns State Park** (Hwy. 1, 37 miles south of Carmel, 831/667-2315 or 800/444-7275, www.parks.ca.gov, www.reservecalifornia.com, $30) has two walk-in environmental campsites perched over the ocean behind McWay Falls. It's a 0.3-mile walk to these two sites, which have fire pits, picnic tables, and a shared pit toilet, but no running water. More importantly, they have some of the best views of the California coast that you can find in a developed state park campground. Fall asleep to the sound of waves crashing into the rocks below. Saddle

Esalen: An Advanced California Experience

The **Esalen Institute** is known throughout California as the home of Esalen massage technique, a forerunner and cutting-edge player in ecological living, and a space to retreat from the world and build a new and better sense of self. Visitors journey from all over the state and beyond to sink into the haven that is sometimes called "The New Age Harvard."

One of the institute's biggest draws, the bathhouse, sits down a rocky path right on the edge of the cliffs overlooking the ocean. The bathhouse includes a motley collection of mineral-fed hot tubs with ocean views—choose the open-air Quiet Side or the indoor Silent Side, and then sink into the water and contemplate the Pacific Ocean's limitless expanse, meditate on a perfect sunset or arrangement of stars, or (on the Quiet Side) get to know your fellow bathers—who will be naked. Regardless of gender, marital status, or the presence of others. Esalen's bathhouse area is "clothing optional"; its philosophy puts the essence of nature above the sovereignty of humanity, and it encourages openness and sharing among its guests—to the point of chatting nude with total strangers in a smallish hot tub.

You'll also find a distinct lack of attendants to help you find your way around. Once you've parked and been given directions, it's up to you to find your way down to the cliffs. You'll have to find your own towel, ferret out a cubby for your clothes in the changing rooms, grab a shower, and then wander out to find your favorite of the hot tubs. Be sure you go all the way outside past the individual claw-foot tubs to the glorious shallow cement tubs that sit right out on the edge of the cliff with the surf crashing just below.

In addition to the nudity and new-age culture of Esalen, you'll learn that this isn't a day spa. You'll need to make an appointment for a massage (at $165 a pop), which grants you access to the hot tubs for an hour before and an hour after your 75-minute treatment session. If you just want to sit in the mineral water, you'll need to stay up late. Very late. Inexpensive ($20) open access to the Esalen tubs begins on a first-come, first-served basis at 1am and ends at 3am. Many locals consider the sleep deprivation well worth it to get the chance to enjoy the healing mineral waters and the stunning astronomical shows.

If you're not comfortable with your own nudity or that of others, you don't approve of the all-inclusive spiritual philosophy, or you find it impossible to lower your voice or stop talking for more than 10 minutes, Esalen is not for you. If you've never done anything like this before, think hard about how you'll really feel once you're in the changing area with its naked hippies wandering about. But if this description of a California experience sounds just fabulous to you, make your reservations now! **The Esalen Institute** (55000 Hwy. 1, 41 miles south of Carmel, 831/667-3000, www.esalen.org) accepts reservations by phone if necessary. Go to the website for more information.

Rock is the better of the two, but you can't go wrong with either. The sites book up far in advance, particularly in summer. Reservations can be made seven months in advance.

A popular U.S. Forest Service campground on the south coast of Big Sur, **Kirk Creek Campground** (Hwy. 1, 58 miles south of Carmel, 805/434-1996, www.recreation.gov, $25) has a great location on a bluff above the ocean. Right across the highway is the trailhead for the Vicente Flat Trail and the scenic Nacimiento-Fergusson Road. The sites have picnic tables and campfire rings with grills, while the grounds have toilets and drinking water.

Plaskett Creek Campground (Hwy. 1, 63 miles south of Carmel, 805/434-1996, www.recreation.gov, $25) is right across the highway from Sand Dollar Beach. The sites are in a grassy area under Monterey pine and cypress trees. There are picnic tables and a campfire ring with a grill at every site, along with a flush toilet and drinking water in the campground.

For the ultimate high-end California green lodging-cum-camping experience, book a yurt (a circular structure made with a wood frame covered by cloth) at the **Treebones Resort** (71895 Hwy. 1, 64 miles south of Carmel, 877/424-4787, www. treebonesresort.com, $300-420). The yurts tend to be spacious and charming, with polished wood floors, queen beds, seating areas, and outdoor decks for lounging, but they are not soundproof. There are also five walk-in campsites ($98-150 for two people, breakfast and use of the facilities included). For a truly different experience, camp in the human nest ($175), a bundle of wood off the ground outfitted with a futon mattress, or a hand-woven twig hut ($215). Any stay includes a complimentary breakfast with make-your-own waffles. In the central lodge, you'll find nice hot showers and clean restroom facilities. There is also a heated pool with an ocean view and a hot tub on the grounds. Treebones has a couple of on-site dining options: the **Wild Coast Restaurant** and the **Oceanview Sushi Bar**.

The campgrounds at Bottchers Gap (Palo Colorado Rd., 805/434-1996, http://campone. com) and Andrew Molera State Park (CA-1, 831/667-2315, www.parks.ca.gov) remain closed due to damage from the 2016 Soberanes Fire.

TRANSPORTATION AND SERVICES

Big Sur can only be reached via Highway 1, which can have one or both lanes closed at times—especially in the winter months when rockslides occur. Check the **Caltrans** website (www.dot.ca.gov) or the **Big Sur California Blog** (www.thebigsurblog.com) for current road conditions.

It is difficult to get around Big Sur without a car. However, **Monterey-Salinas Transit** (888/678-2871, www.mst.org, daily late May-early Sept., $3.50) runs a bus route through Big Sur that stops at Nepenthe, the Big Sur River Inn, and Andrew Molera State Park as it heads to Carmel and Monterey.

Big Sur Station (Hwy. 1, 27 miles south of Carmel, 831/667-2315, 9am-4pm daily) is the closest thing to a visitors center. The staffed building offers maps and brochures for all the major parks and trails of Big Sur, plus a bookshop. This is also where the trailhead for the popular backcountry Pine Ridge Trail is located. Get a **free backcountry fire permit** as well as pay the $5 fee for the Pine Ridge Trailhead parking here.

a yurt at Treebones Resort

Your **cell phone** may not work anywhere in Big Sur. The best places to get cell service are around Andrew Molera State Park and Point Sur, along with the large dirt pullout 0.25-mile south of Big Sur Station on Highway 1. Likewise, GPS units may struggle in this region. It's best to have a map in your vehicle, or pick up a free *Big Sur Guide,* which has a general map of the region.

The **Big Sur Health Center** (Hwy. 1, 24 miles south of Carmel, Big Sur, 831/667-2580, http://bigsurhealthcenter.org, 10am-1pm and 2pm-5pm Mon.-Fri.) can take care of minor medical needs, and provides an ambulance service and limited emergency care. The nearest full-service hospital is the **Community Hospital of the Monterey Peninsula** (23625 Holman Hwy., Monterey, 831/624-5311 or 888/452-4667, www.chomp.org).

Cambria and San Simeon

Cambria owes much of its prosperity to the immense tourist trap on the hill: Hearst Castle. About seven miles north in San Simeon, Hearst Castle, quite frankly, *is* San Simeon; the town grew up around it to support the overwhelming needs of its megalomaniacal owner and never-ending construction.

POINT PIEDRAS BLANCAS

Piedras Blancas Light Station

First illuminated in 1875, the **Piedras Blancas Light Station** (tours meet at the Piedras Blancas Motel, 1.5 miles north of the light station on Hwy. 1, 805/927-7361, www.piedrasblancas.org, tours offered Tues., Thurs., and Sat., adults $10, children 6-17 $5, children under 6 free) and its adjacent grounds can be accessed on a two-hour tour. In 1948, a nearby earthquake caused a crack in the lighthouse tower and the removal of its first-order Fresnel lens, which was replaced with an automatic aero beacon.

Piedras Blancas Elephant Seal Rookery

Stopping at the **Piedras Blancas Elephant Seal Rookery** (Hwy. 1, 7 miles north of San

elephant seals at the Piedras Blancas Elephant Seal Rookery

Simeon, 805/924-1628, www.elephantseal. org, free) is like watching a nature documentary in real time. On this sliver of beach, up to 17,000 elephant seals rest, breed, give birth, or fight one another. The rookery is right along Highway 1; turn into the large gravel parking lot and follow the boardwalks north or south to viewing areas where informative plaques give background on the elephant seals. Volunteer docents are available to answer questions (10am-4pm daily). The beaches themselves are off-limits to humans, since they're covered in the large marine mammals. But thanks to the wheelchair-accessible boardwalks built above the beach, visitors can get just a matter of feet away from the giant creatures. In the fall, most adult seals head out to sea, returning in early to mid-December. Most of the seal births occur between the end of December and the middle of February.

SAN SIMEON

The tiny town of San Simeon was founded primarily to support the construction efforts up the hill at Hearst Castle. The town dock provided a place for ships to unload tons of marble, piles of antiques, and dozens of workers. The general store and post office acted as a central gathering place for the community, and today you can still walk up its weathered wooden steps and make a purchase. Around the corner at the building's other door, buy a book of stamps or mail a letter at the tiny but operational post office.

The **William Randolph Hearst Memorial State Beach** (750 Hearst Castle Rd., 805/927-2035, www.parks.ca.gov, dawn-dusk daily) sits in San Simeon's cute little cove and encompasses what remains of the old pier. Lie on the beach or have a picnic up on the lawn above the sand.

Housed alongside the Hearst Ranch Winery tasting room and the tiny San Simeon post office, **Sebastian's Store** (442 Slo San Simeon Rd., 805/927-3307, 11am-4pm daily, $7-12) showcases tender, juicy beef from nearby Hearst Ranch in burgers, tri-tip, and pulled pork. This is a popular place, and the

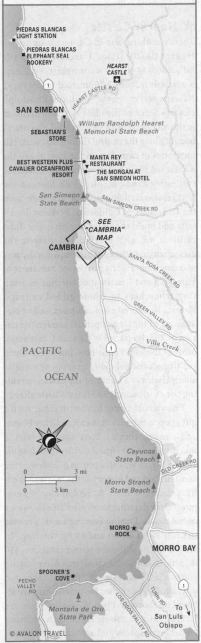

San Simeon to Morro Bay

PIEDRAS BLANCAS LIGHT STATION

PIEDRAS BLANCAS ELEPHANT SEAL ROOKERY

HEARST CASTLE

HEARST CASTLE RD

SAN SIMEON

SEBASTIAN'S STORE

William Randolph Hearst Memorial State Beach

BEST WESTERN PLUS CAVALIER OCEANFRONT RESORT

MANTA REY RESTAURANT

THE MORGAN AT SAN SIMEON HOTEL

San Simeon State Beach

SAN SIMEON CREEK RD

SEE "CAMBRIA" MAP

CAMBRIA

SANTA ROSA CREEK RD

GREEN VALLEY RD

Villa Creek

PACIFIC

OCEAN

Cayucos State Beach

OLD CREEK RD

0   3 mi
0   3 km

Morro Strand State Beach

MORRO ROCK

MORRO BAY

SPOONER'S COVE

PECHO VALLEY RD

TURRI RD

LOS OSOS VALLEY RD

To San Luis Obispo

Montaña de Oro State Park

© AVALON TRAVEL

sandwiches take a few minutes to prepare, so don't stop in right before your scheduled Hearst Castle tour.

★ Hearst Castle

There's nothing else in California quite like **Hearst Castle** (Hwy. 1 and Hearst Castle Rd., 800/444-4445, www.hearstcastle.org, tours daily 8:20am-3:20pm, tour prices vary). Newspaper magnate William Randolph Hearst conceived the idea of a grand mansion in the Mediterranean style on land his parents bought along the central California coast. His memories of camping on the hills above the Pacific led him to choose the spot where the castle now stands. He hired Julia Morgan, the first female civil engineering graduate from the University of California, Berkeley, to design and build the house for him. She did a brilliant job with every detail, despite the ever-changing wishes of her employer. By way of decoration, Hearst purchased hundreds of European and Renaissance antiquities, from tiny tchotchkes to whole gilded ceilings. Hearst also adored exotic animals, and he created one of the largest private zoos in the nation on his thousands of Central Coast acres. Most of the zoo is gone now, but you can still see the occasional zebra grazing peacefully along Highway 1 south of the castle, heralding the exotic nature of Hearst Castle ahead.

The visitors center is a lavish affair with a gift shop, a restaurant, a café, a ticket booth, and a movie theater. Here you can see the much-touted film *Hearst Castle—Building the Dream,* which will give you an overview of the construction and history of the marvelous edifice, and of William Randolph Hearst's empire. (Only daytime tours offer free showings of the movie. During evening tours, a movie ticket is $6 for adults and $4 for children. To see the movie without a tour, tickets cost $10 for adults and $8 for children.) After buying your ticket, board the shuttle that takes you up the hill to your tour. No private cars are allowed on the roads up to the castle. There are several tours to choose from, each focusing on different spaces and aspects of the castle.

Expect to walk for at least an hour on whichever tour you choose, and to climb up and down many stairs.

Even the most jaded traveler can't help but be amazed by the beauty and opulence that drips from every room in the house. Lovers of European art and antiques will want to stay forever. The **Grand Rooms Museum Tour** (45 minutes, 106 stairs, 0.6 mile, adults $25, children $12) is recommended for first-time visitors. It begins in the castle's assembly room, which is draped in Flemish tapestries, before heading into the dining room, the billiard room, and the impressive movie theater, where you'll watch a few old Hearst newsreels. The guide then lets you loose to take in the swimming pools: the indoor pool, decorated in gold and blue, and the stunning outdoor Neptune Pool.

Buy tour tickets at least a few days in advance, and even further ahead on summer weekends. Wheelchair-accessible Grand Rooms and Evening Tours are available for visitors with limited mobility. Strollers are not permitted. The restrooms and food concessions are all in the visitors center. No food, drink, or chewing gum is allowed on any tour.

CAMBRIA

Once you're through with the castle tours, a few attractions in the lower elevations beckon as well. Cambria began as, and to a certain extent still is, an artists' colony. The windswept hills and sparkling ocean provide plenty of inspiration for painters, writers, sculptors, glassblowers, and more. The small beach town becomes surprisingly spacious when you start exploring it. Plenty of visitors come here to ply Moonstone Beach, peruse the charming downtown area, and just drink in the laid-back, art-town feel.

Sights

NITT WITT RIDGE

While William Randolph Hearst built one of the most expensive homes ever seen in California, local eccentric Arthur Harold Beal (aka Captain Nit Wit or Der Tinkerpaw) got busy building the cheapest "castle" he could. **Nitt Witt Ridge** (881 Hillcrest Dr., 805/927-2690, tours by appointment, $10) is the result of five decades of scavenging trash and using it as building supplies to create a multistory home like no other on the coast. The rambling structure is made of abalone shells, used car rims, and toilet seats, among other found materials. Features like the cobblestone archways reveal a true artist's touch. Make an appointment with owner Mike O'Malley to take a tour of the property; don't just drop in.

To find Nitt Witt Ridge, drive on Cambria's Main Street toward Moonstone Beach and make a right onto Cornwall Street. Take the second right onto Hillcrest Avenue and look for the unique structure.

MOONSTONE BEACH

Known for its namesake shimmering stone, **Moonstone Beach** (Moonstone Beach Dr.) is a scenic, pebbly slice of coastline with craggy rocks offshore. Cambria's moonstones are bright, translucent pebbles that can be easiest to find at low tides and when the sun shines, highlighting their features. They are fairly easy to collect, especially after winter storms. The moonstones on Moonstone Beach are not gem quality, but they make a fun souvenir. Many Cambria boutiques and galleries carry moonstone jewelry.

A wooden boardwalk runs along the top of the bluffs above the beach. From here, take in the scenery and watch moonstone collectors with buckets wander below in the tide line. Access is at Leffingwell Landing, Moonstone Beach Drive, and Santa Rosa Creek.

Nightlife

Mozzi's (2262 Main St., 805/927-4767, http://mozzissaloon.com, 1pm-close Mon.-Fri., 11am-close Sat., noon-close Sun.) is a classic old California saloon—there's been a bar on this site since 1866. Old artifacts like lanterns and farm equipment hang from the ceiling above the long redwood bar, jukebox, and pool tables in this historic watering hole. Save some money on "Three Dollar Tuesdays" when all well drinks are just three bucks a pop.

Food

The ★ **Main Street Grill** (603 Main St., 805/927-3194, www.firestonegrill.com, 11am-9pm daily June-Aug., 11am-8pm daily Sept.-May, $4-18) is a popular eatery housed in a cavernous building. The tri-tip steak sandwich—tri-tip drenched in barbecue sauce and placed on a French roll dipped in butter—is

Zebras roam the grounds of Hearst Castle.

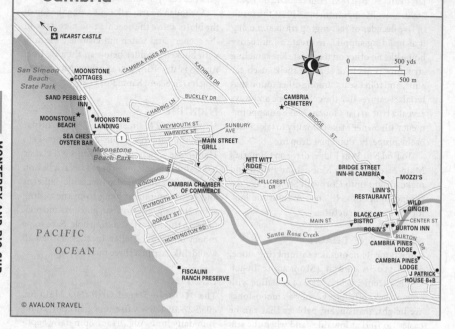

Cambria

a favorite, even though the ABC burger (avocado, bacon, and cheese) puts most burger joints to shame. The giant Cobb salad comes with lots of diced-up bacon and your choice of chicken or steak.

For a seafood dinner, head for the ★ **Sea Chest Oyster Bar** (6216 Moonstone Beach Dr., 805/927-4514, www.seachestrestaurant.com, 5:30pm-9pm Wed.-Mon., $20-30, cash only). The restaurant is in a wooden cottage with great ocean views. Framed photographs on the walls and books on bookshelves add to the homey feel of the place. No reservations are accepted, so expect a long line out the door at opening time, and prepare to get here early (or wait a long while) for one of the window-side tables. Sit at the bar to watch the cooks prepare the impressive dishes like halibut, salmon, and cioppino, which is served in the pot in which it was cooked.

The eclectic menu at **Robin's** (4095 Burton Dr., 805/927-5007, www.robinsrestaurant.com, 11am-9pm Sun.-Thurs., 11am-9:30pm Fri.-Sat., $16-26) features cuisine from around the world, including Thai green chicken, curries, and wild prawn enchiladas, as well as flatiron steak and the signature salmon bisque, all of which are done well. The menu also has vegetarian and gluten-free dishes. The historic building has a large dining room and a deck. Expect fine service from a staff that's proud of their product.

Accommodations

Next to a church, the ★ **Bridge Street Inn-HI Cambria** (4314 Bridge St., 805/215-0724, http://bridgestreetinncambria.com, $50-90) used to be the pastor's house. Now it's a clean, cozy hostel with a dorm room and five private rooms. The kitchen has a collection of cast-iron kitchenware, and there's a volleyball court out front. There's no TV here, but they do offer Wi-Fi and an eclectic book library.

One of the cuter and more interesting options on Moonstone Beach Drive, **Moonstone Cottages** (6580

Moonstone Beach Dr., 805/927-1366, http://moonstonecottages.com, $269-389) offers peace and luxury along the sea. Each of the three cottages has a fireplace, a marble bath with a whirlpool tub, a flat-screen TV with a DVD player, Internet access, and a view of the ocean. Breakfast is delivered to your cottage each morning.

For a great selection of anything from economical standard rooms up to rustic cabins with king beds and a fireplace, pick the **Cambria Pines Lodge** (2905 Burton Dr., 805/927-4200 or 800/927-4200, www.cambriapineslodge.com, $165-365). All rooms have plenty of creature comforts, including TVs, private baths, and, in some cases, fireplaces. There's also a nice garden area with flowering plants, benches, and sculptures.

Her Castle Homestay Bed and Breakfast Inn (1978 Londonderry Ln., 805/924-1719, www.hercastle.cc, $140-170) is a bit different from your average B&B, with only two rooms available and lots of personal attention from the owners. When you make your reservations, ask about a half-day wine tour or dinner reservations. Her Castle can be the perfect hideaway for two couples traveling together who desire the privacy of "their own house."

A stone's throw from Moonstone Beach, the ★ **Sand Pebbles Inn** (6252 Moonstone Beach Dr., 805/927-5600, www.cambriainns.com, $219-369) is a gray two-story building where the clean, tastefully decorated rooms have comfortable beds, mini-fridges, and microwaves. The six rooms facing west have full ocean views, while the bottom three rooms have patios. Expect amenities such as welcome cookies, a better-than-average continental breakfast, coffee and tea served in the lobby, and a lending library of DVDs.

Transportation and Services

Highway 1 travels south through Cambria, the prettiest way to get here. For a quicker route, take U.S. 101 to Paso Robles and then head west on Highway 46 into Cambria. If you use Cambria as a base to explore the Paso Robles wine area or Morro Bay (15 miles), a car will be necessary.

The regional bus system, the **RTA** (805/541-2228, www.slorta.org), connects San Luis Obispo, Morro Bay, Cayucos, Cambria, and San Simeon. Fares are $1.50-3.

If you prefer to travel by rail, take **Amtrak's Coast Starlight** (www.amtrak.com) to either the Paso Robles or the San Luis Obispo (SLO) stations, and make arrangements to rent a car

the Sea Chest Oyster Bar

(easiest from SLO) or get alternative transportation out to the coast.

The **Cambria Public Library** (1043 Main St., 805/927-4336, www.slolibrary.org, 9am-5pm Tues.-Wed., 10am-6pm Thurs., 10am-5pm Fri.-Sat.) offers tourist information and local history, including a map for a self-guided historical walking tour.

Cambria is served by three healthcare facilities: **Twin Cities Hospital** (1100 Las Tablas Rd., Templeton, 805/434-3500, www. twincitieshospital.com) in Templeton, 25 miles inland, and **Sierra Vista Regional Medical Center** (1010 Murray Ave., San Luis Obispo, 805/546-7600, www. sierravistaregional.com) and **French Hospital** (1911 Johnson Ave., San Luis Obispo, 805/543-5353, www.dignityhealth. org), both in San Luis Obispo, 37 miles south. Cambria and San Simeon are policed by the **San Luis Obispo Sheriff's Department** (805/781-4550, www.slosheriff.org).

Sand Pebbles Inn

Santa Barbara and the Central Coast

Look for ★ to find recommended sights, activities, dining, and lodging.

Highlights

★ **State Street:** This 12-block strip, lined with shops, restaurants, bars, and palm trees, is one of coastal California's most inviting and scenic downtowns (page 283).

★ **Santa Barbara Mission:** Graceful architecture, serene surroundings, and an informative museum make this the "Queen of the Missions" (page 283).

★ **Santa Barbara Beaches:** Superb meetings of sand and sea abound in Santa Barbara (page 286).

★ **Channel Islands National Park:** This group of islands has undeveloped beauty, stellar coastal views, and stunning sea caves that can be explored by kayak (page 307).

★ **Montaña de Oro State Park:** This underrated natural treasure comprises 8,000 mostly undeveloped acres of coves, peaks, and canyons (page 313).

★ **Morro Rock:** This 581-foot-high volcanic plug towering over the Pacific and Morro Bay is a natural phenomenon worth seeing (page 313).

★ **Madonna Inn:** The rooms, restaurants, bars—and even the bathrooms—are worth a look at this monument to kitsch in San Luis Obispo (page 322).

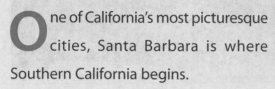

One of California's most picturesque cities, Santa Barbara is where Southern California begins.

It's famous for its pleasant Mediterranean climate and Spanish colonial revival architecture in the style of the Santa Barbara Mission, arguably the most beautiful of the California missions. Along Highway 1 north of Santa Barbara are the popular state parks and beaches of the Gaviota Coast. Places like idyllic Refugio State Beach offer escape from suburban civilization.

South of Santa Barbara, the city of Ventura has a grittier, more urban feel than Santa Barbara. It's charming and walkable, with a historic downtown and popular beach boardwalk, but its biggest attraction is its reliable surf break. Offshore, the Channel Islands hover on the horizon. Commonly reached by boat, these isolated islands offer visitors a glimpse of the wild, undeveloped coastline, as well as amazing recreational opportunities and encounters with rare endemic animal species.

It's worth detouring north to visit college town San Luis Obispo, with its vibrant weekly farmers market, a California mission, and the kitschy but cool Madonna Inn, and nearby Paso Robles' thermal springs and up-and-coming wineries.

PLANNING YOUR TIME

It's possible to explore Santa Barbara in a weekend, or to use the city as a base of operations to enjoy the region, though accommodations can be quite pricey. Those wanting to travel out to more remote places like Channel Islands National Park should add a few days to their stay. Going to the Channel Islands involves getting a space on a boat or plane. In addition, boats travel to some islands only every few days. It's nice to secure a hotel in Ventura or Santa Barbara after a camping expedition on the islands to ease yourself back into civilization before heading on to your next destination.

Previous: Arch Rock off Anacapa Island; Santa Barbara Mission. **Above:** Santa Barbara County Courthouse.

Local Favorites

Knapp's Castle

Santa Barbara and the Central Coast are more than just palm trees and beaches. Here are some quirky sites for those willing to venture off the beaten path:

★ **Knapp's Castle:** In the mountains above Santa Barbara, stone steps, archways, and fireplaces are all that remain of a structure built in 1916 by Union Carbide founder George Owen Knapp. The mansion burned down in a forest fire in 1940 but the stonework remains, along with impressive views of the Santa Ynez Valley and Lake Cachuma.

Reaching Knapp's Castle is a bit of an adventure. From Santa Barbara, take Highway 154 north and drive 10 miles. Turn right onto East Camino Cielo Road and continue three miles to a dirt pullout (look for a big red metal gate across the road to the left). Park your car and walk down the dirt road, passing another metal gate with a sign announcing: "Right to pass revocable by owner." It's a 0.5-mile walk to Knapp's Castle and its fine views.

★ **Ojai:** Ojai (pronounced "oh, hi!") is a scenic and unique little city known for hiking, spas, and New Age activities. Worthwhile stops include perusing **Bart's Books** (302 W. Matilija St., 805/646-3755, www.bartsbooksojai.com), a sprawling outdoor bookstore, and catching sunset atop Meditation Mount. Ojai is a 30-minute drive from Ventura on CA-33.

★ **Morro Bay Skateboard Museum:** (699 Embarcadero, Morro Bay, 805/610-3565, www.mbskate.com, 11am-5pm Mon.-Fri., 10am-5pm Sat.-Sun.) This small museum's collection of more than 200 skateboards includes homemade models and famous brands from the past, including Dogtown and Powell Peralta.

Santa Barbara and Vicinity

Nestled between the Pacific Ocean and the mountains, Santa Barbara is where beach culture meets high culture. You'll find lots of museums, outdoor shopping areas, great restaurants, and four-star resorts. A growing young wine region thrives here, too.

SIGHTS

★ State Street

Though **State Street** (between W. Sola St. and Hwy. 101) travels through different sections of Santa Barbara, the roadway that cuts through 12 blocks downtown is the heart of the city. Wide brick sidewalks on either side are shaded by palm trees and decorated with flowers, giving the city a tropical feel. Clothing stores, restaurants, and bars line the street along with popular attractions including the Santa Barbara Museum of Art.

★ Santa Barbara Mission

It's easy to see why the **Santa Barbara Mission** (2201 Laguna St., 805/682-4713, http://santabarbaramission.org; self-guided tours 9am-5pm daily, adults $9, seniors $7, children $3, children 4 and under free; docent-guided tours 11am Tues.-Fri., 10:30am Sat., adults $13, seniors and military $11, children $8) is referred to as the "Queen of the Missions." It is larger, more beautiful, and more impressive than many of the other missions. When you visit, you'll find the collection of buildings, artwork, and even the ruins of the water system in better shape than at many other missions in the state. The self-guided tour includes a walk through the mission's striking courtyard, with its blooming flowers and towering palm trees, and entrance to the mission museum. Among the museum's displays are a collection of Chumash artifacts and a photo of the church after an earthquake in 1925 toppled its towers. The original purpose of the mission was to transform the native Chumash into Christians. The mission's cemetery is the final resting place of more than 4,000 of these Chumash people.

In late May, the plaza in front of the mission is awash in color during the **I Madonnari Italian Street Painting Festival** (805/964-4710, ext. 4411, www.imadonnarifestival.com, free), inspired by a similar event in Grazie di Curtatone, Italy. The festival benefits the nonprofit Children's Creative Project.

Santa Barbara Maritime Museum

The **Santa Barbara Maritime Museum** (113 Harbor Way, Ste. 190, 805/962-8404, www.sbmm.org, 10am-5pm Sun.-Fri., 9am-3pm Sat., adults $8, seniors and students $5, children 6-12 $4, military personnel in uniform free) sits right on the working harbor. Exhibits tell the maritime history of California, beginning with the local Chumash Native Americans, running through the whaling and fur-hunting eras and up through the modern oil drilling and commercial fishing industries. The children's area features hands-on exhibits that make learning about the sea lots of fun for younger visitors.

Stearns Wharf

Stretching out into the harbor for 2,250 feet, **Stearns Wharf** (State St. and Cabrillo Blvd., www.stearnswharf.org, parking $2.50/hour, first 90 minutes free with validation) was the longest deep-water pier between Los Angeles and San Francisco when it was constructed by John P. Stearns in 1872. A tourist favorite, the wooden wharf hosts candy stores, gift shops, and casual seafood eateries. It is also home to the **Ty Warner Sea Center** (211 Stearns Wharf, 805/962-2526, www.sbnature.org, 10am-5pm daily, adults $8.50, seniors and teens $7.50, children $6), which is operated by the Museum of Natural History.

One Day in Santa Barbara

Begin with coffee and a pastry from **The French Press,** located right on State Street. Take advantage of your hard-won parking space and strike out on foot, with your destination an easy 0.25 mile away: the **Santa Barbara County Courthouse,** one of the finest examples of the city's distinctive Mediterranean architecture. Be sure to climb up to the top of the 85-foot-high **clock tower** for views of the city laid out between the Santa Ynez Mountains and the Pacific Ocean. Wander back down **State Street,** strolling on its wide brick sidewalk and taking some time to enjoy the shops. Follow State Street until it ends at **Stearns Wharf,** the long wooden pier. If you're hungry, take a one-mile walk east of downtown to reach **La Super-Rica Taqueria** and its wonderful Mexican food.

Now fueled up, head back to State Street, pick up your car, and drive to the stunning **Santa Barbara Mission.** Take a self-guided tour through the scenic courtyards and wander among the historic markers in the on-site cemetery. For dinner, climb Highway 154 to **Cold Spring Tavern** for brews, barbecue, and a sunset view from the ridge overlooking Santa Barbara.

Santa Barbara Museum of Natural History

The **Santa Barbara Museum of Natural History** (2559 Puesta del Sol, 805/682-4711, www.sbnature.org, 10am-5pm daily, adults $12, seniors and teens $8, children $7) has large galleries that display stories of the life and times of insects, mammals, birds, and dinosaurs. Of particular interest is a display showcasing the remains of a pygmy mammoth specimen that was found on the nearby Channel Islands. Head outdoors to circle the immense skeleton of a blue whale, and to hike the Mission Creek Nature Trail. The **Gladwin Planetarium** hosts shows portraying the moon and stars, plus monthly star parties and special events throughout the year.

Santa Barbara Botanic Gardens

The **Santa Barbara Botanic Gardens** (1212 Mission Canyon Rd., 805/682-4726, www.sbbg.org, 9am-6pm daily Mar.-Oct., 9am-5pm daily Nov.-Feb., adults $12, seniors and teens $8, children $6) focuses solely on the indigenous plants of California, with plantings from the deserts, chaparral, arroyo, and more. The gardens spread out over many acres and cross several hiking trails. Guided tours are offered on Saturday and Sunday at 11am and 2pm and on Monday at 2pm (included with admission

ticket), or take a self-guided tour with a map and the advice of the docents. The shop offers books and garden-themed gifts, while the nursery sells native Californian plants.

Santa Barbara Museum of Art

The two-floor **Santa Barbara Museum of Art** (1130 State St., 805/963-4364, www.sbma.net, 11am-5pm Tues.-Wed. and Fri.-Sun., 11am-8pm Thurs.; adults $10; seniors, students with ID, and children $6) has an impressive art collection that would make some larger cities envious. Wander the spacious, well-curated museum and take in some paintings from the museum's collection of Monets, the largest collection of the French impressionist's paintings on the West Coast. The museum also has ancient works like a bronze head of Alexander from Roman times and a collection of Asian artifacts including a 17th- or 18th-century Tibetan prayer wheel.

Santa Barbara County Courthouse

If only all government buildings could be as striking as the **Santa Barbara County Courthouse** (1100 Anacapa St., 805/705-5268, http://sbcourthouse.org, 8am-5pm Mon.-Fri., 10am-5pm Sat.-Sun.; free docent-led tours 10:30am and 2pm Mon.-Fri., 2pm Sat.-Sun.). Constructed in 1929, the

Santa Barbara and Ventura

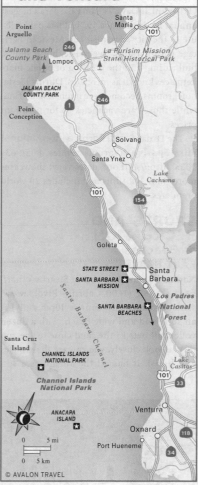

© AVALON TRAVEL

ENTERTAINMENT AND EVENTS

Bars and Clubs

The proximity of University of California, Santa Barbara (UCSB) campus to downtown Santa Barbara guarantees a livelier nighttime scene. Bars cluster on State Street and beyond, and plenty of hip clubs dot the landscape.

The best place to start an evening out on the town is at **Joe's Café** (536 State St., 805/966-4638, www.joescafesb.com, 7:30am-10pm daily). This steak house and bar is known for the stiffest drinks in town. Just go with the classics in this historic establishment, which owes its throwback atmosphere to its checkered tablecloths, tin-paneled ceiling, and framed black-and-white photos of mostly old men adorning the walls.

Tonic (634 State St., 805/897-1800, www.tonicsb.com, 8pm-1:30am Thurs.-Sat.) has a hipster feel, complete with exposed brick walls and a long glass bar. Top-flight DJs spin a mostly hip-hop or house groove, with the occasional mash-up for variety. To cool down, go outside to the huge outdoor patio, which has its own funky octagonal bar.

The **Good Lion** (1212 State St., 805/845-8754, www.goodlioncocktails.com, 4pm-1am daily) utilizes the county's produce to create its finely crafted cocktails. If you get hungry, order some Spanish tapas from adjacent Sama Sama.

In an upstairs suite, **Soho** (1221 State St., Ste. 205, 805/962-7776, www.sohosb.com, 6pm-11:30pm Sun.-Wed., 7pm-1:30am Thurs. and Sat., 6pm-1am Fri.) has hosted big-time touring acts including Jimmy Cliff, Donovan, and Built to Spill. It has live music seven nights a week.

The Brewhouse (229 W. Montecito St., 805/884-4664, www.sbbrewhouse.com, 11am-midnight daily) feels like a neighborhood bar, but it distinguishes itself from other popular watering holes by brewing its own small-batch beers and offering a comprehensive dining menu. Live music takes place in one of the brewery's two rooms Wednesday-Saturday evenings.

courthouse, which is actually four buildings comprising a whole city block, is one of the city's finest examples of Mediterranean-style architecture. The interior's high ceilings, tile floors, ornate chandeliers, and art-adorned walls give it the feel of a California mission. Visit El Mirador, the clock tower, where an open deck 85 feet off the ground provides great views of the towering Santa Ynez Mountains and the Pacific Ocean.

Live Music

Founded in 1873, the **Lobero Theater** (33 E. Canon Perdido St., 805/963-0761, www.lobero.com) is the oldest continuously operating theater in the state. While it used to host entertainers like Tallulah Bankhead and Bela Lugosi, it now welcomes jazz acts like Pat Metheny and Dianne Reeves along with indie rock darling Jenny Lewis and jam band Chris Robinson Brotherhood. The medium-size theater has only one level, and it's filled with cushy red-velvet seats—perfect for a music-filled night out on the town.

The **Santa Barbara Bowl** (1122 N. Milpas St., 805/962-7411, www.sbbowl.com) is a great place to take in a concert during the summer and fall. Built in 1936, it's the largest outdoor amphitheater in the county. It has hosted concerts by Neil Young, Florence & The Machine, and Death Cab for Cutie.

Festivals and Events

Inspired by a similar event in Grazie di Curtatone, Italy, the **I Madonnari Italian Street Painting Festival** (805/964-4710, ext. 4411, www.imadonnarifestival.com, late May, free) finds street painters using Mission Plaza as their canvas. The festival benefits the nonprofit Children's Creative Project.

Fiesta (various venues in Santa Barbara, 805/962-8101, www.oldspanishdays-fiesta.org, Aug., some events free), also known as Old Spanish Days, is Santa Barbara's biggest annual festival. Since 1924, it has paid tribute to the city's Spanish and Mexican heritage with parades, live music, horse shows, bull riding, and the erection of public marketplaces known as mercados. During Fiesta, hotel rooms become near impossible to find, while those rare vacancies go for premium prices.

The 11-day **Santa Barbara International Film Festival** (various venues, 805/963-0023, http://sbiff.org, dates vary) showcases more than 200 films and includes 20 world premieres.

SPORTS AND RECREATION
★ Beaches
EAST BEACH

Named because it is east of Stearns Wharf, **East Beach** (1400 Cabrillo Blvd., www.santabarbaraca.gov, sunrise-10pm daily) is all soft sand and wide beach, with a dozen volleyball nets in the sand close to the zoo (if you look closely, you can see the giraffes and lions). It has all the amenities a sun

Santa Barbara Mission

worshipper could hope for: a full beach house, a snack bar, a play area for children, and a path for biking and in-line skating. The beachfront has picnic facilities and a full-service restaurant at the East Beach Grill.

The **Cabrillo Pavilion Bathhouse** (1119 East Cabrillo Blvd.), built in 1927, offers showers, lockers, a weight room, a single rentable beach wheelchair, and volleyball rental.

WEST BEACH

On the west side of Stearns Wharf, **West Beach** (Cabrillo Blvd. and Chapala St., between Stearns Wharf and the harbor, sunrise-10pm daily) has 11 acres of picturesque sand for sunbathing, swimming, kayaking, windsurfing, and beach volleyball. There are also large palm trees, a wide walkway, and a bike path, making it a popular tourist spot. Outrigger canoes also launch from this beach.

LEADBETTER BEACH

Considered by many to be the best beach in Santa Barbara, **Leadbetter Beach** (Shoreline Dr. and Loma Alta Dr., sunrise-10pm daily) divides the area's south-facing beaches from the west-facing ones. It's a long, flat beach with a large grassy area. Sheer cliffs rise from the sand, and trees dot the point. The beach, which is also bounded by the harbor and the breakwater, is ideal for swimming because it's fairly protected, unlike the other flat beaches. The grassy picnic areas have barbecue sites that can be reserved for more privacy, but otherwise there is a lot of room. The beach and the park can get packed during the many races and sporting events held here. There are restrooms, a small restaurant, and outdoor showers.

ARROYO BURRO BEACH

To the north of town, **Arroyo Burro Beach** (Cliff Dr., 805/687-3714, www.sbparks.org, 8am-sunset daily), also known as Hendry's, is a favorite for locals and dog owners. To the right as you face the water, past Arroyo Burro Slough, dogs are allowed off-leash to dash across the packed sand and frolic and fetch out in the gentle surf. Arroyo Burro is rockier than the downtown beaches, making it less friendly to games and sunbathers. You'll find a snack bar, restrooms, outdoor showers, and a medium-size pay parking lot for your convenience. At peak times, when the parking lot is full, there's no other parking around.

Joe's Café

Santa Barbara

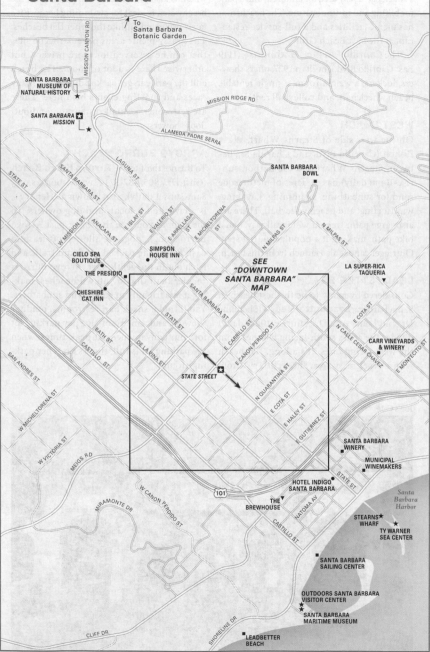

To
Santa Barbara
Botanic Garden

MISSION CANYON RD

SANTA BARBARA
MUSEUM OF
NATURAL HISTORY ★

SANTA BARBARA ★
MISSION ★

MISSION RIDGE RD

ALAMEDA PADRE SERRA

STATE ST

SANTA BARBARA ST

LAGUNA ST

E ISLAY ST

E VALERIO ST

E ARRELLAGA ST

E MICHELTORENA ST

SANTA BARBARA
BOWL

W MISSION ST

ANACAPA ST

N MILPAS ST

N MILPAS ST

CIELO SPA
BOUTIQUE

SIMPSON
HOUSE INN

THE PRESIDIO

LA SUPER-RICA
TAQUERIA ▼

SEE
"DOWNTOWN
SANTA BARBARA"
MAP

CHESHIRE
CAT INN

SANTA BARBARA ST

E COTA ST

STATE ST

DE LA VINA ST

E CARRILLO ST

E CANON PERDIDO ST

N CALLE CESAR CHAVEZ

E MONTECITO ST

CARR VINEYARDS
& WINERY

BATH ST

CASTILLO ST

SAN ANDRES ST

STATE STREET ★

N QUARANTINA ST

E COTA ST

E HALEY ST

E GUTIERREZ ST

W MICHELTORENA ST

W VICTORIA ST

MEIGS RD

W CANON PERDIDO ST

SANTA BARBARA
WINERY

MUNICIPAL
WINEMAKERS

101

HOTEL INDIGO
SANTA BARBARA

STATE ST

Santa
Barbara
Harbor

MIRAMONTE DR

THE
BREWHOUSE

NATOMA AV

CASTILLO ST

STEARNS ★
WHARF ★
TY WARNER
SEA CENTER

SANTA BARBARA
SAILING CENTER

OUTDOORS SANTA BARBARA
VISITOR CENTER
★
SANTA BARBARA
MARITIME MUSEUM

CLIFF DR

SHORELINE DR

LEADBETTER
BEACH

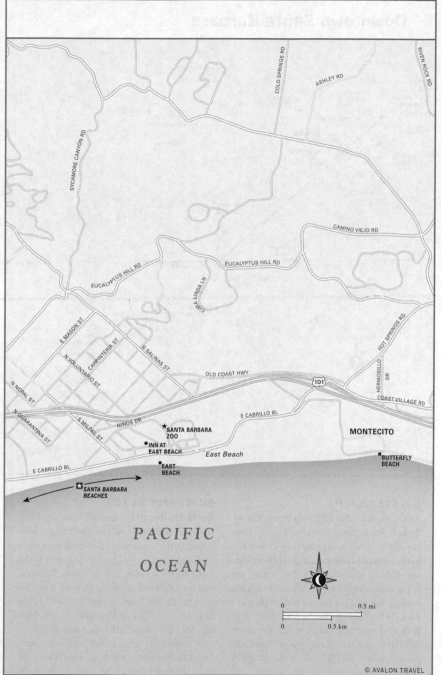

© AVALON TRAVEL

Downtown Santa Barbara

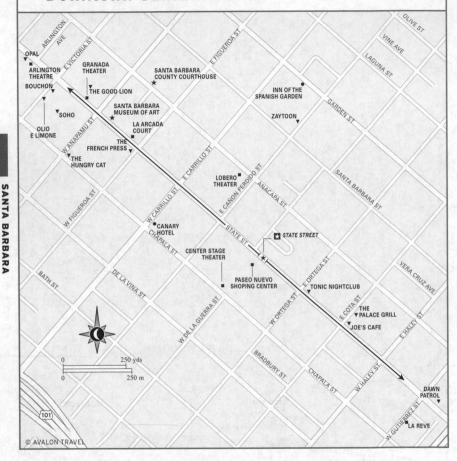

GOLETA BEACH

At the base of the UCSB campus, **Goleta Beach Park** (5986 Sandspit Rd., sunrise-10pm daily) is popular for its picnic tables, barbecue pits, horseshoes, multiple restrooms, and fishing opportunities. The grassy area is partially shaded by trees, and there's also a small jungle gym for the kids. The pier is popular for fishing, and the low breaks make it an easy entry for kayakers. On the mountain-facing side along the bike path are a few platforms for viewing birds in the slough behind the beach.

BUTTERFLY BEACH

Butterfly Beach (Channel Dr., across from the Four Seasons Hotel, Montecito, sunrise-10pm daily) is accessed by a handful of steps leading to the narrow beach. Butterfly is the most west-facing beach in Santa Barbara, meaning that you can actually see the sun set over the Pacific here. To find it, take U.S. 101 to Olive Mill Road in Montecito (a few minutes south of Santa Barbara). At the stop sign, turn toward the ocean (away from the mountains) and follow the road 0.25 miles along the coast; Butterfly Beach is on the left. The beach

Santa Barbara Wine Trail

The wines of Santa Barbara County have been receiving favorable reviews and write-ups in the national media. But not all wine-tasting is done surrounded by vineyards. On the **Urban Wine Trail** (www.urbanwinetrailsb.com) you can sample some of the county's best wines without even seeing a vine. Near Lower State Street, a block from the beach, it's possible to walk to six tasting rooms. Visiting others that are part of the trail will require a little driving.

- **Kalyra Winery** (212 State St., 805/965-8606, www.kalyrawinery.com, 11am-5pm Mon.-Fri., 10am-5pm Sat.-Sun., $12-14) is famous for having been featured in the 2004 movie *Sideways*.

- Once you're done at Kalyra Winery, walk a block down Yanonali Street to **Santa Barbara Winery** (202 Anacapa St., 805/963-3633, www.sbwinery.com, 10am-6pm Sun.-Thurs., 10am-7pm Fri.-Sat., $14), the oldest winery in the county, started in 1962. The tasting bar is just a few feet from the barrel room, and there's a good-size gift shop.

- **Municipal Winemakers** (22 Anacapa St., 805/931-6864, www.municipalwinemakers. com, 11am-6pm Mon., 11am-8pm Tues.-Wed., 11am-11pm Thurs.-Sat., 11am-8pm Sun., $10) is a weekend venture for owner Dave Potter, who will answer your questions and pour his wines.

- **Carr Winery** (414 N. Salsipuedes St., 805/965-7985, www.carrwinery.com, 11am-9pm Mon.-Sat., 11am-6pm Sun., $15-20) has a tasting room in a World War II-era Quonset hut, with a bar up front and tables in the back. The wine bar features live music on Fridays and house wines on tap.

North of Santa Barbara, detour to the Santa Maria Valley to sample wines in the region made famous by the movie *Sideways*. Highways 246 and 154 run through the valley and connect to U.S. 101 in Santa Barbara and north near Solvang for a convenient side trip. For more information, visit www.santaynezvalleywinetrail.com. **Foxen Canyon Road,** off Highway 154, hugs the foothills and is home to a number of wineries.

- **Foxen Winery** has two tasting rooms: the solar-powered **Foxen** (7600 Foxen Canyon Rd., 805/937-4251, www.foxenvineyard.com, 11am-4pm daily, $15-25), where you can sample burgundy, rhones, and chenin blanc, and the rustic, shack-like **Foxen 7200** (7200 Foxen Canyon Rd., 805/937-4251, 11am-4pm daily, $15) for Bordeaux or Tuscan varieties.

- **Rancho Sisquoc** (6600 Foxen Canyon Rd., 805/934-4332, www.ranchosisquoc.com, 10am-4pm Mon.-Thurs., 10am-5pm Fri.-Sun., $10) has a wood-sided tasting room in a setting perfect for some quiet, wine-enhanced relaxation.

- **Presqu'ile Winery** (5391 Presquile Dr., Santa Maria, 805/937-8110, www.presquilewine.com, 11am-6pm Fri., 11am-5pm Sat.-Thurs., $15) pours pinot noir, chardonnay, and sauvignon blanc to enjoy with the wonderful views. They also have 1.5-hour winery tours (11am and 2pm, $45) that include a tasting of pinots with artisan cheeses.

- **Kenneth Volk Vineyards** (5230 Tepusquet Rd., 805/938-7896, www.volkwines.com, 10:30am-4:30pm daily, $10) offers standards like chardonnay, pinot noir, viognier, cabernet sauvignon, and merlot, and is a champion of heirloom varieties: funky, wonderfully oddball wines like the Portuguese grape wine touriga and the jasmine-aroma white wine torrantes.

- **Zaca Mesa Winery** (6905 Foxen Canyon Rd., Los Olivos, 805/688-9339, www.zacamesa. com, 10am-4pm daily, $15-25) is a midsize producer with a modest facility and tasting room. Zaca makes many of the Rhone varietals, such as viognier, roussanne, and syrah. Classics lovers will enjoy the chardonnay, and adventurous types shouldn't skip the syrahs and the Z Cuvee.

is packed most weekends and often weekdays, too, and parking is limited. Park on either side of the street along the beach, or drive up Butterfly Road and park in the nearby neighborhoods. Bring your lunch, water, and sunscreen; there are no public facilities at this beach. Dogs roam freely here.

CARPINTERIA STATE BEACH

Carpinteria State Beach (5361 6th St., Carpinteria, 805/968-1033, 7am-sunset daily, day use $10, camping $35-65) has designated itself the "world's safest beach." Whether that's true or not, this beautiful wide, flat beach is definitely a favorite for locals and visitors alike. With plenty of campgrounds, picnic tables, outdoor showers, RV hookups, and telephones, and a location a short walk to Linden Avenue's restaurants, shops, and grocery store, you'll have everything you need within walking distance. Parts of the campgrounds are tree-lined but right next to the train tracks; passing trains might wake up light sleepers.

Surfing

During the summer months, the Channel Islands block the south swells that would otherwise hit the county. But, during fall and winter, the big north and northwest swells wrap around Point Conception and transform places like Rincon into legendary surf breaks.

Leadbetter Point (Shoreline Park, just north of the Santa Barbara Harbor) is a slow, mushy wave perfect for beginners and longboarders. The locals are reasonably welcoming, and the small right break makes for easy and fun rides.

For a bit more of a challenge, paddle out to the barrels at **Sandspit** (Santa Barbara Harbor). The harbor's breakwater creates hollow right breaks for adventurous surfers. Be careful though: Sandspit's backwash has been known to toss surfers onto the breakwater.

Known as the "Queen of the Coast," **Rincon** (U.S. 101 at Bates Rd. on the Ventura County/Santa Barbara County line) is considered California's best right point break. If you catch a wave outside, there's a chance you can score a memorable-for-life, 300-yard-long ride. But if it's firing, you'll also most likely be sharing the break with lots of other surfers. The time to investigate Rincon is during the winter.

Looking for surfing lessons? Check out the **Santa Barbara Surf School** (805/708-9878, www.santabarbarasurfschool.com, surf lessons $65-85, surf camp $395). The instructors

students at the Santa Barbara Surf School get ready to hit the surf

have decades of surfing experience and pride themselves on being able to get beginners up and riding in a single lesson.

Kayaking and Stand-Up Paddleboarding

One of the best ways to see the Santa Barbara Harbor and Bay is under your own power in a kayak or on a stand-up paddleboard. A number of rental and touring companies offer lessons, guided paddles, and good advice for exploring the region. **Channel Islands Outfitters** (117B Harbor Way, 805/617-3425, www.channelislandso. com, 8am-7pm daily summer, 8am-6pm daily fall and spring, 8:30am-4:30pm daily winter, kayaks $15/hour, SUPs $30/hour) has everything you need to paddle the waters of Santa Barbara and Ventura. Rent a sea kayak or a stand-up paddleboard to take your own ride around the harbor or out into the bay. The company also leads adventurous sea-kayak tours around the nearby Channel Islands.

The **Santa Barbara Sailing Center** (133 Harbor Way, 805/962-2826, www.sbsail.com, kayaks $10-15/hour, SUPs $19-30/hour) also provides kayak rentals and stand-up paddleboard rentals, as well as sea-kayaking tours.

Whale-Watching

Santa Barbara's prime location on the coast makes it a great spot for whale-watching. With its proximity to the feeding grounds of the blue and humpback whales, Santa Barbara is one of the state's best places to spot the marine mammals.

If you're looking for a whale-watching expedition, birding expedition, or dinner cruise, check out the **Condor Express** (301 W. Cabrillo Blvd., 805/882-0088, www. condorexpress.com; whale-watching trips: adults $50-99, children $30-50). In the summertime, cruise out to the Channel Islands to see the blue and humpback whales feed; in the winter, the captain sails into the path of migrating gray whales. The boat is an 88-foot vessel that can seat 68 people. Whale-watching

cruises depart almost daily all year long; call to purchase tickets in advance.

Golf

It might not get the most press of the many golf destinations in California, but with its year-round mild weather and resort atmosphere, Santa Barbara is a great place to play a few holes. There are six public courses within an hour of downtown Santa Barbara—everything from a popular municipal course to championship courses with views of the ocean from the greens.

It's still a golf course, but **Glen Annie** (405 Glen Annie Rd., 805/968-6400, www. glenanniegolf.com, $62-91, carts $15) has worked with Audubon International to create wildlife habitats on its land. Who knows what you might see when you're out walking the lush, green, 18-hole, par-72 course? Well, you'll definitely get great views of Santa Barbara, the ocean, and the Channel Islands on this hilly course. The Frog Bar & Grill, the on-site restaurant, draws any number of non-golfers up to Glen Annie for lunch. Set in a castle-like structure, the Frog serves California cuisine that is a far cry from most clubhouse fare. So come for the golf, but stay for the unusual and delicious fare.

If you're already interested in exploring Santa Barbara's wine country, consider reserving a tee time at **La Purisima Golf Course** (3455 Hwy. 246, Lompoc, 805/735-8395, www. lapurisimagolf.com, $34-75). This golf course, built in 1986, gets high praise for its design and difficulty level—even if you're an expert golfer, "La Piranha" will test your skills. The par-72 course is a 45-minute drive from downtown Santa Barbara, but many locals think it's worth the trip. In addition to the 18 holes, you can access the grass driving range, the short-game practice area, and the pro shop. A number of PGA and LPGA golf pros are on hand to help you improve your game.

The **Sandpiper** (7925 Hollister Ave., 805/968-1541, www.sandpipergolf.com, $150-170, cart $20) boasts some of the most amazing views in all of Santa Barbara. The course is so close to the Pacific Ocean that your ball is in danger of falling into the world's largest water trap. And hey, there's a great championship-rated 74.5, 18-hole, par-72 golf course out there on that picturesque beach too. Take advantage of the pro shop and on-site restaurant, but do be aware of the semiformal, denim-free dress code Sandpiper enforces. It's not cheap, but a long walk on the beach with a great golf game in the middle of it seems well worth it to an endless stream of golfers who rank Sandpiper as one of their favorite courses.

Spas

Folks who can afford to live in Santa Barbara tend to be able to afford many of the finer things in life, including massages, facials, and luxe skin treatments. You'll find a wide array of day spas and medical spas in town.

If you prefer a slightly more natural spa experience, book a treatment at **Le Reve** (21 W. Gutierrez, 805/564-2977, www.le-reve.com, daily 10am-7pm, massages $140-175). Using biodynamic skin care products and pure essential oils, Le Reve makes good on the advertising that bills it as an "aromatherapy spa." Choose from an original array of body treatments, massage, hand and foot pampering, facials, and various aesthetic treatments. If you're up for several hours of relaxation, check out the spa packages that combine facials with massage and body treatments.

Cielo Spa Boutique (1725 State St., Ste. C, 805/687-8979, www.cielospasb.com, daily by appointment only, massages $110-165) prides itself on its warm, nurturing environment. Step inside and admire the scents and the soft lighting and the natural, New Agey decor. Contemplate the colorful live orchids, feel soothed by the flickering candlelight, and get lost in the tranquil atmosphere. The menu of services has an almost Northern Californian flair, with signature champagne treatments and a focus on organics and natural lotions and potions. Check into the luxury packages that combine massages, facials, and more for a full day in the spa.

FOOD
Breakfast and Cafés

The French Press (1101 State St., 805/963-2721, http://thefrenchpress.com, 6am-7pm Mon.-Fri., 7am-7pm Sat.-Sun.) is a long, narrow coffee shop lined with hipsters and couples getting caffeinated and using the free Wi-Fi. The very popular café has a small seating area in front on State Street and out back on Figueroa Street.

Named after the surfing term for waking up early to score waves, **Dawn Patrol** (324 State St., 805/962-2889, www.dawnpatrolsb.com, 7:30am-2pm daily, $6-15) fuels wave riders with fresh juices, coffee, and breakfast options. A unique menu feature is a build-your-own hash with potatoes, a protein, eggs, and a sauce of your choosing. They also serve the intriguing Prisoner Egg Muffin, a soft-baked egg trapped inside a corn-scallion muffin.

Barbecue

★ **Cold Spring Tavern** (5995 Stagecoach Rd., 805/967-0066, https://coldspringtavern.com; restaurant 11am-3pm and 5pm-9pm Mon.-Fri., 8am-3pm and 5pm-9pm Sat.-Sun.; tavern noon-9pm daily; $18-33) is a former stagecoach stop, built in 1886; it hasn't changed much since. The on-site restaurant, in a separate building from the bar, serves up wild game, rabbit, venison, boar, and very good chili. Summer weekends (11am-5pm Sat.-Sun.) feature tender tri-tip sandwiches ($10) grilled outdoors over an open flame. A visit to the tavern is as much about enjoying the charming space as it is about the food. The complex includes an old jail, a one-room wood building that used to hold unruly customers. Rustic and secluded, it hosts live music Friday-Sunday.

California Cuisine

Bouchon (9 W. Victoria St., 805/730-1160, www.bouchonsantabarbara.com, 5pm-9pm Sun.-Thurs., 5pm-10pm Fri.-Sat., $26-42) prides itself on both creative cuisine and top-notch service every night. The wine list

Side Trip to Solvang

Founded in 1911 as a Danish retreat, Solvang makes a fun side trip. It's ripe with Scandinavian heritage as well as a theme-park atmosphere not lacking in kitsch.

In the 1950s, far earlier than other themed communities, Solvang decided to promote itself via a focus on Danish architecture, food, and style, which still holds a certain charm more than 50 years later. You'll still hear the muted strains of Danish spoken on occasion, and you'll notice storks displayed above many of the stores in town as a traditional symbol of good luck.

Solvang draws nearly two million visitors each year. During peak summer season and holidays, people clog the brick sidewalks. Try to visit during off-season, when meandering the lovely shops can still be enjoyed. It's at its best in the fall and early spring when the hills are verdant green and the trees in town are beautiful.

Solvang

The **Elverhøj Museum** (1624 Elverhøj Way, 805/686-1211, www.elverhoj.org, 11am-4pm Wed.-Sun., $5 suggested donation) features exhibits of traditional folk art from Denmark, including paper-cutting and lace-making, wood clogs, and the rustic tools used to create them. It also offers a comprehensive history of the area with nostalgic photos of the early settlers.

The small **Hans Christian Andersen Museum** (1680 Mission Dr., 805/688-2052, www.solvangca.com, 10am-5pm daily, free) chronicles the author's life, work, and impact on literature. Displays include first editions of his books from the 1830s in Danish and English.

Contact the **Solvang Visitor Information Center** (1639 Copenhagen Dr., 805/688-6144, www.solvangusa.com, 9am-5pm daily) for more advice on a Solvang visit.

GETTING THERE

If you're heading from Santa Barbara north to Solvang, you have two choices. You can drive the back route, Highway 154, also known as the San Marcos Pass Road, and arrive in Solvang in about 30 minutes. This is a two-lane road, with only a few places to pass slower drivers, but it has some stunning views of the coast as you climb into the hills. You pass Cachuma Lake, then turn west on Highway 246 to Solvang. The other option is to take U.S. 101, which affords plenty of coastal driving before you head north into the Gaviota Pass to reach Solvang. This route is longer, about a 45-minute drive. Highway 246 is known as Mission Drive in the town, and it connects both to U.S. 101 and Highway 154, which connects to Santa Barbara in the south and U.S. 101 farther north.

consists entirely of wines from Santa Barbara County. The dining room features romantic low lighting, smallish tables, interesting artwork, and an outdoor patio that's perfect for balmy summer nights.

A bit less fancy, **Opal** (1325 State St., 805/966-9969, http://opalrestaurantandbar.com, 11:30am-2:30pm and 5pm-10pm Mon.-Thurs., 11:30am-2:30pm and 5pm-11pm Fri.-Sat., 5pm-10pm Sun., $14-40) is a favorite of Santa Barbara locals. In addition to its eclectic offerings, most with an Asian twist, the stylish eatery serves up gourmet pizzas from a wood-burning oven and fine cocktails from a small bar.

Creole
The Palace Grill (8 E. Cota St., 805/963-5000, www.palacegrill.com, 11:30am-3pm and 5:30pm-10pm Sun.-Thurs., 11:30am-3pm and

5:30pm-11pm Fri.-Sat., $19-37) boasts of being one of Santa Barbara's most popular restaurants and a little piece of old New Orleans in sunny California. The atmosphere gets lively in the evenings, so this isn't the place to come for a quiet meal. The food is pure Louisiana bayou; look for classically prepared étouffées, jambalaya, and gumbo ya-ya. While you dine, take a moment to appreciate the particularly fine service that is a staple of the Palace's reputation.

Italian

For a superb Italian meal and a sophisticated dining experience, ★ **Olio e Limone** (11 W. Victoria St., Ste. 17, 805/899-2699, www.olioelimone.com, 11:30am-2pm and 5pm-9pm Mon.-Thurs., 11:30am-2pm and 5pm-10pm Fri.-Sat., 5pm-9pm Sun., $18-41) is the place to go. Among the specialties of the house are its quail dishes, but the homemade duck ravioli with creamy porcini mushroom sauce is a rich, rave-worthy offering. There's an impressive wine list, or opt for a creative cocktail.

Mexican

Have you ever wanted to know what true, authentic Mexican food tastes like? ★ **La Super-Rica Taqueria** (622 N. Milpas St.,

805/963-4940, 11am-9pm Sun.-Tues. and Thurs., 11am-9:30pm Fri.-Sat., $2.50-5) can hook you up. Of course, you must be prepared to stand in line with dozens of locals and even the occasional Hollywood celeb, all of whom think La Super-Rica's got some of the best down-home Mexican cuisine in all of SoCal.

Middle Eastern

For a Middle Eastern feast, go to **Zaytoon** (209 E. Canon Perdido St., 805/963-1293, www.zaytoon.com, noon-2pm and 5:30pm-9pm Mon.-Thurs., noon-2pm Fri., 1pm-10pm Sat., 5:30pm-9pm Sun., $18-32). This restaurant and hookah bar is popular with groups of friends eager to share a hookah and platters of baba ghanoush, shawarma, and kebabs as talented belly dancers shimmy among the tables. Try to get a table out on the garden patio, a large, softly lit space almost completely enveloped by a living green jungle.

Seafood

It takes something special to make Santa Barbara residents take notice of a seafood restaurant, and **Brophy Brothers** (119 Harbor Way, 805/966-4418, www.brophybros.com, 11am-10pm daily, $19-25) has it. With a prime location looking out over the masts of

Cold Spring Tavern

the sailboats in the harbor, it's no surprise that Brophy Brothers gets crowded at both lunch and dinnertime, especially on weekends in summer. There's also a location in Ventura Harbor.

Yes, they do mean *that* **Endless Summer** (113 Harbor Way, 805/564-4666, http://chuckswaterfrontgrill.com, 11:30am-9pm daily, $11-20); the restaurant is inspired by and named for the famous surfing film. The drinks here are strong, and the menu nods toward burgers and seafood. The sesame-crusted ahi on a warm spinach salad rides the perfect wave of healthy and tasty. Service is friendly, and the atmosphere tends toward casual local hangout.

Tapas

Enjoy classic Spanish tapas at **Loquita** (202 State St., 805/880-3380, http://loquitasb.com, 5pm-10pm daily, $7-44), where you can snack on carpaccio or octopus or go for a heartier meal with one of four paellas. Loquita specializes in sangrias and gin and tonics.

ACCOMMODATIONS
Under $150

Even the hostels in Santa Barbara are upscale, but you'd be hard pressed to find a better room in a better location than at **The Wayfarer** (12 E. Montecito St., 805/845-1000, www.pacificahotels.com/thewayfarer, dorm beds $60-99, private rooms $220-399). In the city's arty Funk Zone, The Wayfarer has unhostel-like features including a heated outdoor pool and a sleek, contemporary decor. Save money by cooking in the communal kitchen and partaking in the morning continental breakfast.

The Presidio (1620 State St., 805/963-1355, www.presidiosb.com, $129-349) has 16 clean and renovated rooms at reasonable prices within walking distance of downtown State Street. The second-floor rooms have vaulted ceilings; all rooms have Wi-Fi and TVs with HBO. The staff is friendly, and the small hotel has unique features like a sun deck and a fleet of beach cruisers for motel guest use.

$150-250

The **Cheshire Cat Inn** (36 W. Valerio St., 805/569-1610, www.cheshirecat.com, $199-400) can provide you with true luxury B&B accommodations. Each room has an *Alice in Wonderland* name but is filled with comfortable Victorian elegance. Rooms are spread out through two Victorian homes, the coach house, and two private cottages. Relax in the evening in the spacious octagonal outdoor spa, or order a massage in the privacy of your own room. Each morning, come downstairs and enjoy breakfast. In addition to the fine facilities, the Cheshire Cat's warm innkeepers will make you feel immediately at home.

Over $250

For a taste of Santa Barbara's posh side, stay at the **Inn of the Spanish Garden** (915 Garden St., 805/564-4700, www.spanishgardeninn.com, $299-580). This building in the historic Presidio neighborhood has the characteristic whitewashed adobe exterior with a red-tiled roof, arched doorways, and wooden balconies. Courtyards seem filled with lush greenery and tiled fountains, while the swimming pool promises relief from the heat. Inside, rooms and suites whisper luxury with fireplaces, deep soaking bathtubs, French press coffee makers, plush bathrobes, and honor bars. The complimentary continental breakfast can be delivered right to your door upon request. The Spanish Inn sits only three blocks from State Street and within walking distance of a number of theaters and historic Santa Barbara attractions.

If you're in Santa Barbara to soak up the sun and sand, book a room at the **Inn at East Beach** (1029 Orilla Del Mar, 805/965-0546, www.innateastbeach.com, $259-389), a block from East Beach. A nice walk along the waterfront boardwalk will take you to Stearns Wharf and downtown. The rooms are clean and stylish with modern furniture and plants, giving them a homey feel. The junior kitchen suites include a full kitchen with a large fridge, oven, and stovetop. The rooms circle a courtyard with a heated pool. Other amenities include a continental breakfast, free parking, flat-screen TVs with 146 channels, and a washer and dryer.

★ **Hotel Indigo Santa Barbara** (121 State St., 805/966-6586, www.ihg.com, $259-359) offers sleek, compact rooms with hardwood floors and a European-style collapsible glass shower wall. Some rooms also have small outdoor patios. Upstairs are two outdoor lounges, a vertical garden, and a library with art-related books. The hotel is in a great location, one block from the beach and two blocks from Santa Barbara's downtown. It's also near the train station, so expect to hear a train roll by occasionally.

The ★ **Simpson House Inn** (121 E. Arrellaga St., 805/963-7067, www.simpsonhouseinn.com, $300-610) is a historic landmark that was built in 1874. Stay in one of the six ornately decorated rooms, one of the four rooms in the reconstructed carriage house, or one of the four garden cottages. The service here is first rate. In the morning, savor a vegetarian breakfast in the main house's dining room or in your own room. The grounds include an acre of English gardens with fragrant flowers, gurgling fountains, fruit trees, and the oldest English oak tree in Southern California.

The ★ **Canary Hotel** (31 W. Carrillo St., 805/884-0300, www.canarysantabarbara.com, $300-600) offers elegant rooms with wooden floors, extremely comfortable canopied beds, and giant flat-screen TVs. While it may be difficult to leave such comforts, the hotel has a rooftop pool and lounge on its sixth floor that offers stunning views of the Santa Ynez Mountains and the red-tiled roofs of the beautiful coastal city. Downstairs, the hotel restaurant and bar **Finch & Fork** serves breakfast, lunch, and dinner.

TRANSPORTATION AND SERVICES

Santa Barbara is on U.S. 101, 325 miles and 5.5 hours south of San Francisco, and almost 2 hours and 95 miles north of Los Angeles. To head out to the Santa Ynez Valley and other local wine regions, take Highway 154 east. This highway connects with U.S. 101 at Santa Barbara and north of Solvang, making it an alternate route to Santa Barbara from the north. Parking can be challenging at the beach on sunny summer weekends. Instead, take the local public streetcar from the downtown area to the beach and leave your car elsewhere.

To reach Santa Barbara by air, fly into the **Santa Barbara Municipal Airport**

Hotel Indigo Santa Barbara

(SBA, 500 Fowler Rd., 805/683-4011, www. santabarbaraca.gov). A number of major commercial airlines fly into Santa Barbara, including United, Alaska, and American Airlines. A more beautiful and peaceful way to get to Santa Barbara is by train. The **Amtrak** *Coast Starlight* (www.amtrak.com) runs into town daily. It travels between Los Angeles and Seattle.

Santa Barbara has its own transit authority. The **MTD Santa Barbara** (805/963-3366, www.sbmtd.gov, regular fare: local service $1.75, waterfront service $0.50) runs both the local bus service and the Waterfront Shuttle and Downtown-Waterfront lines. Have exact change to pay your fare when boarding the bus or shuttle; if transferring buses, ask the driver for a free transfer pass.

The major hospital in town is **Santa Barbara Cottage Hospital** (400 W. Pueblo St., 805/682-7111, www.sbch.org), which includes a full-service emergency room.

THE GAVIOTA COAST

Along a rural stretch of the U.S. 101 coastline north of Santa Barbara are four state parks—Jalama Beach County Park, Gaviota State Park, El Capitan State Beach, and Refugio State Beach. All are typically crowded during the summer months, but also provide a great place to camp for the night.

Jalama Beach County Park

Jalama Beach County Park (9999 Jalama Rd., Lompoc, front gate 805/736-3504, weather and information 805/736-6316, www.countyofsb.org, day use $10) draws families, surfers hoping to score uncrowded waves, anglers hoping to reel in a few fish, and beachgoers who like their beaches undeveloped. Jalama Road winds 14.5 miles toward the park, which includes a playground, a horseshoes pit, a basketball court, flush toilets, and the **Jalama Beach Store and Grill.** From Jalama it's a six-mile beach hike to the east to Point Conception, one of California's best-known maritime landmarks. Check to make sure it's low tide before heading out.

The park has 117 first-come, first-served **campsites** (tent sites $30-45, RV sites with hookups $45-50). There are 12 spots with sites that blend into the beach out front, and a row of RV-friendly sites on a bluff have views of the park below. The amenities here include clean bathrooms with flush toilets, fire pits, picnic tables, and an outdoor shower. The park also rents seven popular **cabins** (805/686-5050, $190-220).

Gaviota State Park

Gaviota State Park (10 Refugio Beach Rd., Goleta, 805/968-1033, www.parks.ca.gov, 7am-sunset daily, $10) is the place for hiking. The park has multiple trails leading into its 2,000 acres of oak woodland and chaparral backcountry, including a strenuous three-mile one-way hike to **Gaviota Peak,** a 2,458-foot peak that offers one of the best views of the Gaviota Coast. Besides the hiking trails, Gaviota State Park has a nice little beach area under the shadow of an 811-foot-high train trestle.

There are 39 **campsites** (800/444-7275, www.reserveamerica.com, $45) in a small loop by Gaviota Creek, just 100 yards from the beach. These sites are mostly open to the elements, including the wind that roars through Gaviota Pass and the heat.

Refugio State Beach

Refugio State Beach (10 Refugio Beach Rd., Goleta, 805/968-1033, www.parks.ca.gov, dawn-dusk daily, $10) is the best place for a beach day. This thin but long finger of beach is lined with scenic palm trees and has a well-protected cove for sea kayaking or stand-up paddleboarding. Beginning and advanced kayak tours, which include kayak usage, are provided by Refugio's park rangers.

There are 67 **campsites** (800/444-7275, www.reserveamerica.com, $45) for crashing out after a day at the nearby beach, which is just feet away from some sites. The sites are fairly close together, and in summer can feel a bit crowded, but this is still a scenic campground with plenty of trees providing shade.

The UFOs of the Gaviota Coast

When spending a night camping at Jalama Beach County Park or another spot on the Gaviota Coast, you may look up and see a strange flying object overhead. Most likely it's not an alien craft searching for humans to probe, but an unmanned satellite or test missile launched from **Vandenberg Air Force Base** (www.vandenberg.af.mil).

Encompassing over 99,000 acres of land on the elbow of the California coast by Point Conception, Vandenberg was initially an Army base called Camp Cooke. In 1965, the Air Force took over the sprawling base and began launching test missiles as a reaction to Russia's Sputnik launch in 1957. The base has the distinction of being the place where the first polar-orbiting satellite was sent into space in 1959.

Vandenberg was also designed to be the West Coast space shuttle launch and landing site. But the site's technical problems and the space program's decision to consolidate shuttle operations at Cape Canaveral in Florida caused the closure of the shuttle program at Vandenberg in 1989.

El Capitan State Beach

El Capitan State Beach (10 Refugio Rd., Goleta, 805/986-1033, www.parks.ca.gov, dawn-dusk daily, $10) offers a narrow, rocky beach with tide pools and the largest campground of the three Gaviota Coast state parks. A stairway provides access from the bluffs to the beach area. Amenities include RV hookups, pay showers, restrooms, hiking and biking trails, a fabulous beach, a seasonal general store, and an outdoor arena.

The **campground** (800/444-7275, www.reserveamerica.com, $45) has 123 campsites strung along multiple loops in the shade or sun. The sites offer a little more privacy than Refugio or Gaviota.

El Capitan Canyon (11560 Calle Real, 866/352-2729, www.elcapitancanyon.com, canvas safari tents $170, cabins $245-795) offers 300 acres of land with private hiking trails and a spa. The accommodations here include canvas safari tents, yurts, and cedar cabins that are like small wooden studio apartments, complete with kitchenettes. In front of each is a picnic table and fire pit for communing with nature. The on-site **Canyon Market** serves a nice selection of breakfast, lunch, and dinner options.

Ventura

Downtown Ventura is compact and easy to walk around; it is three blocks from the beach with buildings that date to the 1800s (a long time by California standards). It's still a bit scruffier than nearby Santa Barbara, with a sizable homeless population for its relatively small area. Farther away, the Ventura Harbor has a cluster of restaurants, bars, and hotels around the harbor, which is the gateway to nearby Channel Islands National Park.

SIGHTS
Mission San Buenaventura

Mission San Buenaventura (211 E. Main St., 805/643-4318, www.sanbuenaventuramission.org, self-guided tours 10am-5pm Sun.-Fri., 9am-5pm Sat., adults $4, seniors $3, children $1) sits right on Ventura's Main Street, just blocks from the beach. A one-room museum on the grounds displays the church's original doors and a collection of native Chumash artifacts. Between

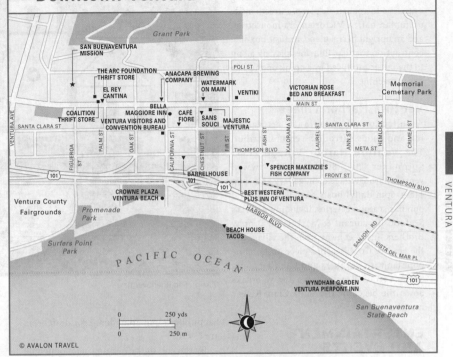

Downtown Ventura

Grant Park

SAN BUENAVENTURA MISSION

THE ARC FOUNDATION THRIFT STORE

ANACAPA BREWING COMPANY

WATERMARK ON MAIN

POLI ST

VENTIKI

VICTORIAN ROSE BED AND BREAKFAST

Memorial Cemetary Park

EL REY CANTINA

COALITION THRIFT STORE

BELLA MAGGIORE INN

VENTURA VISITORS AND CONVENTION BUREAU

CAFÉ FIORE

SANS SOUCI

MAJESTIC VENTURA

MAIN ST

VICTORIA AVE

SANTA CLARA ST

FIGUEROA ST

PALM ST

OAK ST

CALIFORNIA ST

CHESTNUT ST

FIR ST

THOMPSON BLVD

ASH ST

KALORAMA ST

LAUREL ST

SANTA CLARA ST

ANN ST

META ST

HEMLOCK ST

CRIMEA ST

101

BARRELHOUSE

101

CROWNE PLAZA VENTURA BEACH

101

SPENCER MAKENZIE'S FISH COMPANY

FRONT ST

THOMPSON BLVD

Ventura County Fairgrounds

Promenade Park

BEST WESTERN PLUS INN OF VENTURA

HARBOR BLVD

SAN JON RD

Surfers Point Park

BEACH HOUSE TACOS

VISTA DEL MAR PL

PACIFIC OCEAN

WYNDHAM GARDEN VENTURA PIERPONT INN

101

San Buenaventura State Beach

0   250 yds

0   250 m

© AVALON TRAVEL

SANTA BARBARA

VENTURA

the museum and the church is a scenic garden with a tile fountain, an old olive press, and a shrine.

California Street

California Street (end of Figueroa St. to end of California St.), or "C Street," hosted the world's first pro surfing event: 1965's Noseriding International. C Street extends 0.75 mile from Surfer's Point Park to the cove beside Ventura Pier; it's Ventura's recreation hub. Lines of white water streaming off the point entice surfers and stand-up paddleboarders, while longboarders catch waves that can continue for nearly a mile. The vibrant coastal scene includes the Promenade, which bustles with joggers and power walkers, and the popular Omer Rains Bike Trail. Facilities include an outdoor shower, bathrooms, and a picnic area. Parking can be challenging:

There's a free lot that fills up quickly, as well as a pay lot ($2 per day).

Olivas Adobe Historical Park

For a peek into California's 1800s rancho period, take a docent-led tour of **Olivas Adobe Historical Park** (4200 Olivas Park Rd., 805/658-4728, www.cityofventura.net/olivasadobe, guided tours 11am-4pm Sat.-Sun., adults $5, seniors and children $3). Constructed in 1847, the main house on the 4,693-acre Rancho San Miguel was home to Raymundo Olivas, his wife Theodora, their 21 children, and their employees. The 45-minute tour illuminates what life was like during the ranch period, from how the adobe walls were constructed to how bread was baked in outdoor baking ovens. Stops include a bedroom where the eight Olivas daughters somehow managed to live together and an impressive chapel on the second floor of the house. There are also some curiosities on display, including a desk made from an old piano, a wreath made of human hair, a Victorian-era mousetrap, and an upright barrel piano, a music box-like contraption that has figurines playing along to the music produced by a crank on the side of the machine.

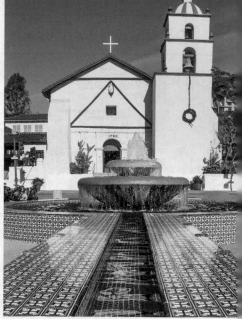

Mission San Buenaventura

Ventura Harbor Village

A collection of restaurants, art galleries, and shops surround Ventura Harbor. The **Ventura Harbor Village** (1583 Spinnaker Dr., 805/642-8538, www.venturaharborvillage.com, gallery and shop 11am-6pm daily) hosts a comedy club and popular seafood eateries, including Andria's Seafood Restaurant & Market and Brophy Brothers. Just feet away from the village are the Harbor Cove Beach, a piece of shoreline popular with kayakers and kite fliers, and Surfer's Knoll Beach, where a wave breaks down the beach by the Santa Clara River's mouth.

ENTERTAINMENT AND EVENTS
Bars and Clubs

Ventiki (701 E. Main St., 805/667-8887, www.ventikiloungeandlanai.com, 11am-11pm daily) brings the South Pacific's tiki culture to downtown Ventura. The bar's waterfall and fire pits prepare you for its many rum-based drinks, including a $25 mai tai. Theme nights include Throwback Thursdays, where the bar focuses on pre-Prohibition cocktails, and Magnum Mondays, an evening full of repeats of the TV series *Magnum P.I.*

True beer connoisseurs flock to **Barrelhouse 101** (545 E. Thompson Blvd., 805/643-0906, www.barrelhouse101.com, 11:30am-10pm Sun.-Mon., 11:30am-10pm Tues.-Thurs., 11:30am-midnight Fri.-Sat.). The 101 beers on tap put them in the rarefied realm of legendary California beer joints. Beers from California and Belgium are strongly represented, but Oregon and the East Coast also make good showings. During happy hour (4pm-7pm Mon.-Fri.), draft beers are $1 off.

By the end of the evening, a lot of people end up at dive bar **Sans Souci Cocktail Lounge** (21 S. Chestnut St., 805/643-4539, noon-2am daily), which stays open late. The small interior with red couches can get crowded; escape to the semi-covered courtyard out front before it fills up with smokers.

Live Music
The Majestic Ventura Theater (26 S. Chestnut St., 805/653-0721, www.venturatheater.net, box office 11am-6pm Tues.-Fri.) gets a variety of pretty big national acts, including many reggae rock acts (J Boog, Tribal Seeds) and rockers (Ministry, Flogging Molly). The 1,200-person-capacity, mission-style theater opened in 1928 as a movie house; decades later it was converted into a concert venue. The old chandeliers still hang in the auditorium, and other details of the 1920s decor remain.

Festivals and Events

In summer, Ventura's art studios and other venues open their doors for a weekend during the **ArtWalk Ventura** (www.artwalkventura. org, Oct.). Some places that participate include the Museum of Ventura County and the Ventura Visitors Center. Other participating venues are restaurants, salons, antiques shops, unique boutiques, and coffee shops—most any place with walls.

The **Ventura County Fair** (10 W. Harbor Blvd., 805/648-3376, www.venturacountyfair. org, Aug.) goes down every summer within the Ventura County Fairgrounds, which is right by the city's main coastal recreation area. Expect the usual attractions: Ferris wheel, cotton candy, livestock exhibits. Live nightly entertainment often features 1980s acts like Chaka Khan and Huey Lewis and the News.

SHOPPING

Main Street in downtown Ventura is home to a surprising number of unique local and specialty stores and has managed to retain a sense of individuality. Thrift stores are popular downtown, including **Coalition Thrift Store** (270 E. Main St., 805/643-4411, www. coalitionthriftstore.com, 9am-6pm Mon.-Sat., 10am-5pm Sun.) and **The Arc Foundation of Ventura County Thrift Store** (265 E. Main St., 805/650-8611, 9am-6pm Mon.-Sat., 10am-5pm Sun.).

SPORTS AND RECREATION

Beaches

SAN BUENAVENTURA STATE BEACH

San Buenaventura State Beach (San Pedro St. off U.S. 101, 805/968-1033, www. parks.ca.gov, dawn-dusk daily, $10) has an impressive two miles of beach, dune, and ocean. It also includes the 1,700-foot Ventura Pier, home to Eric Ericsson's Seafood Restaurant and Beach House Tacos. This is a safer place to swim than some area beaches, as it doesn't get the breakers that roll into the nearby point. Cyclists can take advantage of trails

connecting with other nearby beaches, and sports enthusiasts converge on the beach for occasional triathlons and volleyball tournaments. Facilities include a snack bar, an equipment rental shop, and an essential for the 21st-century beach bum—Wi-Fi (although to pick up the signal, you need to be within about 200 feet of the lifeguard tower).

EMMA WOOD STATE BEACH

Bordering the estuary north of the Ventura River, **Emma Wood State Beach** (W. Main St. and Park Access Rd., 805/968-1033, www. parks.ca.gov, dawn-dusk daily, $10) includes the remnants of a World War II artillery site. There are no facilities, but a few minutes' walk leads to the **campgrounds** (one for RVs and one group camp; first-come, first-served in winter, reservations required spring-fall). At the eastern side of the parking lot, a small path leads out to the beach (and under the overhead train tracks). The beach itself has many rocks strewn about, some nearly the size of footballs.

HARBOR COVE BEACH

Families flock to **Harbor Cove Beach** (1900 Spinnaker Dr., http://venturaharbor.com, dawn-dusk daily), directly across from the Channel Islands Visitors Center at the end of Spinnaker Drive. The harbor's breakwaters provide children and less confident swimmers with relative safety from the ocean currents. The wind can kick up at times, but when it's calm, it's practically perfect. There's plenty of free parking, lifeguards during peak seasons, restrooms, and foot showers. Food and other amenities can be found across the street at Ventura Harbor Village.

FARIA BEACH

Farther north, the Ventura County-run **Faria Beach** (4350 W. U.S. 101, State Beach exit, 805/654-3951, www.ventura.org, 7am-sunset daily, $2-4) is available for tent camping and has 15 RV hookups. The **campground** (sites $35, reservation fee $10) has a playground, horseshoe pits, barbecues, and shower facilities, but is quite small. It's also very crowded with campers, trucks, and people during nice weather because of its proximity to the water.

Surfing

Ventura is definitely a surf town. The series of point breaks referred to as California Street, or **"C Street"** for short, is the best place for consistent right breaks. There are three distinct zones along this mile-long stretch of beach. At the point is the Pipe, with some pretty fast short breaks. Moving down the beach are the Stables, which continue with the right breaks, with an even, low shoulder, and then C Street, breaking both right and left. The waves get mushier and easier for beginners the closer you get to Ventura Pier. There is a pay parking lot right in front of the break across the street from the Ventura County Fairgrounds (10 W. Harbor Blvd.). South of downtown Ventura, **Ventura Harbor** has waves that refract off the harbor's jetties.

SURF CLASSES

Surfclass (805/200-8674, www.surfclass. com, $85) meets at various beaches around Ventura, depending on weather and swells.

They teach everyone from novice landlubbers to rusty shredders. The two-hour class rates are quite reasonable, and they limit class size for individual attention. They will also teach you surf etiquette and lingo.

Ventura Surf School (461 W. Channel Islands Blvd., 805/218-1484, http:// realnetsocial.com/venturasurfschool, private two-hour lesson $125) can also teach you to surf, and they offer a weeklong surf camp and kids-only classes. Beginner lessons are at Mondos Beach.

SURF RENTALS

If you just need gear, swing by **Seaward Surf and Sport** (1082 S. Seaward Ave., 805/648-4742, www.seawardsurf.com, 9am-7pm daily, surfboard rental $15-25/two hours), which is the place to go to buy or rent most anything for the water (including bodyboards and wetsuits). It is half a block from the beach, so you can head straight to the water.

All sorts of gear, including longboards and boogie boards, are available at **Beach Break Surf Shop** (1557 Spinnaker Dr., Ste. 108, 805/650-6641, 10am-6pm daily, surfboard rentals $30-40). It's at the harbor, so pick up your gear, cross the street, and hit the beach.

Ventura Harbor

Whale-Watching

December-March is the ideal time to see Pacific gray whales pass through the channel off the coast of Ventura. Late June-late August is the narrow window for both blue and humpback whales as they feed offshore near the islands. **Island Packers Cruises** (1691 Spinnaker Dr., Ste. 105B, 805/642-1393, www.islandpackers.com, $25-75) has operated whale-watching cruises for years and is the most experienced. It also runs harbor cruises with a variety of options, including dinner cruises and group charters. Most whale-watching trips last about three hours.

Biking

The eight-mile-long, paved **Omer Rains Trail** heads along Ventura's beachfront from San Buenaventura State Beach past the Ventura Pier and Surfer's Point to Emma Wood State Beach. **The Ventura River Trail** (Main St. and Peking St., www.ventura-usa.com) follows the Ventura River inland from Main Street just over six miles one-way, ending at Foster Park. From here it joins the **Ojai Trail,** a two-lane bike path that follows Highway 33 into Ojai (16 miles one-way). If you want to pedal it, **Wheel Fun Rentals** (850 Harbor Blvd., 805/765-5795, www.wheelfunrentals.

com, sunrise-sunset daily, bike rentals $10-40) rents out beach cruisers, surreys, mountain bikes, and low-riding chopper bikes.

FOOD

Anacapa Brewing Company (472 E. Main St., 805/643-2337, http://anacapabrewing. com, 11:30am-9pm Sun.-Tues. and Thurs., 11:30am-9:30pm Wed., 11:30am-10:30pm Fri.-Sat., $11-25) looks like a brewpub should. Regulars sit at a long bar drinking the brewery's Pierpoint IPA, while families eat burgers, salads, and pizzas at booths and tables.

Bolstered by a popular bar, **Café Fiore** (66 California St., 805/653-1266, www. cafefioreventura.com, 11:30am-3pm and 5pm-10pm Mon.-Thurs., 11:30am-3pm and 5pm-11pm Fri.-Sat., 11:30am-3pm and 5pm-9pm Sun., $16-32) is a hot spot for Ventura professionals grabbing a cocktail or meal after work. The food includes Italian favorites like cioppino and osso buco, served in a sleek, high-ceilinged room decorated with furnishings that recall the interior of a Cost Plus World Market. Expect to wait awhile for service on crowded nights and during happy hour.

In a prime spot on the Ventura Pier, ★ **Beach House Tacos** (668 Harbor Blvd., 805/648-3177, www.beach-house-tacos.com,

terrific tacos at Ventura's Spencer Makenzie's Fish Company

11am-8:30pm Mon.-Thurs., 11am-9pm Fri., 8:30am-9pm Sat., 8:30am-8:30pm Sun., $3-8) offers creative options like soy-ginger-lime cream sauce-soaked ahi and ground beef tacos with raisins. Order at the counter and dine at an enclosed seating section on the pier. Expect long lines on summer weekends.

Sleek **Lure Fish House** (60 California St., 805/567-4400, www.lurefishhouse.com, 11:30am-9:30pm Sun.-Thurs., 11:30am-10pm Fri.-Sat., $15-37) is a local favorite for seafood downtown. The menu focuses on charbroiled seafood including fresh and sustainable wild local halibut, wild mahi-mahi, and other tasty morsels from the sea.

Housed in a building that resembles a boat, ★ **Spencer Makenzie's Fish Company** (806 E. Thompson Blvd., 805/643-8226, www. smfishco.com, 11am-8:30pm Sun.-Thurs., 10:30am-9pm Fri.-Sat., $5-13) is known for its giant fish tacos, a tasty fusion of Japanese and Mexican flavors. The sushi-grade fish is hand dipped in tempura batter and then fried. It's topped with the traditional Baja ingredients of white sauce, cabbage, and cilantro. Choose from the array of homegrown sauces along the counter to add splashes of sweet and heat.

ACCOMMODATIONS
Under $150

The ★ **Bella Maggiore Inn** (67 S. California St., 805/652-0277, $75-180) has a great location a few blocks from the beach and just a block off Ventura's Main Street. Some of the rooms are no larger than a college dorm room, but there is a lobby with couches, Italian chandeliers, a piano, and a fireplace. Even better is a courtyard with a fountain and dining area surrounded by vines. The moderate room prices include a tasty hot breakfast in the morning, with omelets, huevos rancheros, and French toast. Free overnight parking is behind the building.

The **Best Western Plus Inn of Ventura** (708 E. Thompson Blvd., 805/648-3101, http:// bestwesterncalifornia.com, $109-200) doesn't look like much at first. But this two-story, U-shaped motel complex has a few pleasant surprises. Ten rooms have partial ocean views (albeit close to the railroad tracks). The clean rooms are all stocked with refrigerators and microwaves, and there's a guest laundry room. The hot breakfast buffet includes eggs, breakfast meats, and make-your-own waffles. There's pool and small hot tub. A Jacuzzi suite is available for those who want to splurge. Across the street from grassy Plaza Park, and just a few blocks to downtown Ventura, it might be the best bang for your buck.

$150-250

If you are traveling to Channel Islands National Park out of Ventura Harbor, the ★ **Four Points By Sheraton Ventura Harbor Resort** (1050 Schooner Dr., 805/658-1212, www.fourpoints.com, $169-199) is a great place to lay your head before an early morning boat ride or to relax after a few days camping on the islands. The rooms are clean and comfortable and have balconies and patios. A few hundred yards from the Ventura Pier and right by the beach, the **Crowne Plaza Ventura Beach** (450 E. Harbor Blvd., 800/842-0800, www.cpventura.com, $139-389) has rooms with ocean-view balconies if you get a room on the fifth floor or higher. It also offers pet-friendly rooms for $75 more.

Set back from San Buenaventura State Beach, **The Pierpont Inn & Spa** (550 Sanjon Rd., 805/947-4757, www.pierpontinn.com, $109-300) is situated on nicely manicured grounds with grassy areas and epic ocean views. The historic property dates to 1910 and has rooms, suites, cottages, and a bungalow. There's a full-service spa on the grounds.

TRANSPORTATION AND SERVICES

Ventura is 34 miles south of Santa Barbara on U.S. 101 and 65 miles north of Los Angeles on the highway. **Amtrak** (Harbor Blvd. and Figueroa St., 800/872-7245, www.amtrak. com) also comes to town.

Community Memorial Hospital (147 N. Brent St., 805/652-5011, www.cmhshealth.org) has the only emergency room in the area.

★ CHANNEL ISLANDS NATIONAL PARK

Only accessible by boat or plane, Channel Islands National Park (1901 Spinnaker Dr., Ventura, 805/658-5730, www.nps.gov, 8:30am-5pm daily) is home to uncrowded trails, isolated beaches, and an extensive marine sanctuary. The most frequented of the park's islands are **Santa Cruz Island,** California's largest island at 24 miles long and up to six miles wide, and **Anacapa,** a dramatic five-mile spine jutting out from the sea. **Santa Rosa** is the second-largest island, but it takes nearly three hours to reach, and the 20-foot steel-rung ladder to access the island is often a deterrent. Wild and windswept **San Miguel** (permit required) is the westernmost island. The southernmost **Santa Barbara Island** is one square mile, but teems with wildlife. Its small size, and distance from the coast, make it a rare stop except for experienced sea-kayakers and avid birders.

Santa Cruz, Anacapa, and, to a lesser degree, Santa Rosa can be visited as day trips. There can be tough weather conditions, and it's often very windy since there's little shelter. Ferries depart from the Ventura Harbor and take between 90 minutes and three hours, depending on the island sailing conditions. Only Santa Cruz and Anacapa can be visited year-round.

Santa Cruz Island

Santa Cruz is the largest of the islands in the park, and by far the most popular island to visit. The environmental organization The Nature Conservancy owns 76 percent of Santa Cruz Island (accessed by special permit only, www.nature.org), while the National Park Service possesses and maintains the remaining 24 percent. This is the only place in the world to see endemic species such as the Channel Islands fox and island scrub jay.

Santa Cruz Island hosted an extensive ranching operation from the mid-1800s up until the 1980s. The **Scorpion Ranch Complex** gives park visitors a glimpse into this isolated way of life, with farming equipment and wooden ranch structures in states of decay. The small visitors center has displays on threatened species, conservation, and the native Chumash people.

A quick introduction to Santa Cruz's cliff-top coastal views and, on clear days, views to the mainland can be found on the moderate **Cavern Point Loop** (2 miles round-trip).

Channel Islands National Park

SANTA BARBARA

VENTURA

If you have more time, the more strenuous **Smugglers Cove Trail** (7.5 miles round-trip) is an old ranch road that cuts across the island's eastern interior to arrive at a south-facing beach. Even if you don't find the elusive island scrub jay on the **Scorpion Canyon Loop** (4.5 miles round-trip) you'll be treated to one of the island's unique canyons, followed by a series of stunning vistas.

The two primary points of entry onto Santa Cruz are **Scorpion Anchorage** and **Prisoners Harbor.** In addition to hiking, the island has two **campgrounds** and an abundance of amazing sea caves that can be explored by sea kayak. Travel time from Ventura is 90 minutes, and travelers offload onto a short pier directly connected to shore, though shore landings from a skiff are possible depending on conditions.

Anacapa Island

Anacapa is actually three islets that are five miles long and a quarter-mile wide. Visitors are able to access **East Anacapa,** a desert-like island with steep cliffs that is home to the stunning Inspiration Point, the **Anacapa Lighthouse,** a two-mile trail system, a small visitors center, a campground, and **Arch Rock,** a 40-foot-high rock window in the waters just east of the island. The easy, flat **Inspiration Point Loop** (1.5 miles round-trip, easy) leads around the island. Even shorter is the walk slightly uphill on the **Lighthouse Trail** (0.5 mile round-trip, easy). The trail doesn't go right up to the lighthouse, but it comes close enough for a great picture and view.

Santa Rosa Island

Rugged and windy **Santa Rosa Island** is less visited than Anacapa and Santa Cruz. Its mountainous spine rises to 1,574 feet at Soledad Peak, with spectacular views of neighboring Santa Cruz Island and the mainland coastline in the distance. The white-sand beaches and coastal lagoons seem virtually untouched, as is the Torrey pine forest, home to some of the rarest pines in the world.

Due to the frequent high winds, sea kayaking, snorkeling, diving, and swimming are only recommended for those with significant experience. But for those who want to explore dry land, Santa Rosa has a handful of trails for hikers who don't mind sweating. The strenuous **East Point Trail** (12 miles round-trip) takes in the Torrey pine forest and some unrestricted beaches. The **Lobo Canyon Trail** (13 miles round-trip) goes to a water-sculpted canyon that looks like it could be in the Southwest. There are also easier outings, including exploring **Water Canyon Beach,** as long as it isn't too windy out.

Travel time is about three hours by boat; you'll need to climb a 20-foot steel-rung ladder to reach flat land.

Kayaking

Santa Cruz Island is pocked with some of the world's most incredible and largest sea caves, and the best way to explore them is by kayak. The easiest way to find some sea caves is to paddle northwest (left) out of **Scorpion Anchorage.**

Anacapa is ripe for exploration by sea kayak. Access to the water is only available from East Anacapa's Landing Cove due to the islands' rugged cliffs. Paddle out to **Arch Rock,** the 40-foot-high rock arch in the waters just east of the islet, or **Cathedral Cove.** This scenic section of coast has an arch known as **Cathedral Arch** as well as **Cathedral Cave,** which can be explored by kayak during higher tides. The cave has five entrances that lead into an impressive chamber.

To book a kayak or tour, contact the **Channel Islands Kayak Center** (3600 S. Harbor Blvd., Ste. 2-108, Ventura Harbor, 805/984-5995, www.cikayak.com, single kayaks $35, double kayaks $55, two-person tour with transportation $200). You must first secure a space for your kayak by calling **Island Packers** (805/642-1393), the concession that takes people out to the island.

Snorkeling and Scuba Diving

Santa Cruz Island offers some fine snorkeling

and scuba diving right where the boat pulls in at Scorpion Harbor. The kelp beds east and west of the Scorpion Anchorage Pier are rich in sealife, while the wreck of the **USS Peacock** 50 yards off Scorpion Rocks in 40 to 60 feet of water captivates divers. The wreck is a fairly intact World War II minesweeper.

To dive the island's other spots, you'll have to have your own boat or be on a charter dive boat to access the sites. Diving trips need to be scheduled from Ventura Harbor. Options include the **Peace Dive Boat** (1691 Spinnaker Dr., G Dock, Ventura Harbor, 805/650-3483, www.peaceboat.com, $115-395) and **Truth Aquatics** (301 W. Cabrillo Blvd., 805/962-1127, www.truthaquatics.com, $100-1,000).

Camping

Multi-day trips allow for extended **camping** (877/444-6777, www.recreation.gov, $15) in the islands' interiors and for visiting several of the islands. The most popular campground on Santa Cruz Island is the **Scorpion Ranch Campground**, a short walk from the pier at Scorpion Anchorage. The lower campground has 22 sites in a eucalyptus-shaded canyon, while the upper loop has three regular sites and six group sites in a meadow. The upper loop is a nice spot, but it's twice as far to lug your camping gear. The campgrounds have a picnic table and food storage box at every site. Pit toilets and water are also available.

There's also camping out of Prisoners Harbor if you hike the strenuous 3.5 miles to the **Del Norte Backcountry Campsite**. This remote spot in an oak grove at 700 feet elevation has picnic tables and a pit toilet.

The **Anacapa Campground** is reachable by a 0.5-mile hike on East Anacapa that includes 154 stairs. This primitive camping area has seven sites with flat spots and picnic tables. There are also some regularly serviced pit toilets. The Anacapa campsites are very exposed to the sun and the wind.

Camping on Santa Rosa can be done at the **Water Canyon Campground**, reached by a level 1.5-mile hike. There are 15 sites with picnic tables and pit toilets. You can do backcountry camping (805/658-5711, free) right on the beach mid-August-December.

Transportation

In preparation for a trip to the islands, visit the **Channel Islands National Park Visitors Center** (1901 Spinnaker Dr., 805/658-5730, www.nps.gov, 8:30am-5pm daily) in Ventura Harbor Village, where you'll find a bookstore, displays of marine life, exhibits, and a 25-minute introductory film on the islands.

The most popular way to get to Channel Islands National Park is by hopping on board a boat run by **Island Packers Cruises** (1691 Spinnaker Dr., Ste. 105B, Ventura Harbor, 805/642-1393, www.islandpackers.com; day trips adults $59-82, seniors $54-74, children 3-12 $41-65; overnight trips adults $79-114, seniors $74-104, children 3-12 $57-90). The boat schedules change according to the seasons, so it's best to visit the website to find out what departing and returning boat times work best with your schedule. It's possible to have a full day on Anacapa Island or Santa Cruz Island by departing at 9am and returning at 4pm. Anacapa is the closest island, and the trip there takes an average of 45 minutes. Santa Cruz has a crossing time of 90 minutes, while Santa Rosa and Santa Barbara islands take 2.5-3 hours to reach.

The Channel Islands' Special Species

Where are you going to find the Santa Cruz Island scrub jay, the island fox, or the island night lizard? The answer is only in the Channel Islands.

Due to its remote location, the five islands of Channel Islands National Park have 23 endemic terrestrial animals and 11 land birds that are now island-only subspecies or races. These animals have evolved and changed from their counterparts on the mainland to adapt to the islands' unique natural habitat.

The island scrub jay has the smallest range of any North American bird species: the 96-square-mile Santa Cruz Island. It is a brighter blue, has a bigger bill, and is larger than its mainland counterpart. Meanwhile, the island fox is the largest of the Channel Islands' native mammals. But the animal is a third smaller than its relatives on the continent.

These special species aren't entirely safe even on the isolated Channel Islands. In the 20th century, habitat destruction, predation by feral cats, and a 1959 wildfire led to the extinction of an endemic subspecies of song sparrow on Santa Barbara Island.

Luckily, the island fox population has recovered since hitting a low of 100 animals on San Miguel, Santa Rosa, and Santa Cruz Islands in 1999. A captive breeding program has now stabilized the animal's numbers, and if you camp in Santa Cruz Island's Scorpion Ranch Campground, be prepared to hide your food from the clever canines.

Pismo Beach

Walking around Pismo Beach feels like you've stepped back in time to a Southern California beach town from 50 years ago. The town's one-way Pomeroy Avenue is lined with beachwear shops, candy stores, and fish-and-chips restaurants. The main attraction—besides the surf and sand—is the 1,200-foot-long Pismo Pier (end of Pomeroy Ave.). The first **Pismo Pier** was built for shipping back in 1881. Though that pier and another were destroyed by storms, the third version, built in 1985 and 1986, still stands today. Walking out on the pier is a great way to get an eyeful of the far-ranging Pismo Beach and the Oceano Dunes to the south. A small concession shack on the pier sells snacks and rents bodyboards and fishing rods.

SIGHTS
Oceano Dunes

It's a rare treat to be able to actually drive on one of California's beaches. It is possible—as long as you have the right vehicle—at the **Oceano Dunes State Vehicular Recreation Area** (3 miles south of Pismo Beach off Hwy. 1, 805/473-7220, www.parks.ca.gov, 6am-11pm daily, $5/day per vehicle). There are 3,600 acres of dunes, beach, wetlands, lakes, and riparian areas to explore by four-wheel drive, dune buggy, four-wheeler, or foot. In the 1930s and 1940s, the dunes were home to the "Dunites," a collective of mystics, nudists, writers, and artists who believed that the dunes were a center for creative energy.

Be careful if you decide to drive on the beach without the proper vehicle: Getting your car stuck in the sand can make for a long afternoon. You can also rent ATVs for the dunes at **B. J.'s ATV Rentals** (197 Grand Ave., Grover Beach, 805/481-5411, www.bjsatvrentals.com, 9am-6pm Mon.-Fri., 8am-8pm Sat.-Sun., $45-300) and **Arnie's ATV Rentals** (311 Pier Ave., Oceano, 805/474-6060, http://pismoatvrentals.com, $60-243).

If you want to explore the dunes but you don't have the proper vehicle, the **Oceano Dunes Preserve Trail** (2 miles round-trip) allows hikers to experience the region without fear of getting run over.

Pismo Beach Monarch Butterfly Grove

Thousands of Monarch butterflies take over a forest of eucalyptus and pine trees in the **Pismo Beach Monarch Butterfly Grove** (Hwy. 1 at the south end of the City of Pismo Beach, 800/443-7778, www.monarchbutterfly. org, Nov. and Feb.). Docents and volunteers are on-site to answer questions (10am-2pm).

Dinosaur Caves Park

Dinosaur Caves Park (Cliff St. and Shell Beach Rd., 805/773-4657, www.pismobeach. org, sunrise-sunset daily, free) offers 11 acres of serious play for the wee ones, with concrete dolphins, an orca, and, best of all, a friendly-looking dinosaur and three cracked dinosaur eggs.

ENTERTAINMENT AND EVENTS

Harry's Night Club & Beach Bar (690 Cypress St., 805/773-1010, www. harryspismobeach.com, 10am-2am daily) has live bands Friday-Wednesday; Thursday is karaoke night. Most acts are classic rock cover bands. Harry's also has big-screen TVs for taking in sporting events and three pool tables.

The **Pismo Beach Clam Festival** (805/773-7034, www.pismoclamfestival.com, Oct.) honors the beach town's clamming past every fall with a clam chowder cook-off and a clam dig. The fest also highlights other aspects of Pismo with surf lessons, live music, and a wine walk.

One of California's largest car shows takes over downtown Pismo and the pier during the **Classic at Pismo Beach Car Show** (909/890-0082, http://theclassicatpismobeach. com, June). More than 1,000 show vehicles are displayed at this free event.

SPORTS AND RECREATION

Fishing

Pismo Pier is the most heavily fished and second-most productive pier on the Central Coast. If you didn't bring a rod, rent one from the small shack on the pier. No license is required for fishing off the pier. To head into deeper waters, contact **Patriot Sportfishing** (805/595-7200, www.patriotsportfishing.com, adults $82/full day, children under 12 $60/full day) out of nearby Avila Beach. Their specialty is rock cod fishing.

Surfing

On either side of the Pismo Pier, waves consistently break for surfers. One of the best aspects of surfing the pier is that the surf is less susceptible to getting destroyed by the winds that wreck waves at other local breaks. Rent a board from **Pismo Beach Surf Shop** (470 Price St., 805/773-2089, www. pismobeachsurfshop.com, 9am-6pm daily, surfboard rentals $20/day).

Horseback Riding

Exploring the coastline just south of Pismo Beach by horseback is possible through the **Pacific Dunes RV Resort and Riding Stables** (1205 Silver Spur Pl., Oceano, 805/489-7787, http://pacificdunesranch.com, $50-75). Their rides (1-1.5 hours) go between dunes and out to the beach.

FOOD

Giuseppe's Cucina Italiana (891 Price St., 805/773-2870, www.giuseppesrestaurant.com, 11:30am-10pm daily, $8-32) began as the senior project of a Cal Poly student. Today, the restaurant still highlights the cuisine of the Pugliese region of Italy with pastas, meat dishes, and wood-fired pizzas, including one topped with clams.

DePalo & Sons (2665 Shell Beach Rd., Shell Beach, 805/773-1589, 7am-10pm daily, $6-13) is a wonderful place to grab a tasty sandwich for a picnic. There's a selection of gourmet goods and fine wine, and a deli counter displays a variety of premade food including pesto artichoke chicken breasts and roasted garlic bulbs. Sandwiches include a Tuscan-roasted sirloin steak sandwich, an Avila crab sandwich, and a pancetta BLT with a slab of homemade mozzarella and pesto mayo.

Sitting by the string of hotels on Price Street, the sleek, stylish ★ **Ventana Grill** (2575 Price St., 805/773-0000, http://ventanagrill.com, 11am-9pm Mon.-Thurs., 11am-10pm Fri.-Sat., 10am-9pm Sun., $14-39) serves up tasty California-Mexican dishes with ocean views. Menu items include entrées like tequila lime chicken, Alaskan halibut ceviche, and crab-encrusted mahi mahi. Ventana also has some darn good margaritas in unique flavors like prickly pear and pineapple.

Run by the same folks behind Ventana Grill, **Oyster Loft** (101 Pomeroy Ave., 805/295-5104, http://oysterloft.com, 5pm-10pm Fri.-Sat., 4pm-9pm Mon.-Thurs., 5pm-9pm Sun., $20-48) serves the fruit of the sea at a location right by the beach. Start with oysters before digging deeper into seafood, meat, or poultry entrées. At happy hour (4pm-5pm Mon.-Thurs.), you can score oysters for $1.50 a pop.

Away from the tourist strip, **Zorro's Café & Cantina** (927 Shell Beach Rd., Shell Beach, 805/773-9676, 7:30am-9pm daily, $10-14) serves Mexican- and American-style breakfasts, lunches, and dinners. Breakfast has unique offerings like chile relleno and eggs, while dinner has more typical items including fajitas and burritos.

On most days a line snakes out of the brightly colored ★ **Splash Café** (197 Pomeroy Ave., 805/773-4653, www.splashcafe.com, 8am-9pm daily summer, 8am-8:30pm Sun.-Thurs., 8am-9pm Fri.-Sat. winter, $6-17). People are waiting for a taste of the rich, buttery clam chowder (served in a cup, bowl, or bread bowl) that utilizes three different types of clams and hits the spot on a chilly day. They also serve fish tacos, burgers, and fried seafood.

Don't wear your best clothes to the **Cracked Crab** (751 Price St., 805/773-2722, www.crackedcrab.com, 11am-9pm Sun.-Thurs., 11am-10pm Fri.-Sat., $12-53). The signature dish is a bucket for two that features three kinds of shellfish steamed with Cajun sausage, red potatoes, and corn. You are given a mallet, a crab cracker, and a bib. If that sounds like too much work, order a seafood sandwich or an entrée like grilled albacore.

ACCOMMODATIONS

Every room at the moderately priced **Kon Tiki Inn** (1621 Price St., 805/773-4833, www.kontikiinn.com, $204-224) has a sweeping view of the ocean as well as a patio or balcony. In front of the large hotel are a heated pool, hot tubs, and a staircase to the beach below. One perk of staying at the Kon Tiki is that guests get full use of the adjacent Pismo Beach Athletic Club.

The exteriors of the buildings at the **Cottage Inn By the Sea** (2351 Price St., 805/773-4617, www.cottage-inn.com, $239-339) conjure images of the English countryside. Rooms have gas fireplaces, a fridge, and a microwave and there's a heated pool and hot tub. Past the small pool deck is a spot on the bluffs over the beach with chairs and tables. In the morning, enjoy the inn's deluxe continental breakfast.

For families or couples who want to stretch out a bit, the ★ **Pismo Lighthouse Suites** (2411 Price St., 805/773-2411, www.pismolighthousesuites.com, $439-529) all have two rooms and two bathrooms, which is a rare hotel luxury. The suites feature nautical decor, like lamps designed to resemble lighthouses and paintings of sea scenes, while the oceanfront suites each include a balcony or patio to take in the fine views of the Pacific or Pismo Beach. Kids will love the family play deck that has a small mini-golf course, table tennis, a badminton course, and a giant chess and checkers set. The hotel also has a heated pool, a spa, and beach access.

At the **Best Western Plus Shore Cliff Lodge** (2555 Price St., 805/773-4671, www.shorecliff.com, $209-519), every room has an ocean view and a patio or balcony. In front of the building is a large, grassy bluff with a gazebo that offers views of Pismo Beach and

Pismo Pier. The Shore Cliff has a swimming pool, soaking tub, and seven pet-friendly rooms, plus a hot breakfast buffet.

Camping

Pismo State Beach has two campground options. The **Oceano Campground** (555 Pier Ave., Oceano, 800/444-7275, www.reservecalifornia.com, tent sites $35, RVs $50) is adjacent to a migratory bird habitat surrounding a lagoon. Also in the park is the **North Beach Campground** (Hwy. 1, Pismo Beach, 800/444-7275, www.reservecalifornia.

com, tent sites $35), which is close to the Pismo Beach Monarch Butterfly Grove.

TRANSPORTATION AND SERVICES

Pismo Beach makes a good stopover along U.S. 101. It is 12 miles south of San Luis Obispo, and 80 miles (1.5 hour) north of Santa Barbara.

For emergencies, visit the nearby **Arroyo Grande Community Hospital** (345 S. Halcyon Rd., 805/489-4261, www. dignityhealth.org/arroyo).

Morro Bay and Vicinity

The picturesque fishing village of Morro Bay is dominated by Morro Rock, a 581-foot-high volcanic plug. The rock was an island until the 1930s, when a road was built connecting it to the mainland. The area around the rock is accessible, but the rock itself is off-limits because it is home to a group of endangered peregrine falcons.

SIGHTS

Morro Bay's most unusual sight is the 16-by-16-foot **Giant Chessboard** (Centennial Pkwy., 805/772-6278). The waist-high chess pieces used in the game weigh as much as 30 pounds. Four picnic tables adjoin the Giant Chessboard; each has a chessboard where the local chess fiends play. Reserve the board for a small fee (8am-5pm Mon.-Fri.) or join the Morro Bay Chess Club when they play on Saturdays starting at noon.

★ Morro Rock

It would be difficult to come to the town of Morro Bay and *not* see **Morro Rock**, which has been called the "Gibraltar of the Pacific." The rock dominates the town's scenery, whether you are walking along the bayside Embarcadero or beachcombing on the sandy coastline just north of the prominent geologic feature. The area around the rock is accessible,

with parking lots, walking paths, and crashing surf.

★ Montaña de Oro State Park

Montaña de Oro State Park (Pecho Rd., 6 miles south of Morro Bay, 805/772-7434, www.parks.ca.gov, 6am-10pm daily, free) is for those seeking a serious nature fix on the Central Coast. This sprawling 8,000-acre park with seven miles of coastline has coves, tide pools, sand dunes, and almost 50 miles of hiking trails. A great way to get a feel for the park's immense size is to hike up the two-mile **Valencia Peak Trail** (4 miles round-trip). In springtime the sides of the trail are decorated with blooming wildflowers, and the 1,347-foot-high summit offers commanding views of Montaña de Oro's pocked coastline and Morro Rock jutting out in the distance. The hike is steep and exposed, so make sure to bring plenty of water on warm days.

For a feel of the coast, park right in front of **Spooner's Cove** and walk out on its wide, coarse-grained beach. On the cove's north end, Islay Creek drains into the ocean. There's also a picturesque arch across the creek in the rock face on the north side. The **Spooner Ranch House Museum** informs visitors about early inhabitants of the park's land, the Spooner family. The small facility also has displays about the area's plants, mountain lions, and raptors.

Morro Bay State Park

Morro Bay State Park (Morro Bay State Park Rd., 805/772-7434, www.slostateparks.com, $8/vehicle) is not a typical state park. It has hiking trails, a campground, and recreational opportunities, but this park also has its own natural history museum, a golf course, and a marina. Just south of town, the park is situated on the shores of Morro Bay. One way to get a feel for the park is to hike the **Black Hill Trail** (3 miles round-trip).

The **Morro Bay Museum of Natural History** (Morro Bay State Park Rd., 805/772-2694, www.ccnha.org, 10am-5pm daily, adults $3, children under 16 free) is small but informative, with displays that explain the habitats of the Central Coast; there are some interactive exhibits for kids. An observation deck hanging off the museum allows for a great view of Morro Bay. Beside the museum is a garden that shows how the area's original inhabitants, the Chumash people, utilized the region's plants.

Play a round of golf at the **Morro Bay Golf Course** (201 State Park Rd., 805/772-1923, http://golfmorrobay.com, $45-54), or head out on the water in a kayak or canoe, or on a stand-up paddleboard rented from **A Kayak Shack** (10 State Park Rd., 805/772-8796, www.morrobaykayakshack.com, 9am-4pm daily Sept.-June, 9am-5pm daily July-Aug., kayaks $14/hour, canoes $18/hour, stand-up paddleboards $16/hour).

ENTERTAINMENT AND EVENTS

Legends Bar (899 Main St., 805/772-2525, daily noon-2am) has a red pool table and a giant moose head poking out from behind the bar. Grab a drink and look at the historic photos covering the walls.

The Libertine Pub (801 Embarcadero, 805/772-0700, http://libertinebrewing.com, 11am-10pm Mon.-Thurs., 11am-11pm Fri.-Sat., 10am-10pm Sun.) is the place for the discerning beer drinker, with 48 rotating craft beers on tap including some made in-house. One of the beers on tap will always be a sour. You can also order craft cocktails (a basil bourbon drink counts marmalade as one of its ingredients) and pub food (including fish tacos, burgers, and *moules frites*). The bartenders also act as DJs, playing selections from the Libertine's stash of vinyl.

Stax Wine Bar & Bistro (1099

a car is dwarfed by Morro Rock

Morro Bay

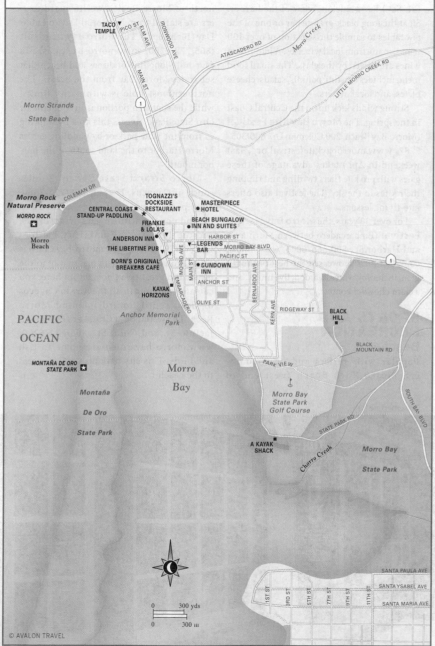

TACO TEMPLE
PICO ST
ELM AVE
IRONWOOD AVE
Morro Creek
ATASCADERO RD
MAIN ST
LITTLE MORRO CREEK RD

Morro Strands
State Beach

COLEMAN DR

Morro Rock
Natural Preserve
MORRO ROCK
Morro Beach

TOGNAZZI'S DOCKSIDE RESTAURANT
CENTRAL COAST STAND-UP PADDLING
MASTERPIECE HOTEL
FRANKIE & LOLA'S
BEACH BUNGALOW INN AND SUITES
ANDERSON INN
HARBOR ST
THE LIBERTINE PUB
LEGENDS BAR
MORRO BAY BLVD
DORN'S ORIGINAL BREAKERS CAFÉ
PACIFIC ST
SUNDOWN INN
ANCHOR ST
KAYAK HORIZONS
OLIVE ST
MORRO AVE
MAIN ST
EMBARCADERO
BERNARDO AVE
KERN AVE
RIDGEWAY ST
BLACK HILL

PACIFIC OCEAN

Anchor Memorial Park

MONTAÑA DE ORO STATE PARK

Montaña
De Oro
State Park

Morro
Bay

BLACK MOUNTAIN RD

PARK VIEW

Morro Bay
State Park
Golf Course

STATE PARK RD

SOUTH BAY BLVD

A KAYAK SHACK

Chorro Creek

Morro Bay
State Park

Morro Bay

SANTA PAULA AVE
SANTA YSABEL AVE
1ST ST
3RD ST
5TH ST
7TH ST
9TH ST
11TH ST
SANTA MARIA AVE

0   300 yds
0   300 m

© AVALON TRAVEL

Embarcadero, 805/772-5055, www.staxwine.com, noon-8pm Sun.-Thurs., noon-10pm Fri.-Sat.) has a sidelong view of the harbor. Sit at the long black-granite bar or one of the few tables to sample the selection of over 100 wines, many from local wineries. A handful of wines are served by the glass. The small food menu includes crostini, paninis, salads, cheese plates, and local oysters.

Strong winds kick up on the Central Coast in the spring. The **Morro Bay Kite Festival** (Morro Bay Beach, 200 Coleman Dr., 800/305-7787, www.morrobaykitefestival.org, last weekend in Apr.) takes advantage of these gales with pro kite fliers twirling and flipping their kites in the sky. The festival also offers kite-flying lessons.

For over 30 years, the **Morro Bay Harbor Festival** (Embarcadero between Marina St. and Harbor St., 800/366-6043, www.mbhf.com, Oct.) has showcased the best of the region, including wines, seafood, live music, and a clam chowder contest.

SPORTS AND RECREATION
Beaches

Popular with surfers and beachcombers, **Morro Rock Beach** (west end of Embarcadero, 805/772-6200, www.morro-bay.ca.us) lies within the city limits, just north of Morro Rock. Two lifeguard towers are staffed from Memorial Day to Labor Day (10am-6pm). The **Morro Bay Sandspit** (805/772-6200, www.morro-bay.ca.us) is a four-mile-long line of dunes and beach that separates Morro Bay from the ocean. The northernmost mile is within city limits, while the southern portion is in Montaña de Oro State Park. Access this area by walking in from the state park or by paddling across Morro Harbor to the land south of the harbor mouth.

Morro Strand State Beach (2 miles south of Cayucos, Hwy. 1, 805/772-2560, www.parks.ca.gov) is a three-mile strand of sand popular with anglers, windsurfers, and kite fliers. **North Point** (Hwy. 1 at Toro Ln., 805/772-6200, www.morro-bay.ca.us) is a bluff-top city park with a stairway to the beach and great tide pools. From here, you can also walk north all the way to Cayucos or head south toward looming Morro Rock. The wetlands at **Cloisters Park** (San Jacinto St. and Coral St., 805/772-6200, www.morro-bay.ca.us) are home to fish and birds. This city park also offers access to the beach.

The Libertine Pub

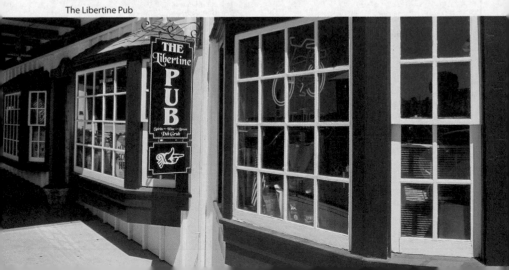

Nine Sisters

Among the distinctive features of San Luis Obispo County are the nine ancient volcanic peaks known as the Nine Sisters of the Morros. These extend from the prominent 581-foot **Morro Rock** of Morro Bay 14 miles south to the 775-foot **Islay Hill,** which is in the city of San Luis Obispo. The highest of the Nine Sisters is 1,559-foot **Bishop Peak,** the top portion of which is part of the 360-acre Bishop Peak Natural Reserve and a popular spot for hikers and rock climbers.

The Nine Sisters make for unique animal and plant habitats. Morro Rock is a nesting place for peregrine falcons, and **Hollister Peak** hosts a colony of black-shouldered kites.

Boat Tours and Fishing

Sub Sea Tours (699 Embarcadero, No. 9, 805/772-9463, www.subseatours.com, adults $16, seniors and students $12, children $8) is like snorkeling without getting wet. The yellow, 27-foot semisubmersible vessel has a cabin outfitted with windows below the water. The 45-minute tour takes you around the harbor in search of wildlife. Expect to see sea lions sunning on a floating dock and sea otters playing in the water. At a much-touted secret spot, fish congregate for feeding. You'll typically see smelt, appearing like silver splinters, and may also catch a glimpse of salmon, lingcod, perch, and sunfish. Kids love it. Sub Sea Tours also schedules **whale-watching excursions** (adults $45, seniors and students $40, children under 12 $35) to see California gray whales and humpback whales.

Rent your own boat to explore the bay through **Bay Cruisers** (845 Embarcadero, 805/771-9337, http://baycruisers.com, 10am-5pm Mon. and Wed.-Thurs., 10am-7pm Fri.-Sun., $85-95/hour). **Chablis Cruises** (800/979-3370, http://chabliscruises.com) are held on a two-story riverboat with a rooftop deck. Options include a two-hour weekly champagne brunch excursion (11am Sat.,

adults $45, children under 12 $23) and two-hour harbor cruises ($20). **Virg's Landing** (1169 Market Ave., 805/772-1222, http://virgslanding.com, $62-92) sends four boats out for daily fishing trips, searching for rock cod, albacore, king salmon, and halibut. They also offer whale-watching excursions (Dec.-Apr.).

Surfing

Morro Rock Beach (west end of Embarcadero, 805/772-6200, www.morrobay.ca.us) has a consistent beach break. It's a unique experience to be able to stare up at a giant rock while waiting for waves. **Wavelengths Surf Shop** (998 Embarcadero, 805/772-3904, 9:30am-6pm daily, board rental $20/day, wetsuit rental $10/day), on the Embarcadero on the way to the beach, rents boards and wetsuits.

Kayaking and Stand-Up Paddleboarding

Paddling the protected, scenic waters of Morro Bay, whether you're in a kayak or on a stand-up paddleboard, is a great way to see wildlife up close. You might observe otters lazily backstroking in the estuary or clouds of birds gliding just above the surface of the water.

Paddle over to the **Morro Bay Sandspit,** a finger of dunes in the northern section of Montaña de Oro State Park that separates the bay from the ocean. Then beach your vessel and climb over the dunes to the mostly isolated beach on the ocean side. Parts of the dunes are sometimes closed to protect the snowy plover. Away from the harbor area, the estuary can be very shallow; plan your paddling at high tide to avoid too much portaging.

Kayak Horizons (551 Embarcadero, 805/772-6444, www.kayakhorizons.com, 9am-5pm daily) rents kayaks ($12-18/hour) and paddleboards ($12/hour) and hosts a three-hour paddle around the estuary ($59). **Central Coast Outdoors** (805/528-1080, www.centralcoastoutdoors.com, kayak tours $55-110 pp) has a range of kayaking tours that depart from the **Morro Bay State Park Marina** (100 State Park Rd.). Options include short paddles, sunset paddles, full-moon paddles, half-day paddles, and a kayak trip to the sandspit for a dinner in the dunes. In Morro Bay State Park, secure a canoe or kayak from **A Kayak Shack** (10 State Park Rd., 805/772-8796, www.morrobaykayakshack.com, 9am-5pm daily late May-early Sept., 9am-4pm daily early Sept.-late May, kayaks $14-18/hour, canoes $18/hour, stand-up paddleboards $16/hour).

Hiking

Morro Bay State Park (Morro Bay State Park Rd., 805/772-2560, www.parks.ca.gov) has 13 miles of hiking trails. The popular **Black Hill Trail** (3 miles round-trip, moderate) begins from the campground road. This climb gains 600 vertical feet and passes through chaparral and eucalyptus on the way to 640-foot-high Black Hill, part of the same system of volcanic plugs that produced nearby Morro Rock.

Montaña de Oro State Park (Pecho Rd., 7 miles south of Los Osos, 805/772-7434, www.parks.ca.gov, 6am-10pm daily) has almost 50 miles of hiking trails. Take in the park's coastline along the **Montaña de Oro Bluffs Trail** (4 miles round-trip, easy). The trailhead begins about 100 yards south of the visitors center and campground entrance and runs along a marine terrace to the park's southern boundary. On the way it passes **Corallina Cove,** where you may see harbor seals and sea otters. Starting at the parking area just south of the visitors center, the **Valencia Peak Trail** (4 miles round-trip, moderate) leads to its namesake 1,347-foot-high peak, which offers a nice view of the coastline spread out below. The **Hazard Peak Trail** (6 miles round-trip, moderate-strenuous) starts at Pecho Valley Road and climbs to the summit of 1,076-foot Hazard Peak, with unobstructed 360-degree views. The **Islay Canyon Trail** (6 miles round-trip, moderate) takes you through the park's inland creekbeds and canyons. Starting at the bottom of Islay

Creek Canyon, this wide dirt path is popular with birders because of the 25-40 different bird species that frequent the area. An abandoned barn makes a good marker to turn back toward the trailhead.

FOOD

The giant parking lot outside **Carla's Country Kitchen** (213 Beach St., 805/772-9051, www.carlaskitchenmb.com, 6:30am-2pm daily, $6-12) attests to the popularity of this breakfast-and-lunch spot. With blue-and-white checkered tablecloths, Carla's serves heaping portions of breakfast classics, including scrambles and omelets, along with sandwiches and burgers. The Pooney scramble is a tasty mess of spinach, cheeses, eggs, bacon, and mushrooms.

Frankie & Lola's (1154 Front St., 805/771-9306, www.frankieandlolas.com, 6:30am-2:30pm daily, $8-17) does breakfast right. Creative savory dishes include the fried green tomato Benedict topped with creole hollandaise sauce and tasty, colorful *chilaquiles* with red chorizo, avocado, and tomatillo salsa. Lunch focuses on salads and sandwiches, with creations including an edamame flatbread and a tri-tip avocado sandwich.

People worship the crab cake and fish tacos at ★ **Taco Temple** (2680 N. Main St., 805/772-4965, http://tacotemple.com, 11am-9pm Wed.-Mon., $13-15). Housed in a big multicolored building east of Highway 1, where colorful surfboards hang on the walls, this is not the standard taqueria. Their California take on classic Mexican dishes includes sweet potato enchiladas and tacos filled with soft-shell crab or calamari. The tacos are served like salads, with the meat and greens piled on tortillas. The chips and salsa are terrific.

Seafood is the way to go when dining in Morro Bay. An unassuming fish house with views of the fishing boats and the bay, ★ **Tognazzini's Dockside Restaurant** (1245 Embarcadero, 805/772-8100, www.morrobaydockside.com, 11am-9pm Sun.-Thurs., 11am-10pm Fri.-Sat. summer,

11am-7pm Sun.-Thurs., 11am-9pm Fri.-Sat. winter, $18-27) has an extensive seafood menu as well as art depicting sultry mermaids hanging on the wall. Entrées include albacore kebabs and wild salmon in a unique tequila marinade. Oyster lovers can't go wrong with Dockside's barbecued oyster appetizer, which features the shellfish swimming in garlic butter studded with scallions. Behind the main restaurant is the **Dockside Too Fish Market** (10am-8pm daily summer, 10am-6pm Sun.-Thurs., 10am-8pm Fri.-Sat. winter), a local favorite with beer, seafood, and live music.

Upscale **The Galley Seafood Bar & Grill** (899 Embarcadero, 805/772-7777, http:// galleymorrobay.com, 11am-2:30pm and 5pm-close daily, $18-46) is popular for items like pan-seared scallops. The menu changes daily depending on the fresh catch.

ACCOMMODATIONS

The **Sundown Inn** (640 Main St., 805/772-3229 or 800/696-6928, http://sundowninn.com, $109-209) is a well-priced motel within walking distance of Morro Bay's downtown and waterfront areas. Rooms have fridges, microwaves, and coin-operated vibrating beds.

The ★ **Masterpiece Hotel** (1206 Main St., 805/772-5633 or 800/527-6782, www.masterpiecehotel.com, $189-300) is a great place to stay for art enthusiasts and lovers of quirky motels. Each guest room is decorated with framed prints from master artists, and the hallways also have prints of paintings by Henri Matisse, Vincent Van Gogh, and Norman Rockwell. There's also a large indoor spa pool decorated like a Roman bathhouse that further differentiates this motel from other cookie-cutter lodging options. Expect a deluxe breakfast in the morning and a wine and cheese serving in early evening.

Built in 1939, the bright ★ **Beach Bungalow Inn and Suites** (1050 Morro Ave., 805/772-9700, www.morrobaybeachbungalow.com, $150-350) has been extensively renovated. The 12 clean, spacious, and modern rooms have hardwood floors, local art on the walls, and flat-screen TVs. Most of the rooms have gas fireplaces. Family suites accommodate four people, while king deluxe suites have full kitchens. Two bicycles are available for cruising around town. There's also a fire pit outside to enjoy the Central Coast evenings. In the morning, a hot breakfast is served to your room.

The family-run **Anderson Inn** (897 Embarcadero, 805/772-3434, www.andersoninnmorrobay.com, $279-429) is an eight-room boutique hotel on Morro Bay's busy Embarcadero. Three of the rooms are perched right over the estuary, with stunning views of the nearby rock. Those premium rooms also include fireplaces and jetted tubs.

Camping

Outside downtown Morro Bay, the **Morro Bay State Park Campground** (Morro Bay State Park Rd., 800/444-7275, www.reservecalifornia.com, tents $35, RVs $50) has 140 campsites, many shaded by eucalyptus and pine trees; right across the street is the Morro Bay estuary. **Montaña de Oro State Park** (Pecho Rd., 6 miles southwest of Morro Bay, 800/444-7275, www.reservecalifornia.com, $25) has more primitive camping facilities. There are walk-in environmental campsites and a primitive campground behind the Spooner Ranch House that has pit toilets.

One mile north of Morro Rock, **Morro Strand State Beach** (Yerba Buena St. and Hwy. 1, 800/444-7275, www.reservecalifornia.com, $35) has over 80 sites right by the beach.

TRANSPORTATION AND SERVICES

From San Luis Obispo, Morro Bay is 13 miles west on Highway 1. Main Street is the main artery through downtown. Highway 41 stretches between Morro Bay and Atascadero, making it a good shortcut if you are coming from San Francisco. If you are heading south from Big Sur, Morro Bay is 30 miles south of Hearst Castle on Highway 1.

The **Morro Bay Trolley** (595 Harbor Way, 805/772-2744, www.morro-bay.ca.us, Mon. 11am-5pm, Fri.-Sat. 11am-7pm, Sun.

11am-6pm, late May-early Oct., $1 per ride, children under 5 free) operates three routes. The **Waterfront Route** runs the length of the Embarcadero, including out to Morro Rock. The **Downtown Route** runs through the downtown (as in uptown) area all the way out to Morro Bay State Park. The **North Morro Bay Route** runs from uptown through the northern part of Morro Bay, north of the rock, along Highway 1. An all-day pass ($3) is not a bad idea if you plan on seeing a lot of sights.

French Hospital Medical Center (1911 Johnson Ave., San Luis Obispo, 805/543-5353, www.dignityhealth.org) and **Sierra Vista Regional Medical Center** (1010 Murray Ave., San Luis Obispo, 805/546-7600, www.sierravistaregional.com) are the closest hospitals. Both are in San Luis Obispo, 13 miles from Morro Bay. If you have an emergency, dial 911. The local police are the **Morro Bay Police Department** (850 Morro Bay Blvd., 805/772-6225).

CAYUCOS

Cayucos is one of California's best little beach towns. There are no real attractions here except for the small strip of a beach between open hillsides and the Pacific. But there are a good number of nice restaurants and places to stay, so it makes a pleasant, less touristy place to spend the night while visiting the area attractions, including Hearst Castle (which is just 30 miles north).

Cayucos is named after the indigenous Chumash people's word for kayak or canoe. One of the early proponents of the town was Captain James Cass, who with a business partner built the pier, along with a store and a warehouse, in the late 1800s. Today the long, narrow pier still stands, while the warehouse is the town's community center and home of the Cayucos Art Society Gallery.

Recreation

The major attraction is **Cayucos State Beach** (Cayucos Dr., 805/781-5930, www.parks.ca.gov, sunrise-sunset daily) and the pier, built in 1875 by Captain James Cass.

The beach has volleyball courts, swing sets, and lifeguard stands, which are staffed during the summer months. The pier is lit at night for fishing. Cayucos is not known for consistent surf, but rideable waves can occur on the south side of the pier. This is a usually mellow beach-break spot good for beginners. The relatively calm waters off Cayucos Beach are a good place to kayak or stand-up paddleboard.

Just a few feet from the beach, **Good Clean Fun** (136 Ocean Front Ln., 805/995-1993, http://goodcleanfunusa.com, 9am-6pm daily) rents out surfboards ($10/hour), wetsuits ($8/hour), bodyboards ($5/hour), stand-up paddleboards ($15/hour), and kayaks ($30-40/hour). They also have surf lessons, a surf camp, kayak tours, and kayak-fishing outings.

Pick up beach equipment at the **Cayucos Surf Company** (95 Cayucos Dr., 805/995-1000, www.cayucossurfcompany.com, 9am-6pm daily summer, 10am-4pm Mon.-Thurs., 10am-6pm Fri.-Sat. winter). They rent wetsuits ($15/day), surfboards ($29/day), bodyboards ($20/day), and stand-up paddleboards ($40/day) and also offer private and group surfing lessons.

Nightlife

The **Old Cayucos Tavern** (130 N. Ocean Ave., 805/995-3209, www.oldcayucostavern.com, 10am-2am daily) is a classic Western saloon, with a poker room in the back and a bar up front. In the barroom, more than 10 beers are available on tap, and paintings of topless cowgirls adorn the walls. There are also two pool tables and a shuffleboard table for those who want to play games without the fear of losing their money in the card room. Western scenes decorate the walls, and wooden barrels serve as tables. Live bands perform on weekends.

Shopping

Cayucos is known for antiques. **Remember When** (152 N. Ocean Ave., 805/995-1232, 10am-5pm daily) is home to antiques and collectibles. The **Lady Spencer Galleria and Distinctive Gifts** (148 N. Ocean Ave.,

805/995-3771, www.ladyspencer.com, 10am-5pm Mon.-Tues. and Thurs.-Sat., 10:30am-4pm Sun.) carries all sorts of unique items from barbed-wire earrings to soy candles and glass tableware.

In a red two-story building on Cayucos's main drag, **Brown Butter Cookie Company** (98 N. Ocean Ave., 805/995-2076, www.brownbuttercookies.com, 9am-6pm daily) bakes and sells original cookie creations, including their original brown butter sea salt cookie and other recipes such as coconut lime and cocoa mint. Witness the delectable creative process as it takes place right behind the counter.

Food

Cayucos is a place for seafood, and nothing is as revered as ★ **Rudell's Smokehouse** (101 D St., 805/995-5028, www.smokerjim.com, 11am-6pm daily, $4-12). Rudell's is little more than a small shack near the beach, but this place serves some of the tastiest fish tacos you'll ever eat, including salmon and albacore variations. The seafood is smoked, and the unexpected but welcome presence of chopped apples gives the fixings a sweet crunch. The seating options are limited to a few outdoor tables, so take your taco to the nearby beach.

Schooners Wharf (171 N. Ocean Ave., 805/995-3883, www.schoonerswharf.com, 11am-10:30pm daily, $12-38) has a serious nautical theme going: It's a two-story compound of corrugated metal and wood decorated with marine flotsam and jetsam. The menu here is seafood-heavy, with a range of items from hearty cioppino to seared ahi. The burgers, made with nearby Hearst Ranch beef, are also worthy of attention. Schooners is one of the only "late-night" spots in Cayucos.

At **Duckies Chowder House** (55 Cayucos Dr., 805/995-2245, www.duckieschowder.com, 11am-8pm daily, $9-13), you can get your chowder New England or Manhattan style and served in a cup, bowl, or bread bowl. Other seafood options are mostly fried; there are also salads and sandwiches on the menu. Pitchers of beer and the company of friends make it all go down easy.

Cayucos has its own **farmers market** (Cayucos Veterans Hall parking lot, 10 Cayucos Dr., 805/296-2056, 10am-12:30pm Fri. summer).

Accommodations

★ **The Saltbox** (150 D St., 800/995-2322, www.thesaltbox.com, $150-220) makes a superb base for exploring the coast. The historic

The Saltbox

blue building, constructed by a ship's captain in the 1880s, is split into three units, each with fully equipped kitchens, private entrances, and a deck or patio. The ground-floor Captain's Quarters can accommodate 6-8 people with three bedrooms, two bathrooms, and an enclosed brick patio area. The Crow's Nest is an upstairs apartment with two bedrooms that can accommodate four people, and it has a nice view of the sea and the pier. The Carriage House is a small studio in the shade of the main house. The place is a bit dated, but that is outweighed by lots of character, a great location, and fair rates.

The **Cayucos Sunset Inn Bed & Breakfast** (95 S. Ocean Ave., 805/995-2500 or 877/805-1076, www.cayucossunsetinn.com, $149-349) has five two-room suites with private balconies, soaking tubs, and fireplaces. The innkeepers provide a full hot breakfast in the morning that is served in the dining room, as well as milk and cookies delivered to your unit every evening.

The **Seaside Motel** (42 S. Ocean Ave., 805/995-3809 or 800/549-0900, www. seasidemotel.com, $110-180) has brightly colored and uniquely decorated rooms with names like "Birdhouse Bungalow" and "Sunflower Surprise." Some rooms have kitchenettes; all have flat-screen TVs and Internet access. Suites are available for larger groups. Guests have access to the on-site garden.

Transportation and Services

Cayucos is right off Highway 1, eight miles north of Morro Bay.

Cayucos by the Sea (www. cayucosbythesea.com) has information on everything from the town's history to its current lodging and restaurant options. Visit the brick-and-mortar location or the website of the **Cayucos Chamber of Commerce** (41 S. Ocean Ave., 805/995-8552, www. cayucoschamber.com, 11am-4pm Fri.-Sun., 1pm-4pm Mon.).

San Luis Obispo and Vicinity

Inland from the coast, San Luis Obispo, otherwise known as SLO (pronounced "slow"), is a worthy home base for exploring nearby Montaña de Oro State Park and Morro Bay. Higuera Street is a one-way, three-lane street lined with restaurants, clothing stores, and bars. A half-block away, restaurant decks are perched over the small San Luis Obispo Creek, a critical habitat for migrating steelhead.

SIGHTS
Mission San Luis Obispo de Tolosa

Founded by Junipero Serra way back in 1772, **Mission San Luis Obispo de Tolosa** (751 Palm St., 805/781-8220, www. missionsanluisobispo.org, 9am-5pm daily summer, 9am-4pm daily winter) was the fifth in the chain of 21 California missions. The church itself is narrow and long, with exposed wooden beams on the ceiling. On the grounds, there is a small **museum** (805/543-6850, 9am-5pm daily summer, 9am-4pm daily winter, suggested donation $5) with artifacts from the Native Chumash people and exhibits on the mission and its missionaries. A nice garden and the Mission Plaza out front of the mission complex are pleasant places to spend the afternoon on a warm day.

★ Madonna Inn

A kitschy attraction worth seeing even if you aren't spending the evening, the **Madonna Inn** (10 Madonna Rd., 805/543-3000, www. madonnainn.com) is a sprawling complex right off U.S. 101 that includes a café, a steak house, a bar, a dance floor, a wine cellar, and a collection of 110 themed rooms like "The Caveman," a unit with a solid-rock wall and a waterfall shower.

Obviously, the rooms are for overnight guests, but there is still a lot to take in if you pull over for a peek. The **Copper Café & Pastry Shop** has copper-plated tables and a copper-plated circular bar, while the **Gold Rush Steak House** is a garish explosion of giant fake flowers and rose-colored furniture. It might remind you of a room in your grandmother's or great-aunt's home—on steroids.

ENTERTAINMENT AND EVENTS

Bars and Clubs

Since San Luis Obispo is a college town, there are plenty of bars in the downtown area. A popular spot with the college students, **Mo/ Tav** (725 Higuera St., 805/541-8733, www.motherstavern.com, 11am-2am daily) has two-for-one-drink nights, karaoke evenings, and weekend dance parties. Across the street is another popular drinking establishment called the **Frog & Peach Pub** (728 Higuera St., 805/595-3764, noon-2am daily). It has live music almost every night, along with a back deck where you can have a drink on a warmer evening.

The **Black Sheep Bar & Grill** (1117 Chorro St., 805/544-7433, www.blacksheepslo. com, 11am-2am daily) has a cozy pub feel on uncrowded nights. This brick-walled, wood-floored tavern has a fireplace and a back patio. It also serves a burger basted in a Guinness beer reduction sauce.

Live Music

The **Performing Arts Center** (1 Grand Ave., 805/756-4849, www.pacslo.org), which is on the California Polytechnic State University campus, hosts live theater events, lectures, concerts, and comedy performances.

SLO Brew (736 Higuera St., 805/543-1843, www.slobrew.com) brings touring acts to San Luis Obispo. It has its own brewery, pub, and second-floor lofts if you want to spend the night.

Cinema

The **Palm Theatre** (817 Palm St., 805/541-5161, www.thepalmtheatre.com) has the unique distinction of being the first solar-powered movie theater in the country. The Palm frequently screens independent, foreign, and art-house films. The **Fremont Theatre** (1035 Monterey St., 805/546-8600, https://fremontslo.com) is an art deco movie house from 1942 that shows new films as well as classic movies.

Madonna Inn

San Luis Obispo and Vicinity

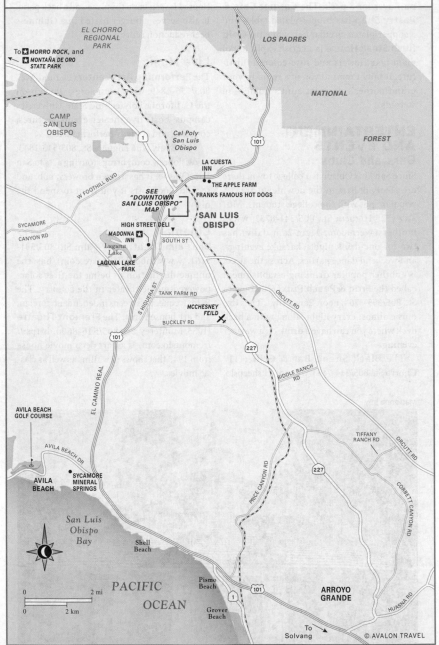

EL CHORRO REGIONAL PARK

LOS PADRES

To ★ MORRO ROCK, and
★ MONTAÑA DE ORO
STATE PARK

NATIONAL

CAMP SAN LUIS OBISPO

FOREST

Cal Poly San Luis Obispo

1

101

LA CUESTA INN

W FOOTHILL BLVD

SYCAMORE CANYON RD

SEE "DOWNTOWN SAN LUIS OBISPO" MAP

THE APPLE FARM

FRANKS FAMOUS HOT DOGS

SAN LUIS OBISPO

HIGH STREET DELI

MADONNA INN

Luguna Lake

SOUTH ST

LAGUNA LAKE PARK

S HIGUERA ST

TANK FARM RD

ORCUTT RD

MCCHESNEY FEILD

BUCKLEY RD

101

227

BIDDLE RANCH RD

AVILA BEACH GOLF COURSE

AVILA BEACH DR

EL CAMINO REAL

PRICE CANYON RD

TIFFANY RANCH RD

ORCUTT RD

227

AVILA BEACH

SYCAMORE MINERAL SPRINGS

CORBETT CANYON RD

San Luis Obispo Bay

Shell Beach

PACIFIC OCEAN

Pismo Beach

Grover Beach

1   101

To Solvang

ARROYO GRANDE

HUASNA RD

0   2 mi

0   2 km

© AVALON TRAVEL

Festivals and Events

The **San Luis Obispo International Film Festival** (817 Palm St. and 1035 Monterey St., 805/546-3456, http://slofilmfest.org, Mar.) screens a range of films at the city's Palm Theatre and Fremont Theatre as well as other county spots including Paso Robles and Avila Beach. The five-day fest draws film folks like Josh Brolin and John Waters.

Festival Mozaic (locations vary, 805/781-3009 or 877/881-8899, www.festivalmozaic. com, July and Nov.) has a winter concert series and a summer music festival. It features chamber music, orchestral performances, and educational events in venues including Mission San Luis Obispo de Tolosa and the Hearst Castle.

HIKING

The 1,546-foot-high **Bishop Peak** (trailheads at the end of Highland Dr. and off Patricia Dr., 805/781-7300, www.slocity.org) is the city's natural treasure. A four-mile round-trip hike to the rocky crown of Bishop Peak offers commanding views of San Luis Obispo and the surrounding area. Named by Spanish missionaries who thought the mountain resembled a bishop's hat, Bishop Peak is the tallest of the morros or "Nine Sisters," a chain of nine volcanic peaks stretching from San Luis Obispo up to Morro Bay. In addition to the fine views, Bishop Peak teems with wildlife, especially birds that float on the mountain's thermals. You might see golden eagles, bald eagles, hawks, owls, vultures, or kestrels. The one-hour hike passes through a forest, by Volkswagen Beetle-sized boulders, and into a series of exposed switchbacks. (Bring water!) Just below the peak are a couple of benches, a dog-watering bowl, and a peak journal in a metal box where you can sign.

FOOD

Being inside **Franks Famous Hot Dogs** (950 California Blvd., 805/541-3488, 6:30am-9pm daily, $3-8) feels a bit like you've traveled back to the 1950s. College students from nearby Cal Poly sit in the red-and-white booths snacking on Franks' daily handmade burgers, fries, or steamed hot dogs. Whether you get a chili cheese dog or a monster burger, the super-low prices recall another era. It's rumored that they have a great breakfast burrito as well.

In a neighborhood a few blocks from downtown, **High Street Deli** (350 High St., 805/541-4738, www.highstdeli.com, 9am-5:30pm daily, $6-9) is worth seeking out if you are a sandwich enthusiast. The "California Turkey" is a heated slab of tastiness with roasted turkey, an Ortega chile, and slices of avocado on toasted sourdough slices. They also sell Italian subs, hot pastramis, and meat loaf sandwiches. After ordering, hunker down on a stool at one of the barrel tables to eat these creations while they're still warm.

The ★ **Firestone Grill** (1001 Higuera St., 805/783-1001, www.firestonegrill.com, 11am-10pm Sun.-Wed., 11am-11pm Thurs.-Sat., $5-18) has a masterpiece in its tender and tasty tri-tip sandwich. Locals swear by it. You'll also find plenty of pork ribs, burgers, and salads topped with grilled meat. Enjoy the goods in a spacious indoor dining room with large TVs or in the outdoor seating plaza. Expect a line out the door.

The place to be is on the deck of **Novo** (726 Higuera St., 805/543-3986, www. novorestaurant.com, 11am-9pm Mon.-Thurs., 11am-1am Fri.-Sat., 10am-10pm Sun., $16-32) overlooking San Luis Obispo Creek. Novo serves tapas including fresh shrimp avocado spring rolls, as well as entrées like a daily fish special. International flavors creep into the menu on items like pork *carnitas sopes,* Thai curries, and a stir-fried noodle dish. They do a late-night limited menu 10pm-1am.

A worthy place for lunch or dinner is the Rachael Ray-approved **Big Sky Café** (1121 Broad St., 805/545-5401, www.bigskycafe. com, 7am-8pm Mon.-Thurs., 7am-9pm Fri., 8am-9pm Sat., 8am-8pm Sun., $9-22). There are plenty of options for carnivores, but Big Sky also has some vegetarian entrées, including a plate of local vegetables served in a variety of preparations.

Bubblegum Alley

Bubblegum Alley (Higuera St. between Broad and Garden Sts.) is a 70-foot-long alleyway that has walls covered in pieces of chewed gum. The newly chewed chunks are bright green, red, yellow, and other such hues, while the older pieces have turned a darker color. Some people have called this oddity an "eyesore," while others have touted it as one of the city's "special attractions." Regardless, Bubblegum Alley, which is rumored to have possibly started as early as the late 1950s, is here to stay. Even after firefighters blasted the alleyway with water hoses in 1985, another layer of gum appeared a little later.

Luna Red (1023 Chorro St., 805/540-5243, www.lunaredslo.com, 11:30am-9pm Mon.-Wed., 11:30am-10pm Thurs., 11:30am-midnight Fri., 9am-midnight Sat., 9am-9pm Sun., $15-32) is in an enviable location between Mission Plaza and bustling Higuera Street. With ample outdoor patio seating, Luna Red serves what it calls "an amalgamation of world cuisines": sashimi, ceviche, lamb kebabs, and a hummus platter.

The ★ **San Luis Obispo Farmers Market** (Higuera St. between Osos and Nipomo Sts., 805/544-9570, www.slocountyfarmers.org, http://downtownslo.com, 6pm-9pm Thurs.) is one of the largest farmers markets in the state. This weekly gathering has the goods of 70 farmers and lots of live music.

ACCOMMODATIONS

A good value, the ★ **Peach Tree Inn** (2001 Monterey St., 800/227-6396, http://peachtreeinn.com, $169-209) has nice rooms, a friendly staff, and a complimentary breakfast. The finest rooms are the Creekside Rooms, each with its own brick patio. The Peach Tree is on the Old SLO Trolley route and is an easy one-mile walk to San Luis Obispo's downtown.

Across the street from the Peach Tree, the **La Cuesta Inn** (2074 Monterey St., 805/543-2777, www.lacuestainn.com, $159-219) has reasonably priced rooms right near U.S. 101. All rooms have microwaves and fridges. This privately-owned hotel has a small heated pool and a hot tub. A deluxe continental breakfast is served; coffee and juice are available in the lobby.

The ★ **Sycamore Mineral Springs Resort** (1215 Avila Beach Dr., 805/595-7302, www.sycamoresprings.com, $195-445) is on 100 acres in a tranquil canyon with mineral springs bubbling beneath it. Accommodations range from cozy rooms with a queen bed to a two-story guesthouse with three bedrooms and three bathrooms. Up on stilts, the resort's West Meadows Suites include a living room with a gas fireplace and a bedroom with a four-poster king bed. The best feature is the back decks, which include large soaking tubs that can be filled with fresh mineral water.

If you ever wanted to know how it feels to spend the night in a cave or in a room inspired by the country of Portugal, plop down some money to spend a whole evening at the ★ **Madonna Inn** (10 Madonna Rd., 805/543-3000, www.madonnainn.com, $199-469). An under-hyped asset on Madonna Inn's 2,200 acres is the pool deck, with a large heated pool, two hot tubs, a poolside bar, and a view of a cascade tumbling down the hillside.

The **Granada Hotel & Bistro** (1126 Morro St., 805/544-9100, www.granadahotelandbistro.com, $209-469) is a 17-room boutique hotel just a half block off Higuera Street. The 1920s-era hotel has been renovated and modernized, with exposed brick walls and hardwood floors. Most rooms also have fireplaces. Attached to the hotel is the **Granada Bistro,** which serves Spanish-inspired cuisine from paella to squash-potato tacos.

Paso Robles

Paso Robles is a popular destination for wine-lovers and day-trippers on U.S. 101. The inland town is a 30-minute drive north from San Luis Obispo.

WINERIES

The densest concentration of wineries cluster along Highway 46 West and the little roads that spring off that main thoroughfare. Many intrepid wine-tasters never make it past this short and easy-to-travel stretch, which locals refer to as the Westside.

- **Rotta Winery** (250 Winery Rd., 805/237-0510, www.rottawinery.com, 11am-5pm Wed.-Mon., tasting fee $10) has been making wine in the region since 1908. It is best known for its estate zinfandel and black monukka dessert wine, which is sweet but not cloying.

- One of the best wineries in these parts is **Hunt Cellars** (2875 Oakdale Rd., 805/237-1600, www.huntcellars.com, 10am-5:30pm daily, tasting fee $10). The friendly and intensely knowledgeable staff members pour some of the finest wines in Paso at this midsize, informal tasting room.

- If you favor small wineries that only produce tiny runs of wine, **Dark Star Cellars** (2985 Anderson Rd., 805/237-2389, www.darkstarcellars.com, 10:30am-5:30pm daily, tasting fee $10) is perfect for you. Ask at the bar about the "synthetic gravity" that is so important to the slow fermentation process used at Dark Star.

- On the Eastside, **Eberle Winery** (3810 Hwy. 46 F., 3.5 miles east of U.S. 101, 805/238-9607, www.eberlewinery.com, 10am-6pm daily Apr.-Oct., 10am-5pm daily Nov.-Mar., tasting fee $15) is one of the pioneers of the Paso wine region. The free cave tour is a great way to escape the heat on a summer's day.

SPA

Even before Paso Robles was known for its wineries, the inland town was a destination for people who wanted to soak in its hot mineral waters. At the **Paso Robles Inn** (1103 Spring St., 800/676-1713, www.pasoroblesinn.com, $199-305), you can splurge on a room with a private mineral tub, or soak in the communal heated pool and spa that date back to 1891.

FOOD

For a bite to eat, grab a taco or two at **Papi's** (840 13th St., 805/239-3720, 11am-9pm daily, $10) or a pint and some pub food at the **Firestone Taproom** (1400 Ramada Dr., 805/225-5913, www.firestonebeer.com, 11am-9pm daily).

TRANSPORTATION AND SERVICES

San Luis Obispo sits squarely on U.S. 101/Highway 1, 230 miles (four hours) south of San Francisco and 95 miles (two hours) north of Santa Barbara. There's an **Amtrak** station in San Luis Obispo (1011 Railroad Ave., www.amtrak.com) where the *Coast Starlight* train stops. Use **SLO Transit** (www.slocity.org, adults $1.25, seniors $0.60) to get around town.

San Luis Obispo is home to two hospitals: **Sierra Vista Regional Medical Center** (1010 Murray Ave., 805/546-7600, www.sierravistaregional.com) and **French Hospital Medical Center** (1911 Johnson Ave., 805/543-5353, www.dignityhealth.org).

Los Angeles

With palm trees lining sunny boulevards, surfers riding the deep-blue Pacific, and unending Hollywood glitz, Los Angeles is the California that lives in our imaginations.

It's true that the Pacific Ocean warms to a swimmable temperature here, there are palm trees, and stars are embedded in the sidewalks on Hollywood Boulevard. But celebrities don't crowd every sidewalk signing autographs, and movies aren't filming on every corner. Instead, L.A. combines the glitz, crowds, and speed of the big city with an easier, friendlier feel in its suburbs. Power shoppers pound the sparkling pavement lining the ultra-urban city streets. Visitors can catch a premiere at the Chinese Theatre, try their feet on a surfboard at Huntington Beach, and view the prehistoric relics at the La Brea Tar Pits. For visitors who want a deeper look into the Los Angeles Basin, excellent museums dot the landscape, as do theaters, comedy clubs, and live-music venues. L.A. boasts the best nightlife in California, with options that appeal to star-watchers, hard-core dancers, and cutting-edge music lovers alike.

In Orange County lies the single most recognizable tourist attraction in California: Disneyland. Even the most jaded local residents tend to soften at the bright colors, cheerful music, sweet smells, and sense of fun that permeate the House of Mouse.

PLANNING YOUR TIME

Los Angeles is enormous, filled with numerous attractions. Try to spend **four days** here in order to soak up all the sights and spend some time at the beach. If you have just one day, focus in on the part of town that interests you the most. Movie fanatics should go to **Hollywood** to wander the **Walk of Fame.** Outdoors lovers should target one of the beach towns (**Malibu, Santa Monica,** or **Venice Beach**) to enjoy the sun and sand. Families will most likely want to head to the house of the mouse (better known as **Disneyland**).

Previous: Hollywood Boulevard at sunset; Santa Monica Pier. **Above:** TLC Chinese Theatre.

Look for ★ to find recommended
sights, activities, dining, and lodging.

Highlights

★ **California Science Center:** Come to see the retired Space Shuttle *Endeavour* and the accompanying exhibit. Stay for displays on the world's ecosystems and humanity's amazing technological innovations (page 337).

★ **Griffith Park:** This large urban park in the Santa Monica Mountains is home to the iconic Hollywood sign and the Griffith Observatory (page 338).

★ **Hollywood Walk of Fame:** Walk all over your favorite stars—they're embedded in the ground beneath your feet (page 339).

★ **The Getty Center:** The art collections alone would make this sprawling museum complex worth a visit. The soaring architecture, beautiful grounds, and remarkable views of the skyline make it a must. And except for paid parking, it's entirely free (page 345).

★ **Santa Monica Pier:** Ride the Scrambler, take in the view from the solar-powered Ferris wheel, or dine on a hot dog on a stick at this 100-year-old amusement park by the sea (page 345).

★ **Venice Boardwalk:** It's hard not to be amused when walking down this paved coastal path in L.A.'s most free-spirited beach community, crowded with street performers, bodybuilders, and self-identified freaks (page 346).

★ **Disney California Adventure Park:** Tour a Disneyfied version of the Golden State, which includes the Pixar-inspired Cars Land (page 372).

★ **The *Queen Mary*:** Take a tour, spend the evening, or stay the night on this huge art deco ocean liner docked in the Long Beach Harbor. Decide for yourself whether it's truly haunted (page 377).

Sights

The only problem you'll have with the sights of Los Angeles and its surrounding towns is finding a way to see enough of them to satisfy you. You'll find museums, streets, ancient art, and modern production studios ready to welcome you throughout the sprawling cityscape.

DOWNTOWN AND VICINITY

Downtown Los Angeles is experiencing serious renewal with streets of new restaurants, new bars, new hotels, and new attractions, including The Broad museum. The initials "DTLA" (which stands for downtown Los Angeles) can be found everywhere: from the sides of buildings to Internet hashtags.

El Pueblo de Los Angeles Historical Monument

For a city that is famously berated for lacking a sense of its own past, **El Pueblo de Los Angeles Historical Monument** (Olvera St. between Spring St. and Alameda St., 213/485-6855, tours 213/628-1274, http://elpueblo.lacity.org, visitors center 9am-4pm daily) is a veritable crash course in history. Just a short distance from where Spanish colonists first settled in 1781, the park's 44 acres contain 27 buildings dating 1818-1926.

Facing a central courtyard, the oldest church in the city, **Our Lady Queen of the Angels,** still hosts a steady stream of baptisms and other services. On the southern end of the courtyard stands a cluster of historic buildings, the most prominent being Pico House, a hotel built in 1869-1870. The restored **Old Plaza Firehouse** (10am-3pm Tues.-Sun.) dates to 1884 and exhibits firefighting memorabilia from the late 19th and early 20th centuries. On Main Street, **Sepulveda House** (10am-3pm Tues.-Sun.) serves as the Pueblo's visitors center and features period furniture dating to 1887.

Off the central square is **Olvera Street,** an open-air market packed with mariachis, clothing shops, crafts stalls, and taquerias. Hidden in the midst of this tourist market is the **Avila Adobe** (9am-4pm daily), a squat adobe structure said to be the oldest standing house in Los Angeles. The home now functions as a museum detailing the lifestyle of the Mexican ranchero culture that thrived here before the Mexican-American War.

Free 50-minute docent-led **tours** (213/628-1274, www.lasangelitas.org, 10am, 11am, and noon Tues.-Sat.) start at the Las Angelitas del Pueblo office, next to the Old Plaza Firehouse on the southeast end of the plaza. Some of the best times to visit are during festive annual celebrations like the Blessing of the Animals, around Easter, and, of course, Cinco de Mayo.

Cathedral of Our Lady of the Angels

Standing on a hillside next to the Hollywood Freeway (U.S. 101), the colossal concrete **Cathedral of Our Lady of the Angels** (555 W. Temple St., 213/680-5200, www.olacathedral.org, 6:30am-6pm Mon.-Fri., 9am-6pm Sat., 7am-6pm Sun., free tours 1pm Mon.-Fri., parking $4-20) is the third-largest cathedral in the world. Every aspect of Spanish architect Rafael Moneo's design is monumental: the 25-ton bronze doors, 27,000 square feet of clerestory windows of translucent alabaster, and the 156-foot-high campanile topped with a 25-foot-tall cross.

Union Station

When **Union Station** (800 N. Alameda St., Amtrak 800/872-7245, www.unionstationla.com, 4am-1am daily) opened in 1939, 1.5 million people supposedly passed through its doors in the first three days, all wanting to witness what is now considered one of the last of the nation's great rail stations. Its elegant mixture of Spanish mission and modern styles—incorporating vaulted arches, marble

Los Angeles Basin

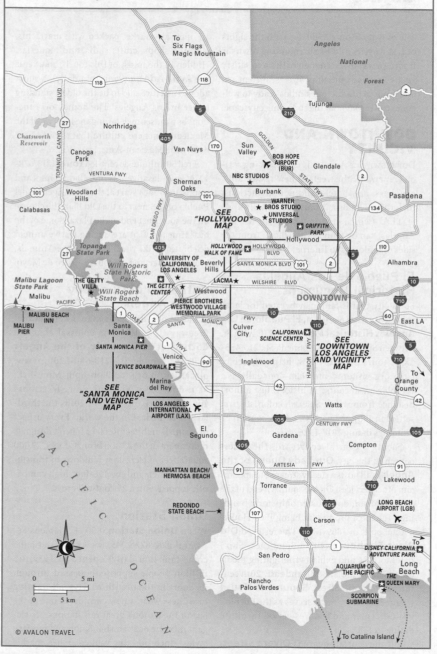

To
Six Flags
Magic Mountain

Angeles

National

Forest

118

118

5

210

Tujunga

2

27

Northridge

GOLDEN

BLVD

Chatsworth
Reservoir

TOPANGA CANYON BLVD

Canoga
Park

405

Van Nuys

170

Sun
Valley

BOB HOPE
AIRPORT
(BUR)

Glendale

2

STATE FWY

Pasadena

VENTURA FWY

NBC STUDIOS

Burbank

101

Woodland
Hills

Sherman
Oaks

101

Calabasas

SAN DIEGO FWY

405

SEE
"HOLLYWOOD"
MAP

WARNER
BROS STUDIO

UNIVERSAL
STUDIOS

GRIFFITH
PARK

134

110

Alhambra

27

Topanga
State Park

Will Rogers
State Historic
Park

UNIVERSITY OF
CALIFORNIA,
LOS ANGELES

Beverly
Hills

HOLLYWOOD
WALK OF FAME

HOLLYWOOD
BLVD

Hollywood

SANTA MONICA BLVD

101

2

5

Malibu Lagoon
State Park

THE GETTY
VILLA

Will Rogers
State Beach

THE GETTY
CENTER

Westwood

LACMA

WILSHIRE   BLVD

10

Malibu

PACIFIC

PIERCE BROTHERS
WESTWOOD VILLAGE
MEMORIAL PARK

DOWNTOWN

MALIBU BEACH
INN

1

COAST

2

710

60

East LA

MALIBU
PIER

Santa
Monica

SANTA   MONICA

FWY

10

Culver
City

CALIFORNIA
SCIENCE CENTER

HARBOR   FWY

110

5

710

SANTA MONICA PIER

1

HWY

Venice

90

Inglewood

SEE
"DOWNTOWN
LOS ANGELES
AND VICINITY"
MAP

To
Orange
County

42

VENICE BOARDWALK

Marina
del Rey

42

SEE
"SANTA MONICA
AND VENICE"
MAP

LOS ANGELES
INTERNATIONAL
AIRPORT (LAX)

Watts

El
Segundo

105

CENTURY FWY

105

405

Gardena

Compton

MANHATTAN BEACH/
HERMOSA BEACH

91

ARTESIA   FWY

91

Lakewood

Torrance

710

REDONDO
STATE BEACH

107

405

LONG BEACH
AIRPORT (LGB)

Carson

110

1

DISNEY CALIFORNIA
ADVENTURE PARK

To
Long
Beach

San Pedro

AQUARIUM OF
THE PACIFIC

THE
QUEEN MARY

Rancho
Palos Verdes

SCORPION
SUBMARINE

PACIFIC

OCEAN

0   5 mi

0   5 km

© AVALON TRAVEL

To Catalina Island

Two Days in Los Angeles

Santa Monica Pier

Los Angeles is notoriously sprawling, but in a couple of days, it is possible to get a serious dose of culture and a few hours on the beach.

DAY 1

Start your morning with coffee and avocado toast at downtown's **Verve Coffee Roasters.** Then browse through the aisles of books at **The Last Bookstore,** including the book art on the 2nd floor. Spend the rest of the morning taking in the sprawling **Los Angeles County Museum of Art,** known as LACMA.

When hunger strikes, head downtown again for some tasty tacos at **B.S. Taqueria.** With your belly full, take a trip to the **California Science Center** to see the Space Shuttle *Endeavour.*

Before the sun drops into the Pacific, rush to the **Ace Hotel's Rooftop Bar** for a fine view of the city's skyline at sunset. Head downstairs for dinner at **L.A. Chapter,** a hip restaurant on the hotel's ground level. End your evening by taking in a movie or a band at a unique venue: the **Hollywood Forever Cemetery.** Or catch an up-and-coming music act at **The Echo and Echoplex.**

DAY 2

Start your beach day at **Cora's Coffee Shoppe** in Santa Monica, a local favorite with a lovely patio. Then walk off that food by taking a half-mile stroll to the **Santa Monica Pier,** where you can ride a Ferris wheel or a roller coaster right over the ocean.

From there, hop in your car and head up the coast toward Malibu. If the waves are breaking, rent a board and wetsuit from the **Malibu Surf Shack** and paddle out into the peeling waves of **Malibu's Surfrider Beach.** Or drive another 20 minutes to **Leo Carrillo State Park,** where you can explore tide pools and coastal caves a world away from urban L.A.

Continue up the coast a few more miles to **Neptune's Net** for lunch. This informal restaurant right on the Pacific Coast Highway has wonderful shrimp tacos topped with pineapple slaw.

Returning south, detour to the **Venice Boardwalk,** where you can be entertained by street performers, bodybuilders, and skateboarders carving the on-the-beach skate park. Finish up with a fine Italian meal and a glass of wine at the **C&O Trattoria,** not far from the Venice Pier.

Near Downtown

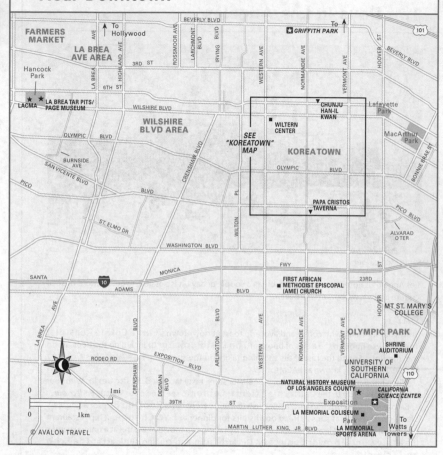

floors, and a 135-foot clock tower—harkens back to a more glamorous era of transportation. The hub for the city's commuter rail network, including L.A.'s first modern subway line, is also a vision of the future: It's slated to be a major hub of the planned California High-Speed Rail System. Two-hour tours of the station's art and architecture happen 10:30am-12:30pm on the second Sunday of the month.

MOCA

The **Museum of Contemporary Art, Los Angeles** (MOCA, 250 S. Grand Ave., 213/626-6222, www.moca.org, 11am-6pm Mon., Wed., and Fri., 11am-8pm Thurs., 11am-5pm Sat.-Sun., adults $15, seniors $10, students $8, children under 12 free) is where you'll see an array of artwork created between 1940 and yesterday afternoon. Highlights include pop art and abstract expressionism from Europe and the United States. Temporary exhibits have displayed the work of Andy Warhol and British artist-turned-Oscar-winning filmmaker Steve McQueen. MOCA has two other locations: The **Geffen Contemporary at MOCA** (152 N. Central Ave., www.moca.org, 11am-5pm

Downtown Los Angeles

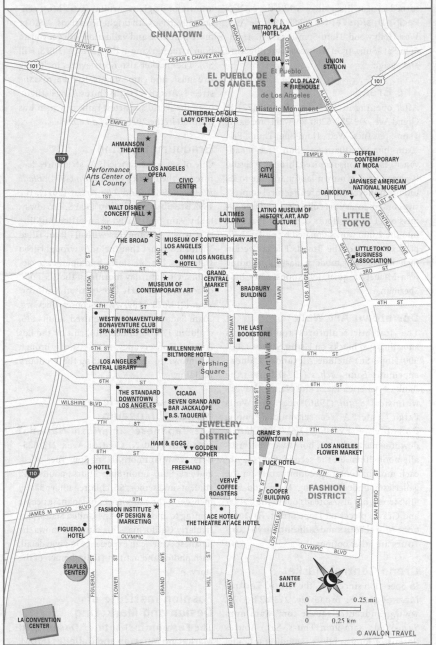

ORO ST
CHINATOWN
SUNSET BLVD
CESAR E CHAVEZ AVE
101
METRO PLAZA HOTEL
MACY ST
LA LUZ DEL DIA
UNION STATION
EL PUEBLO DE LOS ANGELES
El Pueblo
OLD PLAZA FIREHOUSE ★
de Los Angeles
Historic Monument
101
CATHEDRAL OF OUR LADY OF THE ANGELS
TEMPLE ST
110
AHMANSON THEATER ★
Performance Arts Center of LA County
LOS ANGELES OPERA
CIVIC CENTER
CITY HALL
TEMPLE
GEFFEN CONTEMPORARY AT MOCA
JAPANESE AMERICAN NATIONAL MUSEUM
DAIKOKUYA ●
1ST ST
WALT DISNEY CONCERT HALL ★
LA TIMES BUILDING
LATINO MUSEUM OF HISTORY, ART, AND CULTURE
LITTLE TOKYO
1ST ST
CENTRAL
2ND ST
GRAND AVE
THE BROAD ★
MUSEUM OF CONTEMPORARY ART, LOS ANGELES ★
SPRING ST
SAN PEDRO
LITTLE TOKYO BUSINESS ASSOCIATION
AVE
OMNI LOS ANGELES HOTEL ●
3RD ST
3RD ST
FIGUEROA
FLOWER
MUSEUM OF CONTEMPORARY ART ★
HILL ST
GRAND CENTRAL MARKET ■
BRADBURY BUILDING ★
MAIN
LOS ANGELES ST
4TH ST
4TH ST
WESTIN BONAVENTURE/ BONAVENTURE CLUB SPA & FITNESS CENTER ●
BROADWAY
THE LAST BOOKSTORE ■
Downtown Art Walk
5TH ST
LOS ANGELES CENTRAL LIBRARY ★
MILLENNIUM BILTMORE HOTEL ●
Pershing Square
5TH ST
6TH ST
6TH ST
WILSHIRE BLVD
THE STANDARD DOWNTOWN LOS ANGELES ■
CICADA ▼
SEVEN GRAND AND BAR JACKALOPE ▼
B.S. TAQUERIA
SPRING ST
7TH ST
7TH ST
JEWELERY DISTRICT
CRANE'S DOWNTOWN BAR
LOS ANGELES FLOWER MARKET ■
HAM & EGGS ▼
GOLDEN GOPHER ▼
8TH ST
8TH ST
110
O HOTEL ●
FREEHAND ●
TUCK HOTEL ▼
MAIN ST
FASHION DISTRICT
WALL
SAN PEDRO
VERVE COFFEE ROASTERS ▼
COOPER BUILDING ■
9TH ST
JAMES M WOOD BLVD
FASHION INSTITUTE OF DESIGN & MARKETING ★
ACE HOTEL/ THE THEATRE AT ACE HOTEL ●
LOS ANGELES ST
FIGUEROA HOTEL ●
OLYMPIC
BLVD
OLYMPIC BLVD
FIGUEROA ST
FLOWER ST
GRAND AVE
HILL ST
BROADWAY
STAPLES CENTER
SANTEE ALLEY ■
0   0.25 mi
0   0.25 km
LA CONVENTION CENTER

© AVALON TRAVEL

Mon. and Fri., 11am-8pm Thurs., 11am-6pm Sat.-Sun.) is a former police car warehouse turned hangar-like gallery, while the **MOCA Pacific Design Center** (8687 Melrose Ave., West Hollywood, 11am-5pm Tues.-Fri., 11am-6pm Sat.-Sun., free) showcases architecture and design.

The Broad

After opening in 2015, **The Broad** (221 S. Grand Ave., 213/232-6200, www.thebroad.org, 11am-5pm Tues.-Wed., 11am-8pm Thurs.-Fri., 10am-8pm Sat., 10am-6pm Sun., free but advance reservations required through website) is already a downtown landmark due to its unique honeycombed architecture, impressive contemporary art collection, and free admission. The two floors of gallery space dig into the 2,000 works donated by philanthropists Eli and Edythe Broad. The collection includes pieces by modern masters including Jean-Michel Basquiat, Jeff Koons, and Cindy Sherman.

Downtown Art Walk

The dramatic sculptures and fountains adorning two blocks on **Hope Street** (300-500 Hope St.) include Alexander Calder's enormous *Four Arches* (1974) beside the Bank of America Plaza and Nancy Graves's whimsical *Sequi* (1986) near the Wells Fargo Center. A free, self-guided, public **Downtown Art Walk** (213/617-4929, http://downtownartwalk.org, hours vary but usually noon-10pm on the second Thursday of each month) centers predominantly on the galleries bounded by Spring, Main, 2nd, and 9th Streets, but also spreads out to the Calder and Graves pieces on Hope Street. **Historic Core Mural Tours** and **Building on History Tours** are other options.

Grand Central Market

In operation since 1917, the **Grand Central Market** (317 S. Broadway, 213/624-2378, www.grandcentralsquare.com, 8am-6pm Sun.-Wed., 8am-9pm Thurs.-Sat.) houses dozens of food vendors including a falafel stand, a gourmet ice cream booth, and the popular Tacos Tumbras a Tomas, which is known for its giant carnitas tacos. Most vendors advertise with bright neon signs. A $10 or more purchase and validation will get you an hour's free parking at the **garage** (308 S. Hill St.). The market also hosts events including live music and game nights. Right across the street is **Angel's Flight** (https://angelsflight.org), the world's shortest railway, which was featured in the 2016 film *La La Land*.

Bradbury Building

One of several historic L.A. structures featured in the movies *Chinatown* (1974), *Blade Runner* (1982), and *The Artist* (2011), the 1893 **Bradbury Building** (304 S. Broadway, lobby 9am-5pm daily) is an office building that wows filmmakers with its light-filled Victorian court that includes wrought-iron staircases, marble stairs, and open-cage elevators. On Saturday mornings, the 2.5-hour, docent-led **Historic Downtown Walking Tour** (213/623-2489, www.laconservancy.org, 10am Sat., reservations required, adults $15, children 17 and under $10), run by the Los Angeles Conservancy, takes visitors through downtown to sights including the Bradbury Building.

Japanese American National Museum

The **Japanese American National Museum** (100 N. Central Ave., 213/625-0414, www.janm.org, 11am-5pm Tues.-Wed. and Fri.-Sun., noon-8pm Thurs., adults $12, students and seniors $6, children under 5 free) focuses on the experiences of Japanese people coming to and living in the United States, particularly California. This museum shows the Japanese American experience in vivid detail, with photos and artifacts telling much of the story.

Fashion Institute of Design and Marketing

The **Fashion Institute of Design and Marketing Museum and Galleries** (FIDM,

Watts Towers

Watts Towers

With almost 100-foot-tall steel towers decorated with bottles, pottery, seashells, and tile, the **Watts Towers** (1727 E. 107th St., 213/847-4646, www.wattstowers.us, tours 11am-3pm Thurs.-Fri., 10:30am-3pm Sat., noon-3pm Sun., adults $7, seniors and children 13-17$3, children under 13 free) is outsider art on a grand scale. Italian immigrant Simon Rodia spent 33 years building the impressive landscape of spires, walls, birdbaths, and a gazebo without help. The whole structure is meant to resemble a ship stuffed with Rodia's memories. An informative half-hour guided tour is available. Because it's just feet from I-105 and minutes from I-405, a tour of Watts Towers makes a nice break from Los Angeles' crowded freeways.

919 S. Grand Ave., Ste. 250, 213/623-5821, http://fidmmuseum.org, 10am-5pm Tues.-Sat., free) are open to the public, giving costume buffs and clotheshorses a window into high fashion and Hollywood costume design. FIDM pulls from its collection of more than 10,000 costumes and textiles to create exhibits based on style, era, movie genre, and whatever else the curators dream up. Parking is available in the underground garage for a fee. When you enter the building, tell the folks at the security desk that you're headed for the museum. A small but fun museum shop offers student work, unique accessories, and more.

Natural History Museum of Los Angeles County

If you'd like your kids to have some fun with an educational purpose, take them to the **Natural History Museum of Los Angeles County** (900 Exposition Blvd., 213/763-3466, www.nhm.org, 9:30am-5pm daily, adults $12, students and seniors $9, children $5, parking $10 cash only). This huge museum features many amazing galleries; some are transformed into examples of mammal habitats, while others display artifacts of various peoples indigenous to the Western Hemisphere. The Discovery Center welcomes children with a wide array of live animals and insects, plus hands-on displays that let kids learn by touching as well as looking. Admission to the Butterfly Pavilion and special exhibits costs extra.

★ California Science Center

The **California Science Center** (700

Exposition Park Dr., 323/724-3623, www.californiasciencecenter.org, 10am-5pm daily, admission free, parking $10) focuses on the notable achievements and gathered knowledge of humankind. There are many interactive exhibits here, including one that lets visitors "lift" a giant truck off the ground. The Ecosystems section showcases 11 different natural environments, such as a living kelp forest and a polar ice wall.

One major reason people come to the California Science Center is to view the last of NASA's space shuttles, the *Endeavour*. The 132-foot-long shuttle hangs on display in a pavilion and eventually will be shown in its launch position. To see the shuttle exhibit, reserve a timed entry by calling (213/744-2019) or going online (www.californiasciencecenter.org).

Many people also come to the California Science Center for the **IMAX theater** (213/744-2019, adults $8.50, seniors, teens, and students, $6.25, children $5.25), which shows educational films on its tremendous seven-story screen. Your IMAX ticket also gets you onto the rideable attractions of the Science Court.

LOS FELIZ AND SILVER LAKE

East of Hollywood and northwest of downtown, Los Feliz ("loss FEEL-is") is home to an eclectic mix of retired professionals, Armenian immigrants, and movie-industry hipsters lured by the bohemian vibe, midcentury modern architecture, and the neighborhood's proximity to Griffith Park.

★ Griffith Park

Griffith Park (Los Feliz Blvd., Zoo Dr., or Griffith Park Blvd., 323/913-4688, www.laparks.org, 5am-10:30pm daily, free) is the country's largest municipal park with an urban wilderness area. Griffith Park has also played host to many production companies over the years, with its land and buildings providing backdrops for many major films. Scenes from *Rebel Without a Cause* were filmed here, as were parts of the first two *Back to the Future* movies.

If you love the night skies, visit the **Griffith Observatory** (2800 E. Observatory Rd., 213/473-0800, www.griffithobservatory.org, noon-10pm Tues.-Fri., 10am-10pm Sat.-Sun., free), where free telescopes are available and experienced demonstrators help visitors gaze

Griffith Observatory

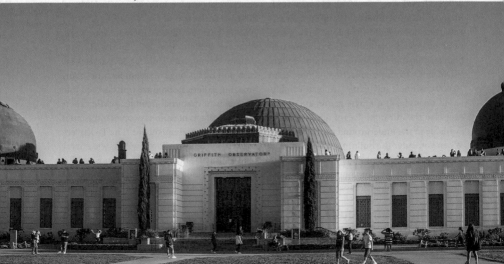

at the stars. Or take in a film about the earth or sky in the aluminum-domed **Samuel Oschin Planetarium** (www.griffithobservatory.org for showtimes, $3-7).

If you prefer a more structured park experience, try the **L.A. Zoo and Botanical Gardens** (5333 Zoo Dr., 323/644-4200, www.lazoo.org, 10am-5pm daily, adults $20, seniors $17, children $15, parking free), where you can view elephants, rhinos, and gorillas. If the weather is poor, step inside **The Autry National Center of the American West** (4700 Western Heritage Way, 323/667-2000, www.theautry.org, 10am-4pm Tues.-Fri., 10am-5pm Sat.-Sun., adults $14, students and seniors $10, children $6), which showcases artifacts of the American West.

Kids love riding the trains of the operating miniature railroad at both the **Travel Town Railroad** (5200 Zoo Dr., 323/662-9678, www.griffithparktrainrides.com, 10am-3:15pm Mon.-Fri., 10am-4:45pm Sat.-Sun. summer, 10am-3:15pm Mon.-Fri., 10am-4:15pm Sat.-Sun. winter, $2.75), which runs the perimeter of the **Travel Town Museum** (5200 Zoo Dr., 323/662-5874, www.traveltown.org, 10am-5pm Mon.-Fri., 10am-6pm Sat.-Sun. summer, 10am-4pm Mon.-Fri., 10am-6pm Sat.-Sun. winter, free), and the **Griffith Park & Southern Railroad** (4730 Crystal Springs Rd., www.griffithparktrainrides.com, 10am-4:45pm Mon.-Fri., 10am-5pm Sat.-Sun. summer, 10am-4:15pm Mon.-Fri., 10am-4:30pm Sat.-Sun. winter, adults and children $2.75, seniors $2.25), which takes riders on a one-mile track.

The **Hollywood Sign** sits on Mount Lee, which is part of the park and indelibly part of the mystique of Hollywood. A strenuous five-mile hike will lead you to an overlook just above and behind the sign. To get there, drive to the top of Beachwood Drive, park, and follow the Hollyridge Trail.

HOLLYWOOD

You won't find blocks of movie studios in Hollywood, and few stars walk its streets except on premiere evenings. But still, if you've ever had a soft spot for Hollywood glamour or American camp, come and check out the crowds and bustle of downtown Tinseltown (and be aware that no local would *ever* call it that). Hollywood is also famous for its street corners. While the most stuff sits at Hollywood and Highland, the best-known corner is certainly Hollywood and Vine.

★ Hollywood Walk of Fame

One of the most recognizable facets of Hollywood is its star-studded **Walk of Fame** (Hollywood Blvd. from La Brea Ave. to Vine St., www.walkoffame.com). This area, portrayed in countless movies, contains more than 2,500 five-pointed stars honoring both real people and fictional characters that have contributed significantly to the entertainment industry and the Hollywood legend. Each pink star is set in a charcoal-colored square and has its honoree's name in bronze. Eight stars were laid in August 1958 to demonstrate what the walk would look like. Legal battles delayed the actual construction until February 1960, and the walk was dedicated in November 1960. At each of the four corners of Hollywood and Vine is a moon that honors the three Apollo 11 astronauts: Neil Armstrong, Michael Collins, and Edwin E. "Buzz" Aldrin Jr. At the edges of the Walk of Fame, you'll find blank stars waiting to be filled by up-and-comers making their mark on Tinseltown.

The complete walk is about 3.5 miles. You'll be looking down at the stars, so watch out for other pedestrians crowding the sidewalks in this visitor-dense area. Careful reading of the information on the Walk of Fame website (www.walkoffame.com) should help you find every star you need to see.

Hollywood Wax Museum

It immortalizes your favorite stars, all right. If you want to see the Hollywood heavyweights all dressed up in costume and completely unable to run away, visit the **Hollywood Wax Museum** (6767 Hollywood Blvd., 323/462-5991, www.hollywoodwaxmuseum.com,

Hollywood

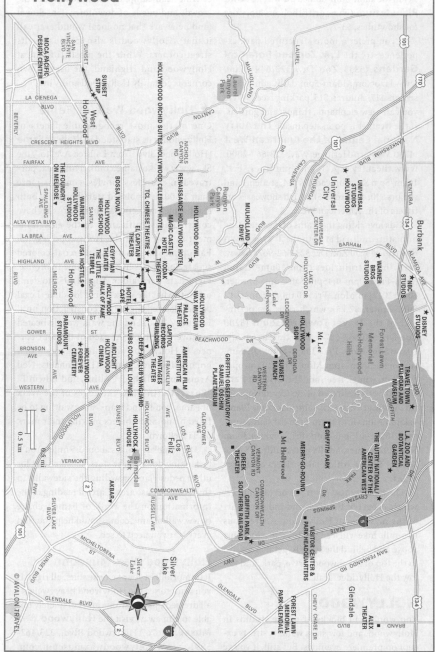

Film Festivals

Home of Hollywood and many of the world's most famous movie stars, Los Angeles is an ideal place to go to the movies. It's even better when you can attend a film festival.

There seems to be an endless array of film festivals in the Los Angeles area. Cofounded by actor Danny Glover, the **Pan African Film and Arts Festival** (310/337-4737, www.paff.org) takes place in February and highlights the works of people of African descent from all over the world.

Movies often debut at the **Los Angeles Film Festival** (866/345-6337, www.filmindependent.org). The LAFF happens in June and includes the screening of 100 films.

Outfest (213/480-7088, www.outfest.org) is the oldest continuous film festival in Los Angeles, and it highlights LBGT-oriented movies in July.

The **Downtown L.A. Film Festival** (www.dtlaff.com), which also happens in July, is for filmgoers who enjoy under-the-radar indie cinema.

The **Sundance Next Fest** (www.sundance.org/next) is a worthy addition to the L.A. film scene. This unique summer fest in August includes movie premieres and concerts by musical acts.

The nonprofit American Film Institute plays some of the biggest pictures of the year at its November **AFI Fest** (866/234-3378, www.afi.com). Come to see what are sure to be some of the year's most talked-about movies.

9am-midnight Sun.-Thurs., 9am-1am Fri.-Sat., adults $23, children 4-11 $13, children under 4 free). The exhibits are re-creations of the sets of all sorts of films, and as you pass through, you'll be right in the action (if staring at eerie, life-size wax likenesses of real people can be called action). You can even get a glimpse of stars on the red carpet at an awards show-style set. Save a dollar by purchasing a ticket online.

TCL Chinese Theatre

You can't miss the **TCL Chinese Theatre** (6925 Hollywood Blvd., 323/461-3331, www.tclchinesetheatres.com) on Hollywood Boulevard. With its elaborate 90-foot-tall Chinese temple gateway and unending crowd of visitors, the Chinese Theatre may be the most visited and recognizable movie theater in the world. Along with the throngs of tourists out front, there are usually elaborately costumed movie characters, from Captain Jack Sparrow to Spider-Man, shaking hands with fans and posing for pictures (for a fee). Inside the courtyard, you'll find handprints and footprints of legendary Hollywood stars. Stop and admire the bells, dogs, and other artifacts in the courtyard; most are the genuine article, imported from China by special permit in the 1920s.

The studios hold premieres here all the time. Check the website for showtimes and ticket information. The Chinese Theatre has only one screen, but seats over 1,000 people per showing. Daily 20-minute **tours** (323/463-9576 or tours@chinesetheatres.com for tickets, adults $18, seniors $14, children $6) featuring anecdotes about the fabled theater are available with a reservation. While you're welcome to crowd the sidewalk to try to catch a glimpse of the stars at a premiere, most of these are private events.

Egyptian Theater

Built under the auspices of the legendary Sid Grauman, the **Egyptian Theater** (6712 Hollywood Blvd., 323/466-3456, www.americancinemathequecalendar.com, adults $12, students and seniors $10) was the first of the grandiose movie houses in Hollywood proper and a follower of those in downtown Los Angeles. King Tut's tomb had been discovered in 1922, and the glorified Egyptian styling of the theater followed the trend for all things Egyptian that came after. The massive courtyard and the stage both boast columns and sphinxes. The first movie to premiere here was *Robin Hood*, in 1922.

Today, get tickets to an array of old-time films, film festivals, and double features, or take a morning tour to get a glimpse of the history of this magnificent theater. Expect to pay $5-20 for parking in one of the nearby lots.

Hollywood Forever Cemetery

The final resting place of such Hollywood legends as Rudolph Valentino, Marion Davies, Douglas Fairbanks, and Johnny Ramone, the **Hollywood Forever Cemetery** (6000 Santa Monica Blvd., 323/469-1181, www. hollywoodforever.com, 8:30am-5:30pm daily summer, 8:30am-5pm daily winter) has received a dramatic makeover and now offers live funeral webcasts. During the summer, the cemetery screens films and holds concerts by national touring acts on its Fairbanks Lawn and in its Masonic Lodge. Visit the website for a list of upcoming events.

Paramount Studios

Paramount Studios (5515 Melrose Ave., 323/956-1777, www.paramountstudiotour. com, tours $58-178) is the only major movie studio still operating in Hollywood proper. The wrought-iron gates that greet visitors were

erected to deter adoring Rudolph Valentino fans in the 1920s. Tours ranging 2-4.5 hours are available. Visit the website or call the studio for tour information.

Mulholland Drive

As you drive north out of central Hollywood into the residential part of the neighborhood, you will find folks on street corners hawking maps of stars' homes on **Mulholland Drive** (entrance west of U.S. 101 via Barham Blvd. exit) and its surrounding neighborhoods. Whether you choose to pay up to $10 for a photocopied sheet of dubious information is up to you. What's certain is that you can drive the famed road yourself. When you reach the ridge, you'll see why so many of the wealthy make their homes here. From the ridgeline, on clear days you can see down into the Los Angeles Basin and the coast to the west, and the fertile land of the San Fernando Valley to the east. Whether you care about movie-star homes or not, the view itself is worth the trip, especially if it has rained recently and the smog is down.

Universal Studios Hollywood

The longtime Hollywood-centric

view from Mulholland Drive

alternative to Disneyland is the **Universal Studios Hollywood** (100 Universal City Plaza, Los Angeles, 800/864-8377, www.universalstudios.com, hours vary, $105-116) theme park. (Save up to $10 by getting tickets online.) Kids adore this park, which puts them right into the action of their favorite movies. Flee the carnivorous dinosaurs of *Jurassic Park*, take a rafting adventure on the pseudo-set of *Waterworld*, quiver in terror of an ancient curse in *Revenge of the Mummy*, or explore the magic of Hogwarts Castle in the *Wizarding World of Harry Potter*. You can also experience the shape-shifting Transformers in a ride based on the movies and the Hasbro toy.

If you're more interested in how the movies are made than the rides made from them, take the Studio Tour with a recorded Jimmy Fallon as host. You'll get an extreme close-up of the sets of major blockbuster films like *War of the Worlds*. Better yet, get tickets at the Audiences Unlimited Ticket Booth and be part of the studio audience of TV shows currently taping. Serious movie buffs can get a VIP pass for $329; a six-hour tour takes you onto working sound stages and into the current prop warehouse.

LA BREA, FAIRFAX, AND MIRACLE MILE

Lined with fabric emporiums, antiques dealers, and contemporary furniture design shops, Beverly Boulevard and La Brea Avenue north of Wilshire Boulevard are increasingly trendy haunts for interior decorators. Along bustling and pedestrian-friendly Fairfax Avenue, kosher bakeries and signs in Hebrew announce the presence of the neighborhood's sizable Jewish population. Around the corner on 3rd Street, The Original Farmers Market is one of L.A.'s historic gathering places. And farther south, Wilshire Boulevard is home to some of the city's many museums, including the Los Angeles County Museum of Art.

La Brea Tar Pits

Nothing can stop the smell of the **La Brea Tar Pits,** where untold thousands of animals became trapped in the sticky tar and met their ancient fate. Paved paths lead around the most accessible pits, while others (mostly those that are in active excavation) are accessible by guided tour only. If what interests you most are the fossilized contents, head for the beautiful **La Brea Tar Pits Museum** (5801 Wilshire Blvd., 213/763-3499, www.

La Brea Tar Pits Museum

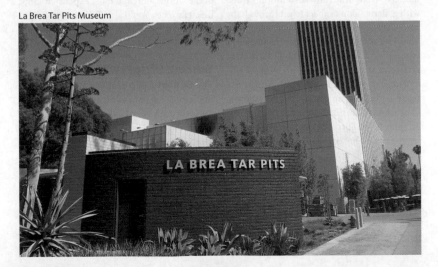

tarpits.org, 9:30am-5pm daily, adults $12, students and seniors $9, children $5, parking $10). The museum's reasonably small size and easy-to-understand interpretive signs make it great for kids. Genuine mammoths died and were fossilized in the tar pits, as were the tiniest of mice and about a zillion dire wolves. For a closer look at how the fossils were buried, get tickets to one of the **Excavator Tours** (noon, 1pm, 2pm, and 3pm daily, free with museum ticket), which are available online.

Los Angeles County Museum of Art

Travelers who desperately need a break from the endless, shiny, and mindless entertainments of L.A. can find respite and solace in the **Los Angeles County Museum of Art** (5905 Wilshire Blvd., 323/857-6000, www.lacma.org, 11am-5pm Mon.-Tues. and Thurs., 11am-8pm Fri., 10am-7pm Sat.-Sun., adults $15, seniors and students with ID $10, children under 17 free), the largest art museum in the western United States. Better known to its friends as LACMA, this museum complex prides itself on a diverse array of collections and exhibitions of art from around the world, from ancient to modern. With nine full-size buildings filled with galleries, don't expect to get through the whole thing in an hour, or even a full day. You'll see all forms of art, from classic painting and sculpture to all sorts of decorative arts (that is, ceramics, jewelry, metalwork, and more). All major cultural groups are represented, so you can check out Islamic, Southeast Asian, European, and Californian art, plus more. Specialties of LACMA include Japanese art and artifacts in the beautifully designed Pavilion for Japanese Art, and the costumes and textiles of the Doris Stein Research Center. Several galleries of LACMA West are dedicated to arts and crafts for children. Perhaps best of all, some of the world's most prestigious traveling exhibitions come to LACMA.

The 120,000 objects at LACMA include pieces by Andy Warhol, David Hockney, and Roy Lichtenstein. Head outdoors for Chris Burden's *Urban Light*, a forest of street lamps, and Michael Heizer's *Levitated Mass*, a giant boulder displayed above a sunken walkway. Moving the rock to its current home was such a feat that it is documented in the 2013 film *Levitated Mass*.

Farmers Market

Begun in 1934 as a tailgate co-op for a handful of fruit farmers, **The Original Farmers Market** (6333 W. 3rd St., 323/933-9211 or 866/993-9211, www.farmersmarketla.com, 9am-9pm Mon.-Fri., 9am-8pm Sat., 10am-7pm Sun.) remains a favorite locale for shopping and people-watching. Along with the adjacent shopping center, The Grove, there are now more than 30 restaurants and 50 shops hawking everything from hot sauce to stickers. Annual events include free summer concerts every Friday.

BEVERLY HILLS AND WEST HOLLYWOOD

Although the truly wealthy live above Hollywood on Mulholland Drive, in Bel Air, or on the beach in Malibu, there's still plenty of money floating around Beverly Hills. Some of the world's best and most expensive shops line its streets. You'll also find plenty of high-end culture in this area, which bleeds into West L.A.

Sunset Strip

The **Sunset Strip** really is part of Sunset Boulevard—specifically the part that runs 1.5 miles through West Hollywood from the edge of Hollywood to the Beverly Hills city limits. The Strip exemplifies all that's grandiose and tacky about the L.A. entertainment industry. You'll also find many of the Strip's legendary rock clubs, such as **The Roxy** and the **Whisky a Go Go** and the infamous after-hours hangout the **Rainbow Bar & Grill.** Over several decades, up-and-coming rock acts first made their names on the Strip and lived at the "Riot Hyatt."

WESTWOOD

Designed around the campus of UCLA and the Westwood Village commercial district, this community situated between Santa Monica and Beverly Hills won national recognition in the 1930s as a model of innovative suburban planning.

University of California, Los Angeles

From its original quad of 10 buildings, the campus of the **University of California, Los Angeles** (UCLA, bounded by Hilgard Ave., Sunset Blvd., Le Conte Ave., and Gayley Ave., tours available at https://connect.admission.ucla.edu/portal/tours, www.ucla.edu) has become the largest in the University of California system, with more than 400 buildings set on and around 419 beautifully kept acres. Today its facilities include one of the top medical centers in the country, a library of more than eight million volumes, and renowned performance venues, including **Royce Hall** and **Schoenberg Hall.**

★ The Getty Center

Located on a hilltop above the mansions of Brentwood and the 405 freeway, **The Getty Center** (1200 Sepulveda Blvd., 310/440-7300, www.getty.edu, 10am-5:30pm Sun. and Tues.-Thurs., 10am-9pm Fri.-Sat. summer, 10am-5:30pm Sun. and Tues.-Fri., 10am-9pm Sat. winter, admission free, parking $15) is famous for art and culture in Los Angeles. Donated by the family of J. Paul Getty to the people of Los Angeles, this museum features European art, sculpture, manuscripts, and European and American photos. The magnificent works are set in fabulous modern buildings with soaring architecture, and you're guaranteed to find something beautiful to catch your eye and feed your imagination. The spacious galleries have comfy sofas to let you sit back and take in the paintings and drawings. There are frequent temporary exhibitions on diverse subjects. Take a stroll outdoors to admire the sculpture collections on the lawns as well as the exterior architecture.

On a clear day, the views from The Getty, which sweep from downtown L.A. clear west to the Pacific, are remarkable. But the museum pavilions themselves are also stunning. Richard Meier's striking design is multi-textured, with exterior grids of metal and unfinished Italian travertine marble. The blockish buildings have fountains, glass windows several stories high, and an open plan that permits intimate vistas of the city below. A stroll through the gardens is a must.

Pierce Brothers Westwood Village Memorial Park

The **Pierce Brothers Westwood Village Memorial Park** (1218 Glendon Ave., 310/474-1579, www.dignitymemorial.com, 8am-6pm daily) is the final resting place of some of the world's most popular entertainers and musicians. Under the shadows of the towering high-rises of Wilshire Boulevard, this small cemetery is the home of **Marilyn Monroe's crypt** (frequently decorated with lipstick marks), as well as Rat Packer **Dean Martin,** author **Truman Capote,** eclectic musician **Frank Zappa,** and the stars of *The Odd Couple,* **Walter Matthau** and **Jack Lemmon.**

SANTA MONICA, VENICE, AND MALIBU

Some of the most famous and most expensive real estate in the world sits on this stretch of sand and earth. Of the communities that call the northern coast of L.A. County home, the focal points are Malibu to the north, Santa Monica, and Venice to the south.

★ Santa Monica Pier

For the ultimate in SoCal beach kitsch, you can't miss the **Santa Monica Pier** (Ocean Ave. at Colorado Ave., 310/458-8901, www.santamonicapier.org, hours vary). As you walk the rather long stretch of concrete out over the water, you'll see an amazing array of carnival-style food stands, an arcade, a small amusement park, a trapeze school, and

Santa Monica, Venice, and Malibu

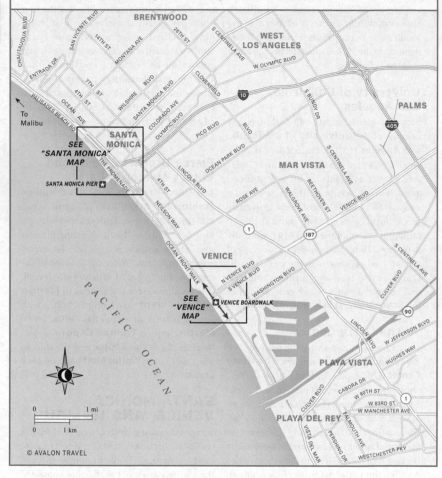

© AVALON TRAVEL

restaurants leading out to the fishing area at the tip of the pier. There's even an aquarium under the pier. The main attraction is **Pacific Park** (310/260-8744, www.pacpark.com, hours vary, $5-10 per ride, all-ride pass $16-30, parking $6-15). This park features a roller coaster, a Scrambler, and the world's first solar-powered Ferris wheel. Several rides are geared for the younger set, and a 20-game midway offers fun for all ages. Free **historic walking tours** (11am-noon Sat.-Sun.) leave from the Pier Shop.

★ Venice Boardwalk

If the Santa Monica Pier doesn't provide you with enough chaos and kitsch, head on down to the **Venice Boardwalk** (Ocean Front Walk at Venice Blvd., 310/396-6764, www.venicebeach.com) for a nearly unlimited supply of both year-round. As you shamble down the tourist-laden path, you'll pass an astonishing array of tacky souvenir stores, tattoo and piercing parlors, walk-up food stands, and more. On the beach side of the path, dozens of artists create sculptures and hawk their wares. This area

Santa Monica

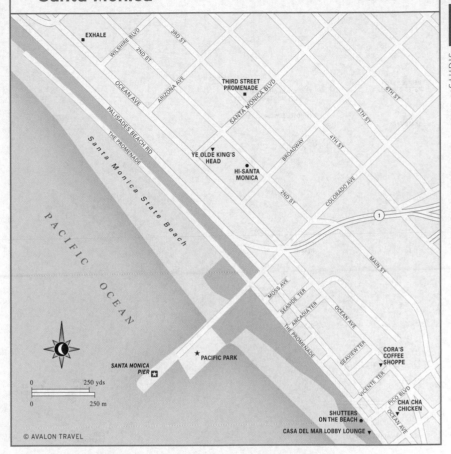

has more than its share of L.A.'s colorful characters, including some who perform for tips. The beach side includes the famous **Muscle Beach** (2 blocks north of Venice Blvd., www. musclebeach.net), an easily distinguishable chunk of sand filled with modern workout equipment and encircled by a barrier, and the **Venice Skate Park** (1500 Ocean Front Walk, 310/650-3255, www.veniceskatepark.com), where skaters get some serious air.

Venice Canals

Take a sedate walk along the paths of the **Venice Canals** (bounded by Washington Blvd., Strongs Dr., S. Venice Blvd., and Ocean Ave.), where locals take a stroll or walk their dogs (Venice is a very dog-oriented town), and enjoy the serenity and peace of the quiet waterways. The home gardens and city-maintained landscaping add a lush layer of greenery to the narrow canals. These paths get you deep into the neighborhood and close to the impressive 20th-century Southern California architecture of Venice.

Malibu Pier

One of Malibu's few sights besides the sand and surf, the **Malibu Pier** (23000 Pacific

Venice

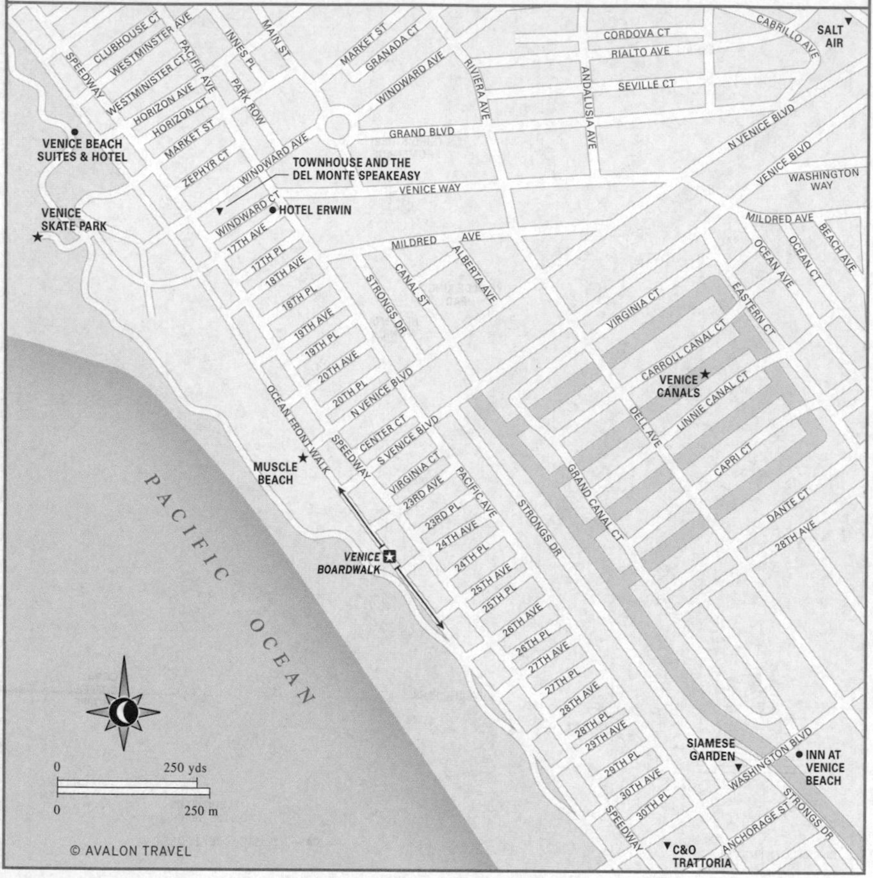

Map labels: CLUBHOUSE CT, WESTMINSTER AVE, MAIN ST, MARKET ST, GRANADA CT, CORDOVA CT, CABRILLO AVE, SALT AIR, SPEEDWAY, WESTMINSTER CT, PACIFIC CT, IRNES PL, PARK ROW, WINDWARD AVE, RIVIERA AVE, RIALTO AVE, HORIZON AVE, PACIFIC AVE, SEVILLE CT, HORIZON CT, ANDALUSIA AVE, VENICE BEACH SUITES & HOTEL, MARKET ST, GRAND BLVD, N VENICE BLVD, ZEPHYR CT, WINDWARD AVE, TOWNHOUSE AND THE DEL MONTE SPEAKEASY, VENICE BLVD, WASHINGTON WAY, VENICE WAY, VENICE SKATE PARK, WINDWARD CT, HOTEL ERWIN, MILDRED AVE, OCEAN AVE, BEACH AVE, 17TH PL, 17TH AVE, MILDRED AVE, ALBERTA AVE, OCEAN CT, 18TH PL, 18TH AVE, STRONGS DR, CANAL ST, VIRGINIA CT, EASTERN CT, 19TH PL, 19TH AVE, 20TH PL, 20TH AVE, N VENICE BLVD, VENICE CANALS, CARROLL CANAL CT, LINNIE CANAL CT, CAPRI CT, CENTER CT, S VENICE BLVD, DEL CAVE, MUSCLE BEACH, OCEAN FRONT WALK, SPEEDWAY, VIRGINIA CT, 23RD AVE, PACIFIC AVE, GRAND CANAL CT, DANTE CT, 23RD PL, VENICE BOARDWALK, 24TH PL, 24TH AVE, STRONGS DR, 28TH AVE, 25TH PL, 25TH AVE, 26TH PL, 26TH AVE, 27TH PL, 27TH AVE, 28TH PL, 28TH AVE, 29TH AVE, SIAMESE GARDEN, WASHINGTON BLVD, INN AT VENICE BEACH, 29TH PL, 30TH AVE, 30TH PL, SPEEDWAY, ANCHORAGE ST, STRONGS DR, C&O TRATTORIA

PACIFIC OCEAN

0   250 yds
0   250 m

© AVALON TRAVEL

Coast Hwy., http://malibupier.com, 6:30am-sunset daily) gets busy in the summer and lonely in the winter, when only die-hard surfers ply the adjacent three-point break and a few anglers brave the chilly solitude. Interpretive signs describe the history of Malibu amid the food stands and sport-fishing and whale-watching charters. A surf museum is planned in the near future. If you'd prefer to hit the waves yourself, you can rent boards and other beach toys.

The Getty Villa

Even driving up to **The Getty Villa** (17985 Pacific Coast Hwy., Pacific Palisades, 310/440-7300, www.getty.edu, 10am-5pm Sun.-Mon. and Wed.-Fri., 10am-9pm Sat. summer, 10am-5pm Wed.-Mon. winter, reservations required, admission free, parking $15) on its Roman-inspired stone driveway will send you back to ancient times. The two-floor villa is modeled after a Roman country house that was buried by the AD 79 eruption of Mount Vesuvius. The architecture and surrounding gardens are a fitting environment for the 1,200 works of art inside, including intact statues and jewelry. Tickets are free, but require advance reservations.

Entertainment and Events

NIGHTLIFE
Bars

Whatever your taste in bars, whether it tends toward hipster dives, old-school watering holes, or beautiful lounges, L.A. can offer its version.

DOWNTOWN

For a money dive bar experience, head to **Crane's Downtown Bar** (810 S. Spring St., 323/787-9966, 5pm-2am Mon.-Thurs., 4pm-2am Fri., 2pm-2am Sat.-Sun.), located inside a former bank vault. There's the occasional DJ spinning and comedy on the second Monday of the month. Next door inside the basement of the NCT Building is the Peking Tavern, if you get hungry for creative dumplings.

At **Seven Grand** (512 W. 7th St., 213/614-0736, http://213hospitality.com/sevengrandla/, 4pm-2am Sun.-Wed., 3pm-2am Thurs.-Sat.), dapper bartenders steer you to the right fermented grain mash—commonly referred to as whiskey. Enjoy it while playing pool, watching live music, or sitting under deer heads mounted on the walls. Deep inside Seven Grand, the exclusive 18-seat **Bar Jackalope** (7pm-2am Sun.-Thurs.) zeroes in on Japanese whiskies.

Under a sign touting breakfast foods, the unassuming **Ham & Eggs Tavern** (433 W. 8th St., http://hamandeggstavern.com, 5pm-midnight Mon.-Thurs., 5pm-2am Fri.-Sat.) serves can beers and wine in one room and hosts music acts next door. The tiny stage has hosted larger-than-expected acts including Nick Waterhouse, The Gooch Palms, and Avi Buffalo.

It may not be as hip as it once was, but the **Golden Gopher** (417 W. 8th St., 213/614-8001, http://213hospitality.com/goldengopher, 5pm-2am daily) jump-started downtown nightlife. It's still a great place to enjoy a drink, with a smoking patio and a liquor store on the premises for bottles to go.

KOREATOWN

R Bar (3331 W. 8th St., 213/387-7227, 7pm-2am Mon.-Tues., 5pm-2am Wed.-Fri., 11am-2am Sat.-Sun.) doesn't look like much from the outside except a dingy corner building with a gold "R" affixed to it. But inside this speakeasy (the password can be found on the bar's Facebook page or on their Twitter page) oozes debauched gothic Victorian decor and a range of events including live music, DJs, storytellers, and karaoke on Wednesday, Thursday, and Sunday nights. There's good beer on tap, cocktails, and a weekly brunch touted by L.A. Weekly as well.

A hidden bar within the Hotel Normandie, **The Walker Inn** (3612 W. 6th St., 213/263-2709, www.thewalkerinnla.com, 6pm-2am Tues.-Sun.) delivers a cocktail tasting menu curated by talented bartenders. Make an advance reservation to ensure you will be one of just 27 guests.

SILVER LAKE AND ECHO PARK

In hip Silver Lake, **The Thirsty Crow** (2939 W. Sunset Blvd., 323/661-6007, www.thirstycrowbar.com, 5pm-2am Mon.-Sat., 2pm-2am Sun.) is a neighborhood bar with 100 different kinds of whiskey, including over 60 small-batch bourbons and a friendly happy hour (5pm-8pm Mon.-Fri., 2pm-8pm Sat.-Sun.).

Echo Park's beer lovers flock to the **Sunset Beer Company** (1498 W. Sunset Blvd., 213/481-2337, www.sunsetbeercompany.com, store hours noon-11pm Mon.-Thurs., noon-midnight Fri.-Sat., noon-10pm Sun.; bar hours 4pm-11pm Mon.-Thurs., 1pm-midnight Fri.-Sat., 1pm-10pm Sun.), an intimate space well-stocked with the latest craft brews from California and beyond. Sip your suds inside over board games or books or outside on a smoker's patio.

BEVERLY HILLS AND WEST HOLLYWOOD

Hit the **Rainbow Bar & Grill** (9015 W. Sunset Blvd., 310/278-4232, www.rainbowbarandgrill.com, 11am-2am daily, cover charge varies) to see an amazing myriad of rock-and-roll memorabilia and get a taste of music history. A group of musicians known as the "Hollywood Vampires," which included Alice Cooper, Keith Moon, John Lennon, Ringo Starr, Harry Nilsson, and Micky Dolenz, congregated here in the 1970s. Today, rockers still drop in after playing shows in the neighborhood. The crowds trickle in as the sun goes down; by the time the shows let out at the nearby Roxy and Whisky a Go Go, your chances of finding a booth diminish significantly. The back rooms also open up late, for dancing, drinking, and smoking (*sh!*). To the surprise of some diners, the hallowed haven also serves a tasty cheeseburger, available until 2am.

They say that Courtney Love used to dance at **Jumbo's Clown Room** (5153 Hollywood Blvd., 323/666-1187, http://jumbos.com, 4pm-2am daily), a one-of-a-kind dive bar with a blood-red interior and a circus theme. They also say David Lynch was inspired to write a section of his film *Blue Velvet* after a visit here.

Located in the Sunset Tower Hotel, **The Tower Bar** (8358 Sunset Blvd., 323/654-7100, www.sunsettowerhotel.com, 6pm-11pm Sun.-Thurs., 6pm-11:30pm Fri.-Sat.) offers a glimpse of old Hollywood. Mobster Bugsy Siegel once had an apartment here. Today, it has walnut-paneled walls, a fireplace, and dim lighting so that celebrities can keep their cool.

Across from the Chateau Marmont, **The Den on Sunset** (8226 W. Sunset Blvd., 323/656-0336, www.thedenonsunset.com, 5pm-2am Mon.-Fri., 3pm-2am Sat., 10am-2am Sun.) has an outside fire pit, while inside there is a collection of board games including Rock 'Em, Sock 'Em Robots. Some nights have DJs and karaoke.

SANTA MONICA, VENICE, AND MALIBU

In Venice beach, head to the **Townhouse and the Del Monte Speakeasy** (52 Windward Ave., Venice Beach, 310/392-4040, www.townhousevenice.com, 5pm-2am Mon.-Thurs., 2pm-2am Fri., noon-2am Sat.-Sun.). Upstairs, enjoy the candlelit tables and pool table of the oldest bar in Venice. Downstairs, the speakeasy is a cellar space that hosts jazz bands, DJs, and comedians.

Casa del Mar Lobby Lounge (1910 Ocean Way, Santa Monica, 310/581-5533, www.hotelcasadelmar.com, 3pm-midnight Sun.-Thurs., 3pm-1:30am Fri.-Sat.) is a dramatic real-life sandcastle on Santa Monica State Beach. Enjoy beautiful ocean views, glittering mosaics, marble floors, romantic piano music, and perhaps the most elegant cocktails in the city.

Also in Santa Monica, **Ye Olde King's Head** (116 Santa Monica Blvd., Santa Monica, 310/451-1402, www.yeoldekingshead.com, 10am-2am daily) is a British pub, restaurant, and gift shop that stretches down a long half block. Crowds of imbibing patrons visit from far and near.

Clubs

Which of the many dance and nightclubs in the L.A. area is the hottest, hippest, or most popular with the stars this week? Ask the locals or check the alternative weekly papers when you arrive. Clubs get crowded on weekend nights, and bouncers take joy in allowing only the chicest hipsters into the sacred spaces beyond the doors. Being young and beautiful helps, of course, as does being dressed in the latest designer fashions.

For those in the know, **Karma Lounge** (3954 Beverly Blvd., 213/375-7141, http://karmarestaurantgroup.com, 5pm-1am Tues.-Thurs., 5pm-2am Fri.-Sat., 10am-9pm Sun.) in Koreatown is a worthy stop for drinks or dancing. Burlesque shows alternate with frequent DJs who spin everything from industrial to Latin. They also serve small plates if you need some fuel.

Dance to world-famous DJs under pulsating lights, falling confetti, or floating bubbles at **Create** (6021 Hollywood Blvd., 323/463-3331, http://sbe.com, 10pm-close Fri.-Sat.). You may catch Kaskade or Afrojack on the turntables at this weekend-only dance club.

The **Three Clubs Cocktail Lounge** (1123 Vine St., Hollywood, 323/462-6441, www.threeclubs.com, 5pm-2am daily, no cover) acts both as a locals' watering hole and a reasonably priced nightclub catering mostly to the collegiate set. Expect to find the dance floor of the rear club crowded and sweaty, with modern dance mixes blaring out over the crush of writhing bodies. Two bars serve up drinks to the masses, and drinks are cheaper here than in the hotter spots. Three Clubs has no decent parking, so you may have to walk several blocks along Hollywood Boulevard long after dark. Bring friends along for safety.

Gay and Lesbian

Sleek, glamorous, and candlelit, **The Abbey Food & Bar** (692 N. Robertson Blvd., West Hollywood, 310/289-8410, www.theabbeyweho.com, 11am-2am Mon.-Thurs., 10am-2am Fri., 9am-2am Sat.-Sun.) is a popular bar with a great outdoor patio and pillow-strewn private cabanas, all of which are usually jam-packed. Savvy bartenders mix 22 different specialty martinis in flavors that include chocolate banana and Creamsicle.

Every Thursday night, **Avalon Hollywood** (1735 Vine St., Hollywood, 323/462-8900, https://avalonhollywood.com, 10pm-3am Thurs., 9:30pm-5am Fri., 9:30pm-8am Sat.) hosts **TigerHeat,** which is said to be the West Coast's largest gay event. Lady GaGa, Britney Spears, and Elton John have made appearances in the club.

An alternative to glammed-up West Hollywood bars, Silver Lake's **Akbar** (4356 Sunset Blvd., 323/665-6810, www.akbarsilverlake.com, 4pm-2am daily) pulls in a gay-friendly crowd with its cozy Moroccan-themed decor, neighborhood vibe, and friendly, unpretentious bartenders.

Live Music

The clubs on the Sunset Strip incubated some of the biggest rock acts of all time. The **Whisky a Go Go** (8901 Sunset Blvd., West Hollywood, 310/652-4202, www.whiskyagogo.com, cover from $10) helped launch The Doors, Mötley Crüe, and Guns N' Roses. Truth be told, it doesn't draw many big names anymore, even though go-go dancers still gyrate on either side of the stage at times. Most nights you'll get a lineup of new bands, sometimes including as many as seven on Tuesday's "Ultimate Jam Night."

Almost next door, **The Roxy Theatre** (9009 Sunset Blvd., West Hollywood, 310/278-9457, www.theroxy.com, cover charge varies) opened in 1973 with a Neil Young performance. Bob Marley, Patti Smith, and Bruce Springsteen have all recorded live albums here since then. Today, it's still relevant, with acts like J. Roddy Walston and The Business. The big black-box theater has an open dance floor, comfy-ish booths (if you can get one), and bare-bones food service. Street parking is nearly nonexistent, and nearby lots will cost $5-15 or more, so think about public transit or a cab. For one of the best after-hours parties on the Strip, try to get into **On the Rox,** located directly above The Roxy. Or stagger next door to the **Rainbow Bar & Grill** (9015 Sunset Blvd., West Hollywood, 310/278-4232, www.rainbowbarandgrill.com, 11am-2am daily).

It's not on the Strip, but **The Troubadour** (9081 Santa Monica Blvd., West Hollywood, 310/276-1158, www.troubadour.com, ticket prices vary) is just as big and bad as its brethren. Over its more than 50 years, Bob Dylan jammed here, Tom Waits was discovered, and Billy Joel opened for somebody else. Countless A-listers have recorded songs in and even about The Troubadour. Buy tickets online; tickets are available at the on-site box office only on the day of the show—unless it's sold out.

With less history under its belt, **The Echo and Echoplex** (1822 W. Sunset Blvd., Echo Park, 213/413-8200, www.spacelandpresents.

com) hosts a lot of up-and-coming indie acts, along with the occasional big act (TV on the Radio) and some impressive coups, including a performance by the Rolling Stones in 2013. **The Theatre at Ace Hotel** (929 Broadway, 213/623-3233, http://www.acehotel.com/losangeles/theatre) has already hosted big acts like Coldplay. The restored 1,600-seat movie theater from the 1920s features more than just rock shows, including lectures, film festivals, and dance productions.

Proclaimed the city's best music venue by the *L.A. Weekly*, **The Fonda Theatre** (6126 Hollywood Blvd., 323/464-6269, www.fondatheatre.com) can accommodate 1,200 people, which is pretty intimate if you're there for a concert by the Rolling Stones, Radiohead, or Lorde.

Comedy

L.A.'s live comedy scene is second only to Manhattan's. More than a dozen major live comedy clubs make their home in the smog belt. Pick your favorite, sit back, and laugh (or groan) the night away.

Located on the Strip, **The Comedy Store** (8433 Sunset Blvd., West Hollywood, 323/650-6268, www.thecomedystore.com, age 21 and older, $15-20) is owned by comedian Pauly Shore's mother, Mitzi. You'll find a show going on at The Store every night of the week; most start at 9pm or later; check the online calendar. In each of three rooms, you'll find a showcase with more than a dozen stand-ups all performing one after another, leaving space for possible celebrity drop-ins. Steve Martin, Whoopi Goldberg, and Yakov Smirnoff got their start here. Buy tickets online for bigger shows, or at the door for shows that don't sell out. Open mics are at 10pm on Sunday.

Will Ferrell, Kristen Wiig, Lisa Kudrow, and Will Forte are alumni of **The Groundlings Theatre and School** (7307 Melrose Ave., 323/934-4747, www.groundlings.com, prices vary). Get tickets to take in some sketch comedy by up-and-coming talents.

THE ARTS
Theater

Even with all the hoopla over film in L.A., there's still plenty of room for live theatrical entertainment in and around Tinseltown.

In addition to the Academy Awards, the **Dolby Theatre** (6801 Hollywood Blvd., 323/308-6300, www.dolbytheatre.com, box office 10am-5pm Mon.-Sat., 10am-4pm Sun.) hosts various live performances, from ballet to shows from music legends like Bob Dylan. Of course, all shows utilize the theater's state-of-the-art Dolby sound system. Half-hour **tours** (on the half hour 10:30am-4pm daily, adults $23, seniors and children $18) that include a view of an Oscar statuette are available daily.

The **Ford Theater** (2580 Cahuenga Blvd. E., 323/461-3673, www.fordamphitheater.org, box office noon-5pm Tues.-Sun. and 2 hours before evening performances, ticket prices vary) takes advantage of Hollywood's temperate climate to bring the shows outdoors in summer. Every sort of theatrical event imaginable can find a stage at the Ford, from jazz, folk, world music, hip-hop, and dance to spoken word.

The **Ahmanson Theater** (135 N. Grand Ave., 213/628-2772, www.centertheatregroup.org, box office noon-6pm Tues.-Sun. and 2 hours before performances, ticket prices vary) specializes in big Broadway-style productions. You might see a grandiose musical, a heart-wrenching drama, or a gut-busting comedy. Expect to find the titles of classic shows alongside new hits on the schedule. With hundreds of seats (all of them expensive), there's usually enough room to provide entertainment, even for last-minute visitors.

The intimate **Kirk Douglas Theatre** (9820 Washington Blvd., Culver City, 213/628-2772, www.centertheatregroup.org) hosts world premieres and edgy productions like David Mamet's *Race*.

Well-known television actors, including Jason Alexander and Neil Patrick Harris, frequently act in the productions at the **Geffen Playhouse** (10886 Le Conte Ave., 310/208-5454, http://geffenplayhouse.org, ticket prices vary). Some shows developed here move on to Broadway.

Classical Music

Although L.A. is better known for its rock than its classical music offerings, you can still find plenty of high-culture concerts as well. The **Los Angeles Opera** (135 N. Grand Ave., 213/972-8001, www.laopera.org, box office 10am-6pm Tues.-Sat., prices vary) has only existed since 1986 but has grown to become one of the largest opera companies in the United States, gaining national recognition. The dazzling performances are held in the Dorothy Chandler Pavilion at the Music Center of Los Angeles County. Grammy-winning singer Placido Domingo has been the opera's general director since 2003.

Better known to its friends as the L.A. Phil, the **Los Angeles Philharmonic** (111 S. Grand Ave., 323/850-2000 or 323/850-2000, www.laphil.com, prices vary) performs primarily at the **Walt Disney Concert Hall** (111 S. Grand Ave.). Concerts can range from classics by famed composers like Tchaikovsky, Bach, and Beethoven to the world music of Asha Bhosle or jazz by Bobby McFerrin. Guest performers are often the modern virtuosos of classical music.

With its art deco band shell set against canyon chaparral, the **Hollywood Bowl** (2301 N. Highland Ave., 323/850-2000, www.hollywoodbowl.com, box office noon-6pm Tues.-Sun.) has long been a romantic setting for outdoor summer concerts by the L.A. Philharmonic and other artists. It also hosts some rock and pop acts.

The **Los Angeles Doctors Symphony Orchestra** (310/259-9604, http://ladso.org, prices vary) has been performing regularly since its inception in 1953. Many, though not all, of the musicians are members of the medical profession. They play everything from Mozart to Schubert.

Cinema

Crowds throng the streets to see stars tromp down the red carpets for premieres at the **Chinese Theatre** (6925 Hollywood Blvd., 323/461-3331, www.tclchinesetheatres.com) and the **Egyptian Theater** (6712 Hollywood Blvd., 323/466-3456, www.americancinemathequecalendar.com, adults $12, students and seniors $10).

The current favorite movie house for star sightings is the **ArcLight Hollywood Cinema** (6360 W. Sunset Blvd., Hollywood, 323/464-1478, www.arclightcinemas.com), where 21-and-older-only screenings allow patrons include beer and wine on sale. Expect the best visual and sound technologies, all-reserved seating, and the updated geodesic Cinerama Dome theater. Make reservations in advance and ask for parking validation for a discount at the adjacent parking structure.

Acclaimed filmmaker and movie enthusiast Quentin Tarantino owns and programs the **New Beverly Cinema** (7165 Beverly Blvd., 323/938-4038, www.thenewbev.com). The slate of 35-millimeter films include spaghetti westerns, horror films, classics, and selections from the filmmaker's personal collection.

Shopping

DOWNTOWN AND VICINITY

Lovers of the written word should not miss **The Last Bookstore** (453 S. Spring St., 213/488-0599, http://lastbookstorela.com, 10am-10pm Mon.-Thurs., 10am-11pm Fri.-Sat., 10am-9pm Sun.). The 22,000 square feet of new and used books include several art pieces and a tunnel made of books, as well as a space devoted to L.A. writers. A full slate of events includes concerts and author readings.

Anyone can come and stroll the narrow aisles of the world-famous **L.A. Flower District** (700 block of Wall St., 213/622-1966, www.laflowerdistrict.com, 8am-noon Mon. and Wed., 6am-noon Tues. and Thurs., 8am-2pm Fri., 6am-2pm Sat., admission $1-2), where just about every kind of cut flower, potted plant, and exotic species can be purchased. One caution: While the flower market itself is safe for visitors, the area to the south is not. Don't wander the neighborhood on foot.

A mix of modern art galleries and fun, touristy gift shops line the 900 block of **Chung King Road** (http://chungkingroad. wordpress.com/galleries), a one-block stretch of Chinatown. Interior decorators often browse the eclectic selection. It can be quiet during the day, but it comes alive during art-opening evenings.

Located in the Fashion District, **Santee Alley** (between Santee St. and Maple Ave. from Olympic Blvd. to 12th St., www. thesanteealley.com, 9:30am-6pm daily) is a bustling outdoor marketplace crammed in an alley. This is the place for deals on everything from dresses to bathing suits to suitcases to cellphone cases.

LOS FELIZ AND SILVER LAKE

Artsy, hip boutiques, cafés, and restaurants line **Sunset Junction** (Sunset Blvd. from Santa Monica Blvd. to Maltman Ave.), a colorful stretch of Sunset Boulevard concentrated around where Sunset meets Santa Monica Boulevard (or, rather, where Santa Monica Boulevard ends). Weekend mornings bring floods of neighborhood locals down from the hills. This strip is also home to the **Silver Lake Certified Farmers Market** (323/661-7771, 2pm-7:30pm Tues., 9am-1pm Sat.).

The fiercely independent **Skylight Books** (1818 N. Vermont Ave., 323/660-1175, www. skylightbooks.com, 10am-10pm daily) in Los Feliz features alternative literature, literary fiction, Los Angeles-themed books, and an extensive film section. It hosts frequent author events and sells signed books.

HOLLYWOOD

The **Hollywood & Highland Center** (6801 Hollywood Blvd., 323/467-6412 or 323/817-0200, www.hollywoodandhighland.com, 10am-10pm Mon.-Sat., 10am-7pm Sun.) flaunts outlandish architecture that's modeled after the set of the 1916 film *Intolerance*. Stroll amid the more than 70 retail stores and 25 eateries that surround the open-air Babylon Court. Save yourself stress and park in the center's lot ($2 for up to 2 hours with validation).

Encompassing an entire city block and two floors, **Amoeba Music** (6400 Sunset Blvd., 323/245-6400, www.amoeba.com, 10:30am-11pm Mon.-Sat., 11am-10pm Sun.) is the world's largest independent music store. This is the place in L.A. to find that rare record or used CD.

LA BREA, FAIRFAX, AND MIRACLE MILE

The stretch of charming and eclectic shops on **West 3rd Street** (between Fairfax Ave. and La Cienega Blvd.) encompasses one-of-a-kind clothing boutiques, home stores, and bath-and-body shops. At one end you'll find

prime shopping at the Hollywood & Highland Center

rodeodrive-bh.com) in Beverly Hills. Among the upscale retailers are **Chanel** (400 N. Rodeo Dr., 310/278-5500, www.chanel.com, 10am-6pm Mon.-Sat., noon-5pm Sun.), **Tiffany's** (210 N. Rodeo Dr., 310/273-8880, www.tiffany.com, 10am-7pm Mon.-Sat., 11am-5pm Sun.), and **Frette** (445 N. Rodeo Dr., 310/273-8540, www.frette.com, 10am-6pm Mon.-Sat., noon-5pm Sun.). The Rodeo Drive Walk of Style salutes fashion and entertainment icons with sidewalk plaques.

Melrose Avenue (between San Vicente Blvd. and La Brea Ave.) is really two shopping districts. High-end fashion and design showrooms dominate the western end, near La Cienega Boulevard; head east past Fairfax Avenue for tattoo parlors and used clothing.

For vintage castoffs, check out **Decades** (8214 Melrose Ave., 323/655-1960, www.decadesinc.com, 11am-6pm Mon.-Sat., noon-5pm Sun.), while **Ron Robinson at Fred Segal** (8118 Melrose Ave., 323/651-1935, www.ronrobinson.com, 10am-7pm Mon.-Sat., noon-6pm Sun.) is a deluxe department store that has everything from the ridiculously trendy to the severely tasteful.

On the strip of Sunset Boulevard famous for nightlife, indie bookstore **Book Soup** (8818 Sunset Blvd., 310/659-3110, www.booksoup.com, 9am-10pm Mon.-Sat., 9am-7pm Sun.) crams every nook and cranny of its space, which includes a strong film section.

The Original Farmers Market and The Grove shopping center; at the other, the Beverly Center.

BEVERLY HILLS AND WEST HOLLYWOOD

Big spenders browse the three-block stretch of luxury stores on **Rodeo Drive** (www.

Sports and Recreation

You'll find an endless array of ways to get outside and have fun in the L.A. area. Among the most popular recreation options are those that get you out onto the beach or into the Pacific Ocean.

TOP EXPERIENCE

BEACHES

Southern California has a seemingly endless stretch of public beaches with lots of visitor amenities, such as snack bars, boardwalks, showers, beach toy rental shacks, surf schools, and permanent sports courts. However, you won't always find clean, clear water to swim in, since pollution is a major issue on the L.A. coast, and water temperatures cool off significantly when you dive into the surf.

Leo Carrillo State Park

Just 28 miles north of Santa Monica on the Pacific Coast Highway, **Leo Carrillo State**

Park (35000 W. Pacific Coast Hwy., Malibu, 310/457-8143, www.parks.ca.gov, 8am-10pm daily, $12 per vehicle) feels like a Central Coast beach even though it's right outside the Los Angeles city limits. Explore the park's natural coastal features, including tide pools and caves. A point break offshore draws surfers when the right swell hits. Dogs are also allowed on a beach at the northern end of the park.

Zuma Beach

Zuma Beach (30000 Pacific Coast Hwy., Malibu, 19 miles north of Santa Monica, surf report 310/457-9701, http://beaches. lacounty.gov, sunrise-sunset daily, parking $3-12.50) is a popular surf and boogie-boarding break, complete with a nice big stretch of clean white sand that fills up fast on summer weekends. Grab a spot on the west side of the Pacific Coast Highway (CA-1) for free parking, or pay for one of the more than 2,000 spots in the beach parking lot. Zuma has all the amenities you need for a full day out at the beach, from restrooms and showers to a kid-friendly snack bar and a beachside boardwalk.

Malibu Beach

Amid the sea of mansions fronting the beach, Malibu Lagoon State Beach (23200 Pacific Coast Hwy., 310/457-8143, www.parks.ca.gov, 8am-sunset daily, $12 per vehicle) and its ancillary Malibu Surfrider Beach offer public access to this great northern L.A. location. Running alongside the Malibu Pier (23000 Pacific Coast Hwy., www.malibupier.com), this pretty stretch of sugar-like sand offers a wealth of activities as well as pure California relaxation. It's likely to get crowded quickly in the summer, so get here early for a parking spot.

Santa Monica State Beach

Santa Monica State Beach (Pacific Coast Hwy., 310/458-8300, www.smgov.net, parking from $7) lines the water-side edge of town. For 3.5 miles, the fine sand gets raked daily beneath the sun that shines over the beach more

than 300 days each year. Enjoy the warm sunshine, take a dip in the endless waves, stroll along the boardwalk, or look for dolphins frolicking in the surf. The best people-watching runs south of the pier area and on toward Venice Beach. For more elbow room, head north of the pier to the less populated end of the beach.

Manhattan Beach

Manhattan Beach (400-4500 The Strand, Manhattan Beach, http://beaches.lacounty. gov) is centered on a fishing pier that is an extension of Manhattan Beach Boulevard, a popular paved path. It's about 12 miles south of Santa Monica.

Hermosa Beach

Hermosa Beach (Hermosa Beach Blvd., Hermosa Beach, http://beaches.lacounty. gov) offers volleyball nets, pristine sand, and wave breaks that surfers love. A paved path is packed with bikers, runners, and in-line skaters. It's two miles south of Manhattan Beach.

Redondo State Beach

The lack of surfers makes swimming a prime activity at Redondo State Beach (400-1700 Esplanade, Redondo, http://beaches.lacounty. gov), complete with lifeguards. You'll find the usual volleyball and beach games, a bike path (which is lit at night), and restaurants on the pier. There's restrooms and showers, and a large multilevel pay parking structure at the pier.

SURFING

The northern section of Los Angeles has some of the region's best surf breaks including County Line, which is on the L.A.-Ventura county line, and Zuma, a series of beach breaks along the beach of the same name. But L.A.'s premier surf spot is Malibu, one of the world's most famous waves. This is where the 1960s surf culture took hold, thanks to legends like Miki Dora, an iconic Malibu-based surfer. The southern section of L.A. County's coastline offers places to surf, but not with the same quality as the breaks around Malibu.

If you've left your board at home, run to the **Malibu Surf Shack** (22935 Pacific Coast Hwy., 310/456-8508, www.malibusurfshack. com, 10am-6pm daily, surfboards $25 per hour, $30-40 per day, wetsuits $10-15) to rent a board. It's walking distance to the break.

Learn to Surf LA (641 Westminster Ave., Ste. 5, Venice, 310/663-2479, www. learntosurfla.com, $130-380) has lessons on the beach near the Santa Monica Pier (near lifeguard tower no. 18), Manhattan Beach's 45th Street lifeguard tower, and Venice Beach's Navy Street lifeguard tower. Each lesson lasts almost two hours and includes all equipment (you'll get a full wetsuit in addition to a board), shore instruction and practice, and plenty of time in the water. Intermediate and advanced surfers can also find great fun with this school, which has advanced instructors capable of helping you improve your skills.

SPECTATOR SPORTS

Los Angeles went from having no NFL teams to being home to the **Los Angeles Rams** (www.therams.com) and **Los Angeles Chargers** (www.chargers.com) in 2017. They will begin playing in the **Los Angeles Stadium** at Hollywood Park in 2020. Until then, the Rams suit up at **Los Angeles Memorial Park** (www.lacoliseum. com), while the Chargers hit the field at the **StubHub Center** (www.stubhubcenter.com) in nearby Carson.

The **L.A. Kings** (http://kings.nhl.com) are no joke now after winning the Stanley Cup in 2012 and 2014. They play lightning-fast NHL ice hockey in downtown L.A. at the **Staples Center** (1111 S. Figueroa St., 213/742-7100, www.staplescenter.com).

The **Los Angeles Lakers** (www.nba. com/lakers) play at the **Staples Center** (1111 S. Figueroa St., 213/742-7100, www. staplescenter.com), along with the often-overlooked **L.A. Clippers** (www.nba.com/ clippers), who are now rising in stature.

The **Los Angeles Dodgers** (http:// losangeles.dodgers.mlb.com) play often and well at **Dodger Stadium** (1000 Elysian Park Ave., www.dodgers.com).

Food

Whatever kind of food you prefer, from fresh sushi to Armenian, you can probably find it in a cool little hole-in-the-wall somewhere in L.A. Local recommendations often make for the best dining experiences, but even just walking down the right street can yield a tasty meal.

DOWNTOWN AND VICINITY

Sure, you can find plenty of bland tourist-friendly restaurants serving American and Americanized food in the downtown area, but why would you, when one of downtown L.A.'s greatest strengths is its ethnic diversity and the great range of cuisine that goes along with it? An endless array of fabulous holes-in-the-wall awaits you. Getting local recommendations is the best way to find the current hot spots. The food stalls at the **Grand Central Market** (317 S. Broadway, 213/624-2378, www.grandcentralsquare.com, 8am-6pm Sun.-Wed., 8am-9pm Thurs.-Sat.) are also fun options.

Classic American

The house specialty at **Langer's Delicatessen and Restaurant** (704 S. Alvarado St., 213/483-8050, www.langersdeli. com, 8am-4pm Mon.-Sat., $12-25), operating continuously since 1947, is a hot pastrami sandwich that some say is the best in the world (yes, that includes New York City). The hot and cold dishes in the traditional Jewish deli style, a vast breakfast menu, and plenty of desserts (noodle kugel, anyone?) will satisfy any appetite level. It's still California, so you can get fresh avocado on your tongue sandwich if you really want to. You can also order in advance and pick up your meal curbside.

Mexican

Chef Ray Garcia puts some twists on the typical taqueria at his ★ **B.S. Taqueria** (514 W. 7th St., 213/622-3744, http://bstaqueria. com, 11:30am-10pm Mon.-Thurs., 11:30am-11pm Fri., 5pm-11pm Sat., 5pm-10pm Sun., $3-15). The menu is heavy on tacos including the famed lardo and clams version, but also includes heartier fare like carne asada. The interior is bright and lively, serving cocktails and craft beer. Make sure to finish with the churros and their spicy melted chocolate dipping sauce.

La Luz del Dia (1 W. Olvera St., 213/628-7495, www.luzdeldia.com, 11am-3:30pm Mon., 10am-8pm Tues.-Thurs., 10am-9pm Fri.-Sat., 8:30am-9pm Sun., $7-10) has been dishing up simple, spicy cafeteria-style Mexican food since 1959. The handmade-to-order tortillas are worth snacking on.

Italian

It seems odd to name a high-end restaurant after a decidedly low-end bug, but that's what the owners of **Cicada Restaurant** (617 S. Olive St., 213/488-9488, www. cicadarestaurant.com, 5:30pm-9pm Tues.-Sat., $24-42) did. Set in the 1920s Oviatt building, decorated in high French art deco style, the beautiful restaurant glitters with original Lalique glass panels—check out the elevator doors. There's a palatial dining room for large parties and balcony seating for intimate duos. The cuisine fuses Italian concepts with California ingredients, techniques, and presentations. Save room for dessert.

Japanese

Even L.A. denizens who've eaten in Japan come back to ★ **Kagaya** (418 E. 2nd St., 213/617-1016, 6pm-10:30pm Tues.-Sat., 6pm-10pm Sun., $40-128) again and again. They also make reservations in advance, because the dining room is small and the quality of the food makes it popular even on weeknights. The *shabu-shabu* (paper-thin slices of beef and vegetables) is but one course in a meal that includes several appetizers, *udon* noodles, and dessert. You can pay a premium for Wagyu beef if you choose, but the king crab legs in season are part of the regular price of dinner. Sit at the counter to watch your food prepared before your eyes.

Busy, noisy **Daikokuya** (327 E. 1st St., 213/626-1680, www.daikoku-ten.com, 11am-midnight Mon.-Thurs., 11am-1am Fri.-Sat., 11am-11pm Sun., under $10) is among the best ramen places in Little Tokyo, hailed by Pulitzer Prize-winning food writer Jonathan Gold. The steaming bowls of hearty pork broth and noodles satisfy even the brawniest appetite.

Coffee and Tea

Santa Cruz chain **Verve Coffee Roasters** (883 Spring St., 213/455-5991, www. vervecoffee.com, 7am-7pm Mon.-Fri., 7am-8pm Sat.-Sun.) feels right at home in DTLA, with a high-tech industrial setting and a small deck shaded with a canopy of tangled vines.

KOREATOWN

Three miles west of downtown, densely populated Koreatown has scores of great restaurants.

Classic American

Old-school gem ★ **Cassell's Hamburgers** (3600 W. 6th St., 213/387-5502, www. cassellshamburgers.com, Sun.-Thurs. 7am-11pm, Fri.-Sat. 7am-2pm, $6-12) has served its famous burgers since 1948. While the original location closed in 2012, it's reopened and modernized inside the Hotel Normandie. The burger is a thing of greasy beauty, still cooked up on the original crossfire broiler, while the can't-miss potato salad has a slight horseradish kick. Just feet from a rotating pie case, a bar serves up craft beers and cocktails.

Follow That Food Truck!

Some of the city's best culinary creations are being served out of food trucks. Gourmet chefs can follow their dreams with little overhead, and the result is some of the L.A. food scene's most blogged-about bites. The annual **LA Street Food Fest** (http://lastreetfoodfest.com) celebrates the rise of this foodie phenomenon.

Websites including **Find LA Food Trucks** (www.findlafoodtrucks.com) and **Roaming Hunger** (http://roaminghunger.com) have sprung up to help you find some of your roving favorites.

Food truck favorite **Kogi BBQ** (twitter @kogibbq, http://kogibbq.com) is still going strong, serving a Mexican-Korean hybrid menu that includes kimchi quesadillas and short-rib tacos.

The owner of **The Grilled Cheese Truck** (twitter @grlldcheesetruk, www.thegrilledcheesetruck.com) was inspired to start a truck selling grilled cheeses after he entered the Annual Grilled Cheese Invitational at the Rose Bowl and realized how many people loved this basic sandwich. His famous item is the cheesy mac and rib, which has barbecued pork tucked into the grilled cheese.

For East Coast meets West Coast fare, search for **Cousins Maine Lobster** (twitter @CMLobster, http://cousinsmainelobster.com), serving lobster rolls and crustacean-stuffed quesadillas.

Happy hunting!

Gastropub

As its name makes clear, **Beer Belly** (532 S. Western Ave., 213/387-2337, www.beerbellyla.com, Sun.-Tues. 11:30am-11pm, Wed.-Thurs. 11:30am-midnight, Fri.-Sat. 11:30am-1am, $9-21) is not for people who are watching their weight. Order a California craft beer for fortification as you try to take down the quadruple-decker grilled cheese sandwich with smoked bacon and maple syrup. Finish the meal with a deep-fried Pop-Tart—and vow to eat nothing but salads for the rest of the week.

Korean

Chunju Han-il Kwan (3450 W. 6th St., 213/480-1799, 8am-11pm Mon.-Sat., 11am-10pm Sun., $10-15) is a casual restaurant in a strip mall with gas burners on the tables that caters primarily to the Korean expat community. You won't find English menus, but helpful waitstaff can guide you through your order. If your server says a dish is spicy, she means it. The menu is eclectic: You can get a hot dog, octopus, fish soup, kimchi, Korean stew (thickened with American cheese), and much more.

Greek

Originally a Greek import company in the 1960s, **Papa Cristos Taverna** (2771 W. Pico Blvd., 323/737-2970, www.papacristos.com, 9:30am-3pm Tues., 9:30am-8pm Wed.-Sat., 9am-4pm Sun., $7-20) still supplies the local Greek community with hard-to-come-by delicacies, which also become ingredients in the cuisine at the Taverna, from the salads to the kebabs to the baba ghanoush.

LOS FELIZ, SILVER LAKE, AND ECHO PARK
Mexican

Not every taco stand wins awards from the James Beard Foundation. ★ **Yuca's** (2056 Hillhurst Ave., 323/662-1214, www.yucasla.com, 11am-8pm Mon.-Sat., $5) received the honor in 2005, confirming what Los Feliz locals have known for decades: This shack serves truly memorable (and cheap) tacos and burritos. Vegetarians beware: Even the beans are made with pork fat.

French

The ★ **Taix French Restaurant** (1911

W. Sunset Blvd., 213/484-1265, http://taixfrench.com, 11:30am-10pm Mon.-Thurs., 11:30am-11pm Fri., noon-11pm Sat., noon-10pm Sun., $13-34) has been serving superb French cuisine in a dimly lit Old World setting in Echo Park since 1927. The menu includes nightly dishes like roast chicken and frog legs Provençal as well as recurring weekly soups and entrées. Enjoy live music or comedy during your dinner at the on-site **321 Lounge.**

Vegetarian

Run by a true Renaissance woman (a spoken word poet, filmmaker, and chef), **Sage** (1700 W. Sunset Blvd., 213/989-1718, www.sageveganbistro.com, 8am-11pm daily, $12-15) keeps Echo Park's hipsters healthy with organic, plant-based cuisine. Order tempura-battered avocado tacos, housemade veggie burgers, flavorful veggie bowls, or butternut squash ravioli at the counter and then wait for your order at a table. (Dining this healthy means you can justify a scoop of gelato after your meal.) There are locations in Culver City (4130 Sepulveda Blvd., 424/228-5835, 11am-11pm Mon.-Thurs., 9am-11pm Sat.-Sun.) and Pasadena (41 Hugus Alley, 626/564-8111, 8am-11pm daily).

Breakfast

A small, colorful eatery in a Silver Lake strip mall, **Trois Familia** (3510 Sunset Blvd., 323/725-7800, www.troisfamilia.com, 9am-2pm daily, $7-15) is helmed by three chefs fusing French, Mexican, and California cuisines to produce tasty and creative breakfasts and lunches. Examples include chorizo crepes and a rich breakfast burrito with French ham, caramelized onions, and truffle salt.

HOLLYWOOD

Hollywood has just as many tasty treats tucked away in strip malls as other areas of Los Angeles. If you want to rub elbows with rock stars, you're likely to find yourself at a big, slightly raunchy bar and grill. For a chance at glimpsing stars of the silver screen, look for upscale California cuisine or perhaps a high-end sushi bar. If all you need is tasty sustenance, you can choose from a range of restaurants.

Classic American

Lit up like a Las Vegas show club into the wee hours of the morning, **Pink's Famous Hot Dogs** (709 N. La Brea Ave., 323/931-4223, www.pinkshollywood.com, 9:30am-2am Sun.-Thurs., 9:30am-3am Fri.-Sat., $3.50-7) is hot

a healthy and tasty meal from Sage

dog heaven. Frankophiles have been lining up at this roadside stand for variations on a sausage in a bun that range from the basic chili dog to the more elaborate Martha Stewart Dog since 1939.

Gastropub

A playful California take on British pub food, **The Pikey** (7617 Sunset Blvd., 323/850-5400, www.thepikeyla.com, 11:45am-2am Mon.-Fri., 10:30am-2am Sat.-Sun., $15-32) has a sense of humor. Case in point: One of its cocktails is named the Divine Brown for the prostitute that actor Hugh Grant was caught with on this same city block back in 1995. The dinner menu is divided into small plates and large plates. The buttery burger with cheddar and Worcestershire aioli is a highlight. It can get loud and crowded at dinnertime.

Italian

The warm but clamorous dining room at **Pizzeria Mozza** (641 N. Highland Ave., 323/297-0101, www.pizzeriamozza.com, noon-midnight daily, $11-29) has been packed since chef Nancy Silverton opened the doors. The wood-fired oven turns out rustic, blistered pizzas with luxurious toppings. Reservations are tough to get, but bar seats

are available for walk-ins. They also have an outpost in Newport Beach and farther away in Singapore.

Brazilian

Need food really, really, *really* late? **Bossa Nova** (7181 W. Sunset Blvd., 323/436-7999, www.bossanovafood.com, 11am-3:30am Sun.-Wed., 11am-4am Thurs.-Sat., $10-20) can hook you up. A big menu of inexpensive entrées can satisfy any appetite from lunch to way past dinnertime. Some of the dishes bear the spicy flavors of the owners' home country of Brazil, but you'll also find pasta, salads, and pizzas. There are two other locations: one at 685 N. Robertson Blvd. (310/657-5070, 11am-11:30pm Mon.-Thurs., 11am-3:30am Fri.-Sat., 11am-midnight Sun.) and one in West L.A. at 10982 W. Pico Blvd. (310/441-0404, 11am-1am Sun.-Thurs., 11am-3:30am Fri.-Sat.). Bossa also delivers.

Breakfast

If you're a flapjack fan, plan on breakfast at ★ **The Griddle Café** (7916 Sunset Blvd., 323/874-0377, www.thegriddlecafe.com, 7am-4pm Mon.-Fri., 8am-4pm Sat.-Sun., $11-30). This hectic, loud breakfast joint serves up creations like a Red Velvet pancake and a

healthy tacos at Trois Familia

pancake with brown sugar-baked bananas. Those who prefer savory to sweet can opt for delicious breakfast tacos or a cobb omelet. The Director's Guild of America is next door, so you may spot a celebrity *auteur*.

LA BREA, FAIRFAX, AND MIRACLE MILE

California Cuisine

Pairing meat and potatoes with a retro-clubby dining room, **Jar** (8225 Beverly Blvd., 323/655-6566, www.thejar.com, 5:30pm-close Tues.-Sun., $21-49) puts a Southern California spin on the traditional steak house. Meats and grilled fishes are served à la carte with your choice of sauce, and the side orders serve two. Jar is also known for its Sunday brunch; try the lobster Benedict. On Sunday, you can order a fried chicken plate, while Tuesday nights feature lobster.

Deli

Midnight snackers unhinge their jaws on the hulking corned beef sandwiches at **Canter's Deli** (419 N. Fairfax Ave., 323/651-2030, www.cantersdeli.com, 24 hours daily, $12-18), in the heart of the Jewish Fairfax district. This venerable 24-hour deli also boasts its share of star sightings, so watch for noshing rock stars in the wee hours of the morning.

BEVERLY HILLS AND WEST HOLLYWOOD

Between Beverly Hills and West L.A. you'll find an eclectic choice of restaurants. Unsurprisingly, Beverly Hills tends toward high-end eateries serving European and haute California cuisine. On the other hand, West L.A. boasts a wide array of international restaurants. You'll have to try a few to pick your favorites, since every local has their own take on the area's best eats.

Italian

If you're looking for upscale Italian cuisine in a classy environment, enjoy lunch or dinner at **Il Pastaio Restaurant** (400 N. Canon Dr., Beverly Hills, 310/205-5444,

popular tapas bar AOC

www.giacominodrago.com, 11:30am-11pm Mon.-Thurs., 11:30am-midnight Fri.-Sat., 11:30am-10pm Sun., $13-45). The bright dining room offers a sunny luncheon experience, and the white tablecloths and shiny glassware lend an elegance to dinner, served late even on weeknights. Il Pastaio offers a wide variety of salads, risotto, and pasta dishes. The blue-painted bar offers a tasteful selection of California and Italian vintages.

Seafood

With a roof that resembles a giant ray gliding through the sea, **Connie and Ted's** (8171 Santa Monica Blvd., 323/848-2722, www.connieandteds.com, 4pm-10pm Mon.-Tues., 11:30am-10pm Wed.-Thurs., 11:30am-11pm Fri., 10am-11pm Sat., 10am-10pm Sun., $12-44) brings the fruit of the sea to West Hollywood. The menu is inspired by New England clam shacks, oyster bars, and fish houses and includes a raw bar of oysters and clams. A West Coast influence creeps in on items like the smoked albacore starter, lobster rolls, and a Mexican shrimp dish.

Tapas

★ **AOC** (8700 W. 3rd St., 310/859-9859, www.aocwinebar.com, 11:30am-10pm Mon., 11:30am-11pm Tues.-Fri., 10am-11pm Sat., 10am-10pm Sun., $14-88) is wildly popular for three reasons: breakfast, lunch, and dinner. Breakfast is served until 3pm and includes fried chicken and cornmeal waffles along with house-made corned beef hash. Lunch features focaccia sandwiches, salads, and plate lunches. At dinner, you can go small (foccacias or salads) or big (roasted fish or meats). Sample from an acclaimed wine list and creative cocktails.

SANTA MONICA, VENICE, AND MALIBU

Yes, there's lots of junky beach food to be found in Santa Monica and Venice Beach, but there is also an amazing number of gems hiding in these towns.

Contemporary

Don't be fooled by the unpretentious exterior of **Cora's Coffee Shoppe** (1802 Ocean Ave., Santa Monica, 310/451-9562, www.corascoffee.com, 7am-3pm Sun.-Mon., 7am-10pm Tues.-Sat., $7-18). The small, exquisite restaurant inside is a locals' secret hiding in plain sight, serving breakfast, lunch, and dinner to diners who are more than willing to pack into the tiny spaces, including the two tiny marble-topped tables and miniature marble counter inside, and a small patio area screened by venerable bougainvillea. The chefs use high-end and sometimes organic ingredients to create typical breakfast and lunch dishes with a touch of the unexpected, including a hamburger salad and a BLT with a smear of goat cheese. The dinner menu includes short rib tacos and all kinds of burgers (including turkey and veggie).

Italian

The ★ **C&O Trattoria** (31 Washington Blvd., Marina del Rey, 310/823-9491, www.candorestaurants.com, 11:30am-10pm Sun.-Thurs., 11:30am-11pm Fri.-Sat., $13-23) manages to live up to its hype and then some. Sit outside in the big outdoor dining room, enjoying the mild weather and the soft pastel frescoes on the exterior walls surrounding the courtyard. C&O is known for its self-described gargantuan portions, which are best shared family-style. Start off with the addictive little garlic rolls. Your attentive but not overzealous server can help you choose from the creative pasta list; the rigatoni al forno is a standout. While C&O has a nice wine list, it's worth trying out the house chianti, where you get to serve yourself on an honor system.

Caribbean

Cha Cha Chicken (1906 Ocean Ave., Santa Monica, 310/581-1684, www.chachachicken.com, 11am-10pm Mon.-Fri., 10am-10pm Sat.-Sun., $7-12) looks just like it sounds: It's a slightly decrepit but brightly painted shack a short walk from the Santa Monica Pier and the Third Street Promenade. The palm tree-strewn patio is the perfect atmosphere to enjoy the Caribbean dishes that come from the fragrant kitchen. The jerk dishes bring a tangy sweetness to the table, while the *ropa vieja* heats up the place. Quaff an imported Jamaican soda or a seasonal *agua fresca* with your meal, since Cha Cha Chicken doesn't have a liquor license.

Seafood

Situated on the Malibu coastline adjacent to the County Line surf break, ★ **Neptune's Net** (42505 Pacific Coast Hwy., Malibu, 310/457-3095, 10:30am-8pm Mon.-Thurs., 10:30am-9pm Fri., 10am-8pm Sat.-Sun. summer, 10:30am-7pm Mon.-Thurs., 10:30am-8pm Fri., 10am-7pm Sat.-Sun. winter, $11-30) catches all kinds of seafood to serve to hungry diners. You'll often find sandy and salt-encrusted local surfers satisfying their enormous appetites after hours out on the waves, or bikers downing a beer after a ride on the twisting highway. One of the Net's most satisfying options is the shrimp tacos: crispy fried shrimp on tortillas topped with a pineapple salsa. The large menu includes a seemingly endless variety of other combinations, à la carte options, and side dishes.

Salt Air (1616 Abbot Kinney Blvd., Venice Beach, 310/396-9333, www.saltairvenice.com, 10am-3pm and 5pm-10pm Sun., 11am-3pm and 5pm-10pm Mon.-Tues., 11am-3pm and 5pm-11pm Wed.-Fri., 10am-3pm and 5pm-11pm Sat., $16-43) is a seafood restaurant with a busy bar. Everyone gets a plate of tasty corn fritters stuffed with cheddar cheese and a dollop of molasses butter to start. The raw bar has oysters from both coasts, while the dinner menu highlights seafood, including slow-cooked cod, seared trout, and olive oil-poached salmon.

Accommodations

From the cheapest roach-ridden shack motels to the most chichi Beverly Hills hotel, Los Angeles has an endless variety of lodgings to suit every taste and budget.

DOWNTOWN AND VICINITY

If you want to stay overnight in downtown L.A., plan to pay for the privilege. Most hostelries are high-rise towers catering more to businesspeople than the leisure set. Still, if you need a room near the heart of L.A. for less than a month's mortgage, you can find one if you look hard enough. Once you get into the Jewelry District and farther south toward the Flower Market, the neighborhood goes from high-end to sketchy to downright terrifying. If you need a truly cheap room, avoid these areas and head instead to the San Fernando Valley.

Under $150

A testament to the DTLA renaissance, ★ **Freehand Los Angeles** (416 W. 8th St., 213/612-0021, www.freehandhotels.com/los-angeles, $55-229) has taken up shop in the old Commercial Exchange Building. The hip 226-room complex splits the difference between hotel and hostel with 167 private rooms and 59 shared rooms with bunk beds. There's much on-site including a communal lobby with

Downtown L.A.'s Freehand Los Angeles

bar, a coffee counter, a home goods store, the Israeli American restaurant **The Exchange,** and the rooftop bar Broken Shaker with an adjacent pool.

Imagine staying at a cute B&B only a mile from the towering skyscrapers. The **Inn at 657** (657 and 663 W. 23rd St., 213/741-2200, https://theinnat657la.com, $140-220) is two side-by-side buildings with one-bedroom guest accommodations and two-bedroom suites, each individually decorated. You'll find a comfortable bed in a room scattered with lovely fabrics and pretty antiques. Each morning, you'll head downstairs for a full breakfast. The inn has a massage therapist on retainer, Wi-Fi, and laundry service.

$150-250

The ★ **Ace Hotel** (929 Broadway, 213/623-3233, www.acehotel.com/losangeles, $199-650) is one of the hippest places to stay in downtown. You can enjoy an evening's entertainment without venturing off the hotel's grounds. The property's 1,600-seat theater hosts the Sundance Next Fest and music performances by big indie acts like Slowdive and Belle and Sebastian. DJs spin poolside at the rooftop bar on the 14th floor, with the downtown skyline as a backdrop. Downstairs, dine at the trendy **L.A. Chapter** (213/235-9660, 7am-3:30pm and 5:30pm-11pm daily, $17-28). The guest rooms, converted from the former offices of the United Artists film studio, feel like arty studio apartments, with concrete ceilings and exposed concrete floors. Some rooms have private terraces; all have Internet radios.

Over $250

For a taste of true L.A. style, get a room at the **Omni Los Angeles at California Plaza** (251 S. Olive St., 213/617-3300, www.omnihotels.com, $276-542). From the grand exterior to the elegant lobby and on up to your guest room, the stylish decor, lovely accents, and plush amenities will make you feel rich, if only for one night. Business travelers can request a room complete with a fax machine and copier, while families can enjoy suites with adjoining rooms specially decorated for children. On-site meals are available at the **Noé Restaurant** (213/356-4100, 5pm-10pm Sun.-Thurs., 5pm-11pm Fri.-Sat.) and the **Grand Café** (213/617-3300, ext. 4155, 6:30am-3pm Mon.-Fri., 7am-3pm Sat.-Sun.). Take a swim in the lap pool, work out in the fitness room, or relax at the spa.

The Standard (550 S. Flower St., 213/892-8080, www.standardhotels.com, $260-1,500) is a mecca for the see-and-be-seen crowd. From its upside-down sign to the minimal aesthetic in the guest rooms, the hotel gives off an ironic-chic vibe. If you're sharing a room, be aware that the shower is only separated from the rest of the room by clear glass. On-site amenities include a gym, a barbershop, and a restaurant open 24-7. The rooftop bar, seen in the 2005 film *Kiss Kiss, Bang Bang*, features spectacular views of the L.A. cityscape.

If you're yearning to stay someplace with a movie history, book a room at the **Westin Bonaventure Hotel and Suites** (404 S. Figueroa St., 213/624-1000, www.starwoodhotels.com, $379-2,500). The climactic scene of the Clint Eastwood thriller *In the Line of Fire* was filmed in one of the unusual elevators in the glass-enclosed, four leaf clover-shaped high-rise building. This hotel complex has every single thing you'd ever need: shops, restaurants, a day spa, and a concierge. Views range from innocuous street scenes to panoramic cityscapes. The **Bona Vista Lounge** (213/612-4743, 5pm-1am daily) slowly rotates through 360 degrees at the top of the building.

The **Tuck Hotel** (820 S. Spring St., 213/947-3815, www.tuckhotel.com, $229-309) is located in a sliver of a building between South Spring Street and South Main Street. It used to house a brothel, but now is home to a small boutique hotel with a lobby bar and restaurant below the rooms. The black walls in the units make it easy to sleep in, while smart TVs and Bluetooth speakers provide entertainment and a soundtrack during your stay.

KOREATOWN

$150-250

★ **Hotel Normandie** (605 S. Normandie Ave., 800/617-4071, www.hotelnormandiela.com, $159-359) has been welcoming guests to Koreatown since opening in 1926, including British author Malcom Lowry, who completed his novel *Under the Volcano* here in the 1930s. Today the building has anything you'd want, including clean rooms, showers with superb water pressure, complimentary continental breakfasts, and complimentary wine in the afternoon. The high-ceilinged lobby leads to the bars at the **Normandie Club** and the exclusive **Walker Inn** with its world, as well as the classic **Cassell's Hamburgers,** gussied-up for modern diners.

Over $250

A block away from the Hotel Normandie, **The Line** (3515 Wilshire Blvd., 213/381-7411, www.thelinehotel.com/los-angeles/, $259-550) is a 1960s hotel spruced up for the modern age. The rooms have floor to ceiling windows, and the restaurants are run by famed chef Roy Choi. There's also a 1980s-throwback bar on-site called Break Room 86.

HOLLYWOOD

If you're star-struck, a serious partier, or a rock music aficionado, you'll want to stay the night within staggering distance of the hottest clubs or the hippest music venues. You might find yourself sleeping in the same room where Axl Rose once vomited or David Lee Roth broke all the furniture.

Under $150

OK, the exterior doesn't look like much, but at the **USA Hostels—Hollywood** (1624 Schrader Blvd., 323/462-3777 or 800/524-6783, www.usahostels.com, dorm $56-59, private room $150), it's what's inside that counts. It still offers the same great prices you'll find at more bare-bones hostels, but you can choose between dorm rooms and private guest rooms. Even the larger dorm rooms have baths attached. (You'll also find several common baths in the hallways, helping to diminish the morning shower rush.) The daily all-you-can-make pancake breakfast is included, along with all the coffee or tea you can drink. Add free barbecue nights on Monday, Wednesday, and Friday, and you've got a great start on seriously diminished food costs for your trip. This smaller hostel also fosters a sense of community among its visitors, with walking tours, a beach shuttle, and free comedy nights.

Hollywood motel rooms for around $100? They exist at the **Hollywood Downtowner Inn** (5601 Hollywood Blvd., 323/464-7191, www.hollywooddowntowner.com, $99-199). Just 1.5 miles from sights such as TCL Chinese Theatre and the Griffith Observatory, this 33-room motel offers basic amenities, including a courtyard pool, complimentary hot breakfast, and, maybe most important, free parking.

$150-250

Named for the world-renowned magic club next door, the ★ **Magic Castle Hotel** (7025 Franklin Ave., 323/851-0800, www.magiccastlehotel.com, $204-399) boasts the best customer service of any L.A.-area hostelry. Sparkling light guest rooms with cushy white comforters and spare, clean decor offer a haven of tranquility. A courtyard pool invites lounging day and night. All suites have their own kitchens, and all guests can enjoy unlimited free snacks (sodas, candy, salted goodies). Enjoy the little luxurious touches, such as high-end coffee, baked goodies in the free continental breakfast, plushy robes, and nightly turndown service. But the most notable perks are free tickets to the exclusive **Magic Castle** (7001 Franklin Ave., 323/851-3313, www.magiccastle.com), although there is a door charge.

The **Hollywood Celebrity Hotel** (1775 Orchid Ave., 323/850-6464 or 800/222-7017, www.hotelcelebrity.com, $169-250) is a nice budget motel that aspires to Hollywood's famed luxury. Guest rooms have mini fridges for leftovers; some have kitchens as well. In the morning, come down to the lobby for a complimentary continental breakfast. Leave your car in the gated, off-street parking lot for just $10 per night, which is a deal.

For film lovers or star seekers, the location of the **Hollywood Orchid Suites** (1753 Orchid Ave., 323/874-9678 or 800/537-3052, www.orchidsuites.com, $179-239) couldn't be better: It's in the Hollywood and Highland Center, right behind the Chinese Theatre and around the corner from the Walk of Fame. Inexpensive parking and proximity to public transit are a bonus. Guest rooms are actually suites; all but the juniors have full kitchens. Don't expect luxury, although you'll get a coffeemaker and free Wi-Fi. The rectangular pool offers cool refreshment after a long day of stalking Brad or Angie.

BEVERLY HILLS AND WEST HOLLYWOOD

If you want to dive headfirst into the lap of luxury, stay in Beverly Hills. Choose wisely and save your pennies to see how the 1 percent lives. West Hollywood, which serves as L.A.'s gay mecca, offers a wider range of accommodations, including budget options, chain motels, and unique upscale hotels.

$150-250

Comfortable and quiet, the ★ **Élan Hotel** (8435 Beverly Blvd., 323/658-6663, www.elanhotel.com, $145-239) has a great location where Beverly Hills and West Hollywood meet. With its friendly staff, this unassuming hotel makes a fine base for exploring Hollywood attractions and the Sunset Strip. The understated rooms are decorated with soothing abstract art. All have mini fridges, coffeemakers, flat-screen TVs; many rooms have small balconies or porches for a breath of fresh air. A complimentary continental breakfast is served every morning.

The affordable **Hotel Beverly Terrace** (469 N. Doheny Dr., Beverly Hills, 310/274-8141 or 800/842-6401, www.hotelbeverlyterrace.com, $220-260) is a spruced-up, retro-cool motor hotel that enjoys a great spot on the border of Beverly Hills and West Hollywood. Lounge in the sun in the garden courtyard or on the rooftop sundeck. In the morning, enjoy a complimentary continental breakfast. The on-site **Cafe Amici** (310/858-0271, 7am-10pm daily) can satisfy your Italian food cravings.

Over $250

The **Beverly Wilshire** (9500 Wilshire Blvd., Beverly Hills, 310/275-5200, www.fourseasons.com, $800-2,000) is the most famous of all the neighborhood's grand hotels. Even the plainest guest rooms feature exquisite appointments such as 55-inch plasma TVs, elegant linens, and attractive artwork. The presidential suite resembles a European palace, complete with Corinthian columns. Enjoy the in-house spa, a dining room, room service, and every other service you could imagine, and you might consider a stay here worth the expense.

In West Hollywood, the **Sunset Tower Hotel** (8358 Sunset Blvd., West Hollywood, 323/654-7100, www.sunsettowerhotel.com, $345-3,000) has a gorgeous art deco exterior and a fully renovated modern interior. Guest accommodations range from smallish guest rooms with smooth linens and attractive appointments up to luxurious suites with panoramic views and limestone baths. All guest rooms include flat-screen TVs, 24-hour room service, and free Wi-Fi.

With architecture like a French castle, **Chateau Marmont** (8221 Sunset Blvd., West Hollywood, 323/656-1010 or 800/242-8328, www.chateaumarmont.com, $450-6,000) looks out on the city from a perch above the Sunset Strip. It has long attracted the in crowd, from Garbo to Leo. It is also where writers from F. Scott Fitzgerald to Hunter S. Thompson have holed up to produce work. The design is eccentric and eclectic, from vintage 1940s suites to Bauhaus bungalows. The hotel was front and center in Sofia Coppola's 2010 film *Somewhere*.

SANTA MONICA, VENICE, AND MALIBU

The best place to stay in Los Angeles is down by the beach. It's ironic that you can camp in a park for $25 in exclusive Malibu or pay over $1,000 for a resort room in "working-class" Santa Monica. Whichever you choose, you'll get some of the best atmosphere in town.

Under $150

The huge **HI-Santa Monica** (1436 2nd St., Santa Monica, 310/393-9913, www.hilosangeles.org, dorm beds $40-71, private rooms $140-230) offers 260 beds right in the thick of downtown Santa Monica, within walking distance of the pier, the Third Street Promenade, and good restaurants. This ritzy hostel offers tons of amenities for the price, including a computer room, a TV room, a movie room, excursions, wheelchair access, sheets with the bed price, and even a complimentary continental breakfast every morning. The local public transit system runs right outside the door.

$150-250

While it's about a 30-minute drive from Santa Monica, the **Hyatt Regency Los Angeles International Airport** (6225 W. Century Blvd., 424/702-1234, https://losangelesairport.regency.hyatt.com/en/hotel/home.html, $229-449) makes an ideal first or last stop in the city. The 580 rooms all have 55-inch HD TVs and soundproof windows. But the property really excels at unexpected amenities including an on-site market open 24 hours a day and a resident dog named Sir Hyatt who is available for petting from travelers who left their own furry friends at home. There's also a bar, a restaurant that serves cuisine inspired by L.A. neighborhoods, an exercise room with views of the LAX runways, a shuttle to the terminals, and a pool deck with cabanas and fire pits.

The surprisingly lovely and affordable **Venice Beach Suites & Hotel** (1305 Ocean Front Walk, 310/396-4559 or 888/877-7602, www.venicebeachsuites.com, $229-349) sits right on the beach, but it's far enough from the boardwalk to acquire a touch of peace and quiet. You can also stroll over to Washington Boulevard to grab a meal or a cup of coffee. Inside, the guest rooms and suites all have full kitchens so you can cook for yourself, which is perfect for budget-conscious travelers. The decor is cuter than that of an average motel; you might find exposed brick walls and polished hardwood floors. Check the website for weeklong rental deals.

Over $250

There's probably no hotel that is a better reflection of Venice's edgy attitude than ★ **Hotel Erwin** (1697 Pacific Ave., 800/786-7789, www.hotelerwin.com, $289-530), just feet from the boardwalk. Graffiti art adorns the outside wall and some of its rooms; all have balconies and playful decor including lamps resembling the barbells used by the weightlifters at nearby Muscle Beach. Sitting atop the hotel is **High,** a rooftop bar that allows you to take in all the action of the bustling boardwalk while sipping a cocktail. The staff is laid-back, genial, and accommodating.

For a charming hotel experience only a block from the ever-energetic Venice Boardwalk, stay at the **Inn at Venice Beach** (327 Washington Blvd., 310/821-2557 or 800/828-0688, www.innatvenicebeach.com, $250-450). The charming orange-and-brown exterior, complete with a lovely bricked interior courtyard-cum-café, makes all guests feel welcome. Common spaces are decorated in a postmodern blocky style, while the guest rooms pop with brilliant yellows and vibrant accents. The two-story boutique hotel offers 45 guest rooms, and its location on Washington Boulevard makes it a perfect base from which to enjoy the best restaurants of Venice. Start each day with a complimentary continental breakfast, either in the dining room or outside in the Courtyard Café. There's complimentary Wi-Fi throughout.

One of this area's best-known resort hotels is **Shutters on the Beach** (1 Pico Blvd., Santa Monica, 310/458-0030, www.

shuttersonthebeach.com, $795-1,165). You'll pay handsomely for the privilege of laying your head on one of Shutters' hallowed pillows. On the other hand, the gorgeous airy guest rooms will make you feel like you're home, or at least staying at the home you'd have if you could hire a famous designer to decorate for you. Even the most modest guest rooms have comfortable beds, white linens, plasma TVs, and oversize bathtubs. Head down to the famed lobby for a drink and people-watching. Get a reservation for the elegant **One Pico** (310/587-1717, 11:30am-2:30pm and 6pm-10pm Mon.-Fri., 10am-3pm and 6pm-10pm Sat.-Sun.) or grab a more casual meal at beachside **Coast** (310/587-1717, 7am-9pm daily).

If you've got silly amounts of cash to spare, stay at the **Malibu Beach Inn** (22878 Pacific Coast Hwy., Malibu, 310/456-6444 or 800/462-5428, www.malibubeachinn.com, $679-1,459), an ocean-side villa on an exclusive stretch of sand known as "Billionaire's Beach." Expect all the best furnishings and amenities. Your guest room will be done in rare woods, gleaming stone, and the most stylish modern linens and accents. A high-definition TV, plush robes, and comfy beds tempt some visitors to stay inside, but equally tempting are the balconies with their own entertainment in the form of endless surf, glorious sunsets, and balmy breezes (every room has an ocean view). Enjoy delicious cuisine at the airy, elegant, on-site **Carbon Beach Club** (310/456-6444, 7am-10pm daily).

Transportation and Services

AIR

L.A. is one of the most commercial airport-dense metropolitan areas in the country. Wherever you're coming from and whichever part of L.A. you're headed for, you can get there by air. **Los Angeles International Airport** (1 World Way, Los Angeles, 855/463-5252, www.lawa.org), known as LAX, has the most flights to and from the most destinations of any area airport. LAX is also the most crowded of the L.A. airports, with the longest security and check-in lines. If you can find a way around flying into LAX, do so.

One option is to fly into other airports in the area, including **Hollywood Burbank Airport** (BUR, 2627 N. Hollywood Way, Burbank, 818/840-8840, http://hollywoodburbankairport.com) and the **Long Beach Airport** (LGB, 4100 Donald Douglas Dr., Long Beach, 562/570-2600, www.lgb.org). It may be a slightly longer drive to your final destination, but it can be well worth it. If you must use LAX, arrive a minimum of two hours ahead of your domestic flight time for your flight out, and consider three hours on busy holidays.

TRAIN

Amtrak (800/872-7245, www.amtrak.com) has an active rail hub in Los Angeles. Most trains come in to **Union Station** (800 N. Alameda St., 213/683-6875, www.unionstationla.com, 4am-1am daily), which is owned by the Los Angeles Metropolitan Transportation Authority (MTA, www.metro.net).

Union Station also acts as a Metro hub, with Metro Rail lines to various parts of Los Angeles. Against fairly significant odds in the region that invented car culture, Los Angeles has created a functional and useful public transit system.

CAR

Los Angeles is crisscrossed with freeways, providing numerous yet congested access points into the city. From the north and south, I-5 provides the most direct access to downtown L.A. From I-5, U.S. 101 south leads directly into Hollywood; from here, Santa Monica Boulevard can take you west to Beverly Hills. Connecting from I-5 to I-210 will take you east to Pasadena. The best way to reach Santa Monica, Venice, and Malibu is via CA-1, also known as the Pacific Coast Highway. I-10 can get you there from the east, but it will be a long, tedious, and trafficked drive. I-710, which runs north-south, is known as the Long Beach Freeway. Along the coast, the Pacific Coast Highway (CA-1) can get you from one beach town to the next.

Parking

Parking in Los Angeles can be as much of a bear as driving. And it can cost you quite a lot of money. You will find parking lots and structures included with many hotel rooms, but parking on the street can be difficult or impossible, parking lots in sketchy areas (like the Flower and Jewelry Districts) can be dangerous, and parking structures at popular attractions can be expensive. Beach parking on summer weekends is the worst, but on weekdays and in the off-season, you can occasionally find a decent space down near the beach for a reasonable rate.

METRO

The **Metro** (323/466-3876, www.metro.net, cash fare $1.75, day pass $7) runs both the subway Metro Rail system and a network of buses throughout the L.A. metropolitan area. Pay on board a bus if you have exact change. Otherwise, purchase a ticket or a day pass from the ticket vending machines at all Metro Rail stations. Some buses run 24 hours. The Metro Rail lines start running as early as 4:30am and don't stop until as late as 1:30am.

Note that the Metro's Expo Line (E) extends to Santa Monica near the pier, saving you a long, congested drive. See the website (www.metro.net) for route maps, timetables, and fare details.

Taxis and Ride Shares

Taxis aren't cheap, but they're quick, easy, and numerous. And in some cases, when you add up gas and parking fees, you'll find that the cab ride isn't that much more expensive than driving yourself.

To call a cab, try **Yellow Cab** (424/222-2222, www.layellowcab.com, L.A., LAX, Beverly Hills, Hollywood) or **City Cab** (888/713-5240, www.lacitycab.com, San Fernando Valley, Hollywood, and LAX), which now has a small fleet of green, environmentally friendly vehicles. Or check out www.taxicabsla.org for a complete list of providers and phone numbers.

Another option is to download a ride-sharing app on your smartphone. Both **Lyft** (www.lyft.com) and **Uber** (www.uber.com) are available all over the city.

TOURIST INFORMATION

The **Hollywood Los Angeles Visitor Information Center** (6801 Hollywood Blvd., 323/467-6412, www.discoverlosangeles.com, 9am-10pm Mon.-Sat., 10am-7pm Sun.) is adjacent to a Metro station and includes a self-serve kiosk where you can purchase discount tickets to area attractions. There are additional self-serve centers at the Los Angeles Convention Center, the Port of Los Angeles (Berth 93), and the California Science Center.

MEDICAL SERVICES

For medical assistance, **LAC & USC Medical Center** (2051 Marengo St., 323/409-1000, http://dhs.lacounty.gov/wps/portal/dhs/lacusc) can fix you up no matter what's wrong with you, or visit the emergency room at the **Long Beach Memorial Medical Center** (2801 Atlantic Ave., Long Beach, 562/933-2000, www.memorialcare.org).

Disneyland Resort

The "Happiest Place on Earth" lures millions of visitors of all ages each year with promises of fun and fantasy. During high seasons, waves of humanity flow through **Disneyland** (1313 N. Harbor Blvd., Anaheim, 714/781-4623, http://disneyland.disney.go.com, 9am-midnight daily, $97-124, Hopper Ticket $166-185), moving slowly from land to land and ride to ride. The park is well set up to handle the often-immense crowds. Despite the undeniable cheese factor, even the most cynical and jaded resident Californians can't quite keep their cantankerous scowls once they're ensconced inside Uncle Walt's dream. It really *is* a happy place.

ORIENTATION

The Disneyland Resort is a massive kingdom that stretches from **Harbor Boulevard** on the east to **Walnut Street** on the west and from **Ball Road** to the north to **Katella Avenue** to the south. It includes two amusement parks, three hotels, and an outdoor shopping and entertainment complex. The Disneyland-affiliated hotels (Disneyland Hotel, Paradise Pier Hotel, and Disney's Grand Californian) all cluster on the western side of the complex, between Walnut Street and **Disneyland Drive (West Street).** The area between Disneyland Drive and Harbor Boulevard is shared by **Disneyland** in the northern section and **Disney California Adventure Park** in the southern section, with **Downtown Disney** between them in the central-west section. There is no admission fee for Downtown Disney. You can reach the amusement park entrances via Downtown Disney (although visitors going to Disneyland or Disney California Adventure Park should park in the paid lots, rather than the Downtown Disney self-park lot, which is only free for the first three hours) or from the walk-in entrance (for those taking public transportation or being dropped off) on Harbor Boulevard. There are also trams from the parking lot to the entrance.

Your first stop inside the park should be one of the information kiosks near the front entrance gates. Get a map, a schedule of the day's events, and the inside scoop on what's going on in the park during your visit.

Tickets

There are as many varied ticket prices and plans as there are themes in the park. A single-day theme park ticket will run from $97 to $124. A variety of other combinations and passes are available online (http://disneyland.disney.go.com).

To buy tickets, go to one of the many kiosks in the central gathering spot that serves as the main entrance to both Disneyland and Disney California Adventure Park. Bring your credit card, since a day at Disney is not cheap. After you've got tickets in hand (or if you've bought them online ahead of time), proceed to the turnstiles for the main park. You'll see the Disneyland Railroad terminal and the large grassy hill with the flowers planted to resemble Mickey's famous face. Pass through the turnstiles and head under the railroad trestle to get to Main Street and the park center. You can exit and reenter the park on the days for which your tickets are valid.

The already expensive regular one-day Disneyland ticket doesn't include Disney California Adventure Park. If you're interested in checking out Disney California Adventure Park as well as Disneyland, your best bet is to buy a **Park Hopper pass** (adults $172-185, children 3-9 $166-178), which lets you move back and forth between the two parks at will for a slight discount. If you're planning to spend several days touring the Houses of Mouse, buy multiday passes in advance online to save a few more bucks per day. It'll help you feel better about the cash you'll spend on junk food, giant silly hats, stuffed animals, and an endless array of Disney apparel.

Fastpasses are free with park admission and might seem like magic after a while. The newest and most popular rides offer Fastpass kiosks near the entrances. Feed your ticket into one of the machines and it will spit out both your ticket and a Fastpass with your specified time to take the ride. Come back during your window and enter the always-much-shorter Fastpass line, designated by a sign at the entrance. If you're with a crowd, be sure you all get your Fastpasses at the same time, so you all get the same time window to ride. It's possible to claim three Fastpasses at a time. Once you've used up your initial allotment, you can visit a Fastpass kiosk to reload.

Rides

In **New Orleans Square,** the favorite ride is the **Pirates of the Caribbean.** Beginning in the dim swamp, which can be seen from the Blue Bayou Restaurant, the ride's classic scenes inside have been revamped to tie in more closely to the movies. Lines for Pirates can get long, so grab a Fastpass if you don't want to wait. Pirates is suitable for younger children as well as teens and adults.

For a taste of truly classic Disney, line up in the graveyard for a tour of the **Haunted Mansion.** The sedate motion makes the Haunted Mansion suitable for younger children, but the ghosts and ghoulies that amuse adults can be intense for kids.

Adventureland sits next to the New Orleans Square area. **Indiana Jones Adventure** is arguably one of the best rides in all of Disneyland, and the details make it stunning. This one isn't the best for tiny tots, but the big kids love it. Everyone might want a Fastpass for the endlessly popular attraction.

In **Frontierland,** take a ride on a Wild West train on the **Big Thunder Mountain Railroad,** an older roller coaster that whisks passengers on a brief but fun thrill ride through a "dangerous, decrepit" mountain's mineshafts.

Fantasyland rides tend to cater to the

younger set. For many Disneyphiles, **"it's a small world"** is the ultimate expression of Uncle Walt's dream, and toddlers adore this ride. Older kids might prefer **Mr. Toad's Wild Ride.** The wacky scenery ranges from a sedate library to the gates of hell. If it's a faster thrill you're seeking, head for the **Matterhorn Bobsleds.** You'll board a sled-style coaster car to plunge down a Swiss mountain on a twisted track that takes you past rivers, glaciers, and the Abominable Snowman.

The best thrill ride of the main park sits inside **Tomorrowland. Space Mountain** is a fast roller coaster that whizzes through the dark. Despite its age, Space Mountain remains one of the more popular rides in the park. Get a Fastpass to avoid long lines.

In 2019, a highly anticipated section of the park inspired by **Star Wars** opens.

★ Disney California Adventure Park

Disney California Adventure Park (http://disneyland.disney.go.com, 8am-10pm daily, ticket prices vary, one-day: children over 9 $99, children 3-9 $93 one-day Park Hopper ticket to both parks: adults $172-185, children 3-9 $166-178) celebrates much of what makes California special. If Disney is your only stop on this trip, but you'd like to get a sense of the state as a whole, this park can give you a little taste.

Disney California Adventure Park is divided into themed areas. You'll find two information booths just inside the main park entrance, one off to the left as you walk through the turnstile and one at the opening to Sunshine Plaza.

Rides

Monsters, Inc. Mike & Sully to the Rescue! invites guests into the action of the movie of the same name. You'll help the heroes as they chase the intrepid Boo. This ride jostles you around but is suitable for smaller kids as well as bigger ones.

Get a sample of the world of tiny insects on **It's Tough to Be a Bug!** This big-group, 3-D, multisensory ride offers fun for little kids and adults alike. You'll fly through the air, scuttle through the grass, and get a good idea of what life is like on six little legs.

For the littlest adventurers, **Flik's Fun Fair** offers almost half a dozen rides geared toward toddlers and little children. They can ride pint-size hot-air balloons known as Flik's Flyers, climb aboard a bug-themed train, or run around under a gigantic faucet to cool down after hours of hot fun.

Paradise Pier mimics the Santa Monica Pier, with thrill rides and an old-fashioned midway. **California Screamin'** is a high-tech roller coaster designed after the classic wooden coasters of carnivals past. This extra-long ride includes drops, twists, a full loop, and plenty of time and screaming fun. California Screamin' has a four-foot height requirement and is just as popular with nostalgic adults as with kids. **Toy Story Midway Mania!** magnifies the midway mayhem as passengers of all ages take aim at targets in a 4-D ride inspired by Disney-Pixar's *Toy Story*.

In **Condor Flats, Soarin' Over California** is a combination ride and show that puts you and dozens of other guests on the world's biggest "glider" and sets you off over the hills and valleys of California. Get Disney's version of a wilderness experience at **Grizzly Peak.** Enjoy a white-water raft ride through a landscape inspired by the Sierra Nevada foothills on the **Grizzly River Run.**

Cars Land was inspired by the hit 2006 film *Cars*. Float on larger-than-life tires on the **Luigi's Flying Tires** ride or be serenaded by Mater as you ride in a tractor on **Mater's Junkyard Jamboree.** The **Radiator Springs Racers** finds six-person vehicles passing locations and characters from *Cars* before culminating in a real-life race with a car of other park visitors.

Parades and Shows

Watch your favorite Pixar characters come to life in the **Pixar Play Parade.** Other regular shows are **Disney Junior—Live on Stage!** and **Disney's Aladdin—A Musical Spectacular.** Both of these shows hark back to favorite children's activities and movies. Check your park guide and *Time Guide* for more information about live shows.

FOOD
Disneyland

One of the few things the Mouse doesn't do too well is haute cuisine. For a truly good or healthy meal, get a hand stamp and go outside the park. But if you're stuck inside and you absolutely need sustenance, you can get it. The best areas of the park to grab a bite are Main Street, New Orleans, and Frontierland, but you can find at least a snack almost anywhere in the park.

For a sit-down restaurant meal inside the park, make reservations in advance for a table at the **Blue Bayou Restaurant** (New Orleans Square, 714/781-3463, $55-59). The best part about this restaurant is its setting in the dimly lit swamp overlooking the Pirates of the Caribbean ride. Appropriately, the Bayou has Cajun-ish cuisine and a reputation for being haunted. You will get large portions, and tasty desserts make a fine finish to your meal. Watch your silverware, though; the alleged ghosts in this restaurant like to mess around with diners' tableware.

If you need to grab a quicker bite, *don't* do it at the French Market restaurant in the New Orleans area. It sells what appears to be day-old (or more) food from the Bayou that has been sitting under heat lamps for a good long time.

Disney California Adventure Park

If you need a snack break in Disney California Adventure Park, you'll find most of the food clustered in the Golden State area. For a Mexican feast, try **Cocina Cucamonga Mexican Grill** ($15). For more traditional American fare, enjoy the food at the **Pacific Wharf Cafe** ($15) or the **Taste Pilots' Grill** ($15).

Unlike Disneyland proper, in Disney

Alternatives to the Mouse

UNIVERSAL STUDIOS HOLLYWOOD

The longtime Hollywood-centric alternative to Disneyland is the **Universal Studios Hollywood** (100 Universal City Plaza, Los Angeles, 800/864-8377, www.universalstudios.com, hours vary, $105-116, parking $10-15) theme park. Kids adore this park, which puts them right into the action of their favorite movies. Flee the carnivorous dinosaurs of *Jurassic Park*, take a rafting adventure on the pseudo-set of *Waterworld*, or quiver in terror of an ancient curse in *Revenge of the Mummy*. If you're more interested in how the movies are made than the rides made from them, take the **Studio Tour.** You'll get an extreme close-up of the sets of major blockbuster films like *War of the Worlds*. Better yet, be part of the studio audience of TV shows currently taping by getting tickets at the Audiences Unlimited Ticket Booth. If you're a serious movie buff, consider buying a **VIP pass**—you'll get a six-hour tour that takes you onto working sound stages, into the current prop warehouse, and through a variety of working build shops that service movies and programs currently filming.

SIX FLAGS MAGIC MOUNTAIN

Six Flags Magic Mountain (Magic Mountain Parkway, Valencia, 661/255-4100, www.sixflags. com, hours vary, adults $85, children $60) provides good fun for the whole family. Magic Mountain has long been the extreme alternative to the Mouse, offering a wide array of thrill rides. You'll need a strong stomach to deal with the g-forces of the major-league roller coasters and the death-defying drops, including the Lex Luthor: Drop of Doom, where you plummet 400 feet at speeds up to 85 mph. For the younger set, plenty of rides offer a less intense but equally fun amusement-park experience. Both littler and bigger kids enjoy interacting with the classic Warner Bros. characters, especially in Bugs Bunny World, and a kids' show features Bugs Bunny, Donald Duck, and more. Other than that, Magic Mountain has little in the way of staged entertainment—this park is all about the rides. The park is divided into areas, just like most other major theme parks; get a map at the entrance to help you maneuver around and pick your favorite rides.

KNOTT'S BERRY FARM

For a taste of history along with some ultramodern thrill rides and plenty of cooling waterslides, head for **Knott's Berry Farm** (8039 Beach Blvd., Buena Park, 714/220-5200, www.knotts.com, hours vary, adults $75, children $45, parking $15). From the tall landmark GhostRider wooden coaster to the 30-story vertical-drop ride to the screaming Silver Bullet suspended coaster, Knott's supplies excitement to even the most hard-core ride lover. For the younger crowd, Camp Snoopy offers an array of pint-size rides and attractions, plus Snoopy and all the characters they love from the *Peanuts* comics and TV shows.

In the heat of the summer, many park visitors adjourn from the coasters to **Knott's Soak City** (www.soakcityoc.com, hours vary daily Memorial Day-Labor Day, adults $48, children $37, parking $15-20), a full-size water park with 22 rides, a kid pool and water playground, and plenty of space to enjoy the O.C. sunshine.

Convenient to the parks, **Knott's Berry Farm Resort Hotel** (7675 Crescent Ave., Buena Park, 714/995-1111, www.knotts.com, $145-215) is a high-rise resort with a pool and spa, a fitness center, and several on-site restaurants.

California Adventure Park, responsible adults can quash their thirst with a variety of alcoholic beverages. If you're just dying for a cold beer, get one at **Bayside Brews.** Or, if you love the endless array of high-quality wines produced in the Golden State, head for the **Mendocino Terrace,** where you can learn the basics of wine creation and production. Have a glass and a pseudo-Italian meal at the sit-down **Wine Country Trattoria at the Golden Vine Winery** (714/781-3463, $15-36).

Downtown Disney

Downtown Disney is outside the amusement parks and offers additional dining options. National chains like **House of Blues** (1530 S. Disncyland Dr., Anaheim, 714/778-2583, www.houseofblues.com, 11am-midnight daily, $15-30) and **Rainforest Café** (1515 S. Disneyland Dr., Anaheim, 714/772-0413, www.rainforestcafe.com, 8am-11pm Sun.-Thurs., 8am-midnight Fri.-Sat., $11-30) serve typical menu staples like sandwiches, burgers, pasta, and steak and seafood entrées, with House of Blues putting a Southern spin on these items and adding live-music shows, while kid-friendly Rainforest Café puts on tropical touches like coconut and mango. **ESPN Zone** (1545 Disneyland Dr., Anaheim, 714/300-3776, www.espnzone.com, 11am-midnight daily, $11-26) has similar offerings with a "sports bar on steroids" restaurant concept.

There are also more individual restaurants, but even these feel a little like chains. The most distinctive of them, **Ralph Brennan's Jazz Kitchen** (1590 S. Disneyland Dr., Anaheim, 714/776-5200, www.rbjazzkitchen.com, 11am-11pm Mon.-Sat., 10am-3pm and 4pm-11pm Sun., $8-37), is meant to replicate the experience of eating in New Orleans's French Quarter. The Cajun menu hits all the staples, including jambalaya, beignets, and various blackened meats and seafood.

The Patina Restaurant Group runs **Catal Restaurant** (1580 Disneyland Dr., Anaheim, 714/774-4442, www.patinagroup.com, 8am-11am and 5pm-9pm daily, $19-41), with Mediterranean fare; **Naples Ristorante** (1550 Disneyland Dr., Anaheim, 714/776-6200, www.patinagroup.com, 8am-10pm daily, $15-46) for Italian food; and **Tortilla Jo's** (1510 Disneyland Dr., Anaheim, 714/535-5000, www.patinagroup.com, 11am-10pm Sun.-Thurs., 11am-11pm Fri.-Sat., $15-21) for Mexican food.

Finally, **La Brea Bakery** (1556 Disneyland Dr., Anaheim, 714/490-0233, www.labreabakery.com, 11am-11pm Mon.-Fri., 9am-11pm Sat.-Sun., $15-35) is the Disney outpost of an L.A. favorite. This bakery, founded by Nancy Silverton, supplies numerous markets and restaurants with crusty European-style loaves. The morning scones, sandwiches, and fancy cookies are superb.

ACCOMMODATIONS

The best way to get fully Disney-fied is to stay at one of the park's hotels.

Disney Hotels

For the most iconic Disney resort experience, you must stay at the **Disneyland Hotel** (1150 Magic Way, Anaheim, 714/778-6600, http://disneyland.disney.go.com, $460-1,016). This nearly 1,000-room high-rise monument to brand-specific family entertainment has everything a vacationing Brady-esque bunch could want: themed swimming pools, themed play areas, and even character-themed rooms that allow the kids to fully immerse themselves in the Mouse experience. Adults and families on a budget can also get rooms with either a king or two queen beds and more traditional motel fabrics and appointments. The monorail stops inside the hotel, offering guests the easiest way into the park proper without having to deal with parking or even walking.

It's easy to find the **Paradise Pier Hotel** (1717 S. Disneyland Dr., Anaheim, 714/999-0990, http://disneyland.disney.go.com, $344-952); it's that high-rise thing just outside Disney California Adventure Park. This hotel boasts what passes for affordable lodgings within walking distance of the parks. Rooms are cute, colorful, and clean; many have two doubles or queens to accommodate families or couples traveling together on a tighter budget. You'll find a (possibly refreshing) lack of Mickeys in the standard guest accommodations at the Paradise, which has the feel of a beach resort motel. After a day of wandering the park, relax by the rooftop pool.

Disney's Grand Californian Hotel and Spa (1600 S. Disneyland Dr., Anaheim, 714/635-2300, http://disneyland.disney.go.com, $417-1,477) is inside Disney

California Adventure Park, attempting to mimic the famous Ahwahnee Lodge in Yosemite. While it doesn't quite succeed (much of what makes the Ahwahnee so great is its views), the big-beam construction and soaring common spaces do feel reminiscent of a great luxury lodge. The hotel is surrounded by gardens and has restaurants, a day spa, and shops attached on the ground floor; it can also get you right out into Downtown Disney and thence to the parks proper. Rooms here offer more luxury than the other Disney resorts, with dark woods and faux-craftsman details creating an attractive atmosphere. Get anything from a standard room that sleeps two up to spacious family suites with bunk beds that can easily handle six people. As with all Disney resorts, you can purchase tickets and a meal plan along with your hotel room (in fact, if you book via the website, they'll try to force you to do it that way).

Outside the Parks

The massive park complex is ringed with motels, both popular chains and more interesting independents. Within walking distance is the **Desert Palms Hotel & Suites** (631 W. Katella Ave., Anaheim, 888/788-0466, www. desertpalmshotel.com, $250-415). The pool and spa provide fun for children and adults alike, and the many amenities make travelers comfortable. Guests with more discretionary income can choose from a number of suites, some designed to delight children and others aimed at couples on a romantic getaway. There are even condo-style accommodations with kitchens.

Away from the Disneyland complex and surrounding area, the accommodations in Orange County run to chain motels with little character or distinctiveness, but the good news is that you can find a decent room for a reasonable price.

The **Hyatt Regency Orange County** (11999 Harbor Blvd., Garden Grove, 714/750-1234, http://orangecounty.hyatt.com, $129-289) in Garden Grove is about 1.5 miles (10 minutes' drive on Harbor Blvd.) south of the

park. The family-friendly suites have separate bedrooms with bunk beds and fun decor geared toward younger guests. Enjoy a cocktail in the sun-drenched atrium, or grab a chaise lounge by the pool or take a refreshing dip.

TRANSPORTATION AND SERVICES
Air

The nearest airport to Disneyland, serving all of Orange County, is **John Wayne Airport** (SNA, 18601 Airport Way, Santa Ana, 949/252-5200, www.ocair.com). It's much easier to fly into and out of John Wayne than LAX, though it can be more expensive. John Wayne's terminal has plenty of rental car agencies, as well as many shuttle services that can get you where you need to go—especially to the House of Mouse.

If you have to fly into LAX for scheduling or budget reasons, catch a shuttle straight from the airport to your Disneyland hotel. Among the many companies offering and arranging such transportation, the one with the best name is **MouseSavers** (www. mousesavers.com). Working with various shuttle and van companies, MouseSavers can get you a ride in a van or a bus from LAX or John Wayne to your destination at or near Disneyland.

Car

Disneyland is on Disneyland Drive in Anaheim and is most accessible from I-5 South where it crosses Ball Road (stay in the left three lanes for parking). The parking lot (1313 S. Disneyland Dr.) costs $20.

Public Transit

If you're coming to the park from elsewhere in Southern California, consider leaving the car (avoiding the parking fees) and taking public transit instead. **Anaheim Resort Transit** (ART, 1280 Anaheim Blvd., Anaheim, 714/563-5287, www.rideart.org, adults $5.50, children $2) can take you to and from the Amtrak station and all around central

Anaheim. Buy passes via the website or at conveniently located kiosks.

Services

Each park has information booths near the park entrance. On the website for **Visit Anaheim** (http://visitanaheim.org), you can plan a trip to the area in advance by looking at the upcoming events and suggested itineraries or by downloading the travel guide.

If you need to stow your bags or hit the restroom before plunging into the fray, banks of lockers and restrooms sit in the main entrance area. If mobility is a problem, consider renting a **stroller, wheelchair,** or **scooter.** Ask for directions to the rental counter when you enter the park.

Disneyland offers its own minor medical facilities, which can dispense first aid for scrapes, cuts, and mild heat exhaustion. They can also call an ambulance if something nastier has occurred. The **West Anaheim Medical Center** (3033 W. Orange Ave., Anaheim, 714/827-3000, www.westanaheimmedctr.com) is a full-service hospital with an emergency room.

Long Beach and Orange County Beaches

The Los Angeles coastline continues beyond the city limits, passing the Palos Verdes Peninsula and stretching farther south to Long Beach, where haunted ships and sunny coasts await.

The Orange County coast begins at Huntington Beach and stretches south across a collection of sunny, scenic beach towns (Newport Beach, Laguna Beach, and Dana Point) until ending at San Juan Capistrano. The surf here is world-renowned. If you've ever seen a surf magazine or surf movie, you've seen surfers ripping Orange County breaks like Salt Creek and Trestles.

LONG BEACH

Long Beach has several worthy attractions befitting its size, including the historic and possibly haunted *Queen Mary* ocean liner and the Aquarium of the Pacific. Long Beach Harbor is also one of the best places to catch a boat ride out to Catalina Island, about 22 miles from shore.

Sights
★ THE *QUEEN MARY*
The major visitor attraction of Long Beach is **The *Queen Mary*** (1126 Queens Hwy.,

877/342-0738, www.queenmary.com, 10am-6pm daily, adults $27-34, children $17.50-24.50, parking $15), one of the most famous ships ever to ply the high seas. This great ship, once a magnificent pleasure-cruise liner, now sits at permanent anchor in Long Beach Harbor. The *Queen Mary* acts as a **hotel** (877/342-0742, $99-389), a museum, and an entertainment center with several restaurants and bars. Book a stateroom and stay aboard, come for dinner, or just buy a regular ticket and take a self-guided tour. The museum exhibits describe the history of the ship, which took its maiden voyage in 1936, with special emphasis on its tour of duty as a troop transport during World War II.

It's not just the extensive museum and the attractive hotel that make the *Queen Mary* well known today. The ship is also one of the most famously haunted places in California. Over its decades of service, a number of people lost their lives aboard the *Queen Mary*. Rumors say several of these unfortunate souls have remained on the ship since their tragic deaths. If you're most interested in the ghost stories of the *Queen Mary*, book a spot on the **Paranormal Ship Walk** (www.queenmary.com, $44), which takes you to the hottest

Orange County

© AVALON TRAVEL

haunted spots; **Dining with the Spirits** (7pm Fri.-Sat., includes three-course dinner, $134), a combination dinner and two-hour haunted tour; or **Paranormal Investigation** (www. queenmary.com, $79), for serious ghost hunters.

The **Queen Mary Passport** (adults $27, children 4-11 $17.50) includes a self-guided audio tour, a look at the vessel's historical exhibits, a viewing of a film showing in the 4-D theater, and admission to the Ghosts and Legends Tour. The **First Class Passport** (adults $34, children 4-11 $24.50) includes all

of the *Queen Mary* Passport attractions along with a ticket to your choice of the Glory Days Historical Tour or the Haunted Encounters Tour.

The *Queen Mary* offers a large paid parking lot near the ship's berth. You'll walk from the parking area up to a square with a ticket booth and several shops and a snack bar. Purchase your general-admission ticket to get on board the ship. It's also a good idea to buy any guided tour tickets at this point. Night tours can fill up in advance, so call ahead to reserve a spot.

AQUARIUM OF THE PACIFIC

The **Aquarium of the Pacific** (100 Aquarium Way, 562/590-3100, www.aquariumofpacific.org, 9am-6pm daily, adults $30, seniors $27, children $18) hosts animals and plant life native to the Pacific Ocean, from the local residents of SoCal's sea up to the northern Pacific and down to the tropics. While the big, modern building isn't much to look at from the outside, it's what's inside that's beautiful—sea stars, urchins, and rays in the touch-friendly tanks, and a Shark Lagoon where you can pet a few of the more than 150 sharks that live here.

Food

Combining elegance, fine continental-California cuisine, and great ghost stories, **Sir Winston's Restaurant and Lounge** (1126 Queens Hwy., 562/499-1657, www.queenmary.com, 5pm-9pm Tues.-Thurs., 5pm-10pm Fri.-Sat., $30-78) floats gently on board the *Queen Mary*. For the most beautiful dining experience, request a window table and make reservations for sunset. Dress in your finest; Sir Winston's requests that diners adhere to their semiformal dress code.

A locals' favorite down where the shops and cafés cluster, **Natraj Cuisine of India** (5262 E. 2nd St., 562/930-0930, www.natrajlongbeach.com, 11am-2:30pm and 5pm-10pm Mon.-Thurs., 11am-2:30pm and 5pm-11pm Fri., 11am-11pm Sat., 11am-9:30pm Sun., $12-20) offers good food for reasonable prices. Come by for the all-you-can-eat lunch buffet Monday-Saturday to sample a variety of properly spiced meat and vegetarian dishes created in classic Indian tradition.

Accommodations

The Varden (335 Pacific Ave., 562/432-8950, www.thevardenhotel.com, $149-199) offers the type of tiny, clean, and modern rooms you'd expect to find in Europe. If you don't mind your bath being a foot or two from your bed, the sleek little rooms in this hotel, which dates back to 1929, are a great deal. The oldest operating hotel in Long Beach, it is named after an eccentric circus performer named Dolly Varden, who is rumored to have hoarded jewels on the premises. The staff is friendly and helpful, and coffee, ice, and fresh fruit are available to guests 24 hours a day. It's also one block from Pine Street, which is lined with restaurants and bars.

Looking for something completely different? At **Dockside Boat and Bed** (Dock 5A, Rainbow Harbor, 562/436-3111 or

the *Queen Mary* in Long Beach

800/436-2574, www.boatandbed.com, $200-350, overnight parking $24, unless you get the $10 discount parking pass from Dockside), you won't get a regular old hotel room, you'll get one of four yachts. The yachts run 38-54 feet and can sleep four or more people each ($25 pp after the first 2). Amenities include TVs with DVD players, stereos, kitchen facilities, wet bars, and ample seating. The boats are in walking distance from the harbor's restaurants and the aquarium. Don't expect to take your floating accommodations out for a spin; these yachts are permanent residents of Rainbow Harbor.

Transportation and Services

Long Beach is about 25 miles directly south of downtown Los Angeles. Head down **I-5 South** for two miles and then merge onto **I-710 South** toward Long Beach. Stay on the roadway for 17 miles, then turn off on Exit 1C for the downtown area and the aquarium.

Long Beach is just 20 miles from Disneyland Resort. Take **CA-22 West** from Disneyland for 12 miles. The roadway turns into Long Beach's East 7th Street, with will take you to the Long Beach city center.

While you can get to the coast easily enough from LAX, the **Long Beach Airport** (LGB, 4100 Donald Douglas Dr., 562/570-2600, www.lgb.org) is both closer to Long Beach and less crowded than LAX.

The **Orange County Transportation Authority** (OCTA, 714/636-7433, www.octa.net, one trip $2, day pass $5) runs buses along the O.C. coast. The appropriately numbered **Route 1** bus runs right along the Pacific Coast Highway (CA-1) from Long Beach down to San Clemente and back. Other routes can get you to and from inland O.C. destinations, including Anaheim. Regular bus fares are payable in cash on the bus with exact change. You can also buy a day pass from the bus driver.

For information, maps, brochures, and advice about Long Beach and the surrounding areas, visit the **Long Beach Convention and Visitors Bureau** (301 E. Ocean Blvd.,

Ste. 1900, 562/436-3645, www.visitlongbeach.com, 8am-5pm Mon.-Fri.).

HUNTINGTON BEACH

This Orange County beach town is known for its longtime association with surfing and surf culture, beginning when Hawaiian legend Duke Kahanamoku first rode waves here back in 1922. Surfers still ride the surf on either side of the **Huntington Beach Pier,** a large concrete pier that offers fine views of the beach scene on both sides. Across the Pacific Coast Highway, Huntington Beach's Main Street is full of restaurants, bars, and shops, including lots of surf shops.

Beaches

Huntington City Beach (Pacific Coast Hwy. from Beach Blvd. to Seapoint St., beach headquarters 103 Pacific Coast Hwy., 714/536-5281, www.huntingtonbeachca.gov, beach 5am-10pm daily, office 8am-5pm Mon.-Fri.) runs the length of the south end of town, petering out toward the oil industry facilities at the north end. This famous beach hosts major sporting events such as the U.S. Open of Surfing and the X Games. But even the average beachgoer can enjoy all sorts of activities on a daily basis, from sunbathing to beach volleyball, surfing to skim-boarding. There's a cement walkway for biking, in-line skating, jogging, and walking. Plus, you'll find a dog-friendly section at the north end of the beach where dogs can be let off-leash.

Food

The Black Trumpet Bistro (18344 Beach Blvd., 714/842-1122, www.theblacktrumpetbistro.com, 11:30am-10pm Tues.-Fri., 4pm-10pm Sat., 4pm-9pm Sun., $12-23) has paintings of jazz legends adorning the walls. The owner wants to represent Mediterranean cuisine from tapas to more substantial entrées. His endeavor has caused The Black Trumpet to be proclaimed one of Huntington Beach's best restaurants by the *OC Weekly.*

For a quick bite to eat, stop off at the **Bodhi**

Tree Vegetarian Cafe (501 Main St., Ste. E, 714/969-9500, 11am-10pm Mon. and Wed.-Sun., $6-10) for vegetarian soups, salads, and sandwiches. **Sugar Shack Café** (213 Main St., 714/536-0355, www.hbsugarshack.com, 6am-2pm Mon.-Tues and Thurs.-Fri., 6am-8pm Wed., 6am-3pm Sat.-Sun., $7-10) is a great place for breakfast, serving omelets and breakfast burritos.

Accommodations

The 17-room **Sun 'n Sands Motel** (1102 Pacific Coast Hwy., 714/536-2543, www.sunnsands.com, $249-399) is a tiny place where you can expect the standard motel room, but the main attraction is across the treacherous Pacific Coast Highway: long, sweet Huntington Beach. Be careful crossing the highway to get to the sand. Find a traffic light and a crosswalk rather than risking life and limb for the minor convenience of jaywalking.

For something more upscale, book a room at the **Shorebreak Hotel** (500 Pacific Coast Hwy., 714/861-4470, www.shorebreakhotel.com, $329-749). Some rooms have private balconies looking out over the beach and pier. Everyone can enjoy the hotel's on-site restaurant, fitness center, and courtyard with fire pits.

Transportation and Services

It can take just 45 minutes to get to Huntington Beach from central Los Angeles. Take **I-5 South** out of downtown for nine miles. Then get on **I-605 South** for 11 miles before merging onto **I-405 South.** Take the Seal Beach Boulevard exit from I-405 and turn left on Seal Beach Boulevard. After 2.5 miles, turn left on the **Pacific Coast Highway,** which you'll take for eight miles to Huntington Beach.

Huntington Beach is one of the closest beaches to Disneyland, just 16 miles away. From Disneyland, get on **CA-22 West** for four miles and then turn on the Beach Boulevard exit. Take Beach Boulevard (CA-39) for eight miles to Huntington Beach.

The beach route between Long Beach and Huntington Beach is the **Pacific Coast Highway (CA-1).** Take it south out of Long Beach for 9.6 miles to reach Huntington Beach. If it's a crowded beach weekend, hop on **CA-22 East** to reach **I-405 South.** Continue for 6.8 miles to the CA-39/Beach Boulevard exit and follow the road to the beach.

Get assistance at the **Huntington Beach Marketing and Visitors Bureau** (301 Main St., Ste. 208, 714/969-3492 or 800/729-6232, www.surfcityusa.com, 9am-5pm Mon.-Fri.), which also has a visitor information kiosk (Pacific Coast Hwy. and Main St., hours vary). Huntington Beach has a **post office** (316 Olive Ave., 714/536-4973, www.usps.com, 9am-5pm Mon.-Fri.) and the **Huntington Beach Hospital** (17772 Beach Blvd., 714/843-5000, www.hbhospital.org).

NEWPORT BEACH

Affluent Newport Beach is known for its beaches, harbor, and The Wedge, a notorious bodysurfing and body-boarding wave.

Beaches

Most of the activity in **Newport Beach** (www.visitnewportbeach.com) centers around Newport Pier (McFadden Pl.) and Main Street on the Balboa Peninsula. This 10-mile stretch of sand is popular for fishing, swimming, surfing, and other ocean activities. On the east end of Balboa Peninsula, **The Wedge** is the world's most famous bodysurfing spot. On south swells, the wave jacks up off the adjacent rock jetty and creates monsters up to 30 feet high that break almost right on the beach. Beginners should stay out of the water and enjoy the spectacle from the sand.

Food

For something French, colorful **Pescadou Bistro** (3325 Newport Blvd., 949/675-6990, www.pescadoubistro.com, 5:30pm-9pm Tues.-Sun., $21-36) fills the bill. Meanwhile, **Eat Chow** (211 62nd St., 949/423-7080, www.eatchownow.com, 8am-9pm Mon.-Thurs., 8am-10pm Fri., 7am-10pm Sat., 7am-9pm

Catalina Island

You can see Catalina from the shore of Long Beach on a clear day, but for a better view, you've got to get onto the island. The port town of Avalon welcomes visitors with Mediterranean-inspired hotels, restaurants, and shops. But the main draw of Catalina lies outside the walls of its buildings. Catalina beckons hikers, horseback riders, ecotourists, and, most of all, water lovers.

The **Catalina Casino** (1 Casino Way, 310/510-7428, www.visitcatalinaisland.com) is a round, white art deco building, opened in 1929 not for gambling but as a community gathering place. Today, it hosts diverse activities, including the Catalina Island Jazz Festival. Stroll through the serene **Wrigley Memorial and Botanical Garden** (Avalon Canyon Rd., 1.5 miles west of town, 310/510-2897, www.catalinaconservancy.org, 8am-5pm daily, adults $7, seniors and veterans with ID $5, children 5-12 and students with ID $3, children under 5 and active military free) in the hills above Avalon.

Outdoor recreation is the main draw. Swim or snorkel at the **Avalon Underwater Park** (Casino Point). A protected section at the north end of town offers access to a reef with plentiful sea life, including bright orange garibaldi fish. Out at the deeper edge of the park, nearly half a dozen wrecked ships await exploration. For a guided snorkel or scuba tour, visit **Catalina Snorkel & Scuba** (310/510-8558, www.catalinasnorkelscuba.com). If you need snorkeling gear, hit up **Wet Spot Rentals** (310/510-2229, www.catalinakayaks.com, snorkel gear $10 per hour, $20 per day).

Descanso Beach Ocean Sports/Catalina Island Kayak & Snorkel (310/510-1226, www.kayakcatalinaisland.com, half-day to full-day $40-72) offers several kayak tours to different parts of the island. **Jeep Eco-Tours** (310/510-2595, www.catalinaconservancy.org, chartered half-day $549 for up to 6 people, chartered full-day $889, nonchartered 2-hour tour $70-109 pp) will take you out into the wilderness to see bison, wild horses, and plant species unique to the island.

The best dining option is **The Lobster Trap** (128 Catalina St., 310/510-8585, www.catalinalobstertrap.com, 11am-late daily, $14-44), which serves up its namesake crustacean in various forms, along with other seafood.

Sun., $9-18) is a local favorite, with items like breakfast *carnitas* tacos and braised short rib burritos.

Expect a line outside **Cappy's Café & Cantina** (5930 W. Coast Hwy., 949/646-4202, 6am-3pm Thurs.-Tues., 6am-8pm Wed., $10-20), a low-slung building that has served breakfast and lunch since 1957. Cappy's serves expand-your-waistband items including a 20-ounce porterhouse steak and eggs and a knockwurst and eggs dish. Enjoy the fare while mellowing out in a beachy atmosphere with plenty of colorful murals.

Accommodations

South of downtown Newport Beach, the **Crystal Cove Beach Cottages** (35 Crystal Cove, 949/376-6200, https://crystalcove.org, reservations 800/444-7275 or www.reservecalifornia.com, dorms $36-108, cottages $179-251) give anyone the opportunity to experience life right on the Southern California sand. Some of the cabins are individual rentals that you can have all to yourself. The dorm cottages offer by-the-room accommodations for solo travelers (linens included; room doors lock). None of the cottages have TVs or any type of digital entertainment. And all the cottages include a common refrigerator and microwave, but no full kitchen, so plan to eat out, perhaps at the adjacent **Beachcomber Cafe** (15 Crystal Cove, 949/376-6900, www.thebeachcombercafe.com, 7am-9:30pm daily, $18-37), where items like breakfast *chilaquiles* and crab-stuffed salmon are served.

Transportation

It takes less than an hour to drive the 40 miles between the L.A. city center and Newport

Catalina Casino

GETTING THERE

The **Catalina Express** (310/519-1212, www.catalinaexpress.com, round-trip: adults $74.50-76.50, seniors $68-70, children 2-11$59-61, children under 2 $5, bike and surfboards $7) offers multiple ferry trips every day, even in the off-season. During the summer, you can depart from Long Beach, San Pedro, or Dana Point. Bring your bike, your luggage, and your camping gear aboard for the hour-long ride.

Beach. Disneyland is even closer, just 26 miles. From either starting point, take **I-5 South** and then merge onto **CA-55 South,** which leads the remaining 10 miles into town. From Huntington Beach, Newport Beach is just a five miles' drive on the **Pacific Coast Highway (CA-1).**

LAGUNA BEACH AREA

Laguna Beach stands apart from other Orange County beach communities with its long-running arts scene, touted fine-dining restaurants, tide-pool-pocked coastline jammed between sandy beaches, and clear ocean water that beckons snorkelers and divers underwater.

Mission San Juan Capistrano

Mission San Juan Capistrano (26801 Ortega Hwy., 949/234-1300, www.missionsjc. com, 9am-5pm daily, adults $9, seniors $8, children 4-11 $6, children under 4 free), in the lovely little town of San Juan Capistrano, has a beautiful Catholic church and extensive gardens and grounds. In late fall and early spring, Monarch butterflies flutter about in the flower gardens and out by the fountain in the courtyard. Inside the original church, artifacts from the early time of the mission tell the story of its rise and fall, as does an audio tour available in the museum.

Beaches

Heisler Park and **Main Beach Park** (Pacific Coast Hwy., Laguna Beach, www. lagunabeachinfo.com) offer protected waterways, with tide pools and plenty of water-based playground equipment. The two parks are connected, so you can walk from one to the other. If you're into scuba diving, there are several reefs right off the beach. You'll find all the facilities and amenities you need at Heisler and Main Beach Parks, including picnic tables, lawns, and restrooms. Park on the street if you find a spot, but the meters get checked all the time, so feed them well.

Laguna Beach has a lot more undeveloped space than other Orange County communities, and **Crystal Cove State Park** (8471 N. Coast Hwy., 949/494-3539, www.crystalcovestatepark.org, 6am-sunset daily, $15 per vehicle) just north of town has 3.2 miles of lightly developed coastline with sandy coves and tide pools. Offshore is the Crystal Cove Underwater Park, which has several snorkeling and diving sites. The park also includes a 2,400-acre inland section with unpaved roads and trails that are open to hikers, bikers, and horseback riders.

At the southern tip of the O.C., Dana Point has a harbor (34551 Puerto Pl., 949/923-2280, www.ocparks.com) that has become a recreation marina that draws locals and visitors from all around. It also has several beaches nearby. One of the prettiest is **Capistrano Beach** (35005 Beach Rd., 949/923-2280 or 949/923-2283, www.ocparks.com, 6am-10pm daily, parking $1-2 per hour). You'll find a metered parking lot adjacent to the beach, plus showers and restrooms available.

Also in Dana Point, **Doheny State Beach** (25300 Dana Point Harbor Dr., 949/496-6172, www.parks.ca.gov, 6am-10pm daily, $15) is popular with surfers and anglers. The northern end of Doheny has a lawn along with volleyball courts, while the southern side has a popular campground with 121 campsites.

Visit **Salt Creek Beach** (33333 S. Pacific Coast Hwy., 949/923-2280, www.ocparks.com, 5am-midnight daily, parking $1 per hour) for a renowned surf break and a great place to spend a day in the sun.

Food

Carmelita's Kitchen De Mexico (217 Broadway, 949/715-7829, www.carmelitaskdm.com, 11am-10pm Mon.-Fri., 9am-9pm Sat.-Sun. $14-28) is a popular local favorite serving upscale Mexican cuisine. The open kitchen puts out terrific entrées including *tampiqueña* (marinated skirt steak) and a seafood trio platter with a lobster enchilada, shrimp taco, and crab relleno. Carmelita's also does some twists on the classic margarita, with cilantro-cucumber and strawberry-jalapeño versions.

Watermarc (448 S. Coast Hwy., 949/376-6272, http://watermarcrestaurant.com, 11am-10pm Mon.-Thurs., 8am-11pm Fri.-Sat., 8am-10pm Sun., small plates $8-18, entrées $29-37), run by executive chef Marc Cohen, focuses on its "grazing plates," from filet mignon potpie to smoked bacon-wrapped dates. The two-story restaurant also has exceptional cocktails. Happy hour (4pm-6pm daily) offers burgers at half price, while all drinks and appetizers are $2 off.

For a casual meal, visitsou **The Stand** (238 Thalia St., 949/494-8101, www.thestandnaturalfoods.com, 7am-8pm daily summer, 7am-7pm daily winter, $7-11), a shack that has lovingly served up vegan food for more than 40 years. Order at the window and dine on the small outdoor porch or take your meal a couple of blocks to the beach.

At **Sapphire Laguna** (1200 S. Coast Hwy., 949/715-9888, www.sapphirellc.com, 11am-10:30pm Mon.-Fri., 9am-10:30pm Sat.-Sun., $24-37), Chef Azmin Ghahreman knows no national boundaries. His international seasonal cuisine might include a Greek octopus salad, Moroccan couscous, a half *jidori* chicken, or Hawaiian-style steamed mahi-mahi.

South of Nick's (110 N. El Camino Real, San Clemente, 949/481-4545, www.nicksrestaurants.com, 11am-10pm Mon.-Thurs., 11am-11pm Fri.-Sat., 10am-10pm Sun., $10-38) offers a menu with an upscale Mexican twist. The bar keeps up with the kitchen's creativity by serving up regular margaritas as well as coconut and cucumber versions.

Accommodations

Perched on a bluff over Laguna Beach's Main

Beach, **The Inn at Laguna Beach** (211 N. Pacific Coast Hwy., 800/544-4479, $289-1,074) is the ideal place to stay for an upscale beach vacation. Half of its rooms face the ocean, and a majority of those have balconies to take in the salt air and sound of the sea. Hit up the inn's beach valet for complimentary beach umbrellas, chairs, and towels. After time on Main Beach, retire to the inn's brick pool deck with its pool and hot tub, or head up to the rooftop terrace and warm up by the fire pit.

The **Laguna Beach House** (475 N. Pacific Coast Hwy., 800/297-0007, www.thelagunabeachhouse.com, $299-559) is a casual, surfing-obsessed motel geared toward wave riders and surf-culture aficionados, with killer decor (including a surfboard shaped by the owner) in each of its 36 rooms and a daily surf report written up on a chalkboard in the lobby. The U-shaped structure surrounds a pool deck with pool, hot tub, and fire pit. Before hitting the waves, enjoy a complimentary breakfast parfait and coffee put out in the lobby.

The **Blue Lantern Inn** (34343 Street of the Blue Lantern, Dana Point, 800/950-1236, www.bluelanterninn.com, $210-585) crowns the bluffs over the Dana Point Harbor. This attractive contemporary inn offers beachfront elegance in 29 rooms boasting soothing colors, charming appointments, and lush amenities, including a spa tub in every bath, gas fireplaces, and honest-to-goodness free drinks in the mini fridge; some feature patios or balconies with impressive views of the harbor and the Pacific. The inn also offers complimentary bike usage, a hot breakfast, and an afternoon wine-and-appetizers spread.

Stay in a historic and stunning Spanish colonial villa at the **Beachcomber Inn** (533 Avenida Victoria, San Clemente, 949/492-5457, http://thebeachcomberinn.com, $280-415). The 10 standard villas and two deluxe villas all come with porches, full kitchens, and full views of the ocean, the beach, and the pier.

Transportation

Laguna Beach is just 50 miles from central Los Angeles, although the highway traffic may make the drive feel a lot longer. Take **I-5 South** for 37 miles and then get on **CA-133 South** for 9.5 miles into town.

If I-5 is jammed up, there's an **alternate route,** but it involves a **toll road,** CA-73, that requires electronic payment. You can register an account or pay a one-time fee online at www.thetollroads.com. From **I-5 South,** merge onto **I-605 South,** following it for 11 miles. Then take **I-405 South** for 14 miles. From there, take **CA-73 South** for 11 miles. Exit on **CA-133** (Laguna Canyon Rd.) and take a right to drive a few miles into Laguna Beach.

The drive from Disneyland to Laguna Beach is only 30 minutes without traffic. Just take **I-5 South** for 13 miles and then get on **CA-133 South** for 10 miles. Laguna Beach is an 11-mile drive south of Newport Beach on the **Pacific Coast Highway (CA-1).**

San Diego

S an Diego is the ideal destination for anyone whose idea of the perfect California vacation is a day lying on a white sand beach, sipping cocktails, and looking out over the Pacific Ocean.

Even though San Diego's physical area seems small compared to other parts of California, it can't be beat for density of things to see. From a world-famous zoo to dozens of museums to the thick layer of military and mission history, San Diego offers education, enlightenment, and fun to visitors with all different interests.

Animal lovers flock to the San Diego Zoo and SeaWorld, while water spirits dive into the Pacific Ocean to catch a wave or examine a variety of sealife in its natural habitat. Travelers who want a little more of the trappings of city life will enjoy the bar and club scene, as well as a thriving theater community.

Across the bay, the long, blue Coronado Bridge connects San Diegans to Coronado, an island-like enclave that beckons beach bums and film aficionados alike to the grandly historic (and reputedly haunted) Hotel del Coronado, where the Marilyn Monroe picture *Some Like It Hot* was filmed.

North of San Diego proper, the towns of La Jolla, Del Mar, Encinitas, and Oceanside offer a more relaxed pace for exploring. Snorkel the azure water of La Jolla Cove or vie for a piece of that pristine sand with the beach crowd. Splurge some of that vacation cash on a horse race at the Del Mar Racetrack, or have an up-close-and-personal interaction with the exotic animals at the San Diego Zoo Safari Park.

PLANNING YOUR TIME

San Diego's major attractions sit relatively close together, and it's easy to get from one place to another. San Diego County has arguably the best **beaches** in the state. If your travel goals are focused on sand and surf, consider staying in **Mission Bay** or **Point Loma**, or farther afield in the North County coastal area. On the other hand, if you're in town to see the zoo or take in some museums, you'll be spending time in **Balboa Park,** which abuts the Old Town and downtown areas. If

Previous: a beach in San Diego's North County; Mission San Diego del Alcalá. **Above:** brown pelicans in La Jolla.

Look for ★ to find recommended
sights, activities, dining, and lodging.

Highlights

★ **Gaslamp Quarter:** This former red-light district is now the hub of San Diego's downtown, filled with restaurants, bars, and shops (page 389).

★ **USS *Midway:*** This aircraft carrier, once the largest ship in the world, served during the Cold War, Vietnam, and Desert Storm. Docents, many of them veterans, vividly recall what life was like on board (page 393).

★ **San Diego Zoo:** The most popular tourist attraction in Balboa Park is home to all sorts of animals, including giant pandas (page 394).

★ **Old Town San Diego State Historic Park:** Wander back into the 1800s when San Diego was the state's first European-settled town in this park enlivened with music, vendors, and people in period dress (page 396).

★ **Hotel del Coronado:** You don't have to stay at the luxurious Hotel del Coronado to enjoy this San Diego landmark. The Del has a historical museum, shopping center, a range of restaurants, and a relaxing beach right out front (page 399).

★ **La Jolla Cove:** Snorkel or scuba dive offshore, kayak through sea caves, or just relax on the sand at this scenic spot (page 401).

★ **Torrey Pines State Reserve:** Take a break from San Diego's beaches at this reserve, which has impressive eroded cliffs, panoramic

coast views, and the nation's rarest pine trees (page 403).

★ **California Surf Museum:** Up in North County, this museum offers homage to the pioneers of the coastal sport with exhibits and regularly occurring summer events (page 429).

you're starting a tour of California missions, head for Old Town first. Military history and navy buffs will be content to spend their whole trip within the city limits of San Diego, dividing their time between the harbor and Point Loma. If you've got an extra couple of hours, take the bridge to Coronado to gawk at the ridiculous exuberance of the Hotel del Coronado.

San Diego makes a perfect **weekend** getaway any time of year, but **summer** lures the most crowds to the city's sandy beaches.

Sights

DOWNTOWN

San Diego's downtown area is small and homey, and the area feels safe to walk in—even if you're a lone woman after dark. The Gaslamp Quarter highlights downtown, offering hundreds of restaurants, dozens of bars and clubs, and a rich history. The area near the airport has a range of hotels and skirts the harbor of San Diego Bay, with its museums and ships and ship museums. The rest of downtown stretches out toward Old Town and Balboa Park.

★ Gaslamp Quarter

The **Gaslamp Quarter** (4th, 5th, and 6th Sts. and Broadway, www.gaslamp.org) has exuded atmosphere since its earliest inception in the 19th century. The 5th Street Pier led sailors right to the area, where saloons and brothels flourished. Ida Bailey—a famous lady of the evening—moved in and cemented the area (then called Stingaree) as a red-light district. Famous Wild West lawman Wyatt Earp ran three gambling halls in the region. After decades of thriving debauchery, a police raid in 1912 heralded the end of the Gaslamp Quarter's popularity. Throughout the first two-thirds of the 1900s, the area decayed, becoming a low-rent district filled with porn theaters and liquor stores. In the mid-1970s, the Gaslamp Quarter Association came to be, and the renewal of this downtown area began.

Today, the Gaslamp Quarter bustles with foot traffic, both locals and tourists. People crowd into the popular and sometimes quirky restaurants, dance like mad at the many bars and clubs, and spend their cash in the shops and boutiques. (But only tourists insist on taking photos under the Gaslamp Quarter sign.) Ghosts reputedly haunt several buildings here; check into a ghost tour or explore on your own to try to see or feel a spook. While the Gaslamp Quarter is quite safe, you will see a scattering of homeless people. In the evenings, the gas lamp-shaped streetlights illuminate the sidewalks and the historic architecture of some of the structures, especially along 5th Street.

Maritime Museum of San Diego

On the downtown waterfront, it's easy to spot the **Maritime Museum of San Diego** (1492 N. Harbor Dr., 619/234-9153, ext. 101, www.sdmaritime.org, 9am-9pm daily Memorial Day-Labor Day, 9am-8pm daily Labor Day-Memorial Day, adults $18, seniors, military, and students $13, children $8): Just look for the tall masts with sails. This museum features a collection of floating historic ships, many of which still sail on a regular basis. The gem of the collection is the famous *Star of India,* which has been plying the high seas since 1863. Other genuine historic ships include the *Medea,* the *Berkeley,* and a Soviet submarine. Another ship that makes regular passenger cruises is the *Californian*—the state's Official Tall Ship. (Yes, California has such a thing!)

Come any day to tour the various ships at dock—on board you'll find a wealth of exhibits depicting the maritime history of San Diego, war at sea in centuries past, and the

San Diego

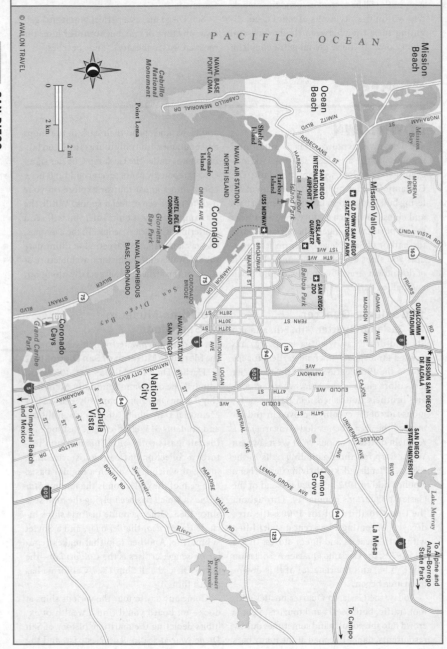

© AVALON TRAVEL

PACIFIC OCEAN

Mission Beach

Ocean Beach

Mission Valley

Mission Bay

MORENA / BLVD

INGRAHAM ST

LINDA VISTA RD

163

FRIARS RD

QUALCOMM STADIUM

8

★ MISSION SAN DIEGO DE ALCALA

SAN DIEGO STATE UNIVERSITY

Lake Murray

To Alpine and Anza-Borrego State Park

8

La Mesa

Lemon Grove

LEMON GROVE AVE

COLLEGE AVE

UNIVERSITY AVE

BLVD

54TH ST

EUCLID AVE

EL CAJON

FAIRMONT AVE

47TH ST

NATIONAL AVE

LOGAN AVE

IMPERIAL AVE

PARADISE VALLEY RD

BONITA RD

Sweetwater

River

Sweetwater Reservoir

125

94

94

805

15

805

To Campo

NAVAL BASE POINT LOMA

CABRILLO MEMORIAL DR

Cabrillo National Monument

Point Loma

Shelter Island

Coronado Island

NAVAL AIR STATION, NORTH ISLAND

Coronado

ORANGE AVE

✚ HOTEL DEL CORONADO

Glorietta Bay Park

CORONADO BRIDGE

NAVAL AMPHIBIOUS BASE, CORONADO

SILVER STRAND BLVD

75

Grand Caribe Park

Coronado Cays

San Diego Bay

75

NAVAL STATION SAN DIEGO

5

NATIONAL CITY BLVD

National City

8TH ST

BROADWAY

E ST

J ST

L ST

H ST

HILLTOP DR

Chula Vista

54

5

To Imperial Beach and Mexico

ROSECRANS ST

NIMITZ BLVD

HARBOR DR

SAN DIEGO INTERNATIONAL AIRPORT ✈

Harbor Island

Harbor Island Park

Harbor

✚ USS MIDWAY

HARBOR DR

5

75

MARKET ST

BROADWAY

✚ GASLAMP QUARTER

1ST AVE

6TH AVE

✚ OLD TOWN SAN DIEGO STATE HISTORIC PARK

✚ SAN DIEGO ZOO

Balboa Park

FERN ST

MADISON AVE

ADAMS AVE

28TH ST

30TH ST

32TH ST

94

15

5

0   2 km
0   2 mi

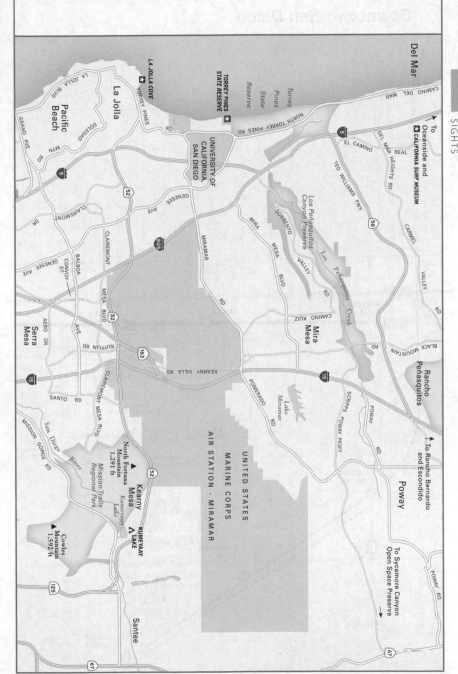

Del Mar

To
Oceanside and
✚ CALIFORNIA SURF MUSEUM

CAMINO DEL MAR
DEL MAR

EL CAMINO
DEL MAR HEIGHTS RD
EL CAMINO REAL

CARMEL VALLEY RD

TED WILLIAMS FWY

Los Peñasquitos
Canyon Preserve

Los Peñasquitos Creek

SORRENTO VALLEY RD

MIRA MESA BLVD

CAMINO RUIZ

Mira
Mesa

BLACK MOUNTAIN RD

Rancho
Peñasquitos

To Rancho Bernardo
and Escondido

SCRIPPS POWAY PKWY

POWAY RD

Poway

To Sycamore Canyon
Open Space Preserve

POWAY RD

67

Santee

125

Cowles
Mountain
1,592 ft

Mission Gorge
Regional Park

MISSION GORGE RD

San Diego River

North Fortuna
Mountain
1,291 ft

Kearny
Mesa

Kumeyaay
Lake

KUMEYAAY
LAKE

CLAIREMONT MESA BLVD

52

SANTO RD

AERO DR

RUFFIN RD

163

KEARNY VILLA RD

POMERADO RD

Lake
Miramar

UNITED STATES
MARINE CORPS
AIR STATION - MIRAMAR

15

15

Serra
Mesa

GENESEE AVE

CONVOY ST

BALBOA AVE

MESA BLVD

CLAIREMONT DR

CLAIREMONT MESA BLVD

MIRAMAR RD

805

52

52

5

GENESEE AVE

Pacific
Beach

GRAND AVE

SOLEDAD MTN RD

LA JOLLA BLVD

La Jolla

LA JOLLA COVE ✚

TORREY PINES

TORREY PINES
STATE RESERVE ✚

Torrey
Pines
State
Reserve

NORTH TORREY PINES RD

UNIVERSITY OF
CALIFORNIA,
SAN DIEGO

✚ CALIFORNIA SURF MUSEUM

5

56

Downtown San Diego

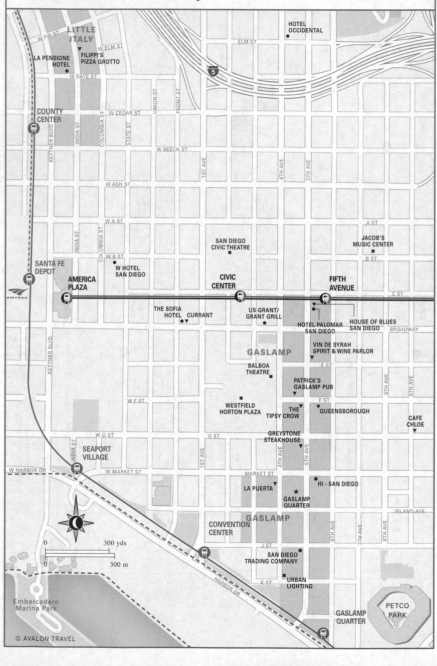

LITTLE ITALY

W FIR ST
W ELM ST
ELM ST

HOTEL OCCIDENTAL

LA PENSIONE HOTEL
FILIPPI'S PIZZA GROTTO

W DATE ST

COUNTY CENTER

W CEDAR ST
W BEECH ST
W ASH ST
W A ST
W B ST

UNION ST
FRONT ST
COLUMBIA ST
STATE ST
INDIA ST
KETTNER BLVD

1ST AVE
4TH AVE
5TH AVE

A ST
JACOB'S MUSIC CENTER
B ST

SANTA FE DEPOT

AMTRAK

AMERICA PLAZA

SAN DIEGO CIVIC THEATRE

W HOTEL SAN DIEGO

CIVIC CENTER

FIFTH AVENUE

C ST

THE SOFIA HOTEL   CURRANT

US GRANT/ GRANT GRILL

HOTEL PALOMAR SAN DIEGO

HOUSE OF BLUES SAN DIEGO

BROADWAY

GASLAMP

VIN DE SYRAH SPIRIT & WINE PARLOR

E ST

BALBOA THEATRE

PATRICK'S GASLAMP PUB

8TH AVE
9TH AVE

F ST

WESTFIELD HORTON PLAZA

THE TIPSY CROW

QUEENSBOROUGH

CAFE CHLOE

W F ST

W G ST

GREYSTONE STEAKHOUSE

G ST

SEAPORT VILLAGE

W HARBOR DR
W MARKET ST

INDIA ST
1ST AVE
4TH AVE
5TH AVE

MARKET ST

LA PUERTA

GASLAMP QUARTER

HI - SAN DIEGO

GASLAMP

ISLAND AVE

CONVENTION CENTER

6TH AVE
7TH AVE
8TH AVE

0   300 yds
0   300 m

J ST

SAN DIEGO TRADING COMPANY

K ST

URBAN LIGHTING

Embarcadero Marina Park

PETCO PARK

GASLAMP QUARTER

HARBOR DR

© AVALON TRAVEL

Two Days in San Diego

While you might not see everything in San Diego within a couple of days, you can see some of the city's best sights and even have a little time to kick back at the beach.

DAY 1

Fortify yourself for a full day of sightseeing at the Hillcrest neighborhood's **Hash House A Go Go** (page 414), where the portions are enormous and tasty. Then head out into nearby **Balboa Park** (page 394), a sprawling urban park with everything from an art museum to a cactus garden. Visit the world-famous **San Diego Zoo** (page 394), home to lots of exotic animals including giant pandas.

From Balboa Park, drive out to Point Loma. This peninsula has the **Cabrillo National Monument** (page 398), which marks where the Spanish explorer first landed on the West Coast, and the **Old Point Loma Lighthouse** (page 398), one of the oldest lighthouses in the state.

For sunset, drive up to the top of the 822-foot-high **Mount Soledad** (page 402) for 360-degree views of the city. While there, take in the sobering veterans' memorial.

Treat yourself to dinner at the elegant **Grant Grill** (page 413) in the **US Grant Hotel** (page 419) or wander a few blocks to **Currant** (page 419) for drinks and snacks. If you still have energy, head out into the surrounding **Gaslamp Quarter** (page 389) for a post-dinner drink. For old-school cocktails in the Gaslamp, order a sipper at **Queensborough** (page 404).

DAY 2

Start the morning right with a tasty French American breakfast in downtown's **Café Chloe** (page 413). Take a few minutes to sip your coffee and read some of the restaurant's magazines or watch people pass by on the sidewalk heading to work.

Get in your car and head out to **La Jolla Cove** (page 401). Snorkel in the offshore marine reserve and then soak up some of Southern California's famous sun on the cove's small, scenic beach.

Dry out by going out to the island-like Coronado for a sunset cocktail at the historic **Hotel del Coronado** (page 399). When hunger strikes, beeline to the **Blue Water Seafood Market & Grill** (page 414), north of downtown, for fish tacos. End the evening with a trip to Old Town for a night tour of the **Whaley House** (page 397), considered to be the most haunted house in America.

---

story of the ship you're on. Make reservations in advance for the historic ship cruises.

★ USS *Midway*

Once the largest ship in the world, the **USS *Midway*** (910 N. Harbor Dr., 619/544-9600, www.midway.org, 10am-5pm daily, adults $21, seniors $18, students $15, military and children 6-12 $8) is now docked along San Diego's Navy Pier. This carrier, which dates to the period just after World War II, served as an active part of the U.S. Navy through Desert Storm in 1991. As you roam throughout the ship, check out the enlisted mess and the dreaded brig as you climb narrow metal steps from deck to deck. Up top, the flight deck includes military planes and helicopters including the F-14 Tomcat, the costar of the 1980s movie *Top Gun*. Consider taking one of the docent-guided tours if you're interested in the realities of life aboard an aircraft carrier; many docents are veterans who served on the ship during the Cold War, Vietnam, or Desert Storm. The self-guided audio tour also makes a good introduction to the ship. Parts of the ship are wheelchair accessible and there are restrooms on board.

BALBOA PARK

The Balboa Park you see today was created for the 1915 Panama-California World Exposition. The Spanish Revival architecture is set amid immense, almost tropical greenery and welcomes visitors with a wealth of museums, halls, exhibitions, gardens, and open spaces. Stop at the **Balboa Park Visitors Center** (1549 El Prado, 619/239-0512, www.balboapark.org, 9:30am-4:30pm daily) for a park map and to plan your visit—there won't be time to see it all!

★ San Diego Zoo

The jewel of San Diego's vast interconnected wildlife park system, the **San Diego Zoo** (2920 Zoo Dr., 619/231-1515, http://zoo.sandiegozoo.org, hours vary seasonally, open daily, adults $54, children $44) lives up to its reputation and then some. The 100-acre zoo actually doubles as the state's largest botanical garden. The zoo grows lovely plants from around the globe that serve as shelter, hiding places, and food for the hundreds of exotic animals that inhabit state-of-the-art enclosures. You'll see perennial zoo favorites including elephants, lions, and polar bears, and you'll also meet a host of other famous and exotic species, such as meerkats, one-foot-tall deer, pythons, and parrots. Other exhibits include two mountain lions and a rare Amur leopard. For the comfort of the human visitors, ample restrooms, benches, concessions, and gift shops are scattered throughout the zoo.

For the best zoo experience, stroll the meandering paved walkways. Some of the paths can be steep—something to remember if you're visiting with kids or folks who have trouble walking; the zoo map can help you find good walking routes. If walking the whole zoo just isn't possible, take a bus ride. The Guided Bus Tour visits many of the zoo's highlights, letting dozens of animals show off for you as you snap photos from the coveted upper deck of the two-story bus. Friendly and knowledgeable docents drive the buses and describe each of the animals and their habitats. If you just want to get from one section of the zoo to another, jump on an Express Bus. For a special treat, take the Skyfari from the front of the park to the rear, where the polar bears play in their pond. You'll get a lovely view of the whole of Balboa Park out to the sea as you traverse the length of the zoo in less than 10 minutes.

Museums and Gardens

Balboa Park is filled with a number of worthy

flamingos at the San Diego Zoo

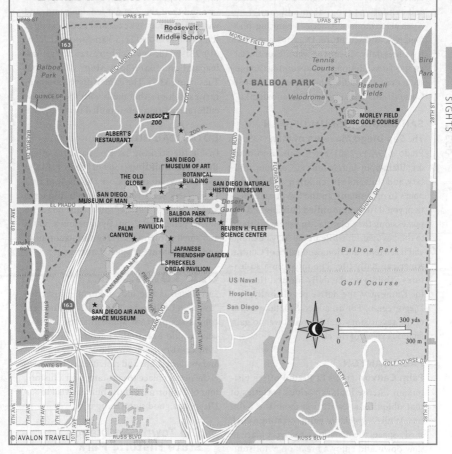

Balboa Park

museums, and meandering paths lead to even more botanical areas and gardens. It's impossible to see everything in one day, but a repeat visit could include the **San Diego Air and Space Museum** (2001 Pan American Plaza, 619/234-8291, https://sandiegoairandspace. org, 10am-4:30pm daily, adults $19.75, seniors, military, and students $16.75, children 3-11 $10.75) for a history of human flight; the **Reuben H. Fleet Science Center** (1875 El Prado, 619/238-1233, www.rhfleet.org, 10am-5pm Mon.-Thurs., 10am-6pm Fri.-Sun., adults $20, seniors $18, children 3-12 $17), where young ones can explore the interactive

science exhibits and everyone can view films in an IMAX dome theater; and the **Natural History Museum** (1788 El Prado, 619/232-3821, www.sdnhm.org, 10am-5pm daily, adults $19, seniors, military, and students $17, children 3-17 $12), which houses a vast collection of fossils and other artifacts presenting San Diego's geologic history.

SAN DIEGO MUSEUM OF ART
The **San Diego Museum of Art** (1450 El Prado, 619/232-7931, www.sdmart.org, 10am-5pm Mon.-Tues., Thurs., and Sat., 10am-8pm Fri., noon-5pm Sun., adults $15, seniors and

military $10, college students $8, children under 17 free) is a highlight. The collections and exhibitions range from old masters to Asian art to modern American painting, photography, and sculpture. Docent tours run a few times daily. Check the website for the latest special exhibitions and upcoming fun museum events including the ongoing Culture & Cocktails that features art, DJs, and drinks.

SAN DIEGO MUSEUM OF MAN

The **San Diego Museum of Man** (1350 El Prado, 619/239-2001, www.museumofman. org, 10am-5pm daily, adults $13, seniors, military, and students $10, children under 5 free) hones in on humans. In the Egyptian collection, you'll find mummified humans and the possessions they planned to take with them to the next world, while in the Maya exhibit, you'll see reproductions and relics of Central American daily life. The museum also features exhibits on the daily life and times of the Kumeyaay, the native people of the San Diego region. For an added $10, take a tour of the seven-story California Tower to gain fabulous views of the city.

PALM CANYON

Palm Canyon (1549 El Prado) offers visitors an intense look at various varieties of that ubiquitous California icon: the palm tree. With 58 species of palms creating a cool, shady space, the canyon is a perfect place to slow down and enjoy a break on a hot summer day. The Mexican fan palms at the center of the garden have lived here almost 100 years. The groomed paths connect the canyon to the Old Cactus Garden; the Alcazar Garden also sits adjacent to the palms, and a tram stop nearby makes access a breeze.

JAPANESE FRIENDSHIP GARDEN

The **Japanese Friendship Garden** (2125 Park Blvd., 619/232-2721, www.niwa.org, 10am-7pm daily, adults $10, seniors, military, and students $8, children under 6 free) began as a teahouse during the 1915-1916 Panama-California World Exposition and grew over the years to include many elements of a traditional Japanese formal garden. Enjoy the tranquility of the Zen garden, koi pond, and wisteria arbor, or take tea and noodle soup at the **Tea Pavilion** (2215 Pan American Way, 619/231-0048, www.cohnrestaurants.com/teapavilion, 10am-3pm Mon., 10am-4pm Tues.-Sun., $3-7). The garden displays temporary exhibitions that mesh with the Japanese cultural traditions exemplified here.

BOTANICAL BUILDING

Inside the striking lattice structure of the **Botanical Building** (1549 El Prado, 619/239-0512, www.balboapark.org, 10am-4pm Fri.-Wed., free) are 2,100 plants including ferns and orchids. A carnivorous plant bog with pitcher plants and Venus flytraps and a "touch and smell garden" with fragrant lemon mint and chocolate are of special interest.

OLD TOWN

San Diego is the oldest European-settled "town" in California. The Old Town area encompasses the first Spanish settlements of what would eventually become California, 19th-century homes and businesses, parks, and modern shops and restaurants. Old Town is the perfect place to get started on a historic tour of California, a ghost-hunting visit to San Diego, or a good sightseeing trip.

★ Old Town San Diego State Historic Park

The **Old Town San Diego State Historic Park** (corner of San Diego Ave. and Twigg St., 619/220-5422, www.parks.ca.gov, visitor center and museums: 10am-5pm daily May-Sept., 10am-4pm Mon.-Thurs., 10am-5pm Fri.-Sun. Oct.-Apr., free) makes a great place to start exploring the history of California's first town. The park hosts many events over the course of each year. The state park visitors center sits in the **Robinson Rose House,** first built in 1853 as a family home and set of offices by attorney James Robinson. Another major home, the **McCoy House** was built in 1869 and now serves as the park's interpretive center. Each room details different eras in San Diego history with displays, interpretive plaques, and re-created scenes. Move on to the early-19th-century Mexican pueblos, including La Casa de Machado y Stewart; this adobe structure contains many artifacts that would have been part of the daily life of San Diego citizens in 1821-1872. Enjoy period music, pet the burros, and observe the park staff engaging in activities folks might have done 150 years ago. If you're more into the afterlife of the residents of Old San Diego, visit the El Campo Santo Cemetery—the oldest cemetery in the city. The park also includes a number of known haunted sites, including the Robinson-Rose House, Casa de Bandini, and La Casa de Estudillo.

There are shops and restaurants within the park at **Fiesta de Reyes** (2754 Calhoun St., 619/297-3100, http://fiestadereyes.com, 10am-9pm Mon.-Thurs., 10am-10pm Fri.-Sat., 9am-9pm Sun.). In the center of the colorful courtyard is **Casa de Reyes** (2754 Calhoun St., 619/220-5040, http://casadereyesrestaurant.com, 10am-9pm Mon.-Thurs., 10am-10pm Fri.-Sat., 9am-9pm Sun., $10-19), recommended for its potent margaritas, strolling mariachis, and terrific atmosphere rather than its food.

Whaley House

Billed as the most haunted house in the United States, the **Whaley House** (2476 San Diego Ave., 619/297-7511, www.whaleyhouse. org, 10am-9:30pm daily Memorial Day-Labor Day; 10am-4:30pm Sun.-Tues., 10am-9:30pm Thurs.-Sat. Labor Day-Memorial Day; adult $8-13, seniors and children $6-8) was built by Thomas Whaley in 1856. Over the century it was inhabited, many members of the Whaley family lived and died inside the brick-constructed Greek Revival mansion. Before Whaley built the house on the corner of San Diego Avenue and Harney Street, the spot was used for at least one recorded public hanging. If you love a good ghost story, call ahead to book one of the 90-minute **Ghost-Hunting Tours** (10:30pm-midnight select evenings, $50). Self-guided tours are enhanced by the wandering docents, who can answer questions about the house.

Presidio Park

One of the early Mexican settlements in San Diego was a military installation, now **Presidio Park** (2811 Jackson St., 619/525-8213, www.sandiego.gov). Inside the park, the **Junípero Serra Museum** (2727 Presidio Dr., 619/232-6203, www.sandiegohistory.org,

the allegedly haunted Whaley House

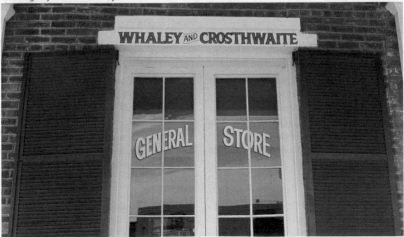

10am-1pm and 1:30pm-5pm Fri.-Mon. June-Sept., 10am-1pm and 1:30pm-4pm Sat.-Sun. Sept.-June, adults $6, seniors and students $4, children $3) sits on the spot where Father Junípero Serra and Captain Gaspar de Portolà established the Presidio fort. Its collections include housewares, artifacts, and a cannon; the exhibits span eras from the Mexican occupation through the early California period of San Diego and through 1929. Outside, stroll along the more than two miles of trails winding through the acres of gardens and wild areas of the park.

Mission San Diego del Alcalá

The first mission erected in California, **Mission San Diego del Alcalá** (10818 San Diego Mission Rd., 619/281-8449, www.missionsandiego.com, 9am-4:30pm daily) was blessed by Father Junípero Serra in 1769, making it the first Christian church in California. Inside, you'll see evidence of the life of the Franciscan monks who operated the mission until 1834, and of the native Kumeyaay people who lived here before the Europeans came. The church you see is actually the fifth church built on this site; one of the bells in the tower is original (dating to 1801). It still operates as an active Catholic church today, and visitors should respect the mission as a house of worship. They offer guided **tours** (9am, 11am, and 1pm Mon.-Fri., $2).

POINT LOMA

Point Loma is at once one of the most beautiful and one of the most important pieces of land in the San Diego region. It proved the perfect place to build defenses for the harbor and the settlements beyond, and has since served as a military installation for more than 200 years. From the tip of the point, you can see from the Cuyamaca Mountains to Mexico and down into the harbor of San Diego Bay.

Fort Rosecrans Military Reserve

San Diego has historically hosted an extensive military presence. Fort Rosecrans began as a Spanish presidio that was fortified against imminent British threat in the late 1700s. After California became a state, the U.S. government refurbished the fort to protect the San Diego harbor. It was rechristened Fort Rosecrans and parts of it are still in use for Army Reserve activities.

When you visit the parklands of Cabrillo National Monument, you can see remnants of old buildings belonging to the fort, many used during the two World Wars. The highlight of any visit is the **Fort Rosecrans National Cemetery** (1880 Cabrillo Memorial Dr., 858/658-7360, www.cem.va.gov, sunrise-sunset daily). In addition to the haunting rows of stark white tombstones marching in dressed line across green lawns, you'll find graves here from combatants who fought wars of the California Republic. The grounds include monuments to fallen soldiers from little-known battles and near-forgotten tragedies such as the 1905 boiler explosion on the USS *Bennington*.

Cabrillo National Monument

Cabrillo National Monument (1800 Cabrillo Memorial Dr., 619/557-5450, www.nps.gov, 9am-5pm daily, $15/vehicle, $10/motorcycle, $7 bike-in/walk-in) celebrates the initial encounter of San Diego Bay by Spanish explorer Juan Rodríguez Cabrillo in the mid-16th century. Today, a large statue of Cabrillo stands within the monument lands overlooking the San Diego Bay. At the visitors center, learn more about the history of Cabrillo's life and explorations.

The wildlife and the scenery are other great reasons to visit the national monument. The parkland of Cabrillo offers hiking trails through the southern coastal scrub ecosystem so precious and unique to this part of the state. Enjoy the wildlife and lovely plants, and come in spring for the best profusion of wildflowers.

OLD POINT LOMA LIGHTHOUSE

Among the oldest lighthouses in California, the **Old Point Loma Lighthouse** (1800 Cabrillo

Memorial Dr., 619/557-5450, www.nps.gov, 9am-5pm daily) began its watch over San Diego Bay in 1855. Unfortunately, the light was often dimmed by pernicious fog, and a new lighthouse went into operation in a better location in 1891. Luckily for visitors, the old lighthouse remained untouched. Come in to peruse the exhibits and imagine what life was like on the site back in the 1880s. Stop in the old assistant keeper's house for information on all the lighthouses of the Point Loma area. Old Point Loma Lighthouse is part of the Cabrillo National Monument (covered in its admission fee).

Sunset Cliffs Natural Park

Sunset Cliffs Natural Park (west of Sunset Cliffs Blvd. between Adair and Ladera Sts., 619/525-8213, www.sandiego.gov and www.famosaslough.org/sc.htm) is a 68-acre parcel with 1.5 miles of shoreline on the western flank of Point Loma, one of San Diego's best coastal areas. The steep coastal bluffs showcase panoramic views and sometimes passing California gray whales, while the sandy coves and rocky reefs below lure surfers, tide poolers, and sunbathers. A mile-long trail crowning the bluff heads from Osprey Point south to eroded sandstone badlands.

Sunset Cliffs Natural Park

CORONADO
★ Hotel del Coronado

When it opened in 1888, the **Hotel del Coronado** (1500 Orange Ave., 619/435-6611 or 800/468-3533, www.hoteldel.com) was the largest hotel resort in the world. Since then, it has hosted a parade of presidents and movie stars. The Del, as it's called by some, has also had its influence on popular culture. It's where author L. Frank Baum wrote some of *The Wonderful Wizard of Oz,* while the Stephen King story *1408,* which later became a film, was partially inspired by a supposed haunting in the hotel. But the Del might be best known as the setting of the 1959 comedy *Some Like It Hot,* which starred Marilyn Monroe, Tony Curtis, and Jack Lemmon.

Today, even though it's not the largest resort in the world, the Del's stately red-shingle-roofed buildings still sprawl over a couple of blocks. Even if you are not staying over at the hotel, it's worth a visit to imagine the glamour of days gone by. You can also wander around the resort's historic buildings, go shopping in its shops, dine in its restaurants, grab a drink in one of its bars, or just sit on the beach out front.

MISSION BAY

Mission Bay offers serene waters untroubled by the sometimes-pounding Pacific surf. It's a perfect place to center your family vacation, take in the natural wonders of Mission Bay Park, or head for the colorful fun of SeaWorld. While the main attractions are the wide expanses of beach, the area's three beach communities are worth a visit. The farthest south of these is **Ocean Beach,** which is centered on Newport Avenue. Ocean Beach has a bit of a countercultural feel. On the north side of the San Diego River estuary is **Mission Beach,** home to Belmont Park, a beachfront amusement park. Between La Jolla and Mission Beach is **Pacific Beach.** In summer, the three-mile-long boardwalk and beach are filled with sunbathers, runners, and surfers.

Mission Bay Park

The more than 4,000 acres of **Mission Bay Park** (Mission Blvd., 619/276-8200, www. sandiego.gov) encompass the largest artificially made aquatic park in the country. Among the beach and land formations are 19 miles of charming sands perfect for sunbathing, sandcastle making, and beach volleyball, as well as 14 miles of bike paths. Half of the designated parkland is actually off the shore, in the abundant calm waterways. Swim in one of the eight designated, lifeguard-protected areas throughout the park, or take a deeper dive out into the channel to kite surf or water-ski. Several areas have become significant wildlife preserves.

Belmont Park

Belmont Park (3146 Mission Blvd., 858/228-9317, www.belmontpark.com, hours vary seasonally, rides $3-6, unlimited ride wristbands $17-27) is a Mission Beach amusement park that was initially built in the 1920s. The only remnants of the original park are the **Giant Dipper** roller coaster and plunge pool. There's also a vertical plunge, bumper cars, and a carousel.

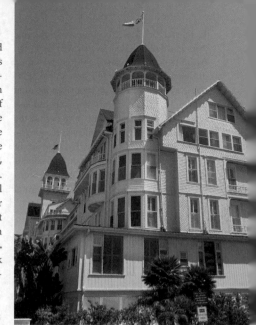

Hotel del Coronado

SeaWorld San Diego

SeaWorld San Diego (500 SeaWorld Dr., 619/222-4732, https://seaworld.com/san-diego, hours vary, $70) is notable for its captive killer whales. Kids can meet Shamu in the killer whale pool just inside the park entrance. You'll also see sharks, endangered sea turtles, dolphins, and other denizens of the deep. On hot days, the river ride and splashdown roller coaster cool off overheated park visitors. Plenty of food concessions (including a coffee stand) revive weary families, prepping them for animal shows and action-packed rides. If you want to have breakfast or dinner with Shamu at the restaurant looking out into the killer whale tank, advance reservations are recommended. If you go, buy your tickets online to save some significant money.

LA JOLLA
Sunny Jim Cave

Of the seven sea caves in the La Jolla cliffs, **Sunny Jim Cave** (1325 Coast Blvd., 858/459-0746, www.cavestore.com, 10am-5:30pm

La Jolla

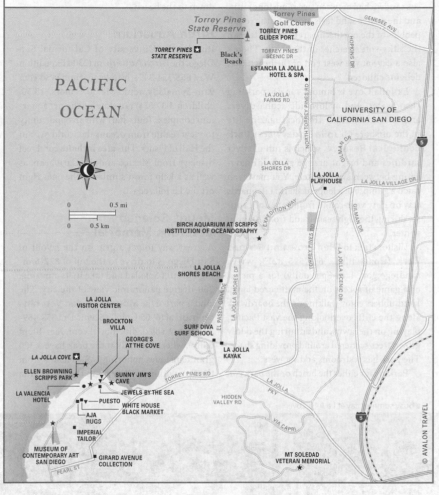

PACIFIC OCEAN

Torrey Pines State Reserve

Torrey Pines Golf Course

GENESEE AVE

TORREY PINES GLIDER PORT

TORREY PINES SCENIC DR

TORREY PINES STATE RESERVE ★

Black's Beach

ESTANCIA LA JOLLA HOTEL & SPA

HOPKINS DR

NORTH TORREY PINES RD

LA JOLLA FARMS RD

UNIVERSITY OF CALIFORNIA SAN DIEGO

LA JOLLA SHORES DR

GILMAN DR

LA JOLLA PLAYHOUSE

LA JOLLA VILLAGE DR

EXPEDITION WAY

GILMAN DR

0   0.5 mi
0   0.5 km

BIRCH AQUARIUM AT SCRIPPS INSTITUTION OF OCEANOGRAPHY ★

TORREY PINES RD

LA JOLLA SCENIC DR

LA JOLLA SHORES BEACH

EL PASEO GRANDE

LA JOLLA SHORES DR

LA JOLLA VISITOR CENTER

BROCKTON VILLA

GEORGE'S AT THE COVE

SURF DIVA SURF SCHOOL

LA JOLLA KAYAK

LA JOLLA COVE ★

ELLEN BROWNING SCRIPPS PARK ★

SUNNY JIM'S CAVE

TORREY PINES RD

LA JOLLA PKY

LA VALENCIA HOTEL

JEWELS BY THE SEA

HIDDEN VALLEY RD

PUESTO

WHITE HOUSE BLACK MARKET

AJA RUGS

IMPERIAL TAILOR

VIA CAPRI

MT SOLEDAD VETERAN MEMORIAL ★

MUSEUM OF CONTEMPORARY ART SAN DIEGO

GIRARD AVENUE COLLECTION

PEARL ST

© AVALON TRAVEL

SAN DIEGO
SIGHTS

Mon.-Thurs., 9am-5:30pm Fri.-Sun., adults $5, children under 17 $3) is unique. Purchase admission at the weathered, shingle-fronted Cave Store, then climb carefully down the 145 steps to the cavern proper to see a sizable sea cave of sandstone, carved over the millennia by the Pacific into the cliffside. Look from inside the cave out toward the ocean—an interesting and eerie view.

But how did the tunnel get built? Gustav Schultz, a retiree and painter, hired laborers to hand-dig the tunnel in 1903 as a tourist attraction. L. Frank Baum, the author of *The Wonderful Wizard of Oz*, named the cave "Sunny Jim's" after a cartoon breakfast cereal mascot. Schultz painted local landscapes in the Cave Store until his death in 1912.

★ La Jolla Cove

One of the most photographed beaches in the state, **La Jolla Cove** (1100 Coast Rd., 619/221-8899, www.sandiego.gov, 8am-8:30pm daily summer, 9am-5:30pm daily winter) differs from other San Diego beaches. The small cove sits sandwiched between two sandstone cliffs, and the coarse sand feels more like the rough pebbles of the northern part of the state than the silky-soft stretches of the south. There's also a cave at the west end of the beach that delights children.

La Jolla Cove is famous for its sparkling clear water, and at low tide scuba divers and snorkelers enjoy the local marine life in the offshore **La Jolla Underwater Park Ecological Reserve,** which is full of silver sardines and bright orange garibaldi navigating between swaying kelp. You may even catch a glimpse of a leopard shark. Lifeguards stay on duty year-round from 9am until sunset during the high season and from 10am in winter.

Visitors trek to **Ellen Browning Scripps Park** (Coast Blvd., 619/525-8213, www. sandiego.gov, 4am-8pm daily) for a picnic or a game of soccer on the manicured lawn. Landlubbers enjoy walking on the boardwalk along the cliffs overlooking the vast Pacific, playing on the lawns, and admiring the oddly grown trees scattered around providing shade. The park has restrooms and showers.

Parking for either the beach or the park can be tough, especially in the summer. Consider parking in a pay lot downtown and hoofing it down to the beach.

Birch Aquarium

Run by the University of California, San Diego, the **Birch Aquarium** (2300 Expedition Way, 858/534-3474, http://aquarium.ucsd.edu, 9am-5pm daily, adults $18.50, seniors $15.50, children 3-17 $14) is a state-of-the-art aquarium complex. Tours start with an opportunity to view sealife from oceans the world over in the Hall of Fishes. This area includes coral reef displays from Mexico and the Caribbean, as well as a kelp forest similar to the ones right off the La Jolla coast.

Mount Soledad Veterans Memorial

A great way to get a grip on the layout of San Diego is to drive to the top of 822-foot-high Mount Soledad and take in its amazing, 360-degree panoramic view of the city. The land is part of the **Mount Soledad Veterans Memorial** (6905 La Jolla Scenic Dr., 858/459-2314, www.soledadmemorial.com, 7am-10pm daily), where six walls at the peak have 3,300 granite plaques honoring U.S. veterans from the Revolutionary War up to the recent Iraq

a busy summer day at La Jolla Cove

War. The highest point of the small mountain above the walls and plaques is a large concrete cross. Superb views of San Diego include downtown, Scripps Pier, and on clear days, the Coronado Islands off the coast of Baja California.

★ Torrey Pines State Reserve

Most outdoor recreation opportunities in San Diego center on the city's fine beaches, but the **Torrey Pines State Reserve** (12600 N. Torrey Pines Rd., 858/755-2063, https://torreypine.org, www.parks.ca.gov, 7:15am-sunset daily, $10-15/vehicle) has beaches along with miles of hiking trails, maritime chaparral, a lagoon popular with migrating birds, and sculpted bluffs. The stars of the reserve are its Torrey pines, the rarest species of pine tree in the nation, found only here and on the Channel Islands. Just 10,000 of the trees exist in their native habitat.

The best way to experience the 2,000-acre reserve is to head out on one of its trails. The paths are not long (just 1.75 miles at the most) but offer an introduction to this dramatic collision of desert and coastal habitats. Before or after your hike, stop by the **visitors center** (9am-6pm daily summer, 9am-4pm daily

winter) in the adobe Torrey Pines Lodge to learn more about this unique ecosystem. Or join a free **docent-led hike** (10am and 2pm Sat.-Sun. and holidays).

The reserve offers some beautiful wilderness trails. Look for *Pinus torreyana*—the rarest species of pine tree in the nation. The shortest walk is the **High Point Trail,** only 100 yards up to views of the whole reserve, from the ocean to the lagoon to the forest and back. For an easy, under-one-hour walk, take the **Guy Fleming Trail** for a level 0.66 mile through forest, wildflower patches, and views of the ocean. A slightly longer excursion, the **Razor Point Trail** (1 mile round-trip) descends a sandy path to a bluff-top lookout with a fine view of waves rolling onto the coast below. For a longer walk, leave the visitors center by the road, then take the **North Fork Trail** west to the **Broken Hill Trail,** which will bring you right down to the beach stairway and a great view of Flat Rock.

Torrey Pines State Reserve is one of just 16 state reserves in California. There are stricter regulations in place to preserve its natural features. No dogs are allowed anywhere, and no food or drink (except water) is allowed in the reserve above the beach.

Torrey Pines State Reserve

Entertainment and Events

NIGHTLIFE

Bars and Clubs

The Gaslamp Quarter is the hottest part of downtown San Diego for the young and energetic nighttime crowd. Getting into the ultra-hip **Vin De Syrah Spirit & Wine Parlor** (901 5th Ave., 619/234-4166, www.syrahwineparlor.com, 5pm-midnight Tues.-Wed. and Sun., 5pm-2am Thurs.-Sat.) is an adventure. Walk down a graffiti-covered staircase to a subterranean area with an unmarked, vegetation-covered door. That's the entrance. Sip creative cocktails or wine while taking in the bar's eclectic décor, which includes grapevines, lots of mirrors, and umbrellas hanging from the ceiling.

Queensborough (777 5th Ave., 619/546-4995, www.queensboroughsd.com, 7pm-2am Wed.-Sat., 6pm-2am Sun.) brings New York City to the Gaslamp. The Big Apple-inspired cocktails include the Lower East Side and I Only Do Brooklyn on Weekends. Sip them in the elegant, high-ceilinged bar.

The Tipsy Crow (770 5th St., 619/338-9300, http://thetipsycrow.com, noon-2am Mon.-Sat., 9am-2am Sun.) offers three different bar experiences in a building that dates to 1874. The Lounge is a place to, well, lounge while sipping drinks, such as signature cocktail the Salty Dog (grapefruit juice and vodka with a salted rim). Drink craft beers in The Main at the large room's 40-foot mahogany bar. For live entertainment, including bands and comedians, head downstairs to The Underground.

A refreshingly unassuming bar in the Gaslamp Quarter, **Patrick's Gaslamp Pub** (428 F St., 619/233-3077, http://patricksgaslamppub.com, 10am-2am Mon.-Fri., 9am-2am Sat.-Sun.) has been serving drinks and fun since the 1930s. The bartenders are friendly, the vibe is low-key, and there's a small stage where bands perform nightly.

A locals' favorite, **Hamilton's Tavern** (1521 30th Ave., 619/238-5460, http://hamiltonstavern.com, 3pm-2am Mon.-Fri., 1pm-2am Sat.-Sun.) is in a neighborhood near Balboa Park. The tavern serves a range of 28 craft beers on tap and a creative bar food menu.

Enjoy a fine whiskey at **Seven Grand** (3054 University Ave., 619/269-8820, http://213hospitality.com, 4pm-2am Mon.-Sat., 8pm-2am Sun.) in the hip North Park neighborhood. Seven Grand has a 15-page menu devoted to whiskey, though they also have craft beers on tap and cocktails, and many of the libations are based around whiskey.

Gay and Lesbian

With a young, hip scene and a significant gay presence, nightlife in the Hillcrest neighborhood is happening most every night of the week. **The Brass Rail** (3796 5th Ave., 619/298-2233, www.thebrassrailsd.com, noon-2am Mon.-Sat., 9am-2am Sun.) is one of San Diego's oldest gay venues. Offerings include drag shows, DJs, and happy hours. **Urban Mo's** (308 University Ave., 619/491-0400, www.urbanmos.com, 9am-1:30am daily) describes itself as a "hetero-friendly gay restaurant." It has everything from line dancing nights to all-you-can-eat spaghetti nights with show tunes as a soundtrack.

Live Music

The **San Diego Reader** (www.sandiegoreader.com) and the **San Diego CityBeat** (www.sdcitybeat.com) have comprehensive guides to upcoming concerts by local and touring bands.

Since 1989, **The Casbah** (2501 Kettner Blvd., 619/232-4355, www.casbahmusic.com, 8:30pm-2am daily) snags some of the biggest national touring acts in indie rock, punk, and metal. The bands play in a small, dimly lit room to crowds of just 200 people, which

San Diego Brewery Tour

San Diego is a craft brew capital, with 130 craft breweries around the county. Newcomers join longtime legacy brewers Stone Brewing Co., Ballast Point, AleSmith Brewing Company, and Green Flash Brewing Company. Local breweries are primarily known for creating potent and flavorful India pale ales and double India pale ales, but with so many breweries there are plenty of suds to suit your taste.

The **San Diego Brewers Guild** (www.sdbeer.com) is a good place to check to plan your brewery visits. It has a map of the area's breweries and a list of upcoming events.

Behemoth **Stone Brewing Co.** (1999 Citracada Pkwy., Escondido, 760/294-7866, www. stonebrewing.com, 11am-11pm daily) is the largest brewery in Southern California. The North County location is the site of the actual brewery. You can embark on **tours** (noon, 2pm, 4pm, 6pm Mon.-Fri., hourly noon-6pm Sat.-Sun., adults $5, nondrinkers and children $1) that include a beer tasting at the end. Or just post up in the Stone Brewing World Bistro and Gardens (2816 Historic Decatur Rd., 619/269-2100, 11:30am-9pm Sun.-Thurs., 11:30am-10pm Fri.-Sat.) in San Diego and order their very popular Stone Pale Ale and food.

A heavyweight brewery and local favorite, **Port Brewing Co.** (http://portbrewing.com) sprang out of a local pizza parlor in 1992. Sip on suds like the Wipeout IPA while enjoying pizza at one of their five San Diego County locations including in **Ocean Beach** (1956 Bacon St., 619/224-4700, www.pizzaport.com, 11am-10pm Sun.-Thurs., 11am-midnight Fri.-Sat.).

For a beer with a view, head to **Amplified Ale Works** (4150 Mission Blvd., #208, 858/270-5222, www.amplifiedales.com, 11am-11pm Mon.-Wed., 11am-midnight Thurs.-Sat., 11am-11pm Sun.) where you can sip on their Electrocution IPA or Whammy Bar Wheat from a perch with a view of the ocean.

Modern Times focuses on complex session beers along with hybrid brews. Their **North Park Flavordome** (3000 Upas St., 619/269-5222, http://moderntimesbeer.com, noon-10pm Mon.-Thurs., noon-midnight Fri., 11am-midnight Sat., 11am-10pm Sun.) has fanciful decor befitting their creative brews. They also have the **Lomaland Fermentorium** (3725 Greenwood St., Point Loma, 619/546-9694, noon-10pm Mon.-Thurs., noon-midnight Fri., 11am-midnight Sat., 11am-10pm Sun.), where they brew their beer and have 16 varieties on tap.

In the mountain community of Alpine, the **Alpine Beer Company** pours terrific beers, including their superb Duet IPA, at their **Tasting Room** (2363 Alpine Blvd., Alpine, 619/445-2337, http://alpinebeerco.com, noon-7pm Tues.-Sun.) and at **The Pub** (1347 Tavern Rd., Alpine, 619/445-2337, http://alpinebeerco.com, 4pm-9pm Tues.-Wed., 11am-9pm Thurs.-Sun.).

means that it is a great place to see a rowdy rock show.

The music venue chain **House of Blues** (1055 5th Ave., 619/299-2583, www.houseofblues.com) hosts shows by national touring acts. The Casbah even books some performances here.

The Observatory North Park (2891 University Ave., 619/239-8836, http://observatorysd.com) is a restored 1930s theater that brings big indie acts including Queens of the Stone Age, Ja Rule, and Dan Auerbach to perform in the North Park area. No alcoholic drinks can be brought in, though you can enjoy a preshow libation at the adjacent West Coast Tavern.

The Soda Bar (3615 El Cajon, 619/255-7224, www.sodabarmusic.com) gets smaller national touring acts and local bands in a dive bar atmosphere. The 20 craft beers on tap complement the music.

In Point Loma, head to **Humphreys Backstage Live** (2241 Shelter Island Blvd., 619/224-3577, www.humphreysbackstagelive.com), a lounge-style venue with live music or DJs. In summer, buy tickets in advance for the **Humphreys Concerts by the Bay** (800/745-3000, www.humphreysconcerts.com) series.

National acts play against the backdrop of the marinas of Shelter Island as the sun sets over San Diego Bay.

Performing Arts

THEATER

Live theater lives well in San Diego. If you're in the city for more than one night, it will be worth your while to take in a show at The Old Globe, the La Jolla Playhouse, or one of the innumerable repertory theaters.

The **Old Globe** (Copley Plaza, Balboa Park, 619/234-5623, www.theoldglobe.org, patron services noon-6pm Tues.-Sun.) is one of the most famous theater complexes in California. Originally constructed to produce abbreviated Shakespeare plays for the 1935 California Pacific International Exposition, the magnificent Old Globe was remodeled to permanence in 1937. It has been producing a full season ever since, growing to add two auxiliary theaters: the **Sheryl and Harvey White Theatre** and the **Lowell Davis Festival Stage.** The Old Globe seats almost 600 people and has produced world premieres of plays such as *Into the Woods* and *The Full Monty.* Today the Globe puts on 15 plays and musicals a year.

The huge outdoor **Lowell Davis** facility can seat almost 700 spectators and presents shows during the summer and fall festival season. The smaller **Sheryl and Harvey White Theatre** presents theater in the round, in an intimate black-box-style setting.

For a night of high-budget, fabulous Broadway theater, check out the **La Jolla Playhouse** (2910 La Jolla Village Dr., La Jolla, 858/550-1010, www.lajollaplayhouse. com, box office hours: noon-6pm Mon., noon-7:30pm Tues.-Wed., noon-8pm Thurs.-Sat., noon-7pm Sun.; non-show hours: noon-6pm Mon.-Sat.). This top-tier theater company produces big musicals, small experimental plays, historical dramas, and everything in between. The playhouse encompasses a building complex with three separate theaters.

CLASSICAL MUSIC

Every week of the year for almost a century, the **Spreckels Organ Society** (619/702-8138, http://spreckelsorgan.org) has serenaded the Spreckels Organ Pavilion of Balboa Park (Pan American Rd. E.) with beautiful music. Concerts happen Sunday (2pm-3pm) and Monday (7:30pm) in the summer.

Originally created to produce San Francisco Opera productions in the 1950s, the **San Diego Opera** (box office 619/533-7000, www.sdopera.org, 8:30am-4:30pm Mon.-Fri.) quickly grew into an independent production company to rival even its famed neighbor to the north. In addition to the regular season filled with original productions of famous operas, the San Diego Opera hosts international stars at special concerts and presents a variety of musicals to the San Diego community. Productions usually take place at the **San Diego Civic Theatre** (1100 3rd Ave.).

Cinema

Built in 1912, the single-screen **Ken Cinema** (4061 Adams Ave., 619/283-3227, www. landmarktheatres.com) specializes in independent and foreign films and restored classics. Happily, the seats are not the same vintage as the rest of the theater—updated, comfortable theater chairs were installed in 2004. There's no parking lot, so try your luck on the street with the locals who come to the Ken regularly.

FESTIVALS AND EVENTS

Adams Avenue Street Fair

This long-running street fair is one of the largest in California. The **Adams Avenue Street Fair** (http://adamsaveonline.com, Sept.) features 100 music acts performing on eight stages, carnival rides, and 300 craft and food vendors.

LGBT Pride Parade and Festival

There's nothing sexier than loving yourself. To celebrate being yourself, San Diego hosts the annual **San Diego LGBT Pride** (Balboa Park, 619/297-7683, www.sdpride.org, July), one of the city's biggest annual celebrations. The weekend is packed with events and attractions, from a 10K run to a Ferris wheel. Almost a dozen stages offer music from hip-hop to acoustic to Latino to lavender. One of the biggest events is the Saturday Pride Parade featuring creative floats, music, and wildly celebratory people.

The parade and festival spill out to the Hillcrest neighborhood in the evening. Check the website for information about park-and-ride services, parking, bicycle parking, and public transit, and to purchase tickets in advance.

San Diego Bay Fair

Mission Bay revs up and gets loud when hosting the supercharged powerboat-racing event **San Diego Bay Fair** (858/578-7454, www.sandiegobayfair.org, Sept.). Watch drag boat racing, Formula One, cracker box inboards, and more. Stands on beaches around the bay allow people the best views of the races—buy tickets in advance to get a good seat. Bring earplugs and money for parking if you want a space anywhere near the bay.

Shopping

Shopping in San Diego runs primarily to malls and shopping centers that offer a good, if selective, experience. Downtown, wander the Gaslamp Quarter for San Diego-grown clothing or hit the immense Horton Plaza for stores you know. Old Town is fun for unique Mexican souvenirs and is a short jump from Mission Valley where the mall is king. Farther north, La Jolla provides a more relaxed, upscale experience.

DOWNTOWN
Gaslamp Quarter

The Gaslamp Quarter is home to local chains like the **San Diego Trading Company** (376 5th Ave., 619/696-9581, www.sandiegotradingcompany.com, 9am-8pm Mon.-Sat., 10am-6pm Sun.). Jeans, jackets, and accessories are found at the chain **Lucky Brand Jeans** (621 5th Ave., 619/230-9260, www.luckybrandjeans.com, 10am-9pm Mon.-Sat., 11am-7pm Sun.). Specialty items are available at **Urban Lighting** (301 4th Ave., 619/232-6064, www.urbanlighting.net, 9am-5pm Mon.-Fri., 10am-4pm Sat.).

Westfield Horton Plaza
Westfield Horton Plaza (324 Horton Plaza, 619/239-8180, www.westfield.com, 10am-8pm Mon.-Sat., 11am-6pm Sun.) gathers all your favorite shops into one place with standard mall amenities, including day spas, salons, and plenty of food options. Many midrange to upscale chain boutiques make a home at Horton Plaza, such as Gap, Bebe, Guess, and Victoria's Secret.

OLD TOWN
Bazaar del Mundo

Old Town's cheerful and colorful **Bazaar del Mundo** (4133 Taylor St., 619/296-3161, 10am-5:30pm Sun.-Mon., 10am-9pm Tues.-Sat.) shopping center, easily accessed from I-5 and I-8, brings the best of Mexico across the border. From the familiar figures in the **Laurel Burch Gallerita** to the unusual and often elegant imports of **Artes de Mexico,** you'll find perfect gifts for everyone on your list (and for yourself, of course). When you come down to the bazaar, come hungry: Some of the best and most visitor-friendly Mexican food is served here.

Fashion Valley

A bit higher-end than Horton Plaza, the **Fashion Valley** (7007 Friars Rd., 619/688-9113, www.simon.com, 10am-9pm Mon.-Sat.,

11am-7pm Sun.) mall focuses on the home with some designer boutiques, as well as men's and women's clothing chains.

LA JOLLA

This upscale suburb prides itself on its walking-and-shopping, much of which is centered on Prospect Street.

Prospect La Jolla

Big-name and upscale chain stores rent space on Prospect, as do locally owned one-of-a-kind boutiques. Look for monochromatic womenswear at **White House/ Black Market** (7925 Girard Ave., 858/459-2565, www.whitehouseblackmarket.com,

Mon.-Sat. 10am-7pm, Sun. 11am-6pm), or a matching men's tuxedo at **Imperial Tailor and Formal Wear** (7744 Fay Ave., 858/459-8891, 9:30am-4pm Mon.-Fri., 10:30am-1pm Sat.). For local fine jewelry, visit **Jewels by the Sea** (1237 Prospect St. B, 858/459-5166, www.jewelsbythesea.biz, noon-6pm Mon. and Wed.-Sat., 1pm-6pm Sun.).

Elegant antiques stores cluster in La Jolla. Pick up a great new piece at shops such as **AJA Rugs** (955 Prospect St. E, 858/459-0333, http://ajadesign.com, 10am-7pm Mon.-Sat., 11am-6pm Sun.) or the **Girard Avenue Collection** (7505 Girard Ave., 858/459-7765, http://girardavenuecollection.com, 10:30am-5:30pm daily).

Sports and Recreation

San Diego has more than its share of sunny days year-round, so get outside! In an area with dozens of miles of beaches, zoos, parks, trails, and endless opportunities for recreation, even the most dedicated couch potatoes can find something great to do under the famed California sun.

TOP EXPERIENCE

BEACHES

From Encinitas and Del Mar down almost to the Mexican border, the California coast shows off its best beaches. They all seem to be 100 yards wide, perfectly flat, entirely composed of pale, soft, sugar sand, and run as far in either direction as the eye can see. Bring a towel, umbrella, sunscreen, swimsuit, and surfboard. And if it's a weekend in summer, come early in the morning to stake a prime spot in the sand.

Most of the beaches in San Diego County maintain a lifeguard presence in summer, and many have lifeguards patrolling in winter as well. Look for the light blue towers on the beach to find the nearest available lifeguards, or for permanent buildings bearing a large red cross.

Ocean Beach

Ocean Beach (1950 Abbot St., Ocean Beach) is a one-mile stretch of sand broken up by several rock jetties. It beckons locals and visitors alike with its lifeguard-protected waters, multiuse areas, and famous **Dog Beach** (north end of Ocean Beach), where dogs are allowed off-leash. Farther south are designated areas for fishing, surfing, and swimming. (Be aware that rip currents can be strong at Ocean Beach.) At the south end of the beach, walk out on the Ocean Beach Municipal Pier. The main lifeguard station at Abbot Street has restrooms and showers. Lifeguards stay on duty from 9am until dusk daily. Ample parking can be found at three lots that range from the south to the north end of the beach. The smallest lot is the one by the lifeguard station; go north or south for better parking opportunities.

Black's Beach

Locals' favorite **Black's Beach** (north of downtown La Jolla and south of Torrey Pines State Beach) has fame as a surf break. A deepwater canyon offshore acts as a wave magnet, pulling in any swell from a westerly direction. But pause a second before grabbing your board and clambering down the 300-foot cliffs: Black's doubles as a well-known nude beach.

The difficulty with Black's Beach is getting here. The unofficial beach has no permanent lifeguard station or parking lots; do the best you can on the street. No stairways lead down to Black's, so either scramble down the cliff paths or take your chances with the tides and enter from an adjacent beach to the north or south. Lifeguards are stationed here in the summer only and the waters are unregulated, so be extremely careful of your fellow surfers and swimmers.

Coronado Main Beach

The Hotel del Coronado marks the **Coronado Main Beach** (Ocean Blvd.). Anyone can walk through the outdoor common areas of the Del to reach this charming sandy beach to relax. Yet another fabulous, sun-drenched chunk of coastline, the Coronado Main Beach gets ultra-crowded in the summer; come early if you want a prime spot of your own. Do pay attention to the signs and flags—a nasty breakwater of large boulders hides under the water just in front of the Del at high tide. Also take a look at the odd-shaped dunes; from the air, they spell out "Coronado."

SURFING AND STAND-UP PADDLEBOARDING

San Diego offers some of the best surfing in California. The temperate water (averaging 65-70°F in the summer) allows surfing year-round, although wetsuits are a good idea in winter. San Diego is also an ideal place to learn how to stand-up paddleboard (SUP). The calm waters of Mission Bay are ideal for beginners, while the waves at La Jolla Shores are usually not too big for those who want to try riding a wave on a SUP.

Surf Breaks

San Diego boasts plenty of classic Southern California surfing. In La Jolla, **Black's Beach** is the best beach break in the county, but access to the spot involves hiking down the twisting path of a 300-foot-high cliff face. **Mission Beach** has year-round waves as well as lifeguards, restroom facilities, and about a zillion tourists and sun worshippers in the summer. If you're serious about surfing, check out **Windansea Beach** (6800 Neptune Pl.), which has a heavy shore break and a rockier coastline with a reef that produces one of the region's most revered waves. You will find dense crowds of fellow surfers, so this isn't the best spot for beginners. The small, consistent waves at **La Jolla Shores** (8200 Camino del Oro, La Jolla) bore the hard-core masters but are perfect for novice surfers. Just stick within the lifeguard-designated surfing areas to avoid the swimmers and scuba divers.

Surf Lessons and Rentals

Check out one of San Diego's many surf schools: you'll go to a small-wave beach, learn the basics on dry land, and then paddle out for the first time. Most schools promise to get you up and riding (if only for a few seconds) the very first time. If you've come to Southern California specifically to surf, check with the schools about multiday, all-inclusive (lodging too!) "surf camps" that get you surfing all day, every day. Most surf schools rent and sell boards, leashes, wetsuits, board-care equipment, and repair and replacement equipment.

Competitive surfer Rick Gehris started **Surfari** (3740 Mission Blvd., Mission Beach, 858/337-3287, www.surfarisurfschool.com, $55 group lesson, $85 private lesson, start times 9am, 11am, 1pm, 3pm), which operates at Mission Beach. Each 2.5-hour lesson includes land instruction, interactive in-the-water instruction, and an hour afterward on your own to play. Regular group lessons happen almost every day of the year.

The first women-centered surf school in the world, **Surf Diva** (2160 Avenida de la Playa, La Jolla, 858/454-8273, www.surfdiva. com, $90/hour private lessons, $160/two-day clinic, $375/week clinic) creates an estrogen-friendly, supportive atmosphere for girls ages five and up to learn the ins and outs of the waves at La Jolla Shores. They also offer SUP rentals and lessons, as well as classes for the whole family. Book a private lesson, or take a 2-5-day clinic to get serious about the sport.

Stand-Up Paddleboarding

Learn on land before stand-up paddleboarding into the water with a two-hour beginner course at **Mission Bay Aquatic Center** (1001 Santa Clara Pl., Mission Beach, 858/488-1000, www.mbaquaticcenter.com, $55). They also take paddlers out on moonlight tours ($55) and for yoga sessions ($35), with the boards taking the place of yoga mats.

BOATING

The calm waters of Mission Bay and San Diego Bay make all forms of boating great fun. Kayaking is a favorite pastime, especially for would-be explorers of the famous La Jolla Caves.

Powerboating and Waterskiing

On the calm waters of the two bays, you can water-ski and wakeboard, dash around on a Jet Ski, or just cruise offshore in a speedboat. **Seaforth Boat Rentals** (888/834-2628, www.seaforthboatrental.com, $65-1,500) has four locations: in Mission Bay (1641 Quivira Rd.), downtown San Diego (Marriott Hotel and Marina, 333 W. Harbor Dr., Gate 1), Harbor Island (955 Harbor Island Dr., Ste. 130), and Coronado (1715 Strand Way). If you're planning to cruise, rent one of the large speedboats, which range up to 50 feet and have plenty of room for passengers, coolers, and snacks. If you've got an athletic crew, reserve a ski boat. For a more motorcycle-like on-the-water experience, pick up a modern, powerful Jet Ski that rides 2-3 people.

Action Sport Rentals (619/241-4794, www.actionsportrentals.com, $85-185) is a multi-boat rental outfit with several locations. Rent a three-seater Jet Ski or 6- to 12-passenger speedboat and tool around the bays. For a bigger party, Action offers 13-passenger power pontoon boats. If you want to water-ski

or wakeboard but don't have anyone to drive the boat, reserve some time with Action's professional driver.

Sailing

Seaforth Boat Rentals (888/834-2628, www.seaforthboatrentals.com, $45-350) offers 16- to 54-foot rental sailboats. You can also book a sailing lesson, or even hire a captain to take care of the practicalities while you and your party enjoy a glass of wine and a meal or snack on the water.

Kayaking

San Diego boasts some of the best sea kayaking in the state. The most popular spots to paddle are the La Jolla Caves, part of the larger **La Jolla Cove Ecological Reserve** (1100 Coast Blvd., www.sandiego.gov). **La Jolla Kayak** (2199 Avenida de la Playa, 858/459-1114, www.lajollakayak.com, single kayaks from $45, double kayaks from $59, tours $59-109) rents kayaks and does a two-hour tour of the caves and underwater park of La Jolla.

SNORKELING AND SCUBA DIVING

The reefs and wrecks off San Diego offer amazing sights, clear waters, and brightly colored sealife. A great place to enjoy a calm snorkel is **La Jolla Cove.** Make a reservation with a professional outfit such as **Scuba San Diego, Inc.** (619/260-1880, www.scubasandiego.com, $75) to take a guided tour of the La Jolla Cove Ecological Reserve. They also offer an exciting night dive; a Scuba Adventure trip for new divers who are not yet certified; and a dive trip to Wreck Alley, where eight shipwrecks rest on the ocean floor, including an almost-400-foot-long destroyer. Or bring your own (or rent some) equipment and kick offshore on your own (with at least one friend, of course).

FISHING

Charter companies offer half- to full-day deep-sea fishing trips for everything from rock cod to yellowfin tuna and mahi-mahi,

Local Favorites

With warm ocean water and lots of sunny beaches, it can be difficult to leave San Diego's sand. Here are a few places off-the-beaten shore to explore:

★ **Spruce Street Suspension Bridge:** (Spruce and First Sts.) This vertigo-inducing suspension bridge hangs 70 feet above the ground across Sessions Canyon.

★ **Niki de Saint Phalle's Queen Califia's Magical Circle:** (Kit Carson Park, 3333 Bear Valley Pkwy., Escondido, 760/839-4000, www.escondido.org, 9am-noon Tues. and Thurs., 9am-2pm second Sat. of the month) Reminiscent of architect Antoni Gaudí's fanciful creations in Barcelona, Spain, this sculpture garden features nine large-scale pieces, a snake-inspired wall, and a maze.

★ **Self-Realization Fellowship Meditation Gardens:** (215 W. K St., Encinitas, www.encinitastemple.org, 9am-5pm Tues.-Sat., 11am-5pm Sun., free). Take in the flowers, stare into koi ponds, linger at ocean views, and sample moments of meditation at these peaceful gardens.

depending on the season. Most companies include both Mexico and California fishing licenses with your charter as needed, as well as rental or included tackle and fish cleaning and filleting services. The tuna season (for fishing well offshore for large tuna) runs from early summer through the fall most years.

Leaving out of the San Diego harbor, **H&M Landing** (2803 Emerson St., 619/222-1144, www.hmlanding.com, half-day adults $52, seniors, military, and children $42, tackle rental $12-50) offers half-day, three-quarter-day, overnight, and multiday trips year-round. Shorter trips ply the Point Loma kelp beds, while longer trips can head out to the Coronado Islands or farther into the open water.

Seaforth Sportfishing (1717 Quivira Rd., 619/224-3383, www.seaforthlanding.com, half-day adults $48, seniors, military, and children $38, tackle rental $14) offers fishing trips for most of the major sport species in the San Diego area. Seaforth's half-day trips (five hours, morning or afternoon year-round) allow the catching of more than a half dozen types of fish, and are perfect for families with children or new anglers. Three-quarter-day trips last all day (eight hours) and can range

as far as the Coronado Islands in Mexico. The Overnight Mexico and Multi-Day Tuna trips are best for experienced anglers. On any trip, expect a full galley with snacks, meals, and beverage service.

Point Loma Sportfishing (1403 Scott St., 619/223-1627, www.pointlomasportfishing.com, half-day adults $48, seniors and military $40, children $35, tackle extra) offers 18 boats and an extensive list of fishing options. Hard-core anglers can book a two-week cruise that ranges more than 1,000 miles from San Diego, going after enormous deepwater tuna and other major-league sport fish. Several of Point Loma's boats offer sedate, family- and beginner-friendly half-day (6 hours) and three-quarter-day (8-10 hours) trips for rockfish, sea bass, barracuda, and yellowtail near the San Diego and northern Mexico coastlines. Private charter boats are available for parties of 5-25.

For small groups looking to fish together, **Dana Landing Market & Fuel Dock** (2580 Ingraham St., Dana Landing, 619/226-2929, www.danalanding.com) maintains a fleet of six-passenger fishing boats that can handle half-day to two-day fishing trips. **Action Sport Rentals** (619/241-4794, www.actionsportrentals.com, $85-185) offers bay-safe skiffs, tackle, and bait year-round. You'll also find a boat launch here.

AERIAL SPORTS

Book a tandem flight with **Torrey Pines Glider Port** (2800 Torrey Pines Scenic Dr., La Jolla, 858/452-9858, www.flytorrey.com, paragliding $175, hang gliding $225) on either a hang glider or a paraglider with only 20 minutes of preflight instruction. The specialty of the house is paragliding, and you can sign up for lessons and get certified to paraglide all on your own.

Ever wanted to take flight like Superman? Fly over the bay propelled by a state-of-the-art jetpack at **Jetpack America** (Mission Bay Sports Center, 1010 Santa Clara Pl., Mission Beach, 888/553-6471, www.jetpackamerica. com, 10am-5pm daily, $97-699). They offer everything from 10-minute tandem flights to pricey Rockstar and Superhero jetpack experiences.

GOLF AND DISC GOLF

With fabulous, sunny weather year-round, San Diego and its surrounding countryside are a golfer's dream. Wherever you go, you'll find a course or two awaiting you, from easy nine-holers up to U.S. Open hosts. If you're new to the area, consider calling **Showtime Golf** (866/661-2334, www.showtimegolf. com). This golf service provider can get you advance or last-minute tee times, book you into local tournaments, and answer all your questions about the vast range of golfing options in the San Diego area.

If you know anything about golf in San Diego and La Jolla, you know that the One True Golf Course here is **Torrey Pines** (11480 N. Torrey Pines Rd., La Jolla, 858/452-3226, www.torreypinesgolfcourse.com, 18 holes $110-252). Home of the 2008 U.S. Open, the Torrey Pines Golf Course has two championship 18-hole courses on coastal cliffs with views of the ocean. Plan to book well in advance for a tee time at this gorgeous course.

San Diego can lay claim to one of the oldest disc golf courses in the world with the **Morley Field Disc Golf Course** (3090 Pershing Dr., 619/692-3607, www.morleyfield.com, sunrise-sunset daily, Mon.-Fri. $4, Sat.-Sun. $5). The course might be considered posh to some disc golfers with its greens fees, maintained grounds, and pro shop that rents discs.

SPECTATOR SPORTS

The **San Diego Padres** (http://sandiego. padres.mlb.com) play throughout the regular season (and hopefully into the World Series) at **Petco Park** (100 Park Blvd., 619/795-5000) in downtown San Diego. Few rainouts mar the Padres' home season, and in addition to the game, you can view Balboa Park, the cityscape, and San Diego Bay from the lovely and spacious modern stadium. Sit back with a brew or a soda, enjoy the extra legroom, and bask in the perfect spring baseball weather of San Diego.

Petco Park is well situated for fans who prefer to avoid the inevitable parking nightmares by taking public transit to the game. The MTS trolleys and buses have multiple stops within a block or two of the ballpark, and the Coaster rail line offers extra trains on game nights for fans coming in from the North County towns. If you're staying in the Gaslamp Quarter, consider just walking over to the stadium from your lodgings. If you must drive, prepare to pay $8-15 for downtown lot parking and $20 for a slot right by the park.

Food

DOWNTOWN

California Cuisine

A local legend, the ★ **Grant Grill** (326 Broadway, 619/744-2077, www.grantgrill.com, 6:30am-10pm daily, $28-52) has been serving upscale cuisine since 1951. The wonderful ambience of the posh dining room makes even the most casual of diners feel wealthy and "part of the crowd." The Grant Grill, part of the US Grant Hotel, serves breakfast, lunch, and dinner daily, and offers a full-service **lounge** (2:30pm-close daily) with live music where you can nibble on bar food accompanied by fine cocktails.

Casual

The Crack Shack (2266 Kettner Blvd., 619/795-3299, www.crackshack.com, 9am-10pm Sun.-Thurs., 9am-11pm Fri.-Sat., $9-29) does not sell anything illicit unless you consider poultry a drug. Fried chicken is served along with creative items such as a crispy chicken sandwich enhanced with a fried egg and miso-maple butter.

French

★ **Café Chloe** (721 9th Ave., 619/232-3242, www.cafechloe.com, 4pm-9:30pm Tues.-Thurs., 9am-10pm Fri., 8:30am-10pm Sat., 8:30am-9:30pm Sun., $21-32) transports diners and coffee sippers to a Parisian café. While Chloe's intimate café feel and attentive service should be noted, it's the food here that truly stands out. Brunch is served all day, every day. The dinner menu changes according to what's fresh and could include entrées like duck confit or salmon and morels.

★ **Currant** (140 W. Broadway, 619/702-6309, www.currantrestaurant.com, 7am-10am, 11am-2:30pm, and 4:30pm-10pm Mon.-Fri., 9am-2:30pm and 4:30pm-10pm Sat.-Sun., $15-28) is an eclectic French American eatery on the ground floor of The Sofia Hotel. In the tile-floored dining room or at the oval bar, start the morning with their house-made beignets with a range of dipping sauces. The playful "Popcorn of the Moment" appetizer is based on what the chef feels like creating that day. Past versions have included feta with chorizo and bacon with blue cheese. Among the dinner choices are a burger with Irish white cheddar and a croque monsieur. There's also a good bar with a daily happy hour (3pm-7pm) and Wine Wednesdays, when bottles of wine are half price.

Italian

For comfortable, warm Italian food without high prices or pretense, go to **Filippi's Pizza Grotto** (1747 India St., 619/232-5094, www.realcheesepizza.com, 11am-10pm Sun.-Thurs., 11am-11pm Fri.-Sat., $10-15). The tempting Italian market and dimly lit restaurant enjoy a classic atmosphere, complete with red-and-white checkered tablecloths. Order a pizza, lasagna, a giant meatball sandwich, or classic and uncomplicated pasta. Filippi's serves late into the evening—until almost midnight on weekends. You'll have to jostle the local crowd for a seat on Friday and Saturday nights. Filippi's has locations in other parts of San Diego County, but the original is this one.

Mexican

La Puerta (560 4th Ave., 619/696-3466, www.lapuertasd.com, 11am-2am Mon.-Fri., 10am-2am Sat.-Sun., $9-14) offers a unique take on Mexican food and cantina cuisine. Inside, the dark and cool interior is dimly lit with orange lightbulbs and candles. La Puerta doesn't do typical Mexican fare—the menu includes carnitas pancakes and the popular surf-and-turf tacos stuffed with steak and shrimp and grilled vegetables. The guacamole is terrific. The bar serves more than 100 varieties of tequila, and the margaritas are made with freshly squeezed lime juice.

Steak and Seafood

The Mission Hills neighborhood has a popular local eatery worth seeking out. The ★ **Blue Water Seafood Market & Grill** (3667 India St., 619/497-0914, http://bluewaterseafoodsandiego.com, 11am-9pm Mon.-Thurs., 11am-10pm Fri., 11:30am-10pm Sat., 11:30am-9pm Sun., $9-27) has a simple concept done well. First, pick the fresh seafood you want, then choose the marinade you'd like it cooked in. Finally, select it as a sandwich, salad, plate, or taco. Or opt for the cioppino, a lobster taco, or a tuna melt. Expect to wait in a long line out the door if you come during busy hours.

For a rich slab of beef after a long day playing outside, head for the **Greystone Steakhouse** (658 5th Ave., 619/232-0225, www.greystonesteakhouse.com, 4pm-10:30pm Sun.-Thurs., 4pm-11:30pm Fri.-Sat., $28-52) in the heart of the Gaslamp Quarter. At this upscale eatery, white tablecloths light up the dim interior, where the dining area surrounds a staircase leading down into the belly of the restaurant. The menu includes steakhouse standards—great cuts of beef, lobster and tuna, and an array of yummy sides—as well as some interesting California-style entrées and appetizers. Portions are big, so consider splitting an entrée so you can enjoy an appetizer and some dessert. The wine list focuses on California wines, and the full bar offers cosmos and martinis. The service can be a bit slow during the dinner hours, but it's friendly.

BALBOA PARK, HILLCREST, AND NORTH PARK
American

The local breakfast favorite is **Hash House A Go Go** (3628 5th Ave., Hillcrest, 619/298-4646, www.hashhouseagogo.com, 7:30am-2:30pm Mon., 7:30am-2pm and 5:30pm-9pm Tues.-Thurs., 7:30am-2pm and 5:30pm-9:30pm Fri., 7:30am-2:30pm and 5:30pm-9:30pm Sat., 7:30am-2:30pm and 5:30pm-9pm Sun., breakfast and lunch $8-17,

Currant

dinner $15-39). The Hash House puts its own spin on casual American food, including a variety of fresh local ingredients that take the oversized dishes up a notch. You'll dine in a modern atmosphere with industrial-urban decor, complete with brushed-metal tabletops.

For a quiet dinner, try the **Crest Café** (425 Robinson Ave., 619/295-2510, www.crestcafe.net, 7am-midnight daily, $8-16). This colorful, cheerful diner welcomes a more sedate crowd with a bright dining room and three wonderful meals per day. Among the traditional diner fare are a few upscale dishes and a wide array of Mexican-inspired entrées.

To find ★ **Carnitas' Snack Shack** (2632 University Ave., 619/294-7675, http://carnitassnackshack.com, 11am-9pm Sun.-Thurs., 11am-10pm Fri.-Sat., $8-10), look for the pig atop its roof or the line of people spilling down the sidewalk in front. The menu changes daily, but needless to say the fare is pig-heavy. The Triple Threat Pork Sandwich includes pork schnitzel, pulled pork, and bacon, while the juicy carnitas tacos are about the best you'll find anywhere. There is a small, shaded place to eat on the side of the building, but if there's a long line, get your food to go.

Coffee and Tea

Round out your Balboa Park experience with a cup of tea and a meal at the **Tea Pavilion** (2215 Pan American Plaza, 619/231-0048, www.balboapark.org, 10am-3pm Mon., 10am-4pm Tues.-Sun., $6-8). You can also get a bowl of noodles, some sushi, or a quick snack. If all that tromping around the park has tired you out, perk up with an espresso drink, plain ol' coffee, tea, or pastries from **Daniel's Coffee Cart** (1770 Village Pl., www.balboapark.org, 7am-6pm daily).

A favorite Hillcrest coffee shop is **Gelato Vero Caffe** (3753 India St., 619/295-9269, 6am-midnight Mon.-Thurs., 6am-1am Fri.-Sat., 7am-midnight Sun., $10), which serves the workday-morning caffeine-jonesing crowd *and* the late-night dessert and coffee hounds. The gelato is all made in-house, and the owners and fans assert that you won't find any better this side of Italy.

Gastropub

It seems like every block of North Park has its own brewery, and **Waypoint Public** (3794 30th St., 619/255-8778, www.waypointpublic. com, 4pm-10pm Wed.-Thurs., 4pm-midnight Fri., 9am-midnight Sat., $12-19) capitalizes on this phenomenon with a menu that zooms in on food paired with craft beer. Brisket, grilled cheese, and mussels with pork belly are ideal counterparts to IPAs and lagers. The brews include 30 on tap and more than 100 in bottled form. They even have a breakfast beer menu. Hipster crowds enjoy the fare in a space with reclaimed wood and decorated with old kitchenware.

OLD TOWN

In Old Town's little corner of Mexico, Bazaar del Mundo, you'll find some great south-of-the-border eats in a variety of styles and price ranges. At **Casa Guadalajara** (4105 Taylor St., 619/295-5111, www.casaguadalajara.com, 11am-9pm Mon.-Thurs., 11am-10pm Fri., 10am-10pm Sat., 10am-9pm Sun., $10-33), the low, whitewashed, adobe-style building with the red-tiled roof exudes a Mexican atmosphere. Inside, enjoy the music of strolling mariachis as you sip a margarita and dine on excellent regional Mexican cuisine. The seafood-heavy menu features Mexican classics as well as the chef's unique creations.

Carnitas' Snack Shack

POINT LOMA

Japanese

For some amazing sushi, go to **Umi Sushi** (2806 Shelter Island Dr., 619/226-1135, www.umisushisandiego.com, 11:30am-2:30pm and 5pm-10pm Mon.-Sat., 5pm-10pm Sun., $4-16). Choose from among the three dozen rolls on the menu, plus plenty of nigiri, sashimi, specialty platters, and "sushi boats." Umi also offers hot entrées, noodle dishes, and salads. Sit at the sushi bar or pick a table in the classically Japanese-styled dining room.

Mediterranean

Looking for a respite from the endless seafood of Point Loma? Grab a bite at the **Fairouz Cafe and Gallery** (3166 Midway Dr., 619/225-0308, http://fairouzcafeandgallery.com, 11am-9pm Sun.-Thurs., 11am-10pm Fri.-Sat., $15-20). The bright, cheerful dining room features the original artwork of Al Nashashibi, a painter with roots in Jerusalem. On the menu, you'll find meat and vegetarian entrées in the Middle Eastern tradition, with lots of lamb and chicken, plus several Greek specialties.

Steak and Seafood

For the best of the land out by the sea, visit ★ **Island Prime** (880 Harbor Island Dr., 619/298-6802, www.cohnrestaurants.com, 5pm-9pm Sun.-Thurs., 5pm-10pm Fri.-Sat., $27-54). This huge house of steak and fish seats more than 600 on a busy evening. Ask in advance for a window seat or a table out on the deck overlooking the harbor and the San Diego skyline. The simple decor makes use of the wooden architectural features of the building, and the menu boasts shellfish, finned fish, and hearty meats in a classic steak house-meets-California style. Start (or finish) your meal with a martini or another fabulous cocktail.

In addition to high-octane libations, the **C Level Cocktail Lounge** (11:30am-9pm Sun.-Thurs., 11:30am-10pm Fri.-Sat., $10-38) serves a light dinner menu.

Enjoy a fabulous meal while looking out over the harbor or the ocean at **Humphreys Restaurant** (2241 Shelter Island Blvd., 619/224-3577, www.humphreysbythebay.com, 11:30am-2pm and 5:30pm-9pm Mon.-Thurs., 11:30am-2pm and 5:30pm-10pm Fri.-Sat., 10am-2pm and 5:30pm-9pm Sun., $14-29). This hotel-based restaurant serves three meals daily, plus brunch on Sunday. On the dinner menu, seafood reigns, though various land-based entrées get their due as well. At lunchtime, upscale sandwiches and salads make the most of lighter midday standards. The breakfast menu includes all the egg-based standards, fresh fruits, and pastries, plus a few scrumptious surprises. Sunday brunches are buffet-style, with plenty of made- and carved-to-order specialties.

For the freshest slab of fish on Point Loma, eat at the aptly named **Point Loma Seafoods** (2805 Emerson St., 619/223-1109, www.pointlomaseafoods.com, 9am-8pm Mon.-Sat., 10am-7pm Sun., $5-14). Much of the fish sold here, either as a hot meal to eat right here or chilled in paper and ready to cook, comes straight off the fishing boats in the harbor. Shellfish, including local spiny lobster, is fresh, top quality, and sold only in season. Hot food and sandwiches come with slaw and fries. The cold foods include seafood salads plus a small array of sushi and sashimi. The atmosphere makes it perfect for visitors looking for reasonable prices and truly great fish.

CORONADO

American

If you're a night owl looking for nourishment after hours, you'll find it at the **Night & Day Café** (847 Orange Ave., 619/435-9976, 6am-1pm Mon., 6am-11pm Tues.-Wed., 6am-4am Fri.-Sat., 6am-midnight Thurs. and Sun., $7-15). This small, hole-in-the-wall diner will make you feel right at home. The menu has a wide range of pancakes, omelets, and burgers, and lots of Mexican food from huevos rancheros to churros. Tacos are just $2 (2pm-10pm daily).

Dinner Cruises

An unforgettable way to dine in this coastal community is to take a dinner cruise in the calm waters of San Diego Bay. While you shouldn't expect the food on these cruises to be the best for the price, the atmosphere and scenery make up for any culinary deficiencies. Be forewarned that the drinks tend to be a bit weak as well; if you love a strong cocktail, plan to hit one of the many downtown bars before or after your cruise.

The juggernaut of the dinner- and event-cruise industry in California, **Hornblower** (1 Hornblower Ave., 619/686-8700, www.hornblower.com, daily boarding 6:30pm, dinner $79, brunch $63) offers a popular three-hour dinner cruise every night. Pick up a glass of complimentary champagne as you walk down the gangplank and onto the yacht. Enjoy your three-course dinner (or more, if you pay extra) as the sun drops below the horizon. Take a constitutional on the deck and then return for dessert, or make for the entertainment deck and dance the evening away as the yacht slowly makes its way around the bay. If you prefer a daytime cruise, book passage for a Sunday champagne brunch.

Flagship Cruises & Events (1050 N. Harbor Dr., 800/442-7847, www.flagshipsd.com, dinner adults $70-85, children $42-51, brunch adults $65, children $39) also has nightly dinner cruises and Sunday champagne brunches out on the bay. The company offers a fun cruise and a tasty meal. Reserve your place at the table a few days in advance for Friday and Saturday nights and for Sunday brunches in summertime.

French

Chez Loma French Bistro (1132 Loma Ave., 619/435-0661, www.chezloma.com, 5pm-8:30pm Mon.-Wed., 5pm-9pm Thurs.-Fri., 9:30am-2pm and 5pm-9pm Sat., 9:30am-2pm and 5pm-8:30pm Sun., $26-37) is a charming restaurant in the historic Carez Hizar House, a white-frame building with warm, red dining rooms. The cuisine tends toward the classic French brasserie style, with the occasional hint of California color. The wine list shows off the best of California and France, including a large selection of flights. Chez Loma has been highly praised and presented with a number of regional restaurant awards.

Thai

Off the main tourist drag, **Swaddee Thai Restaurant** (1001 C St., 619/435-8110, 11am-3pm and 5pm-10pm Tues.-Sat., 5pm-10pm Sun., $13-25) is something of a hidden gem. They serve typical Thai fare like pad Thai as well as tasty green and red curry dishes.

MISSION BAY
Burgers

Regularly proclaimed one of the best burger joints in the country, ★ **Hodad's** (5010 Newport Ave., Ocean Beach, 619/224-4623, www.hodadies.com, 11am-10pm daily, $5-10) has been serving burgers in San Diego's Ocean Beach neighborhood since 1969. A line snakes out the door at mealtimes as people attempt to get inside the license plate-decorated shack to munch delicious burgers, including the worth-the-wait single bacon cheeseburger with perfectly crispy bacon. You can also find their burgers at their downtown location (945 Broadway, 619/234-6323, 11am-9pm Sun.-Thurs., 11am-10pm Fri.-Sat.) and within Petco Park.

Seafood

At the boastfully named **World Famous** (711 Pacific Beach Dr., Pacific Beach, 858/272-3100, www.worldfamouspb.com, 7am-11pm daily, $10-55), you can enjoy breakfast, lunch, or dinner with a view. Fish is the specialty of the house and is purchased fresh daily. Preparations range from classic American to a variety of ethnic stylings. Grab a drink at the bar and take a seat indoors in the Vegas-inspired dining room or outdoors on the seaside patio.

LA JOLLA

California Cuisine

★ **George's at the Cove** (1250 Prospect St., 858/454-4244, www.georgesatthecove.com, 11am-3:45pm and 4:30pm-10pm daily) is a La Jolla institution. The complex includes three separate restaurants. The favorite, **Ocean Terrace** (lunch and dinner daily, $16-39) offers unpretentious and delicious cuisine in casual outdoor seating on the roof of the building. Downstairs, you'll find the ultra-urban **California Modern** (dinner daily, $28-36). The dining room's industrial design precedes the chic, if sometimes overwrought, dishes on the menu. Windows offer views of La Jolla Cove while diners settle in for a multicourse dinner. If you're looking for a cocktail on the balcony, **George's Bar** (lunch and dinner daily, $16-39) has just what you seek. Order from the Ocean Terrace menu, or just sip your drink as you enjoy the warm evening air.

Mexican

Puesto (1026 Wall St., 858/454-1260, http://eatpuesto.com, 11am-9pm Sun.-Thurs., 11am-10pm Fri.-Sat., $13-18) is all about The Taco. It begins with a handmade, stone-ground tortilla topped with choices like Maine lobster, filet mignon, and octopus. (Puesto sells three tacos for $15; these are not taqueria prices.) The Puesto empire started here, two blocks from La Jolla Cove; today, it's a Southern California mini-chain. They also have a location downtown (789 W. Harbor Dr., 619/233-8880, 11am-10pm daily).

Seafood

For good seafood and a fabulous view, dine at **Brockton Villa** (1235 Coast Blvd., 858/454-7393, www.brocktonvilla.com, 8am-9pm daily, $14-32), which dates from the late 1800s. Here you can enjoy classic American dishes with a California twist, plus plenty of fish, of course. The casual atmosphere of this beach bungalow blends perfectly with the sugar-sand beaches of San Diego. Wooden tables, funky mismatched chairs, and bright white paint evoke a casual resort atmosphere.

Accommodations

On summer weekends, some hotels in the popular beach neighborhoods of Point Loma, Mission Bay, and Coronado may require a two- or three-night minimum.

DOWNTOWN

Acres of hotels cluster throughout downtown San Diego—from budget hostels to high-end luxury resorts and national chains. For a more interesting experience, look to the smaller chains and the independents.

Under $100

For budget accommodations in the heart of San Diego, call the **HI-San Diego** (521 Market St., 619/525-1531, www.sandiegohostels.org, dorm beds $60, private rooms $129). Get just about anywhere from this almost-elegant youth hostel right in the middle of the Gaslamp. (Bring your HI card for lower rates.) Inside, you'll find private and double rooms, as well as dorm rooms that sleep 4-10 people in single beds. Amenities include standard hostel fare: coin-op laundry, an open kitchen, a common room with a TV, and a courtyard area. Plan to bring or buy a lock for the lockers in the dorm rooms.

$150-250

La Pensione Hotel (606 W. Date St., 619/236-8000, 800/232-4683, www.lapensionehotel.com, $150-220) prides itself on offering the best value in the best location in downtown San Diego. The exterior blends the look of a Mediterranean home with the Spanish colonial revival style of Southern California. A standard room has one queen-sized bed, unusual photographic wall art, and a clean bathroom. Work out in the fitness center (daily 24 hours), and wake up to complimentary coffee and a pastry at the on-site Caffe Italia. The hotel is in Little Italy, within easy walking distance of great restaurants and cafés, and only blocks from the Gaslamp Quarter. La Pensione does not have as many off-street parking spots as rooms, so parking is first come, first served during the high season. If you're bringing your kids, be aware that trundle beds are not available; the hotel requests that only two people stay in any one room.

★ **The Sofia Hotel** (150 W. Broadway, 619/234-9200, 800/826-0009, https://thesofiahotel.com, $202-339) is an imposing Gothic revival-style building in downtown San Diego, with metal fire escapes plunging down its front like giant zippers. The comfortable rooms feel classic with their mahogany-stained furniture and armchairs with ottomans, but they also have contemporary amenities including TVs with HBO. The hotel puts on complimentary yoga classes every morning and guided walking tours on weekends. A plus is the on-site **Currant** restaurant, which serves food and drinks.

Over $250

To stay in *the* classic San Diego hotel, book a room at the ★ **US Grant Hotel** (326 Broadway, 619/232-3121, 866/837-4270, www.theusgrant.com, $369-989). Built in 1910, the US Grant has anchored the Gaslamp Quarter for more than a century. Inside, you'll be showered with luxury, from the elegant lobby to the in-house spa to the gorgeous rooms and luxurious showers. Even the standard rooms have plush linens, nine-foot ceilings, original artwork, and all the amenities. All the restaurants of the Gaslamp are within staggering distance, or stay in the hotel and dine at the upscale California-style Grant Grill.

For a great view of downtown, book a room on one of the top floors at ★ **Kimpton Hotel Palomar San Diego** (1047 S. 5th Ave., 619/515-3000 or 888/288-6601, www.hotelpalomar-sandiego.com, $300-460). Besides lots of windows, these elegant, modern rooms have wood floors and stone washbasins in the bathroom. Amenities include a heated rooftop swimming pool, a spa, and the on-site restaurant **Curadero,** which serves Mexican street food. The friendly staff host a daily wine-tasting (5pm-6pm); guests can borrow surfboards and bikes.

The Sofia Hotel

BALBOA PARK, HILLCREST, AND NORTH PARK
$150-250

Stay just a block and a half from a row of Hillcrest restaurants with an evening at the **Hillcrest House Bed and Breakfast** (3845 Front St., 619/990-2441, www. hillcresthousebandb.com, $159-229). The seven rooms are named for San Diego attractions, with the Zoo room featuring animal prints. A stay includes a continental breakfast and 24-hour beverages. A big plus is the free off-street parking.

OLD TOWN
$100-150

The **Kings Inn** (1333 Hotel Circle S., 619/297-2231, www.kingsinnsandiego.com, $99-300) offers spacious, nonsmoking motel rooms at affordable prices. Rooms are done in florals with jewel-colored carpets and light walls, with either one king or two queen beds. Outside, take a dip in the cute, apostrophe-shaped pool or accompanying spa. The location is convenient to sightseeing and transportation. Attached are two family restaurants: The **Amigo Spot** serves authentic Mexican cuisine, while the **Waffle Spot** has waffles, as well as breakfast dishes and a kids' menu.

For thrift, exterior charm, and location, location, location, you can't beat the **Old Town Inn** (4444 Pacific Hwy., 800/643-3025, www.oldtown-inn.com, $104-204). Built to resemble a rancho, this motel sits across the street from the Old Town Transit Center, so you can get virtually anywhere in San Diego County. The white-painted, red-tile-roofed exterior gives way to plain motel rooms inside, with muted pastels, dark carpets, and floral bedspreads. Deluxe rooms include a two-burner stove, refrigerator, and microwave. Grab a DVD or two from the inn's library to watch a flick in your room. This family-friendly motel has a heated pool, free parking, and a free daily continental breakfast.

POINT LOMA
$100-150

For the cheapest accommodations near the beach, book a bed or room in the ★ **HI-San Diego, Point Loma Hostel** (3790 Udall St., 619/223-4778, www.sandiegohostels.org, dorm beds $35-40, private rooms $69-120). A short drive from famous Ocean Beach, this charming, bright-red hostel sits in the midst of Point Loma. The proprietors provide ample bike racks for secure storage. A bus stop is only a block away from the hostel, making it easy to get to the zoo, Old Town, or the beaches. Inside, you'll find 4-10-bed dorms and private or family rooms that have linens, Internet access, and storage lockers. Common areas include a common kitchen, living room, courtyard, and laundry. This is a great place to stay for a truly inexpensive family beach vacation.

The family-owned **Dolphin Motel** (2912 Garrison St., 619/758-1404 or 866/353-7897, www.dolphin-motel.com, $79-149) offers comfortable rooms at reasonable rates in two modest white buildings. The white walls match the pristine white bedspreads, daring you to find fault with the cleanliness at this budget motel. Rooms aren't huge, but you'll get a comfortable bed, TV with basic cable, air-conditioning, free Wi-Fi, and a fridge. You're a short walk from the harbor, and fishing, kayaking, and water sports are easily accessible. Enjoy a complimentary pastry and a morning cup of coffee in the attractive courtyard.

A budget option in Point Loma is **The Pearl Hotel** (1410 Rosecrans St., 619/226-6100, www.thepearlsd.com, $110-250), a hip and lively boutique hotel with a happening social scene. The 33 rooms horseshoe around a saltwater pool that's home to "Dive-In" movie nights on Wednesdays. The decor evokes a cool 1960s vibe. Guests get complimentary use of the property's bikes. The hotel is home to **EAT at The Pearl**, a popular restaurant.

$150-250

A Shelter Island charmer, **The Bay Club**

Hotel and Marina (2131 Shelter Island Dr., 800/672-0800, www.bayclubhotel.com, $209-289) provides bay and harbor views, comfortable rooms, and charming amenities. You'll find a funky geometric swimming pool with matching spa and a fitness center.

Over $250

On Shelter Island, **Humphreys Half Moon Inn & Suites** (2303 Shelter Island Dr., 800/542-7400, www.halfmooninn.com, $249-434) looks out over the bay toward the city skyline with its own private marina and a lush tropical garden. Large, home-styled rooms might have views of the greenery or the great blue bay. For luxury, add an "enhancement," such as champagne and strawberries or an in-room massage. Amenities include a pool, poolside bar, an on-site gourmet restaurant, and live music at the hotel's own club. In the summer, get tickets to one of the famed outdoor concerts held on the resort property.

The exterior of the **Kona Kai Resort** (1551 Shelter Island Dr., 619/221-8000 or 800/566-2524, www.resortkonakai.com, $309-376) evokes the legendary Hotel del Coronado—but you'll find a sense of peace and tranquility that feels more like a Hawaiian resort. With a fitness center, a pool, and a full-service spa,

you won't lack for amenities as you bask in the Shelter Island sunshine. Inside, rooms feature soft neutral tones and colorful accents. The Kona Kai has its own private beach by the marina.

CORONADO
$150-250

Literally across the street from the Del, the stately **Glorietta Bay Inn** (1630 Glorietta Blvd., 619/435-3101, www.gloriettabayinn.com, $199-700) was the dream mansion of San Diego legend John D. Spreckels. Today, the lovely structure oozes charm, even as the less-glamorous motel buildings behind it offer spacious budget accommodations. For a premium, book a room inside the mansion proper; each is uniquely decorated and includes upscale services and amenities. The Inn Rooms behind the mansion are spacious, with adequate amenities and cheerful tropical-resort decor. For families, the Inn Suites offer a full kitchen and a living room as well as one or two bedrooms. A free continental breakfast is served each morning in the mansion's breakfast room. The mansion's common rooms boast photos commemorating the history of the house and the Spreckels family.

At **Villa Capri By the Sea** (1417 Orange

Dolphin Motel

Ave., 800/231-3954, www.villacapribythesea.com, $219) you get all the benefits of staying right at the hot center of Coronado (that is, near the Del), without the costs or the ghosts. Rooms are dimly lit but comfortable with light and homey kitchens and bright bedrooms perfect for a sunny beach vacation. Suites sleep up to six people and include a full kitchen. You'll appreciate the air-conditioning, cable TV, and Wi-Fi after hours out on the sand with on-loan beach toys. There's a 3- to 4-day minimum in summer.

Over $250

★ **Hotel del Coronado** (1500 Orange Ave., 800/468-3533, www.hoteldel.com, $400-1,869) dominates the landscape of Coronado Island. The white-painted, red-roofed mammoth sprawls for acres from the beach to the road, taking up a couple of blocks. Inside, the Del is at once a historical museum, shopping mall, food court, and, oh yeah, a hotel. Famously haunted, the Del offers almost 700 rooms, plus another 70-plus individual cottages at Beach Village. Your best bet to catch a ghost in action is to book a room in the Victorian Building. For a more modern hotel experience, stay in the Ocean Towers or California Cabanas. Room sizes and decor vary, from smaller Victorian-decorated rooms to expansive resort-themed suites; ocean-facing rooms cost extra.

MISSION BAY
$150-250

Almost-affordable rates seem a surprise at oceanside **The Dana on Mission Bay** (1710 W. Mission Bay Dr., 800/445-3339, www.thedana.com, $189-339). It's so close to SeaWorld that you can walk to the park, and it has its own private marina for serious sea lovers. Pick from two blocks of rooms: The Marina Cove section offers less-expensive rooms without views of the ocean. Inside, Marina Cove rooms are fairly small, with brightly colored, tropical-themed decor. The Water's Edge premium rooms have wonderful views out over the Pacific and a subtler, elegant design scheme. Rent a personal watercraft or a boat directly from The Dana or stay on the 10-acre resort property and splash in one of the two large swimming pools.

Mission Bay Motel (4221 Mission Blvd., 866/649-5828, www.missionbaymotel.com, $159-219) offers clean, comfortable accommodations near the beach and Mission Bay Aquatic Park. This cheerful, white-and-blue motor hotel makes a perfect base from which to enjoy the many sights and sun-drenched beaches. Choose from rock-bottom-priced singles (which sleep two people) to multi-bed rooms with kitchenettes that can accommodate the whole family. The residential Pacific Beach neighborhood offers local restaurants, a beach one block away, and public transit access.

Over $250

If you came to San Diego to loll about on the beach sipping fruity cocktails, the **Bahia Resort** (998 W. Mission Bay Dr., 800/576-4229, www.bahiahotel.com, $250-609) is the perfect place to stumble out of your room onto a strip of Mission Bay's sun-warmed sugar sand. Inside, understated rooms are done in a variety of styles. Enjoy the comfort of the plush beds, overstuffed furniture, and the homey touches in the larger apartment-like suites. Charming Moroccan decor surrounds the large pool and tremendous (30-person) spa. The hotel restaurant, Café Bahia, offers tasty traditional breakfast, lunch, and dinner with a touch of Middle Eastern flavor. Order from the café and waiters will deliver to you poolside.

Sleep over the ocean at the **Crystal Pier Hotel** (4500 Ocean Blvd., 800/748-5894, www.crystalpier.com, $330-415), where cottages and suites are perched right on Pacific Beach's Crystal Pier above the crashing surf. Each room has a fully equipped kitchenette and private deck over the beach. A guaranteed parking space helps to seal the deal.

LA JOLLA
Over $250

In La Jolla, upscale accommodations abound. One of the most charming is the ★ **Estancia La Jolla Hotel & Spa** (9700 Torrey Pines Rd., 858/550-1000, www.estancialajolla.com, $299-1,000). Built on a historic Mexican rancho, the traditional arrangement of buildings and courtyards gleams with restoration and vitality. (When driving in, look for the resort name on a standard cross-street sign.) Palm trees and succulents grace the landscape. Inside, spacious rooms in neutral tones are accented with bright oranges, yellows, and greens. Beds offer an extra-comfy night's sleep, made even better by a visit to the spa or a day spent lounging under a cabana by the vast swimming pool, sipping drinks from the poolside bar. The hotel offers many of the amenities of a full-scale resort, including a restaurant and wine bar. As you stroll the groomed paths through the endless gardens dotted with native plants, you'll also find the main lobby and the main sitting room, complete with huge stone fireplace and all the help you need from friendly concierges at the desk.

The candy-colored **La Valencia Hotel** (1132 Prospect St., 858/454-0771, www. lavalencia.com, $285-3,500) has it all: ocean views, high-end restaurants, sumptuous rooms, and a great downtown location. Rooms, suites, and villas are decorated tastefully in earth tones with splashes of bright color. Downstairs, take advantage of the state-of-the-art workout room, then cool off in the large, sparkling blue pool. Walk to the cliffside boardwalk or down to the beach from the La Valencia, and enjoy the shopping and restaurants of Prospect Street.

The Lodge at Torrey Pines (11480 N. Torrey Pines Rd., 858/453-4420, www. lodgetorreypines.com, $400-3,500) offers luxury, service, amenities, and access to the amazing Torrey Pines Golf Course. The classic Southern California craftsman architecture is a work of art in itself. The craftsman elegance continues into the rooms, with designer fabrics, tasteful appointments, gorgeous marble bathrooms, and views of the golf course and ocean. Golfers should check the golf packages and arrange tee times through the hotel. Book an appointment at the full-service spa, rent one of the charming cabanas at the beach, or take a guided hike at the state reserve. There are numerous kids' activities and amenities available at the resort.

Transportation and Services

If you're coming to San Diego from Los Angeles, you'll be relieved by the easing of traffic. If you're coming from anyplace else, you may be horrified by the packed highways. In the grand scheme of California transit, San Diego isn't the worst place to try to get around. The highway network makes some sense, there's almost adequate in-town public transit, and the rail and air travel centers bustle with activity.

GETTING THERE
Air

The **San Diego International Airport** (SAN, 3665 N. Harbor Dr., 619/400-2404, www.san.org) is right along San Diego Bay, convenient to downtown, Coronado, and most San Diego attractions. Short-term parking ($1 per hour) sits adjacent to the terminals. Long-term lots surround the airport. A 60-minute maximum, free "cell phone lot" lets drivers wait for incoming passengers.

Train

From the north or the east, the **Amtrak *Pacific Surfliner*** (800/872-7245, www. amtrak.com) runs a dozen times daily from Paso Robles along the Pacific Coast down to

San Diego. Boarding is easy from most major California destinations in the area, including San Luis Obispo, Santa Barbara, Los Angeles, and Anaheim. Check into transfers from the *Coast Starlight* and the *Capitol Corridor* routes as well. Amtrak services the **Santa Fe Station** (1050 Kettner Blvd., midnight-1am and 3am-11:59pm daily) and the **Old Town Transit Center** (4005 Taylor St.).

For a reliable local commuter train, jump on board **The Coaster** (760/966-6500, www.gonctd.com/coaster, daily in summer, Sat.-Sun in winter, adults $4-5.50 one-way, seniors and people with disabilities $2-2.75 one-way, children under 6 free). The Coaster runs from Oceanside south into downtown San Diego and back Monday-Friday with four trains on Saturday and Sunday, plus special-event and holiday service. Purchase tickets from the vending machines in every train station. In San Diego proper, catch the trolley or the bus from either the Old Town Transit Center or the Santa Fe station.

Car
Most visitors drive into San Diego via the heavily traveled I-5 from the north or south. I-805 runs parallel to I-5 at La Jolla and leads south into Mission Valley. Both I-805 and I-15 cross I-8, which runs east-west through Mission Valley. The smaller yet surprisingly pretty Route 163 runs north-south from I-5 in Balboa Park north to I-15 in Miramar.

GETTING AROUND
Parking
Parking is the hardest at the beaches in summer. Everyone else seems to be trying to find a parking spot close to the sand between June and September. If you can, find another way to get from your accommodations to the beach, be it bicycle, public transit, or your own two feet. If you must drive, check the parking situation ahead of time (most beach websites offer parking information). Bring cash for pay parking, come early in the morning, and be prepared to walk up to a mile from your parking spot down to the beach itself.

In the downtown areas, you'll find fairly average city parking issues. Happily, San Diego's major attractions and event venues tend to be accompanied by large parking structures, but be prepared to pay a premium.

Bus and Trolley
In downtown San Diego, Coronado, and La Jolla, the **MTS** (619/233-3004, www.sdmts.com, bus ticket $2.25, trolley ticket $2.50) operates both an extensive bus system and trolley routes. If you plan to make serious use of the trolleys and buses, use the vending machines at trolley stations to get a day pass—a regular day pass ($5) is a bargain, and two-, three-, and four-day passes can save you more money. Day passes work on NCTD Breeze buses as well as most MTS routes.

If you plan to pay your fare for buses or trolleys on board, have exact change available. The vending machines are more forgiving, as many take $1 and $5 bills and make change.

Hop onto the **Old Town Trolley** (866/754-0966, www.trolleytours.com, $35) for a great look at the highlights of San Diego without the headaches of parking and traffic. The trolley can take you in a loop through downtown (including the Gaslamp Quarter), Old Town, out over the bridge to the Del on Coronado, and around the harbor. Get on and off the trolley at any time to visit a museum, go shopping, or grab a bite to eat. On board, the driver will narrate, pointing out sights and stopping along the way. While the Old Town Trolley is too expensive to use in place of public transportation, it's a great way to get out and see the highlights in a day.

Tours
Several fun, unique tours show off different sides of the city. **Flagship Cruises & Events** (990 N. Harbor Dr., 800/442-7847, www.flagshipsd.com, adults $25-30, seniors and military $22-28, children $13-15) offers one-hour boat tours of the north and south ends of the bay, and a two-hour tour that covers the bay in full. You'll see some of the most famous

San Diego sights from a new perspective: the Maritime Museum ships, the USS *Midway,* the Coronado Bay Bridge, and Fort Rosecrans. This excursion company also provides regular dinner and brunch cruises; reservations are recommended.

Hitch a ride on the **Old Town Trolley Tours** (888/910-8687, www.trolleytours.com, $35) for travel and entertainment. This fleet of orange-and-green trolley-like buses hits San Diego's major sights including Balboa Park, the Hotel del Coronado, and Old Town San Diego.

For a unique look at San Diego Bay, add a **Seal Tour** (800/868-7482, www.sealtours. com, adults $37.80, children 4-12 $22.50) to your Old Town Trolley ticket. You'll get a ride on a strange-looking amphibious contraption that will take you from the road around the harbor out into the harbor itself to look at the city from the water.

Take your own tour of San Diego with a cute talking **Go Car** (2100 Kettner Blvd., 800/914-6227, www.gocartours.com, 8am-7pm daily, $110-150/hour). In your Go Car, you'll be directed through town by a talking GPS navigation unit that also knows stories about the sights of San Diego. With a Go Car,

you can take a standard tour or program your own routes through the area.

Looking for something fun and a little spooky? The two-hour **Haunted San Diego Ghost Tour** (619/255-6170, www. hauntedsandiegotours.com, $35), a combined bus and walking tour, includes stops at haunted sites in the Gaslamp Quarter, downtown, and Old Town. Highlights include a historic cemetery and the notorious Whaley House.

SERVICES

If you get sick, the **UCSD Medical Center-Hillcrest** (200 W. Arbor Dr., 619/543-6222, http://health.ucsd.edu) offers emergency and clinic services, as does **Scripps Mercy Hospital** (4077 5th Ave., 619/294-8111, www.scripps.org). The **Kaiser Permanente Medical Center** (4647 Zion Ave., 619/528-5000, https://thrive.kaiserpermanente. org) includes a full-service, 24-hour emergency room. La Jolla also has a number of hospitals, with **Scripps Green Hospital** (10666 N. Torrey Pines Rd., 858/554-9100, www.scripps.org) and **Scripps Memorial Hospital** (9888 Genesee Ave., 858/626-4123, www.scripps.org).

North County

As you drive north up the Pacific Coast Highway from downtown San Diego, you begin to see where all the legends about California beaches and surfing came from. The sun shines down over desert plants, pale sands, little surf towns, the mountains to the east, and the glittering blue sea to the west. If you want a movie-style California beach vacation, you can't do better than a weekend in Encinitas, Del Mar, Carlsbad, or Oceanside. At the same time, the north end of San Diego County offers some great sights and activities, from the Safari Park to Mission San Luis Rey.

DEL MAR
Del Mar Racetrack and Fairgrounds

In horse-racing season, you'll find significant crowds descending on the tiny town of Del Mar and the famous **Del Mar Fairgrounds** (2260 Jimmy Durante Blvd., 858/755-1161, www.delmarfairgrounds.com), where some of the finest thoroughbreds ever to grace a track have raced to victory. The track was built in the late 1930s, with Bing Crosby supplying both funds and fame to create the glorious equestrian facilities that continue to delight race and horse fans. The structures at the fairgrounds are built in the style of various California missions, and careful attention to detail has created possibly the most beautiful permanent indoor-outdoor exhibition facilities in the state.

Races usually run July-early September. Wagering rules can be found at the track or on the fairgrounds website, as can information about the off-season telecast racing series. Show up on some Friday and Saturday afternoons to enjoy the **Del Mar Summer Concert Series,** where you can see acts like Eagles of Death Metal, Steel Pulse, and Steve Aoki.

If you prefer a different style of equestrian event, come to Del Mar a little bit earlier in the year for the **Del Mar National Horse Show** (858/792-4288, www.delmarnational.com). This event lasts three weeks each spring, with a full week each devoted to Western events, dressage, and hunter/jumper activities. Book your room and buy tickets in advance, as this is one of the most popular horse shows in the western United States each year.

Any number of other events take place at the fairgrounds every month of the year. Ample pay parking surrounds the fairgrounds, or if you're taking the train, grab a free shuttle from the Coaster straight to the racetrack.

Del Mar City Beach

Running the length of downtown Del Mar, **Del Mar City Beach** (15th St. and Coast Blvd. to the Rivermouth) is touted as one of the best beaches in an area famous for its welcoming sands. With the exception of easy parking, this huge strip of coastline has it all. The soft sand invites sunbathers, who can spend all day soaking up rays. The ocean beckons, the cool Pacific making a perfect counterpoint to hot summer days. A decent **surf break** near the center of City Beach beckons to new and experienced wave riders alike. Dogs are allowed on a section of the beach north of 29th Street. Lifeguards protect the shores, complete with the towers that mark all guarded county beaches. Pay attention to the colored flags on

the beach: Blue means swimming is okay, and a red flag means the water in front is a surfing area.

Once you park (bring quarters for the meters), getting onto the beach is easy. The area is flat and simple to access, and in some places boardwalks and paths make beach access even simpler. Just off the beach, the **Powerhouse Community Center** (1658 Coast Blvd.) offers restrooms, restaurants, and a stage.

Entertainment and Events

The **Belly Up Tavern** (143 S. Cedros Ave., Solana Beach, 858/481-8140, www.bellyup. com, hours vary) regularly scores legends including Willie Nelson, Toots & the Maytals, and Buddy Guy to perform for just 600 lucky folks. They also have up-and-comers and indie favorites.

For a charming night out, grab a seat at the **North Coast Repertory Theater** (987 Lomas Santa Fe Dr., Solana Beach, 858/481-1055, http://northcoastrep.org, box office noon-4pm daily, $49). The North Coast Rep produces about eight shows annually, including musicals, dramas, comedies, and family favorites. The theater at Lomas Santa Fe Plaza is conveniently located near I-5 and the Del Mar Racetrack.

The **San Diego County Fair** (2260 Jimmy Durante Blvd., Del Mar, 858/755-1161, www. sdfair.com, June-July) runs several weeks in summer and is one of the best in the state. It's held at the famed Del Mar County Fairgrounds.

Food

For elegant yet casual beach-town dining, try famed **Arterra** (11966 El Camino Real, 858/369-6032, www.arterrarestaurant.com, 6:30am-10:30am, 11am-2pm, and 5:30pm-10pm Mon.-Fri., 7am-11am and 5:30pm-10pm Sat., 7am-11am Sun., $16-32). Located inside the San Diego Marriott Del Mar, Arterra offers great service and top cuisine created from fresh local and organic ingredients. Start with a drink and a seafood appetizer in the modern, comfortable outdoor lounge. Inside the

Juanita's Taco Shop in Encinitas

get a studio or a one-bedroom or two-bedroom private unit in condo-style accommodations. The meticulous landscaping makes the whole complex lovely. For a modest extra fee, your unit will face the near-enough-to-touch Pacific Ocean. Perhaps the only downside (or upside) is the resort's proximity to the rail line and the highways—which provides both easy transportation and noise.

For a tip-top resort experience, book a room at **L'Auberge Del Mar** (1540 Camino Del Mar, 800/245-9757, www.laubergedelmar.com, $399-799). Enjoy the elegant rooms, posh spa, upscale dining, and superior amenities, all with glorious views overlooking the ocean. Float in the leisure pool or work out in the lap pool, or book time at a tennis court. They also have a unique beach valet service.

ENCINITAS

In the sunny surf town of Encinitas, surfers swarm to **Swami's** (1298 Hwy. 101), a legendary right point break in front of a gold-domed temple.

plush, red-splashed dining room, tasting menus (with or without wine pairing) are a popular option.

Accommodations

Built in the charming Spanish colonial revival style, **Les Artistes** (944 Camino Del Mar, 858/755-4646, www.lesartistesinn.com, $180-280) offers something different from the standard chain-motel experience. Each room is named for and decorated in the style of a particular artist or theme, from the French countryside of Monet to the peace of Zen. Despite its unique and fun decor, this is a budget motel; the nonsmoking rooms are small and you won't trip over your doorsill and fall into the ocean. But the beach and downtown restaurants and shops are only a few blocks away. Families and pets receive a warm welcome.

If you want a beach house of your own, book a bungalow or suite at the **Wave Crest Resort** (1400 Ocean Ave., 858/755-0100, www.wavecrestresort.com, $210-495). You'll

San Diego Botanic Garden

Plant and garden lovers come from around the world to visit the **San Diego Botanic Garden** (230 Quail Gardens Dr., 760/436-3036, www.sdbgarden.org, 9am-5pm daily, adults $14, seniors, military, and students $10, children 3-12 $8). The 30-plus-acre spread is home to sub-gardens highlighting rare plant species from almost every continent. View the famous Bamboo Garden, the Undersea Succulent Garden, the waterfall in the Rainforest Garden, and plump offerings in the Subtropical Fruit Garden. A coffee cart offers minimal refreshments, or bring a picnic to enjoy on the grounds. Restrooms hide delicately among the plants, but the visitors center and gift shop sit at the center of the gardens. The grounds also host the West Coast's largest interactive children's garden.

Sports and Recreation

Paddle Planet (996 N. Coast Hwy., Leucadia, 760/602-9767, www.paddleplanet.net,

9am-5pm Wed.-Sat., 10am-5pm Sun.-Mon., $59-149) conducts stand-up paddleboarding instruction at North County beaches including Cardiff State Beach, San Elijo State Beach, Ponto State Beach, and the South Carlsbad Campground. Lessons range from beginning paddling to ocean paddling and ocean paddle surfing.

Food

For haute cuisine with an Italian flair, have dinner at **Vivace** (Four Seasons Aviara, 7100 Aviara Resort Dr., Carlsbad, 760/603-3773, www.vivace-restaurant.com, 6pm-9:30pm Mon.-Sat., $46-76). A perfect restaurant for a romantic night out, Vivace offers contemporary Italian cuisine and a wine list with selections from California and regions of Europe including Italy. Admire the elegant tropical-themed decor throughout the several interconnected dining spaces. (Look down; the floor is gorgeous!) Plan at least an hour and a half so that you can enjoy the whole dining experience.

A favorite of local surfers, ★ **Juanita's Taco Shop** (290 N. Coast Hwy., Encinitas, 760/943-9612, 7am-midnight Sun.-Thurs, 7am-3am Fri.-Sat., $5-14) serves tasty Mexican food, especially the juicy carnitas burrito. The windows of this small taqueria are plastered with surf stickers; inside, an ocean mural covers the walls and ceiling of the small dining area.

CARLSBAD
Legoland

Now let your little builders see Legos on a grand scale at **LEGOLAND** (1 Legoland Dr., 760/918-5346, http://california.legoland.com, hours vary, adults $91-115, children $85-109). Peer at dinosaurs built from Lego bricks on Coastersaurus, a roller coaster that reaches the relatively benign speed of 21 miles per hour. The main attraction is Miniland, which has reproductions of seven places in the country (including San Francisco and New York City) made with Lego bricks. Don't worry; there

are plenty of shops here to purchase the latest Lego toys.

Food

Started by a German immigrant in 1967, **Tip Top Meats** (6118 Paseo Del Norte, 760/438-2620, www.tiptopmeats.com, 6am-8pm daily, $5-15) is a butcher shop, specialty market, deli, and restaurant. Tip Top makes its own sausages and does hefty dinners including stuffed pork chops and veal cordon bleu. Despite this, it might be best known for the Big John Breakfast, consisting of three eggs, home fries, and all of the breakfast meats you can eat.

Our earliest ancestors discovered fire and used it to cook food. **Campfire** (2725 State St., 760/637-5121, https://thisiscampfire.com, 11:30am-2:30pm and 5pm-10pm Tues.-Fri., 10am-3pm and 5pm-10pm Sat.-Sun., $22-27) keeps that spark of knowledge alive with a menu based on flame-cooked meals. Start with chargrilled oysters and end with s'mores. In between, enjoy blistered veggies and hearty seafood and meats.

Accommodations

For a classic luxury-resort experience complete with a golf course, multiple swimming pools, ocean views, and almost every service you can dream up, stay at the **Four Seasons Aviara** (7210 Blue Heron Pl., 760/603-3700, www.fourseasons.com, $352-525). Rooms include L'Occitane toiletries, specially made comfy beds, and tasteful tropical decor. Downstairs, the lobby and common areas shine with marble floors and columns. Indulge at the various shops, including a wonderful little jewelry store that specializes in unique colored gems. The friendly and helpful concierge and desk staff can get whatever you want whenever you want. On the Four Seasons property are a golf course, tennis court, a spa, a family swimming pool, an adults-only pool, and three on-site restaurants. There are a number of activities tailored for the younger set, or enjoy some of the more adult aspects of the resort.

OCEANSIDE

★ California Surf Museum

It's impossible to think of California without thinking of the state's surf culture. At the legendary **California Surf Museum** (312 Pier View Way, 760/721-6876, www.surfmuseum. org, 10am-4pm Fri.-Wed., 10am-8pm Thurs., adults $5, seniors, military, and students $3, children under 12 free), you'll see and pay homage to all that has gone into the California surf scene over its many decades. One exhibit on the history of board shaping shows the progression of the surfboard from the wooden Hawaiian models to the lightweight foam boards used today. Among the boards showcased are world-champion surfer Andy Iron's thruster (a modern surfboard with three fins) and a five-fin board used by 11-time world-champion Kelly Slater. Also on display is the shark-bitten board of Bethany Hamilton, a pro surfer who lost her left arm in 2003 after a shark attack while surfing.

Mission San Luis Rey

Sometimes referred to as the "King of the Missions," **Mission San Luis Rey** (4050 Mission Ave., 760/757-3651, www. sanluisrey.org, self-guided tours 9:30am-5pm Mon.-Fri., 10am-5pm Sat.-Sun., adults $7, seniors $5, children 3-18 $3) is the biggest of the California missions and one of the most lavishly restored. Visit the stately formal gardens, complete with manicured lawns, roses, antique sculptures, and ruins of structural elements of the mission buildings, or take a tour of the museum and church, both of which relate the history of Mission San Luis Rey through interpretive panels and artifacts. Special **Behind the Scenes Tours** (reservations 760/757-3651, ext. 170, times and prices vary) occur once a week. In front of the mission, explore the ruins of the Lavanderia, a large open space where Native Americans once bathed and washed clothes outside of the mission grounds. (Take the stairs down to find the remains of the gargoyles that once sprayed water for laundry.) The cemetery is one of the largest and best maintained in the mission system, with memorials dating from the earliest days of this 1798-founded Franciscan church.

Sports and Recreation

The **San Diego Surfing Academy** (760/230-1471 or 800/447-7873, www.sandiegosurfingacademy.com, private lessons $120/person, group lessons $100/person) runs year-round at the Oceanside Harbor. You must make an appointment to take lessons with the SDSA, but the quality of instruction makes it worth the bother. With two-hour group classes and by-the-hour private lessons, this safety-oriented school makes certain you'll know what you're doing out there in the surf. Relive the moment you stand up for the first time again and again with a complimentary GoPro video of your accomplishment. All equipment is included in the fee.

ESCONDIDO

San Diego Zoo Safari Park

The San Diego Zoo doesn't keep too many large animals in the confines of its limited site. To see and experience the life and times of giraffes, lions, and elephants, visit the wildly popular **San Diego Zoo Safari Park** (15500 San Pasqual Valley Rd., 619/231-1515, www. sdzsafaripark.org, 9am-5pm daily, adults $54, children $44, parking $15). Deliberately set well away from urban San Diego, this huge park gives a variety of animals the space they crave to live more naturally. Walking trails offer miles of adventure through different areas of the park, such as Condor Ridge, Lion Camp, Gorilla Forest, and the African Plains, or take a "Safari" tour out into different areas of the park in colorful vehicles, as docents describe the wildlife. Experience the thrill of seeing a cheetah run full-speed, grazers enjoying an afternoon munching grasses and leaves, or the vista of the park from the air by zip line or from the ground by electric trike. The San Diego Zoo Safari Park caters both to families and to adults seeking a more grown-up experience. Check your map for the location of playgrounds and family-themed attractions. Ample food, restrooms, and concessions cluster around the entrance area, but services get thinner as you get farther out into the park.

TRANSPORTATION AND SERVICES

The North County is served by the North County Transit District (NCTD). **NCTD Coaster Connecter** (760/966-6500, www. gonctd.com/coaster, Mon.-Sat., adults $4-5.50 one-way, seniors and people with disabilities $2-2.75 one-way, children under 6 free) bus routes connect to the **Santa Fe Station** (1050 Kettner Blvd.) in downtown San Diego.

To drive between the North County and San Diego, take I-5 north along the coast, which reaches Del Mar in 20 miles, Encinitas in 26 miles, and Carlsbad and Oceanside in about 40 miles. Escondido sits farther inland via Highway 78.

In the North County area, the only trauma center is within the **Palomar Medical Center** (2185 Citracado Pkwy., 442/281-5000, www.palomarhealth.org) in Escondido. Get regular hospital services at the **Scripps Memorial Hospital** (354 Santa Fe Dr., 760/633-6501, www.scripps.org) in Encinitas.

Background

The Landscape

GEOGRAPHY

California's geographic profile is as diverse as its population. At nearly 159,000 square miles, California is the third-largest state in the United States, stretching 770 miles from the Oregon state line to the Mexican border. California includes the Sierra Nevada mountain range, numerous national parks and monuments, coast and giant redwoods, volcanoes, and the tallest mountain in the contiguous United States, Mount Whitney, at 14,505 feet. In addition, two major tectonic plates—the north-moving Pacific and south-moving North American Plate—give California a reputation for shaking things up a bit.

Mountain Ranges

The California coast is characterized by craggy cliffs, rocky beaches, and enormous coast redwoods *(Sequoia sempervirens)* that reach heights up to 380 feet. The coast is bounded by the aptly named Coast Range, ruggedly steep mountains formed 30 million years ago when part of the Pacific Plate jammed, folded, and compressed to form the Coast Range and Transverse Range. In addition to the Coast Range, there are two other significant high-elevation regions in the state. In the north, the Cascade Mountains evolved through volcanic activity 10 million years ago when the Juan de Fuca Plate—earth's smallest tectonic plate, caught between the North American and Pacific Plates—collided with the North American Plate and was forced under the larger plate. Magma from the melting plate raised a series of mountains, including California's two active volcanoes—Mount Lassen and Mount Shasta. Mount Lassen (10,462 feet) last blew its top in 1915; today, the surrounding national park offers a glimpse into the earth's formation. Majestic Mount Shasta, along I-5 north of Redding, has not erupted in quite some time. At 14,179 feet, Mount Shasta's extreme height creates its own weather system.

To the east is the Sierra Nevada, stretching 400 miles north-south and forming the eastern spine of the state. Its peaks and valleys include Mount Whitney, Lake Tahoe, Yosemite, and the giant sequoias *(Sequoiadendron giganteum)* in Sequoia and Kings Canyon National Parks. The Sierra Nevada formed 60 million years ago when magma seeped up between the Pacific and North American Plates. It created a massive pool of granite that slowly cooled to form a batholith, a massive dome-shaped formation of intrusive igneous rock. For the past 12 million years, the formation has been pushing upward.

Earthquakes and Faults

Earthquakes occur when the tectonic plates that compose the earth's crust shift along faults, the boundaries between the plates—and California's seat on the Pacific Ring of Fire is well established. The North American Plate and Pacific Plate came together about 150 million years ago, causing the compression and folding of the earth's crust that ultimately created the Sierra Nevada; meanwhile, the area west of the Sierra eroded and filled with sediment, forming the Central Valley. About 30 million years ago, a ridge of the Pacific Plate became jammed and caused the folding and compression that formed the Coast and Transverse Ranges. More importantly, the contact caused the Pacific Plate to change direction and move northward, forming the San Andreas Fault. This infamous strike-slip fault, where two tectonic plates

---

Previous: a trail paralleling the Big Sur coastline; Glass Beach, Fort Bragg.

move horizontally—the North American Plate moving mostly southward and the Pacific Plate moving mostly northward—runs from along the North Coast, down near San Francisco, and then east of Los Angeles before branching off into Mexico and the Pacific Ocean.

The plates frequently catch as they move past each other, storing energy and causing tension to build. When the plates jolt past one another, they release this energy in the form of an earthquake. Earthquakes along numerous faults happen daily, a total of 10,000-37,000 times each year. Most register less than magnitude 3 and go unnoticed by Californians used to the shake, rattle, and roll. However, there have been several significant earthquakes in California history. The 1906 San Francisco earthquake had a magnitude of 7.7-8.3 and involved the "rupturing" of the northern 300 miles of the San Andreas Fault from San Juan Bautista to Cape Mendocino. The 1989 Loma Prieta earthquake, with an epicenter near Loma Prieta Peak in the Santa Cruz Mountains, was small by comparison at magnitude 6.9 and with only 25 miles of ruptured fault. California's stringent building codes, developed in the wake of deadly and destructive earthquakes, include an extensive seismic retrofit program that has brought older buildings, overpasses, bridges, and other structures up to stringent standards.

CLIMATE

Vast in size and varied in geography, California also has a vastly varied climate, from boiling heat in the Central Valley to subarctic temperatures at mountain summits.

Along the North Coast, the weather stays fairly constant: chilly, windy, and foggy. Summer days rarely reach 80°F, and winter rainstorms can pound the area. San Francisco shares its cool and foggy climate, with temperatures in the 50s and 60s well into summer. South on the peninsula or across the Bay in Marin County and the East Bay, the temperature may rise 20-30°F, and the fog often makes way for sun. North of San Francisco, the Wine

Country is graced with milder weather and warm summers, perfect for growing grapes.

The Central Coast is a bit warmer than the San Francisco Bay Area, but still, expect cool temperatures and fog in summer. A chilly wind accompanies the rain in winter, often closing mountain roads and highways, including Highway 1.

From the Los Angeles Basin down to San Diego and up the coast to Santa Barbara, temperatures are mild all year long. Expect fog on the beaches during the summer, cool days in the wintertime, and hotter temperatures in the inland valleys and at Disneyland. For the best summertime beach weather in the state, head for San Diego.

ENVIRONMENTAL ISSUES

Californians face several major environmental issues. The state battles drought, and water for crops, farms, and human consumption is always in short supply. Conservation measures can include limiting development and urban sprawl, restricting water usage, and designating set periods for personal and recreational use, such as watering lawns.

Weather extremes include massive wildfires and floods. In 2017 alone, California suffered major wildfires in Napa, Sonoma, and Ventura.

Water pollution is also an issue. Most tap water is safe to drink, but swimming in California's plentiful bays, lakes, and rivers as well as the Pacific Ocean requires more caution. Pollution may cause *E. coli* outbreaks at beaches, affecting wildlife and beachgoers alike. Fishing is no longer permitted in San Francisco Bay due to high mercury levels in the Bay's fish.

Many of the state's grand oak trees have succumbed to sudden oak death, a disease that spreads through spores to eventually kill live oaks, black oaks, and tan oaks. To control its spread, travelers are advised to clean all camping equipment thoroughly and to buy and burn local firewood rather than importing it from elsewhere.

Plants and Animals

PLANTS

Redwoods

A visit to California's famous redwoods should be on every traveler's list. The coast redwood *(Sequoia sempervirens)* grows along the North Coast as far south as Big Sur. Coast redwoods are characterized by their towering height, flaky red bark, and moist understory. Among the tallest trees on earth, they are also some of the oldest, with some individuals almost 2,000 years old. Coast redwoods occupy a narrow strip of coastal California, growing less than 50 miles inland to collect moisture from the ocean and fog. Their tannin-rich bark is crucial to their ability to survive wildfires and regenerate afterward. The best places to marvel at the giants are within the Redwood National and State Parks, Muir Woods, and Big Basin State Park.

The giant sequoia *(Sequoiadendron giganteum)* grows farther inland in a 260-mile belt at 3,000-8,900 feet elevation in the Sierra Nevada mountain range. Giant sequoias are the largest trees by volume on earth; they can grow to heights of 280 feet with a diameter up to 26 feet and can live for thousands of years. Giant sequoias share the ruddy bark of the coast sequoia as well as its fire-resistant qualities. The best places to see giant sequoias up close are at Sequoia and Kings Canyon National Parks, Calaveras Big Trees, and the Mariposa Grove at Yosemite National Park.

Oaks

California is home to many native oaks. The most common are the valley oak, black oak, live oak, and coastal live oak. The deciduous valley oak *(Quercus lobata)* commonly grows on slopes, valleys, and wooded foothills in the Central Valley. The black oak, also deciduous, grows throughout the foothills of the Coast Range and Sierra Nevada; it is unfortunately one of the victims of sudden oak death. The live oak habitat is in the Central Valley, while the coastal live oak occupies the Coast Range. The acorns of all these oaks were an important food supply for California's Native American population and continue to be an important food source for wildlife.

Wildflowers

California's state flower is the California poppy *(Eschscholzia californica)*. The pretty little perennial grows just about everywhere, even on the sides of the busiest highways. The flowers of most California poppies are bright orange, but they also appear occasionally in white, cream, and an even deeper red-orange.

ANIMALS

Mountain Lions

Mountain lions *(Felis concolor)* are an example of powerful and potentially deadly beauty. Their solitary territorial hunting habits make them elusive, but human contact has increased as more homes are built in mountain lion habitat throughout California. Many parks in or near mountain lion territory post signs with warnings and advice: Do not run if you come across a mountain lion; instead, make noise and raise and wave your arms so that you look bigger. The California Fish and Game Department (www.dfg.ca.gov) offers a downloadable brochure with other tips.

Black Bears

Don't take the name black bear *(Ursus americanus)* too literally. The black bear can actually have brown and even cinnamon-colored fur, sometimes with a white patch on the chest. The black bear is pretty common throughout North America, including in the forests of Northern California south to Sonoma County, the Sierra Nevada, and the Transverse Range. They are also frequently spotted on the North Coast's Lost Coast Trail. While the black bear can appear cuddly from a distance, distance is exactly what should separate bears and humans—at least 25 feet or more. These are wild animals; do not attempt to feed or approach them, and never come between a mama bear and her cubs. Bears can run up to 30 mph, and they can definitely outrun you. Campers should use bear-proof food lockers at campgrounds or a bear canister in the backcountry; never keep food or any scented products (toothpaste, energy bars, hair products) in a tent or in view inside a car. Bears can be crafty and destructive—some have broken into cars and shredded the interiors looking for food. Bears are mostly nocturnal but can be seen out during the day, and they do not always hibernate in winter.

Whales

The massive, majestic gray whale *(Eschrichtius robustus)* was once endangered, but its numbers have rebounded with international protection. The gray whale measures about 40 feet long and has mottled shades of gray with black fins; its habitat is inshore ocean waters, so there is a chance to get a glimpse of them from headlands up and down the coast. Gray whales generally migrate south along the coast November-January, and closer to shore February-June when they migrate northward. Mendocino County is a perfect place to watch the water for a glimpse of whales breaching.

Perhaps a more recognizable behemoth is the humpback whale *(Megaptera novaeangliae)*. At 45-55 feet long, the humpback is the only large whale to breach regularly; it then rolls and crashes back into the water, providing one of the best shows in nature. The whale also rolls from side to side on the surface, slapping its long flippers. Humpbacks generally stay a little farther from shore, so it may be necessary to take a whale-watching cruise to catch a glimpse of them, but their 20-foot spouts can help landlubbers spot them from shore. Look for humpbacks April-early December off the coast near Big Sur, particularly at Julia Pfeiffer Burns State Park.

The blue whale *(Balaenoptera musculus)* is the largest animal on earth. At 70-90 feet long, the blue whale even exceeds dinosaurs in size.

With a blue-gray top and a yellowish bottom, the blue whale has a heart the size of a small car, along with two blowholes; alas, it does not breach. They can be seen June-November off the California coast, especially at Monterey and north of Point Reyes.

California Sea Lions

Watching a beach full of California sea lions *(Zalophus californianus)* sunning themselves and noisily honking away can be a pleasure. Sea lions are migratory, so they come and go at will, especially in the fall when they head to the Channel Islands for breeding. If you have a serious hankering to see California sea lions, try Pier 39 near Fisherman's Wharf or on the coast at Seal Rocks, both in San Francisco.

Sea Otters

Much higher on the cuteness scale is the sea otter *(Enhydra lutris)*, which can be spotted just offshore in shallow kelp beds. Once near extinction, the endearing, playful sea otter has survived; now there are more than 2,000 in California waters. It can be a bit mesmerizing to witness a sea otter roll on its back in the water and use a rock to break open mollusks for lunch. Sea otter habitat runs mainly from Monterey Bay to Big Sur, but they have also been spotted in the waters near Mendocino.

Birds

California has a wide range of habitat with accessible food and water that makes it perfect for hundreds of bird species to nest, raise their young, or just stop over and rest during long migrations. Nearly 600 species have been spotted in California, so it may be just the place for a bird-watcher's vacation.

Among the most regal of California's bird species are raptors. The red-tailed hawk *(Buteo jamaicensis)* is found throughout California and is frequently sighted perched in trees along the North Coast highway, in the Central Valley, and even in urban areas such as San Francisco. The red-tailed hawk features a light underbelly with a dark band and a distinctive red tail that gives the bird its name.

Although not as common as it once was, Swainson's hawk *(Buteo swainsoni)* has been an indicator species in California's environment. The Swainson's hawk population has declined due to loss of habitat and excessive pesticide use in agricultural lands in the Central Valley; its main diet consists of the locusts and grasshoppers that feed on the area's crops, passing the contaminants on to the birds. These hawks are smaller than the red-tailed hawk, with dark brown coloring and some white underparts either on the chest or under the tail.

With wings spanning 10 feet from tip to tip, the California condor *(Gymnogyps californianus)* is the largest flying bird in North America. In the recent past, the condors' population had plummeted due to its susceptibility to lead poisoning, along with deaths caused by electric power lines, habitat loss, and gunshots from indiscriminate humans. In 1987, there was only one California condor left in the wild; it was taken into captivity as part of a breeding program. In 1997, the Monterey County-based nonprofit the Ventana Wildlife Society (VWS) began releasing the giant birds back into the wild. Currently, 70 wild condors soar above California's Central Coast. The species' recovery is one of conservation's great success stories.

Reptiles

Several varieties of rattlesnakes are indigenous to the state. The northern Pacific rattler makes its home in Northern California, while more than half a dozen different rattlesnake varieties live in Southern California, including the western diamondback and the Mojave rattlesnake.

If you spot California's most infamous native reptile, keep your distance. All rattlesnakes are venomous, although death by snakebite is extremely rare in California. Most parks with known rattlesnake populations post signs alerting hikers to their presence; hikers should stay on marked trails and avoid tromping off into meadows or brush. Pay attention when hiking, especially when negotiating rocks and woodpiles, and never put a foot or a hand down in a spot you can't see first. Wear long pants and heavy hiking boots for protection from snakes as well as insects, other critters, and unfriendly plants you might encounter.

Butterflies

California's vast population of wildflowers attracts an array of gorgeous butterflies. The Monarch butterfly *(Danaus plexippus)* is emblematic of the state. These large orange-and-black butterflies have a migratory pattern that's reminiscent of birds. Starting in August, they begin migrating south to cluster in groves of eucalyptus trees. As they crowd together and close up their wings to hibernate, their dull outer wing color camouflages them as clumps of dried leaves, thus protecting them from predators. In spring, the butterflies begin to wake up, fluttering lazily in the groves for a while before flying north to seek out milkweed on which to lay their eggs. Pacific Grove, Santa Cruz, and Pismo Beach are great places to visit these California "butterfly trees."

History

EXPLORATION

Juan Rodríguez Cabrillo, a Portuguese explorer and adventurer, was commissioned in 1542 by the Viceroy of New Spain (Mexico) to sail into what is now San Diego Bay. He continued north as far as Point Reyes before heading to Catalina Island in late November 1542 to winter and make repairs to his ship. On Christmas Eve, Cabrillo tripped, splintering his shin, and the injury developed gangrene. He died on January 3, 1543, and is buried on Catalina. The rest of his party arrived in Barra de Navidad on April 14, 1543. Having found no wealth, advanced Native American civilization or agriculture, or Northwest Passage, Portuguese interest in exploring California lapsed for more than 200 years.

English explorer Francis Drake claimed a chunk of the Northern California coast in 1579. It is thought that Drake landed somewhere along Point Reyes to make extensive repairs to his only surviving ship, *The Golden Hind*. Drakes Bay, just east of Point Reyes, is marked as the spot of his landing, but the actual location is disputed. Drake eventually left California and completed the second recorded circumnavigation of the world (Ferdinand Magellan's was the first).

THE MISSION PERIOD

In the mid-1700s, Spain pushed for colonization of Alta California, rushing to occupy North America before the British beat them to it. The effort was overly ambitious and underfunded, but missionaries started to sweep into present-day California.

The priest Junípero Serra is credited with influencing the early development of California. A Franciscan monk, Serra played an active role in bringing Christianity and European diseases to Native American people from San Diego north to Sonoma County. The Franciscan order built a string of missions; each was intended to act as a self-sufficient parish that grew its own food, maintained its own buildings, and took care of its own people. However, mission structures were limited by a lack of suitable building materials and skilled labor. Later, the forced labor of Native Americans was used to cut and haul timbers and to make adobe bricks. By the time the missions were operating, they claimed about 15 percent of the land in California, or about one million acres per mission.

Spanish soldiers used subjugation to control indigenous people, pulling them from their villages and lands to the missions. Presidios (royal forts) were built near some of the missions to establish land claims, intimidate indigenous people, and carry out the overall goal of finding wealth in the New World. The presidios also housed the Spanish soldiers who accompanied the missionaries. The cities of San Francisco, Santa Barbara, San Jose, and later Santa Cruz grew from the establishment of these missions and the presidios.

In 1821, Mexico gained independence from Spain along with control of Alta California and the missions. The Franciscans resisted giving up the land and free labor, and Native Americans continued to be treated as slaves. From 1824 to 1834, the Mexican government handed out 51 land grants to colonists for land that had belonged to Native Americans and was held by nearby missions. From 1834 to 1836, the Mexican government revoked the power of the Franciscans to use Native American labor and began to redistribute the vast mission land holdings.

In the 20th century, interest in the history of the missions was rekindled, and funds were invested to restore many of the churches and complexes. Today, many of the missions have been restored as Catholic parishes, with visitors centers and museum displays of varying levels of quality and polish. Some have been restored as state parks.

THE BEAR FLAG REVOLT

Mexico gained independence in 1821, claiming the Spanish lands that would become California and the U.S. Southwest. Hostilities between U.S. and Mexican troops began in April 1846 when a number of U.S. Army troops in the future state of Texas were attacked and killed. The first major battle of the Mexican-American War was fought the following month, and Congress responded with a declaration of war.

Rumors of possible Mexican military action against newly arrived settlers in California led a group of 30 settlers to seize the small Sonoma garrison in 1846. The uprising became known as the Bear Flag Revolt after a hastily designed flag depicting a grizzly bear and a five-point star was raised over Sonoma as the revolutionaries declared independence from Mexico. John A. Sutter, who had received a land grant near present-day Sacramento, and his men joined and supplied the revolt.

Captain John C. Frémont, who was leading a U.S. Army Corps of Topographical Engineers Exploratory Force, returned to Northern California when he received word that war with Mexico was imminent and that a revolt had occurred. The Bear Flag Revolt was short-lived; Frémont took over the rebellion and replaced the Bear Flag with the U.S. flag. Without orders and without knowing about the declaration of war, Frémont went on to the San Francisco Presidio to spike, or disable, the canons there. More U.S. ships, marines, and sailors arrived and took control of California ports up and down the coast. Frémont's forces grew into the California Battalion, whose members were used mainly to garrison and keep order in the rapidly surrendering towns.

THE GOLD RUSH

James Marshall was a carpenter employed by John Sutter to build a sawmill in Coloma near Placerville. Marshall made a glittery discovery on January 24, 1848, in a nearby stream: gold. Soon news spread to Sacramento and San Francisco that chunks of gold were on the riverbeds for the taking, and the Gold Rush was on. Thousands of people streamed into Northern California seeking gold. After panning streams and water-blasting hillsides for gold, the famous hard-rock mines of California began construction. Although panning continued, by the 1860s most of the rough men had taken jobs working in the dangerous mines. The most productive region was a swath of land nearly 200 miles long, roughly from El Dorado south to Mariposa, known as the Mother Lode or Gold Country. Mining towns such as Sonora, Volcano, Placerville, Sutter's Creek, and Nevada City swelled to huge proportions, only to shrink back into obscurity as the mines eventually closed one by one. Today, Highway 49 winds from one historic Gold Rush town to the next, and gold mining has mostly given way to tourism.

As American and European men came to California to seek their fortunes in gold, a few wives and children joined them, but the number of families in the average mining town was small.

Another major group of immigrants came to California from China—not to mine but to labor and serve the white miners. Most were forced to pass through the wretched immigration facilities on Angel Island in the middle of San Francisco Bay before being allowed onto the mainland; others were summarily shipped back to China. San Francisco's Chinatown became a hub for the immigrants, a place where their language was spoken and their culture understood. Thousands headed east into the Sierra foothills, becoming low-level laborers in the industry surrounding the mines or workers on the railroads continuously being built to connect Gold Country to the rest of the country.

The dramatic population boom caused by the Gold Rush ensured that California would be on the fast track to admission into the United States, bypassing the territorial phase. California became a state in 1850—it had gone from a Mexican province to the 31st U.S. state in little more than four years.

THE RAILROADS

California's population swelled to more than 250,000 within three years of the Gold Rush. To help settlers avoid the grueling cross-country trip, Eastern industrialists pushed for a railroad to open the West. While politicians argued, Theodore D. Judah got to work. Judah came to California from New York at the bidding of the promoters of the Sacramento Valley Railroad. The route linked the Embarcadero along the Sacramento River to Folsom, the jumping-off point to the goldfields. When the Sacramento Valley Railroad project ended in 1856, Judah became a passionate advocate for a transcontinental railroad. He lobbied in Washington DC, and in 1861 convinced a group of merchants—men who would become known as the Big Four—to incorporate the Central Pacific Railroad in Sacramento.

The Big Four were Leland Stanford, Charles Crocker, Collis Huntington, and Mark Hopkins, and they were instrumental in developing the state railroad system between 1861 and 1900. Stanford operated a general store for miners before becoming an American tycoon, industrialist, politician, and the founder of Stanford University. Crocker founded a small, independent iron forge, invested in the railroad venture, and eventually gained a controlling interest in Wells Fargo Bank before buying the rest of the bank for his son. Huntington was a Sacramento merchant who later went on to build other railroads. Hopkins was another Sacramento merchant who formed a partnership with Huntington before joining him in investing in the transcontinental railroad.

In mid-1862, President Abraham Lincoln signed the Pacific Railroad Act, giving the Central Pacific Railroad the go-ahead to build the railroad east from Sacramento and the Union Pacific Railroad to build west from Omaha. The government used land grants and government loans to fund the project. Workers for the two companies met May 10, 1869, at Promontory Summit, Utah, to complete the nation's first transcontinental railroad with a ceremonial golden spike.

THE GREAT DEPRESSION

The stock market crash of 1929 led to the Great Depression. Many property owners lost their farms and homes, and unemployment in California hit 28 percent in 1932; by 1935, about 20 percent of all Californians were on public relief.

The Great Depression transformed the nation. Beyond the economic agony was an optimism that moved people to migrate to California. Settling primarily in the Central Valley, these Midwest transplants preserved their ways and retained identities separate from other Californians. The Midwest migrant plight was captured in John Steinbeck's 1939 novel *The Grapes of Wrath*. Steinbeck, a Salinas native, gathered information by viewing firsthand the deplorable living and labor conditions under which Okie families existed. The novel was widely read and was turned into a movie in 1940. Government agencies banned the book from public schools, and libraries and large landowners campaigned to have it banned elsewhere. That effort lost steam, however, when Steinbeck won the 1940 Pulitzer Prize.

Even during the worst economic depression in U.S. history, Californians continued to build and move forward. The San Francisco-Oakland Bay Bridge was completed in 1936 and the Golden Gate Bridge in 1937, connecting the land around San Francisco Bay and putting people to work. The 1939 Golden Gate International Exposition on Treasure Island in San Francisco Bay helped show the Great Depression the door.

WORLD WAR II

During World War II, San Francisco became home to the Liberty ships, a fleet of like-design ships built quickly to help supply the war effort. Some Liberty ships, known as the Mothball Fleet, are now tied together farther up Carquinez Strait and can be seen while driving south on I-680 near one of the state's first capitals, Benicia.

Unfortunately, California was also home to a deplorable chapter in the war—the internment camps for Japanese people and Japanese Americans. In reaction to the attack on Pearl Harbor, President Franklin Roosevelt signed Executive Order 9066 in 1942, creating "military exclusion zones" for people of Japanese ancestry. Approximately 110,000 Japanese Americans were uprooted and sent to relocation camps in desolate areas such as Manzanar, in the dry basin of the eastern Sierra; Tulelake, in the remote northeast corner of the state; and as far away as North Dakota and Oklahoma.

In San Francisco, the immigration station on Angel Island became a deportation center in addition to interning Japanese prisoners of war. Today, examples of their carved inscriptions on the prison walls remain as part of the museum in the old barracks building.

THE 1960S

Few places in the country felt the impact of the radical changes of the 1960s more than California. It's arguable that the peace and free-love movements began here, probably on the campus of the indomitable University of California, Berkeley. Certainly Berkeley helped to shape and foster the culture of hippies, peaceniks, and radical politics. The college campus was the home of the Black Panthers, anti-Vietnam War sit-ins, and numerous protests for many progressive causes.

If Berkeley was the de facto home of 1960s political movements, then San Francisco was the base of the era's social and cultural phenomena. Free concerts in Golden Gate Park and the growing fame of the hippie community taking over a neighborhood called Haight-Ashbury drew young people from across the country. Many found themselves living on Haight Street for months and experimenting with the mind-altering chemicals emblematic of the era. The music scene became the stuff of legend. The Grateful Dead—one of the most famous and longest-lasting of the 1960s rock bands—hailed from the Bay Area.

CALIFORNIA TODAY

The spectacular growth of the electronics industry started in Silicon Valley, south of San Francisco. Many firms settled in the area of Palo Alto, Santa Clara, Sunnyvale, and San Jose, producing innovations such as personal computers, video games, and networking systems at an incredible pace. All these firms were based in the Santa Clara Valley, dubbed Silicon Valley after the material used to produce integrated circuits. Hewlett-Packard and Varian Associates were among the early companies that grew here. Even today, the tenant list is impressive: Facebook, YouTube, LinkedIn, Adobe Systems, Apple, Cisco Systems, Intel, Oracle Corporation, SanDisk, and Symantec.

The demand for skilled technical professionals was so great in the high-tech industry that firms had difficulty filling openings and began lobbying to have visa restrictions eased so they could recruit professionals from abroad. Later, however, the dot-com financial bubble that formed in the mid-1990s burst, and tech-industry stock values plummeted in April 2000; many tech companies went into bankruptcy or were sold for a fraction of their worth, and jobs evaporated overnight. Within a few years, it seemed that many of the coveted high-tech jobs were "off-shored" (sent to India for 10 percent of the U.S. labor cost) or "on-shored" by recruiting among newcomers from China and India.

Despite the dot-com bust, the nation's electronics industry has bounced back, and Silicon Valley continues to be the technological hub of the state. Among metropolitan areas, Silicon Valley has the highest concentration of tech workers, with nearly 286 out of every 1,000 private-sector jobs. And the money is good too—the San Jose-Sunnyvale-Santa Clara metropolitan area has the most millionaires and billionaires per capita in the United States.

Local Culture

INDIGENOUS CULTURES

The diverse ecology of California allowed Native Americans to adapt to the land in various ways. Communities settled from the border of present-day Oregon south through the mountain ranges and valleys, along the coast, into the Sierra Nevada, and in the arid lands that stretch into Mexico. These groups include the Maidu, Miwok, Yurok, and Pomo. More than 100 Native American languages were spoken in California, and each language had several dialects, all of which were identified with geographic areas. There are about two dozen distinct Native American groups in the Del Norte-Humboldt-Mendocino area alone.

The following is an overview of the groups most commonly encountered when traveling around the state.

Yurok

The Yurok people are the largest Native American population in California, and they continue to live along the Klamath River and the Humboldt County coast near Redwood National Park, north of Eureka and south of Crescent City. Spanish explorers arriving in 1775 were the Yurok's first contact with Europeans. Fur traders and trappers from the Hudson's Bay Company arrived around 1827, but it wasn't until gold miners arrived in 1850 that the Yurok faced disease and destruction that diminished their population by 75 percent. Researchers put the 1770 population at 2,500-3,100, which dropped to 669-700 by 1910. Today, there are more than 5,000 Yurok living in California and about 6,000 in the United States overall.

Pomo

The name for the Pomo people and their language first meant "those who live at the red earth hole," possibly referring to the magnesite the tribe used for its red beads or the reddish earth and clay mined in the area. It was also once the name of a village near the present-day community of Pomo in Potter Valley. The Pomo territory was large, bounded by the Pacific Ocean to the west and extending inland to Clear Lake in Lake County. Today, the territory includes present-day Santa Rosa and much of the Sonoma County wine country.

In 1800 there were 10,000-18,000 Pomo living in approximately 70 communities that spoke seven Pomo languages. But as the Pomo interacted and traded with the Russians at Fort Ross, added pressure came from the Spanish missionaries and American settlers pressing in from the south and east. European encroachment may have been the reason Pomo villages became more centralized and why many Pomo retreated to remote areas to band together in defense.

The Pomo suffered not only from lifestyle changes and loss of territory but from diseases for which they had no immunity. Missionaries, traders, and settlers brought with them measles, smallpox, and other diseases that devastated indigenous populations. In 1850 miners began settling in the Russian River Valley, and the Lake Sonoma Valley was homesteaded. As a result, the U.S. government forced the Pomo off their land and onto reservations. Historians believe there were 3,500-5,000 Pomo in 1851, but only 777-1,200 by 1910. There were nearly 5,000 Pomo by the early 1990s.

Miwok

Before contact with white settlers in 1769, the Miwok people lived in small bands in separate parts of California. The Plains and Sierra Miwok lived on the Sacramento-San Joaquin Delta, in parts of the San Joaquin and Sacramento Valleys, and in the foothills and western slopes of the Sierra Nevada. The Coast Miwok—including the Bodega Bay Miwok and the Marin Miwok—lived in what is now Marin and southern Sonoma Counties.

Lake Miwok people were found in the Clear Lake Basin of Lake County. The Bay Miwok were in present-day Contra Costa County. Miwok domesticated dogs and grew tobacco but otherwise depended on hunting, fishing, and gathering for food. Miwok in the Sierra exploited the California black oak for acorns, and it is believed that they cultivated the tree in parts of what is now Yosemite National Park.

Like so many indigenous people in California, the Miwok suffered after explorers, missionaries, miners, and settlers arrived. Historians estimate there were at least 11,000 Miwok in 1770, but in all four regions there were only about 671 Miwok in 1910 and 491 in 1930. Today, there are about 3,500 Miwok.

Ohlone

The Ohlone people once occupied what is now San Francisco, Berkeley, Oakland, Silicon Valley, Santa Cruz, Monterey, and the lower Salinas Valley. The Ohlone (a Miwok word meaning "western people") lived in permanent villages, only moving temporarily to gather seasonal foods such as acorns and berries. The Ohlone formed an association of about 50 different communities with an average of 200 members each. The villages interacted through trade, marriages, and ceremonies. Basket weaving, ceremonial dancing, piercings and tattoos, and general ornamentation indicated status within the community and were all part of Ohlone life. Like other Native Americans in the region, the Ohlone depended on hunting, fishing, gathering, and agrarian skills such as burning off old growth each year to get a better yield from seeds.

The Ohlone culture remained fairly stable until the first Spanish missionaries arrived to spread Christianity and to expand Spanish territorial claims. Spanish explorer Sebastián Vizcaíno reached present-day Monterey in December 1602, and the Rumsen group of Ohlone were the first the Spanish encountered. Father Junípero Serra's missionaries built seven missions on Ohlone land in the mid-18th century, and most of the Ohlone people were brought to the missions to live and work. For the next 60 years, the Ohlone suffered, as did most indigenous people at the missions. Along with the culture shock of subjugation came the diseases for which they had no immunity—measles, smallpox, syphilis, and others. It wasn't until 1834 that the California missions were abolished and the Mexican government redistributed the mission land holdings.

The Ohlone lost the vast majority of their population between 1780 and 1850 because of disease, social upheaval from European incursion, and low birth rates. Estimates are that there were 7,000-26,000 Ohlone when Spanish soldiers and missionaries arrived, and about 3,000 in 1800 and 864-1,000 by 1852. There are 1,500-2,000 Ohlone people today.

Yokuts

The Yokut people have inhabited the Central Valley for at least 8,000 years; they may even have been the first people to settle here. The Yokuts lived in the San Joaquin Valley from the Sacramento-San Joaquin River Delta south to Bakersfield and east to the Sierra foothills. Sequoia and Kings Canyon National Parks are included in this area, as are the cities of Fresno and Modesto. Like other Native Americans, the Yokuts developed water transportation, harvesting abundant tule reeds to work them into canoes.

Spanish explorers entered the valley in 1772 and found 63 different Yokut groups scattered up and down the Central Valley. Many of the Yokuts were taken to the various missions, where they suffered from European subjugation and diseases. Later, as miners entered the region, the Yokut people were forced from their lands. There may have been as many as 4,500 Yokuts when the Spaniards arrived, but the last full-blooded member of the Southern Yokuts is said to have died in 1960. Yokut descendants today live on the Tule River Reservation near Porterville and at the Santa Rosa Rancheria near Lemoore.

Paiute

The Paiute people are grouped by their language—despite location, political connection, or even genetic similarity. For the Northern Paiutes and the Southern Paiutes, that language is the Numic branch of the Uto-Aztecan family of Native American languages. The Northern Paiutes live in the Great Basin; the Southern Paiutes lived in the Mojave Desert on the edge of present-day Death Valley National Park. Between the Northern Paiutes and the Southern Paiutes are the Mono Lake Northern Paiutes and the Owens Valley Paiutes.

The Northern Paiute lifestyle was well adapted to the harsh environment of the Great Basin. Each band occupied a territory usually centered around a lake or other water source that also provided fish and waterfowl. Food drives to capture rabbits and pronghorn were communal and often involved nearby bands. Piñon nuts were gathered and stored for winter, and grass seeds and roots were part of the diet. Because of their remoteness, the Northern Paiutes may have completely avoided the hardships of the mission period. Their first contact with European Americans may have occurred in 1820, but sustained contact did not happen until the 1840s; several violent confrontations over land and other conflicts occurred in this period. In the end, smallpox did more to decimate the Northern Paiutes than warfare. The Northern Paiutes established colonies that were joined by Shoshone and Washoe people and eventually received recognition by the federal government.

The Southern Paiutes were not as fortunate as the Northern Paiutes. The first contact with Europeans came in 1776, when the priests Silvestre Vélez de Escalante and Francisco Atanasio Domínguez met them while seeking an overland route to the California missions. The Southern Paiutes suffered slave raids by the Navajo and Ute before Europeans arrived, and the raids increased afterward. In 1851, Mormon settlers arrived and occupied local water sources, and the slave raids ended. Settlers and their agrarian practices such as cattle herding drove away game and limited the Southern Paiutes' ability to gather food, disrupting their traditional lifestyle.

Chumash

The Chumash lived on land from Malibu up to Paso Robles, but they also traveled out to the northern Channel Islands. Before the Mission Period, they had over 20,000 people living in 150 independent villages scattered along the coast.

The Chumash were a maritime culture that built large wooden canoes called tomols, which they used to fish and travel among their coastal enclaves. They are also known for their cave paintings in places like Santa Barbara's Painted Cave State Historic Park.

During the Mission Period, five missions were built in Chumash territory. Shortly after the foundation of these missions, European diseases wiped out a large number of the Chumash. By 1831, there were fewer than 3,000 Chumash on this section of the California coast. Today there is a band of Chumash living on a reservation in Santa Barbara's Santa Ynez Valley.

Essentials

Transportation

AIR
San Francisco Bay Area
San Francisco's major airport is **San Francisco International Airport** (SFO, U.S. 101, San Mateo, 650/821-8211 or 800/435-9736, www.flysfo.com), located approximately 13 miles south of the city. Plan to arrive at the airport up to three hours before your flight leaves. Airport lines, especially on weekends and holidays, are notoriously long, and planes can be grounded due to fog.

To avoid the SFO crowds, consider booking a flight into one of the Bay Area's less-crowded airports. **Oakland International Airport** (OAK, 1 Airport Dr., Oakland, 510/563-3300, http://oaklandairport.com) serves the East Bay with access to San Francisco via the Bay Bridge and commuter trains. **San Jose International Airport** (SJC, Airport Blvd., San Jose, 408/392-3600, www.flysanjose.com) is south of San Francisco in the heart of Silicon Valley. These airports are quite a bit smaller than SFO, but service is brisk from many U.S. destinations.

AIRPORT TRANSPORTATION
Several public and private transportation options can get you into San Francisco. **Bay Area Rapid Transit** (BART, www.bart.gov, one-way ticket to any downtown station $8.95) connects directly with SFO's international terminal, providing a simple and relatively fast (under one hour) trip to downtown San Francisco. The BART station is an easy walk or a free shuttle ride from any point in the airport. **Caltrain** (800/660-4287, www.caltrain.com, tickets $3.25-15) is a good option if you are staying farther south on the peninsula. To access Caltrain from the airport, you must first take BART to the Millbrae stop, where

the two lines meet. This station is designed for folks jumping from one line to the other. Caltrain tickets range in price depending on your destination.

Shuttle vans are another cost-effective option for door-to-door service, although these make several stops along the way. From the airport to downtown San Francisco, the average one-way fare is $17-25 per person. Shuttle vans congregate on the second level of SFO above the baggage claim area for domestic flights, and on the third level for international flights. Advance reservations guarantee a seat, but these aren't required and don't necessarily speed the process. Some companies to try include **Quake City Shuttle** (415/255-4899, www.quakecityshuttle.com) and **SuperShuttle** (800/258-3826, www.supershuttle.com).

For **taxis,** the average fare to downtown San Francisco is around $40. Or use a smartphone app to hitch a ride with **Uber** (www.uber.com, airport to downtown $27-85) or **Lyft** (www.lyft.com, airport to downtown $28-41).

Los Angeles Basin
The greater Los Angeles area is thick with airports. **Los Angeles International Airport** (LAX, 1 World Way, 855/463-5252, www.lawa.org) serves the greater Los Angeles area and is about 10 miles south of the city of Santa Monica. If you're coming in from another country or from across the continent, you're likely to find your flight coming into this endlessly crowded hub. If you're flying home from LAX, plan plenty of time to get through security and the check-in lines—up to three hours for a domestic flight on a holiday weekend.

To miss the major crowds, consider flying

ESSENTIALS
TRANSPORTATION

into one of the many suburban airports. **John Wayne Airport** (SNA, 18601 Airport Way, Santa Ana, 949/252-5200, www.ocair.com) serves Disneyland perfectly, and the **Long Beach Airport** (LGB, 4100 Donald Douglas Dr., Long Beach, 562/570-2600, www.lgb.org) is convenient to the beaches. **Hollywood Burbank Airport** (BUR, 2627 N. Hollywood Way, Burbank, 818/840-8840, http://hollywoodburbankairport.com) is 12 miles from downtown Los Angeles, while the **Ontario Airport** (ONT, 1923 E. Avion Dr., Ontario, 909/937-2700, www.flyontario.com) is farther east. Either BUR or ONT can be a good option for travelers planning to divide their time between Los Angeles, Palm Springs, and the deserts.

AIRPORT TRANSPORTATION

In Los Angeles, free shuttle buses provide service to the Los Angeles County Metropolitan Transportation Authority **Metro Rail** (323/466-3876, www.metro.net), accessible at the Green Line Aviation Station. Metro Rail trains connect Long Beach, Hollywood, North Hollywood, Downtown Los Angeles, and Pasadena. Passengers should wait under the blue "LAX Shuttle Airline Connection" signs outside the lower-level terminals and board the "G" shuttle. Passengers may also take the "C" shuttle to the **Metro Bus Center** (323/466-3876, www.metro.net), which connects to buses that serve the entire L.A. area. Information about bus service is provided via telephones on the Information Display Board inside each terminal.

Shuttle services are also available if you want to share a ride. **Prime Time Shuttle** (800/733-8267, www.primetimeshuttle.com) and **SuperShuttle** (800/258-3826, www.supershuttle.com) are authorized to serve the entire Los Angeles area out of LAX. These vans can be found on the lower arrivals deck in front of each terminal, under the orange "Shared Ride Vans" signs.

Taxis can be found on the lower arrivals level islands in front of each terminal, below the yellow "Taxi" signs. Only licensed taxis are allowed into the airport; they have standard rates of about $40 to downtown and $30 to West Los Angeles. Or opt for ridesharing services **Uber** (www.uber.com) and **Lyft** (www.lyft.com), which can cost $27-155 to get downtown from LAX. Look for signs reading "Ride Service Pick Up."

San Diego

San Diego International Airport (SAN, 619/400-2404, www.san.org) is a centrally located urban airport a mere three miles from the city center. While the location makes it a little noisy for those living in neighborhoods under the flight path, it makes getting to and from the airport a quick trip from most parts of the city. The airport is split into two major terminals plus a small commuter terminal, hosting 20 airlines and subsidiaries.

Regional Airports

Domestic flights can be an economical and faster option when traversing between major cities within the state. San Francisco International Airport (SFO, www.flysfo.com), Oakland International Airport (OAK, http://oaklandairport.com), and San Jose International Airport (SJC, www.flysanjose.com) connect with several smaller regional airports. These include the **Monterey Regional Airport** (MRY, www.montereyairport.com), the **Santa Barbara Airport** (SBA, www.santabarbaraca.gov), the **San Luis Obispo County Regional Airport** (SLO, www.sloairport.com), and the **Arcata-Eureka Airport** (ACV, http://co.humboldt.ca.us). **Southwest Airlines** (www.southwest.com) provides affordable flights among the larger airports, while **United Airlines** (www.united.com) has regular flights to regional airports. Geared toward commuters, flights are generally frequent but a bit pricey.

TRAIN

Several long-distance **Amtrak** (www.amtrak.com) trains rumble through California daily. There are eight train routes that serve the region: The *California Zephyr* runs from Chicago and Denver to Emeryville; the *Coast Starlight* travels down the West Coast from Seattle and Portland as far as Los Angeles; the *Pacific Surfliner* will get you to the Central Coast. There is no train depot in San Francisco; the closest station is in Emeryville in the East Bay. Fortunately, comfortable coach buses ferry travelers to and from the Emeryville Amtrak station, with many stops in downtown San Francisco.

BUS

A very affordable way to get around California is on **Greyhound** (800/231-2222, www.greyhound.com). The San Francisco Station (200 Folsom St., 415/495-1569) is a hub for Greyhound bus lines. Bus routes generally follow the major highways, traveling U.S. 101 and stations line the coast from Crescent City to San Diego. Most counties and municipalities have bus service with routes to outlying areas.

Megabus (https://us.megabus.com) stops in San Francisco (Townsend St. at 5th St.) with intercity connections to Caltrain and Muni. From San Francisco, Megabus travels south to Los Angeles (Union Station, 8 hours, $21 one-way) and north to Sacramento (6740 Q St., 2 hours, $5 one-way) multiple times daily.

Boltbus (https://www.boltbus.com) departs from San Francisco (200 Folsom St.) three times daily with transportation to Los Angeles (Union Station, 8-9 hours, $25 one-way).

CAR

California is great for road trips. Scenic coastal routes such as Highway 1 and U.S. 101 are often destinations in themselves. **Highway 1,** also known as the Pacific Coast Highway, follows the North Coast from Leggett to San Luis Obispo on the Central Coast and points south. Running parallel and intertwining with Highway 1 for much of its length, **U.S. 101** stretches north-south from Crescent City on the North Coast through the Central Coast, meeting Highway 1 in San Luis Obispo.

Road closures are not uncommon in winter. Highway 1 along the coast can shut down due to flooding or landslides. I-5 through the Central Valley can either close or be subject to hazardous driving conditions resulting from tule fog, which can reduce visibility to only a few feet.

Traffic jams, accidents, mudslides, fires, and snow can affect highways and interstates at any time. Before heading out on your adventure, check road conditions online at the **California Department of Transportation** (Caltrans, www.dot.ca.gov).

Common-sense maintenance consciousness is required on the road. If the car gets hot or overheats, stop for a while to cool it off. Never open the radiator cap if the engine is steaming. After the car has sat, squeeze the top radiator hose to see if there's any pressure in it; if there isn't, it's safe to open. Never pour water into a hot radiator—you could crack your block. If you start to smell rubber, your tires are overheating, and that's a good way to have a blowout. Stop and let them cool off. In winter in the high country, a can of silicone lubricant such as WD-40 will unfreeze door locks, dry off humid wiring, and keep your hinges in shape.

Car and RV Rental

Most car-rental companies have locations at each of the major California airports. To reserve a car in advance, contact **Budget Rent A Car** (U.S. tel. 800/218-7992, outside U.S. tel. 800/472-3325, www.budget.com), **Dollar Rent A Car** (800/800-5252, www.dollar.com), **Enterprise** (855/266-9289, www.enterprise.com), or **Hertz** (U.S. and Canada tel. 800/654-3131, outside U.S. tel. 800/654-3001, www.hertz.com).

To rent a car, drivers in California must be at least 21 years of age and have a valid driver's license. California law also requires that all vehicles carry liability insurance. You can purchase insurance with your rental car, but it generally costs an additional $10 per day, which can add up quickly. Most private auto insurance will also cover rental cars. Before buying rental insurance, check your car insurance policy to see if rental-car coverage is included.

The average cost of a rental car is $40 per day or $210 per week; however, rates vary greatly based on the time of year and distance traveled. Weekend and summer rentals cost significantly more. Generally, it is more expensive to rent from car rental agencies at an airport. To avoid excessive rates, first plan travel to areas where a car is not required, then rent a car from an agency branch in town to further explore more rural areas. Rental agencies occasionally allow vehicle drop-off at a different location from where it was picked up for an additional fee.

Another option is to rent an RV. You won't have to worry about camping or lodging options, and many facilities, particularly farther north, accommodate RVs. However, RVs are difficult to maneuver and park, limiting your access to metropolitan areas. They are also expensive, both in terms of gas and the rental rates. Rates during the summer average $1,300 per week and $570 for three days, the standard minimal rental. **Cruise America** (800/671-8042, www.cruiseamerica.com) has branches in San Francisco, San Jose, San Mateo, San Luis Obispo, Los Angeles, Costa Mesa, Oceanside, and San Diego. **El Monte RV** (888/337-2214, www.elmonterv.com) operates out of San Francisco, Santa Cruz, Los Angeles, Newport Beach, and San Diego, among other places.

Another way to get around is with **Jucy Rentals** (800/650-4180, www.jucyrentals.com), rental minivans with pop-up tops. The colorful vehicles are smaller and easier to manage than large RVs, but still come equipped with a fridge, a gas cooker, a sink, a DVD player, and two double beds. Rental locations are in San Francisco and Los Angeles.

Visas and Officialdom

PASSPORTS AND VISAS

If you are visiting from another country, you must have a valid passport and a visa to enter the United States. If you hold a current passport from one of the following countries, you may qualify for the Visa Waiver Program: Andorra, Australia, Austria, Belgium, Brunei, Chile, Czech Republic, Denmark, Estonia, Finland, France, Germany, Greece, Hungary, Iceland, Ireland, Italy, Japan, Latvia, Liechtenstein, Lithuania, Luxembourg, Malta, Monaco, the Netherlands, New Zealand, Norway, Portugal, San Marino, Singapore, Slovakia, Slovenia, South Korea, Spain, Sweden, Switzerland, Taiwan, and the United Kingdom. To qualify, you must apply online with the Electronic System for Travel Authorization and hold a return plane or cruise ticket to your country of origin dated less than 90 days from your date of entry.

Holders of Canadian passports don't need visas or visa waivers.

In most other countries, the local U.S. embassy should be able to provide a tourist visa. The average fee for a visa is US$160. While a visa may be processed as quickly as 24 hours on request, plan at least a couple of weeks, as there can be unexpected delays, particularly during the busy summer season (June-Aug.).

EMBASSIES

San Francisco and Los Angeles are home to embassies and consulates from many countries around the globe. If you should lose your passport or find yourself in some other trouble while visiting California, contact your country's offices for assistance. To find an embassy, check online at www.state.gov, which lists the websites for all foreign embassies in the United States. A representative will be able to direct you to the nearest embassy or consulate.

CUSTOMS

Before you enter the United States from another country by sea or by air, you'll be required to fill out a customs form. Check with the U.S. embassy in your country or the **Customs and Border Protection website** (www.cbp.gov) for an updated list of items you must declare.

If you require medication administered by injection, you must pack your syringes in a checked bag; syringes are not permitted in carry-ons coming into the United States.

Also, pack documentation describing your need for any narcotic medications you've brought with you. Failure to produce documentation for narcotics on request can result in severe penalties in the United States.

If you're driving into California along I-5 or another major highway, prepare to stop at Agricultural Inspection Stations a few miles inside the state line. You don't need to present a passport, a visa, or even a driver's license; instead, you must be prepared to present all your fruits and vegetables. California's largest economic sector is agriculture, and a number of the major crops grown here are sensitive to pests and diseases. In an effort to prevent known pests from entering the state and endangering crops, travelers are asked to identify all produce they're carrying in from other states or from Mexico. If you've got produce, especially homegrown or from a farm stand, it could be infected by a known problem pest or disease. Expect it to be confiscated on the spot.

You'll also be asked about fruits and veggies on your U.S. Customs form, which you'll be asked to fill out on the airplane or ship before you reach the United States.

Travel Tips

TOURIST INFORMATION

When visiting California, you might be tempted to stop in at one of several Golden State Welcome Centers scattered throughout the state. In all honesty, these visitors centers aren't that great. If you're in an area that doesn't have its own visitors center, the State Welcome Center might be a useful place to pick up maps and brochures; check www.visitcwc.com to find a local Welcome Center wherever you're visiting. Otherwise, stick with local, regional, and national park visitors centers, which tend to be staffed by volunteers or rangers who feel a real passion for their locale.

If you are looking for maps, almost all gas stations and drugstores sell maps both of the place you're in and of the whole state. **California State Automobile Association** (CSAA, https://calstate.aaa.com) offers free maps to auto club members.

Many local and regional visitors centers offer maps, but you'll need to pay a few dollars for the bigger and better ones. But if all you need is a wine-tasting map in a known wine region, you can probably get one for free along with a few tasting coupons at the nearest regional visitors center. Basic national park maps come with your admission payment. State park maps can be free or cost a few dollars at the visitors centers.

The state's **California Travel and Tourism Commission** (877/225-4367, www.visitcalifornia.com) also provides helpful and free tips, information, and downloadable maps and guides.

California is in the Pacific time zone (PST and PDT) and observes daylight saving time March-November.

Money

California businesses use the U.S. dollar ($). Most businesses also accept the major credit cards Visa, MasterCard, Discover, and American Express. ATM and debit cards work at many stores and restaurants, and ATMs are available throughout the region. In more remote areas, such as the North Coast, some businesses may only accept cash, so don't depend entirely on your plastic.

You can exchange currency at any international airport in the state. Currency-exchange points also crop up in downtown San Francisco and at some of the major business hotels in urban areas.

California is not a particularly expensive place to travel, but keeping an eye on your budget is still important. San Francisco and the Wine Country are the priciest regions for visitors, especially with the amount of high-quality food and luxury accommodations. Advance reservations for hotels and marquee restaurants in these areas are recommended.

Banks

As with anywhere, traveling in California with a huge amount of cash is not recommended, which may make frequent trips to the bank necessary. Fortunately, most destinations have at least one major bank. Usually Bank of America or Wells Fargo can be found on the main drags through towns. Banking hours tend to be Monday-Friday 8am-5pm, Saturday 9am-noon. Never count on a bank being open on Sundays or on federal holidays. If you need cash when the banks are closed, there is generally a 24-hour ATM available. Furthermore, many cash-only businesses have an on-site ATM for those who don't have enough cash ready in their wallets. The unfortunate downside to this convenience is a fee of $2-4 per transaction. This also applies to ATMs at banks at which you don't have an account.

Tax

Sales tax in California varies by city and county, but the average rate is around 7.5 percent. All goods are taxable with the exception of food not eaten on the premises. For example, your bill at a restaurant will include tax, but your bill at a grocery store will not. The hotel tax is another unexpected added expense to traveling in California. Most cities have enacted a tax on hotel rooms largely to make up for budget shortfalls. As you would expect, these taxes are higher in areas more popular with visitors. In Wine County you can expect to add an additional 12-14 percent onto your hotel bill, while in San Francisco the tax tops 15 percent. Some areas like Eureka have a lower hotel tax of 10 percent.

Tipping

Tipping is expected and appreciated, and a 15-20 percent tip for restaurants is about the norm. When ordering in bars, tip the bartender or waitstaff $1 per drink. For taxis, plan to tip 15-20 percent of the fare, or simply round up the cost to the nearest dollar. Cafés and coffee shops often have tip jars out. There is no consensus on what is appropriate when purchasing a $3 beverage. Often $0.50 is enough, depending on the quality and service.

Communications and Media

With the exception of rural and wilderness areas, California is fairly well connected. Cellphone reception is good except in places far from any large town. Likewise, you can find Internet access just about anywhere. The bigger cities are well wired, but even in small towns you can log on either at a library or in a café with a computer in the back. Be prepared to pay a per-minute usage fee or purchase a drink.

The main newspapers in California are the *San Francisco Chronicle* (www.sfchronicle.com) and the *Los Angeles Times* (www.latimes.com). Of course, there are other regional papers that may offer some international news in addition to the local color. As for radio, there are some news stations on the FM dial, and in most regions you can count on finding a National Public Radio (NPR, www.npr.org) affiliate. While they will all offer some NPR news coverage, some stations will be more geared toward music and local concerns. **KCRW** (89.9 FM, www.kcrw.com) is a particularly good NPR station serving the greater Los Angeles region.

Because of California's size both geographically and in terms of population, you will have to contend with multiple area codes—the numbers that prefix the seven-digit phone number throughout the state. The 800 or 866 area codes are toll-free numbers. Any time you are dialing out of the area, you must dial a 1 plus the area code followed by the seven-digit number.

To mail a letter, find a blue post office box; these are found on the main streets of any town. Postage rates vary by destination. You can purchase stamps at the local post office, where you can mail packages. Stamps can also be bought at some ATMs and online at www. usps.com, which can give you the location and hours of the nearest post office. Post offices are generally open Monday-Friday, with limited hours on Saturday. They are always closed on Sunday and federal holidays.

Conduct and Customs

The legal **drinking age** in California is 21. Expect to have your ID checked if you look under age 30, especially in bars and clubs, but also in restaurants and wineries. Most California bars and clubs close at 2am; you'll find the occasional after-hours nightspot in San Francisco.

Smoking has been banned in many places throughout California. Don't expect to find a smoking section in any restaurant or an ashtray in any bar. Smoking is illegal in all bars and clubs, but your new favorite watering hole might have an outdoor patio where smokers can huddle. Taking the ban one step further, many hotels, motels, and inns throughout California are strictly nonsmoking, and you'll be subject to fees of hundreds of dollars if your room smells of smoke when you leave.

There's no smoking in any public building, and even some of the state parks don't allow cigarettes. There's often good reason for this; the fire danger in California is extreme in the summer, and one carelessly thrown butt can cause a genuine catastrophe.

Recreational **marijuana** became legal in California in 2018. It is now legal for adults age 21 and older to possess, transport, or share up to one ounce of cannabis and eight grams of cannabis concentrate. Local governments and the state's **Bureau of Cannabis Control** (http://bcc.ca.gov) decide where products are sold. Be aware that the drug is still illegal under federal law, setting up a possible legal fight between the federal government and the state.

ACCESS FOR TRAVELERS WITH DISABILITIES

Most California attractions, hotels, and restaurants are accessible for travelers with disabilities. State law requires that public transportation must accommodate the special needs of travelers with disabilities and that public spaces and businesses have adequate restroom facilities and equal access. This includes national parks and historic structures, many of which have been refitted with ramps and wider doors. Many hiking trails are also accessible to wheelchairs, and most campgrounds designate specific campsites that meet the Americans with Disabilities Act standards. The state of California also provides a free telephone TDD-to-voice relay service; just dial 711.

If you are traveling with a disability, there are many resources to help you plan your trip. **Access Northern California** (http://accessnca.org) is a nonprofit organization that offers general travel tips, including recommendations on accommodations, parks and trails, transportation, and travel equipment. **Gimp-on-the-Go** (www.gimponthego.com) is another travel resource. The message board on the **American Foundation for the Blind** (www.afb.org) website is a good forum to discuss travel strategies for the visually impaired. For a comprehensive guide to wheelchair-accessible beaches, rivers, and shorelines from Santa Cruz to Marin County, including the East Bay and Wine Country, contact the **California Coastal Conservancy** (510/286-1015, www.scc.ca.gov), which publishes a free and downloadable guide. **Wheelchair**

Getaways in San Francisco (800/642-2042, www.wheelchairgetaways.com, $80-145 per day) and Los Angeles (800/638-1912) rents wheelchair-accessible vans and offers pickup and drop-off service from airports ($100-300). Likewise, Avis Access (800/669-9585, www. avis.com) rents cars, scooters, and other products to make traveling with a disability easier; click on the "Services" link on their website.

TRAVELING WITH CHILDREN

Many spots in California are ideal destinations for families with children of all ages. Amusement parks, interactive museums, zoos, parks, beaches, and playgrounds all make for family-friendly fun. On the other hand, there are a few spots in the Golden State that beckon more to adults than to children. The North Coast's focus on original art and romantic B&Bs brings out couples looking for weekend getaways rather than families. In fact, before you book a room at a B&B that you expect to share with your kids, check to be sure that the inn can accommodate extra people in the guest rooms and that they allow guests under age 16.

WOMEN TRAVELING ALONE

California is a pretty friendly place for women traveling alone. Most of the major outdoor attractions are incredibly safe, and even many of the urban areas boast pleasant neighborhoods that welcome lone female travelers. But you'll need to take some basic precautions and pay attention to your surroundings, just as you would in any unfamiliar place. Carry your car keys in your hand when walking out to your car. Don't sit in your parked car in a lonely parking lot at night; just get in, turn on the engine, and drive away. When you're walking down a city street, be alert and keep an eye on your surroundings and on anyone who might be following you. In rural areas, don't go tromping into unlit wooded areas or out into grassy fields alone at night without a flashlight; many of California's critters are

nocturnal. Of course, this caution applies to men as well; mountain lions and rattlesnakes don't tend to discriminate.

SENIOR TRAVELERS

California makes an ideal destination for older or retired folks looking to relax and have a great time. You'll find senior discounts nearly every place you go, including restaurants, golf courses, major attractions, and even some hotels, although the minimum age can range 50-65. Just ask, and be prepared to produce ID if you look young or are requesting a senior discount. You can often get additional discounts on rental cars, hotels, and tour packages as a member of AARP (888/687-2277, www.aarp. org). If you're not a member, its website can also offer helpful travel tips and advice. Road Scholar (800/454-5768, www.roadscholar. org) is another great resource for senior travelers. Dedicated to providing educational opportunities for older travelers, Road Scholar provides package trips to beautiful and interesting destinations. Called "Educational Adventures," these trips are generally 3-9 days long and emphasize history, natural history, art, music, or a combination thereof.

GAY AND LESBIAN TRAVELERS

California is known for its thriving gay and lesbian communities. In fact, the Golden State is a golden place for gay travel—especially in the bigger cities and even in some of the smaller towns around the state. As with much of the country, the farther you venture into rural and agricultural regions, the less likely you are to experience the liberal acceptance the state is known for. The International Gay and Lesbian Travel Association (www.iglta.org) has a directory of gay- and lesbian-friendly tour operators, accommodations, and destinations.

San Francisco has the biggest and arguably best Gay Pride Festival (www.sfpride.org) in the nation, usually held on Market Street on the last weekend in June. Meanwhile, San Diego has a large celebration called San

Diego LGBT Pride (https://sdpride.org) in July. Year-round, San Francisco's Castro District offers fun of all kinds, from theater to clubs to shopping, mostly targeted at gay men but with a few places sprinkled in for lesbians. If the Castro is your primary destination, you can even find a place to stay in the middle of the action.

West Hollywood in Los Angeles has its own upscale gay culture. Just like the rest of L.A.'s clubs, the gay clubs are havens of the see-and-be-seen crowd.

Santa Cruz on the Central Coast is a quirky town known for its lesbian-friendly culture. A relaxed vibe informs everything from underground clubs to unofficial nude beaches to live-action role-playing games in the middle of downtown. Even the lingerie and adult toy shops tend to be woman-owned and -operated.

Health and Safety

MEDICAL SERVICES

For an emergency anywhere in California, **dial 911.** Inside hotels and resorts, check your emergency number as soon as you get to your guest room. In urban and suburban areas, full-service hospitals and medical centers abound, but in more remote regions, help can be more than an hour away.

If you're planning a **backcountry expedition,** follow all rules and guidelines for obtaining **wilderness permits** and for self-registration at trailheads. These are for your safety, letting the rangers know roughly where you plan to be and when to expect you back. National and state park visitors centers can advise in more detail on any health or wilderness alerts in the area. It is also advisable to let someone outside your party know your route and expected date of return.

Being out in the elements can present its own set of challenges. Despite California's relatively mild climate, **heat exhaustion** and **heat stroke** can affect anyone during the hot summer months, particularly during a long, strenuous hike in the sun. Common symptoms include nausea, lightheadedness, headache, or muscle cramps. **Dehydration** and loss of electrolytes are the common causes of heat exhaustion. If you or anyone in your group develops any of these symptoms, get out of the sun immediately, stop all physical activity, and drink plenty of water. Heat exhaustion can be severe, and if untreated can lead to heat stroke, in which the body's core temperature reaches 105°F. Fainting, seizures, confusion, and rapid heartbeat and breathing can indicate the situation has moved beyond heat exhaustion. If you suspect this, call 911 immediately.

Similar precautions hold true for **hypothermia,** which is caused by prolonged exposure to cold water or weather. For many in California, this can happen on a hike or backpacking trip undertaken without sufficient rain gear, or by staying too long in the ocean or another cold body of water without a wetsuit. Symptoms include shivering, weak pulse, drowsiness, confusion, slurred speech, or stumbling. To treat hypothermia, immediately remove the wet clothing, cover the person with blankets, and feed him or her hot liquids. If symptoms don't improve, call 911.

WILDERNESS SAFETY

Many places are still wild in California, making it important to take precautions with regard to wildlife. While California no longer has any grizzly bears, **black bears** thrive and are often seen in the mountains foraging for food in the spring, summer, and fall. Black bears certainly don't have the size or reputation of grizzlies, but there is good reason to exercise caution. Never get between a bear and her cub, and if a bear sees you, identify yourself as human by waving your hands above your head, speaking in a calm voice, and backing away slowly. If a bear charges, do not run. One of the best precautions against an unwanted bear encounter is to keep a clean camp; store all food in airtight, bear-proof containers; and strictly follow any guidelines given by the park or rangers.

Even more common than bears are **mountain lions,** which can be found in the Coast Range as well as in grasslands and forests. Because of their solitary nature, it is unlikely you will see one, even on long trips in the backcountry. Still, there are a couple things to remember. If you come across a kill, probably a large, partly eaten deer, leave immediately. And if you see a mountain lion and it sees you, identify yourself as human, making your body appear as big as possible, just as with a bear. And remember: Never run. As with any cat, large or small, running triggers its hunting instincts. If a mountain lion should attack, fight back; cats don't like to get hurt.

The other treacherous critter in the backcountry is the **rattlesnake.** They can be found in summer in generally hot and dry areas from the coast to the Sierra Nevada. When hiking in this type of terrain—many parks will indicate if rattlesnakes are a problem in the area—keep your eyes on the ground and an ear out for the telltale rattle. Snakes like to warn you to keep away. The only time this is not the case is with baby rattlesnakes that have not yet developed their rattles. Unfortunately, they have developed their fangs and venom, which is particularly potent. Should you get bitten, remain calm and seek immediate medical help.

Mosquitoes can be found throughout the state. At higher elevations they can be worse, prompting many hikers and backpackers to don head nets and apply potent repellents, usually DEET. The high season for mosquitoes is late spring-early summer.

Ticks live in many of the forests and grasslands throughout the state, except at higher elevations. Tick season generally runs late fall-early summer. If you are hiking through brushy areas, wear pants and long-sleeve shirts. Ticks like to crawl to warm, moist places (armpits are a favorite) on their host. If a tick is engorged, it can be difficult to remove. There are two main types of ticks found in California: dog ticks and deer ticks. Dog ticks are larger, brown, and have a gold spot on their backs, while deer ticks are small, tear-shaped, and black. Deer ticks are known to carry Lyme disease. While Lyme disease is relatively rare in California—there are more cases in the northernmost part of the state—it is very serious. If you get bitten by a deer tick and the bite leaves a red ring, seek medical attention. Lyme disease can be successfully treated with early rounds of antibiotics.

There is only one major variety of plant in California that can cause an adverse reaction in humans if you touch the leaves or stems: **poison oak,** a common shrub that inhabits forests throughout the state. Poison oak has a characteristic three-leaf configuration, with scalloped leaves that are shiny green in the spring and then turn yellow, orange, and red in late summer-fall. In fall, the leaves drop, leaving a cluster of innocuous-looking branches. The oil in poison oak is present year-round in both the leaves and branches. Your best protection is to wear long sleeves and long pants when hiking, no matter how hot it is. A product called Tecnu is available at most California drugstores—slather it on before you go hiking to protect yourself from poison oak. If your skin comes into contact with poison oak, expect a nasty rash known for its itchiness and irritation. Poison oak is also extremely transferable, so avoid touching your eyes, face, or other parts of your body to prevent spreading the rash. Calamine lotion can help, and in extreme cases a doctor can administer cortisone to help decrease the inflammation.

CRIME AND SAFETY PRECAUTIONS

The outdoors is not the only place that harbors danger. In both rural and urban areas, theft can be a problem. When parking at a trailhead or in a park or at a beach, don't leave any valuables in the car. If you must, place them out of sight, either in a locked glove box or in the trunk. The same holds true for urban areas. Furthermore, avoid keeping your wallet, camera, and other expensive items, including lots of cash, easily accessible in backpacks; keep them within your sight at all times. Certain urban neighborhoods are best avoided at night. If you find yourself in these areas after dark, consider taking a cab to avoid walking blocks and blocks to get to your car or to wait for public transportation. In case of a theft or any other emergency, call 911.

Resources

California Department of Transportation
www.dot.ca.gov
Check here for state map and highway information before planning a coastal road trip.

Visit California
www.visitcalifornia.com
Before your trip, visit the official tourism site of the state of California.

California Outdoor and Recreational Information
www.caoutdoors.com
This recreation-focused website includes links to maps, local newspapers, festivals, and events as well as a wide variety of recreational activities throughout the state.

California State Parks
www.parks.ca.gov
The official website lists hours, accessibility, activities, camping areas, fees, and more information for all parks in the state system.

SFGate
www.sfgate.com
This website affiliated with the *San Francisco Chronicle* offers information on activities, festivals, and events in the city by the bay.

SF Weekly
www.sfweekly.com
This website for one of the city's weekly alternative papers has a strong arts and entertainment emphasis.

WineCountry
www.winecountry.com
This tourism website offers information on all of California's wine regions, including Napa, Sonoma, Mendocino, Carmel Valley, Paso Robles, Santa Barbara, and Temecula.

LATourist
www.latourist.com
This informative visitors website is dedicated to the City of Angels.

Los Angeles Times
www.latimes.com
This daily newspaper for Los Angeles covers Southern California and the world.

L.A. Weekly
www.laweekly.com
One of the best alternative weeklies out there, the *L.A. Weekly* has superb arts, music, and food coverage.

Los Angeles Convention and Visitors Bureau
www.discoverlosangeles.com
It's the official website of the Los Angeles Convention and Visitors Bureau.

Disneyland
http://disneyland.disney.go.com
Find information on all things Disney here.

Index

List of Maps

Photo Credits

MAP SYMBOLS

≡≡≡ Expressway	○ City/Town	✈ Airport
--- Primary Road	◉ State Capital	✈ Airfield
— Secondary Road	⊛ National Capital	▲ Mountain
---- Unpaved Road	★ Point of Interest	✦ Unique Natural Feature
— Feature Trail	• Accommodation	⚲ Waterfall
---- Other Trail	▼ Restaurant/Bar	♠ Park
.... Ferry	▪ Other Location	☯ Trailhead
═══ Pedestrian Walkway	⋀ Campground	⚡ Skiing Area
▥▥▥ Stairs		

⚑ Golf Course	
℗ Parking Area	
▟ Archaeological Site	
⛪ Church	
⛽ Gas Station	
⟅⟆ Glacier	
▦ Mangrove	
⟋ Reef	
⊟ Swamp	

CONVERSION TABLES

°C = (°F - 32) / 1.8
°F = (°C x 1.8) + 32
1 inch = 2.54 centimeters (cm)
1 foot = 0.304 meters (m)
1 yard = 0.914 meters
1 mile = 1.6093 kilometers (km)
1 km = 0.6214 miles
1 fathom = 1.8288 m
1 chain = 20.1168 m
1 furlong = 201.168 m
1 acre = 0.4047 hectares
1 sq km = 100 hectares
1 sq mile = 2.59 square km
1 ounce = 28.35 grams
1 pound = 0.4536 kilograms
1 short ton = 0.90718 metric ton
1 short ton = 2,000 pounds
1 long ton = 1.016 metric tons
1 long ton = 2,240 pounds
1 metric ton = 1,000 kilograms
1 quart = 0.94635 liters
1 US gallon = 3.7854 liters
1 Imperial gallon = 4.5459 liters
1 nautical mile = 1.852 km

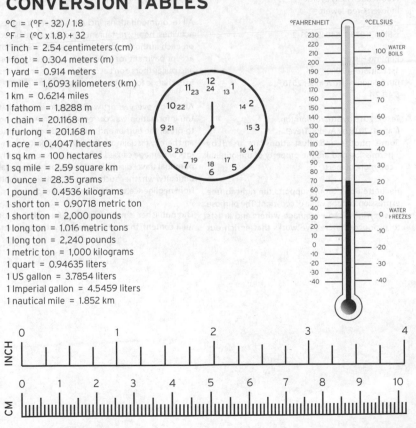

MOON COASTAL CALIFORNIA

Avalon Travel
Hachette Book Group
1700 Fourth Street
Berkeley, CA 94710, USA
www.moon.com

Editor: Sabrina Young
Series Manager: Kathryn Ettinger
Copy Editor: Linda Cabasin
Production and Graphics Coordinator: Darren Alessi
Cover Design: Faceout Studios, Charles Brock for
  Handbooks
Interior Design: Domini Dragoone
Moon Logo: Tim McGrath
Map Editor: Albert Angulo
Cartographers: Brian Shotwell, Albert Angulo, and
  Karin Dahl
Proofreader: Kelly Lydick
Indexer: Greg Jewett

ISBN-13: 978-1-64049-291-2

Printing History
1st Edition — 2000
6th Edition — November 2018
5 4 3 2 1

Front cover photo: Big Sur coast © Dennis Frates /
  Alamy Stock Photo
Back cover photo: San Diego skyline © Sean Pavone
  | Dreamstime.com

Printed in China by RR Donnelley